D1691957

ANIMAL TRAINING

Successful Animal Management
THROUGH
Positive Reinforcement

By Ken Ramirez

Shedd Aquarium
The World's Aquarium

Shedd Aquarium
1200 South Lake Shore Drive
Chicago, IL 60605

www.shedd.org

© **1999 by Kenneth T. Ramirez and Shedd Aquarium.** All rights reserved. No part of this book may be reproduced, stored in a retrieval system, or transmitted, in any form or by any means (electronic, mechanical, photocopying, recording, or otherwise) without the prior written permission of the publisher. No patent liability is assumed with respect to the use of the information contained herein. Although every precaution has been taken in the preparation of this book, the publisher and author assume no responsibility for errors or omissions. Neither is any liability assumed for damages resulting from the use of the information contained herein.

Library of Congress Cataloging-in-Publication Data:
Ramirez, Ken   1957 -
    Animal Training: Successful Animal Management through Positive Reinforcement / Ken Ramirez
        p.   cm.
    Includes bibliographical references and index.
    ISBN: 0-9611074-9-9
        1. Training - Animals - Marine Mammals - Aquarium - Zoo.   2. Animal Training.   3. Positive Reinforcement
I. Title.
SF408.R173 1999
636.08RAM

                                                                                            CIP

Printed in the United States of America

10 9 8 7 6 5 4 3 2 1

ANIMAL TRAINING: Successful Animal Management through Positive Reinforcement represents the philosophy of the marine mammal training program at John G. Shedd Aquarium in Chicago, IL., a not-for profit education, conservation, and research organization. The articles herein are the property of their respective authors or their respective publications and are included by special permission.

Soundings, IMATA Conference Proceedings, and *Marine Mammals: Public Display and Research* are publications of the International Marine Animal Trainers Association, 1200 S. Lake Shore Drive, Chicago, IL 60605. © 1977, 1978, 1979, 1980, 1981, 1982, 1983, 1984, 1985, 1986, 1987, 1988, 1989, 1990, 1991, 1992, 1993, 1994, 1995, 1996, 1997, 1998, and 1999.

AZA Conference Proceedings are publications of the American Zoo and Aquarium Association, 8403 Colesville Rd., Suite 710, Silver Spring, MD 20910-3314. © 1991, 1993, & 1995.

Articles by Karen Pryor are published by Sunshine Books, 49 River St., Waltham, MA 02453. © 1994, 1995, and 1996.

Articles by Gary Wilkes, are copyrighted by Mr. Wilkes, all rights reserved © 1994, 1999.

ABA-SIG Newsletter is published by the Animal Special Interest Group of the Association for Behavior Analysis. © 1995 and 1996.

Every Animal is the Smartest: Intelligence and the Ecological Niche by Marian Breland Bailey from *Animal Intelligence: Insights into the Animal Mind* edited by R.J. Hoage and Larry Goldman; © 1986 by the Smithsonian Institution.

Article from the *Chicago Tribune* published by the Tribune Publishing Company. © 1996.

Article by Fran Pennock Shaw from *Dog World* a PJS Publication. © 1996.

Some of the images used herein were obtained from IMSI's MasterClips® and MasterPhotos™ Premium Image Collection, 1985 Francisco Blvd. East, San Rafael, CA 94901-5506, USA.

Additional images obtained from T/Maker Company/Brødrbund Software, Inc., P.O.Box 6121, Novato, CA 94948-6121.

Photo Credits:
Cover Photos: Trainer with beluga © John G. Shedd Aquarium, photo by Edward G. Lines, Jr.; Dog, ANIMALS ANIMALS © Barbara Wright; Killer whale, ANIMALS ANIMALS © James Watt; Gorilla, ANIMALS ANIMALS © John Chellman; Elephant, ANIMALS ANIMALS © D. Allen; Dolphin © Chicago Zoological Society, Mike Greer; Sea lion, ANIMALS ANIMALS © Barbara Reed.
Photos © John G. Shedd Aquarium: page 41, 421, 519, and back cover by Edward G. Lines, Jr.; page 275 by Steve Bubalo.
Photos © Chicago Zoological Society: page 65 and 113 by Jim Schulz; page 255 by Mike Greer; page 531 by CZS AV Service.
Photo © E.P.Associates, Inc: page 21 by Todd Robeck
Photos from ANIMALS ANIMALS: page 1 © Bradley Smith; page 133 © Miriam Agron; page 213 © Ted Levin; page 361 © David C. Fritts; page 391 © Zig Leszczynsk; page 557 © L.L.T. Rhodes.

Cover & Chapter Heading Design: Karen Kohn & Associates, LTD.
Book Design: K. Ramirez

Table of Contents

Preface	xii
Acknowledgements	xiv
Chapter 1 – Introduction	**1**
Using this Manual	**2**
Logical flow of information	2
Small manageable pieces	2
Don't Shoot the Dog	2
Other references	3
Theory vs. applications	4
Experience is the best teacher	5
History of Animal Training	**5**
Menageries	5
Domestication	5
Work animals	5
Performers	6
Research	6
Animal welfare	6
Modern training	7
What is Training?	**8**
Definition of training	8
Why we train	9
Primary reasons	9
Secondary reasons	10
Understanding the reasons	12
The complete professional	12
How We Train (A Simplified Version)	**12**
Learning about the animal	12
Operant conditioning	13
Gaining the animal's trust	13
Rules of the game	13
Positive reinforcement	13
Bridging	14
Behaviors not tricks	14
Scanning	14
How fast can they learn?	15
Stimulus control	15
Targeting	15
Successive approximations	16
Being creative	16
Summary	16
Featured Articles	**17**

Chapter 2 - Knowing the Animal — 21

Understanding the Species — 22

Specific Animal History & Behavior — 23
Acquisition — 23
Previous human interaction — 24
Observations & ethograms — 25

Proper Diet & Nutrition — 25
A healthy animal is a happy animal — 25
Base diet — 25
Varied diet — 26
Quality diet — 26
Supplements — 26

The Environment — 26
Space — 26
Social structure — 27
Water quality — 27
Other environmental conditions — 28
Terrain & foliage — 28
Animal care staff needs — 28
Public needs — 28
Regulations and the law — 28

Record Keeping — 29
Non-training records — 29
Training records — 30
Planning & summary records — 32
The computer age — 33

Developing Trust Through Interaction — 35
Trust a step toward relationship building — 35
Determining type of contact — 36
Learning an animal's preferences — 38
Trust takes time — 38

Featured Articles — 39

Chapter 3 – The Human Element — 41

Intelligence — 42
Definitions — 42
Studying intelligence — 43
Cognition studies — 43
All animals can learn — 43
How smart is a dolphin? — 44
Intelligence is a matter of perspective — 44

Anthropomorphism (A Trainer's Biggest Stumbling Block) — 45
- Definition — 45
- Thinking for the animal — 46
- Making excuses for the animal — 46
- Health concerns — 46
- "Three's Company" syndrome — 46
- We will always anthropomorphize — 47
- Compromise — 47

Compassion & Emotion — 48
- Compassion is good — 48
- Keep your emotions in check — 48

Featured Articles — 50

Chapter 4 – Basic Operant Conditioning — 65

Getting used to the Lingo — 66
- Technology — 66
- Defining the audience — 66
- Learning basic terms — 67

Operant vs. Classical Conditioning — 68

Positive Reinforcement — 69
- Primary reinforcers — 69
- Secondary reinforcers — 69
- Timing — 69

Bridging Stimulus — 69
- Conditioned reinforcer — 69
- Selecting a bridge — 70
- Teaching the bridge — 70
- Why a bridge? — 70

Shaping — 71
- Successive approximations — 71
- Selective reinforcement — 71
- Black and white (establishing criteria) — 71
- Number of trainers — 71

Shaping Techniques — 72
- Scanning — 72
- Targeting — 72
- Modeling — 73
- Mimicry — 73
- Abstract learning — 73
- Pryor's 10 laws of shaping — 73

Stimulus Control   **74**
    Discriminative stimulus   75
    Choosing the cue   75
    Consistency   75
    Changing a cue   75
    Pryor's rules of stimulus control   75

Superstitious Behavior   **76**
    Poor bridging   76
    Poor observation   76
    Sloppy cues   76
    Using superstitious behavior   76

Dealing with Incorrect Responses   **77**
    Ignore the behavior - LRS   77
    Time outs   77
    Deprivation is not the answer   78
    Negative reinforcement & punishment   78

Have a Training Plan   **78**
    Map your behavior   78
    Be flexible   79
    Stay focused   79
    Keep good records (communicate)   79

Summary   **79**

Featured Articles   **80**

Chapter 5 –
Non-Formal Interactions   113

Formal Training   **114**

Technique vs. Instinct   **115**

Developing a Relationship   **115**
    Caring about the animal   115
    Polarized camps   116
    Building the relationship   116
    Play   117

Animal Observations: Ethograms   **117**

Featured Articles   **118**

Chapter 6 Husbandry Training
(A Training Program's First Steps)   133

Cooperative Behavior — **134**
- Stationing — 134
- Targeting — 135
- A to B — 136
- Gating — 136
- Taction — 136

Desensitization — **137**
- Training through desensitization — 137
- Habituation & counter-conditioning — 137
- Generalization vs. discrimination — 137

What is Husbandry Training? — **138**
- Definition — 138
- Basic husbandry principles — 138
- Advantages to training — 138
- The veterinarian's role — 138
- Desensitize, desensitize, desensitize — 139
- Precise bridging — 139

General Body Exams — **139**
- Tactile work — 139
- The Layout — 140

Blood Sampling — **140**
- Where to draw — 140
- Take your time — 141
- The one stick rule — 141
- Helpful hints — 141

Working around the Mouth & Head — **141**

Removal from their Environment — **142**
- Stretcher/cage/kennel training — 142
- Other removal methods — 142
- Non-voluntary removal — 143

Summary – Other Husbandry Behaviors — **144**

Featured Articles — **145**

Chapter 7 – Social Animals (Working with More than One) — **213**

One-on-One Training — **214**
- Ideal situation — 214
- Community groups — 214
- When one-on-one fails — 215

Dealing with Changing Social Situations — **215**

Gating & Separation Training	**215**
What if Separation is not Possible?	**216**
Group Training	**216**
Stationing	216
Fairness	217
Bridging in a group	218
Introducing New Animals to the Group	**218**
Featured Articles	**220**

Chapter 8 – Variety   255

The Spice of Life	**256**
Session Structure	**256**
Length	256
Location	256
Behavior selection	257
Pace	257
Companion animals	257
Trainers	257
Reinforcers	257
Caution	257
"I can't provide variety"	258
Session Type	**259**
Exercise sessions	259
Play sessions	259
Innovative sessions	259
Focus sessions	259
Be creative	259
Enriching the Environment	**260**
Behavioral enrichment	260
The animal's home	260
Environmental conditions	260
Social structure	260
Habitat configuration	260
Enrichment devices	261
Consistency	**261**
Featured Articles	**262**

Chapter 9 – Advanced Techniques & Concepts   275

What is an Advanced Concept?	**276**
Easy as 1, 2, 3	**276**
Cautions about use of Advanced Concepts	**277**
Black & White: Where's the Gray?	**278**
Right or wrong	278
Gray area	278
Large staff	279
Setting clear expectations	279
Secondary Reinforcers	**280**
Punishment, Negative Reinforcers, & Aversive Stimuli	**280**
Varied concepts	280
Definitions	280
Using the terms in the real world	283
Schedules of Reinforcement	**286**
Looking at it simply	286
It's an alphabet soup	286
Implementing a variable schedule	288
How long does it take?	288
Variety is the goal	289
Recall, Delta, and "No"	**289**
Different concepts	289
Recall	289
Delta	290
The "No" signal	290
Effective tools	291
Chained Behaviors	**291**
Technical chains	291
Common chains	291
"Continue" Signal	**292**
Combination Behaviors	**292**
End of Session Signal	**293**
Other Advanced Concepts	**293**
Featured Articles	**294**
Chapter 10 Aggression	**361**

A Natural Phenomenon	**362**
Dealing with Aggression Operantly	**362**
Operant Principles	**363**
Turner's Rules on Dealing with Aggression	**363**
When to Intercede	**364**
Trainer directed	364
Animal directed	364
Putting Aggression on Cue	**365**
Jaw pop study	365
Protection dogs	365
Featured Articles	**366**

Chapter 11 – Problem Solving   391

Planning	**392**
Identify the problem	392
Determine the cause	392
Implement the plan	392
Constant monitoring	392
Determining the Cause	**393**
Environmental	393
Social	394
Psychological	394
Physical	395
Trainer	395
Session use	395
Regression	396
Desensitization	396
Implementing the Plan	**396**
Untraining Undesirable Behavior (Pryor's Eight Methods)	**396**
Shoot the animal	396
Punishment	397
Negative reinforcement	397
Extinction	397
Train incompatible behavior (DRI)	398
Put the behavior on cue	398
Shape the absence of the behavior (DRO)	398
Change the motivation	398
Complex Problems	**399**

| Featured Articles | 400 |

Chapter 12 – Complex Training & Modern Applications — 421

Putting all the Theory Together	422
Getting to know the animal	422
Expand your knowledge	422
Practice and gain experience	422

| Interactive Programs | 422 |

| Protected Contact Training | 423 |

| Other Zoo Applications | 424 |

| Research Training | 424 |

| Training Pets & Other Domestic Animals | 426 |

| Featured Articles | 428 |

Chapter 13 – The Professional Trainer (Resources & Getting a Job) — 519

Knowledge + Practice = Experience	520
Working in the Field	520
Professional Zoological Organizations	520
Other Professional Resources	522
Featured Articles	525

Chapter 14 - Glossary — 531

Index — 557

Author - Title Index	559
Facility/Organization Index	568
Subject Index	570
Animal Index	574
Bibliography	576

Preface

Aren't there enough books on animal training? Why should anyone want to read this one? Honestly, there are hundreds of readily available books about animal training, ranging from housebreaking your puppy to scientific books on animal behavior and textbooks about operant conditioning. Each has its own focus and intended audience. This book was written as a manual for marine mammal trainers with a focus on the use of proven principles of operant conditioning. My hope is that professional animal trainers will find this manual to be a useful reference and teaching tool. Although the animals most frequently discussed are marine mammals (whales, dolphins, seals, otters) the manual covers the training of animals as diverse as the largest elephant in the zoo to the smallest cocker spaniel pup at home.

I have been a "professional" animal trainer for more than 20 years – that is, I have had a job as a trainer for that amount of time. But a true professional should be much more than just someone who is paid to teach an animal to do tricks or to perform an unusual behavior. A real professional is a trainer with extensive knowledge of the animals and their natural behavior, together with a combination of experience and skill in modifying behavior. Even the most accomplished biologist or behaviorist is not automatically a good trainer. In fact, animal training is a unique discipline in its adaptation of a broad range of knowledge and skills to enrich the life of animals in the trainer's care.

This manual had its genesis as far back as 1981, when I was a young trainer suddenly thrust into a position of authority over a marine mammal program. I had been training dolphins for nearly four years in which I had the opportunity to see and experience a great deal. But I did not feel I was prepared to be in charge of an entire training program. I had also been fortunate to work for a short time with guide dogs for the vision impaired. I was truly fascinated by training and had studied psychology, behavior, biology, and many other disciplines; but putting it all together to train an animal was something I had learned entirely on the job. Then one day, when my supervisor, the head trainer, quit his job, I found myself standing uneasily in his shoes. A group of younger and less experienced trainers suddenly looked to me for guidance and expected me to teach them to be professional animal trainers.

As I attempted to rise to this new challenge, I searched the local libraries but found relatively little useful information. There were technical texts on operant conditioning that were so confusing that I thought I would need an advanced degree even to get past the title page. There also were countless books on training a pet dog, but few of them discussed why their advice worked; they just gave you the steps to accomplish your goal. It was then that I began collecting articles that seemed to pertain to the training of dolphins, sea lions, birds, and other exotic animals. I had also worked with many talented trainers over the years, so I reviewed with a new sense of urgency a notebook I had kept of their "words of wisdom," training secrets, and anything else they had ever said to me about training. I realized that I had, in fact, already started my own training manual!

Then two important, yet unrelated events, occurred. First, I discovered a book by Karen Pryor called *Lads Before the Wind*, which recounted her experiences when *she* found herself suddenly in charge of a marine mammal training program with little previous formal experience. I certainly could relate to that. At the same time, I learned about an organization called the International Marine Animal Trainers Association (IMATA), a group of marine mammal professionals who shared information about the career and the animals I had grown to love. Suddenly I was finding lots of really useful information about animal training, especially about the training of marine mammals. I joined IMATA, devoured every issue of their newsletter *Soundings*, and finally, in 1984, made it to my first IMATA conference. It immediately became an addiction; I have never missed a conference since that first one. You might say I went overboard, I joined committees, became active in the organization, and even had the privilege of serving as IMATA's president. Through IMATA I made new friends and discovered colleagues who shared my passion for and knowledge of marine mammal training. I have never been the same since.

Throughout all this, I still faced an ever-growing challenge of teaching eager young employees the skills necessary to train and care for a variety of animal species. IMATA became an invaluable resource, as I used articles and papers from their publications to teach myself and my staff about emerging trends and new applications in the field of marine mammal training. Meanwhile, Karen Pryor had written another book, *Don't Shoot the Dog*, which is referenced throughout this manual. I quickly made that book required reading for everyone on my staff. It remains one of the most clearly written explanations about the use of operant conditioning in a non-technical and easy-to-understand style.

As a consultant, I traveled to many zoological facilities and found young trainers asking the same questions I had asked and looking for resources that would help them apply operant conditioning properly. I used *Don't Shoot the Dog* combined with articles I had collected over the years from IMATA and other sources as references for these young trainers. This manual is a combination of those sources interwoven with my own explanations about how this theory and experience can be combined into a cohesive training program. In 1996, Western Illinois University asked me to develop a graduate level course on animal training. I used the training program I had developed for my own staff, the collection of articles I had used as references over the years, and combined them into a textbook. In essence, this book is that textbook and also the training manual I use to guide my staff at the John G. Shedd Aquarium in Chicago. Finally, it is a reference book or a reader that collects in one place what I consider to be some of the most important articles to have been written about training.

Rather than try to reinterpret what others already have written so well, I have obtained permission to reprint more than 100 articles (by more than 150 writers) throughout this manual. I have tried to put each article into a context that explains why I believe each article is worthwhile. The order and manner in which I have interpreted the material is certainly the result of my own perspective. But I hope that others in the animal training field will find it a useful reference. For me, this will always be a work in progress, as new things are learned and new articles written. Someday, I hope others will compile similar volumes sharing their favorite articles and their own perspectives about how to implement and manage training programs. For it is only through this kind of sharing that we all will become better trainers. In the end, it is the animals under our care that will benefit most from this knowledge.

Ken Ramirez
Chicago, Illinois
June, 1999

Acknowledgements

Although the writing of this manual has been a single-minded goal of mine for many years, it might never have been completed had many individuals not contributed their valuable time and talents to helping me make this dream a reality. A special thanks must go to four individuals who read the entire text and provided valuable technical and critical comments. The first three – Cheryl Messinger, John Kirtland, and Randy Brill – are talented trainers and all former presidents of the International Marine Animal Trainers Association (IMATA) who read the entire book, provided valuable feedback, and endless encouragement to complete this project. The fourth individual, Lisa Takaki, has read the book more times than anyone else, providing practical and technical feedback almost daily. Lisa has been my assistant, my friend, my colleague and my companion throughout this journey and the manual could never have been completed without her professional and personal support.

I am indebted to the many authors and publishers of the numerous articles that have been included in the text. Their cooperation in allowing their work to be reprinted here has made this manual possible. Because I have relied so heavily on the various publications of IMATA, I am grateful to IMATA's board of directors, and its editors for their kind permission to use so many articles from their many publications. In particular, I must thank Bud Krames and Ted Turner for allowing my requests to be heard at board meetings during their tenures as president.

Carolyn Donaldson of McGraw-Hill has provided professional guidance and advice to keep me on the right track throughout this writing. The thankless task of editing, proofing, indexing, and reading this material over and over fell on the shoulders of nine individuals who volunteered countless hours to complete this monumental task. I will forever be indebted to them all: Jennifer M. Dailer, Liz Deatherage, Lisa M. Gibler, Jessica T. McClure, Erin L. McEntee, Jill A. Moyse, Sarah E. Potchebout, Josh Rosenberg, and Kristina Wilhemon. My sincere gratitude goes to Clarence G. Petersen for donating his valuable time to handling the daunting professional copy editing chores.

It is also important to single out those individuals who were instrumental at the very start and end of this project. In many ways, I must thank Dr. Jeanette Thomas of Western Illinois University for first inspiring me to publish this manual as a book; Jeanette's encouragement to teach a graduate course on animal training is what really kick-started this project. Finally, getting the book into print was made so much easier by the support, financial and otherwise, of the John G. Shedd Aquarium, especially Ted Beattie, president and CEO, for his leadership and vision, and most important Jan Powers, information management director, for pushing the project to completion.

I must also thank the countless colleagues who have shaped my understanding of operant conditioning and guided me throughout my career. It would take an entire chapter to list them all by name, but every coworker and fellow professional with whom I have dealt has played a part, large or small, in making me a better trainer. Certainly the staff of the Shedd Aquarium is owed the most sincere thanks of all. We are each influenced by our environment; I have spent the last decade working at the aquarium and nowhere have I experienced a better work place or a more dedicated staff than at the Shedd Aquarium. Finally, of course, I would have learned nothing and consequently written nothing if it had not been for the many animals that I have had the pleasure of knowing over the years. It is to each of them that I dedicate this book and owe the greatest amount of gratitude. Any errors that remain in the text rest entirely on my shoulders. – KTR.

Introduction 1

Using this Manual

Logical Flow of Information

This manual is organized from the simplest and most basic concepts in animal training to the most complex and advanced. It follows the sequence of training that we use in teaching the animal care staff at the John G. Shedd Aquarium. Many of the theories and principles described will overlap. In those cases, concepts are grouped into the earliest section in which that concept might need to be used by a trainer. In an effort to reduce redundancy, if a topic or concept is pertinent to more than one section, it will be explained only in the section where its use is most critical. All other references to the topic will refer to the section where the detailed information is first presented.

Small Manageable Pieces

Like the animals we are learning to train, we learn best in small increments. Therefore, each subject in this manual is presented in small, easily digestible pieces. Each section (in many cases each paragraph) is given a title so that you will know what to expect in the section that follows. This should also provide a quick reference for trying to locate information at a later date. This manual is not complete in itself. It was originally designed for our marine mammal training staff and was meant to be integrated with seminars, practice sessions, demonstrations, and other texts. Training is a dynamic process that must be practiced constantly; reading one book will not make anyone a good trainer. However, this manual is intended to be a reference for the beginner as well as the experienced trainer; it is assumed that this will not be the reader's only source of information or guidance.

Don't Shoot the Dog

One of the best books ever written about positive reinforcement and training is Karen Pryor's *Don't Shoot the Dog*, first published in 1984. This book is required reading for the marine mammal staff at the Shedd Aquarium and will be referenced throughout this manual. Karen's writing is fun to read and easy to understand. Her book is designed for anyone who wants to learn to use positive reinforcement techniques effectively, on animals or people. Because the entire book is loaded with useful information, it will be referenced throughout the manual simply as (*DOG*). For example, if I wanted you to read the foreword to her book to understand her reasons for writing it, I would end the sentence with this reference: (*DOG*, pp. ix - xv). In the summer of 1999, Karen revised and updated her book, so all page references correspond to those of the revised edition. For those of you with the original version of *Don't Shoot the Dog*, chapter subjects remain the same. But Karen has rewritten significant portions of the text, so I highly recommend the newer edition. It's hard to believe that she could make such a valuable resource even better! The 1999 edition is technically more accurate, while retaining her lively writing style and excellent real life examples. You will likely want to read the book many times and refer to it often throughout your training career; I know I do.

Speaking of Karen Pryor, another excellent resource is her 1975 book *Lads Before the Wind*, which chronicles her experiences at Sea Life Park in Hawaii. She was in charge of the marine mammal training program when the park opened in the early 1960s. Though she had no formal training then, Karen built a program that paved the way for much of her later writing about the use of positive reinforcement. *Lads Before the Wind* is fun and full of great anecdotal information about training techniques and their application.

Other References
At the end of each chapter, I have included a selection of articles from many excellent books and other professional training sources, both technical and popular. Young trainers sometimes find it a challenge to apply the information from these varied sources to specific training situations. Here, articles have been selected that describe a specific technique, term, concept, or problem. I do not necessarily agree with every technique or description that is included, but in every case I believe important points are made. Whenever I refer to an article that is included in the manual, I will direct the reader to it by its title and indicate the page number where that article will be found.

Each chapter ends with articles that pertain to the subjects described and referenced in that particular chapter. I have introduced each article with an introductory comment that indicates why I believe the article is noteworthy. You will note that certain resources are used frequently; what follows is a description of the primary sources:

IMATA – The International Marine Animal Trainers Association is an organization of professional trainers. Its members are leaders in animal training techniques and their application. The organization publishes a variety of materials that are referenced throughout the manual.

Conference Proceedings – Each year IMATA holds a conference at which trainers from all over the world share training experiences. Many papers from these conferences are used in this manual.

Trainer's Forum – This is a regular question and answer column that appears in IMATA's quarterly magazine *Soundings*. Readers submit questions seeking advice on training specific behaviors or solving particular problems. What I like best about this column is the opportunity it offers to read responses (sometimes contradictory) from a variety of trainers and facilities. I encourage you to read all the entries and compare the similarities and differences among training programs.

Feature Articles – *Soundings* often features training articles written by IMATA members. These articles often contain interesting and valuable training information.

Marine Mammals: Public Display and Research – This is a relatively new peer-refereed journal that IMATA publishes.

AZA Conference Proceedings – The American Zoo and Aquarium Association is a professional organization of zoological institutions. Their annual conferences focus on all aspects of zoo management and animal care. Although training is not the primary focus of this organization, there are often articles about the application of training in a zoological environment.

Karen Pryor's book *On Behavior* – In addition to *Don't Shoot the Dog*, Karen has written countless articles about training. *On Behavior* is a collection of some of her best writing about behavior.

Gary Wilke's book *A Behavior Sampler* – Gary is an award-winning syndicated pet columnist who uses principles of operant conditioning to explain pet behavior and training. *A Behavior Sampler* is a collection of his articles, and I highly recommend reading the entire book. His short and often humorous articles are fun to read and they offer sound behavioral advice.

ABA – The Association for Behavior Analysis is devoted to the use of behavioral analysis in many applied settings. The majority of its books and articles are about the use of behavior analysis to study and teach humans. But the organization has a special interest group devoted to applications of behavioral analysis to animals.

Theory vs. Application

These two terms are used throughout the manual; while they work hand in hand, it is important to understand the difference between theory and application. For our purposes theory includes operant principles and concepts, while application refers to the techniques and use of those principles.

Experience is the Best Teacher

It is important to point out that no matter how well you understand the concepts in this manual, knowledge alone will not make you a trainer. Understanding a technique does not mean you will be able to apply it properly. Many years of practice are usually needed before a trainer is considered skilled. Training is such a dynamic process that good trainers will finally learn by doing. What's more, they will never know it all, but will continue growing by adding to their training knowledge and experience.

History of Animal Training

Menageries

Humans have interacted with animals at least as far back as we have historical records. In fact, evidence suggests that people have always been fascinated with animals of all types. Ancient kings and pharaohs maintained large menageries as a sign of their wealth and power. These menageries, while a far cry from modern zoos, were early examples of maintaining and caring for wildlife.

Domestication

Over time, as many animals were bred for food and work, a process of domestication took place. Animals specifically and selectively bred for desirable traits (tractability, speed, strength, etc.) over time go through an evolutionary process until they're said to be domesticated. Through this interaction, animals invariably become comfortable in the presence of humans, and it is natural that people would seek ways of interacting more closely with these animals.

Work Animals

For centuries humans have trained animals to assist them in their day-to-day lives. Dogs were trained for hunting prey or herding livestock. Horses, camels, and oxen were trained for riding and hauling. Birds were trained as messengers. The variety and scope of animal training to assist humans has been limited only by the imagination of the people doing the training. It has been said that a talented trainer can train any animal to do anything that the animal is mentally and physically capable of doing. Gary Wilkes describes a few of the more modern and unusual applications of animal training in *Amazing Feats of Animal Learning*, on page 17.

Performers

There is some indication that animals have been used to entertain people almost as long as they have been trained as work animals. Circuses, fairs, and carnivals have used animal performers for centuries. The demand for more entertaining and unique "tricks" eventually elevated the skill level of those doing the training. But as new training techniques were developed, they remained closely guarded secrets. Trainers did not want their rivals to learn how to train "trademark" behaviors. This is still true in some corners of the circus world.

Meanwhile, zoos were becoming increasingly popular. They had become much more of a scientific enterprise than in their earliest days, but they did little in the way of formal training. Dolphins and whales were the animals that would eventually begin to bridge the gap between performance and science. Modern training of dolphins began only in the late 1940s. But in a relatively short time, marine mammal trainers were breaking new ground in exotic animal training. The very nature of dolphins, unable to be leashed or forced to perform, led to many innovative training techniques.

Research

The ability to train these huge, wild, aquatic mammals without coercion or force started a training revolution. The animals were even trained to cooperate in their own care. They could also be trained to cooperate in research projects that would help people to understand more about their physiology, anatomy, and natural behavior. In essence, marine mammal training played an important role in discovering a new way to manage zoological collections by teaching animals to take part in their own care. This change did not come about overnight. In fact, it has been a slow process that continues to evolve.

Animal Welfare

Perhaps one of the most important aspects of animal training is its ability to provide for the animals' overall physical and mental welfare. We will discuss the benefits of a successful training program in later sections. However, it is important to point out that not everyone understands or recognizes that training is beneficial to animal care. You will read many articles in this manual about the introduction of training to the zoological community.

One of my favorite stories about the importance of training is a study commissioned by one of the humane societies in London in the 1970s.

The society was determined to shut down the traveling circuses of England, asserting that training "demeaned" the animals. The society thus commissioned a group of scientists from Cambridge University to do a comparative study of animals in zoos and in circuses. They were hoping to show that the zoo animals were healthier specimens than those in the circuses. When the study was complete, it concluded that the circus animals were far healthier in every respect. Circus animals were of a better weight and more physically fit than most of their zoo counterparts; they were bright-eyed and alert; and they exhibited little to no stereotypical behavior. (I will digress to say that I have no idea about the conditions of traveling circuses in England at the time. Perhaps they deserved to be shut down, but certainly not because they trained their animals; training would be one of the best things that circuses could do for their collections). The university study specifically mentioned the training of the animals to be the single most important aspect in improving the condition of the animals. The humane society chose not to publish the study.

There is no doubt that in today's zoological environment training has evolved from the animals' being taught to perform solely for entertainment to the animals' being trained to cooperate in their own care. This transition was not always easy or planned, but in the end it has proven beneficial to the animals. Training today is the cornerstone of a good animal care program.

Modern Training

Still, our knowledge and understanding of animal training is in its infancy. What we know today will continue to expand as we begin to learn more about how and why animals behave the way they do. The marine mammal training community is often considered the leader in progressive animal training techniques. Operant conditioning techniques were not discovered or first defined by marine mammal trainers, however. That was done by the behavioral psychologist B.F. Skinner in the 1930's. Marine mammal trainers were not even the first to apply the techniques accurately to animal training. But marine mammal trainers were the first to put the techniques to widespread use in the zoological community. In fact, many of these techniques are not in widespread use in society as a whole, Ted Turner comments on this in his article *Letting Go of Our Humanism*, on page 18.

What is Training?

There probably are as many ways to train an animal as there are trainers attempting the task. What makes our job even more confusing is that there are many correct ways to go about teaching an animal a behavior. Likewise, there are numerous wrong ways and mistakes that can be made. It is important that trainers realize that there are many pitfalls that may lie in the way of successful training. Recognizing those pitfalls is a key to being a good trainer. Throughout this manual you will find suggestions that will help you to avoid them.

Definition of Training

Before we go any farther, we should define the word *training*. Everybody's definition will certainly be different. In fact, much of what you'll be reading in this manual represents just one way of looking at the process we call training — just one philosophy. As a trainer or behaviorist, you will gain many insights through your own experiences and develop your own philosophy. Ultimately, it is through the combined experiences and philosophies of many trainers that new ideas are formed and take hold. In the long run, this is in the best interest of the animals under our care.

So what is training? Simply put, training is teaching. Certainly many books on training, psychology, operant conditioning, or behavioral analysis will give you a more complex definition. But those definitions, while technically accurate, can often lead us astray of our real goal: animal care. Later, we will explore more detailed definitions and discuss conditioning theory. However, we should never lose sight of the simple one-word definition: training is *TEACHING*.

We are teaching animals to live in their new environment. It is not unlike children in school, who are taught and/or trained to live in the real world. In the zoo or aquarium, we are the animals' teachers, parents, doctors. Our animals look to us for many of their needs and we must learn how to provide them. One way to do that is to teach the animals to cooperate in that process.

Note: There are those who would argue with this definition of training, suggesting that conditioning and teaching are quite different. The belief is that teaching implies certain cognitive processes that may not always be present when an organism is conditioned. Although this argument may be true, and even technically accurate, it makes the training process appear cold and mechanical. The term teaching implies shared experiences and goals between trainer and animal. This is a distinction that I believe is important, even fundamental, to the attitude trainers should bring to the process.

Why We Train

As teachers or trainers, we must know why we are training. There must be a purpose behind what we do – and let's hope none of us have chosen to train animals without knowing why we do it. Often, if a visitor is asked, "Why do you suppose they train dolphins?" The normal reply is frequently, "So they can jump through hoops and do shows!" Nothing could be, or should be, farther from the truth. Certainly, if an animal is going to perform it must be trained, but that should not be the main reason for establishing a good training program.

Far more important reasons for training are those that directly benefit the animal being trained. Reasons that serve other functions, such as benefiting the species and advancing our own knowledge are important, too, but not the principle reason for training. What is crucial is that trainers have their priorities straight. As long as our priorities are in order, we can always be sure of providing our animals with the best care possible.

Primary Reasons for Training

Let's first examine the primary reasons for training. They fall into three categories:
- Physical exercise
- Mental stimulation
- Cooperative behavior

These three objectives are so important to an animal's well-being that it is hard to believe that some zoos have no behavioral enrichment programs for their animals. Training is a means of providing an animal with a more fulfilling life. Those of us who work as animal behaviorists, don't look at training as a luxury or fringe benefit; it is an essential part of an animal's life.

Physical Exercise – When we build an exhibit, we build it with an animal's needs in mind. But no matter how large the exhibit, it will never be the Pacific Ocean, the African Savannah, or the Brazilian rain forest. It isn't meant to be. In the wild, when an animal travels great distances, it is usually in search of food, a better climate, or a means to avoid predators. Animals do not face these problems in the protected care of an aquarium or zoo. For this reason, we must find other ways of providing our animals with exercise. Training gives us a means to provide needed exercise in an enriching and challenging way. We will discuss this in more detail throughout the manual.

Mental Stimulation – As described in the preceding paragraph, animals in nature face a good many problems. Life in the wild is not easy. In eliminating many of the worries and problems that otherwise would face our animals, we leave them free to occupy their time in other ways. As trainers, we must continually provide new and interesting stimulation to their environment and to their lives. Training itself provides our animals with challenges. The imaginative trainer can enhance an animal's life in ways that we will explore throughout this manual.

Cooperative Behavior – Many trainers will refer to cooperative behaviors as "husbandry behaviors," "medical behaviors," or "veterinary procedures." However, the term *cooperative behavior* itself, though less specific, is more to the point. To provide our animals with the best care possible, we must be able to provide medical care, move them from place to place, or separate them when necessary. If they are taught how to give blood or how to move from one enclosure to another, life is easier for both animal and trainer. Teaching cooperative behavior is an essential component of good animal care. Chapter 6 is devoted to the topic of husbandry and other cooperative behaviors.

Secondary Reasons

What about secondary reasons for training? Where do they fit into the program? Secondary reasons are usually the ones that are more obvious to the public: entertainment, education, research, work.

Please don't confuse these secondary reasons for training with the reasons for public display. Many of the things that come out of training further the very real and important goals that zoos and aquariums have set out to accomplish. The display of animals to the public educates visitors about animals they seldom, if ever, get to see. It provides visitors with an awareness of animals and gives us a unique opportunity to teach them about the plight these animals face in the wild. Ultimately, this will aid in conservation efforts going on around the world. These issues are not within the scope of this manual but are important to understand. As trainers, we must be intimately aware of the reasons our animals are in our care. We must be equally aware of our role as animal care specialists, and of the importance of putting an animal's individual needs above all else. It is for that reason that we must understand the difference between primary and secondary reasons for training.

Entertainment and Education – The public probably perceives entertainment as one of the main reasons we train animals. Some people no doubt think the only reason we train animals is so they can perform in a show – and shows, as we've said, certainly serve a valuable purpose. Today we know that training serves a much greater purpose than simply teaching animals a few "tricks." So even though public presentations are a secondary reason for training that does not diminish the important role engaging presentations play in educating the public.

Research – The very term often conjures up images of laboratory animals being dissected for scientific study. However, some of the best research is observational or behavioral and not invasive at all. In fact, much of what we know today about many animals has come from what we have learned by observing and training them in zoos and aquariums. Training provides us with a means of teaching the animals to cooperate in research projects that can ultimately help their species, their conservation, and their care.

Other Reasons – Obviously, this category covers any other reasons you may think of for training an animal. In some cases, we train animals to help us or to work for us as with guide dogs for the disabled, or as plow horses, etc. Animals have also been trained to participate in sporting events, such as horse and dog racing. Most of these applications have been applied primarily to domestic animals.

Although many of the other reasons for training have their purposes, too, they will not be the focus of this manual. (Several good books are listed in the bibliography that can tell you more about training animals for these other purposes).

Understanding the Reasons

The list of types and reasons for training could go on and on. As trainers, we must simply keep in mind what we're here for, what is in the best interest of the animals under our care. Keeping in mind the primary reasons for training can make those priorities clearer.

The Complete Professional

It is probably evident by now that being a trainer is a complex job. If you're going to succeed in teaching your animals to live in a zoological environment, they must be happy, healthy animals. A trainer must know much more than just behavioral theory. To be a good trainer you must understand the natural history and biology of the animals. You must also have an understanding of veterinary care, nutritional and dietary needs, water quality, and all other aspects of animal care. You are a keeper, a biologist, a mammalogist, an ethologist, and much more. In essence, a trainer must be a complete animal care professional.

How We Train (A Simplified Version)

Before we jump headlong into a detailed account of training methods, terms, and theories, perhaps it would be wise to pause for a brief and simple overview of training. In fact, this section will deliberately be over-simplified. It is intended to give a general overview in layman's language of training a wild animal, in this case, a dolphin. This may be the best approach simply because newcomers bring to their own training a variety of talents, backgrounds, and experiences with animals. For the beginner, this section will serve as a good introduction to the basics of how we train animals. For the more experienced trainer, it may serve as a narrative to help you describe training to the public. Since this section is designed for the novice, many important training steps will be skipped, and terminology will be kept simple and in some cases overly anthropomorphic.

Learning About the Animal

So, how does one begin to train an animal like a dolphin? To start, we must know as much about our animals as possible. Not only must we

understand its individual characteristics, its likes and dislikes, but we must also be knowledgeable about the animal's natural history and biology. We should constantly ask ourselves questions about each animal under our care:
- Where does it normally live?
- What is its social structure like?
- What does it eat?
- What animals does it encounter in the wild and how do they interact?
- What other factors are important to its life?

The importance of these and similar questions will be the subject of chapter 2, "Knowing the Animal." This information will prove invaluable to you as you begin to interact with your animals.

Operant Conditioning

The techniques we use to train our animals have a foundation in the science of psychology and behavior analysis. The many complex principles that we use to teach the animals are referred to as operant conditioning. That will be defined and described in chapter 4, "Basic Operant Conditioning."

Gaining the Animal's Trust

The first step to positive interaction with a dolphin is to gain the animal's trust. This can be accomplished through the daily interactions of feeding, playing with, and caring for the animal. Like first impressions, the first steps toward establishing that trust can be of critical importance. Animals are very sensitive and perceptive creatures, and trust is a two-way street. You must trust that they will not bite you, just as they must trust that you won't hurt them. This trust will build over time as you interact with the animal.

Rules of the Game

Once trust has been established, you can begin to teach the dolphin about the tools of training and the rules of the game. At the Shedd Aquarium we like to think of training as a game. By looking at it from that perspective, it is easy to remember that for training to succeed it should be fun. Therefore, we must find some way of letting the dolphin know that it is doing well, or playing the game correctly. We do that through the use of a whistle. Each time we blow the whistle, it is our way of saying "Good" or "You did well" or "That was excellent."

Positive Reinforcement

But how does the animal know that the whistle means "Good"? We teach it the meaning of the whistle in the early phases of training by pairing the whistle with something the animal likes, such as food. This is the start of positive reinforcement training – that is, each time we blow the whistle, we immediately follow the sound of the whistle by giving the animal a fish. Because we know that dolphins like fish, we call the fish a primary reinforcer. As we get to know this dolphin better, we learn about other things that it seems to like and enjoy. Many dolphins like being rubbed on the back or belly; they sometimes like their tongue scratched, or they enjoy playing with a toy. These can be used as reinforcers, too, and they are referred to as secondary reinforcers.

Bridging

Each time you blow a whistle, follow it immediately with a positive reinforcer. Before too long, the animal will realize that every time it hears the whistle, something good is going to happen! We call this whistle a bridging stimulus, or simply a bridge. The reason for the term "bridge" will be explained later. The choice of a whistle as a bridge is somewhat arbitrary. Anything that the animal can recognize with consistency can be used as a bridge to let the animal know it has done well. We use a whistle because it can be blown with consistency by each trainer and its sound carries well under water.

Behaviors Not Tricks

Once you are certain that the dolphin understands the meaning of the whistle, you can begin teaching a variety of behaviors. You'll notice that we use the term *behavior* instead of *trick*. A trick is something a magician does with a deck of cards. There is really nothing magical about the things we train dolphins to do. Most trained behaviors are extensions of natural behaviors. When we see a person stand, talk, walk, or run, we would not say, "Hey! That was a neat trick!" Of course not, those are all things we do quite naturally. Likewise, when dolphins jump, spin, breach, lob their tail, or make noise, they, too, are behaving naturally.

Scanning

One way to begin teaching a dolphin to exhibit natural behaviors on cue is simply to sit back and watch the dolphin play, watching it naturally jump, spin, and flip. We call this "scanning for behavior" or "capturing behavior." As you watch the animal play, you will see it exhibit behavior that you would like it to perform on cue. If you would like the animal to jump, for example, each time the animal leaps into the air, blow the whistle. Since the animal has learned that the whistle means "good," it will likely swim over for a fish, its reinforcer. At first, the animal may not realize that the whistle was blown because it was jumping. But if the dolphin jumps with any regularity, it will soon associate the whistle with jumping if you consistently blow the whistle each time it jumps. Before long, the dolphin will start jumping more and more, hoping to hear the whistle.

How Fast Can the Dolphin Learn?
How long does this learning process usually take? That all depends on the dolphin. If the dolphin is young and new to the training game, it could take a long time. On the other hand, if the animal is more experienced and knows the "rules of the game," it is possible that it might make the connection between its behavior and the whistle almost immediately. In either case, the timing of the whistle can be critical. By bridging at the precise moment, you are telling the dolphin exactly what you want it to do.

Stimulus Control
By pairing the behavior with some sort of audible, visual, or tactile cue, the animal will begin to associate the cue with that specific behavior. Once the animal understands that the cue means "jump," you only reinforce the dolphin's jumping if the cue has been given first. This is known as bringing the behavior under stimulus control. The choice of a cue, whether it be visual, audible, or tactile, can be somewhat arbitrary. The most important thing is that you choose a cue that you can re-create consistently and that the animal will be able to differentiate from other cues.

Targeting
Scanning can be fun and effective, but it can take a very long time. And because there are many behaviors that the animal may not offer voluntarily, we often invent games to encourage new behavior. One of the most useful games is one we call "targeting." Targeting means teaching an animal to touch some part of its body to another object. One example would be to teach the dolphin to touch its rostrum to our hand. The simplest way to teach targeting is for you to do the targeting first. Reach down and touch the dolphin's rostrum with your hand. As you touch the dolphin, blow the whistle, then reinforce. After repeating this action several times, the dolphin becomes aware that each time you touch its rostrum, it hears the whistle. When you are relatively certain the dolphin understands that concept, reach down, but stop your hand an inch away from its rostrum. When the dolphin realizes that you are not going to touch its rostrum, it will usually reach up and touch your hand itself. When that happens, you are ready to move on.

Successive Approximations

Now that the dolphin is initiating the touching, or "targeting," itself, you have the basis for training many other behaviors. The target, in this case your hand, has become a valuable training tool. You can use the target to guide the dolphin into many diverse behaviors. For example, once the dolphin is touching your hand reliably, you can begin to move your hand to various positions around the animal's head. You can begin to slowly raise your hand higher. You can also place a ball or buoy in your hand to get the dolphin used to targeting on other objects. Then, by attaching the buoy to a long pole, you can guide the dolphin, step by step, higher into the air. These steps are called successive approximations. Eventually, as you raise the target high out of the water, the dolphin will begin to jump in order to touch the buoy. Through creative use of buoy movement, you can guide the dolphin into even more leaps, jumps, or flips.

Being Creative

Targeting can be done with any part of the dolphin's body, and the target may be any object or prop. With a little imagination on the part of the trainer and the dolphin, the possibilities are endless. Training is a very dynamic process. It is not a one-way activity. As a trainer, you must be acutely aware of your animal's attitude toward training. Perhaps one of the most important keys to successful training is making it fun for the dolphin and for you. Never allow a training session to go on too long, or get boring. If your animal is having fun, it will look forward to each session.

Summary

In a nutshell, that's how training is done. The process, however, is considerably more complex. The differing personalities of each animal and each trainer make training even more complex – an inexact discipline at best. There are many good rules that help make training easier. Applying the rules will vary from one species to another, but the basic operant conditioning concepts are the same whether you are training your dog at home, a dolphin in the aquarium, a tiger in the zoo, or even a child in school. As soon as you learn the rules, you'll learn that there are numerous exceptions. Training is certainly challenging and fun but most important, training is a way of enhancing the quality of life for each of the animals under your care.

A Behavior Sampler by Gary Wilkes

Here is a brief look at some unusual ways that animals have been trained to help humans. This article demonstrates that with a little imagination you can train almost anything.

Amazing Feats of Animal Learning

by Gary Wilkes

During the Gulf War in Iraq, news programs flooded viewers with videotape of hi-tech "smart bombs" that unerringly hit their targets. It might surprise you to know that during World War II, a group of scientists invented the first "smart bomb," that could guide itself to the target. Over 50 years ago, behavioral scientists developed a bomb that had the "inhuman" accuracy of over 90%. This skill level was 30% better than the best bombardiers had achieved. The generals who were shown the "smart bomb" were fascinated by it, until they learned its secret. Inside the bomb were three pigeons trained to peck at keys that could change the bomb's course. The generals were afraid to develop the bomb because they believed that the public might assume that the pigeons were not the only "bird brains" connected with such a venture.

Although this "smart bomb" project was judged to be a wacky idea, the truth is that it probably would have worked. When humans combine good training techniques with animal "know-how," many amazing things can be accomplished. A variation of the pigeon bomb is used in rescue attempts at sea. The method utilizes a bird to spot the yellow life vests of pilots who have been lost at sea. This bird sits perched in a small observation window on a naval airplane. When the bird spots something yellow, it pecks a key to alert the crew. Pigeons can see yellow at distances far beyond the range of the human eye.

Pigeons are not the only animals that have been taught to do unusual things. Recent developments in arson investigation include dogs that sniff out the burned remains of flammable substances. The dogs allow investigators to quickly pinpoint the focus of an investigation and save hundreds of man-hours. Other novel uses for canine noses include termite-sniffing dogs and U.S. Customs Service dogs that can detect contraband fruit, vegetables and plants.

Another unusual animal task is the practice of using dolphins and seals to find objects underwater. Free-swimming marine mammals can identify objects at depths of over 800 feet. Recent advances in this behavioral technology allow dolphins to be fitted with miniature video cameras that allow humans on the surface to see exactly what the animal sees. In a single day, seals and dolphins can cover an area that would require weeks of searching by human divers.

This cooperative nature of the human/animal bond is not exclusively established by the human partner. Small groups of dolphins along the Atlantic coast of Brazil herd fish into the waiting nets of fishermen. The fishermen do not deliberately reinforce the dolphin's behavior, yet this phenomenon has been observed for over 100 years. It is possible that the dolphins instigated this relationship. Several generations of dolphins and fishermen have each passed the behavior along to their young.

Developing new roles for animals in human society is not without controversy. In Australia, pigeons were taught to peck a key to reject defective parts on a production line. This project was developed as a way to relieve human workers from the tedium of the job. The project was stopped by protesters who said that reinforcing birds to do such a tedious task was inhumane. The result was that humans were rehired to take over the "inhumane" work.

A group of trainers working for the government developed a crow that could follow a red laser dot and carry a miniature camera to photograph whatever was there. The animal was then recalled with a blue recall beacon, so that the bird and film could be recovered. In a similar project, a bird was taught to wear a harness that held a tiny microphone and transmitter. The red laser spot would be aimed at a window ledge near someone who was being watched. The bird would fly to the spot and then pull a retaining pin that dropped the transmitter on the ledge. The suspect could be "bugged" in almost any location and few people would suspect a crow of being a spy.

As modern training techniques create more ingenious animal skills, our social contact with animals will increase. It is no longer remarkable to see animal-assisted therapy in hospitals or service dogs helping their masters in public. This development can both enhance our lives as well as give new meaning to everyday occurrences. For instance, the next time someone says, "a little bird told me," it just could be the truth.

VOL 23, NO 3, 1998. The following article was written as a "President's Corner," a regular feature of IMATA's magazine *Soundings*. Ted Turner, president of IMATA in 1998, wrote this very perceptive article about the positive nature of our methods of animal training as contrasted by the more negative ways we have been brought up to deal with human behavior. The article goes to the very heart of what makes positive reinforcement such a special and effective tool; it is really too bad that more people don't use these tools in their interactions with each other. I have included it in the book's introduction, because Ted writes so well about the importance of our profession and our training techniques.

Letting Go of Our Humanism

by Ted Turner

As young children, we are introduced to the dichotomy of learning. The contrast of doing something "right" versus doing something "wrong" is often dramatically represented to us by those that want us to learn this difference; our teachers, our parents, our peers. As we begin to assimilate this information, we attempt to practice and replicate these skills we've observed and experienced repeatedly. As adults, we operate on our environment by applying learning principles that bring attention and focus to incorrect, inappropriate, or anti-social actions and behaviors. We develop a system of policies, rules, and laws that provide a punishing consequence for those whose behavior patterns do not comply. This, we believe, will stop the "incorrect" and "inappropriate" from occurring.

We believe this principle to be true and this gives us comfort and security. Because of the enormity of the task, little time is left to develop a similar system of incentives, motivators, and rewards. As we mature, we remain ever vigilant and become exceedingly skilled at finding and pointing out the "wrong." These skills are perfected in some workplaces, and the style of management that results is one replete with tension and stress as attempts to maintain "compliance" become the driving focus, while at the same time, an increasing number of behavior problems build. More rules, policies, and discipline are employed ... the cycle continues.

For those of us lucky enough to get out of the traditional workforce and into the animal field, we experience an over-whelming sense of satisfaction and spend countless hours interacting with our animals. We find that animals, like humans, also behave in the same dichotomous pattern. That most express themselves in behaviors that appear appropriate for a particular species. Yet, we also observe some "inappropriate" behaviors as well. This disturbs us greatly and we often employ our ingrained, humanistic approach for the purpose of suppressing and controlling these inappropriate, and sometimes destructive, behavior patterns. What else can we do?

The marine mammal training field has been an enigma to many other fields of animal training. The principles employed by most marine mammal behaviorists have never complied with the traditional use of discipline. In fact, the lack of punishment and discipline has drawn criticism in the past. Yet many cannot explain the enormous success the marine mammal field has experienced in all aspects of behavior. From formal shows to husbandry, from birth and breeding to intimate guests encounters, the marine mammal trainer continues to set the standard for a positive, enriching, and effective animal training program. Our success is easily explained; we focus on the positive, pure and simple. We establish programs that diversify reinforcement. We make learning fun for our animals and remove focus on the "incorrect." When asked, "What do you do when an animal does something wrong?" most of us answer simply, "Nothing." This usually causes the person asking the question great anxiety (much to our delight!), because we are often misunderstood.

But our positive programs are being studied, replicated, and utilized by all forms of animal training with all species of animals. Our trainers are involved with every type of animal known and these positive principles continue to be most effective ways of decreasing inappropriate behavior while, at the same time, increasing more appropriate behavior. We have overcome our humanistic habits that "catch them doing something wrong" and instead we "catch them doing something right." We've broken the humanistic cycle to the benefit of our animals. A difficult thing to overcome for most of us and impossible to some of us. Congratulations IMATA, you're a special group of trainers!

Knowing the Animal 2

While the subject of this chapter is one of the most critical in providing good animal care, most of the principles discussed in this chapter are a part of most zoo or aquarium husbandry protocols. At Shedd Aquarium, for example, we rely on our *Husbandry and Daily Procedure Manual*. The concepts are presented briefly here because they are an integral part of any successful training program. In fact, they must be in place before training can even begin.

Understanding the Species

Before you attempt to train an animal, you should know as much as possible about the natural history, anatomy and physiology of the species. The more you know about its natural habitat, social structure, feeding habits, and natural behavior, the better equipped you'll be to provide the animal with a safe and comfortable environment. As elementary as it may seem, once you understand that a dog naturally likes to dig and most birds like to fly, the less likely you will be to waste your time trying to teach your dog to fly. Each species has specific behaviors that come more naturally to them than others. Each of these behavioral differences is based on their anatomy, physiology, or natural history. It requires a deep understanding of the differences between two breeds of dog or two species of dolphin to recognize differences more subtle than the fact that dogs don't fly. Here are a few basic examples:

Pinnipeds
Seals are widely thought of as popular performing animals in zoos and in some circuses. However, the animal normally used and referred to as a seal is actually a sea lion. These two animals, although closely related, are anatomically very different, and many of their natural behaviors are distinctly different, too. Without understanding such basics you can easily frustrate yourself and your animal, as demonstrated in *Are We Talking Seals or Sea Lions?* (T. Forum, 1989), on page 39.

Beluga Whales
Due to their natural swimming speed and size, beluga whales are not acrobatic animals like many of the dolphin species. It is not impossible to teach them to leap and flip, but they will never attain the height nor demonstrate the energy of a small dolphin. If you are not aware of these basic facts, you could waste valuable training time trying to teach a beluga to do a difficult or impossible task.

Otters

River otters are energetic and highly trainable animals. Just like dolphins and sea lions they can be taught to follow and touch a target with their nose. In fact, because they rely on their olfactory senses so heavily, it is natural for them to examine objects (such as a target) with their nose first. However, when we tried to introduce a target to our Alaskan sea otters, we found that their natural foraging and exploratory instincts caused them to use their paws first. It took much longer to teach them to touch a target with their nose; teaching them to touch a target with their paws was a cinch. Understanding the natural abilities and tendencies of a species will greatly improve a trainer's chances for success.

Specific Animal History & Behavior

Once you understand the species as a whole, you must then get to know the individual. It is not impossible to start training without specific individual histories, but it can certainly make life easier. Many teachers will often get to know the backgrounds of their students to help understand unusual behavior in class. With animals this information becomes so much more difficult, because you can't ask animals about their past and expect to get an answer. Even when teaching people, you can't always count on getting an honest or complete answer.

Acquisition

How, when, and from where an animal came is vital information to a trainer. It can help you to understand many aspects of the animal's behavior.

Born in the wild – Knowing at what age an animal was brought into a zoological setting can be important. The older it was, the more experiences it may have had that will affect your decision-making when it comes to breeding or to anticipating the animal's reaction to other species.

Born under human care – The details of an animal's birth and rearing when young are helpful throughout its life. For example, was the animal raised by its mother or was it hand-raised?

Rehabilitated animal – Any animal that has been stranded or rehabilitated, then brought under human care may have specific medical needs. The intensity of care during the rehabilitation process may dramatically affect its interactions with people. The same is true of pets that may have come from a shelter, which often suggests that the animal's history is not fully known.

Transfer from another facility – All of the above information and details of the animal's previous care and training are critical. You can never overestimate the importance of having as much information about an animal's past as possible.

Previous Human Interactions

Even if an animal has been in the same facility all its life, a good understanding and knowledge of its past training and care is extremely important. You cannot rely on generalized species information or recent memories of an individual trainer to help you understand all the things that an animal may need or experience. Here are two examples to illustrate this point:

Magellanic playtime - At some of the Sea World parks, the animal care staff will select a few recently hatched Magellanic penguins and hand-raise them. These young birds will invariably imprint on the staff and become easy to handle. The birds are used in many of Sea World's educational outreach programs. One member of Sea World's education staff visited Shedd Aquarium and was taken into our penguin exhibit for a visit. We introduced him to one of our rockhopper penguins, and as I started scratching the rockhopper on the neck, the Sea World visitor said, "Oh, I don't trust rockhoppers, they're so mean! I much prefer the Magellanics." As he said this he reached down to pet one of our Magellanic penguins. I screamed and stopped him just in time to keep him from losing a finger! Our Magellanic penguins were *not* hand-raised, and are quite aggressive, with very sharp beaks. Our rockhoppers, on the other hand, have been a part of our training program and are very gentle when touched. This is an example of generalizing about a species without knowing the individual animal's history.

Zsa Zsa the retired dolphin – An old, retired show dolphin at Marineworld of Texas named Zsa Zsa had not performed in years. To keep her occupied, young trainers were encouraged to play with her, providing her with as much enrichment as possible. Swimming with staff members seemed to be one of Zsa Zsa's favorite pastimes. Trainers always swam in full uniform (polo shirt and shorts), partly to comply with a strict dress code the park followed. One of the newer female trainers decided to engage in a swim session at a time when few park visitors were present. She removed her polo shirt, under which she wore a bikini top with string ties in the back. The new trainer was unaware that one of Zsa Zsa's old behaviors had been to seize a string or rope and continue pulling it until a release bell sounded. No sooner had the trainer entered the water than Zsa Zsa pulled and untied the young woman's bikini top, refusing to give it back until cued. To make matters worse, a group of young boys happened along and just stared at the topless trainer for several minutes before another staff member came along to render assistance. So knowing your animal's history can be very important (following park rules wouldn't hurt either).

Observations & Ethograms

Understanding the behavior of your animals can also come from systematic daily observations. A well developed, scientifically designed observation log known as an ethogram can give the trainer invaluable data about an animal's behavior. However, even informal observations can prove to be very helpful. An in-depth discussion of the importance of keen observation can be found in chapter 5, "Non-Formal Interactions."

Proper Diet & Nutrition

A Healthy Animal is a Happy Animal

It may not be possible to truly quantify the happiness of the animals under our care. But it's safe to say that an animal that is not eating properly will not stay healthy or happy for long. A key element to a successful training program is a healthy, well-fed animal. The idea that an animal must be hungry or food deprived to perform well is simply not true. Certainly an overweight and overfed animal may lack motivation, but an overweight animal is not healthy, either. When we eat too much, isn't it usually difficult to get ourselves motivated to do anything but take a nap? Many animals are the same way; it is the role of the animal care staff to provide a proper balance.

Base Diet

Most animals will have food prepared in excess of their base nutritional requirements. This is like dessert or the extra order of fries that we might eat from time to time. The base diet of an animal is carefully calculated to provide the proper total weight, calories, protein, and fat for each individual. It is important that animals receive their base diet daily. But because most animals are opportunistic feeders – they eat whenever food is available – the average daily intake over a month is more important to its health than that single day's intake. For that reason, fluctuations in each animal's daily consumption, within limits, is normal.

Varied Diet

All animals should be offered a varied diet that includes more than one type of food. This provides the animal with variety and a balanced diet and it assures that they are accustomed to eating more than one thing in the event that a particular food becomes unavailable.

Quality Diet

Within the marine mammal community we use only foods that are fit for human consumption. Our standards for freshness and quality are unequalled even by most restaurants. Before using any kind of food, it is standard practice to have it analyzed and tested for nutritional content, caloric value, protein, and other important dietary parameters.

Supplements

Because most animals in a zoological setting do not eat live food, vitamin supplements are often helpful. Live fish, for example, are often carriers of parasites that can be debilitating for many marine mammals; freezing fish right after it is caught kills most parasites. Any nutrients that might be lost in freezing and subsequent thawing can be replaced through vitamin supplements.

The Environment

The single most important and constant element in an animal's life is the environment in which it lives. An uncomfortable or unpleasant environment is not conducive to learning and training. More important, poor care of the animal's home is unhealthy.

Space

Creating enough space for all the animals you hope to house is a major consideration. The size and number of animals are important, as is consideration of future population growth. Knowledge of the movement in and use of the species' natural habitat is important, as well. Information from other facilities that have housed the species in question is also vital.

Not an exact replica of the wild – Sometimes people mistakenly believe that a zoo should try to replicate as many aspects of an animal's natural habitat as possible. Not only is that unrealistic, it is also unwise. Along with the beneficial elements of an animal's natural habitat come predators, pollution, and the need to search for food. The space needed for these endeavors does not always need to be replicated. Training is an important way to provide the mental stimulation and physical exercise an animal would normally get in the wild.

Understanding natural behavior – Just because an animal may swim thousands of miles in the wild, or live for a time in very deep water, does not always mean that those conditions are vital. For example, let's examine the beluga whales that spend the summer in the Churchill River in Manitoba, Canada. During the summer they will remain for months in the river, which in some areas is less than three feet deep. As the river freezes over in the winter, the belugas are forced to leave, not only to avoid getting trapped by the forming ice but also to follow the fish that are their food supply. In the aquarium, we often give the belugas access to any of our four cetacean habitats. They invariably choose the smaller, shallower pools, an indication that they do not need the great depth offered by our largest habitat.

Social Structure

An important element in determining habitat size and creating the right environment for any animal is determining its social needs. The training aspects of this topic will be covered in depth in chapter 7, "Social Animals." Consideration of the population size, breeding plans, sex ratio, and separation capabilities are important elements of the animal's environment.

Water Quality

For aquatic animals, healthy water quality is an essential component of their environment. The entire life-support system must be carefully designed and monitored. Critical elements that must be monitored several times daily include salinity, temperature, bacteria (coliforms), pH, and chemical additives (chlorine, ozone, copper, iron, silver, etc.). It is important that whatever is added to the water must be monitored regularly. The more delicate the needs of an animal, the more detailed the monitoring that must occur. Although water clarity is not always a health issue, it is certainly an aesthetic one. But murky water can be an indication of potential problems, as well as a detriment to observing and training animals.

Other Environmental Conditions
In addition to the water, the weather and all other ambient conditions must be considered, especially for land animals. Lighting can be a particularly important element of indoor habitats, but it is important to outdoor habitats as well. Protection from the elements must also be considered. If an animal needs shelter from the sun, wind, or rain, adequate cover should be available. Temperature considerations, too, are important, especially in locations that endure extreme conditions at certain times of the year.

Terrain & Foliage
The landscaping of the animal's habitat is important for all species, terrestrial, aquatic and avian, and is an important consideration in their care. Trees, bushes, dirt, sand, hills, valleys, and all other elements that go into making a habitat complete are more than just decorative. Each species has specific needs that can be addressed through habitat design.

Animal Care Staff Needs
Ideally, animal care personnel will be intimately involved in the design of an animal's home. Certainly the animal care staff will be the most familiar with their needs in caring for the animal each day. Even staff members working with animals in an old, established facility should be familiar with all these environmental needs. Trainers must be intimately familiar with the environmental factors that affect the animals they're teaching. Knowledge of a habitat's weaknesses and strengths will help you as a trainer in all your interactions with the animals.

Public Needs
In a zoological setting, exhibits are designed so the public can view the animals. Great care must be taken to ensure that the safety of the public and the animals is given serious attention. It is always important, for example, to give the animals a quiet space away from the public when they need it.

Regulations and the Law
The modern zoo employs animal care personnel who are committed to the animals' well being. Most zoos and aquariums have animal care and use committees who are responsible for overseeing animal activities and are good at self-regulation. On a larger scale, profes-

sional organizations such as the American Zoo and Aquarium Association (AZA) and the Alliance for Marine Mammal Parks and Aquariums set guidelines and standards that members are expected to follow. Finally, a number of government agencies have been established to regulate and monitor animal care. The Animal Welfare Act was enacted to provide guidelines for the care, keeping, and transportation of many species of wildlife. Other laws strictly govern minimum habitat size and other standards for the care of many species. For example, marine mammal facilities in the United States regularly undergo surprise inspections by the Animal and Plant Health Inspection Service (APHIS), a division of the Department of Agriculture (USDA). It is important to be familiar with all the laws and regulations that govern the care and housing of your animals.

Record Keeping

An area often overlooked in discussing important elements of training is a good record keeping system. Whether you're training your dog at home or a dolphin at the aquarium, conscientious record keeping will help you identify trends and keep track of the animals' progress in training. For a large staff working in a zoological environment, it is also important to keep records for communication and consistency. No two training programs maintain their records in quite the same way; however, they all have several elements in common. At Shedd Aquarium we keep more than 50 types of records. While that may seem excessive, it helps us to keep track of a large animal collection cared for by a large staff. What follows are some highlights of our most important records.

Non-Training Records
Trainers must be acutely aware of all aspects of their animals' lives. The more information that is available, the more tools you can use to solve problems and make sound decisions. A few examples of these critical non-training records include:

Environmental – The importance of the environment to an animal's well being was described previously. A trainer should be aware of changes in that environment and be conscious of trends or dramatic shifts in temperature, water quality, salinity, or any other factor that may affect the animals.

Beluga Rake Log
This log is maintained at Shedd Aquarium to monitor skin abrasions or lesions that are common with cetaceans. Many of these marks are teeth marks (rakes) from other animals. The rake log helps us monitor social aggression as well as follow the healing process.

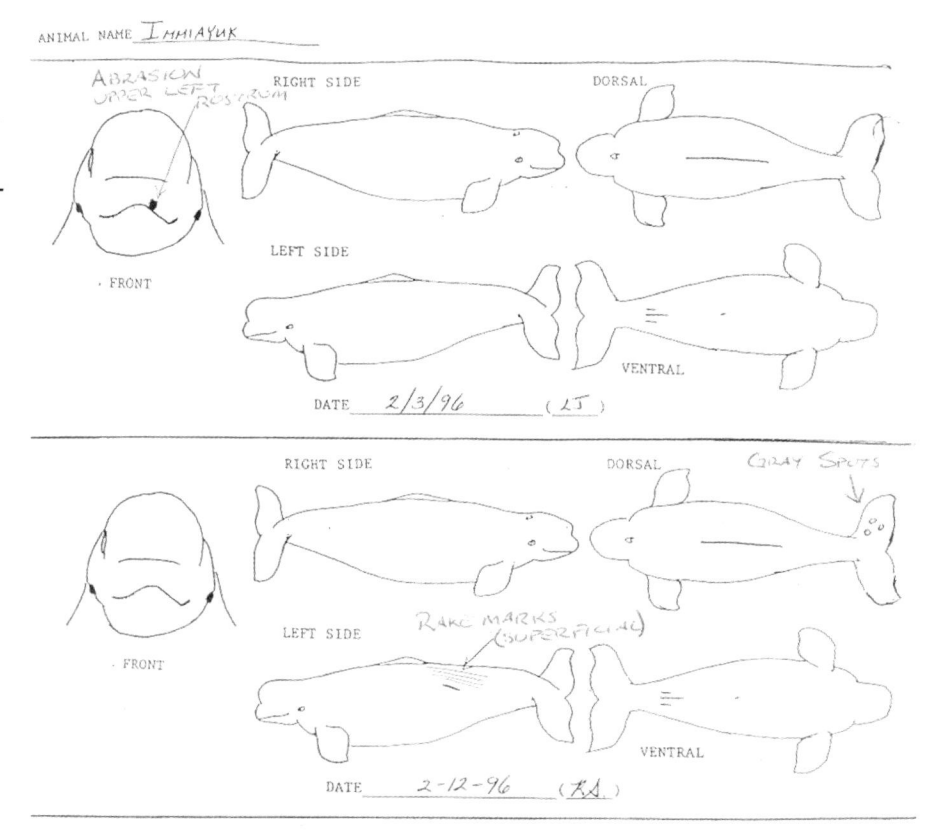

Medical – The veterinarian usually will keep detailed medical records, but it is always wise for trainers to keep their own medical logs. This is important in tracking trends that might affect an animal's behavior. Health records that a trainer might maintain include a weight log, a respiration log, a molting log, or a rake log (see sample above).

Observation – General observational records are helpful in monitoring animals when they're not in a training session. This will be discussed in more detail in chapter 5, "Non-Formal Interactions."

Training Records

There is much information that can be helpful in tracking animal behavior on a daily basis. The most important elements are described below. Included on the next page are samples of our weekly animal log and our behavioral log, which give a clearer understanding of each element.

Date – Obviously, you want to keep track of dates, so that you can monitor how long training projects have taken. Sometimes this will help you to identify seasonal trends or to pinpoint patterns of good or poor behavior.

Time – The time of day can be important in monitoring trends. Some animals work best at a certain time each day.

Who – The trainer should be identified. This is especially important when several trainers work with one animal.

Location – Even if there are few options available, it is good to keep track of where each session took place – which habitat, or even which part of each habitat. I have known pet owners who discovered that their dog did better at new training in very specific parts of a room, but the owners did not notice that until they began keeping precise records.

Weekly Animal Log
This is only a fragment of this record. It is packed full of information about every interaction in a given week. Special notations (*) indicate to look at the behavioral log or medical log for more detail

Behavioral Log
This type of log allows trainers to write as much information about a session as they need. The portion of the log to the left corresponds to the weekly log above.

Chapter 2 - Knowing the Animal

Behavioral rating – It is helpful to track behavior by developing an objective rating system. Assigning a ranking for a session will help to monitor trends in the animal's attentiveness and interest in sessions. While such ratings are subjective, it is good to try to set criteria that help to make the rating system standard among all trainers working together. (An example of one facility's ranking system is described on pages 331-332).

Comments – Finally, it is important to take the time to describe in detail the progress or setbacks encountered during a session. Any notes that might be relevant when looking back at the session in the future should be included. The comments should be clear enough that they will make sense the day after they were written as well as be clear to someone reading them ten years later.

Can you keep too many records? – It is doubtful that you could keep too many records. However, an important aspect of good record keeping is being able to access information when you need it. If there is an overwhelming amount of data, it must be organized so that it, too, can easily be referenced. In addition, if record keeping becomes too cumbersome it will become a nuisance to maintain and easier to gloss over or skip. Keeping it simple has its advantages.

Planning & Summary Records

One of the advantages to a systematic record keeping system is its use in planning ahead or looking back at the past. Two examples of these kinds of records are on the next two pages.

Pre-training plan/Goal sheet – Planning the steps you will take to train a behavior is an essential part of training. It serves as a road map (pre-training plan – page 33) that you will follow as you train a behavior. As with any journey, there may be detours along the way, but the map is your guide. As you change your plans, you can keep track of those changes on your goal sheet (see page 34). At the Shedd Aquarium we use the same form for our pre-training plan and our goal sheet. One is an overview of the proposed steps. The second is a realistic description of what you're planning and what you're actually doing.

Monthly diet summary – Assessing the overall progress of an animal is dependent on looking at trends. Health and nutrition are critical aspects of the general state of your animal. A monthly summary of your animal's daily diet trends can be very helpful (see example on page 35).

TRAINING/GOAL/BEHAVIOR SHEET   X PRE-TRAINING PLAN
                                 ___ GOAL SHEET
ANIMAL NAME Tique   ___ FINISHED BEHAVIOR SHEET
BEHAVIOR Pec Wave / Slap
CUE: _____

STEPS: (If used as a goal sheet, please start each step with the date)   LEAD | MGR | SUP

1. Begin with Tique in ultrasound position.
2. Touch my hand to top of her pec bridging as I touch.
3. Approximate hand away from pec so that she moves the pec to touch my hand
4. Once she is lifting pec as far as possible begin bridging movement of pec back to water
5. Alternate bridging for full lift with slapping the water, shaping for big movement + slap
6. Once lifting + slapping well, increase the number of lifts + slaps before bridging
7. As step #6 progresses, start holding the target hand forward toward head to encourage forward motion while slapping
8. Slowly fade hand away from her + incorporate it into SD.
9. When complete, approximate the opposite pec in the same manner.

Pre-Training Plan
This is a sample plan for training a pec wave with one of our dolphins at the Shedd Aquarium. Each time a new behavior is planned the trainer should develop a road map or a plan of the steps he or she hopes to follow. The trainer may change the plan as training proceeds, but the pre-training plan gets them started. As they actually train the behavior, trainers will fill out a goal sheet. An example of a goal sheet for the pec wave can be found on the next page.

The Computer Age

As we move into the 21st century, computers are having a dramatic impact on the way we maintain records. Computerized records have begun to revolutionize animal tracking systems. Trends in behavior or health can be spotted and tracked automatically; cross-referencing of data is easier; and historical records can be available at the touch of a button. Pictures, video, and sound can be incorporated, and future applications will be limited only by the imagination. Although several marine mammal facilities are tracking animal behavior by

Goal Sheet
This is page one of the goal sheet that was used to actually train the behavior outlined in the pre-training plan on the previous page. As you will note, the pre-training plan is only used as a guide by the trainer. The goal sheet, on the other hand, is filled out during each step of the training. It allows the trainer to plan out each approximation. Later, when the behavior is complete there will be an accurate record of all the steps, progress, and set-backs for each behavior trained.

```
TRAINING/GOAL/BEHAVIOR SHEET          ___ PRE-TRAINING PLAN
                                       ✓  GOAL SHEET
ANIMAL NAME  Tique                    ___ FINISHED BEHAVIOR SHEET
BEHAVIOR  Pec Wave
CUE: _____
     _____
     _____
     _____
```

STEPS: (If used as a goal sheet, please start each step with the date)

1. (2-14-94) While in ultrasound position (w/ head to my left), touch right hand to top of exposed left pec, bridging each time hand touches pec.

2. (2-14-94) After multiple bridging of hand touching pec, place hand near pec and bridge any voluntary movement of pec up toward hand, especially if pec actually touches hand.

3. (3-2-94) Slowly approximate hand farther away causing pec to come up.

4. (3-5-94) Each time layout SD is given, the training hand will wave just a little, slowly approximating toward the final SD.

5. (3-13-94) Use exaggerated pec wave SD, fading away layout SD, until she rolls onto her side reaching to touch my hand. Bridge for touching hand.

6. (3-20-94) REGRESS. Give clear layout SD. Roll into U/S position. Then get her to target to my hand. (She got confused during step #5).

7. (4-10-94) Attempt to fade out layout SD. More slowly than before.

8. (4-27-94) After she touches hand moving up, move hand to surface of water & bridge her for any movement of pec back down. Alternate this step with occasional bridge of just the upward movement of pec.

9. (5-12-94) Alternate between bridging for touching hand on the upward motion and bridging after touching the hand both up then down. Continue until both are consistent.

10. (5-15-94) Fade out target for downward motion as soon as possible, bridging her for bringing (slapping) pec onto water on her own.

11. (5-29-94) Temporary hold on behavior. New labs being mixed...

Goal sheets can continue for many pages, documenting the continued progress of the training. The section to the right is part of the second page of the goal sheet above.

18. (1-19-95) Approximate toward continuous slaps until bridged. If she offers forward motion bridge it, but don't expect forward motion.

19. (2-8-95) REGRESS. Use target again to get bigger motion on her upward swing. Continue to work toward multiple slaps using hand target every time.

20. (2-22-95) Fade out hand target, reintroduce it whenever needed.

21. (3-1-95) REGRESS. Make hand signal more distinct so as not to confuse it with lob tail. Do not work the two behaviors back to back.

22. (3-18-95) Continue to work behavior once each session.

23. (4-5-95) Start working behavior in opposite direction. Try early steps and see how she responds.

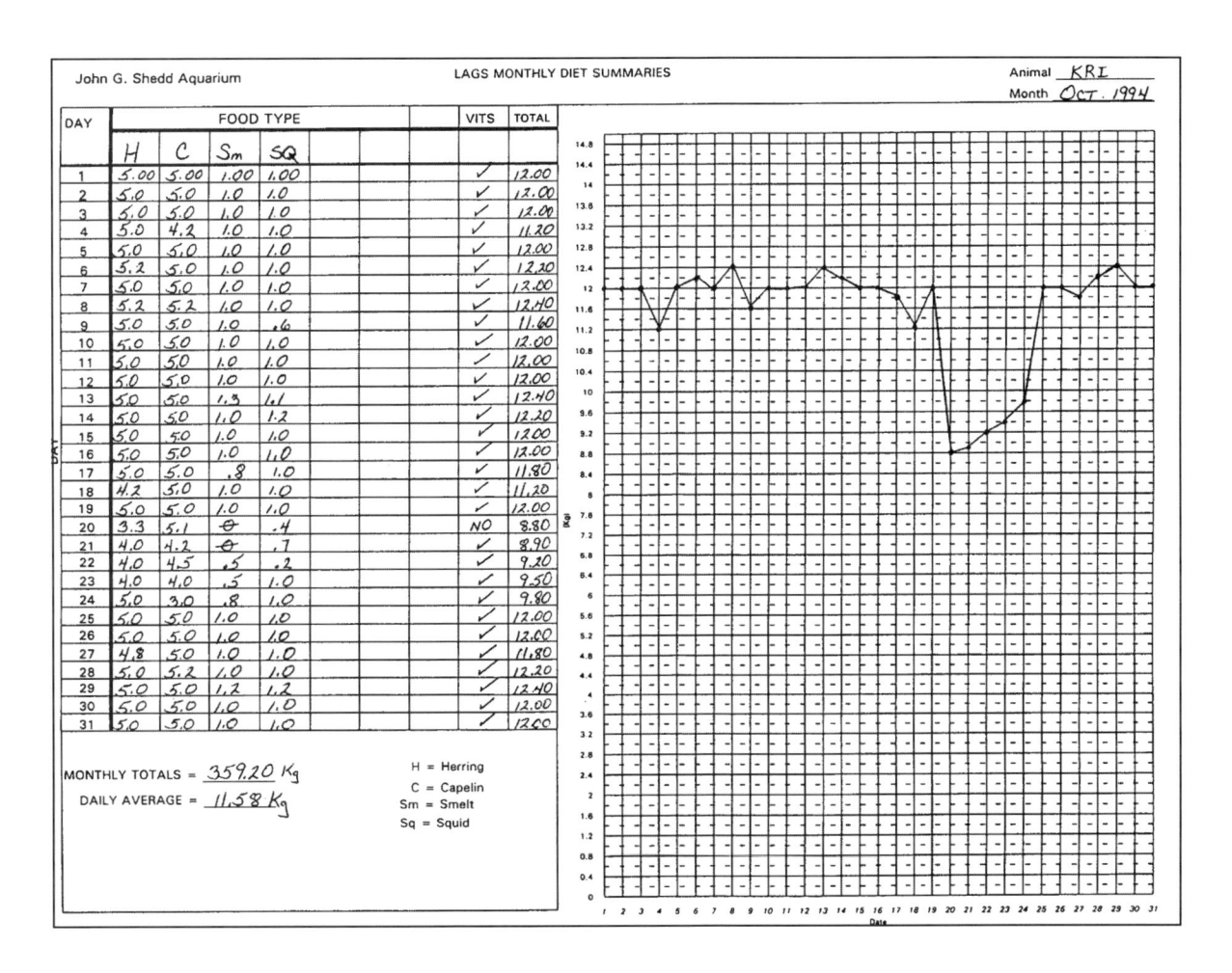

DAY	FOOD TYPE				VITS	TOTAL
	H	C	Sm	Sq		
1	5.00	5.00	1.00	1.00	✓	12.00
2	5.0	5.0	1.0	1.0	✓	12.00
3	5.0	5.0	1.0	1.0	✓	12.00
4	5.0	4.2	1.0	1.0	✓	11.20
5	5.0	5.0	1.0	1.0	✓	12.00
6	5.2	5.0	1.0	1.0	✓	12.20
7	5.0	5.0	1.0	1.0	✓	12.00
8	5.2	5.2	1.0	1.0	✓	12.40
9	5.0	5.0	1.0	.6	✓	11.60
10	5.0	5.0	1.0	1.0	✓	12.00
11	5.0	5.0	1.0	1.0	✓	12.00
12	5.0	5.0	1.0	1.0	✓	12.00
13	5.0	5.0	1.3	1.1	✓	12.40
14	5.0	5.0	1.0	1.2	✓	12.20
15	5.0	5.0	1.0	1.0	✓	12.00
16	5.0	5.0	1.0	1.0	✓	12.00
17	5.0	5.0	.8	1.0	✓	11.80
18	4.2	5.0	1.0	1.0	✓	11.20
19	5.0	5.0	1.0	1.0	✓	12.00
20	3.3	5.1	0	.4	NO	8.80
21	4.0	4.2	0	.7	✓	8.90
22	4.0	4.5	.5	.2	✓	9.20
23	4.0	4.0	.5	1.0	✓	9.50
24	5.0	3.0	.8	1.0	✓	9.80
25	5.0	5.0	1.0	1.0	✓	12.00
26	5.0	5.0	1.0	1.0	✓	12.00
27	4.8	5.0	1.0	1.0	✓	11.80
28	5.0	5.2	1.0	1.0	✓	12.20
29	5.0	5.0	1.2	1.2	✓	12.40
30	5.0	5.0	1.0	1.0	✓	12.00
31	5.0	5.0	1.0	1.0	✓	12.00

John G. Shedd Aquarium — LAGS MONTHLY DIET SUMMARIES — Animal KRI — Month Oct. 1994

MONTHLY TOTALS = 359.20 Kg
DAILY AVERAGE = 11.58 Kg

H = Herring
C = Capelin
Sm = Smelt
Sq = Squid

computer, the trend seems slow to spread. But as young trainers enter the field, computers are becoming a way of life, and the speed, storage capacity and flexibility of computers will enhance our ability to care for our animals.

Developing Trust through Interaction

Trust as a Step Toward Relationship Building

An important but difficult to define aspect of knowing your animals lies in your developing a relationship with each of them. Some trainers rely too heavily on this part of training; others ignore it altogether. These differences are discussed in more detail in chapter 5, "Non-Formal Interactions." A good relationship will not take the place of good technique, but it is an important part of understanding the animal. The basis for this understanding is trust – mutual trust. You must be secure in the knowledge that the animal won't (or can't) bite you; the animal must know that you will not hurt it. Trust is developed through feeding, playing with, and caring for the animal. It is during these early stages of getting to know an animal that you must determine how you will interact with it. What types of contact will you use?

Determining Type of Contact
The goal here is to choose a mode and level of interactivity that will allow you to safely train, feed, and care for your animals. There are no industry wide definitions for each of the six categories about to be described here, but the explanations provided are fairly common. Keep in mind that there are no definitive boundaries that tell you where one mode of contact ends and another one begins. Many training programs may rely on several types of contact, not just one.

Free contact – The animal and trainer have equal access to the work area. The animal is not restrained, muzzled, or confined in any way. It is believed by some trainers that free contact is the only way to build true trust between trainer and animal. But many training programs have proved that's not true. Free contact can also be the most dangerous way to interact with wild animals because it offers little or no protection. Some free contact training is done with clearly established escape routes and barriers available to trainers if they need protection. A few examples of free contact training include:
- Dogs & Cats: Most people work with their pets unleashed and in their home or yard. The animals can climb, lick, and touch their trainers at will. This is the ultimate in free contact training. Many other domestic animals are worked in this mode, too.
- Dolphins: Any time trainers get in the water with the animals would be considered free contact training.
- Rodeo Clowns: When a bull rider in a rodeo falls off the bull, the clowns (whose job is to help distract the bull from hurting the cowboy) will run around in front of the bull trying to attract its attention. This seemingly foolish endeavor is definitely free contact interaction, although no formal training is taking place. However, a number of escape routes are usually in place, including an easily climbed fence and a padded barrel.

Semi-protected contact (Semi-free contact) – This is a fairly common type of contact in which the trainer is partially protected or isolated from the animal. The high degree of flexibility in this system offers wonderful opportunities for interaction. Examples:
- Leashes & Muzzles: These devices respectively restrict

the animal's movements and ability to bite. Depending on their size, strength, or speed, the animals still may be able to cause injury. Plenty of contact can still be made, and training can take place with relatively few restrictions.
- Dolphin Training: Much of the interaction between dolphin and trainer takes place in separate mediums – the animal in the water, the trainer on land. When the animal is unable to leave the water, and the trainer chooses to remain on land, their contact would be considered semi-free. The animal can still bite or bump the trainer, but since this type of training usually is done for convenience rather than protection, the emphasis is on "semi-free" rather than "semi-protected." The concepts are the same; the differences are simply a matter of perspective.

Protected contact – In this type of contact the trainer is virtually protected from the possibility of injury by the animal. Contact is made only with a portion of the animal's body at a time. The animal is trained to present one part of its body against, for example, a fence or through a small window or door, allowing access by the trainer. Recent innovations in this type of training have proven that well-designed protected contact systems can allow animal and trainer interactions while still providing protection. Several articles about protected contact training with elephants can be found in chapter 12, "Complex Training: Modern Applications."

Confined contact – This form of contact is usually reserved for medical procedures that might cause the animal discomfort. Confined contact can be used in concert with any of the other contact modes described. The animal may be maneuvered into a restraint chute, a squeeze cage, or other restraining mechanism. This can often be accomplished through proper conditioning techniques. Some examples of confined contact devices include cetacean stretchers, pinniped squeeze cages, and elephant restraint chutes. Chemical restraint, such as general anesthesia, is considered by some to fall into the category of confined contact.

Hands-off training – While this is certainly a protected form of interaction (and is referred to as protected contact by some trainers), it entails no physical contact of any kind. However, when voice contact and eye contact can still be made, relationships and trust can still be established. The term "no-contact" training is sometimes used in discussing hands-off training; however, the same term is sometimes applied to remote training, described below. Many zoo animals are conditioned to move from enclosure to enclosure using this technique. No physical contact takes place, but trainers may throw food to the animals, call their names, and make eye contact. The lack of physical contact does not prevent training from taking place.

Remote training – This is truly no contact training. In remote training an attempt is made to remove the human element entirely from the picture. Needless to say, no relationship or trust can be developed through this type of training (although it could take place at other times). Remote training is sometimes used when developing automatic feeding devices or enrichment devices for animals. If an animal paws against a tree, for example, a mechanism may dispense food from above, perhaps on a random basis. If an animal crosses a light beam, it may cause a fish to be injected into the water. A description of this type of training is presented in an article by Gary Priest in chapter 11, "Problem Solving."

Learning an Animal's Preferences

During the early stages of getting to know an animal, many of its preferences will become obvious. Favorite foods, preferred resting sites, choices in companion animals, and details of how it occupies its time will be invaluable as you implement your training program. The learning process should continue throughout your relationship with each animal. But it is during the formative stages of training that this information can be most valuable.

Trust Takes Time

As you will see in later sections, trust is not developed overnight. Relationship building takes time and is a dynamic process. What you get out of gaining the animal's trust will be directly proportional to the amount of effort you put into it. This subject will be discussed again in later chapters.

Trainer's Forum

VOL 14, NO 3, 1989. Believe it or not, the question below was seriously submitted to *Trainer's Forum*. It is understandable that the public may not know the difference between seals and sea lions, however trainers should certainly know better. This question emphasizes the importance of knowing the natural history, anatomy and physiology of an animal. The first answer takes a serious approach to answering the question while the second response is more humorous.

Are We Talking Seals or Sea Lions?

QUESTION: I have tried for two years to get our 7-year-old harbor seal to do the classic front flipper walk that most seals at other zoos do. I don't think she's overweight or too young, but her flippers seem awfully small. She will lift up her tail, but I can't seem to progress from there. Do any of IMATA's members have any hints?

ANSWER 1: After pondering this question I wonder whether the animal in question may possibly be a sea lion rather than a harbor seal. Although sea lions can perform front flipper stands (walks) quite easily, I've never seen or heard of a true seal performing such a feat. Anatomically the seal may not possess the musculo skeletal properties necessary to support its own weight on its front flippers.

If this animal is a member of the sea lion or fur seal species the front flipper stand is easily attained through a program of strength conditioning. We find it easier to initiate this behavior from the animal's seat or pedestal. While on its seat, condition the animal to use its chest as a fulcrum and raise its hind quarters off the seat proper with the use of a target. Once the animal understands the principal of raising its hind quarters upon the touch of a target, transfer the behavior to the deck. Strengthening the chest muscles is essential at this point. Short sessions every day will strengthen its upper body and soon endurance can be achieved. Important aspects to look for are: keep the animal's head up and chest off the ground, keep the front flippers tucked in close to the chest, and attempt to distribute the animal's weight directly over the front flippers.

Pat (Bucko) Turley
MarineWorld Africa, U.S.A.

ANSWER 2: Possibly taking the seal to a neighborhood bowling alley and stationing her in the gutter may help. If that gets no results, you may try getting her to stand on her hind flippers.

Jim Alexander
St. Louis Zoo

The Human Element 3

Before we actually begin training an animal, we must recognize that we bring many biases to a training session. Some are personal and others are part and parcel of being human. These traits are not in and of themselves a bad thing, but we must know how to recognize them and understand how they affect our ability to train the animals under our care. This chapter will touch on several important and interesting topics that I like to refer to as the human element.

Intelligence

It sometimes surprises new trainers to find out that the intelligence of an animal may have very little to do with how trainable it is. Yet, as humans, the subject of intelligence continues to fascinate us. It is frequently the subject of debate among scientists, too. Trainers, after successfully training a new behavior, will often comment on how smart their animal is! But was the animal exhibiting truly intelligent behavior or was the trainer simply using good operant conditioning techniques? Could it have been a little of both or was the trainer being too anthropomorphic? We'll look at the subject of anthropomorphism later in this chapter, but since the topic of intelligence seems to intrigue us so much, let's examine it first.

Definitions

Sometimes the biggest debates over animal intelligence start because those discussing the topic can't agree on terms. Words like *intelligence*, *think* and *reason* seem to have many interpretations. As defined by *The American Heritage Dictionary, Second Edition*, the following definitions and interpretations seem to be the most common.

Intelligence – "The ability to acquire and apply knowledge; the faculty of thought and reason; superior powers of the mind." Even these basic definitions can be open to interpretation.

Think – "To formulate in the mind; to reason about, to reflect on, to decide." Thinking usually implies a conscious thought, one that is analytical in nature.

Reason – "The capacity for rational thought, inference, or discrimination."

Studying Intelligence

The investigation of animal intelligence has grown to become a respected and important field. However, the fact that humans are doing the investigations means that many of the methods of study must take a uniquely human approach to the subject. As we study animal behavior, we find that traits we thought to be uniquely human (and signs of our intelligence) are in fact shared by many other animals. Traits such as tool use, play, cooperative behavior, deception, creativity, and language are just a few examples of behavior that once was thought to be unique to humans. The discovery that these traits can be seen in animals as diverse as honey bees, snakes, and crows, has caused many to take notice and to re-examine our beliefs about animal intellect.

Cognition Studies

One of the areas that seems to attract the most attention, especially among those interested in working with primates and cetaceans, is the study of animal cognition. It is particularly fascinating for trainers in that many of these studies involve training animals to cooperate in the study. Several articles on this topic appear in chapter 12, "Complex Training and Modern Applications." Some of the most famous cognition studies include Lou Herman's work with bottlenose dolphins (*Tursiops truncatus*), Ron Schusterman's work with California sea lions (*Zalophus californianus*), Irene Pepperberg's work with African gray parrots (*Psittacus erithacus*), and the many studies teaching sign language to primates. These studies are some of the most high-profile intelligence investigations in the animal behavior field, but they also have been greeted with the most skepticism: are the animals exhibiting intelligent behavior, or are they just extremely well trained?

All Animals Can Learn

Although all animals have the capacity to learn, the question may be how and why do they learn? Any system that we develop to test intelligence will be biased in some way. The challenge lies in determining what each test really means or indicates. Two primary factors will influence accuracy in the interpretation of any test for animal intelligence – an understanding of the animal's natural history and an understanding of the limits of the test. An animal will naturally show an aptitude for a concept it needs or uses regularly in the wild. If a human has lived in the woods and has needed to hunt for his food from a very young age, that individual can develop an aptitude for hunting that one who has lived a lifetime in the city may never acquire. Both individuals may have equal mental capacity, but the former would score better on a test that requires tracking wild game, while the latter might excel at navigating the subway system in a big city. Each test is biased toward one individual or the other. It is almost impossible to develop a test that fairly takes into account species differences as well as individual experiences.

Past experiences play a big role in how well any individual can be evaluated in a test. When trainers play a role in teaching animals behavior for cognitive studies, questions will often arise about how well the animals were taught. Does the animal do well because the trainer was exceptionally skilled at using operant techniques? Can two individuals really be compared without asking if the differences are due to their training, their past experience, or their species-specific traits? But sometimes those questions are not the ones the studies are trying to answer. Sometimes investigators are simply trying to understand the cognitive process or to discover if an animal can learn in a certain way.

How Smart is a Dolphin?

Karen Pryor takes a unique approach to answering this question in her 1981 article *Why Porpoise Trainers are not Dolphin Lovers*, on page 50. So how smart *is* a dolphin? Those of us who work with dolphins regularly get the question in this form: "How does dolphin intelligence compare to that of a human, a chimp, or other animals?" It is not an easy question. At Shedd Aquarium we respond by pointing out that scientists and educators have yet to agree on how to gauge and measure human intelligence. Educators argue over the merits of various testing techniques, such as IQ tests. If we are unable to agree on a system for quantifying human intelligence, how can we begin to accurately assess the intelligence of an animal so different from ourselves? What we do know is that each animal is as smart as it needs to be to survive in its natural habitat.

Intelligence is a Matter of Perspective

Marian Breland Bailey and Bob Bailey write about this concept in their article *Every Animal is the Smartest*, on page 54. Animals possess the skills they need to survive in the wild. Intelligence might be viewed as simply another adaptive trait such as vision, sense of smell and speed that animals possess in varying degrees as needed in their particular environmental niche. Sometimes the argument or question about animal intelligence is posed as if to put animals in some pre-conceived position or hierarchy. It is as if the answer to the question of intelligence gives added importance to an animal's very existence. But all animals have intrinsic value. Each is a critical part of the ecosystem and should be valued on its own merits, not based on some comparison or contrast to humans or other animals. Intelligence should not make one animal any more or less important than another.

Although the subject will probably continue to fascinate us forever, and will continue to be a worthwhile avenue of study, trainers should not allow the issue of intelligence to overshadow the importance and effectiveness of using good operant conditioning techniques. Don't forget that these techniques have been proven effective on everything from the simplest earthworm to the smartest Harvard graduate.

...ONE THING ABOUT DOLPHINS WE MUST REMIND THOSE OF YOU WITH EXPENSIVE CAMERAS, THEY SEEM TO ENJOY GETTING PEOPLE WET...

Anthropomorphism
(A Trainer's Biggest Stumbling Block)

Definition
When we assign human qualities, characteristics, or motivation to animals, it is referred to as anthropomorphism. The public does it, trainers do it, and so do some scientists. Yet, we find ourselves constantly fighting the urge to use anthropomorphic language. We are constantly told it is bad. Why is that? I believe it is because anthropomorphic thinking can be a trainer's biggest stumbling block. Otto Fad (1994) writes about the subject in his article, *Anthropomorphism, the Natural Enemy Within?* on page 59.

Thinking for the Animal

I am constantly amazed at how often trainers will say, "The animal knows what I want." Or, "I think the animal thought I was going to do such and such so I..." Although we all make these comments, it is a major mistake to use them in our training decisions. We cannot allow ourselves to make decisions based on what we believe an animal is thinking. It will backfire on us 95% of the time. Training is successful because we reinforce good behavior, as it occurs, not from reinforcing good thoughts or intentions.

Making Excuses for the Animal

A similar situation occurs when we try to justify the animal's error with a well-intentioned excuse. The following statements are all too common among some trainers:

- "The animal's not feeling well, but he made a good effort."
- "I don't think my cue was clear, so I gave him the benefit of the doubt."
- "The other animal got in the way, so I reinforced him – It wasn't his fault."

While these excuses may indeed be valid, they do not justify reinforcing poor behavior. When we reinforce an incorrect response based on such excuses we are anthropomorphizing. Reinforcement of this sort mistakenly assumes that the animal will understand why you reinforced its substandard behavior. So, when you later expect the animal to perform up to par, the animal may become confused or frustrated.

Health Concerns

What if we know the animal is sick or that its substandard performance is not the animal's fault? In those cases, we simply should refrain from requesting the problem behavior until the obstacle (illness or pesky other animal) has been resolved. We can even give the animal other opportunities to receive reinforcement. However, we should not reinforce incorrect behavior just because the animal is ill; this will ultimately send mixed messages to the animal. We should also be careful about making husbandry decisions based on anthropomorphic thinking. In that area, too, this may cause us to make decisions for the wrong reasons as pointed out by Gary Wilkes in his article, *Anthropomorphism: A Case of Mistaken Identity*, on page 62.

"Three's Company" Syndrome

When I think of the problems trainers create for themselves by making anthropomorphic decisions, I am reminded of the television situation comedy "Three's Company," popular in the 1970's. In every episode the comedy was based on multiple misunderstandings. "He thought that she thought that you were upset because you frowned when you walked in the door, so he quit his job!" That's the plot of an entire episode, full of funny misunderstandings that get resolved in the end. Every episode revolves around misunderstandings and actions based on what one character assumes the other is thinking.

The point is, we constantly get into fights and have disagreements with friends, partners, and coworkers because we misinterpret an expression or a "look." If we can't accurately gauge the thoughts or intentions of other people, how can we pretend to understand the thoughts of animals? We shouldn't try. Not, at least, when trying to reinforce behavior.

We Will Always Anthropomorphize
Why won't we ever get rid of anthropomorphic references? Simply put, because it's easy and because we're human. The fact is that we are people trying to relate animal behavior to other people. What concepts and the language that describes them do we understand better than human feelings, emotions, and thoughts? It is easier to say that the two dogs were playing than to say that the two dogs were engaged in interactive behavior. "Playing" conjures up an image we can all understand. However, many wild animals engage in behaviors that are not easily defined in human terms. It is in those instances that we must be careful.

Compromise
Perhaps the best solution is compromise. As long as we understand why anthropomorphism is hazardous, and use it with the full understanding of what we are doing, we can avoid most of the pitfalls. The topic will always spark controversy, but that is usually based on a lack of understanding of the pros and cons of using anthropomorphic references. As trainers, we can still show compassion and feeling for the animals under our care, we can even use anthropomorphic references if we desire, but we can not afford to make reinforcement decisions based on anthropomorphic thinking.

Compassion & Emotion

This section will focus on the most volatile of human elements, emotions and feelings. I will avoid discussing the subject of animal emotions, because even the best trainers will have opposing views on that subject. The previous section on anthropomorphism speaks to my thoughts on using intangible elements such as emotion when reinforcing behavior. However, the trainer's emotional state can have a dramatic effect on the success of a training session.

Compassion Is Good

Most animal trainers are very compassionate individuals. We get into this profession because of a deep love for the animals we work with. We care a great deal about each animal under our care and will do almost anything for those animals. Trainers who work with pets are usually not shy about expressing the love they have for their animals; often wearing their emotions on their sleeves (I mean that in only the nicest way). In the zoological community, we have a unique mix of scientists, educators, behaviorists, veterinarians, and specialists in many other disciplines who have come together to provide for our animals' care. This unique mix of individuals have diverse ways of looking at and talking about animals. Discussions about the dangers of anthropomorphism often create uncertainty among young trainers about what is appropriate to say or feel about the animals.

I have been a member of IMATA for many years, and can tell you that marine mammal trainers love the animals they work with. You can eavesdrop on any conversation at an IMATA gathering and hear trainers talking affectionately about their animals. There is no conflict between the scientific need for objectivity when observing animals for a research project or when clearly defining criteria in shaping a behavior, and having fun when playing with your animals. Each situation is different, and a good trainer can wear many different hats; in fact, the best trainers usually do. We will explore this subject in a little more detail in chapter 5, "Non-Formal Interactions."

Keep Your Emotions in Check

Unfortunately, the part of us that gives us compassion can also make us highly emotional creatures. Emotion is a powerful force within each of us that, when out of control, can ruin a training session. The very humanity that makes us compassionate and caring individuals, and thus better trainers, can work against us, too. We all know parents who care deeply for their children but sometimes get angry when their kids forget to clean their room, get home after curfew, or fail to get good grades in school. The parents feel so invested in their children's lives that they sometimes take their children's failings personally. Those reactions can be so emotional that good decision-making goes out the window. Trainers can make the same mistake.

Operant conditioning works so well because it entails no emotional decision-making, but instead uses scientifically proven principles to modify behavior. Trainers who get angry or frustrated during a session will likely let emotion cloud their decision-making abilities. Even if the trainer's emotional state is not related to the animal being trained, problems can arise. A trainer who has had a disagreement with his boss, endured a terrible traffic jam on the way to work, or received an emotional phone call from a loved one may not be in any condition to be blowing a whistle that will shape an animal's behavior. It is imperative that we keep our emotions under control when training our animals.

Even positive and happy events can create an emotional overload that will make trainers lose focus and reinforce undesirable behavior. Several years ago, the boyfriend of one of the aquarium's trainers asked if he could propose to his girlfriend during one of our dolphin presentations. We agreed, and carefully set up the session so that she would not suspect a thing. The proposal took her by such surprise that she was overcome with such emotion and literally forgot she had an animal in front of her. Moments later, when she vaguely realized that a dolphin was staring at her, she dumped a handful of fish into the water, while still staring misty-eyed at her fiancé. She reinforced the dolphin without having a clue to what the dolphin had just done! Fortunately, we had anticipated her reaction and were able to get another trainer to step in and take over. Every trainer must be aware of that powerful emotional force bottled up in each of us and be prepared to deal with it.

Karen Pryor

On Behavior
Essays & Research

In the forward to Karen Pryor's book *On Behavior* Ellen P. Reese writes about this article stating, "terrible title, but important message." I couldn't agree more. Karen presented the following paper as a talk to the New York Academy of Science Conference on Animal Communication. Her desire was to dispel many of the popular myths about dolphins. The important message was that perhaps much of what we think of as communication may simply be a result of advanced operant conditioning techniques, which have helped us to understand our animals better.

Why Porpoise Trainers are not Dolphin Lovers
Real and false communication in the operant setting

by Karen Pryor

DOLPHIN LOVERS ABOUND. Everyone who has ever seen "Flipper" on television, visited an oceanarium, or read John Lilly's books thinks that dolphins are cute, playful, friendly, harmless, and affectionate to each other and to man, that they save drowning people, and that they are possessed of extraordinary intelligence and a rich communication system comparable perhaps to our own.

Porpoise trainers know otherwise (many prefer the word "porpoise" to "dolphin" because it differentiates the mammals from a pelagic fish, *Coryphaena hippurus,* which is also called "dolphin.") The novice trainer quickly learns that porpoises can be very aggressive. They are highly social animals, to which rank order is a matter of considerable importance. Aggressive interactions between porpoises, usually during dominance disputes, include striking, raking with the teeth, and ramming with the beak or rostrum, sometimes with serious consequences, such as broken ribs or vertebrae, or punctured lungs, in the rammed animal. A dolphin that has become accustomed to humans shows no hesitance in challenging the human for dominance, by means of threat displays and blows; a person who is in the water with an aggressive porpoise is at a dangerous disadvantage. The sentimental view that these animals are harmless stems at least in part from the fact that they are usually in the water and we are usually on boats or dry land; they can't get at us.

Interaction with porpoises in a training situation, usually with the trainer at tank-side, also brings their vaunted intelligence under pragmatic scrutiny. A poll of experienced trainers reveals that some trainers, after working with many individual animals of several species for five years or more, were not willing to place porpoise intelligence levels above that of dogs; the majority of the respondents, however, agreed with the dictum that porpoise intelligence is "between the dog and the chimpanzee, and nearer to the chimpanzee" (by no means, however, does it appear to trainers to be equal to or superior to that of the great apes.)

A confounding effect of this question is that most of the porpoises kept in captivity are Atlantic bottlenosed porpoises, *Tursiops traucatus,* a coastal species which is highly adaptable, plastic in its behavior, and an opportunistic feeder, showing a marked tendency to play with and to manipulate objects, and some tolerance for solitude. Other genera of Delphinidae, such as pilot whales, belugas, and the small, pelagic, white-sided, spinner and spotter porpoises, exhibit quite different behavioral profiles. Spinner porpoises (*Stenella longirostris*), for example, show very little tendency to play and high avoidance of foreign objects. They have difficulty negotiating barriers and or obstacles, seldom learn to tolerate (much less solicit) human touch, and become inappetent and in fact rapidly moribund if kept in isolation from species mates. It is perhaps unfortunate that the popular view of porpoises is based on the genus *Tursiops,* the bottlenose, which is in fact a rather anomalous member of the Delphinidae, behaviorally.

Nevertheless, whether the subject is an inactive pilot whale, a very active but timid spinner, or a bold, aggressive bottlenosed dolphin, the trainer can train it: not by loving it, or even liking it – one may find oneself cordially despising a particular individual – but by operant conditioning (Defran and Pryor 1980).

People often ask a working trainer about "communication." John Lilly having established an apparently ineradicable mystique by holding that there is something unusual about dolphin communication (Lilly, 1961). The flippant answer is that anyone can communicate just fine with a whistle and a bucket of fish.

In fact what is "different" about porpoises, compared to other frequently trained animals, is the manner in which they are trained. Aversive methods are virtually unavailable. The porpoise trainer cannot use the choke chain, the spur, the elephant hook, the cattle prod, or even a fist, on an animal that can swim away if alarmed. As they cannot "get at" us, so we cannot "get at" them.

The laboratory psychologist's mind may at once turn to devising some arcane method of punishment. In fact, punishment is unnecessary. Other than the mild negative reinforcement of a brief interruption of the training session, (a "time-out") porpoise trainers achieve highly disciplined and complex responses entirely with positive reinforcement.

The proliferation of trained porpoise shows, as well as some rather limited use to trained porpoises as a domestic animals working in the open sea, has paralleled in time the promulgation and increasing public awareness of the laws of operant conditioning described by B.F. Skinner and others. Unlike traditional animal trainers, porpoise trainers are not only at the mercy of these laws, they are aware of them, and use them consciously. The jargon of the porpoise trainer is a jargon of the laboratory: successive approximation, conditioned stimuli, variable schedules of reinforcement, and so on. Unlike the shaper working under laboratory conditions, however, the porpoise trainer, in addition to being largely limited to positive reinforcement, is interacting with the animal; he or she can see the animal, the animal can see him or her, and both can introduce changes in the training process, at will. It is a situation, both rigorous and admitting of spontaneity: a game.

The game has "rules" on both sides: "I will reinforce you only for jumps in which you do not touch the hoop as you pass through it;" "I have come to expect a fish for at least every three or four jumps, and will stop jumping if you let eight or ten responses go unrewarded." It is a game in which challenge is always present, as the trainer, mindful of the various techniques for maintaining response levels, raises criteria or introduces new criteria; but, at least in the hands of a skilled trainer, it is a game that the animal always, eventually, wins.

A dog or a horse learns responses because it must do so to avoid aversive stimuli; a pigeon in a Skinner box must work, because it is hungry; and when we train people, we generally use a mix of positive and negative, of praise and coercion, though sometimes covert. There is little coercion, however, in the porpoise-trainer interaction (even food deprivation is hazardous, and seldom used) and this has an effect upon both trainer and animal. The animal is, as it were, training the trainer to give fish, and thus is shaped towards finding new ways to elicit fish; it is shaped in fact towards innovative response. The trainer in turn may become a very skilled and imaginative user of Skinner's laws. Porpoise trainer shoptalk (as opposed, let us say, to racehorse trainer shoptalk) is generally concerned with ingenious shaping programs, or novel use of operant conditioning techniques and not with the personalities or achievement of individual animals. It is the fascination of the game that keeps porpoise trainers in their strenuous, low-paying jobs, year after year, and not the fascination of the animals themselves. Many trainers in fact come to prefer the more reliably conditionable pinnipeds, and some greatly enjoy working with birds, another group that cannot be trained aversively.

This is not to say that every porpoise trainer is a walking compendium of Skinnerian laws. The less educated trainer, or the self-taught trainer working in isolation, may be full of superstitious behaviors ("You have to wear white; dolphins like white") or may be unable to say how he is cueing his animals, and thus fall victim to Clever Hans phenomenon, maintaining, for example, that his animals respond telepathically. The animals of course quickly develop superstitious behavior too; for example, only responding to trainers in white clothes.

The nontrainer, interacting with dolphins, is also apt to misinterpret, especially in the matter of social signaling. He may, for example, interpret the gaped jaw, a threat display, as a "smile," or touches and jostling as affectionate play, when they are often dominance challenges. Dr. Lilly made much of anecdotes concerning a male porpoise making sexual advances to a human female, but male bottlenosed porpoises in captivity may exhibit sexual behavior towards almost anything; and it is behavior which, after all, we do not find intelligent or endearing in male dog (Lilly 1978).

The interactive, positive-reinforcement training setting is an excellent way to become acquainted with the nature and function of social signals in an unfamiliar species. You do no not need months or years of observation to discover which gesture, postures, and acts are aggressive, which affiliative, and so on. For example, in spinner porpoises, an extremely loud echo-location click-train is a threat display. This may not be obvious the first time you swim with spinners; if it is immediately followed by a sharp blow of a dorsal fin to your upper arm, you will recognize it the second time you hear it, and prepare to take evasive action.

In the operant setting, most large mammals quickly direct their intraspecific social signals at the trainer. They are not begging; begging does not work; they are exhibiting frustration, making submissive or aggressive displays, and so on, both giving and garnering information. One of the commonest trainer-directed social signals is sudden eye contact, which can be described metaphorically as the "Am I on the right track?" eye contact. Verifying that the trainer is indeed watching, the animal then escalates the vigor or duration of the response, and thus earns reinforcement. This is not a behavior seen only in porpoises, although they make eye contact more often than many other mammals; I have experienced this specific social interchange of information in an operant conditioning setting with an elephant, a wolf, a hyena, several polar bears, and primates.

The wise trainer makes use of whatever social signaling he feels he can accurately interpret. The animal can make use of this communication link too. Porpoises, for example, probably do not care what we think of them, and according to Gish, do not necessarily, in their own acoustic social signaling, increase volume to add emphasis; nevertheless porpoises can learn that human increased volume – yelling – means "I mean it!" and respond appropriately, not from fear or a desire to please, as a dog might, but from having gleaned the appropriate information in training interaction (Gish 1979).

The richness and detail of information available in the operant setting enables communication to occur on a level considerably exceeding that of the usual interactions between man and beast. The porpoise trainer, for example, can change his tankside location to indicate when he wants previously conditioned responses, and when the animal is at liberty to earn reinforcement through new responses. A porpoise can indicate through a series of totally wrong responses that the quality of the fish reward is not satisfactory; this device is not uncommon in research animals being fed from feeding machines, in which fish may dry out or spoil. The porpoise, through actions, and with eye contact, may deliberately test the trainer's criteria: take, for example, this episode (Pryor 1975):

> Two false killer whales (*Pseudorca crassidens*) have been trained to jump a hurdle simultaneously, in opposite directions. The behavior, used in daily public performances, has deteriorated, due to trainer carelessness. One whale now always jumps too late, spoiling the effect of the mid-air crossing of trajectories. A corrective training session was held, as follows:
> 1. Trainer presents cue (an underwater sound). Both animals approach hurdle. Animal A jumps from the left; the conditioned reinforcers (a whistle) is sounded, and the cue is turned off; animal B then jumps from the right. Animal A receives a handful of fish. Animal B returns to trainer but is not reinforced.
> 2. Trainer presents cue. Both animals approach the jump, jump simultaneously in opposite directions, hear the whistle, the cue is turned off, and both are awarded with 2 pounds of fish, many small fish (>10) dumped directly into the animals' large mouths. These are very large animals, and that constitutes the usual reinforcement.
> 3. Trainer presents cue, and the first episode is repeated, with animal B jumping late, after the cue is off, getting no whistle, and no fish.
> 4. Trainer presents cue and animal B does something quite unprecedented; it switches sides and jumps in synchrony

with animal A, but from the left or same side, hearing the cue, and the whistle, but getting no fish.
5. Trainer presents cue. Both animals jump, and from opposite directions, and animal B is just slightly late. Animal A receives 2 pounds of fish, and animal B gets one little 2-ounce smelt. Animal B physically startles, and makes eye contact with the trainer.
6. Trainer presents cue. Animal B increases swimming speed and makes perfect jump, opposite to and in synchrony with animal A. Both animals are given 4-pound reward. Both animals henceforth perform the response correctly, eight times a day.

Does this demonstrate these large delphinids' "intelligence?" Perhaps: One would not expect such methodical testing of the criteria by a spinner porpoise, which has a behavioral repertorie generally more limited and rigid that that of *Pseudorca*. However, the anecdote may demonstrate the kind of communication that can arise purely through operant conditioning and through using positive reinforcement flexibly. Nothing in the "rules" suggests that half a reinforcement should convey the information, "You're about half right." But whether or not that interpretation represents what truly happened, there was information in the unusually tiny reinforcement, information that the animal, to all pragmatic intents and purposes, recognized and made note of.

Gregory Bateson has stated that operant conditioning is a method of communicating with alien species (Bateson, pers. comm.) Others have suggested that the various language acquisition experiments with apes are nothing more than glorified operant conditioning.

Whether what the apes do is related to language, as we use language, is beside the point to a porpoise trainer. Like the porpoises, the apes have experienced very elaborate operant conditioning programs, in a setting conducive to interchange of social signals and a setting which, while rigorous, is admitting of spontaneity on both sides. It is a training circumstances that is rather rare in the world at large. What seems evident, and is taken now almost for granted by many researchers, is that at least chimpanzees are capable of assimilating enormous numbers of signs – conditioned stimuli, if you will – and of attaching correct meanings to these signs. A signing chimp, or even an ape that merely recognizes some signs (such as some orangutans or gorillas now do at the National Zoo) is capable both of giving and receiving information that is far more subtle than that normally conveyed between a person and a pet animal or a caged specimen. Something is developed; it may or may not be language; it is certainly heightened communication.

Innovative responses, and increased communication, thus may be not so much an indication of unusual or near-human capabilities in a species, but rather an artifact of the effect of advances techniques ("glorified," if you like) of operant conditioning in opening pathways for communication, including two-way and unpremeditated communication, between other species – perhaps many other species – and man.

REFERENCES

Defran, R.H. and K. Pryor. 1980. The behavior and training of cetaceans in captivity. In *Cetacean Behavior,* L. Herman, Ed., Wiley-Interscience, New York, N.Y.

Gish, S.I., 1979. *Quantitative Analysis of two-way Acoustic Communication between Captive Atlantic Bottlenosed Dolphins (Tursiops truncatus* Montagu). Ph.D. dissertation. Univ. of California at Santa Cruz.

Lilly, J. 1961. *Man and Dolphin.* Doubleday and Co., New York, N.Y.

Lilly, J. 1978. *Communication Between Man and Dolphin.* Crown, New York, N.Y.

Pryor, K. 1975. *Lads Before the Wind.* Harper & Row, New York, N.Y.
[Also 1987, Sunshine Books, North Bend WA].

Marian Breland Bailey and her late husband Keller Breland together formed a unique company called Animal Behavior Enterprise (ABE) in Hot Springs, Arkansas in 1946. After Keller passed away, Marian continued her creative animal training with Bob Bailey (they were among the most innovative animal trainers anywhere). Their most visible work has been seen at state fairs for decades, the "Tic-Tac-Toe Playing Chicken," the "Basketball Playing Raccoon," or the "Piano Playing Rabbit." However, in the training community they are best known for their innovative and excellent training skills. They are frequently hired as consultants to help train animals for some very difficult tasks. Their exposure to so many types of animals, and to so many different training situations, combined with their study of animal behavior make them uniquely qualified to discuss the subject of intelligence. This article from the book *Animal Intelligence: Insights into the Animal Mind* is straightforward and easy to understand. Its lack of scientific jargon makes it one of the clearest descriptions of the subject.

Every Animal Is the Smartest: Intelligence and the Ecological Niche

by Marian Breland Bailey and Robert E. Bailey
Animal Behavior Enterprises

Let me begin by asking a question: What do the "nest" building of a bower bird, the tail wagging of a dog, tool use by humans, and the dance of the bees have in common? Each is a example of animals behavior, more specifically of *adaptive* behavior that helps the animal survive in its environment. There are, of course, many kinds of adaptive behavior. As Gould, Beck, and others (this volume) have warned, many highly adaptive behaviors are genetically determined and cannot be considered "intelligent." But intelligent behavior, as difficult as it is to define, is almost always adaptive for an animal in its natural environment.

Such things as the ability to *discriminate* – to tell one object from another object, or to make the right response in a certain situation, which is perhaps what we mean by *judgment* – as well as the ability to remember and the ability to use symbols, all have been considered part of intelligence, and all are adaptive. But one other stands out that often determines which animal survives in a niche occupied by competitors, namely, *flexibility*. Flexibility is one of the dictionary definitions of intelligence; it is basically what psychologists means by the ability to generalize – that is, to vary behavior in the face of changing environmental conditions, to transfer to a new set of conditions useful responses learned in other circumstances, or to see similarities between one set of stimuli and another. For example, a dolphin trained to retrieve a ring from the water's surface will readily retrieve a hat, a doll, or any similar object on the water's surface. If trained to toss a basketball with its nose, the dolphin will also use a flipper or its tail. In the long run, the flexible animal has a profound advantage when environmental changes call for a complementary rapid change in behavior.

Since 1947, our company, Animal Behavior Enterprises (ABE), has been conditioning (or training, as most people would say) animals to respond to different kinds of stimuli. Often this training has been "to order." A client might ask, "Can you train a cat to turn on a television set and play a piano?" or "Can you train a dolphin to carry packages in the open ocean?"

In the past 36 years we have been asked many questions. The two most common are "What do you think is the most intelligent animal?" and "What animal is the easiest to train?" Of course, these are almost different forms of the same questions, and both are almost impossible to answer, at least as stated. To the second we must always reply, "Train to do what?" and to the first, our first answer is always, "Every animal is the smartest for the ecological niche in which it lives – if it were not, it would not be there." This is admittedly an oversimplification, but let me elaborate a bit.

Even in man's early history, animal intelligence was thought of in the context of man's own behavior – a rather anthropomorphic way of thinking. If an animal could learn tasks set for it by humans and solve human-oriented problems, it was considered intelligent; if it could not, it was stupid. But it is also common knowledge that animals are superior to humans in many abilities. Dogs, cats rats, mice, bats, and dolphins, to name a few, hear sounds much higher in pitch than we can; bats can emit very high-pitched sounds and analyze their echoes, which helps the bat catch flying insects and avoid obstacles in flight; and dogs can sniff out the trail of prey that may be out of sight and hearing. All these characteristics influence what people think of an animal's intelligence.

There are also differences between individuals and species in the ability to associate certain stimuli with certain responses *(connectability)*. These are by no means as clear to the casual observer as are the other differences I have mentioned in regard to sensory and motor abilities. However, if a dog can learn to come to its master when it hears a certain whistle, and almost always does so, that dog is considered "smart." If it cannot, it is considered "dumb." Pigs are sometimes thought "stupid" because they are "stubborn" – that is, they do not always go in the direction the farmer would like them to go. Thus, connectability certainly seems to be an important part of "intelligence," and of adaptability.

It was once believed by a large number of behavioral psychologists that any animal could learn anything, provided the correct methods were used, and that the differences between species were relatively insignificant. B. F. Skinner has pointed out that under certain laboratory conditions, all animals produce very similar patterns or responses. He writes:

> Pigeon, rat, monkey, which is which? It doesn't matter…Once you have allowed for differences in the ways in which they make contact with the environment (the stimuli they respond to), and in the ways in which they act upon the environment (the responses they make), what remains of their behavior shows astonishingly similar properties (Skinner 1959).

And from another behavioral scientist:

> We arbitrarily choose almost any act from the animal's repertoire and reinforce it with food, water, or whatever else the animal will work to obtain…The same act can be used for any reinforcement…In any operant situation, the stimulus, the response, and the reinforcement are completely arbitrary and interchangeable. No one of them bears any biologically fixed connection to the others (Teitelbaum 1966).

Statements like these were commonly made in the 1950's and early 1960s; they resulted principally from the narrow concentration on a limited number of species – especially white rats and pigeons – and from the ardent belief of many early behaviorists that all animal and human behavior could be summarized and explained by a few basic principles.

In the late 1940s and early 1950s Keller Breland and I, like many other psychologists, confidently thought we could train any animal to do anything – although we cagily inserted in our first proposal the phrase "within the physical and neurological limits of the animal." It was well we did. For in a very few months it became clear that not all animals would condition with equal ease to react in certain ways to certain stimuli. Our paths were strewn with records of pigs that would readily pick things up but only reluctantly put them down; with cows that would *not* hurry to food, no matter how hungry they were; with chickens that would not stand still, when that is all they were required to do to get food (for which we replaces them with rabbits, animals that can sit still); with raccoons that delayed reinforcement by "washing" everything they got their paws on; and with chickens that caused the same kind of delay by shaking and cracking the plastic capsules that earned their rewards. We reported a few of these "misbehaviors" in a paper published in the *American Psychologist* (Breland and Breland 1961).

While all this was going on, we became aware of a breath of fresh air blowing across the ocean from European ethologists – zoologists who study animal behavior. The psychologist Verplanck published an article about some of the ethologist's early work on instinctive behavior patterns (Verplanack 1955). Here at last were possible answers to some of our dilemmas, and ethology has radically altered the viewpoint of many psychologists. The last twenty years or so have seen widespread acceptance of the notion that species differences are behaviorally significant: that animals differ in their capacities to react to certain stimuli, and that not all responses are possible for all animals. But most important is the understanding that the idea of a general "learning ability" is the understanding that the idea of a *general* "learning ability" is inappropriate. It is now clear that there is a qualitative difference in the types of associations the various species are capable of forming – a particular animal might make some connections readily, some with great difficulty, and some not at all. Examples have been steadily accumulating from modern psychological laboratories. Garcia and his colleagues found that with rats, food avoidance learning using taste is very fast, but food avoidance using visual or auditory stimuli is very slow (Garcia and Koelhing 1966; Garcia, McGowan, and Green 1972). On the other hand, other researchers have found that visually oriented birds quickly learned food avoidance using visual cues, but not with auditory cues (Shettleworth 1972).

All these findings from various sources have some bearing on judgments of an animal's intelligence. To be "intelligent" an animal must at least be capable of making the associations or connections that determine its survival in its niche. Simply because an animal cannot with ease make a certain kind of connection does not necessarily mean that the animal is stupid; perhaps in that animal's niche that kind of connection is simply not required.

Since the 1960s we at ABE have made a regular practice of studying an animal ethologically before we start a training program. We find out what types of behaviors the animal uses in its niche, what is easy to condition, what is hard. And so we trained an ungulate to use a grazing response to play a harmonica, a pig to "play a piano" by moving its feet along the keys (figure 1), a duck to paddle a boat, and a goat to "use its head" to ring a bell. For the Montreal World's Fair, Expo 67, the Canadian government asked us to show the public how various domestic animals make their living in a common ecological niche – the barnyard. The particular behaviors involved crossing a stream of water, getting food, and returning home. A pigeon flew across the stream, lighted on a small building (where it rang a bell), and flew back. A chicken walked across a log, chased a butterfly in a tree, and returned to its chicken house. A rabbit crossed the stream by going through the log, scratched in a garden and returned to its burrow. And a duck slid down through a waterfall, dabbled in a pool for a fish, and then returned to its nest. All this was completely automated – controlled completely by timers and the sequence of events.

Here we need to sound a word of warning: using an animal's natural behavior in a situation like this does not necessarily demonstrate a high degree of intelligence on the part of the animal, although people generally tend to read intelligence into such a situation. Thus intelligence, in this instance, is in the eye of the beholder. We hear comments such as "Look at the smart pig playing the piano!" "I never knew a chicken was smart enough to use a computer," and so on.

For some training programs, we can also make use of the animal's ease in making certain connection. For example, a project for the U.S. Army involved training birds to fly down the road ahead of a convoy and detect camouflaged troops in ambush on the side of the road. The bird of choice here was the homing pigeon, because of its strong

Figure 1 *Piano-playing pig. The piglet uses its feet to play the piano; however, the rooting and biting responses in food getting situations are very strong and often interfere with foot movements. (Illustration by Richard Swartz.)*

flight capabilities and inbred tendencies to return to the home loft (in this case a mobile loft mounted on one of the convoy's trucks). In another Army project, the assignment was to train a dog to detect buried antipersonnel mines. A hunting dog (with a keen nose) was the obvious choice; the dog was trained to sit at the location where it sniffed out a mine.

Seabirds have been scanning the ocean for fish for thousands of years. Could they also be trained to scan for other objects? Could a herring gull, for example, spot a downed flier wearing a life jacket? We decided we would find out. We started with chicks a few hours old, and raised them from infancy with human trainers. The training started in flight pens, moved to sheltered bays and small boats, and finally to the open ocean. And our hunches were right: because of the birds' strong natural hunting behavior it was easy to train them to scan for life jackets, which, through our conditioning, became associated with food.

Another aspect of behavior ABE has used to advantage is the relationship between connectability and the flexibility, or generalizing ability, which I have already mentioned. The more variable the niche, the more types of connections the animal may be required to make. We are all familiar with the countless stories of "smart" dogs locating lost masters or their belongings. We once trained a crow to retrieve a small object. On one occasion, when it could not locate the article (which was not there), it spent several extra minutes hunting, and finally returned with another article of similar size and shape.

We have, over the years, studied and trained many animals, both flexible and rigid. Some of the more inflexible are the peafowl, the swan, and the booby. The last bird is an interesting case, because in spite of relative inflexibility – as far as conditioning new behaviors – it is superbly adapted, in its flight abilities particularly, to its own niche. Some of the most flexible birds (one is tempted to say "the smartest") are the crows and their relatives, and the parrot family. In a comparative study of long-distance pattern vision, the raven proved able to master the problem readily, while the seagull, with perhaps very similar visual abilities, was a total "dunce."

One interesting contrast occurs when two different species are trained on the same type of response – a chicken, for example, makes a fine visual discrimination in picking the face card of a group of five. It is much more difficult to teach the same type of discrimination to a macaw, but the macaw can learn essentially the same behavior making a tactile discrimination (figure 2). For the chicken, the face card is marked with a tiny black dot; for the macaw, the face card bears a small indentation for which the bird feels with its tongue. Ducks, although in many ways quite different from chickens, can also learn fine visual discriminations – for example, a duck can be trained to select a picture of another duck of its own kind. This does not mean that the duck really sees this two-dimensional drawing as a real duck; it has simply been conditioned to make a certain type of dabbling response to a certain visual pattern.

Actually, the ability to form discriminations

Figue 2 *A macaw picks out the ace of hearts by feeling with its toungue a small indentation on the back of the card. (Illustration by Richard Swartz.)*

does not seem to be one of the main facets of intelligence. Many people assume that the chicken must after all be very smart because we have been able to train so many fine visual discriminations. We feel the ability to generalize, to be flexible, and to make many kinds of connections is much more "intelligent" than the capacity for forming discriminations. Among the mammals, the raccoon shows this flexibility of behavior (figure 3). This animal, like monkeys and apes, has very dextrous hands that make possible many skills. But such dexterity is not a prerequisite for flexible, "intelligent" behavior. Some of the most interesting of all the animals, to us as well as to the general public, have been the dolphins and whales: great generalizers, tremendously flexible in their behavior, and extremely well adapted to their watery niche.

I do not pretend to have provided the last work on animal intelligence, but perhaps I have been able to communicate the complexity of the problem. And, perhaps the animals described here have themselves told us something about how "smart" they are. Of course, in the long run, animals have taught us more than we have taught them.

Figure 3 Basketball-playing raccoon. Raccoons, among mammals, are good generalizers. They exhibit a great deal of varied, flexible behavior and can use their hands (or forepaws) very much as primates do. (Illustration by Vichai Malikul.)

SELECT BIBLIOGRAPHY

Alcock, John. 1979. *Animal behavior: An evoluntionary approach.* Sunderland, Mass.: Sinauer.

Breland, K., and M. Breland. 1961. The misbehavior of organisms. *American Psychologist 16: 681–84.*

———. 1966. *Animal behavior.* New York and London: Macmillan

Garcia, J., and R.A. Koelling. 1966. Relation of cue to consequence to avoidance learning. *Psychonomic Science* 4:123–24.

Garcia, J., B.K. McGowan, and K.M. Green. 1972. Biological constraints on conditioning. In *Biological boundaries of learning,* ed. M.E.P. Seligman and L.L. Hager. New York: Appleton-Century-Crofts.

Lorenz, K. 1952. King Solomon's ring. New York: Crowell.

Seligman, M.E.P., and J.L. Hager, eds. *Biological boundaries of learning.* New York: Appleton-Century-Crofts.

Shettleworth, S.J. 1972. Conditioning of domestic chickens to visual and auditory stimuli: Control of drinking by visual stimuli and control of conditioned fear by sound. In *Biological boundaries of learning,* ed. M.E.P. Seligman and J.L. Hager. New York: Appleton-Century-Crofts.

Skinner, B.F. 1959. A case history in scientific method. In *Psychology – A study of a science,* ed. S. Koch. Vol. 2. New York: McGraw-Hill.

Teitelbaum, P. 1966. The use of operant methods in the assessment and control of motivational states. In *Operant behavior; Areas of research and application,* ed. W.K. Honig. New York: Appleton-Century-Crofts.

Verplanck, W. 1955. Since learned behavior is innate and vice versa, what now? *Psychological Review* 62:139–44.

VOL 19, NO 4, 1994. Anthropomorphism, what's the big deal? Do we make too much of this issue? Otto Fad of Sea World explores the ideas and controversy surrounding the topic in this well researched article. While not all trainers may agree with all of the points discussed in this article, you cannot help but come away with some interesting food for thought. I believe this article should be required reading for all trainers.

Anthropomorphism: The Natural Enemy Within?

by Otto Fad
Sea World of Florida

Anthropomorphism is the assigning of human qualities to...oh, we all know all about the "A-word," right? Since "dolphinism" has become the totemism of our time, perhaps some discussion is warranted.

None of us can escape the effects of anthropomorphism. It is culturally hammered into us from childhood. But instead of accepting this as a mere fact of life, let's inspect the issue and introspect our role in its promulgation.

Although our livelihoods are based on compassion for other species and we are driven to provide our charges with the best care possible, anthropomorphism is not to be thoughtlessly invoked. Formal anthropomorphic declarations dent our professionalism and bludgeon the credibility of ethology as a legitimate science.

Anthropomorphism is a well-established cultural phenomenon and, as individuals, we can trace our indoctrination to our first post-natal hours. Before we are even capable of discussing animals, adorable, large-eyed plush replicas of them (usually of the genus Ursus) are thrust into our laps. We soon graduate to cartoon capers in which the star may be a wisecracking bipedal rabbit or a turtle with an attitude and a semiautomatic weapon. We read of scholarly owls and deceitful wolves, and watch movies about lions with dignity (an adaption of questionable benefit in times of severe drought). From here it's a mere hop, skip, and a leap-of-faith to remedial cows and dolphin geniuses.

Anthropomorphic language is a double-edged sword. On the one side, it is colorful, easy, comfortable, easy, familiar, easy, convenient, and of course, easy. On the other side, it infers purpose and intent even where there is none. As long as we're on the sword analogy, you know what they say about people who "live by the sword." For a marine mammal trainer, to speak in anthropomorphic terms to the scientifically illiterate is to use that "sword" on oneself. In behavioral terminology, using cute, cuddly words reinforces those who think in cute, cuddly ways.

Portraying our animals in anthropomorphic terms provides fodder for animal rights extremists. The enormous popularity of dolphins in our society has given captivity considerations a religious dimension. The conservation creed of the nineties has created dolphin deities. As one author (Vicchio, 1986) points out deifying to demonizing others. Contrast the spiritualization of the dolphin with the torture we have visited upon cats and sharks, among others. Some of the "sport" killing of cat and shark species (whether for trophy hunting, predator elimination, or some other euphemism) has been perversely justified by the view that these animals are evil incarnate. Even cuddly killer whales, which afterall are just big dolphins, were (although in some areas that should be in the present tense) routinely shot at by people who bestowed upon them the decidedly anthropomorphic moniker of "devilfish."

Our discussion to this point notwithstanding, anthropomorphism is not a dirty word. When used by our ancestors it helped answer questions about the world and our place in it. Great writers use it to paint vivid pictures. When used with regard to the weather or computers, anthropomorphism can help us to understand how some systems work. In a curious indication that scientific thinking has matured over the milennia, Carl Sagan and Ann Druyan (1992) turn the tables, using a computer model and free market economic system to explain the evolution of human consciousness (p. 403). It is curious indeed, that authors would choose twentieth century technology which is often explained to novices via anthropomorphism to discuss that part of us which is the seat of all anthropomorphic thought.

Even in oceanaria, anthropomorphism is not the plague. For example, character development can have its place in marine mammal education. After all, you've got to get people's attention if you want to teach them, and entertainment is one way of grabbing their ears. Characterization like that utilized in shows is consistent with many other stimuli to which we adults expose kids. That is, it is very unintimidating. Instead of fighting the anthropomorphic saturation of our cultural fabric, it may serve us better to "go with the flow" in general presentations. After all, even a cursory conservation message or brief introduction to marine mammal appreciation is better than nothing. There are guests who are ready to discuss marine mammal topics in greater depth. For them we like to provide opportunities to satisfy their curiosity without turning off or turning away the masses who might otherwise have no live exposure to marine mammals. One of the best times to accomplish this is immediately after shows, when trainers can meet guests and answer questions informally. This is a time when it is critical to avoid being overly anthropomorphic. Chances are that the people who take advantage of these opportunities are perhaps a little more curious than your average guest, and they may even be critical thinkers who don't believe everything that they read or see on TV.

Some scientists use anthropomorphic language. Some unwittingly slip into its use, while others engage in what is called "mock anthropomorphism." This is a strategy wherein the author (sometimes with and sometimes without a disclaimer) knowingly anthropomorphizes in an attempt to simplify an explanation. That underscores the awkwardness of some "science speak," the terminology of behaviorism being one good example. Probably many of us use "mock anthropomorphism" to take verbal shortcuts. To maintain integrity and not allow our words to affect our thinking we must be aware that this is indeed what we are doing. When conversing with others not familiar with our day-to-day "trainerspeak," we should issue a disclaimer to that effect. However, in a professional context, anthropomorphic terminology should be avoided as much as possible.

For the most part, anthropomorphism is unscientific. Anytime we ascribe a more complicated explanation for a response or group of responses in the face of a simpler explanation (like talking about "motivation" instead of reinforcement histories, balance of reinforcement, stimulus generalization, etc.) we are waxing anthropomorphic. Unfortunately, using exclusively acceptable behavioral terms would alienate some of our guests. In fact, J.S. Kennedy attributes much of the new "anthropomorphism" to a backlash against radical behaviorism.

For us, eliminating all anthropomorphic terms may be not only an impractical goal, but also an undesirable one. Most of us engage in little pure science-we function to bridge the gap between science and lay people in one very specific area. Obviously, it behooves us to be familiar with the language of both the ethologist and the zoogoer. In **Marine Mammals and Man**, Forrest G. Wood elucidates some stumbling blocks in spanning this chasm in his discussion of the popular press' generally awe-filled reports on John Lilly's work.

For millions of people, we are the medium for the delivery of information from the sender (scientists) to the receiver (public). For those of us working with marine mammals in the United States, this is our educational responsibility as mandated by the Marine Mammal Protection Act. But as many well-meaning statesmen can attest, translating from one language to another can be perilous indeed to one's message.

Consider the difference between saying that a dolphin "likes" a particular reinforcer versus the dolphin "responds well" to it. The intended message may be the same, but the interpreted messages are quite different. The former describes the effectiveness of a reinforcer as a product of conscious thought, while the latter allows an explanation of an established reinforcement history with identical or similar stimuli.

A corollary of anthropomorphism is the "training is an art, not a science" mindset. We have enviable careers, but they are tarnished when we mystify our jobs. As with any job, there are identifiable skills that good trainers possess. Some of these are keen observational skills, a thorough knowledge of marine mammal natural history, a disciplined commitment to positive reinforcement, and a critical, analytical mind. Certainly, there are other talents and traits that an individual can develop and, as in other vocations, dedication and hard work do pay off in the long haul. Good training is a product of mastering a short list of talents. It only seems magical when not examined analytically. By mystifying our jobs, we do ourselves no favor and we add to that "dolphin mystique."

By becoming very familiar with the natural history of our animals, we become able to explain their behavior from an adaptive point of view. Decisions that have their genesis in an "if I were a dolphin..." mindset are inherently faulty. Unscientific thinking all too quickly attributes a cause-and-effect relationship to unrelated or only temporally-related events.

Of course, we can't expect to go "cold turkey" and eschew our familiar phraseology in favor of a better justified jargon. But by being more aware of our use of anthropomorphic terms, we run less risk of being misinterpreted and fueling the fire of animal rights extremism.

In conclusion, here are the thoughts of two distinguished contemplators of the anthropomorphism issue. Stephen J. Vicchio (1986): "Much of the anthropomorphizing of animals, I suspect, comes from a lack of knowledge about them...zoological programs that are careful to avoid these stereotypic and anthropomorphic sentiments are sorely needed." J.S. Kennedy (1992) adds that although anthropomorphism "is probably programmed into us genetically as well as inoculated culturally, that does not mean that the disease in incurable."

REFERENCES / FURTHER READING

Griffin, D.R., (1986). **The Question of Animal Awareness**. New York: Rockefeller University Press.

Kennedy, J.S., (1992). **The New Anthropomorphism**. Cambridge: Cambridge University Press.

Sagan, C. and A. Druyan, (1992). **Shadows of Forgotten Ancestors**. New York: Random House.

Vicchio, S.J., (1986). *From Aristotle to Descartes: making animals anthropomorphic*, in R.J. Hoage and L. Goldman (Eds.) **Animal Intelligence** (pp. 187-207). Washington, D.C.: Smithsonian.

Wood, F. G., (1973). **Marine Mammals and Man**. New York: Robert B. Luce.

A Behavior Sampler by Gary Wilkes

Gary Wilkes often uses anthropomorphic references to get his point across to his readers. He "thinks" for the dog or cat to illustrate, usually quite humorously, why certain training techniques do or don't work. However, here he illustrates one of the dangers of carrying anthropomorphism too far. Using anthropomorphic terms to describe or talk about animal behavior is very different from using those same ideas to make important training or husbandry decisions.

Anthropomorphism: A Case of Mistaken Identity

by Gary Wilkes

A few days ago, I spoke with a man whose male dog was lifting his leg and urinating in the house. I asked if he had considered neutering the dog as a first step toward solving the problem. He seemed offended at the idea and told me, "No animal of mine is going to lose his manhood." He reacted exactly as if I had suggested neutering him, rather than the dog. He apparently did not understand that dogs do not have a "manhood."

It is common among humans to treat an animal exactly as if it were a furry little human. This practice is called anthropomorphism. Often anthropomorphism is as harmless as talking to your pet as you would a person, for instance, we believe that Fifi "knows exactly what we are saying" because she cocks her head while she listens to us. Because the position of the dog's head looks exactly like a human pose of intense listening and concentration, we believe that she must also understand what she hears. The trouble with this practice begins when you start to base your decisions about your animal's care as if it were truly human.

Cats are often the victims of inappropriate anthropomorphic attitudes. Because humans assume that cats are aloof and uncontrollable, they are often allowed to roam and breed freely. A mother cat may be completely wild, starving and parasite ridden and still be praised for "being a good mother." Because her behavior with her kittens appears to mimic human nurturing she will gain the sympathy, but not the assistance, of her human observers. Conversely, if the animal abandons her kittens, she is a "bad mother" - even though the kittens may be genetically defective.

Female dogs are not immune to anthropomorphic treatment. Many dogs are forced to have a litter of puppies in tribute to the supposed benefits of motherhood. While the general belief is that one litter will calm the dog down and make her better with kids, it is actually spaying that is more likely to cause those changes in behavior. Maternity in dogs can actually awaken undesirable behavior such as biting people in order to defend the pups.

The sex lives of dogs are also often treated as if they are identical to humans in their desires and practices. To better understand why this is inappropriate, we have to look at the process of domestication. To start with, dogs are not natural creatures. They have been systematically shaped through selective breeding for thousands of years. Not only do they not resemble humans in their sexual behavior, they no longer resemble their ancestors, the wolves.

When men first started to breed domestic dogs, they ran into a major problem. Most wolves are monogamous and usually mate for life. The first dog breeders could not simply mate wolves together. They had to play a Love Connection-style game of matching a suitable pair that also happened to "fall in love" with each other. So, one of the first changes caused by selective animal breeding was to make dogs as promiscuous as possible. If an animal was willing to mate with any other wolf it was a prime breeding animal. After ten thousand years, this behavior is retained in the rampant sexuality of the typical male dog.

So, the sex drive of dogs is not a natural phenomenon. This once necessary trait is now a major liability. When thousands of dogs are packed into relatively small areas they often react erratically because of this sexual tension. Males will jump over and dig under fences to find a female in heat. Once on the street they are in danger of automobiles, disease and the attacks of other animals. In an effort to protect the dog's libido, his owner stands a good chance of losing the animal to theft, injury and death.

In all its forms, anthropomorphism is a risky practice. Holding an animal to the same standards as a human sets them up for constant failure. Rather than attempting to force pets into a human mold, it is far more interesting to appreciate them as they are and celebrate the differences.

Basic Operant Conditioning 4

This chapter will cover basic operant conditioning techniques needed to begin training. The concepts here are building blocks, fundamental to all effective training. Our philosophy at Shedd Aquarium is to teach training slowly, building your knowledge without rushing ahead of your skill level. The techniques throughout this manual are organized with that progression in mind. As previously noted, Karen Pryor has written some wonderful descriptions of many of the concepts outlined here. So it is recommended that you read chapters 1 to 3 of her book *Don't Shoot the Dog* (*DOG*, pp. 1-97), before continuing with this chapter. What follows are particulars about how to apply that information to marine mammal training and to indicate where our philosophies may differ.

Getting used to the Lingo

Technology
Training is a technology, a science with proven principles applied to modifying the behavior of an organism. If applied properly, these applications of science to behavior can be very effective. So often, training is thought of as an art or a creative endeavor; consequently, the scientific principles that underlie behavior are sometimes overlooked. While a good trainer may indeed be creative and artistic in his or her approach to training, the reasons why operant conditioning works are based on scientific principles. If we look at these principles as a science and their applications as a technology, we may be less likely to forget why training works. However, since training is used in many different applications, many diverse ways of speaking about training have developed. Not all trainers think about training in the technical or scientific sense but that does not mean they have nothing to teach us; therefore, one must be well versed in the unique jargon that is part of this field.

Defining the Audience
The terminology used in discussing training tends to vary with the audience. Understanding the differences between audiences will help you to identify not only the meaning but also the intent of various terms. Generally, training terms fall into several categories; it is helpful to understand all of these:

Technical – These are terms as defined in the operant textbooks and behavior journals. They have been derived from psychology labs and the study of operant learning and behavior analysis. Unfortunately, there are still discrepancies among psychologists about many of these terms, but most of those discrepancies are in complex learning principles that are outside the scope of this manual.

Industry – Within each training community, there are terms that relate specifically to that field. For the sake of precision, the marine mammal community is making a concerted effort to use more and more technical terms. However, there will always be the need to define terms that are specific to each field. Horse trainers will have terms that are unique to their work, as will dog trainers, marine mammal trainers and many other specialists.

Common – The terminology used by the public is the most widely used and understood. Karen Pryor uses a combination of common and technical terms in her book *Don't Shoot the Dog*. Because many of us deal with the public, we, too, must be able to describe what we do in common terms.

Slang – Finally, slang creeps into everyone's vocabulary. They are the only terms we will avoid in this manual. It is important to recognize, however, that slang is frequently used by almost every discipline, often as a shorthand for longer words or complex phrases.

Learning Basic Terms

Since there is no universally agreed upon set of terms, definitions will be included in the text, as well as in a consolidated list of terms in chapter 14, "Glossary." An introduction to basic terms can be found in the 1996 Trainer's Forum article *Basic Marine Mammal Training Terminology*, on page 80. The more familiar you are with terminology of all kinds, the more easily you will be able to communicate with trainers from other disciplines and facilities.

I remember that I was once at a conference where a trainer said, "We quit using rears in favor of CR when our KW husbandry broke down." I nodded my head knowingly, tried desperately to process what I had just heard, and finally I said, "Huh?" The trainer, I would discover, had combined slang for an acronym with another acronym (an incorrect one at that), then with yet *another* acronym – and he succeeded in losing me completely. "Rears" was slang for "R.I.R.," an acronym for "Random and Interrupted Reinforcement." "CR" should have been "CRF," a fairly common acronym for "continuous reinforcement." But "KW"? He *really* stumped me with that one. It turned out to be slang for "killer whales" – slang that had yet to travel far beyond the facility where the trainer worked. Fortunately, most trainers don't use that much slang – at least not in the same sentence. Still, knowing the basics is certainly important.

Operant vs. Classical Conditioning

These two conditioning techniques are often confused and misunderstood by the public. Most training that we will discuss will be based on operantly conditioned behavior.

Operant Conditioning

This is learning in which behaviors are altered by the consequences that follow them. If a dog pokes its nose into a water fountain, gets sprayed with cold water, and enjoys the experience, it is likely to repeat the behavior. On the other hand, if the spray of cold water frightens or annoys the dog, it will be less likely to repeat the behavior. These responses were operantly conditioned. B.F. Skinner first coined the term in 1938 in his book *The Behavior of Organisms*. Operant conditioning is sometimes referred to as Skinnerian conditioning or instrumental conditioning. The animal or person being conditioned is the operator, or operant. The animal or person chooses to engage in the activity, thus the term "operant." Much of our learning is operantly conditioned; we make choices about our actions based on our past experiences. The principles of operant conditioning as applied to animal training will be the focus of this manual.

Classical Conditioning

Classical conditioning describes an involuntary, or automatic, response to a stimulus. This type of conditioning is sometimes called respondent conditioning, or Pavlovian conditioning as a result of Pavlov's famous experiment with dogs. If a dog is regularly given food immediately following the sound of a bell, the dog will begin to anticipate the arrival of the food. At the sound of the bell, the dog may begin to salivate, even though the food has not yet been presented. The dog did not choose to salivate; therefore it was a reflexive response, classically conditioned. This type of behavioral response occurs all the time, but we will not focus on it in this manual. Our goal is to teach the animals to respond consciously to each of our interactions with them. Nevertheless, it is still wise for the trainer to understand classical responses and the effect they have on behavior.

Positive Reinforcement

Positive reinforcement is the basis of all conditioning (*DOG*, pp. 1-4), particularly as we apply it to marine mammal training. The difficult thing for many trainers to learn is how to make sense of the countless reinforcement options.

Primary Reinforcers
A primary reinforcer is something that an animal finds inherently reinforcing. Usually, this is something that satisfies a basic biological need. Consequently, food is one of our strongest reinforcers.

Secondary Reinforcers
A secondary reinforcer is something that has acquired reinforcing value through its association with a primary reinforcer. Wild animals can learn that petting and other human interactions are reinforcing once the animal has come to associate people with their feeding and care. The concept and use of secondary reinforcers are an important part of training, but they should be reserved for trainers with a more complete understanding of operant conditioning techniques, we'll explore the use of secondary reinforcers in greater depth in chapter 9, "Advanced Techniques and Concepts."

Timing
The most important aspect of good training is precise timing of reinforcement. For reinforcement to have the desired effect, it must be delivered to an animal the moment the desired behavior occurs. One second too late or too early and you may be reinforcing a different behavior (*DOG*, pp. 7-10).

Bridging Stimulus

Conditioned Reinforcer
To help in the timing of reinforcement, a conditioned reinforcer should be taught to the animal. Some signal that means, "*That* was good." Such a signal indicates to the animal the precise moment at which it did the correct behavior (*DOG*, pp.13-17). In the marine mammal community this type of conditioned reinforcer is called a bridging stimulus. The bridging stimulus is actually the first of the secondary reinforcers that we teach our animals. It is a secondary reinforcer with a very specific meaning, referred to by some as an

"event marker," precisely indicating (marking) the behavior (event) that was offered correctly.

Selecting a Bridge

With marine mammals, a dog whistle is often used because its sound travels well above and below the water. However, a bridging stimulus can be audible, visual, or tactile. It can be anything the animal can easily distinguish and a trainer can deliver in a timely manner. At Shedd Aquarium we use a variety of bridging stimuli to suit varying needs. Whatever the chosen bridge, it should be a distinct stimulus that serves no other purpose in the animal's environment, otherwise it might confuse the animal. The bridge draws an animal's attention away from food and focuses its attention on the task at hand. Another advantage to using a bridging stimulus is that it is easily transferred from trainer to trainer, allowing a number of trainers to let an animal know it did well. Using a vocal bridge, such as saying "good" can be effective, but some animals will not immediately recognize it when said in a deeper or higher voice or with a different accent than those of the primary trainer. The selection of a bridge should be made with all of those factors in mind.

Teaching the Bridge

The process of teaching an animal that the whistle means "good" is a relatively easy one. We simply pair the whistle with a primary reinforcer. In time, the animal will associate the sound of the whistle with the delivery of food. Once that association is made, the bridge can be a very effective tool. In essence, that's why the bridge, a conditioned reinforcer, becomes the first of your secondary reinforcers. Gary Wilkes examines the benefits of using a bridging stimulus with pets in his article *Primarily, Secondary Reinforcers End on a Good Note*, on page 84.

Why a Bridge?

The bridge becomes useful when you cannot deliver a primary reinforcer at the precise moment you would like. Instead, you must deliver a secondary (or conditioned) reinforcer, which bridges the gap between the completion of the behavior and the delivery of the primary reinforcer. Because the animal learns to generalize that the whistle is good, you will sometimes hear it called a generalized reinforcer. Throughout the manual, we will usually refer to it as a bridge or a whistle. The timing and consistency of the bridge is extremely important and worthy of further exploration; a more detailed discussion can be found in *Bridging Basics: How to Maintain Consistency* (T. Forum, 1997), on page 86. For a more advanced look at bridging, particularly with multiple animals, see chapter 7, "Social Animals."

Shaping

The term "shaping" refers to the various techniques used to actually train a behavior (*DOG*, pp.35-67). A few important terms should be understood before diving into the articles about shaping techniques.

Successive Approximations

Because these are the small steps that move in the direction of a desired behavior when training, they are called approximations of that behavior. If you think of training as climbing a ladder, you must take one rung at a time. The rungs of the ladder, then, are successive approximations of the behavior we wish to train: reaching the top. A fine example of successive approximations with elephants is described by Gary Wilkes in *Elephants Go from Carrot and Stick to Carrot and Click*, on page 90.

Selective Reinforcement

This is the process of reinforcing only those responses that move in the direction of the desired behavior. When teaching ladder-climbing, you would reinforce a step up the ladder while ignoring a step down the ladder. That is the essence of selective reinforcement.

Black and White (Establishing Criteria)

This is the important concept of recognizing that a behavior is either right or wrong – there's nothing in between. While we all know that there is plenty of gray area, it is recommended that only experienced trainers try to judge those in-between regions. That will be discussed in detail in chapter 9, "Advanced Techniques and Concepts." A new trainer should understand that for an animal to learn, expectations should be clearly communicated; criteria cannot be vague. A trainer who constantly changes the criteria, sets the animal up for failure. An animal that clearly understands what is expected, black and white (right and wrong), will learn faster and be less frustrated.

Number of Trainers

Many of the concepts discussed in this manual are based on the assumption that there will be a large staff working with the animals being trained. Employing many trainers in a single program necessitates increased precautions to help prevent communication and behavioral breakdown. Even training the house pet can become complicated if everyone in the family is trying their hand at training it.

New training – When a behavior is being trained for the first time, only one trainer should be assigned to that behavior. This is critical in assuring consistency.

Behavioral maintenance – In a large facility, many trainers will eventually work with the animals. Each animal may interact with two or more trainers in a given day. Because of this diversity, stricter rules must apply to behavioral maintenance than would apply to an individual who is the animal's only trainer and caregiver.

Communication – Behavior will evolve over time, and shaping occurs every time we interact with an animal, even if we are simply feeding it. When large numbers of trainers interact with an animal, good communication is critical, a subject discussed in chapter 2, "Knowing the Animal."

Shaping Techniques

The literature written about various shaping techniques is fairly comprehensive. Targeting is the technique most used by dolphin trainers, but we will touch on each of the techniques that can be used to shape behavior.

Scanning

This technique – the act of reinforcing behavior that is naturally offered by an animal – is considered old-fashioned and not widely used except with certain types of behaviors. A more detailed account of scanning (also called capturing) can be found in *Scanning or Capturing Behavior: A Necessary Tool, an Outdated Technique, or a Lost Art* (Ramirez, 1996), on page 92. Austin McDevitt (1982) in *Random Reinforcement of Spontaneous Behavior* describes another use of this technique, on page 95.

Targeting

Teaching an animal to touch some part of its body to an object is called targeting. Descriptions of basic uses of targeting can be found in chapter 6, "Husbandry Training" (see pages 135-136). To get you started understanding the concept please read Karen Pryor's description (*DOG*, pp.58-62) and Gary Wilkes' article, *Training by Pushing and Tugging is "Off-Target,"* on page 97.

Modeling

This technique is not often used with dolphins, but is frequently used in training pets. It entails "showing" the animal how to do the behavior. Sometimes it is referred to as "molding," because trainers will physically mold the behavior as in training sign language to apes by putting the animals' hands in the desired position, then reinforcing them for allowing it. This concept is briefly described in the two suggested readings listed under targeting.

Mimicry

A common use of mimicry is in training birds to talk. But mimicry can be a behavior in itself. Teaching an animal to mimic the behavior of another animal has been used in research and enrichment training. Young animals will sometimes mimic older ones, which was the subject of a 1995 Trainer's Forum article, *Calf Mimicry: To shape or to Capture?* on page 98. In some technical circles, mimicry is considered a type of modeling; however, the concepts have been separated in this manual.

Abstract Learning

When two separate concepts are put together for the first time to form a new idea or behavior, this is considered abstract learning. It is the method most used in teaching people in school. This is not truly considered shaping; it is actual teaching. But the fact is that shaping can be used as the foundation for abstract learning. That topic will not be explored in this manual.

Pryor's 10 Laws of Shaping

These laws are very well thought out and described by Karen Pryor (*DOG*, pp.38-52). Learn them. Know them. Live them. Every training program will develop its own set of rules and laws, but Karen has summed up the most important basics very well. Paraphrased they are:

1. **Raise criteria in small increments.** By using successive approximations you will set the animal up to succeed.

2. **Train one criterion at a time**. Keep your goals clear and remember the concept of black and white. When we train a dolphin to give us its tail so that we can take a voluntary blood sample, there are multiple criteria. The dolphin must allow us to touch its tail, then hold its tail; it must remain calm, allow lengthy touching, accept pressure on the tail, and eventually accept the insertion of a needle. These are just a

few of the steps, each with its own criterion. We must be careful not to overwhelm an animal with too much all at once.

3. **Vary reinforcement before moving to next approximation.** Although we do not recommend that new trainers use a fully variable schedule of reinforcement until they gain experience (see chapter 9), this is still an important rule. Reinforcement can be varied in many ways including varying magnitude of reinforcement, type of reinforcers, or requiring longer duration or repetition of the behavior being trained.

4. **Relax old criteria when introducing new criteria.** When an animal is being introduced to something new, it is not unusual for an animal to fail to meet all previously learned criteria. This is acceptable at first.

5. **Plan ahead.** Have a training plan in mind and know the eventual goals.

6. **Don't change trainers in mid-stream.** For consistency it is not wise to have different people training the same behavior.

7. **If a plan doesn't work, change the plan.** Training is a dynamic process, so don't be afraid to change the plan if needed.

8. **Don't stop a session gratuitously.** Stay focused, don't get distracted, and don't end a session without a reason.

9. **Regress when behavior deteriorates.** Animals can forget or get confused. Taking a few steps backward can refresh their memory and get them back on the right track.

10. **End on a positive note.** Keep training fun. Don't end a session if the animal is frustrated; end with success.

Stimulus Control

Once you have trained a behavior, you will want to be able to ask the animal to perform the behavior on a specific cue or signal. This is called bringing the behavior under stimulus control (*DOG*, pp. 68-97).

Discriminative Stimulus
This is the technical name for a cue or signal. Trainers will often refer to it as simply an "SD." It is often written S^D.

Choosing the Cue
Signals may be auditory, visual, or tactile. The choice should be based on what the animal will clearly understand and not confuse with any other signal. As Gary Wilkes writes in *What's in a Name*, on page 100, animals can easily misinterpret cues we give them. In addition, the choice of an S^D may depend on how the behavior is going to be used. For example, animals trained for work in films often must rely on visual cues, because the trainer should not be heard directing the animal off-screen.

Consistency
As with all elements of training, consistency is very important. How the cue is given and what the cue means should not vary over time. Trainers, when maintaining behavior, will often get sloppy in giving the animal a signal. A sloppy S^D is the equivalent of developing a speech impediment. Mild variations in pronunciation are usually understood, but the more severe the impediment, the more difficult the words are to understand. When animals have difficulty understanding, they will often try to "guess" what is meant. We should not put our animals in that position.

Changing the Cue
Sometimes during the course of training you may want to change the S^D being used. This can be done through a process called fading (*DOG*, pp. 77-79).

Pryor's Rules of Stimulus Control
Karen provides a good list and description of how to determine if a behavior is truly under stimulus control (*DOG*, pp. 73-74). These four rules sum it up pretty well:

1. The behavior always occurs immediately upon presentation of the conditioned stimulus (the dog sits when told to).
2. The behavior never occurs in the absence of the stimulus (during a training session the dog never sits spontaneously).
3. The behavior never occurs in response to some other stimulus (the dog does not sit when you say "lie down").
4. No other behavior occurs in response to this stimulus (the dog does not lie down when you say "sit").

Superstitious Behavior

The phenomenon of superstitious behavior occurs all the time when training (*DOG*, pp. 26-29). We must constantly be aware of superstitious behavior as Gary Wilkes points out in *Superstitious Behaviors*, on page 101.

Poor Bridging
One of the primary causes of superstitious behavior is a poorly timed bridge. Once an animal has learned the meaning of the bridging stimulus, it will respond to that bridge very precisely. If the bridge occurs a second too early or too late, you may get unwanted behavior.

Poor Observation
Sometimes superstitious behavior occurs because the trainer is not observing closely. In some cases, the trainer may not be able to see the undesired behavior. A dolphin being trained to roll on its side for a medical exam, might inadvertently close its right eye during the procedure. If the bridge occurs while the eye is closed, the animal may always close that eye during the behavior even though it was never the trainer's intention to shape the behavior in that way.

Sloppy Cues
When an S^D is not distinct, the sloppy signal may inadvertently become the new cue. After a time the animal may no longer respond to the original S^D. The animal will have developed a superstitious behavior (learning the sloppy cue in place of the actual cue), a case of inadvertent fading.

Using Superstitious Behavior
Just because a behavior was accidentally shaped doesn't mean it might not be useful. If a trainer is aware of how and when an animal superstitiously exhibits a specific behavior, the trainer might take advantage of the behavior. This is one of the methods described in the section on scanning for getting behaviors that were spontaneously offered. Trainers will often use their own superstitious behavior to try to recreate the circumstances under which an animal previously offered a desired response. We are just as capable of superstitious behavior as our animals.

Dealing with Incorrect Responses

Ignore the Behavior – LRS

A basic principle in operant conditioning is to reinforce desired behavior and ignore unwanted behavior. Theoretically, the way to accomplish this is to provide the least reinforcing stimulus possible to the animal following an incorrect response; a least reinforcing stimulus is called an LRS. However, many trainers have difficulty ignoring bad behavior, because their emotions get in the way. A technique used successfully by many facilities is referred to as a 3 to 5 second "no response," or neutral response. In 1991 Mike Scarpuzzi and his colleagues at Sea World wrote about the application of this principle in *Decreasing the Frequency of Behavior through Extinction*, on page 103. The basic idea is simply to follow an incorrect response with no reaction of any kind. In short, an attempt is made to make as little change in the animal's environment as possible for a brief period (3 to 5 seconds). Although it is impossible to provide a truly neutral response, the idea is to come as close to a neutral response as possible at the point where reinforcement normally would be given.

Time-outs

A time-out is the removal of the opportunity for positive reinforcement. This is a common technique in training and teaching and is still widely used by many trainers, especially with terrestrial animals. The neutral response, or LRS, is actually a very brief time-out. But, many trainers make a distinction between the two terms. There is no doubt that a time-out can be effective, but the frequency of misuse of the traditional time-out created a need for a more focused and effective technique that could be easily understood and applied by young trainers. Often, trainers would implement a time-out by turning their back on an animal or walking away from a session. This was sometimes coupled with an angry or frustrated state of mind by the trainer, and the results were ultimately not always effective. The LRS is an attempt to define a specific type of time-out that can be implemented easily by everyone on a training staff. Experienced trainers may find uses for the longer time-out, but for the novice a lengthy tme out is usually self-defeating. Perhaps the one situation when a lengthy time-out may be warranted is when the animal initiates it. If an animal chooses not to participate in a session or frequently leaves, you cannot force it to participate, so it may eventually be appropriate to end the session and leave. For a more in-depth look at the *Proper Use of a Time Out* (T. Forum, 1999), see page 108.

Deprivation is not the Answer

Because food is a primary reinforcer, it is easy for a young trainer to mistakenly believe that the way to "get an animal's attention," if it is not cooperating, is to cut back the animal's daily rations. This method of trying to motivate an animal is called food deprivation, and is *not* an appropriate technique for dealing with incorrect responses. Although food deprivation may get an animal's attention, it can have severe aversive ramifications – causing anxiety, frustration, aggression, or other problems. Trainers should look for positive alternatives to solving behavioral problems. The LRS, described previously, is a good solution, because it is essentially neutral. Although reinforcement is not offered after an incorrect response, the animal will get other opportunities to earn reinforcement later in the session. It is important to remember that an animal should receive its base diet every day. Additional thoughts about the problems with deprivation can be found in Chapter 9, "Advanced Techniques and Concepts," and more solutions for dealing with undesirable behavior are described in chapter 11, "Problem Solving."

Negative Reinforcement & Punishment

These two concepts are often looked at as solutions for correcting incorrect behavior. New trainers should not consider these techniques until they have gained more experience and understand them thoroughly. In fact, I will not even define them now, because I believe it requires a more complete understanding of operant conditioning to fully appreciate the nuances of these principles. These concepts, along with other means to correcting problem behavior, will be discussed in detail in chapter 9, "Advanced Techniques and Concepts" and in chapter 11, "Problem Solving."

Have a Training Plan

Map Your Behavior

As described in chapter 2, "Knowing the Animal," a training plan is very important. Following a step-by-step procedure will assure that you have a clear idea of your goals. This will set the animal and you up for success. Many experienced trainers map out their training plan in reverse: the planning starts with the finished behavior and they plan the steps backwards. This technique helps them to avoid training themselves into a corner or a dead end.

Be Flexible
Your training plan, like a map, is only a guide. Training is a dynamic process that requires you to respond to your animal's needs. Because every animal will respond differently to a situation, you must be prepared to adjust your plan accordingly. Gary Wiles describes the need for planning (as well as other basic concepts) in *How to get Your Dog into Carnegie Hall*, on page 110.

Stay Focused
It is easy to get distracted and sidetracked. If you want to train a specific behavior, you must be constantly aware of your ultimate goal. Revisit your plan often, change it when needed, reassess goals frequently.

Keep Good Records (Communicate)
This can never be mentioned too often. Keeping a record of each step taken, each setback, and each success will prove beneficial long after the behavior has been trained. Systematic records also can keep a staff informed and provide a historical document that can help track problems and trends.

Summary

This chapter has focused on basic techniques, the essentials of operant conditioning. This is all you need to know to effectively train any animal, right? Well, not quite. Once techniques have been learned, they must be applied properly. To do this, the trainer must gain experience. Training is an interactive process in which you must react and respond to the animals; the animals will respond by presenting you with new challenges. Dealing with these challenges will be the subject of the chapters that follow.

VOL 21, NO 1, 1996. Understanding the lingo of operant conditioning is the first step to applying it and communicating about it effectively. The following article is one of the few *Trainer's Forum* columns that does not take a question and provide answers. It is a printed version of a video presentation compiled by trainers from S.A.I.C., Sea World, Brookfield Zoo, and Shedd Aquarium. They have tried to explain, in simple terms, the most important or often used terms in marine mammal training.

Basic Marine Mammal Training Terminology

At the 1995 conference in Las Vegas, the Animal training Advisory Committee presented the first of many papers focusing solely on training. Presented by committee chair Mark Beeler of SAIC, the presentation, Basic Marine Mammal Training Terminology and Techniques Defined and Explained, is reprinted here in *Trainer's Forum* as a service to the membership. Keep in mind that the presentation was a paper and video presentation, and our technology has not progressed far enough to present the video portion here in the magazine! Also, remember that training methods vary from facility to facility, and the methods presented here are across-section and not IMATA's dictate on how to train. We hope that you find it informative and useful. Enjoy!

**BASIC MARINE MAMMAL
TRAINING TERMINOLOGY AND
TECHNIQUES DEFINED AND EXPLAINED**

*by Mark C. Beeler (SAIC)
and the
IMATA Animal Training Advisory Committee
(Contributing authors: Eric Bogden, Sea World of California, Pete Davey, Shedd Aquarium, and Tim Sullivan, Brookfield Zoo)*

[Mark Beeler]: The understanding of basic marine mammal training terminology and techniques is considered a necessity for the novice to succeed within the marine mammal training industry. Common terminology and techniques of particular usefulness will be defined and explained.

The success of the novice marine mammal trainer relies heavily upon a firm foundation in both levels of practical experience and the understanding of the basic concepts of operant conditioning. It is the combination of the two that improves training technique and, therefore, aids in the success of training sessions. It is the duty of marine mammal facilities to provide novice trainers with the resources to become more knowledgeable and skilled. However, building a foundation is ultimately the responsibility of the individual trainer. Attending conferences such as this can be a key element in the novice trainer's educational process. To begin, we will go to Sea World of California, and a closer look at some beginning fundamentals of their conditioning process.

[Text of video/ Eric Bogden narrating]: Hi. I'm here poolside at Sea World of California. The understanding of basic marine mammal training technology is essential to the trainer. I'd like to explain some common terminology and show you how they are used here with our killer whales.

Terminology discussed will be operant conditioning, primary reinforcement, conditioned reinforcers, bridging stimulus, targeting, successive approximations, and shaping. Let's begin with the definition of operant conditioning.

Operant conditioning is a type of learning in which the likelihood of behavior is increased or decreased by the consequences that follow. So, we can say that the likelihood of behavior, or the chances of an animal repeating a desired behavior, depends on what happens after it.

For example, a whale is asked to perform a

back breach. The whale completes the behavior and returns to the trainer; the trainer then offers a consequence to the whale. The consequence that the trainer offers depends on whether the trainer wants the frequency of a behavior to increase or decrease. In the case of the back breach, the trainer wants the whale to repeat that behavior, so the trainer offers a consequence that is rewarding to the whale (some type of reinforcement). There are different types of reinforcement. We'll try by defining primary reinforcement.

Primary reinforcement is reinforcement provided by a stimulus that the organism finds inherently rewarding, usually stimuli that satisfy biological drives such as hunger or thirst. Thus, food is a primary reinforcement; fish is a stimulus that is inherently rewarding to the killer whales.

Food, or primary reinforcement, is just one way to reward an animal. Other types of rewards can be used to increase the frequency of behavior. These rewards fall into the category of conditioned reinforcers.

A **conditioned reinforcer**, is any stimulus that has acquired its reinforcing properties through association with primary reinforcement. A conditioned or secondary reinforcer is any stimulus that is paired with primary reinforcement. Eventually, through repeated pairings, the new stimulus takes on positive characteristics and becomes a reinforcer, such as ice, rubdowns, toys, water, et cetera.

Choosing when to use reinforcement is also important, as a delay of a few seconds may accidentally reinforce an undesired behavior. Since it is not always possible to instantly reinforce an animal while it is performing, a signal is useful to tell the animal that it has performed correctly and it will receive further reinforcement. This signal is called a bridge signal.

A **bridge signal** is a conditioned reinforcer that communicates to the animal that it is performing the correct behavior. It is also a discriminative stimulus to return to the trainer for another signal. The bridge signal, usually a whistle or a light touch with the killer whales, communicates to the animal that "yes, you are doing the behavior correctly." It is very important that when we use a bridge signal (for example, with a bow behavior) to bridge at the highest point, or apex, of the bow. If the bridge comes early, the whale is rewarded at a lower point, and if bridged late, the whale is rewarded on the way down. The topography, or shape of the behavior will change depending on when the trainer uses the bridge signal.

So far the terminology defined has to do with increase frequency of behavior. Now let's define some common terms used in training a behavior.

One term used when training marine mammals is **target**. Targeting is simply asking an animal to station--or target--on an object. The object could be a trainer's hand or foot, or it could be a float mounted to a pole, which is called a target pole. The target pole may be used to lead an animal through a series of steps to gradually perform a complex behavior. This step-by-step process is called successive approximation.

Successive approximations are small changes in behavior in the direction toward the desired response. For example, a trainer asks a whale to follow a target. The desired response is a forward dive. By rewarding each step that is closer to the forward dive (i.e: the desired response to the target) the trainer is shaping the beginning steps, or changes, toward a forward dive.

As you can see, understanding basic marine mammal training terminology is essential to the trainer. Terms such as operant conditioning, primary reinforcement, secondary reinforcement, conditioned reinforcers, bridge stimulus, targeting, successive approximations, and shaping are used day-to-day when interacting with the killer whales at Sea World of California.

[Mark Beeler]: To continue the novice trainer on the path towards understanding, we now move to Chicago to find additional information and demonstrations of terms and techniques as applied by trainers at the Brookfield Zoo.

[Text of video/ Tim Sullivan narrating]: Hello to IMATA from the Windy City, Chicago. The staff and animals of Brookfield Zoo's Seven Seas Panorama are pleased to present this next segment. We will attempt to define and demonstrate the following training terminology: selective reinforcement, differential reinforcement, and reinforcement schedules.

Starting with the first term, **selective reinforcement** is the process of only reinforcing responses that approximate the desired behavior. For example, if you were to bridge a sea lion for looking into a camera [demonstrated on video] and not bridge when it looks away, you will be using selective reinforcement to train the animal to look directly into the lens.

Our next term will be **differential reinforcement**, which involves two or more physically different behaviors; one is reinforced and the other is extinguished. [As demonstrated on the video, two trainers work with a walrus on voluntary blood sampling. When the second trainer sticks the flipper, the walrus flings the first trainer into the air and onto the rocky shoreline.] (Incidentally, this is a very special effect, don't try it at home!) You would not want to reinforce the unwanted behavior. The desired behavior is for the walrus to remain relaxed for the stick, and when she does so, the trainer reinforces. Not reinforcing the "fling the trainer through the air," but reinforcing the desired behavior, is differential reinforcement.

Our next term is **schedules of reinforcement**, which are the rules that govern the delivery of reinforcement. When a given schedule is in effect, the reinforcement can only be attained by meeting the requirements of the schedule. There are two basic types of reinforcement schedules: continuous reinforcement schedule and intermittent reinforcement schedule.

The first is considered the traditional reinforcement schedule, so let's start with that one. A **continuous reinforcement schedule** states that each correct behavior is reinforced each time it is performed. For example, each time a walrus allows ear medication to be applied, he is reinforced for each relaxed response.

The next four schedules are categorized as **intermittent reinforcement schedules**. They are: fixed interval schedule, variable interval schedule, fixed ratio schedule, and variable ratio schedule.

A **fixed interval schedule** states that a reinforcement is only available after a pre-determined amount of time has elapsed after the last reinforcement. For example, you would reinforce an animal on a three second fixed interval.

A **variable interval schedule** requires reinforcement to be available after varying amounts of time have elapsed between each reinforcement. In this case, the time of each interval changes, but still ends up at a three second average.

A **fixed ratio schedule** states that a reinforcement is available after a predetermined number of responses. For example, a sea lion targets on a buoy, then vocalizes, then waves. You reinforce after every third behavior and this is a fixed ratio interval.

A **variable ratio schedule** requires a reinforcement to be available after a varying number of correct responses. So a sea lion would bark, get a reinforcement, bark, then wave, then porpoise, and get a reinforcement, and so on.

There is a variation of the variable ratio schedule which incorporates the use of conditioned or secondary reinforcers. In the 1970's, R.I.R. stood **for Random and Interrupted Reinforcement**. In the '80s it **was Reinforcers delivered Intermittently in a Randomized order** (still R.I.R). And most recently, **the variable ratio with reinforcement variety** (V.R.R.V.); which is basically using a fluctuating combination of primary and secondary reinforcers throughout a training session. All of this is an oversimplification for a very complex but highly effective form of variable ratio reinforcement and we highly recommend you do some homework before implementing this or any other technique.

We hope this has adequately defined some basic terms and that you find it a useful basic primer or a nice refresher course. Thank you.

[Mark Beeler]: The final segment, from the John G. Shedd Aquarium, shows through the training of the gating behavior an overall look at the application of the basic terms and techniques interpreted by the previous two facilities.

[Text of video/ Pete Davey narrating]: Basic maintenance behaviors can make life much easier on both trainers and animals. Perhaps one of the most commonly used of these if the gating behavior. After all, if you would like a three-quarter ton beluga whale to move from one habitat to another, it would be really nice if he went on his own! Solid gating behavior can also prevent a race for the gate, which you would definitely lose with a fast moving dolphin. The basic concept is to get the animals to go through the gate to another pool, both on their own and when we ask them to. In technical terms, we want to put gating under stimulus control.

Speaking of technical terms, let's define a few before putting them to work.

Stimulus: Any physical event, condition, or object which may or may not alter the behavior of an organism.

Stimulus control: refers to the high probability of an emitted behavioral response in the presence of a distinct stimulus.

Discriminative stimulus: A stimulus in the presence of which a given response is reinforced, with the result that the response is more likely to occur in the presence of this stimulus than in its absence.

Got all that? Okay, with these definitions in mind, let's go back to actually training the behavior. We want an animal (cetacean, pinniped, or other) to go from one pool to another. In essence, we're asking the animal to go from point A to point B and there just happens to be an open gate in the middle. Sounds simple, right? Well, it can be if good training techniques are utilized.

The first step is to teach the animal to target. Presenting the target is our key stimulus at this point. Keep in mind that there are actually many other stimuli present: the gate, the trainer, other animals, et cetera. We introduce the stimulus—the target—and touch it to the animal's rostrum, bridging and reinforcing the animal for allowing this to occur. We repeat this until the animal understands that when that stimulus is presented it is to touch the target.

We can then approximate the target away from the animal so that wherever we present that particular stimulus, the animal responds by touching it or "targeting" on it. Targeting can now be said to be under stimulus control.

The next step is to introduce a new stimulus, which will mean "go to the target." This can be done by introducing a second trainer. The primary trainer can point to the animal and then sweep his arm in the direction of the second trainer who is presenting the target by slapping it on the water. In this manner, the animal learns to move several feet to touch the target and receive reinforcement. The animal associates the new stimulus—a point and arm sweep—with the presentation of the original stimulus—the target. We now have introduced an S^D, a discriminative stimulus.

Once the animal understands that the S^D means to search for and touch the target, we will have established stimulus control. Using successive approximations, we can slowly increase the distance from point A (the first trainer) to point B (the second trainer). At the same time, we can increase the amount of time the animal will stay at point B before returning to point A.

After firmly establishing the A to B behavior, we must add a critical new stimulus: going through a gate. Eventually the animal must go from point A through a gate to point B, and stay in the new location while the gate is closed. Moving through the gate can be accomplished through successive approximations. Point B can be gradually approximated toward the gate, into the threshold or channel, and finally through the gate. With the exception of actually closing the gate, the rest of the behavior has already been conditioned.

Although each of these steps seems pretty straightforward, there is more to training than just good technique. Establishing a positive relationship with each animal is very important. Caring for the animal, feeding it, playing with it, and making every session positive are keys to building trust and developing a good relationship. If a positive relationship has been developed between animal and trainer, going through a gate may not be as difficult to condition. Part of maintaining the relationship is not to push a new behavior along too quickly, making sure that each step is positive.

Allowing the animal to be very familiar with each habitat on his or her own is important before conducting a formal training session. If the animal can explore and swim back-and-forth through the open gate on its own, it will be much more accepting of the gating behavior. Once the animal is moving through the gate under stimulus control, allow the animal to be completely comfortable with this step before trying to close the gate. Once you do close the gate, do so only briefly, opening it again immediately. Always reinforce the animal for allowing the gate to close, never allowing the animal to feel trapped. The animal should move voluntarily and remain under stimulus control throughout the process. Desensitize the animal to noises associated with the gate, and any other changes in the environment that might be associated with the gate closing. Small steps like this are time-consuming, but keep the sessions positive. By being patient and making every small step a positive one, the gating behavior can be established and maintained for many years to come. Good luck!

[Mark Beeler]: Understanding the concepts explained in each segment are important to the novice trainer, as they will provide basic training tools that will be used over and over throughout careers, from the position of assistant trainer to training supervisor.

To gain further understanding of operant conditioning terminology and techniques, I would like to offer this suggestion to interested novice trainers. Utilize the International Marine Animal Trainers Association's greatest resource—people! Approach one of the many outstanding trainers that are a part of this organization, introduce yourself and ask for a small bit of their time. Most will be willing to oblige. Then, through simple question and answer dialogue, seek to increase your knowledge about marine mammal training. Seek in order to learn. Learn in order to grow. Grow in order to succeed.

Thank you.

SUGGESTED READING:

A Primer of Operant Conditioning. G.S. Reynolds. Glenview, Illinois: Scott, Foresman, and Company. 1975 ed.

Schedules of Reinforcement. C.B. Ferster & B.F. Skinner. New York: Appelton-Century-Crofts. 1966.

A Behavior Sampler by Gary Wilkes

The power of the bridging stimulus (which is a conditioned or secondary reinforcer) is obvious to most marine mammal trainers. Surprisingly, many pet owners are not aware of this technique. The use of a bridging stimulus and the importance of timing it well is described below.

Primarily, Secondary Reinforcers End on a Good Note

by Gary Wilkes

Ming, the Greyhound, likes to play fetch with her master, Bill. She runs swiftly for any object that he tosses - and then refuses to bring it back to him. She has the same problem when he calls her to come. She makes a good start but fizzles out before she gets back to him. Bill can't figure out why she will not respond. The solution is simple but subtle. Bill must stop encouraging her to come, and start reinforcing her for coming.

You may wonder how encouraging the dog to come could possibly stop her from performing the behavior. The secret to this puzzle lies in understanding how praise and encouragement work to change behavior.

When a sound is linked to an actual positive reinforcement, such as food or physical affection, it takes on all or part of the power of the actual reinforcer. Ivan Pavlov's research at the beginning of this century confirmed this phenomenon. He linked the sound of a bell to the presentation of food. Soon the dog would start to drool at the sound of the bell - even if no food was present. While the bell was not the actual food that the animal craved, it had the power to trigger the same complex reactions in the dog. When a sensation is associated with an actual reinforcer, this way, it is called a secondary reinforcer.

This information was a novel piece of trivia until the 1930's, when B.F. Skinner showed the world the power of these associations. Skinner proved that you could do much more than make dogs drool with a secondary reinforcer. He discovered that while the actual food reinforcer strengthens the odds that a behavior will occur, the secondary reinforcer is critical to telling the animal which behavior should be strengthened.

For instance, when Shamu is learning to do a back flip it is impossible to shove a fish in his mouth (the actual reinforcement) at the exact instant he performs the behavior correctly. Instead, the trainer blows a whistle (the secondary reinforcer) that means, "YES! I liked THAT!" The whistle bridges the gap from the instant the behavior occurs to the time it takes for the animal to receive his actual reward.

While this may seem like a lot of psychobabble, the correct application of this theory can have big benefits in practice. Bill's problem with Ming is a good example of the misuse of secondary reinforcement.

When Ming gets the ball, Bill attempts to encourage her by saying "Good girl," and "Way to go!" To Ming, the sounds of "good girl" and "way to go!" mean that she has done something correctly (get the ball), she can expect some kind of reward, and that behavior is over. This is like the whale trainer's whistle. She translates the praise exactly as Shamu translates the whistle. (YES! I liked THAT!)

Because Bill does not understand how secondary reinforcers work, he has no idea of why Ming will not return. The first problem is with his timing. Bill's timing of the praise has consistently been at the instant Ming starts to come back. When he says "good girl", she thinks she has been reinforced for picking up the ball - only! Since the behavior of returning has not yet occurred, she cannot understand that Bill is trying to reinforce that behavior as well. Bill has inadvertently reinforced her for starting the behavior, but not for finishing it.

To solve the problem, Bill must wait until the behavior is finished before he praises her. His mistaken belief that chanting encouragement will cause her to return to him has actually reinforced her for staying away. A quick solution will be to wait until Ming is very close to him and say "Come." Then Bill offers her a very palatable treat. He waits until she has come as close as she is going to and then says "Good girl" - at the end of the sequence. After a few repetitions she will be able to respond to his command by returning all the way. By giving her an accurate indication of what she must do to be reinforced, he will counteract his previously ineffective training.

Praise and encouragement are powerful tools for changing behavior. Correct timing is an important factor in using them correctly. If an animal has trouble finishing a behavior, try this unlikely advice - make sure you start with a good ending.

VOL 22, NO 3, 1997. Precise bridging is a fundamental component to all good training programs. However, once we arm our trainers with a whistle or a clicker, we sometimes forget that we must continue to refine and monitor their use of the bridge. It is particularly important that the use of the bridge be consistent among all trainers at a facility. This article provides five different answers to a great question about bridging and how to introduce the bridge to new trainers.

Bridging Basics: How to Maintain Consistency

QUESTION: At our facility, everyone bridges differently at various times. Dog whistles are used for a bridge. Sometimes a bridge is short and precise while others, perhaps when an animal has just learned something new, are loud and long. Some behaviors are bridged, and some are not, either because it is a consistent behavior, or the bridge distracts during a presentation. Does this confuse the animals? Does your staff have guidelines to follow when bridging? When do you allow a new trainer to bridge?

ANSWER 1: Over the course of the last year, we have had a 100% turnover in our marine mammal staff. Because this new staff has no history with each other or the animals, we needed to establish clear lines of communication not only for each other but also for the animals in our care. Consistency was paramount! One way to accomplish this goal was to establish specific criteria for every behavior our animals performed and then accurately bridge every response that met or exceeded that criteria. Since, by definition, the bridge is a secondary reinforcer that is used as a signal to instantly reinforce and animal, the timing and method of delivery of this reinforcement will affect the animal's behavior. Yes, we do bridge every correct response but not always with just a whistle. Depending on the species, we have conditioned a visual bridge (an enthusiastic point at the animal), a tactile (2 gentle taps) and 2 other auditory bridges (a clicker and the verbal "good"). By using these alternate bridges, we can consistently bridge our animals yet avoid some of the reasons you mentioned for not bridging.

Your animal's behavior will be the clearest indicator of whether your bridging strategy is confusing or not. Do their behaviors remain solid or do they regularly break down? Do successive approximations of a new behavior progress predictably or stall for no apparent reason? Although we know there are many factors at work, certainly how and when we bridge should be one of the first things we look at when dealing with training challenges.

In general, a short precise signal is preferred since this allows you to communicate with pinpoint accuracy the exact moment an animal elicits a response you want to reinforce. I think we are all guilty from time to time of offering the excited "long blast" bridge, but whether or not this is detrimental is context dependant. Consistently using the long bridge while training a dolphin to bow might reinforce the beginning, middle, and end of the behavior which is problematic if you are trying to increase the height of the bow. A long blast on the whistle offered immediately after a dolphin successfully swats a ball with its flukes probably won't affect the desired criteria of this particular behavior. We have a relatively small staff so we have not had to establish formal guidelines for bridging. For now, we just monitor each other. We are careful to be unpredictable as to the timing of when we bridge so that our animals cannot anticipate when the bridge will occur; will it be on the 4th or 10th rotation of a barrel swim, on the take off, or after 3 laps of a perimeter swim; after 1 second or 30 seconds of a vocal; etcetera? When we allow a new trainer to bridge depends on the individual, the animal, and how solidly that animal performs a particular behavior. We usually start with a new trainer delivering the S^D while a more experienced trainer bridges the behavior until the new kid can get into the timing and rhythm of bridging. Another way to add reinforcement variety is to add your bridges into your repertoire of secondary reinforcer to be used after your animal returns to station to receive reinforcement. For example: a dolphin is bridged using a whistle for performing a behavior correctly, it returns to station and you offer a quick point at the animal (a visual bridge) as a secondary. Two taps on a walrus's back are used to bridge the animal for a nice layout, and when it returns to station, you click your clicker as a secondary and so on.

Certainly there are instances when we do not always bridge correct responses, such as when two or more animals are performing a synchronous behavior and one of the animals did not meet the criteria, or if an animal retrieves a foreign object and you choose to deliver food instantly upon receiving the object, etcetera.

Tracy Belting
Point Defiance Zoo and Aquarium

ANSWER 2: The bridge is probably one of the single most important tools used in training, if used correctly. Not only is it a secondary reinforcer, but it is as important to shaping behavior as the target pole. With the many dolphins I have worked with at M.A.P., I have noticed that how you bridge is definitely noticed by the animal. When shaping a particular behavior, just a normal whistle blast is used unless the animal goes above and beyond what is expected, at which point a louder and longer blast is used.

Although the dolphin's response to a longer bridge seems more enthusiastic, perhaps the above par behavior was due to a higher level of energy or enthusiasm to begin with. This, in turn, leads to a more excited trainer, and thus a longer, louder bridge. But, even with small behaviors, the dolphin's reaction is different with the longer bridge.

All trainers use the bridge in different ways, some bridge after every given behavior, some only during shaping, some bridge random behaviors at random times. Most show behaviors need a bridge to terminate the desired behavior such as bows, wave, sing, etcetera (behaviors trained to be continued until bridged). The dolphins I work with get bridged continuously when shaping a new behavior or when improving an old one. With behaviors that are already learned and are not terminated by a bridge, the bridge is saved for those moments when the animal comes up with a tremendous energy and really nails it! I have found this works well for flips, target jumps, spinners, etcetera, without any breakdown in consistency. The amount of reinforcers used following one of these behaviors (primary and/or secondary) is a good indicator to the animal of the quality of the given behavior. Personally, I have noticed animals that are bridged continuously for every behavior do not respond as well to the bridge as when it is used sparingly. Our staff has strict guidelines when using the bridge. Senior Trainers are in charge of teaching the staff the proper use of the bridge. A new trainer spends a great deal of time just watching other trainers bridge. As they learn to work the animals themselves, a senior staff member bridges for them. As they start by bridging small behaviors such as stationing, waves, etcetera. This gives them the opportunity to become comfortable with working with the animals as well as with looking for criteria. They then move on to bridging bows with the senior staff present. Bridging bows gives them the eye to whistle coordination, trying to nail the peak of each bow. They spend a long time working with senior staff on eye to whistle coordination along with bridging criteria.

Trainers are brought on slowly in adding to the behaviors they bridge, after working with senior staff on each behavior. The best way to learn the importance of a bridge as a tool is to watch and assist in training sessions. By having senior staff explain the purpose of each bridge, the trainers gain a better understanding of the shaping processes as well as the importance of using the bridge properly, even with completed behaviors.

Timothy Hoffland
Marine Animal Productions

ANSWER 3: At our facility, we use dog whistles as a bridge. New trainers are allowed to bridge as they are introduced to the behaviors they can ask for. The criteria for each new behavior is explained to them, and they are told when they should bridge. By critiquing different sessions we will hopefully catch any poor bridging and correct it.

We prefer the bridge to be a short, crisp "toot" of the whistle, but it does sometimes vary depending on the excitement of the trainer. Most of our behaviors are bridged with the exception of when an animal clearly understands a behavior and its criteria. For example, if the animals are asked for a high jump, and they hit the target, then there does not need to be a whistle. This is also true for behaviors like going through a hoop, where the criteria are very clear. These behaviors are also self-terminating, successful or unsuccessful, so not bridging does not leave the animal trying endlessly to meet criteria.

Marine Mammal Staff
Indianapolis Zoo

ANSWER 4: Dolphin Research Center has not collected or acclimated wild dolphins for many, many years. In the past, working with a green, untrained dolphin, we practiced very consistent bridging techniques. An animal that has never learned the "training game" needs fairly accurate information. Generally we would only have one or two trainers work with the dolphin until it understood the bridge. Even the time of the sessions was kept the same from day to day. We were building a sense of security, understanding, and consistency.

I do not believe that variable sounds of the bridge affects a training-wise dolphin. We use Acme Thunderer police whistles at DRC, since we explain training and it is an advantage for the guests to hear the bridge. We train our trainers to make a short, loud blast on the whistle, but it doesn't always end up that way. As described in the question, sometimes in new training, and exuberant trainer will blast an "exclamation point" whistle...one that is longer and louder than usual as if to say "YES, YES, THAT'S IT!" I see the dolphins responding with excitement to these unusual bridges. We also have a trainer who is soft spoken and it reflects in her whistle-blowing style. We've worked on it, yet she is still a softer "tooter" than the rest of us. The great thing is, the dolphins know it and respond to her quiet whistles very well, while if I bridge that lightly they continue doing the behavior ("I didn't hear anything, did you?"). I give the animals a lot of credit for understanding our communication. We have some behaviors that we bridge verbally or by touch, like the hug, where the bridge is a kiss on the cheek (as it should be).

We have never practiced the technique of not bridging a behavior, just because it is consistent. Our dolphins seem excited to hear the bridge, and it is a goal to reach each time they begin a behavior. It is probably an expectation on their part that they will be bridged if they do their job well, and I think that's a fair expectation. If a behavior cannot be bridged for presentation or filming reasons, we work the same behavior in other sessions where it can be bridged to reinforce it specifically. In some film work an audible bridge is not possible so we use hand gestures to end the behavior and call the animal back to the station. Our dolphins were initially a bit confused when we didn't bridge the same way during film work, but they soon caught on. Now we are convinced that they know when it's a "shoot." They get very excited when they see the big cameras and all of the people milling around their pool. They no longer are confused with the style of film work sessions and seem to take it all in the context of the environment.

DRC's guidelines for bridging are based more on when you bridge rather than how long or short the sound itself is. New trainers watch sessions to learn criteria for different dolphin behaviors. At first they learn the signals or cues, while an experienced trainer does the bridging from behind them. Once they are good with the signals, they begin bridging in their sessions as well, again with an experienced trainer watching and giving feedback. How long it takes depends on each individual's abilities. They are learning not only how to bridge, but more importantly, how to interact with the dolphin. Being comfortable touching the dolphins, making eye contact with them, taking to them, playing with them...these are all components needed before we move into training or bridging with the dolphins. Good timing on bridges is important, whether it is a new behavior or one the dolphin has done for years. We have almost extinguished some great behaviors by letting them fade away...the flip becomes a bit less tucked over time, the visible part of a speed run becomes shorter and shorter. We've all seen this happen and it is almost always due to inconsistent bridging. If a behavior cannot be bridged once in a while (like the film work described earlier) then it is important that in other sessions the dolphin does hear a bridge to remind them what a "perfect" response is.

Linda S. Erb
Dolphin Research Center

ANSWER 5: The science of operant conditioning states that reinforcing a behavior at the precise moment the behavior is done correctly will increase the frequency of that behavior. If we accept this to be true, how often can we give a dolphin a fish or rub-down at the height of a bow or flip? The nature of many of the behaviors our animals do prevents us from being able to give a reinforcer at precisely the moment the behavior is done correctly, so we developed a way of signaling that what you did was correct. We call this signal a bridging stimulus because it bridges the gap between when the animal does the behavior correctly and when they receive reinforcement. This is the most powerful training tool we have at our disposal, and in the hands of a good trainer it can produce some amazing behaviors, but likewise, if used incorrectly, or even inconsistently, it can break down behavior very quickly.

In order for the bridge to be an effective training tool, it needs to be used consistently. Probably the most common use of the whistle as a bridge is a short, loud blast. If a whistle bridge is too long, what part of the whistle is the animal listening to? The beginning, or the end? And what are you actually reinforcing? For example, if we wanted to teach a dolphin to jump high, we would bridge the animal at the precise moment the behavior was done correctly, at the height of the jump. But if we are not careful and start blowing the whistle at the height of the animals jump, not ending it until they reenter the water, is the animal being conditioned to jump high, or to renter the water? Only further observation of the behavior will tell if the criteria is maintained. We have found that by keeping the bridge as short as possible, while still allowing the animals ample opportunities to hear it, allows us to be more precise with our approximations. Keep in mind that, as a group, your staff should try to delive the bridge the same way. Inconsistent use of the bridge (some long and some short) can lead not only to break down in behavior, and frustration, but even to aggression. Used consistently, the animal can learn easily and quickly and what you're looking for can be much clearer. When an animal returns following the bridge, you can choose the type and magnitude of reinforcement warranted by the animal's response. When the animal responds incorrectly or performs the behavior below criteria, it does not receive a bridge.

At Seven Seas we bridge our animals for all correct responses. In addition to the whistle bridge we also utilize a tactile bridge ("good") for the pinnipeds. Any incorrect or below criteria response, and the animal is not bridged and receives the least reinforcing thing we can do, which is a no-response, or neutral response for 3 – 5 seconds. After that we have the option of asking the behavior again or we can move onto something different. We try to make learning as black and white as possible for the animal.

New trainers are allowed to bridge behavior when they show and understanding of basic operant principles, can present S^Ds correctly and consistently, and know behavioral criteria. Generally new trainers start out watching and following experienced staff for weeks. The next step is for the new trainer to start working basic or strongly conditioned behaviors with only one animal, and with only an experienced trainer next to them. The experienced trainer is there primarily to watch and evaluate whether or not the bridging stimulus is being applied correctly and consistently with the guidelines of the department. They new trainer graduates to working the animal solo only when the experienced trainer is comfortable with the new trainer's abilities. Over the course of the new trainer's first year they will not train any new behaviors, instead learning how to maintain behavior, as an individual, and as part of a team. Bringing on a new trainer is a very slow process with consistency and communication being the key to our training program.

Seven Seas Staff
Brookfield Zoo

A Behavior Sampler by Gary Wilkes

A full description of protected contact training with elephants can be found in chapter 12, "Complex Training and Modern Applications." However, this short article is an example of shaping through successive approximations described in easy to understand terms. It is always a challenge to find easy ways to describe operant techniques. Gary does a great job of this in all his articles.

Elephants Go from Carrot and Stick to Carrot and Click

by Gary Wilkes

Question: Of all careers, which is most likely to get you killed?

Need a hint? It is not the obviously risky professions, such as smoke jumper, secret service agent, or paparazzi. The most dangerous job in America is that of an elephant keeper.

From Hannibal's war elephants to logging operations in Thailand, humans have controlled these largest of land mammals. Over the millennia, techniques of training and control have changed a little. A short, wooden rod with a small hook on one end is the primary tool. The handler uses the hook to pull a leg or the trunk, to get the animal to move in a particular direction, or to signal the animal to turn left or right. Confining the animal is achieved by chaining the animal's feet to the ground. Chaining is still a popular method of controlling captive elephants.

While some elephants adapt readily to this system, others do not. In the past, the primary means of controlling "bad" elephants has been to simply increase the amount of force. One danger with this technique is that the force needed to "impress" an elephant runs dangerously close to hurting or terrifying the animal. While intimidation may work for the short run, the old saying about an elephants memory seems true - they certainly never seem to forget those who have hurt them. It is so easy for an elephant to "accidently" crush a human that it is not a good idea to be around one that doesn't like you. Untrustworthy elephants are often left chained almost continuously or simply confined in isolation.

To provide proper health care, even chained, dangerous elephants must occasionally be handled. At the San Diego Zoo, behavior specialist Gary Priest is routinely faced with developing novel and humane ways to control these animals. One of Priest's challenges was a male elephant with a history of serious aggression and desperately in need of having his feet groomed. In captivity, elephants build up calluses on the bottoms of their feet. If the calluses are not periodically removed, the animal is eventually unable to walk.

The bull elephant had not had his feet groomed in almost ten years. The traditional method of removing the calluses requires that a keeper stand underneath the elephant and shave the calluses with a sharp tool. In such a vulnerable position, the animal can kill the keeper at any time, either accidentally or intentionally. This animal would have loved the opportunity to "accidentally" squash one of those little "man-critters." For such an openly dangerous elephant, a new "hands-off" approach was necessary.

First, the keepers built a large, seven ton steel gate at one end of the compound. In the center of the gate a hole was cut out - about the size of an elephant's foot. On the "people side" of the gate, a steel stirrup was constructed. Now all that had to be done was to ask a violent, bull elephant to daintily put his tootsies through a blank wall and let strange little creatures hack away at his feet with knives. That's where Gary Priest and his trainers stepped in.

Using methods originally developed for marine mammals, Priest's first job was to teach the animal a signal that means "Good boy." A small tin cricket, or clicker, was associated with carrots. Every time the elephant did something right, he would hear the click that meant "Soup's on!" and then receive a piece of carrot. By timing the clicks correctly, the trainers gradually shaped the behavior, one step at a time. If the animal failed to get it

90   ANIMAL TRAINING

right, the absence of the click told him that he would not get the carrot.

First the animal got clicks and carrots for simply approaching the gate. If he stood still for a couple of seconds he would get another click and treat. Two seconds was parlayed into ten seconds, and then into twenty. Next the trainer snapped the clicker when the animal's left front foot was off the ground one inch. Soon the inch was six inches, and then two feet in the air. A little to the left and the animal's foot was in the stirrup. The elephant was then taught to place each of his other feet into the hole. Soon the animal would voluntarily walk to the gate and out one foot after another into the mysterious hole. He would hold it there while the keeper trimmed the pads of his feet and groomed the animal's nails.

After their success with his feet, the keepers then taught the elephant to allow them to pull his ear through a slot in the gate. The veins on the back of an elephant's ears are convenient for taking blood. Now they could check his health more closely while getting him periodically groomed. The zoo keepers got an unexpected bonus as well. The animal's temperament changed. The level of aggression dropped dramatically. He seemed to enjoy the daily training sessions and stopped charging the gate.

It is too often assumed that the best means of handling an animal is with force and punishment. Behavior programs like the San Diego Zoo's not only solve the immediate issue of control, but build toward an overall improvement in the animal's life. With elephants, traditional "carrot & stick" methods are best replaced with "carrot & click!"

VOL 21, NO 1, 1996. Scanning for behavior is one of the techniques used to train most of the dolphin aerial behaviors at the John G. Shedd Aquarium. This step by step account describes how this training technique was utilized. This paper was first presented at the 20th Annual IMATA Conference in the Bahamas.

Scanning or Capturing Behavior: A Necessary Tool, an Outdated Technique, or a Lost Art?

by Ken Ramirez
John G. Shedd Aquarium

INTRODUCTION

When reading the title of this paper there are many questions that may come to mind. First, what exactly is scanning or capturing behavior? Second, once trainers realize what it is, they often ask why we would want to train that way! And finally, why should we write a paper on scanning? After all, it's not a new technique for training, it's been around forever. It certainly isn't the best way to train most behaviors. Yet, at the John G. Shedd Aquarium we choose to use scanning quite extensively with our Pacific white-sided dolphins (*Lagenorhynchus obliquidens*), particularly with their aerial behaviors. There have been drawbacks in training this way, but we've also seen some real benefits.

USES OF SCANNING

In the 1960's, Karen Pryor and Ingrid Kang reported on the training of a rough toothed dolphin (*Steno bredanensis*) that was required to invent a new behavior every session. All in all, the dolphin created numerous behaviors during the brief project. A form of scanning was used to teach the dolphin to participate in that project. Today, many trainers use innovative sessions, allowing animals to be creative. Some facilities actually have an "innovative" S^D, which asks the animal to either do anything it wants, or in some cases, create a new behavior. These concepts are what scanning is all about.

Most trainers use some form of scanning. When training an animal to vocalize, one usually waits for the animal to vocalize on its own. When the vocal behavior is displayed, it is bridged and reinforced. Most animals catch on quickly and begin vocalizing often. The final step is to pair the behavior with a cue. A behavior trained in this manner is often referred to as a captured behavior or a scanned behavior.

When I was first exposed to dolphin training in the mid-1970's, I learned from a man who trained everything that way. He would sit back, with a whistle in his mouth and a bucket of fish next to his chair, and just stare at the pool. If a dolphin did anything that remotely resembled a desired behavior, he blew the whistle and threw a fish at the dolphin. With good use of selective bridging he shaped amazing behaviors: tailwalks, leaps, flips, pec slaps, and tail waves. There wasn't a target in sight. The man never left his chair. I couldn't decide if he was a genius or just lazy. In fact, it was a long time before I ever saw a trainer use a target. When I discovered the use of targeting, it was like someone had just invented the wheel. I used targeting for everything. It wasn't until I started working with our Pacific white-sided dolphins many years later, that I brushed the cobwebs off my memories of that man sitting in his chair scanning.

THE LAGS

Prior to the John G. Shedd Aquarium's opening of the Oceanarium, our Pacific white-sided dolphins, or Lags, were housed at the University of California at Santa Cruz – Long Marine Lab. They stayed at the lab for over two years where their acclimation and early training took place. Due to our agreement with Long Marine Lab and Dr. Ken

Norris, we were not allowed to begin formal training for the first year after their arrival at the Lab. Because one of Dr. Norris's graduate students was working on a social pattern study, they requested that little formal training be conducted. We sat at Long Marine Lab, hands tied behind our backs, itching to take out our targets and begin training.

The year long observation period turned out to be a wonderful opportunity. The Lags proved to be quite active and playful animals. Throughout the day we noticed a lot of aerial activity. We would see flips, breaches, corkscrews, barrel rolls, high leaps, and quick porpoising. Interestingly, this aerial activity came in spurts. Once one animal began leaping, they all joined in. These aerial bouts lasted form ten to thirty minutes at a time.

GAME PLAN

Once we were able to begin training, we focused our attention on the basics and concentrated on husbandry training. Bridging was established quickly, and formal training progressed rapidly. Between sessions, we continued to be impressed with the Lag's activity level, and their apparent enthusiasm for jumping. We finally decided to try capturing their aerial behaviors. We had noticed a pattern to their aerial activity, which often occurred at specific times of the day. We watched the animals closely and selected specific behaviors, bows or high leaps and breaches, that we felt we could easily catch them doing. We then began watching them unobtrusively, with fish available at pool side, at those times when they were likely to exhibit aerial activity.

When an animal offered a desired behavior, we bridged and threw a fish to them. At first, this simply interrupted the activity. The animal would stop what it was doing and come over and stare. In the beginning, to alleviate that problem, we found it useful to stay out of sight, even as we reinforced. This kept the animals from focusing on us and encouraged them to continue with their aerial activity. At the outset, we might get the desired behavior only once in an entire session.

Since aerial bouts lasting at least twenty minutes were common, we planned scanning sessions daily. They became the highlight of our day. The Lags caught on to the game quickly. Once they realized they were being reinforced for a specific jump or flip, they began offering the behavior repeatedly. At that point we no longer threw fish at them, but instead waited for them to come over for reinforcement. It was then that we introduced an S^D.

We arbitrarily selected distinct and unique hand signals. We often used very exaggerated cues to avoid confusion with established S^Ds. Once the animal caught on to the rules of the game, we know they were likely to repeat the desired behavior again and again. Thus, after each reinforcement we presented the new S^D, then backed away from pool side. Inevitably the animal exhibited the aerial again. It took time for the animal to understand and pair this S^D with the desired behavior, but it was a natural progression.

When we were convinced that the dolphin understood the S^D, we were ready to try it outside of a scanning session. We usually tried it during a formal session immediately following a scanning session. As soon as we called the animals to the station we would try the new S^D. In time, we moved the behavior to different parts of a session until the animal perceived it as just another behavior.

We found ourselves guilty of exhibiting a lot of superstitious behavior. Since the animal invented the behavior, we had no way of knowing what prompted the behavior nor on what cues the dolphin relied. At the beginning, we carefully kept track of which trainer reinforced, where they stood, what they wore, and even the time of day. We wanted to be able to recreate the scene precisely to increase our chances of getting the behavior again. Eventually we found that most of those details were not important. In fact, if we dwelled on them for too long we ran the risk of conditioning the animal to expect those things.

SHAPING THE BEHAVIOR

Once an animal had learned to exhibit a behavior regularly and consistently on cue, we became more selective with our bridging. At first, the animal determined its own criteria for each behavior, but we wanted to be able to shape height, body position, and pool location. Since we had not used any specific steps to get the behavior, we shaped many criteria simultaneously. For each behavior we set priority levels for all criteria. For example, with bows we concentrated on bridging for height and waited to work on pool locations later. For breach behaviors, we focused on how and where they landed first, and later we worried about height.

The key to shaping a scanned behavior is very precise bridging. Even after the behavior is finished in the trainer's mind, it probably isn't complete in the dolphin's mind. After all, they were encouraged to be creative at the start, so they often continue to be creative later. Therefore, good, precise bridging is still critical, even while simply maintaining a behavior. An excellent example of this occurred when we scanned a tail lobbing behavior. At the outset we accepted lobtails in either the ventral up or down position. Once we decided we preferred the ventral up, we had to be very careful with our bridging choices. In one instance, we were so unclear about our criteria that the dolphin began alternating between ventral up and ventral down positions between each slap of her tail. In other words, she was spinning as she slapped. We eventually had to use a target to fix the behavior. Only after an animal was solid on a behavior did we move forward and try extending distance and height, or try paring animals together, or even try group behaviors.

DISADVANTAGES

Because we have successfully trained many behaviors using scanning, we are strong proponents of using this training techniques in certain circumstances. There are some definite disadvantages, however, and scanning for behavior is not advisable for all situations. The most obvious disadvantage is having no approximations to fall back on. If you teach an animal to do a flip using a target, and the animal forgets the behavior years later, your can pull out your target and regress until the animal remembers. With scanning, it all happens in the animal's head, so you have nothing to go back to.

We experienced that very problem with one of our female dolphins. She had developed an incredible corkscrew, or air spin behavior which we scanned for and had firmly established on an S^D. We had even incorporated it into our public presentations. One day she quit doing the behavior. To get the behavior back we recreated the exact circumstances under which we had originally scanned for it, but nothing worked. We finally gave up. Then months later she offered the corkscrew again. By the end of the day she was corkscrewing reliably on S^D again. However, that same day she lost a firmly established breach behavior. She does not seem capable, or willing, to differentiate between more than two aerials at a time.

Specific criteria are also more difficult to maintain with scanned behaviors. A targeted behavior can be positioned, defined, and shaped with good use of a target, but a scanned behavior must be approximated slowly through precise bridging. Poor bridging is always a bad practice, but in a scanned behavior it can also be dangerous. The animal is keenly paying attention to our whistle, and is often very trusting of our decisions. Poor bridging can lead an animal into a dangerous location or position. Likewise, changing the rules or criteria of a behavior must be done through slow shaping procedures if the behavior was scanned, but could often be redefined quickly if it had been targeted.

ADVANTAGES/CONCLUSION

Used carefully, scanning can be a wonderful tool for training. It allows the animals to be creative and invent their own behavior. It also helps a staff understand the need for precise bridging, since poor bridging causes scanned behavior to change quickly. Scanning does not exclude targeting; a target can easily be added to a behavior that the animal first created on its own. And finally, scanning makes the animal go through a different thought process as it learns. Unlike targeting, which is like taking them by the hand and guiding through a behavior, scanning forces the animal to interpret information given to them through our bridge. This thought process constantly keeps the animal more in tune and focused on what we, as trainers, are doing.

In conclusion, we wouldn't suggest throwing your targets away. Nor would we advocate scanning with all animals in all situations. There is a certain amount of control lost when behaviors are scanned, and that is not to our advantage with certain behaviors. Additionally, we might not accomplish very much if we always waited for an animal to show us a behavior first. However, when the opportunity presents itself, as it has with our Lags, you might want to consider scanning as a possible training tool. We have been pleased with the results and plan to continue using scanning to capture behavior spontaneously offered by our animals. It's been challenging and fun for us, and we think it's been fun for the animals, too.

1982 IMATA Conference, Honolulu, Hawaii, USA. This paper describes another approach to using the concept of scanning or capturing behavior. Here the trainers at the Minnesota Zoo used it as a component to their variable reinforcement schedules.

Random Reinforcement of Spontaneous Behavior

by C. Austin McDevitt
Minnesota Zoological Garden

ABSTRACT

In order to promote increased animal activity throughout the day, a program of random reinforcement of spontaneous behavior was instituted at the Minnesota Zoo in May 1982. Initially, only our bottlenose dolphins, Mindy and Rio, were exposed to this form of reinforcement. In August 1982 we expanded the program to include our beluga whales, Anana (Little Girl) and Nukilik (Big Mouth). A measured amount of each animal's diet is set aside each day to be used for spontaneous behavior reinforcement. At random times throughout the day (not including scheduled training sessions), the trainer takes a position near the pool where he or she can observe the animals, but the animals cannot observe the trainer. When one or the other of the animals performs a behavior spontaneously, a fish is thrown to that animal (like manna from heaven). This program with the dolphins has resulted in an increase in the desired animal activity and increased attentiveness during regular training sessions.

INTRODUCTION

It is important to put the evolution of the Minnesota Zoological Garden's program of Random Reinforcement of Spontaneous Behavior into historical perspective.

In 1969, Pryor, Haag, and O'Reilly described a method of training for novel behaviors. Simply described, the animals in the program were, during a specific time period, reinforced for spontaneously emitting novel behavior; "novel" was defined as any behavior that had not previously been reinforced. The results of this program showed that the animals would not only emit novel behaviors during the training sessions, but that there was an increase in the general activity level of the animals involved.

In 1974, Dave Butcher described a method of conditioning, which came to be known as Random and Interrupted Reinforcement or RIR. This program initially involved changing the standard fixed ratio of reinforcement (usually 1:1 or continuous reinforcement) commonly being used at the time to one of a variable or intermittent ratio of reinforcement. In this way the animal involved could not anticipate when or for what behavior it was going to be reinforced. In the years following its original presentation, RIR has been expanded to include not only the use of a varied schedule of reinforcement but also a variety of reinforcers. These reinforcers run the gamut from the standard use of food to allowing the animal to choose its own form of reward (Brill 1981). What we have done at the Minnesota Zoo is to combine both forms of conditioning into what we feel is a successful marriage.

METHODS AND PROCEDURE

As this program was one that evolved over a period of months rather than one that was planned, I will present it in the chronological order of events.

In November 1981, we began to expand our RIR program by using novel stimuli as conditioned reinforcers. These novel stimuli included the use of a squirt bottle, a brush and sponge as tactile reinforcers, and extension of the amount of time spent in the water with the animals as social reinforcement. In December 1981, we began performing unscheduled training sessions with the animals. We varied the number of these unscheduled sessions from zero to three times per day. We felt that this would break the monotony of the daily routine to which both the animals and the trainers had become accustomed. At this time we also began to leave props in the pool between training sessions for added diversion. Because of my previous bad experiences at another institution, these props were things that the animals could not lift or throw to the public; they included a belly board, an inner tube, and heavy ring. In February 1982, I spent three days with Randy Brill and his staff at the Seven Seas Panorama, Brookfield Zoo, to get more firsthand experience in RIR's application. Upon my return, and after much discussion with my staff, I reluctantly agreed to place objects in the pool, which the animals could throw to the public so that interaction could take place. These objects included an assortment of balls and rings. My staff and I closely observed the interactions that were taking place to be sure that members of the public were in no way abusing the animals, that is, throwing the props back at the animals in a way that could injure them. Happily, no such incidents occurred. During this period of time (which initially lasted from the 6t to the 13th of March), no reinforcement was provided during this interaction period other than the reinforcement of the interactions themselves. During this eight-day period the amount of interaction between the public and the animals was at a consistently high level.

From March 14th to the 30th, the dolphins were confined to their holding pool because of renovation work talking place in the exhibit pool. To provide diversions during this period, members of the zoo's volunteer corps were permitted in the holding area to play with the dolphins. We also varied the feeding times, again as a means of providing variety while the animals were in the smaller holding pool.

Following their reentry into the exhibit pool we noted a decline in the dolphins' interaction with the public. Because of this, we started to reinforce this interaction with fish which were thrown to the dolphins from the poolside and not from their regular feeding station. As might be expected, this caused an increase in interactive behavior, but we also began observing an increase in novel behavior by the animals. It should be pointed out that, during this time, we were continuing our program of random training sessions and water time with the animals.

Throughout March and April we continued to evaluate and reevaluate where our program was going and what effect it was having on the animals. Our conclusions were that overall activity had increased dramatically, and that attentiveness during training sessions were greatly improved. However, when we were reinforcing interactive behavior from the poolside the animals would orient toward us when they became aware of our presence. Because of this, we decided to provide this reinforcement from a location where the animals could not see us. This was above the pool, among the shrubbery and rock facade which form the back wall of the pool. In addition, we began randomly to reinforce not only interactive behavior, but any spontaneous behavior that the animals emitted. This led to a dramatic increase in activity throughout the day, with the animals performing a variety of previously reinforced or shaped behaviors such as ball tossing, tail walking, porpoising, dorsal tail lob, and vocalizations. In addition, novel behavior increased with the animals producing behaviors such as ventral tail lobs, corkscrew swimming, pirouettes and body slams, and a combination of shaped and novel behaviors such as starting to tail walk and ending in a pirouette.

CONCLUSION

Our experience leads us to believe that a program of Random Reinforcement of Spontaneous Behavior is of value in a training program for the following reasons: (1) it provides the animals with additional stimuli that help relieve the stress of confinement, (2) it allows more innovation on the animal's part and many of the novel behaviors can be incorporated into show formats, and (3) we gain another tool in an ever-expanding RIR program.

It must be said that we do not feel that this program is an end in itself but something that must be built upon. Each trainer must decide how a program of Random Reinforcement of Spontaneous Behavior can be incorporated into his or her show and training programs. Finally, the evolution of the RIR program has shown us all that our art must constantly change. We have seen that the use of various stimuli and reinforcers keep both the animals in our trust and the trainers who work with them in a healthier state of mind.

REFERENCES

Brill, Randy. "Dolphin Training Does a Flip-Part II." Bison (December 1981/January 1982).

Butcher, Dave. "The Trainer as the Trainee." In Fourth Annual Conference Proceedings of the International Marine Animal Trainers Association, 1974, Orlando, Florida, edited by Rusty White and Bill Scronce. Orlando, FL: Sea World of Florida, 1974, pp. 107-15.

Pryor, K. W., R. Haag, and J. O'Reilly. "The Creative Porpoise: Training for Novel Behavior" Journal of Exp. Anal. Behav. 12 (1969): 653-61.

A Behavior Sampler by Gary Wilkes

While targeting has been used effectively by most professional trainers, it is a relatively recent discovery for pet owners. Some of the examples below might be more accurately termed "baiting" by marine mammal trainers (a practice we usually avoid), but the general concepts below are worth understanding.

Training by Pushing and Tugging Is "Off-Target"

by Gary Wilkes

Over the years, Bob Hope has become linked with golf. In movies and on stage, he has often held his arms around a beautiful woman and guided her arms through the motion of swinging a club. I think we can agree that teaching golf was the last thing on his mind.

Bob may not know it, but pushing, tugging or guiding someone through a behavior is called modeling. It is the primary way that people teach animals. If you want Spot to sit, shove down on his rear while tugging his neck upward. If Fifi won't come, put a rope on her and reel her in like a tuna. Of you want Bruno to sit parallel with you, nudge him with your foot. While these examples are all too common, they are usually quite inefficient. All animals possess an innate resistance to being pushed, shoved or tugged.

A more flexible system of teaching utilizes an animal's instinctive ability to target and track prey. To see this system at work, toss your pet's favorite toy across the room. Aha! The same dog that cannot follow you while on a leash can track the toy perfectly and is suddenly skidding across the kitchen floor at almost 20 miles per hour - with no help from the leash.

Now grab the toy and touch Fido's nose. As he tries to bite it, move it back over his forehead. Keep it low enough that he does not try to jump up to get it. He will either back up or sit. Next, try your luck at getting Fido to lie down. Touch the toy to his nose and move it in a straight line to his front paws. As Fido tries to grab the toy, move it slowly along the ground away from him. To follow the toy, he must gradually stretch until he is lying down. If he stands up instead, go back to the sitting position and try again. If he succeeds, give him lots of treats and affection.

Controlling a dog's ability to target can go much farther than just laying down or sitting. Most small dogs learn to dance by trying to target a treat over their head. Targeting is the primary behavior used by herding dogs, retrievers and other working animals.

Gunther Gabel-Williams, master circus trainer, uses targeting with his tigers. He uses a stick equipped with a small nail that holds a bit of meat. When he moves the stick, his tigers follow the bit of meat and then receive a reward for the correct action.

House cats adapt readily to training that uses targeting rather than modeling. Pulling and tugging your cat will merely frustrate both of you. Teaching a cat to sit, lie down or roll over can be easily accomplished through targeting.

While many trainers continue to use the age-old method of modeling, targeting reflects a more natural and efficient way to teach. Besides the challenge and enjoyment of teaching without force, your pet's behavior will soon be right on target too!

VOL 2O, NO 4, 1995. Scanning or capturing behavior always seems to take a back seat to targeting in most training programs. But what do you do when desired behavior is being offered? The subject of capturing behavior is not discussed frequently in the literature, so the six responses below are a unique opportunity to get some diverse opinions.

Calf Mimicry:
To Shape or to Capture? - That's the Question

QUESTION: We often observe young dolphins born in our facility mimicking their mothers while their mothers do trained behaviors. Would you reinforce these mimicked behaviors during training sessions and place them under stimulus control or would you wait and shape these behaviors through successive approximations?

ANSWER 1: When training behaviors with animals, the trainer usually shapes these through successive approximations, or he could "capture" the behavior and associate an S^D with it. The problem with captured behaviors is that if the criteria begins to diminish, or the behavior doesn't occur at all, then you have no steps to fall back on in order to regain that behavior. You must wait until it happens again (if it happens again) on its own in order to capture it again.

So what about calves mimicking the mother's behavior? Should these be reinforced even though they were not shaped? We believe the answer is yes. This is not necessarily to "get" behaviors on the animals, for the same behaviors may need to be shaped in the future, but there are many advantages to capturing these behaviors at an early age.
1. It gets the calves thinking and is mentally stimulating.
2. It solidifies the understanding of the bridge and the use of a variety of reinforcements.
3. It helps to build a relationship between the calf and the trainer, since the trainer will need to be there to reinforce and combine the behavior with an S^D.
4. It also allows the trainer to reinforce teamwork with the other dolphins, which is very important since the calves are a new member of the same pod.

The only disadvantage is if the trainer thinks he can keep this behavior up to criteria when it is captured, and then he'll need the best of luck, for if the behavior ever falters, he's stuck with nothing.
Training staff
Dolphin Quest Hawaii

ANSWER 2: To shape or to capture...that is the question. Whether 'tis nobler in the mind to suffer the slings and arrows of outrageous training techniques or...As far as I know, this is one debate that some marine mammal trainers will never agree upon. Most trainers probably can't even tell if a specific behavior was trained originally by capturing or through shaping. Where the difference is first noticed is when the behavior begins to break down. As the animal begins to offer incorrect responses to a specific S^D, the trainer may decide to back up or "go back to kindergarten" with the behavior. By backing up, the trainer hopes to remind the animal of the steps leading up to the completed behavior. If the behavior was initially trained via successive approximations, this should be pretty easy. If the behavior was initially captured, however, it may be more difficult to recreate the scenario in which the calf offered the behavior (mimicry). Of course, the animal can be retrained using successive approximations, but that could take significantly longer than if the behavior were originally trained through approximation.

Comparing the two methods, we see that a young animal tends to learn a captured behavior faster than a shaped one. However, the behavior trained using shaping will be easier to maintain and troubleshoot. The creative trainer can establish stimulus control using either method while an animal is young. One can concentrate on completing mimic learned behaviors, as well as training most new behaviors by using as much successive approximation training as possible.

Greg Biedenbach
National Aquarium in Baltimore

ANSWER 3: Yes, we do capture some behaviors that are mimicked by the calves and place them under stimulus control. Several behaviors, such as bows and vocals, are usually captured when training any animal. If the calves are mimicking their mothers, all the easier for us to get the behavior on an S^D. Even gate training can be easy!

We don't like to depend too much on mimicking, however, and recommend training as many behaviors as possible. As any experienced trainer knows, capturing a mimicked behavior is easy and fun, but if the behavior deteriorates you can't go back a step and rework it.

So take advantage of some of the mimicking, train the rest, and you can enjoy quality behaviors by utilizing both methods of training.

Debbie Marrin-Cooney
Marine World Africa USA

ANSWER 4: We have a rule of thumb—if you see something you like, reinforce it! If a young dolphin is mimicking its mother, great! Think of all the training time that is being saved. Sooner or later that animal will realize that there is a "key" to being reinforced on various behaviors. That "key" is the signal or S^D. Sooner or later the young dolphin will figure it out.

Training Staff
Dolphin Quest Moorea

ANSWER 5: Successive approximations and reinforced mimicked behaviors both result in behaviors that are brought under stimulus control in some form. However, the key to the question of which of the two concepts should be used is dependent on the behavioral objective. Quite often both traditional and innovative training principles can be used successfully. Traditional shaping is good when you need to correct aspects of behaviors that become lost or need to be strengthened. However, many steps are added to the training process (e.g.: The prompting and fading of targets) which often are not prominent in the end result.

Compare this to reinforcing the response of a young animal that bows with its mother. When the S^D has been reinforced (for the calf). Mimicking, in essence, is successive approximations of a different and less traditional type. In the end, the choice between reinforcing mimicked behavior or shaping through successive approximation is yours. A healthy blend of both are employed successfully in Sea World of Australia's overall training program.

Jeff Murphy
Sea World of Australia

ANSWER 6: You hate to stifle the little tikes creativity by not reinforcing mimicked behaviors. This is a natural learning process the calves would go through in the wild. Go ahead and "catch" the behavior, but we strongly suggest you go through the appropriate approximations for each behavior later so that you have something to fall back on when confusion arises (and it will!)

Tracy Belting
Minnesota Zoo

A Behavior Sampler by Gary Wilkes

This humorous article gives great examples of what happens when S^Ds are not clearly thought out and taught to an animal. Most importantly it demonstrates that cues, whether audible, tactile, or visual, can easily be misinterpreted if the trainer is not clear and consistent in training and maintaining a behavior.

What's in a Name?

by Gary Wilkes

I was in the market the other day when I saw a little book of potential names for new babies. Inside were over 1000 names and their meanings, with things like - Peter comes from a Greek word that means "rock" and Winifred is Old English for "washed ashore after a squall." While humans can obviously understand names that describe personal attributes or conditions, have you ever wondered what your animals might imagine their names mean? Here's a simple multiple-choice question that can help you find out.

Your pet should think its name means...
 a) absolutely nothing
 b) come
 c) NO!
 d) stop, look, wait for the next command.

The correct answer for this test is "d" - which is also the least likely to be true.

One reason for this paradox is that while humans think of a name in terms of identity, animals respond to names as signals associated with certain behaviors. A human names a Schnauzer "Blitz" to describe the Germanic heritage of his breed type, while Blitz thinks his name means "Run away, before the two-legged giant whacks you with a newspaper."

The reason for this discrepancy is simple - Blitz has inadvertently learned that his name actually means 'no!" For instance, when Blitz moves to raid the trash, his owner is far more likely to yell "Blitz!" rather than a simple "no!" If his owner consistently uses his name and then scolds or punishes him, an association between the sound "Blitz" and scolding is inevitable. Soon the dog will flinch and run when he hears his name.

Some owners go even farther in teaching this association. The most common variation on this theme is to yell the dog's name and then scream NO! ("Blitz, NO!") Supposedly, this practice allows you to punish one dog while sparing another. The reasoning is that if Witchy, the Wheaton Terrier, is minding her own business, yelling "Blitz, no!" will effect him but not her. While this may be logical for humans, a closer look shows that it is confusing for dogs.

First, if Witchy knows her name correctly, she is not going to be listening when you call "Blitz." The first thing she is going to hear is the word "NO!" screamed at her. Though she may be perfectly innocent of any offense, she will assume she is being punished for whatever she is doing when she hears the word "NO!"

From Blitz's view, the scene is equally confusing. Just as he picks up a bedroom slipper, he hears his master call his name. He drops the slipper and responds promptly by turning to face his master - that's when he hears the word "NO!" Instead of thinking that picking up the slipper was the bad behavior, Blitz is now convinced that looking at his owner was the evil act. The dogs have each learned different lessons from this experience. From now on, Witchy may become generally leery of her owner, and Blitz will start purposely avoiding his name.

Another common misuse of a dog's name is when it ultimately means "come," rather than "attention." The easiest way to teach this is to yell the dog's name when you want to discover his location. If Fido is out of sight, the easiest way to find him is to call the dog's name. As he shows up to investigate your call, it is natural for you to praise him for coming. A few weeks of enthusiastic greetings and the dog has figured out that his name means "come and get it."

While many owners do not see the harm in using an animal's name in place of the word "come," the practice hides a dangerous possibility. If Fido runs out the front door and across the street, you may have a serious problem. If there are cars whizzing by, you must have a way to warn Fido and tell him to stay. The problem is that he thinks "Fido" means "come." In this scenario, you cannot get his attention without also triggering the command to "come" - which may cause an accident.

For those of you who answered that a dog's name means "absolutely nothing," you have astute powers of observation - many animals do not react to their names at all. One reason for this is the common practice of constantly, and inappropriately, using the dog's name. "Fifi, sit!, Fifi come, Fifi, this, Fifi, that, Fifi, Fifi, FIFI!" The owner simply tacks the name onto everything, but never waits to see if the dog responded correctly. Soon the name has less and less meaning for the dog.

Teaching your pet to stop, look and listen is an important behavior. It allows you to control your pet from a distance and insure that he will focus on you in an emergency. Regardless of the fancy-sounding name you pick for your pet, make sure your pet knows what it really means - stop, look and listen!

A Behavior Sampler by Gary Wilkes

Even the most experienced trainer can fail to prevent an animal from occasionally learning superstitious behaviors. The following examples demonstrate how easily animals can make totally unplanned (and often unwanted) associations.

Superstitious Behaviors

by Gary Wilkes

Many people are cautious about letting a black cat walk across their path. I know a black cat who is absolutely terrified of anyone who bakes cookies. Sam is a superstitious cat.

About 60 years ago, the behaviorist, B.F. "Fred" Skinner, invented an interesting machine. It was a complex box that could provide a variety of conditions to test how animals learn. The major advantage of the "Skinner box" was that the animal was allowed to participate in the experiment without the interference of the human experimenter. A simple setup included a colored light and typewriter key. If the pigeon pecked the key while the light was on, a mechanism could both count the peck and drop some corn into a hopper. By adapting to the box, the pigeon could figure out what "caused" the corn. The pigeon's behavior would change in order to get the corn. The ability to count how often the pigeon pecked, and the rate at which corn was delivered was a scientific breakthrough.

Soon after Skinner started using his box, he discovered something remarkable. He set the mechanism to dump corn into the hopper at random times. There was no connection between the appearance of the corn and any particular behavior that the pigeon might perform. The pigeon could do anything, or nothing and still get fed - at random times. The pigeon amazed the researcher by developing new behaviors anyway.

To appreciate this, it is necessary to imagine the pigeon's point of view of the process. Gertrude, the pigeon, is moving slowly around the box. She hears the sound of corn falling into the hopper. She gobbles greedily but is still hungry. Gertrude may now ask herself, "What caused the corn, and can I make it happen again?" You and I know that her quest is hopeless. Gertrude knows something that we don't, however. Just before the corn fell into the hopper, Gertrude had turned to her left. After eating, she turned to her left again. Gertrude was now convinced that if she just kept turning to the left she would receive a treat. She was absolutely right. Because the box is set up to reinforce her randomly, any behavior that she selects will eventually lead to more corn. Even though her behavior has nothing to do with when and how she gets corn, she will end up performing useless behaviors over and over again.

About a year ago, Sam's owner was baking some cookies. Naturally curious, Sam decided to investigate. As he approached the kitchen, his owner was sliding a hot batch of cookies from the oven. As she lifted the hot cookie sheet, her potholder slipped. The hot metal burned her hand. The sheet of cookies flew from her hand and clattered loudly against the counter and then onto the floor. Sam cleared out and hid in the bedroom. Whatever made the loud noise did not follow Sam under the bed. Sam learned his lesson well. If he smells cookies he knows that the cookie monster is loose in the house. The only safe place to be is under the bed. Even though the connection between cookies and flying cookie sheets was accidental, Sam isn't taking any chances.

Many people know of an animal that is displaying superstitious behavior. Dogs that are afraid of new things in their environment often fall into this category. The instinctive fear reaction to anything new can develop a permanent aversion to a part of the yard, or to something as harmless as a spare tire. If a loud noise occurs at the instant that Rover is investigating the tire, he may develop a fear of all tires, or the spot in the yard where the tire lies. Even removing the tire may not change this attitude. To Rover, tires are unlucky.

Ken and Melrene Wasserman, of Everett, Washington, own a Labrador Retriever named Jayboo. Whenever someone laughs, Jayboo spins in circles, as fast as he can. Ken did not set out to teach him the behavior. It happened the same way Gertrude learned to turn left. The first time Jayboo spun, it was to bite a flea on his tail. He spun so fast that he became dizzy, and staggered like a drunk. The behavior was so humorous that Ken and Melrene laughed and patted Jayboo on the head. A few more repetitions and the behavior not only happened more often, but it became connected to the sound of laughter. Friends and neighbors helped to perpetuate the behavior until it became a regular part of Jayboo's repertoire. The apparent mysterious development of the behavior makes it even funnier and keeps people laughing and Jayboo spinning.

As a pet owner you can use this knowledge to your advantage. Creating associations between particular behaviors and some reinforcement can keep a dog out of the trash or teach him to spin three times before getting a treat. In essence, all training relies on an animal's willingness to connect unrelated but reinforced events. If a behavior seems unusual, ask yourself how the pet could have gained some payoff by performing it. Experiment by using affection and treats to shape and select a small tendency in your animal that can turn into an interesting and unique behavior.

Conference Proceedings

1991 IMATA Conference, Vallejo, California, USA - One of the basic premises of operant theory is that to extinguish a behavior you should ignore it (provide no reinforcement). Time-outs were considered by many as the most effective way to accomplish this task. A modified time-out was developed in the form of a neutral response, a type of least reinforcing stimulus or "LRS." In 1985 Sea World began to implement a three-second no response (a neutral response) as their LRS. The success they have seen from the use of this technique is outlined in this paper. Trainers utilize the LRS in a variety of ways to decrease undesirable behavior, however, there is limited literature available about its use.

Decreasing the Frequency of Behavior through Extinction: An Application for the Training of Marine Mammals

by Michael R. Scarpuzzi[1], Clinton T. Lacinak[2], Ted N. Turner[3], Charles D. Tompkins[4], and David L. Force[5]
[1]Sea World of California, [2]Sea World, Inc., [3]Sea World of Ohio, [4]Sea World of Florida, and [5]Sea World of Texas

ABSTRACT

Many techniques and methods have been used to decrease the frequency of behavior. Historically these techniques have included food deprivation, S-delta, pre-aversive stimuli, and aversive stimuli. Extinction is an empirically derived decrease procedure for use in behavior modification programs. During extinction, reinforcement is no longer delivered for a previously reinforced response. Our objective was to apply extinction as a consequence for behavior without producing the behavioral manifestations of punishment or negative reinforcement. In 1985, we redefined a practical application of true extinction for the training of marine mammals. Our application consists of a three-second period of time in which the trainer applies the least reinforcing stimulus (LRS) to the animal's environment as a consequence of an undesired response. We use the LRS at all four Sea World parks and currently apply it to a variety of marine mammals species including killer whales (*O. orca*), California sea lions (*Z. californianus*), Pacific Walrus (*O. rosmarus divergens*), Atlantic bottlenose dolphin, (*T. truncatus*), Pacific white-sided dolphin (*L. obliquidens*), common dolphin (*D. delphis*), Stenella dolphin (*S. frontalis*), Commerson's dolphin (*C. commersoni*), beluga whale (*D. leucas*), pilot whale (*G. macrorhynchus*), and false killer whales (*P. crassidens*). The animals represent all age groups and include both males and females. In marine mammals, the LRS will effectively decrease undesired behavior without the side effects of punishment or negative reinforcement. The application of the LRS also maintains the integrity of a completely positive reinforcement schedule.

INTRODUCTION

Some of the methods that have been used in the past to decrease the frequencies of behavior include:
- A stimulus delta
- A verbal "No"
- A pre-aversive stimulus
- Conditioned aversive stimulus (shield, net)
- Backing away or taking a "time-out"
- Physically removing reinforcement
- Putting the animal back into the holding facility
- Physical punishment

All of these consequences will eventually, and in some cases, immediately, produce negative side effects such as a conditioned "emotional" response.

At Sea World in 1985, we wanted to find a way to teach the animals that it was "okay" to make a mistake, how to behave after a mistake is made, and to reduce the number of mistakes without producing negative side effects.

In order to accomplish this we wished to find a way to respond to the animal when an unacceptable behavior was elicited, at the same time avoiding any negative consequences. More specifically we were searching for a stimulus that was indeed positive, yet would hold only minimal reinforcing properties.

As marine animal trainers, we recognize the reinforcing property that a stimulus can produce. By definition a stimulus, which is any physical event or condition, may take several forms (Ferster and Culbertson, 1982). Secondary reinforcers (conditioned) and primary reinforcers (unconditioned) are stimuli which follow an operant behavior and increase its frequency. A discriminative stimulus precedes an operant behavior and sets the stage for a behavior or performance to be reinforced. An aversive stimulus will increase the frequency of a behavior through its termination (negative reinforcement). As you can see, everything we do and everything in the environment is a stimulus.

The role of the Reinforcing Stimulus is the key to increasing frequencies of Behavior.

Sea World uses a variable ratio (VR) schedule of reinforcement. Reinforcements come in a variety of forms including primary reinforcement (food) and secondary reinforcement (toys, games, taction, excitement, or other "conditioned reinforcers"). This provides an ever changing and interesting environment for the animals.

We know that to "reinforce," is to follow a behavior with a reinforcing stimulus. The reinforcing stimulus is the event which increases the frequency of the behavior that it follows (Ferster and Culbertson, 1982). However, any stimulus may or may not increase the frequency of the behavior it follows. This depends upon what the animal perceives or has previously learned. Therefore, to be most effective in decreasing the frequency of a behavior, we use a stimulus that will hold the least reinforcing property.

Predictable and constant reinforcement of the same type will eventually result in the loss of its reinforcing characteristics through satiation and will serve to decrease the frequency, intensity, and/or duration of a behavior instead of increasing it, (Nye, 1979). Predictability also plays an important role in decreasing the frequency of behavior through the process of extinction. When a behavior no longer produces a reinforcing stimulus, the behavior will decrease in frequency. When the operant performance occurs sufficiently often without being reinforced, its frequency may drop to the original unconditioned level. The procedure of discontinuing reinforcement is called extinction. This procedure of not delivering reinforcement is the most effective way of reducing the frequency of a previously conditioned performance (Ferster and Culbertson).

Traditional behavior modification recognizes four major principles used to reduce or increase the frequency of a behavior. These stimuli include two types of reinforcement (positive and negative) and two types of punishment (also positive and negative). At Sea World, we directly apply only one of these four principles: positive reinforcement.

Punishment is never used as a consequence of behavior for many reasons. The use of punishment will result in "avoidance" behaviors, "escape" behaviors and many other conditioned "emotional" responses associated with frustration, including aggression (Nye 1979).

Negative reinforcement is also not practiced, although there are many examples of this occurring naturally in the animals' environment. For example, a group of sea lions are swimming when a pod of killer whales attack the group. The sea lions hopefully swim in to the shore away from the killer whales. The sea lions are negatively reinforced for swimming away through the termination of the aversive stimulus, (killer whale attack).

OBJECTIVES

We hoped to reduce the frequencies of behavior and, at the same time avoid producing the negative side effects of true extinction. The overriding goal is to build even stronger positive relationships with the animals. We are able to accomplish this task through the application of a stimulus that held minimal positive reinforcing properties.

METHODS

Our application consists of a period of time in which the trainer applies the *least reinforcing stimulus(LRS)* to the animal's environment as a consequence of an undesired response. We implemented the LRS in all four Sea World parks to various species of animals (a total of over 240 animals). We have applied this technique to animals of all ages, from a one-year-old Atlantic bottlenose dolphin to a 30-year-old killer whale. The entire staff, a total of over 100 trainers, consistently applied this reduction technique exclusively over the last six years. The LRS provides the minimum amount of reinforcement possible, and when applied consistently after an undesired behavior, the LRS will reduce the frequency, intensity, and duration of a behavior.

In our application it could be stated that the Least Reinforcing Stimulus (LRS) is an event which, when presented as a consistent consequence of specific behavior, decreases the probability of the response it follows. The LRS is a 2-3 second pause, with eye contact, by the trainer. It is not a fixed or pre-determined posture that the trainer assumes after an undesired response. If, for example, the trainer is in the water when the undesired response is exhibited, the trainer pauses (LRS) in the water. If he/she is standing when the undesired behavior occurs, the trainer pauses 2-3 seconds in that position. This provides minimal positive or negative environmental change for the animal which otherwise may accidentally reinforce the undesired behavior or some other behavior.

As a general rule, the LRS should occur at the point in time when the <u>actual</u> reinforcement is applied <u>most often</u> for a particular behavior. For example, if an animal does an incorrect "breach" behavior, the LRS should replace the act of rubbing, touching, feeding, etc. It should not begin during the time the animal is returning to the stage <u>unless you normally deliver reinforcement at that time.</u>

Because behavior and learning is based on frequencies, the LRS will aid in the animal's learning if it replaces the point at which you most frequently apply the actual reinforcement. It is not used in place of the "Bridging Stimulus." The principle here is, bring attention to correct behavior, bring as little attention as possible to incorrect behavior and then go on as normal.

The animal's response to the application of LRS must be conditioned and maintained through intermittent reinforcement. Although this may sound contradictory, this is the key to avoiding the negative effects that may occur during true extinction. This is where the animal learns the concept of "it's okay to make a mistake." This can be easily understood when we use a human model. When a child exhibits a series of behaviors known as "tantrum" (after he doesn't get what he expects or makes a mistake) it is often because he has not learned an appropriate or socially acceptable behavior, or has been some how reinforced for producing tantrums. However, if the parent brought little attention to the tantrum and brought more attention to the behavior he exhibits that is more controlled, the controlled behavior would increase in frequency. The parent, hopefully, will acknowledge this and reinforce it. An aggressive response or "tantrum" by our animals is dangerous to our animals, the surrounding environment, and us. We must provide intermittent reinforcement for calm relaxed responses after applying LRS. This will provide the animal with an appropriate behavior, "calmness," as a response to the extinction process that will gain it access to possible intermittent reinforcement. When proper intermittent reinforcement is applied, the animal will avoid frustration and learn that (through an incorrect performance) it's "okay" to make a mistake.

The LRS provides an opportunity for the animal to learn to terminate the response it is given, think about the criteria and to try another behavior the next time. This is a very effective and non-frustrating way of communicating to our animals, and is related closely to Differential Reinforcement of Incompatible behavior (DRI) (Kazdin, 1988). For example, if you reinforce the animal for remaining calm, the animal is less likely to perform the incompatible behavior of getting upset. It is behaviorally incompatible to remain calm and also be upset.

Figure 1 will help illustrate where an LRS is positioned on a Punishment-Reinforcement continuum. The LRS falls on the perceived positive side

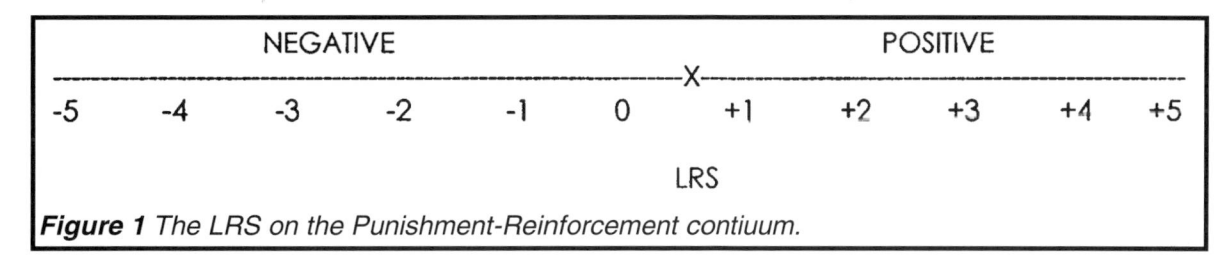

```
        NEGATIVE                                    POSITIVE
----------------------------------------------X---------------------------------------------
 -5     -4     -3     -2     -1      0     +1     +2     +3     +4     +5
                                          LRS
```

Figure 1 *The LRS on the Punishment-Reinforcement contiuum.*

of the punishment-reinforcement continuum because of the conditioning process of intermittent reinforcement.

We have found through experience, that the application of a 2-3 second pause by the trainer, after an undesired response (behavior) by the animal, will eventually decrease the undesired behavior. This "pause" (LRS), when <u>consistently</u> applied after an incorrect response, offers the least reinforcing stimulus possible without being aversive (due to its passive nature and the intermittent reinforcement of its acceptance) and thus avoids frustration by the animal. It allows the animal to better understand the contingencies of reinforcement without using aversives.

SUMMARY

- The LRS (Least Reinforcing Stimulus) is a discriminative stimulus.
- The LRS (Least Reinforcing Stimulus) is the consequence delivered by the trainer to an incorrect or undesired behavior.
- The LRS is a calm, passive 2-3 second pause by the trainer, and is not some fixed or predetermined posture.
- The LRS should be applied at the point at which a trainer would normally deliver primary or secondary reinforcement.
- The positive conditioning or "acceptance" of the LRS (by the animal) is done through periodic reinforcement of calm, non-reactive behaviors and attitude thus avoiding any future frustration in the animal.

CONCLUSION

Because the LRS contains reinforcing properties, it must be noted that it will not immediately eliminate any undesirable behavior. Using a purely "positive," system requires more time, patience, accuracy, diligence, and hard work on our part. Ours is not a science of "quick fixes" that may frustrate our animals, but instead we provide a positive, clear contingency which, over time, will shape strong relationships and safe environments, and equally important, communicate that it is "okay" to make a mistake. Because of scrutiny by our beloved detractors it is essential for our survival to seriously consider these methodologies. If we do not continue to improve our animal training techniques, that would be a mistake that would not be "okay."

GLOSSARY

aversive event - A stimulus that suppresses a behavior that it follows or increases a behavior that results in its termination.

conditioned aversive stimulus - An initially neutral event that acquires aversive properties by virtue of being paired with other aversive events or with a signal that no reinforcement will be forthcoming.

conditioned emotional response - A learned emotional response elicited by a perceived aversive stimulus.

discriminative stimulus (S^D) - An antecedent event or stimulus that signals that a certain response will be reinforced. A response is reinforced in the presence of an S^D. After an event becomes an S^D by being paired with reinforcement, its presence can increase the probability that the response will occur.

extinction - A procedure in which the reinforcer is no longer delivered for a previously reinforced response.

extinction burst - An increase in the frequency and intensity of responding at the beginning of extinction.

fixed-interval schedule - A schedule of administering reinforcement. In an FI schedule, reinforcement is given to the first occurrence of the target response after a fixed time interval elapses.

fixed-ratio schedule - A schedule of administering reinforcement. In an FR schedule, an unvarying number of occurrences of the target response is required for reinforcement.

negative punishment - The removal of a positive event after a response.

negative reinforcement - An increase in the frequency of a response that is followed by the termination or removal of a negative reinforcer.

operant conditioning - A type of learning in which behaviors are altered primarily by regulating the consequences that follow them. The frequency of operant behaviors is altered by the consequences that they produce.

positive punishment - An aversive event is presented after a response.

positive reinforcement - An increase in the frequency of a response that is followed by a positive reinforcer.

primary reinforcement (primary reinforcer) - A reinforcing event that does not depend on learning to achieve its reinforcing properties. Food, water, and sex are primary reinforcers.

punishment - Presentation of an aversive event or removal of a positive event contingent upon a response that decreases the probability of the response.

schedule of reinforcement - The rule denoting how many or which responses will be reinforced.

secondary reinforcer - The rule denoting how many or which responses will be rein forced.

stimulus delta - An antecendent event of stimulus that signals that a certain response will not be reinforced.

time out from reinforcement - A punishment procedure in which contingent upon behavior, access to positive reinforcement is withdrawn for a brief period. Isolation from a group exemplifies time out from reinforcement.

variable Interval schedule - A schedule of administering reinforcement. In VI sched ule, the first occurrence of the target response after a given interval has elapsed is reinforced. However, the time interval changes each time that reinforcement is delivered; the interval is variable. The schedule is denoted by the average time that must elapse before a response can be reinforced.

variable-ratio schedule - A schedule of administering reinforcement. In a VIR schedule, a number of occurrences of the target response are required for reinforcement. The number of required responses varies each time that reinforcement is delivered. The schedule is denoted by the average number of times that the response must occur before reinforcement is delivered.

REFERENCES

Ferster, C. B. & Culbertson, S. A. (1982). Behavior Principles, (3rd Edition) pp. 6, 374-375, 84, 87-89,127). New Jersey: Prentice-Hall, Inc.

Kazdin, R. D. (1989). Behavior Modification in Applied Settings, pp. 35, 337-338, 340-341, 348-349. Wadsworth, Inc.

Nye, R. D. (1979). What is B. F. Skinner Really Saying. Pp. 32, 33, 41-49. New Jersey: Prentice-Hall, Inc.

VOL 24, NO 2, 1999. Because the time out is a common method for dealing with incorrect responses, it is surprising that a *Trainer's Forum* column did not deal with the following question sooner than it did. All three responses are thoughtful and provide good feedback to the question, yet each is quite diverse in the style of answer. The first and last responses deal with the time out as a technique to be used only when absolutely needed, while the second response simply discusses how to use a time out.

Proper Use of a Time Out

QUESTION: Can someone please tell me the proper use of a time out? What behavior constitutes a time out, how long, and how often? I'm concerned that our staff has overused it and that it may become ineffective.

ANSWER 1: If you are concerned that you are overusing it, you probably are! When developing a plan for the appropriate use of a time out, your ultimate goal is to avoid using it altogether. By definition, a time out is a form of punishment. By removing ourselves, reinforcement opportunities, and any other positive interactions with the animal we are hoping to decrease the frequency, intensity, or duration of undesirable behavior. Therein lies the problem. When using time outs, we are focusing on punishing problem behavior instead of directing our attention to reinforcing the good stuff!

Defining exactly when you would use a time out is tricky because once you identify those behaviors your animals will ultimately figure them out too. If the use of a time out has become predictable, your animals can end a session any time they want by offering the undesirable behaviors.

If previously established behaviors are breaking down (behaviors are not being performed up to criteria, the animal is offering incorrect behaviors, or the animal is refusing to perform certain behaviors), there may be other factors at work. If you can rule out health problems or other major behavioral influences such as breeding season or changes in group dynamics, then it's time to look in the mirror (ouch!) and evaluate your training program. Is the staff communicating well to ensure consistency when interacting with the animals? Are you providing your animals with a stimulating dose of fun and unpredictability? There are so many ways to vary the daily experiences of the animals in our care, from the delivery of food to environmental enrichment to training sessions and schedules of reinforcement.

Instead of concentrating on the undesirable behavior or behavior pattern, step back and look at the big picture. Can you identify what factors precede the inappropriate behavior(s)? Does the problem occur when the animal is in a certain part of the exhibit? Does the behavior occur at a predictable point in time? Is the behavior more likely to occur when certain animals work together? This may seem vague, but if you can identify what potentially elicits the problem behavior or what might be inadvertently reinforcing it, you can avoid those situations and start replacing them with opportunities to reward appropriate behavior.

Instead of the use of a time out, there are other effective techniques for dealing with undesirable behavior including DRI, DRO, and DR-(insert favorite letter here) which involve differentially reinforcing one behavior instead of another (i.e. a dolphin can't successfully perform a calm fluke presentation at pool side and chase another dolphin at the same time, therefore, you are differentially reinforcing the calm fluke presentation). The use of an LRS (least reinforcing stimulus) to decrease the frequency of behavior through extinction has become an industry standard (Scarpuzzi, et. al., 1992 IMATA Conference). So RSVP by using these techniques ASAP to see positive results PDQ or you may be SOL, OK?

When all is said and done, the application of

any effective training technique is founded on the premise that the animal is paying attention. If that's not the case, take a time out!

Traci Belting
Point Defiance Zoo & Aquarium

ANSWER 2: At our facility, a time out may be used following the incorrect response to a cue, no response to a cue, or a response that does not meet the behavioral criteria. Generally speaking, our first response to one of the above conditions is a three-second neutral response. This simply means that the trainer reacts neutrally - not responding positively or negatively - for a period of about three seconds. At this time, the trainer may then decide to repeat the cue, ask for another behavior or terminate the session. If the animal continues to respond incorrectly, a longer time out may be used. This may involve either a longer duration neutral response or termination of the session, with either the animal being returned to its enclosure or the trainer leaving the animal area. The duration of the time out depends on several factors, including the behavioral reason for it and the trainer's schedule. It is important to remember that time outs are training tools, not punishment. One of the most important reasons for the effectiveness of a time out is its neutrality. Sometimes a trainer may unwittingly be reinforcing incorrect behavior by reacting to it (i.e. tensing up their body, talking to the animal, etc.), which may unintentionally reinforce the undesired response. If time outs are being used continuously without improvement in the animal's behavior, look to see if they are being used neutrally and not negatively. It might also be helpful to examine the training steps and techniques being used, to see if the animal might be confused as opposed to uncooperative. If you feel that time outs are being used too often, try keeping a log of when they are used and the animal's response following them. Then the training staff can look at this information to track not only the frequency of time out use but also its effectiveness. Good luck.

Training Staff
Loon Mountain Wildlife Theater

ANSWER 3: A time-out has been defined as the removal of the opportunity for positive reinforcement and in the jargon of operant psychology it is a form of negative punishment. Punishment is a technique that will decrease the probability of a response occurring over time, and negative punishment is the removal of a positive stimulus – something the animal seeks to encounter – from the animal's environment, thereby decreasing the frequency of the response that proceeded it. When an animal is misbehaving or is not responding to cues, the trainer has the option of taking the food and leaving the training session for a period of time. Both the trainer and the food are positive stimuli that the animal seeks to encounter; by taking a time-out following undesired behavior, the trainer has removed the positive stimuli – the food and himself – from the animal's environment, thereby decreasing the likelihood of that undesired behavior occurring when he returns. This technique can be an effective tool for decreasing unwanted or inappropriate behavior.

Having said that, it is also a technique that is frequently misused, particularly by inexperienced trainers. Too often, trainers in the throes of frustration over an animal that is not responding in the manner that they had envisioned will choose to walk away. This is an easy solution and takes less effort than trying to determine *why* the animal is responding in an inappropriate manner. It may be that the animal wants to respond correctly but is confused, taking a time-out in this situation will only add to the confusion and will very likely create frustration in the animal as well. Consequently, it is recommended that a time-out be used only by experienced trainers (or under the supervision of an experienced trainer), and even then it should be used only rarely. One instance where a time-out is probably appropriate is when the animal chooses not to participate in a session. The animal cannot be forced to participate, so in this situation it may be appropriate to simply end the session and leave.

The challenge in situations where animals are responding incorrectly, inappropriately, or not at all is to not walk away but to find a way to work through the problem, to find a solution that is acceptable to both the animal and the trainer. There are alternatives to time-outs available to the trainer. One of the most commonly used is to provide the animal with only the minimum of reinforcement following an undesired behavior. Known as an LRS, this is generally defined as a period of time in which the trainer applies the least reinforcing stimulus (LRS) to the animal's environment as a consequence of an undesired response. This technique provides the minimum of reinforcement possible and will reduce the frequency, intensity, and duration of a behavior.

There are several descriptions of LRS and its use in the literature and, if the trainer is unfamiliar with this concept, it is suggested that these articles be researched.

The LRS technique – and others – when properly applied are generally as or more effective in correcting undesirable behavior than is the use of a time-out. If you feel that the time-out is already being overused, it almost assuredly is. The focus of any animal training program should be on positive reinforcement, and punishment techniques such as a time-out should be used rarely and only in extreme cases.

John Kirtland
International Wildlife Resources

A Behavior Sampler by Gary Wilkes

Although this story utilizes a variety of training techniques, I prefer to emphasize the element of planning. To solve the problem described, a training plan had to be developed and carefully followed. Often it is the lack of clear goals and a well formulated training plan that prevents trainers from making good progress.

How to Get Your Dog Into Carnegie Hall

by Gary Wilkes

There is an old joke about a visitor to New York City who asks a local how to get to Carnegie Hall. The New Yorker's wry answer is "Practice, practice, practice."

Most people understand that to become skillful at anything, one must practice. This is assumed to be true for behaviors such as playing the violin, flying an airplane, or performing brain surgery. It is ironic that this belief stops short when we consider our pets.

For instance, Cliff has a St. Bernard named Mortimer, who embarrasses him whenever a guest comes into the house. At first sound of the doorbell, Mort bellows like a bull and charges the door. When Cliff opens the door, he holds Mort by the collar while the guest tries to slip past. When the guest finally sits down, Mortimer shoves his face in the lap of his newest friend.

In case you do not know, most St. Bernards carry a load of drool in their mouths at all times. Mortimer is no exception. Mortimer's victim now has several large strings of slime smeared across his legs. Mortimer is not a big hit with Cliff's friends.

Cliff has always tried to get Mortimer to be nice when people come over. He waits on pins and needles as his guests sit on the couch and then begins his apology, as Mort approaches the guest. Just as Mort slimes the person, Cliff yells at the dog and bodily drags him off to his kennel. On the surface it looks as if Mort has failed again - but a closer look shows that the problem is elsewhere.

Cliff has forgotten that learning requires repetitions. Each time a guest comes over, Mortimer gets only one chance to succeed or fail. Sometimes it is as much as a week between visitors. The few successful repetitions are so far apart that Mortimer forgets what he has learned from week to week.

To help Mort through this dilemma, Cliff must restructure the situation to allow for many repetitions in a short amount of time. The following is an example of a typical training session.

The doorbell rings - Mortimer races to the door. Cliff tells Mort that he is wasting his time. No one is coming into the house until Mort sits. Mort barks for a few seconds and then realizes that Cliff isn't going to answer the door. Cliff's accomplice waits until Mortimer is quiet and then rings the doorbell again. The process is repeated until the sound of the doorbell fails to elicit a response from Mort. After Mort's initial reaction is extinguished, it is time to get a little tougher. This time, as the bell rings, Cliff stands and walks toward the door. Mort returns instantly to his old behavior, as if it had never been extinguished. As Mort starts to go wild, Cliff says "Wrong" in a normal tone of voice and sits back down. The "doorbell" person waits until Mort shuts up.

Each time Mort breaks and rushes to the door, Cliff says "Wrong." Soon even the entrance of the guest does not cause Mort to go crazy. Each failure leads to the word "wrong" and the quick exit of the guest. Mort soon learns that barking, sliming or jumping causes people to leave.

On his first day of training, Mort saw this pattern unfold about 50 times over about 30 minutes. On the first repetition, Mort gave his typical wild reaction. By the time he had heard the bell ring for the 50th time, he did not charge the front door, jump on the guest or slime the person's lap. Cliff had taught him the first step toward politeness without lifting a finger.

Later that afternoon, Cliff's friend comes for a second round of training. Mort acts like an idiot for the first three repetitions and then settles down - much faster than usual. On the fourth repetition, Mort is perfectly behaved. Cliff praises him and gives him a doggie treat for a great performance.

After several training sessions, Mort became quite consistent in his correct response to the door. Without resorting to harsh treatment, Cliff had changed Mort's behavior through consistent reinforcement over many repetitions.

Cliff is so pleased with Mort's behavior he's thinking of getting him into show-biz - now that he knows how to get into Carnegie Hall.

Non-Formal Interactions

5

Let's take a break from talking technique specifically. Theory will always be important, but we must regularly step back and look at the animals and the other interactions that we have with them.

Formal Training

When we refer to formal training we're talking about the act of consciously and deliberately shaping a behavior. However, training goes much deeper than formal interactions. *Every interaction we have with an animal has some kind of reinforcing value* (whether it be positive or negative). That statement is so important and fundamental in understanding non-formal training that it can hardly be said too often. Seldom, if ever, is an interaction completely neutral. For that reason, we must consciously be aware of what we are doing any time we are near or around our animals. Here are three examples of unintentional shaping:

Children in the Next Room
Sometimes parents will argue while their children are in the next room. Because the discussion is not directed at the children, parents may even forget that they are there to overhear the argument. No formal interaction is taking place between the parents and the children, but the ominous tone of the argument may make a young child scared to come into the room.

Beluga Spitting Behavior
When the Shedd Aquarium beluga whales were housed at the Point Defiance Zoo and Aquarium in Tacoma, they developed the habit of spitting huge streams of cold water at trainers as they passed by. Each time the cold water would hit a trainer, the trainer would scream, giggle, or run away. That human reaction must have been very reinforcing for the whales, because within a month the spitting had all but gotten out of hand. Without formally training it, we had quickly taught the belugas to spit at us. So we had to examine and adjust our own behavior as we passed the whales' habitat to solve the problem. We found that if we ignored the behavior by not reacting or responding to the cold water as it hit us, the behavior eventually subsided.

Epileptic Dolphin
At another facility a dolphin appeared to have an epileptic seizure. Everyone sprang into action, running to get the vet, jumping into the

pool, and eventually moving the dolphin to a shallow pool, where it would receive round-the-clock care. After two weeks in which no seizures and no other health problems were discovered, the dolphin was moved back to its normal home. Within days it started having more seizures. As before, the staff mobilized quickly, and as soon as everyone was attending to the dolphin, it seemed fine. This time the animal care staff decided not to move the dolphin. Instead, a 24-hour watch was placed on the animal, but the observers remained out of sight. They quickly discovered that the dolphin began to exhibit seizures only if someone was present but not paying attention to the animal! The staff's actions, although not in a training session, had shaped this unusual behavior. To solve the problem the trainers increased their play and other interactions with the dolphin when formal training was not taking place.

Technique vs. Instinct

What role does instinct or being "good with animals" play in being a good trainer? Gary Wilkes examines that question in *Were You Born "Good with Animals?" or Did You Learn it?* on page 118. Certainly, technique is critical to being a good animal trainer, but to apply technique effectively you must know the animal and understand its needs. Each of these elements can be learned. Good sense (or instinct) comes from experience. These experiences can be gathered and learned during non-formal interactions. Play sessions, observations, feedings, and other types of exposure to your animals will help your understanding of each individual animal to grow. These non-formal interactions will add to your animal "instincts" and help you apply good technique.

Developing a Relationship

Caring about the Animal

Is loving your animal a bad thing? Of course not! Being caring and compassionate is part of developing a good relationship with each animal. Some trainers refuse to talk about relationships, focusing only on technique, stimulus response, and reinforcement, but it is doubtful that they achieve good responses from their animal if they're not responsive to the animal's needs. Gail Laule (1989) touches on that subject as well as others in *If My Friends Could See Me Now*, on page 119.

Polarized Camps
In truth, there are two distinct extremes in the training community, or at least they always seem at odds with each other. There are those who focus only on technique, stating that if reinforcement is used properly you do not have to like or care about your animal. At the other extreme there are those who feel that as long as you love your animal, technique is unimportant. The real answer is somewhere in between, a balance of technique and caring. All good trainers have both, even though they may not know it or admit it.

Technique rules – If you ever meet a good trainer who talks about nothing but operant principles, watch the way he or she treats the animal. Invariably good trainers will still talk to their animal or offer soothing tactile reinforcement. If their animal is sick, they will call the vet at the drop of a hat. They will handle the animal with great care. These individuals may not even realize how much they care about the animal, but the animal responds nevertheless.

Love conquers all – "Affection is all an animal needs." Trainers who make that statement and are still successful are either practicing good public relations, or they actually don't realize that they use operant principles every day. After all, the concept of positive reinforcement fits right into caring for an animal, whether the trainer knows that he's using the technique or not.

True extremists – Those who truly fit into the extremes of the two beliefs described will ultimately fail as trainers. If technique is all that's used, the animal certainly will become ill, as many of its needs will not be met. If affection is the only component of training, the animal will become an unruly, misbehaved yet well-loved animal. In 1998 Ted Turner wrote a wonderful essay that describes the importance of non-formal interactions in an animal's life; see *Have You Been too Busy?* on page 122.

Building the Relationship
As you learn more about an individual animal, trust will develop. Preferences will become obvious and you can use that information in developing a training plan or looking for new reinforcers. Recognizing when an animal is having an off day is also important. It can lead to faster detection of a medical concern, but it can also change the way you approach and evaluate a training session. Gary Wilkes

discusses that in *Animals Can Make Mistakes*, on page 123. Trust and relationship building take time. At first the animal will not be aware of your intentions, so trust will take a while to develop. Patience is a virtue in all aspects of an animal care program.

Play

Perhaps play would be better termed unstructured interactions. But, no matter how the animal perceives an unstructured interaction, if your intent is play, then it can be called play. Formally, play sessions are defined as interactive sessions in which the animal's cooperation is voluntary and not contingent on any primary reinforcement. Play sessions are important in the development of trust. They can help you discover favorite toys, preferred games, and favored tactile spots. These sessions will shape interactive behavior and can be the start of great relationship building.

Animal Observations - Ethograms

Is Observation an Interaction?

Animal observations do not normally constitute an interaction of any kind. However, one of the advantages of regular observations of the animals that you train is the extra knowledge that you gain about them. This information can be useful in all future interactions. A well-documented observation program can be an invaluable tool in caring for and training your animals.

Looking at Two Examples

The best proof is in reading what others have written about their observation programs. The Brookfield Zoo in *Trainer Involvement in Behavioral Observations* (Gifford, 1990), on page 125 and EPCOT's Living Seas Pavilion in *The Ethogram: Present and Future Applications* (Rector, 1986), on page 127. Both facilities employ structured observations as part of their daily care program.

A Behavior Sampler by Gary Wilkes

Practice, along with knowledge, does make perfect. Animal training is a skill and a technology that can be learned.

Were You Born "Good with Animals?" Or Did You Learn it?

by Gary Wilkes

There are quite a few people out there who consider themselves "naturally good with animals." It is a rare shock to one of these people when they meet an animal who happens to be "naturally bad with people who are naturally good with animals." The inevitable result is a nasty bite wound and a shattered ego. The belief that being good with animals is an innate quality can give false confidence to some, while excluding others from the enjoyment of animal companionship.

The term "naturally good with animals" should really refer to a level of expertise rather than genetic endowment. Usually the person in question just happens to have been raised on a farm, competed in rodeos, 4-H, dog shows, or is the child of an animal lover. The fact that the person handles animals well is invariably the result of a simple formula - the person has handled lots of animals. Conversely, people who are not good with animals are primarily those with the least experience.

For people who are not good with animals, encounters with non-humans can range from mild annoyance to true terror. For some, a petting zoo or pony ride is as frightening as a real-life Jurassic Park. A popular, but mistaken belief that displaying fear can cause an animal to attack complicates this reaction. For someone who is terrified of animals, hiding the fear is impossible. The only solution is to avoid their fear by avoiding animals entirely.

Ironically, it is often the person who tries to ignore animals that seems to attract them most. The reason for this reaction is simple. Many animals perceive direct eye contact as a threat or challenge. People who try to ignore animals intentionally avoid eye contact. This passive display acts as a lure to most animals. Despite human complaints about simply wanting to be left alone, the animal views passive behavior as an open invitation for greeting and affection.

The first step toward becoming good with animals is to realize that good handling is a simple matter of expanding your knowledge. The first thing to know is that different species may react differently to the same situation. For instance, a dog is usually pleased to have its belly rubbed. Doing the same thing to a cat may cause the animal to grab you with its claws and either bite or scratch you.

Another important consideration when handling pets depends on the age of the animal. Both dogs and cats move their young by picking them up by the scruff of the neck. Though both species tolerate this behavior as infants, only cats will allow you to do this to them as adults. Many dogs react to someone grabbing their scruff by inflicting a bite to the offending wrist.

While there are many differences among species, some reactions are almost universal. Most species react to eye contact as a threat or challenge. This common reaction is responsible for the belief that animals will attack if they sense fear. In reality, the animal attacks because it perceives the fearful human stare as a threat. If the frightened human avoids staring "wide-eyed" at the beast, his chances of getting bitten are greatly reduced. By using peripheral vision, the person can still watch the animal without triggering a bite.

One of the most important general rules for handling animals is to give them plenty of warning before you touch them. This rule is especially important if you know nothing of the animal's temperament. In public, it is both dangerous and rude to assume that you may interact with someone's pet. If you don't wait to find out if the "little dog bites," you may find out the hard way.

For those of you who are intimidated by strange animals, there are plenty of opportunities to learn better handling skills. Many animal shelters, veterinary hospitals and kennels accept volunteer help or would be willing to give you instruction. Almost every city has clubs for lovers of purebred dogs and cats that can help you learn sage and humane handling skills. Attending dog, cat and livestock shows can put you in touch with people who are both skilled and humane in their treatment of animals. The more you work at it the faster you may become "unnaturally good with animals."

Conference Proceedings

1989 IMATA Conference, Amsterdam, Holland. The topics covered in this paper are varied and quite basic, applying marine mammal techniques in a zoo setting. However, when discussing technique the subject of building relationships with our animals is sometimes skipped. This element of animal care and training is difficult to quantify but its importance is brought out at the end of this paper.

If My Friends Could See Me Now

by Gail Laule
Active Environments Inc.

ABSTRACT

The author takes a look at her experiences over the last ten years, from training marine mammals, to baboons, to a variety of terrestrials including cheetah, raccoons, and a squirrel named Alvin. Among the similarities and differences lie some universal truths about technique, desensitization, enrichment, flexibility, sensitivity, and plain old common sense. This presentation is further enhanced and enlightened by videotape.

IF MY FRIENDS COULD SEE ME NOW

I trained marine mammals for eight-and-a-half years. In that time I worked with a variety of species - harbor seals, walrus, sea lions, dolphins, and whales, including the Rolls Royce of them all, killer whales. During that time I trained the usual flips, spins, and roll-overs. But I also had the opportunity to train sea lions to work in the public and off-grounds, to help train Corky, our killer whale, to chase and present her mammaries to an artificial calf, and to train husbandry behaviors such as tube insertions and blood collecting. Through these experiences, my training skills expanded and grew.

Then Marineland closed and I moved to the Los Angeles Zoo where, for the last two years, I've been doing special training projects and developing new shows. My animals are no longer aquatic, unless you count our water-loving raccoons and coyote. There are no more fins and flippers, just paws, hands and feet, and facial expressions. In that time I've trained sloth bears to gate, orangutans to urinate on cue, and drill baboons to socialize and voluntarily participate in artificial insemination procedures. One show includes raccoon, coyote, opossum, and owl. The other has more exotic species such as lemurs, coatimundi, serval, caracal, and a bat-eared fox who doubles as compound watch dog. There are also more dangerous animals such as mountain lions and cheetahs.

This all sounds pretty neat, and it is. But it's a far cry from my days with the sea lions, dolphins, and whales. So much so that I worried that my training skills that I worked so hard to develop were evaporating before my very eyes. After all, just how much conditioning can you do with an opossum?

And then it struck me one day, while training our squirrel Alvin to sing, that my training skills really haven't suffered, and, in fact, the opposite is true. My time with these species has forced me to become more flexible and innovative than ever before. My problem-solving skills have been taxed to the max. After all, I've had to work with an owl, that majestic symbol of learning that actually has a brain the size of a pea, and is a whole lot denser than the rather bright common crow. I've also discovered that the cheetah's awesome physical presence is in part a cover for a brain whose most complex analysis is: if it's food, (e.g.: gazelle, rabbit, or children), run after it; if it's not, run away from it. On the plus side, I've discovered that lemurs, who are known for their lack of smarts are trainable. We've been able to train a number of behaviors in four individuals, of two different species with good reliability.

The challenge with these animals is that their instinctive behavior is equal to or greater than their ability to learn new behavior. In contrast, cetacean's and pinniped's ability to learn far surpasses their instincts or hard wiring. Try this analogy. Animals present you with a window of opportunity, that part that makes them accessible to learn. With killer whales that window is the size of this room. We haven't even begun to tap the limits of orca cognitive ability. With a small cat, like the caracal, it's the size of my fist. So you have a peephole to work through, and the rest of the room, their instincts, to contend with. And those instincts are ever present. For instance, "Walk across that open space? Are you crazy? You might get jumped!" You won't change that hard wiring, so you learn to work around it.

So, how does all this apply to marine mammals? Well, my recent experiences have led me to some thoughts that I believe apply to all training, and I'd like to share these with you now. First, operant conditioning works. I know you're not surprised, but these days it fills me with this sense of wonder and exhilaration. Maybe it's a sense of power, that with a clicker and food, anything is possible. But I think it's because when you work with marine mammals, it's so easy, you take it for granted. But try going out into the zoo world, and coming face-to-face with a sloth bear that doesn't want to gate. Standing there with your clicker and handful of grapes, you feel real silly. But then two months later when he willingly gates anytime of the day, well, that's where the wonder and exhilaration comes in. So I would suggest that operant conditioning provides the tools, how you use them provides endless opportunities. So, be creative.

Okay, thought number two. A clicker or whistle, properly applied, is an awesome weapon in the fight against loss of control. This struck me one day when I realized that I feel safer working our 75 pound cheetah with a clicker and food, than with food alone. All the animals I work with are potentially dangerous, relatively unpredictable, and highly instinctual. When annoyed or stressed, their normal reaction is to lash out, and usually that means either biting or scratching the trainer. So, we continually bridge routine behaviors, like putting leashes and collars on and off, because there will be days when the coyote or raccoon just doesn't want to be leashed or collared, and a well-established and consistent bridge can get you the behavior you need while avoiding the injury you don't.

Now I realize that with marine mammals, the issue of control is different than the terms in which I describe it here. With highly instinctual animals, from big cats to little lemurs, it is important that we, the trainers, be in charge. If their role is to be dominant, aggression is an integral part of that role. Therefore, we set clear-cut rules on acceptable and unacceptable behavior, and bridge and reinforce accordingly. With smarter animals, like dolphins and killer whales, the combination of good training skills, a positive relationship with the animal, and the animal's own cognitive ability comprise your measure of safety. You, the trainer, are not dominant. Rather, you function with the animal in a cooperative, more equal partnership, which is designed to meet the training agenda and the animal's needs concurrently.

Smart animals need control over their own lives, especially dominant animals. Their misbehavior, like their intellect, is more complex and can be a way of communicating need. So their behavior needs to be interpreted and your guesses empirically tested.

Although control is not the goal, skillful bridging with marine mammals is very important, and a critical element in some situations. For example, socialization issues like dominance can be mitigated by reinforcing a dominant animal for allowing a subdominant animal to eat and work. Exactly how and when you bridge the dominant animal tells him clearly what he is being reinforced for. Precise bridging is also crucial in training husbandry behaviors. Bridging just when the dolphin feels the needle prick, and not as she is pulling away is an important distinction, with long-lasting effects if you miss the right second. Of course, good bridging while training show behaviors provides clarity and helps the animal figure out just what the trainer is looking for. Finally, desensitizing animals to novel situations or events requires good bridging skills.

Which brings me to my next observation: desensitization, which is often taken for granted, is a significant component of any good training regimen.

With the animals I train now, desensitization is a daily event. In fact, it probably comprises about 80% of the training we do. Each day presents more opportunities for desensitization work. That stump the coyote sat on yesterday is suddenly a spot to be avoided at all costs; the audience laughs too loud and the raccoon that has been working for five months straight is off-stage like a shot; the serval suddenly thinks he sees something, I certainly don't, but the rest of the training session is an exercise in futility. These scenarios, and hundreds like them, occur everyday at the compound. So, consequently, desensitization has taken on new meaning for me. Sometimes I feel like I'm desensitizing the animals to life itself. Operationally, however, it has sharpened my eye for anticipating problems, and improved my skills in heading them off before disaster strikes.

I think that marine mammal trainers often take desensitization for granted. We use it with sea lions to prepare them for work in the public. Husbandry training is, in fact, desensitization to an unpleasant stimulus, a needle or a tube. But there are all sorts of other little situations that happen in the midst of training that may warrant some desensitization, like: an animal's apprehension of a new prop or toy, reacting to a strange sound, or an immediate flight response to the sight of the veterinarian approaching. Formally desensitizing animals to these little scary things, instead of assuming they'll go away, is time well spent.

My last observation is the simplest, but perhaps the most profound. A meaningful relationship between animal and trainer is what makes all this worthwhile. Ultimately, every training decision and aesthetic consideration we make should have the animals' best interests at heart. You can't make the best decisions for the animals if you don't truly care. And the kind of relationship I'm talking about doesn't happen in a day. It takes time and effort, but it's worth the wait.

This idea, although accepted in the oceanarium community, is still often resisted in the zoo world. A lot of zoos have hands-off policies that discourage keepers from having any direct contact, besides cleaning and feeding, with their animals. At the L.A. Zoo this is changing, but I think some people envy the trainer's opportunities for human-animal contact. With some of our animals, building a relationship has added importance. With the mountain lions and cheetah, it is critical to establish strong bonds with them as babies if you want to be able to work them as adults. Therefore, we hand raise them, including taking them home with us at night for as long as possible, usually about four months. In that time we build a bond and also set ground rules for what is acceptable behavior and what is not. With the other animals, because of their unpredictability, knowing them well is critical to avoiding problems or injury. But besides all the practical reasons for building relationships, it feels real good.

So in closing, I'd just like to say this. We're a privileged few here. We get to work and play with animals for a living. All we owe in return is to share our love and respect for these creatures with everybody else. Our job, therefore, is to skillfully train and then effectively present these animals to the public. Unfortunately, man's inhumanity to nature provides us with endless material: gill nets, whaling, the incidental take of dolphins, poaching, habitat destruction, pollution, the fur and pet trade, and on and on and on. Depressing to say the least. But, if we do our job well, we can make a difference. My little pea-brained opossum can present a conservation message as effectively as your big-brained bottlenose dolphin. I just have to work a little harder.

VOL 23, NO 4, 1998. During Ted Turner's tenure as president of IMATA (1997-1998) he took the opportunity to use the president's quarterly column in the magazine *Soundings* to write some very good essays that celebrated IMATA's members and the importance of our profession. Here he relates a story about animal-human interactions and the importance of non-formal interactions. It is an important lesson from which we can all learn a great deal.

Have you been too busy?

by Ted Turner
Sea World of Ohio

An experiment was conducted at Ohio State a few years back where two groups of rabbits were being tested for their response to specific environmental deprivation. The animals were housed in modest cages and placed on shelving units stacked on top of one another. On the top shelf, the control group was given fresh food and water every day, their substrate changed, and they had access to natural sunlight. On the bottom shelf the experimental group was subject to harsh conditions. These unfortunate subjects went days with limited water, food was scarce, and cleanliness was poor. But, as time went by, the expected results were not obtained much to the disappointment of the researchers. In fact the opposite effect occurred! The animals on the top shelf deteriorated while the animals on the bottom shelf thrived! "How could this be?" the researchers asked, and determinedly they tried the experiment again, this time, using different animals. Unfortunately, they obtained the same confusing results.

After commiserating with their advisor, they were encouraged to try once more but this time they were instructed to switch the cages on the shelves. Finally, the data made sense and the expected results were achieved. A conclusive statement was developed for the write up that said, rabbits deprived on the top shelf deteriorated, while rabbits with access to clean housing and fresh food and water on the bottom shelf thrived. A neat, fundamental piece of science, definitively recorded. "Cha-ching!"

Just to be certain, (and mostly because their advisor made them), the researchers now switched the housing conditions but did NOT move the cages (standard scientific protocol in controlling for error), so that the thriving, bottom-shelf rabbits were now subject to the harsh conditions, and the final conclusions could be replicated and verified with one small glitch: it didn't work. As before, the top-shelf rabbits deteriorated despite the optimal conditions and the bottom-shelf rabbits, subject to severe conditions, thrived. Quite perplexing-

Late into the evening the researchers sat in the lab, trying to analyze what went wrong with this simple, idiot proof cause and effect study. "We've controlled for everything," they whined. "How can the data be all over the place!" As they continued to postulate, the night janitor came in. A small, kind woman she said, "Do you mind if I take my break in here again? I love to visit the animals," she stated, as she began to pet and touch the rabbits through the cage wire. The researchers slowly looked at each other as the significance of this variable began to sink in. "I spend just about every night in here but I wish I could reach the ones on the top shelf, they look like they could use some attention too," and she smiled warmly at the young students.

The power of affection, the time spent just sitting, the touch, the relationship we know that is critical for developing a strong level of trust between animals and their trainers does much more that just demonstrate to the show audience or zoo visitor that we care, it changes animals' lives quite literally. This is as fundamental as food and water and sunlight. But ironically, it is the first to go when we get busy "caring" for our animals, when responsibilities inundate us with paperwork and e-mail and phone calls. When administrative duties, or inclement weather, or low gaffing, or the boss, or well, there will always be a million reasons why we just "can't." We'd love to, but we just don't have the time. So instead, here's a boomer ball and a ten-million dollar facility.

Why do some animals in large, state-of-the-art facilities still deteriorate even with a multitude of environmental enrichment opportunities? My guess is that they need the same thing that a rich but unhappy child needs affection, attention, and interaction with the person who cares for them. When the affection and positive attention goes, in so many cases, so does appropriate behavior and optimal health. If you don't believe me, try it yourself for a year.

Why do some animals in small, antiquated facilities thrive? It's the people. Good people, simple as that. People that love to just sit with their animals, who know every detail of their moods, who invent games and train interesting things. People who know what their animals really like, their personalities, their individual characteristics. These kind of dedicated people know, (or have a strong desire to know) exactly how their animals learn best, what gets them enthusiastic, and what they don't like. And, their animals give back. They give back many times over with amazing behaviors, long lives, many babies, and reciprocal affection. This is what makes up IMATA. People who spend time making a real difference in the lives of the individual animal; a different type of busy person who WILL put the time in no matter what the priority. To all of you, you have my admiration and all of my affection!

A Behavior Sampler by Gary Wilkes

The moral of this story is tolerance. We often expect a great deal from our animals, which is fine. However, when they do make mistakes, it may not mean that a major behavioral problem is imminent. It could simply be a mistake!

Animals Can Make Mistakes

by Gary Wilkes

Recently I was at the San Diego Zoo, watching a "Birds of Prey" animal show. A trained hawk was released from a cage, high over the audience's heads. The planned routine called for the hawk to swoop over the crowd to display his fantastic flight abilities. That is what was supposed to happen, but did not. What happened was that a wild hawk flew over the amphitheater and distracted his captive cousin. The "trained" hawk flew off and perched in a tree and refused to return to its handler. The lesson to learn from this experience is that when you are working with animals, don't expect perfection.

There is a tendency on the part of humans to assume that animals are capable of behavioral perfection. We rarely imagine a majestic cougar misjudging a leap and landing on a cactus rather than a deer, but it can happen. Wildlife movies and films tend to reinforce an image of infallible animals until we incorrectly assume that all animals have the ability to do what they want, when they want, flawlessly.

Far from being perfectly robotic, animals survive in an environment that abhors consistency. If all zebras automatically turned left when chased by lions, the lions would be ecstatic - unless all lions automatically turned right when attacking zebras. These absurd examples display an obvious fact; nature requires animals to vary their behavior. The human goal of repetitive, identical behaviors, such as in dog obedience competitions, is actually unnatural and generally unattainable. Expecting a dog to perform the same twelve behaviors in the same order with the same level of enthusiasm in exchange for the same reinforcements is unrealistic. If the same goals were applied to professional baseball, we would expect all players to bat .500, all pitchers would win 50% of their games and spectators would flock to watch more exciting games, such as televised golf.

Obedience competitors are not the only ones with unrealistic expectations of dog perfection. Many owners are startled that their wonderfully trained, six-year old Schnauzer suddenly fails to come when called. The owner's refrain of "He's never done that before," implies the belief that Fritzi's behavior is unchanging and unchangeable. Taking a dog's good behavior for granted is the quickest way to ruin it. Behaviors that are never reinforced often decay and fall apart. Assuming that Fritzi will always come simply because he has always done so is risky thinking. A better approach would be to give Fritzi a treat every once in awhile, for correct behavior.

Another feature of this belief in behavioral perfection, is the idea that an animal may be a "perfect failure." This assumption of perfect failure may be an artificial limitation on a dog's learning potential. If Rover has jumped on some guests, it does not mean that he will jump on all guests. The perfectionist's solution is to confine Rover when guests arrive, rather than teach him correct behavior. A more realistic approach recognizes that Rover is capable of improving his method for greeting guests. Replacing the jumping with an acceptable behavior may solve the greater problem. Allowing Rover to be "less than perfect" during his initial training and gradually increasing his level of competence will usually solve the problem quickly.

Expecting a dog to walk perfectly at heel, at all times, is another example of pet perfectionism. Most dogs are supremely challenged when expected to ignore every new sight and smell that they come in contact with. Wise owners limit the enforced heeling aspects of a walk and allow for periods of loose-leash sniffing and sight-seeing. Periodically expecting perfectionism for a limited period of time is a much more realistic goal for your pet.

One of the pleasures of owning a pet is the animal's ability to offer unique and interesting behavior. Allowing animals to be themselves includes occasionally letting them behave erratically. Demanding robot-like performance or assuming that any mistakes are signs of spite or malice denies their basic nature. When living with pets it is important to accept their mistakes as part of their total personality and to remember, "they're only non-human."

1990 IMATA Conference, Chicago, Illinois, USA. To be a successful trainer, one must know the animal well. Observations of animal interactions and activities when the trainer is not present are a valuable tool to the trainer. Informal observations are useful, but they can be difficult to interpret and quantify. Tara Gifford describes the benefits of a formal observational program.

Trainer Involvement in Behavioral Observations

by Tara Gifford
Chicago Zoological Society

ABSTRACT

Dolphins exhibit complex behavior, which many marine mammal facilities formally document. Such documentation has been conducted by trainers and researchers over the last four years at Brookfield Zoo's Seven Seas. Observations are conducted four days a week and focus on aggressive, submissive, amicable, sexual, and synchronous behaviors. The investment of time and commitment yields a number of benefits, Including the trainers' improved insights into behaviors which are observed outside of a training situation. Observation methods and the additional benefits of trainers' involvement are discussed.

INTRODUCTION

Most of the interaction that trainers have with animals is during shows or as casual observers. But is this a true reflection of what is going on in the animal's social grouping? Over the past four years trainers and researchers at the Brookfield Zoo have studied our dolphins' behavior and discovered that there is a thrilling soap opera happening among us. There is plenty of romance, men, fighting, and sleeping around. This paper discusses the observation methods, the categories of behavior focused on, the value of doing observations and their future at the Brookfield facility.

Behavioral observations have been done on many different animals. At Seven Seas we have been studying dolphins, but pinnipeds would be interesting subjects as well. Amy Samuels of the Brookfield Zoo's Conservation Biology Department set up the observation protocol and then taught the trainers how to do the data collection. The dolphins are observed early in the morning before the days' events begin, for once fish buckets appear and people are present with which to interact, the animals tend to watch the people. Part of the observations are to watch how the dolphins and people relate to each other.

SAMPLING TECHNIQUE

The sampling technique consists of focal animal sampling; i.e., one animal in the group is chosen as the focal animal and observed for a ten-minute period, three times a week. This reduces the difficulty in recording all animals during an aggressive outbreak. Individual dolphins are observed in a pre-determined order so that sampling is not biased. This avoids a situation where the focus might be on individuals who are social, but to the exclusion of the loners. Good observation technique requires that within a group of animals all members should be examined methodically and uniformly.

INFORMATION GATHERED

Two types of information are recorded during each ten-minute focal sample. The first piece of information is obtained every minute, on the minute recording who the focal animal's neighbors are, the activity at the moment, and who is where in the pool system. These "point" samples provide, among other information, an estimate of how much time each animal spends with others or alone (e.g. in a holding pool). The second type of information collected is a continuous recording of all social interactions of the focal animal. This data provides a detailed record of what kinds of interactions in which each animal is involved, with whom, and how often.

Social behaviors have been divided into the following categories: amicable, aggressive, submissive, sexual, posturing, swim types, synchronous behavior, use of holding areas, and the all-inclusive "other" (for the things that are not easily classified). These general categories each contain a sub-list of behaviors. Individual behaviors must always be looked at in context. For example, a mouth open is typically aggressive, but it could also be placed into a sexual category when an animal is swimming with its snout near a female's genitals.

There are so many behaviors in each category that codes are used to describe the common ones. Therefore, it is crucial to have descriptive, precise definitions of what each behavior is. Up to seven people have participated in our observation program and without precise definitions, many interpretations of the same interaction could occur.

To enable the observer to keep constant observation on the interactions (sometimes they happen very quickly), a tape recorder is used to recreate a play-by-play record. After the sample, the data is then transcribed onto data sheets. Observation data is collected and entered into the computer and monthly summaries are created to identify patterns of association. A more technical analysis of the data is done by Amy Samuels.

PURPOSE

The primary purpose for the observations is to help collect data for research into dolphin behavior. Currently, the observations and information collected are being revised to help better manage the dolphins. The observations could also be used to investigate specific trainer concerns by focusing on an aggressive animal or a female in estrus.

In addition to the morning observations, the dolphins are also observed for a different purpose. Five-minute respiration rates, three times a day, are taken on each animal. This data will be used to establish a normal baseline for each animal, in case of respiratory ailments. In the process of this observation, the animal's general appearance and any unusual behavior is noted.

Time is involved in learning the observation protocol and in doing the actual observations and data collation. Observational opportunities are well spent, giving a trainer a set, consistent time to watch an animal without interruption. Secondly, it provides an opportunity to see what the animals do outside of show and training situations where reinforcements are involved. Thirdly, collated data can show long-term changes in behavior as well. For example, when the facility had Mindy and Rio from the Minnesota Zoo last fall and winter on a breeding loan, observations on the Minnesota dolphins were done before, during and after introducing them to Brookfield's dolphins. It could clearly be seen how their behavior toward each other had changed after introduced to Brookfield' dolphins. Last but not least, the observations can be a useful baseline for other research. Seven Seas has worked with Peter Tyack of the Woods Hole Oceanographic Institute on his vocalight research for several years. Dr. Tyack is studying signature whistles of the bottlenose dolphin. The dolphins wore a vocalight that lit up when they whistled - each dolphin having their own color. While a hydrophone taped the whistles, trainers noted, via underwater viewing, which color light blinked, thus identifying the dolphin. Dr. Tyack would now like to collect data on dolphin whistles using data loggers in conjunction with our behavioral observations. Each animal would wear a mini-computer data logger. The loggers can then be synchronized and the whistles traced to each dolphin in relation to the others. To have behavioral data collected at the same time would provide a more complete picture, linking the whistles and the dolphins' interactions.

As stated earlier, the observation procedures have been continually evolving. As more is learned about the dolphins, new questions arise and the protocol has been modified many times. There is so much more to learn about the animals' social structure and behavior that this project will probably go on for a long time. Over time, many factors affect behavior: e.g., animal maturation, introduction of new animals, births and hormonal cycles, to name a few. The more information that can be gathered, the more pieces of the puzzle we will have and the more insightful will be the management of the animals.

SUMMARY

Trainers, researchers and experimenters all can learn a great deal from observing the animals. It takes time and commitment, but there are many benefits to be obtained. Our observations will continue to change as we learn more about our animals and find more efficient ways to study them. Meanwhile, at Seven Seas every morning we stay tuned as the soap opera unfolds.

1986 IMATA Conference, Vancouver, Canada. Once you have committed to watching and observing your animals regularly, it is only a small step to formalizing the process in the form of an ethogram. Scientists utilize ethograms to characterize behavior patterns in animals. The benefits of using ethograms as a tool for trainers and others in a zoological setting are discussed in the following paper.

The Ethogram: Present and Future Applications At The Living Seas Pavilion

Deidre A. Rector, Gretchen S. Jacobs, and Thomas G. Hopkins
The Living Seas Pavilion, Walt Disney World
EPCOT Center

ABSTRACT

The ethogram will be discussed as a tool for studying marine mammals in a variety of environments typical of zoos and oceanaria. Ethogram design and methodology will be outlined, as well as some problems encountered. Use of the ethogram at the Living Seas to establish behavioral baselines with *Tursiops truncatus* prior to the implementation of environmental changes in the Research Module is one application. Future plans for utilizing this procedure to study main task behavior of not only *Tursiops*, but also other marine creatures will be presented. Suggestions for the use of ethograms in other settings and species suited to this type of study will also be discussed.

THE ETHOGRAM...AT LIVING SEAS

In researching this paper, I came across a quote from Eiseley in The Unexpected Universe: "One does not meet oneself until one catches the reflection from an eye other than human" (Lehner, 1979). This does not refer to the stern gaze of your boss; but rather has a special meaning to us as trainers, who meet quite a different gaze every day. We turn our skilled observational eye to the behavior of our animals, applying what we learn from these observations to helping our charges learn their research and show behaviors. Carefully we watch not only what they learn, but how -- their motivational state, their response to reinforcers, and their psychosocial status as they learn. Our approach is derived primarily from the field of psychology: the study of behavior both elicited and emitted.

There is however another field of the study of behavior from which we could benefit as well, and that is the field of ethology. Ethology examines animal behavior through, as Konrad Lorenz defined, "the application of orthodox biological methods," focusing on the animal's behavior *per se* (Lehner, 1979). Ethologists study what an animal does --not only what, but also when, how, why, and where: Is the behavior a function of age, time of day, or season; physically, how is it accomplished, what are the evolutionary and phylogenetic components; why is it engaged and how does it help the animal to survive; and where in the environment and social system does it occur?

Some ethologists specialize in animal communication, or zoosemiotics; while others concentrate on social organization and social systems, or sociobiology. But whatever their specialty, their aim is to describe and quantify the behavior of animals (Hailman, 1985).

One tool for this purpose is the ethogram, a set of comprehensive descriptions of characteristic behavior patterns of a species. The animals' behavioral repertoire is all of the behavior of which it is capable; a behavioral catalog is a subset of repertoire, that is, all behavior that has been observed. An ethogram, then, is a catalog which approaches repertoire in its comprehensiveness (Lehner, 1979).

To begin building an ethogram, the units of

behavior (sometimes called beunits) must be selected, described, and finally defined - preferably, operationally defined. Some of you already may be familiar with this process, having provided data for Hull's study of *Tursiops* and *Orcinus* (Hult, date unknown). In his study, Hult has already identified 213 beunits for Tursiops through observations of 140 investigators with both captive and wild animals.

Those of you familiar with the ethogram have probably begun to acknowledge its utility to our profession. For the unfamiliar, think back for a moment to your last "shop talk" session -with a trainer from another oceanarium -- there you were, talking about this problem you had with Sparky's "high swans" and suddenly, your companion's eyes are glazed over with that "I-have-no-idea-what-you're-talking-about" look. You realized then that your "high swan" was something else to the other trainer, and set about describing the behavior, developing between you a common, operational definition of just what the animal was doing. And then you ordered another round of drinks.

Aside from providing a common behavioral terminology, and, commensurately, increasing communication; what other purposes might the ethogram serve? By operationally defining beunits, subjectivity is reduced. With increased objectivity, trainers' observations would become more amenable to empirical examination.

During the 1979 IMATA Conference, Bruce Stephens challenged us to consider *everything* an animal does, to go beyond the trained behaviors, and look at even the subtleties. He cautioned against being daunted by the enormity of this exercise, against being put off by the complexity and volume of an individual's behavior (Stephens, 1979). Certainly the animals with which we work have extensive behavioral repertoires, expanding daily through our efforts as trainers, as well as through their own considerable behavioral plasticity. What they do can tell us volumes about "who" they are --and this is the basic premise behind The Living Seas' Ethogram Program.

At The Living Seas there is no show pressure, nor are there behavioral deadlines. We are in the process of establishing a research facility, yet in no hurry to leap in until we have first established behavioral baselines on each animal. These baselines, obtained via the ethogram tool described later, are considered to be the foundation for any research which may be conducted at the Seas.

The concept of behavioral baselines is not a new one, and many of you may have experience with this tool from working in the mental health profession. Often, human subjects (or clients) are observed to determine the frequency, duration, and severity of a behavior problem before treatment programs or acquisition programs are designed and implemented.

So, in our first year of operation at the Seas, we have chosen to assess these baselines as a first step to research. In developing the original procedure for the ethogram, we enlisted the assistance of Jeffrey C. Norris, doctoral candidate in wildlife at the University of Florida (Norris, 1986).

The procedures were tailored to the environment in which we would begin ethogram data collection: the 200,000-gallon Marine Mammal Research Module. This area is one of two habitats at the Seas for our Atlantic bottlenose dolphins *(Tursiops truncatus);* the other being the 5.7 million gallon Coral Reef Environment. The Research Module has both underwater and topside viewing areas, accessible to guests from 9:00 AM to 8:00 PM. The underwater area has a concave observation "tube" which yields the optimum view of the front pool, as well as the gate leading to a backstage holding pool.

Originally, we planned to use a headset microphone and Sony cassette tape recorder to document behavior with voice-notes, using only one person to collect data. Practice sessions proved this apparatus to be not as effective as videotaping the sessions. Using videotape, we still had the advantage of voice-notes on the audio channel of the VCR, but also gained visual documentation of each session --useful in assessing inter-rater reliability (IRR), as well as a permanent record of behavior for training future data collectors.

Data collection sessions were run for five minutes per animal per hour from 9:00 AM until 5:00 PM. The original design called for sessions from 8:00 AM -8:00 PM, abut this proved impractical due to staffing limitations. The first focal animal for each session was determined by coin toss before the session. Over a week's period, data would be collected for the first twenty minutes of every hour, then replication sequences would be run for both the middle-and last-twenty minutes of each hour. Only the five most experienced staff members functioned as data collectors. Topside support staff merely clarified behaviors not visible to the data collector; for example, when the focal animal actually breathed vs. just bobbing to surface without a breath. This information was conveyed by stage microphone through the guest PA system to the data collector downstairs. Additional sound data was provided by having the hydrophones on and piped to the guest PA, so that vocalizations would be recorded concomitant with other behaviors.

Set-up, data collection, log-keeping, and equipment tear-down took about twenty minutes each session. A typical session is something like this. After flipping a coin to determine first focal animal, the data collector sets up the portable VHS video recorder and camera in the observation tube. Once the camera is rolling, voice-notes describing data, time, observer's name, focal animal, time elapsed since last training session, and any other pertinent factors are recorded; then the time clock in the camera is started and the data collection on the first animal begins. The voice-notes are recorded on the audio channel of the VCR via a shotgun microphone attached to the camera. Voice-notes are phrased in "subject -verb -object – modifier" format, such as: "TOBY SOCIAL-SWIM," "TOBY RUBS TYKE," "TOBY ERECTION." Behaviors are noted only when they began, so if only one behavior occurs continuously for the data session, it is mentioned only once. As the camera's clock rolls to the 5:00 minute mark, the data stops for the first focal animal, and the observer prepares to repeat the process for the next animal.

We encountered problems of all kinds during our first few sessions, anything from video gremlins to guest interference. Equipment failure sometimes caused a loss of a session (or sessions); those were made up the next day if possible. We found we were being too complex with our descriptions, necessitating reassessment of earlier tapes, and simplifying our voice-note procedures. Gathering data in full view and earshot of guests also presented challenges. Ultimately, we had to block off the observation area with clip-on ropes, after several data collectors were mauled by pushy parents and knee-high video saboteurs. Still, guests insisted upon asking questions of the data collector, oblivious to the fact that this person was concentrating very hard on the task --this was resolved in a very un-Disneylike manner: we ignored them until after the session. Anatomical terminology and sexual beunits presented yet another problem to our Disney data collectors, which we solved by voice-noting initials of the anatomy or behavior,

NOT by cutesy code words like "pink-coral." ("TOBY ERECTION" became "TOBY E").

Just as guests interfered on one side of the pool, our own staff presented a problem on the other, backstage side. Often during early ethogram sessions, staff from other departments were found interacting with the focal animal backstage. Signs and frequent temper tantrums proved to deter this source of interference.

As for the analysis of the data, it must be entered into our Sperry PC as a first step. 'Me programs are being refined at present so that this data can be entered as quickly as possible, analyzed by a variety of statistical programs, and then graphed. Earlier programs proved cumbersome in the number of steps required to input data.

Earlier I mentioned the nuisance factor of guests, but let's face it, they pay our salaries in the park business. We have found many guests to be curious about "doing research," and, once exposed to some of the problems involved, more understanding of the current state of information on marine mammals. Guests can become a part of the process, calling out behaviors right along with the topside trainer. While their data has no meaning to us, their experience of role-playing data collector certainly is effective audience involvement. Guests also seem to get excited about interacting with the staff, and this opens up some dialogs which are quite enjoyable for both trainer and guest.

The ethogram also has proved useful to our Visiting Student Scientists who are interning with The Living Seas to get hands-on cetacean research experience. Eventually they will run a very simple auditory threshold study, but prior to this they are collecting ethogram data. Part of their study will examine whether the ethograms from before the experiment differ significantly from tile ethograms after.

Ethograms can provide clues to rates, frequencies, and duration of behaviors. Ethograms make accessible to us information on behavioral sequences of animals, how they use their time (time budgets), and their social/environmental standing as they behave. In describing the animal, ethograms go beyond stimulus-response, putting its behavior into the social, psychological and environmental contexts. As the data continues to be collected over time, a catalog of behavior develops which more closely describes "repertoire."

At the Seas, these catalogs will provide a continuum of information about the behavior of normal, healthy individuals, and how this changes as the subject ages, sexually matures, is introduced to different societal configurations, meets new animals, bears young, and loses a companion. Questions amenable to study include; will ethograms change as the Marine Mammal Research Module changes with the addition of gravel bottom, more species of fish, and redirected lighting? Will time budgets be affected by the inception of the Responsive Environment Computer System, whereby dolphins manipulate environmental factors via computer mediated stimuli? Can the ethogram help us recognize sickness earlier in its onset, as suggested by observational data from a captive killer whale indicating that the animal's peak respiration rate declined systematically as sickness came on (Ray, 1980)?

Comparisons between beunits exhibited in our two very different habitats could be made also, once a Coral Reef Environment ethogram procedure is created. Using four SCUBA divers as data collectors, and dividing the larger habitat into quadrants, the ethogram in 5.7 million gallons of water becomes manageable. A fifth, topside observer could document holding pool behavior. Observers would rotate positions each session, and every tenth session would test IRR positioning by two observers together in two quadrants and comparing their results. Data collection could be either "occur/not occur" format or general behavior tallies on underwater slates, for predetermined beunits. Sessions would be five-minute segments timed by watches with elapsed time beepers ("synchronize your Casios!"). Replications for each subsequent third of an hour would resemble the procedure used for the Marine Mammal Research Module.

A design like the one described above would provide the opportunity to observe oral manipulation of non-food items, for example. Such oral manipulation may be a part of a normal, healthy dolphin's need to explore its environment however, this behavior could lead to ingestion of the non-food object. While this behavior seems to occur in both wild and captive animals, and can be hazardous to the animals' health, the antecedents for the beunit of object-ingestion are not clearly understood. Is the actual ingestion a function of sickness or competition, or a "neurosis" manifested in an unstimulating environment, or a combination of all of these things? Observations of normal, healthy dolphins in a controlled, yet complex environment might at least provide us with an idea of how frequently the animals "naturally" engage in the oral manipulation beunit, and if it seems to be related to the dolphins' social status.

Another area for future study via the ethogram at the Seas could be multi-species interaction; that is, social relationships between dolphins and sharks, or divers, or sea lions, etc. The future also holds the possibility of applying this technique-to cataloging sharks' and other large fishes' adaptation and maintenance behaviors.

In closing, I hope that by sharing our experiences (and problems), and future plans at the Seas, I have sparked some interest in the ethogram as a tool. It is not a complicated procedure, nor an extremely time-consuming method. 'Me procedures are adaptable to fit a variety of environments: from training tanks, to research areas, to feeder pools. Ethograms need not require a big-bucks budget, nor an investment in complicated equipment: data collection can be done simply on a divers' slate or notepad. Data analysis can be simplified by computer software, but is manageable without such equipment as well.

On an institutional level, this tool can be useful to us in defining what a normal, healthy dolphin is, at each of our different facilities. With this tool, we can assess the effect of social and environmental changes, and perhaps anticipate the onset of sickness a little better than we can now with our subjective data.

On a professional level, the ethogram tool could benefit us, too. If we adopted this procedure as widely as the VRRV system, envision the database we could create of empirically derived information about a particular species! The increased number of subjects and beunits documented would not only expand the generalization of our species' information, but would also bring us closer to truly describing the repertoire of the subjects and their society. Gathering data on all species of marine mammals with whom we have contact would enable us to develop delphinid behavioral catalogs, cetacean catalogs, and to compare/contrast different species. By monitoring the naturally occurring vocalizations as part of the process, we may prepare the way for future zoosemiotic studies of cetacean communication. By combining our efforts, working as an international team of behaviorists, we could develop a body of information which goes far beyond "best guess" and approaches "repertoire" for each species in our care.

ACKNOWLEDGEMENTS

I would like to thank John Gale of Active Environments for his unceasing technical and emotional support, as well as Jeffrey Norris, Gretchen Jacobs, Thomas Hopkins, and Drs. Pete Schroeder, Jay Sweeney, Rae Stone, Bob Stevens, Dan Odell, and Paul Cardeilhac for their input.

REFERENCES

Cardeilhac, Paul T., DVM, University of Florida, personal correspondence.

Hailman, Jack P. *Ethology, Zoosemiotic and Sociobiology.* Amer, Zool., 25, 1985, pp 695-705.

Hult, Robert W. *Tursiops and Orcinus Behavioral Repertoire Comparisons.* Transcript of paper submitted for publication, Cetology, date unknown.

Hult, Robert W., Dupey, Steve E., and Badley, Ron W. *Mortalities Associated With Pre Ingestion by Small Cetaceans.* Cetology, 38, 1980, pp. 1-3.

Lehner, Philip N. Handbook Of Ethological Methods. Garland STPM Press, New York NY, 1979.

Martinez, David R. and Klinghammer, Erich. *Partial Ethogram. of the Killer Whale (Orcinus Orca L.)* Carnivore, Part 3, 1978, pp. 13-27.

Norris, Jeffrey. *Suggested Procedures for Preliminary Dolphin Behavioral Research a The Living Seas Pavilion.* Personal correspondence to The Living Seas' Technical Library, 1986.

Odell, Daniel K., University of Miami (FL), personal correspondence.

Ray, Roger D., Carlson, Mark A., Carlson, Milo L., and Carlson, Timothy. *Social Organization and Synchrony in a Pair of Killer Whales.* Annual Proceedings of IMATA Conference, 1980, pp. 32-54.

Schroeder, Pete, DVM, NOSC (Hawaii), personal correspondence.

Stephens, Bruce. *Marine Mammals & Emotion: Human Involvement in Conditioning.* Annual Proceedings. Of Conference 1979, pp. 14.

Stevens, Robert, DVM, personal correspondence.

Stone, L. Rae, DVM, personal correspondence.

Sweeney, Jay, VMD. personal correspondence.

Husbandry Training 6

A Training Program's First Steps

So far, we have looked at many techniques for training animals. As we start applying these techniques it is very important that each animal develop a solid training foundation. Before husbandry behaviors can take place, basic cooperative behaviors must have been taught. So before defining husbandry, let's examine cooperative behaviors first. The early steps, as described previously, should occur in roughly this order:
- Know the species
- Know the individual
- Develop trust and establish mode of contact
- Determine reinforcers
- Condition the bridging stimulus
- Establish cooperative basics
- Begin husbandry training

Cooperative Behavior

One of the three primary reasons for training is cooperative behavior. Husbandry behaviors are what most people consider cooperative behavior. However, husbandry is just one part of the bigger concept of cooperative behavior (albeit one of the most important parts). Many of the basic behaviors that we often take for granted (a good attentive animal, for example) are needed to maintain control during training. The importance of these basic behaviors is often forgotten, until an animal begins performing poorly. Without these early building blocks, very little training can progress. Before jumping into a discussion of what is traditionally meant by husbandry, let's talk about other cooperative behaviors that must also be established.

Stationing

It is very important that an animal know where you expect it to be during a session. A child in school has a seat assignment, a bird will often have a perch, and film animals will usually have a specific spot (a swatch of carpet or some other marker) indicating where the animal should stand. During the early stages of training it is important to condition the animal to pay attention to you and to know where to be. We teach dolphins to "station" vertically in front of us so that they can easily see us and we can easily provide reinforcement. Stationing should be strictly maintained and used as the basis for all other behaviors. With few exceptions, all behaviors start and finish at station. A cue is not presented unless an animal is properly at station. Reinforcement is not offered unless the animal is at station. Through selective reinforcement, an animal can learn good stationing fairly quickly. A more detailed look at stationing alternatives can be found in chapter 7, "Social Animals."

Targeting

Although the concept of targeting was discussed in the Introduction and in chapter 4, "Basic Operant Conditioning," we said little about how to apply the concept. To start, there are a number of basic targeting maneuvers that will help in many training situations. By simply touching a buoy, or any object, to the animal's head or rostrum, then bridging and reinforcing, the animal will quickly be conditioned to initiate the touching (targeting) on its own. From there it is a matter of successive approximations to get the animal to understand the basics that follow. A truly target-trained animal should understand all these variations:

Simple targeting – You should be able to present the target anywhere in the vicinity of the animal's head, and it should move to touch the target. As the animal becomes more comfortable moving in all directions you can increase the distance from the animal's head.

Complex targeting – Teaching an animal to touch a target relatively high over it's head can be more difficult than it first appears, because the animal must learn to exert the extra energy to jump or lift its head up to touch the target. Once the animal has mastered this feat, you might try putting the target under or below it. Then place it to the far right, the far left, behind the animal; and continue to get more creative. The animal should readily touch the target wherever it is presented.

Follow target – The next step is to get the animal to follow the target wherever you take it. As the animal is about to touch the target, move it just out of reach. This encourages the animal to follow it a short distance. Eventually you can teach an animal to follow for very long distances just about anywhere you choose to go.

Extended target – Another basic targeting concept is to teach the animal to keep touching a target until it hears the bridge. Sometimes it is useful to have the animal remain on a target for minutes on end. Lengthy targeting duration must, of course, be approximated slowly.

A Variety of targets – The animal should also understand that it can target on various types of objects: your hand, the end of a stick, a buoy, or any other object. Some trainers, have creatively used items as diverse as a laser pointer for a target; by aiming the pointer at different areas of an animal's habitat, the trainer can ask an animal to move to new locations, while the trainer can remain outside the habitat. Trainers should be creative and adapt targets for the situation and species of animal being trained.

Whole body – In time, you will want to condition the animal to target any part of its body to a variety of targets. This will facilitate many husbandry procedures.

Multiple targets – As you begin to train more complex behaviors, you will need the animal to understand the idea of maintaining contact with one target while trying to touch another one with a different part of its body. The first time a second target is introduced, the animal may get confused and abandon the first target to touch the second. Carefully planned approximations will eliminate that problem.

A to B

Another basic concept that starts with targeting is teaching an animal to move from point A to point B on cue. This is a helpful behavior that will serve multiple purposes and is useful when training almost any animal. This process is described in the article referenced under desensitization below (Ramirez, 1991).

Gating

The process of gating (getting an animal to move through a gate, a door, or any other opening) can be taught using the A to B behavior. Management of a large animal collection requires the ability to separate and move animals easily. So gating is a most important cooperative behavior. But it's not always a simple behavior to train – it takes time. Too often, trainers take gating for granted. This usually occurs when young trainers join a training staff where all the animals are already gate-trained. Once the behavior is well established and maintained it seems very simple. To emphasize the importance of this behavior, four articles about gate training (and animal separation) can be found in chapter 7, "Social Animals."

Taction

An animal that has become accustomed to being touched will always be easier to manage. Basic tactile interactions can often start with the targeting process. Even aggressive or unpredictable animals can be desensitized to human touch by having the trainer work through a fence or other form of protection. The importance of an animal's acceptance of being touched, rubbed, massaged, and handled should be obvious, but it should never be taken for granted. That some animals seem to solicit petting and other types of tactile interaction doesn't mean they will automatically accept tactile interactions needed for some medical procedures. It is a process that requires constant attention and desensitization.

Desensitization

Training through Desensitization

Desensitization is the process of getting an animal used to a new stimulus through gradual exposure to it. The stimulus may be people, other animals, noises, lighting, or anything the animal may perceive as new or frightening. Anytime something new is added to the animal's environment, it is wise to expose the animal to it gradually, if possible. A slow, calm introduction to new things will maintain the animal's trust and facilitate better care. Ultimately, desensitization is the key to good tactile interactions, which are critical for good husbandry. First, look at the application of desensitization techniques with a variety of animals in some unique situations at the Shedd Aquarium, in *Using Desensitization Techniques to Prepare Animals for Transport* (Ramirez, 1991), on page 145.

Habituation & Counter-Conditioning

Throughout this manual we use the term desensitization. However, as you read more about training and how animals learn you will encounter the terms habituation and counter-conditioning. Often, these terms are used interchangeably. By definition, habituation and counter-conditioning are distinct types of desensitization. Hurley and Holmes (1998) describe the differences and explore the topic in depth in *A Review of the Psychological Principles and Training Techniques Associated with Desensitization*, on page 150. In essence, habituation is passive desensitization, during which an animal gets used to new stimuli over time without its being followed by reinforcement from a trainer. On the other hand, counter-conditioning is active desensitization, meaning that the animal gets used to a new stimulus when it is paired with or followed by reinforcement.

Generalization vs. Discrimination

For a desensitization program to be effective, an animal must learn to generalize certain stimuli and discriminate between others. When training husbandry behaviors, for example, it is helpful for animals *not* to discriminate between the veterinarian and the staff used in practice – we want the animal to generalize the presence of extra people as being non-threatening. Meanwhile, we *do* want the animal to discriminate one S^D from another – we do not want the animal to generalize that every hand signal means the same thing. While this may seem obvious, there's more to be said about the distinction between the two concepts in Gary Wilkes' *Generalization and Discrimination: Fraternal Twins*, on page 157.

What is Husbandry Training?

The dictionary defines husbandry as:
- The cultivation of crops and the breeding and raising of livestock.
- The application of scientific principles to animal breeding.
- The careful management of resources.

In a zoological setting, husbandry is the careful management (using the best scientific principles and knowledge) of our animals.

Basic Husbandry Principles
The basic principles of good animal husbandry go far beyond the training program. They include:
- A healthy environment
- Proper nutrition
- Proper social structure
- Sound behavioral management
- Professional veterinary care
- Systematic record keeping

Advantages to Training
All of those principles can be met more easily through a training program. By teaching an animal to cooperate in its own health care, life becomes less stressful for the animal and the trainer. It is this kind of cooperative behavior that we call husbandry training. Husbandry training facilitates good health care by allowing the veterinarian better access to the animal. Animals can be taught to position themselves properly for an exam, including moving from one enclosure to another. Innovative husbandry training is taking place every day, many examples are included in the articles at the end of this chapter.

The Veterinarian's Role
Since veterinarians must be comfortable with every voluntary medi-

cal procedure, they should be included in the planning of all husbandry training. What equipment will they use? How hard or soft is their touch? Will they want to do anything more than you had planned with the behavior once it is trained? How long does the vet need to perform the procedure or test? Will any additional people be needed during the procedure? Does the equipment used make noise? These questions and many more should be discussed with the veterinarian. The vet should understand the care that goes into training a medical behavior; each trainer should understand the needs and complexities of the veterinarian's job. Preparing for every contingency is an important part of husbandry training. Developing a good relationship with your veterinarian is vital to success.

Desensitize, Desensitize, Desensitize

It would be difficult to overemphasize how much desensitization training must take place to prepare an animal for voluntary medical behaviors. Continue to vary the method and manner of practicing the behavior to expose the animal to every contingency. If the vet cannot be a part of the training, use individuals that the animal does not see daily to play the role of the doctor. The more accurately every step of the process is practiced, the more likely you will be to succeed. Desensitization is a process that will continue throughout the life of the animal.

Precise Bridging

Finally, as with all training, precise bridging can make or break husbandry training. It is imperative that an animal be calm and relaxed during any medical procedure. Therefore, the trainer must take great care to bridge and reinforce calm behavior only. If the animal is exhibiting the proper body position; but is tense or nervous when we bridge, we may be reinforcing for behavior that will get worse over time. Grey Stafford discusses this important aspect of husbandry in his 1996 article *Husbandry Training*, on page 159.

General Body Exams

Tactile Work

Again and again throughout this section on husbandry the same words will pop up: "relaxed," "calm," "desensitize," and "tactile." If an animal does not allow you to touch it, few husbandry behaviors are possible. Good tactile manipulation allows you to look at an animal's skin, fur, or feathers. It allows you to feel for muscle tone, get a heart rate, and take important measurements. For an overview of marine mammal husbandry at Sea World, read *Sea World's Husbandry Training Program: Update* (Lacinak, 1996), on page 160.

The Layout

Most husbandry behaviors require that the animal be in a specific position where it can remain calm for an extended period. The basic position for many cetacean husbandry behaviors is called the layout. Through targeting, the dolphin or whale can be taught to lie motionless at the surface of the water in a horizontal position directly in front of you. At the slightest touch or push, you should be able to roll or otherwise maneuver the animal into any position. First, the animal should be taught to respond to the layout cue. Once in the layout position the animal should wait for further instruction, usually tactile cues that let it know what you want next. The animal should remain calm throughout the process. Some of the husbandry behaviors that rely on the layout include:

- Blood sampling
- Urine sampling
- Semen collection
- Fecal sampling
- Body measurements
- Ultrasound exams
- Heart rate monitoring
- Milk collection (breast pump)
- Eye & ear exams
- Body exam (topical treatments)

Blood Sampling

The process of taking blood begins with venipuncture – puncture of a vein. It is imperative to work closely with the veterinarian or health technician who will be drawing the blood. Because animals cannot tell us where they feel pain or whatever bothers them, we must rely very heavily on blood samples to determine if they are ill. That makes blood sampling the single most important medical behavior we can train.

Where to Draw

Knowing where to take the sample is the first step to desensitization. In some cases there are multiple locations where blood can be drawn. However, the restrictions of a voluntary sample will often dictate the best location. Some examples:

- PINNIPEDS – Rear flippers or lower back
- PARROTS – Toe nails
- CETACEANS – Tail
- ELEPHANTS – Ear

Take Your Time
I am a firm believer in taking successive approximations slowly with any behavior. A slow desensitization process is critical in training husbandry behaviors because they have the potential to cause the animal discomfort. Rushing to get your first voluntary blood sample may make it your last sample as well. Taking blood too often can have the same effect; it may break down the animal's trust in the trainer. I have always believed that for a potentially uncomfortable husbandry behavior (like blood sampling) to be successful, it must be practiced at least a hundred times for every real sample taken!

The One Stick Rule
Always remember, if you insert the needle and the animal remains calm, the behavior has been done correctly. The vet may have missed the vein and got no blood, but if the animal remained calm, bridge and reinforce. At Shedd Aquarium we follow a policy of not trying again the same day (or for several days). We refer to that as the "one stick rule." Certainly there are exceptions to the rule, but seldom. If you have successfully trained this behavior, why push a good thing by asking for it too often? Getting that one extra sample today may not be worth regressing several months if the animal becomes frustrated. When special circumstances require more frequent sampling, the animals can be conditioned to accept that, too, but it's more difficult. The trainer must approximate the desired frequency of collection, training the animal step-by-step to accept it. Animals involved in research projects or animals in a breeding program may require more frequent monitoring than normal. As long as you take the time for appropriate approximations, you should be able to take blood as often as necessary.

Helpful Hints
Every trainer who has successfully trained an animal for blood sampling has his or her own special secret to success. Mine is the one stick rule. Fortunately, when trainers share their knowledge and experience they can be combined to form new ideas and methods. Five trainers share their own secrets in the article, *How to Maintain Voluntary Blood Sampling with Dolphins* (T. Forum, 1992), on page 169.

Working Around the Mouth & Head

The most important aspect of deciding whether to work around the head or mouth of an animal is trainer safety. If you feel you can safely gain access to the eyes, mouth, ears, or other parts of the head, many beneficial husbandry behaviors can be trained. However, it is never worth the risk of getting bitten by an unpredictable animal. Knowing your animal is the key to determining whether to proceed. Many trainers will rely on a protected contact system for working in these highly sensitive areas. A full description of protected contact training of elephants can be found in several articles at the end of chapter 12, "Complex Training and Modern Applications." Sea otters are a good example of an unpredictable and potentially dangerous animal when working near the mouth. At Shedd Aquarium we have successfully worked unprotected around the heads of our otters. But it took us quite some time to get to that point, as described in *Initiation of a Sea Otter Training Program* (Ramirez, 1992), on page 172.

Removal from their Environment

Some husbandry procedures may require that an animal be removed from its normal enclosure or home. There usually are many options available. Creative trainers can often find solutions to seemingly impossible situations.

Stretcher/Cage/Kennel Training

With the proper equipment, animals can be trained to swim into a stretcher or walk into a squeeze cage voluntarily. The behavior does not have to be permanently associated with a medical or unpleasant procedure. If the behavior is used regularly as a part of the animal's daily activity, the behavior can be reliably maintained. A description of stretcher training for cetaceans, written in 1987 by Debra Skaar, can be found in *Stretcher Training for Handling Whales and Dolphins*, on page 176.

Other Removal Methods

Sometimes animals can be removed from their environment without the use of a cage, kennel, or stretcher. Cetaceans can be taught to slide onto a platform or a boat. Terrestrial animals can be taught to follow a target or walk on a leash to new locations. This type of training takes time and careful attention to desensitization steps. A discussion of teaching a sea lion to leave its home environment (to work in public) can be found in *Teaching Pinnipeds to Work in Public Areas* (T. Forum, 1989), in chapter 11, "Problem Solving." Although the article does not discuss the topic with medical behaviors in mind, the techniques described are appropriate whenever you wish to walk an animal into a new environment.

Non-Voluntary Removal

When it is necessary to remove an animal that hasn't been trained to cooperate, there can be a fear on the part of the trainers that the animal will make an unpleasant association between the staff and the procedure. That is certainly possible, but many steps can be taken to decrease the chances of that occurring.

Don't trick an animal – When an animal is tricked, fooled, or baited into cooperation, trust is broken – the animal will have been "punished" for trusting you. Avoid this at all costs, or recognize the consequences if you feel compelled to use that method. A more detailed discussion of the uses and pitfalls of punishment can be found in chapter 9, "Advanced Techniques and Concepts."

Avoid direct associations – Refrain from pairing a negative experience directly with a well-trained behavior, it may extinguish the well-trained behavior. Example: A dolphin has been trained to do a voluntary slide-out for simple visual and tactile exams. The animal has never been out of the water for more than a few minutes and has always been well reinforced for the behavior. Should you suddenly choose to use the slide-out behavior to restrain the animal for a lengthy medical exam, chances are it won't slide-out again for weeks, months, or even years. However, a gradual process of desensitization to restraint during slide-outs could eventually condition the animal to accept exams in this manner. In *Passive Restraint Training in Tursiops truncatus* (page 178), Rita Stacey and her colleagues describe an excellent example of using reinforcement to maintain voluntary restraint under difficult circumstances.

Desensitize the Precursors to Removal – Even if you cannot train an animal to leave its home voluntarily, you can desensitize it to many of the experiences that precede the process. If moving into a restraint box, dropping the pool level, or the presence of a dart gun causes an animal to become uncomfortable, expose the animal to these things daily (or as frequently as possible) without the negative consequences that normally follow. Chip Harshaw describes this in *Extended Separation and Targeting of North American River Otters (Lontra canadensis) for Sedation Purposes*, on page 181.

Use Your Knowledge of Basic Operant Techniques – It really is as simple as that. You have many techniques at your disposal to shape a desired behavior and avoid negative associations. Even if you are not engaged in formal training, you should keep your training tools handy. They are valuable allies in caring for your animals and shaping cooperative behavior.

Summary
Other Husbandry Behaviors

There are many types of husbandry behaviors that can be trained, you are limited only by your own creativity. Husbandry behaviors lead to better animal management and stress-free interactions for both animal and staff. The important steps are:
- Plan carefully
- Progress slowly
- Desensitize all stimuli
- Bridge precisely
- Maintain trust
- Apply proven operant techniques

At the end of this chapter, in addition to the articles already referenced, are a variety of other excellent articles about husbandry training. Some of the husbandry topics covered in these articles include:
- Cat husbandry (Krueger, 1996), page 164.
- Cystoscopy (deSousa, 1998), page 185.
- Dental work (Lacinak, 1996), page 160.
- Dog husbandry (Teuscher, 1996), page 163.
- Forced exhale (Krames, 1984), page 189.
- Gastric tube/Endoscopy (Ramirez, 1996), page 192.
- Girth measurements (Ramirez, 1996), page 192.
- Horse husbandry (Teuscher, 1996), page 163.
- Mammary presentation/Milk collection (Kamolnick, 1994), page 198; (Krames, 1986), page 189; (Ramirez, 1996), page 192.
- Nail clipping (T. Forum, 1997), page 205.
- Pinniped husbandry (T. Forum, 1993), page 201; (T.Forum, 1997), page 205.
- Semen collection (Keller, 1986), page 203.
- Stranded animal husbandry (Schofield, 1995), page 207.
- Urine Sampling (Krames, 1986), page 189; (Ramirez, 1996), page 192; (T. Forum, 1990), page 197.
- Ultrasound exams (T.Forum, 1993), page 201; (Ramirez, 1996), page 192.

1991 IMATA Conference, Vallejo, California, USA. The following paper was awarded the outstanding husbandry/research award for 1991. The unusual circumstances surrounding the construction of the John G. Shedd Aquarium's oceanarium presented unique opportunities to desensitize various animals to the rigors of transport. These were the formative years of Shedd Aquarium's training program.

Using Desensitization Techniques to Prepare Animals for Transport

Ken Ramirez, Cynthia Alia, Connie Arthur, Pete Davey, Greg Dye, Faith Dunham, Chip Harshaw, Pam Herman, Meg Hudson, Donnarose Janosek-Christakis, Manny Onate, Jim Robinett, Suzie Rogers, Mark Ryan, & Lisa Takaki
John G. Shedd Aquarium

ABSTRACT

On April 27, 1991 the new oceanarium at the John G. Shedd Aquarium opened to the public. The aquarium's marine mammal collection was housed all over the United States during the construction of the new pavilion. In an effort to reduce the potential acclimation problems, a training program was introduced to prepare each of the animals for the transport to the oceanarium. Three different desensitization techniques were used to prepare three separate animal groups for the move. This paper will focus on the success of these techniques in transporting two beluga whales (*Delphinapterus leucas*) five Alaskan sea otters (*Endhyra lutris*), and four Pacific white-sided dolphins (*Lagenorhynchus obliquidens*).

INTRODUCTION

On April 27, 1991, the John G. Shedd Aquarium opened its new oceanarium to the public. This was the culmination of many years of planning and hard work. The oceanarium houses a variety of animals including harbor seals, Pacific white-sided dolphins, a variety of penguins, Alaskan sea otters, and beluga whales. Many of these animals were acquired prior to the completion of the new facility. Each of the animal groups were housed at various locations around the country, where their initial acclimation and training was begun.

In each case our training program focused on two main goals, the start of basic husbandry training as well as preparation for the move to Chicago. There were a number of unique factors about our facility and our animals that made it imperative that extra care be taken to insure a smooth and quick transition from their temporary home to their new one that was still under construction. It seemed only natural that we felt there was no more important goal than to teach the animals about the transport and their new facility. Interestingly, factors ranging from species differences to habitat size and configuration presented us with individual concerns that required special training considerations.

This paper will focus on three of our animal groups. We will present the methods we used to prepare our otters, whales, and dolphins for the move to the John G. Shedd Aquarium. Since each animal group posed some different challenges, we will discuss the preparation, implementation, and results of each desensitization plan.

OTTERS

The first group of animals we will discuss are our Alaskan sea otters. Originally, we had not planned to acquire our otters until construction of our new facility was complete. However, in the Spring of 1989 the *Exxon Valdez* struck Bligh Reef in Prince William Sound and rendered many otters homeless. The U.S. Fish and Wildlife Service requested that a number of zoos and aquariums give the unreleasable otters a home. The Shedd Aquarium was one of those facilities. However, since our new oceanarium was over a year-and-a-half away for completion, a temporary facility was set up in one of the current Aquarium galleries. While far from being a perfect sea otter home, it proved quite comfortable for our four new residents. In fact, one year later, a fifth orphaned otter was added to the group.

Since the otters were with us well ahead of schedule, we had to begin planning for their long-term care sooner than we had expected. Most of us had come from a background in dealing with animals that were regularly trained for basic cooperative behaviors. We saw no reason to treat our otters any differently. For those of you who have never worked with sea otters, we were naively going where few trainers had gone before! Even had we realized the seemingly impossible road that lay ahead, I am certain we would have proceeded with just as much enthusiasm (albeit skeptical enthusiasm).

It is probably important to point out that all five of our otters were orphaned, and thus hand raised. This is a critical point in understanding the amount of tactile interaction we were able to use with these otters. It should also be pointed out that had these pups not been hand-raised we would have had to approach their training in a much different manner. From the outset, we decided that we would maintain as much of a hands-on approach as possible. We wanted to begin basic husbandry training, and felt that a very tactile receptive animal would certainly facilitate that training. Throughout the early stages of working with each sea otter, we handled them daily. We encouraged hand feeding and scheduled regular play sessions in their exhibit. These included providing them snow to play in, giving them ice cubes, introducing toys, or simply sitting with them in the exhibit. In time, we began to include more formalized sessions.

Formal sessions consisted of bringing the animals into a work or training area. In our case, we chose a table about waist high that allowed us easy access to the animals. We could carry out one animal at a time, work them in pairs, or bring out the whole group. Our primary purpose for these sessions was to gain some control over the otters' work environment and allow us to explore the possibilities of formal training. Since these animals were rescued from the oil spill, there were a number of medical concerns that we had to face. We felt it important to pursue a few basis husbandry procedures, these included: tubing for medication and vitamin supplementation, thermometer insertion for temperature taking, general body exams, positioning for voluntary blood sampling, and handling for taking of regular weights.

Although husbandry was the focus of most of our training, we also started training a number of other behaviors. We began conditioning a bridging stimulus (a dog whistle for two of them and a verbal bridge for the others), started basic targeting and following, we introduced a kennel, reinforced name recognition, and taught them the concept of gating. We found the sea otters to be very curious and inquisitive animals (and that's an understatement)! In many ways, we found them to be so enthusiastic about sessions that they were at times unpredictable. When working with otters there is certainly never a dull moment.

As the oceanarium construction drew closer to completion, we began considering the different methods we might use to move the animals. Obviously, moving a small animal like a sea otter is not difficult. But with the positive rapport that we had built with these otters, we had the potential of making the transition seem almost effortless to these animals. Since the otters seemed to enjoy tactile interactions, and were used to being handled, we decided to carry the otters by hand to their new exhibit. We approximated this process for many months before ever making the real move. Each session consisted of progressively longer walks. We took them down new corridors and hallways, desensitizing them to every possible type of doorway and lighting. Another factor we had to deal with was their size. A young 10-pound otter can be quite a handful, but as the otter grows and becomes a juvenile of 50-plus pounds, carrying him can be nearly impossible. Their spine is so flexible you would swear they were invertebrates; infact, we affectionately referred to them as slinky with fur. To help in making the move positive for both trainer and animal we established rest stations along the route to their new home. This gave our backs a rest while allowing us to provide the animals with a variety of reinforcers, including ice, krill, towels, shellfish, or toys.

On the day of the move to the oceanarium, we carried all five animals in an otter parade to their new habitat. They made the transition well, and their natural curiosity had them exploring the new facility for hours. They ate well immediately and we were pleased with the smooth transition. Little did we know that we were going to make that move several more times. Because of their curiosity, the otters managed to dismantle many parts of their new home. Electric drills and power tools are no match for the paws of an otter, they found weak spots in the exhibit quickly and we were soon carrying them back to their temporary home while their new habitat was being repaired. This process was repeated several times before they finally took up permanent residence in the oceanarium (we hope).

There is no doubt that we could have easily put each otter in a kennel to carry them back and forth each time we needed to move. But we felt that because these animals had been desensitized to being handled and were trained for the move, it made each move a fun, stress-free experience.

CETACEANS

The other two groups of animals that we decided to desensitize for the move were our two beluga whales and four Pacific white-sided dolphins. These animals were acquired well before construction was complete to give us time to prepare them for life in the new oceanarium. We felt that bringing naïve animals, a new staff, and a new facility together all at once was a recipe for disaster. By bringing the animals and staff together gradually before moving into the building, it gave everyone ample time to learn about the facility, the animals, and each other. In the long run, we feel that this time was a real asset in making the transport and acclimation so easy for each of our cetaceans.

The beluga whales were housed at the Point Defiance Zoo and Aquarium in Tacoma, Washington, while the dolphins were housed at the University of California at Santa Cruz' Long Marine Lab. Training for each animal group was carefully coordinated to insure consistency in training style and philosophy at each facility. Our first goal was to desensitize each of the animals to things they might face once at the Shedd Aquarium. We set basis husbandry behaviors as a top priority. We concentrated on fluke presentations for taking blood, stomach and fecal tube insertion, general body exams, and ultra-sound positioning.

Another major concern was gating. The Shedd Aquarium has four interconnected cetacean habitats, the largest one containing two million gallons of water. Since there would be a need to rotate animals from habitat to habitat, it would be imperative that every animal be a consistent gater. Due to the naturalistic design of our facility, the medical pool is hidden beneath a forest-covered mountain. Thus, even more critical, was the need for each animal to be comfortable gating through a tunnel. The medical pool has three large gates leading to the other three habitats. But to get through the gates the animals would be required to swim through a channel that is covered by a low hanging bridge, forming a virtual tunnel.

Since gating was obviously a high priority, we chose to approach training it in three basic steps. First we would teach all of the animals a basic "A to B" cue. We would tap the animal's melon or rostrum and point to a person or target several feet away. We increased the distance and direction of this "A to B" behavior until each animal was consistently moving from point A to point B without hesitation.

Step two was to approximate the B location into other pools. We placed particular emphasis on the importance of taking our time. We always made the gating sessions just a small part of an entire session. During gate training we did not close the gate until we were certain the animals had become very comfortable with the process. An even then we at first only closed the gate for very brief periods.

Finally, once we felt that gating was consistent, we placed plywood over the existing channels. The first time we tried covering the entire channel, the animals were hesitant to pass underneath. So we regressed and simply covered small sections at a time. Within a month the animals were negotiating the tunnel without a problem, and since we made the move to Chicago both the belugas and the dolphins are gating regularly.

Another factor that was important in preparing the animals for easy acclimation to the environment at Shedd was the exposure to other animals and species. At both west coast facilities our animals shared the pool complex with other animals. We used that to our advantage in rotating animals from pool to pool. And in the case of the belugas we even mixed the Point Defiance adult belugas and harbor porpoise with our whales. Aside from introducing our animals to new species, these situations also added the concept of other animals on opposite sides of a gate, which we think helped in their social adjustment once at the aquarium.

One other preparation that we considered critical was desensitizing the animals to having the trainers' feet and legs in the water. Most of our working spaces at the aquarium are under ten inches of water, so we gradually acclimated our cetaceans to having our feet in the water throughout a session. In Santa Cruz we literally approximated our work platform from above the pool level, down to pool level, then slightly below pool level. This process was essential in desensitizing the animals to what became a normal working condition.

BELUGAS

But there were other transport issues that concerned us, too. The marine mammal community has successfully transported cetaceans for over 25 years. Modern techniques using wet transports and high speed jets have made transport a more comfortable experience for the animals. Today it is usually the trainers and veterinarians that experience the stress of transport. Most of the literature and personal communications with those who have worked with beluga whales indicate that belugas transport comfortably; they ride well and seem to make a move without incident.

However, several reports have indicated a reluctance for belugas to eat readily after a transport. While not true in all cases, several facilities have reported animals more interested in their new surroundings than in food. Although this might be a perfectly understandable situation, it was not a predicament in which we wanted to find ourselves.

We reviewed the papers of those who had dealt with delayed eating in beluga whales, and we discussed the matter with many who had worked with belugas, to try to pinpoint the causes. The one common thread in every case seemed to be an abundance of new stimuli that surrounded the animals upon arrival at their new location. This included everything from simply being in a new pool, to new personnel, different fish, different training props, new sounds and lighting, different water chemistry, and the list goes on. Some things were beyond our control to change. But an attempt was made to make things in Tacoma as much like Chicago as possible. One specific thing that seemed to be constant in every single problem case that we examined was the need to constantly drop the water to handle the animal. Even animals that were well trained for husbandry behaviors might be uncooperative while acclimating to a new environment. This, of course, would be very inconvenient, since it is usually after a transport that several phyical exams are required. We decided to desensitize our belugas to this process. Several times a week we scheduled "water down" sessions. We would lower the level of their habitat and do several training and play sessions with the water at waist level. We conditioned them to a variety of water down situations, including being handled as if for a tube feeding, always making each session as positive as possible. Within a month, the animals no longer associated the pool level dropping with being handled for a physical exam. Instead, it was just another type of training session.

As with the otters, our training was put to the test with beluga whales. Our meticulously planned 10-hour transport turned into a 27-hour marathon. Bad weather delayed us slightly, but once we were finally loaded and ready to go, we were only an hour or so behind schedule. Once we were all buckled in and ready for take off, the plane suddenly lurched backward. We thought we were on our way, wrong! An unmanned airport service truck somehow slipped into reverse and ran right into our plane's right wing. It would be many hours before a new part could be flown in to replace the damaged wing flap. We considered moving the animals back to Tacoma and rescheduling the transport. But, because the belugas were resting comfortably, we finally decided to stay where we were. Although we were very concerned about the delay, the belugas had no idea how long the transport was supposed to be, so they were fine.

Over 24 hours after leaving Tacoma our two five-year-old female beluga whales arrived at their new home in Chicago. We placed them in the medical pool with water at waist level just as we had practiced so often in Tacoma. The same trainers, same bucket, same wet-suits were all used (we were a living definition of the term superstitious behavior)! Within half an hour of placing the whales into their new habitat they were eating and exhibiting behavior just like they had in Tacoma.

Within two weeks both whales were eliciting all of their previously trained behaviors and seemed very comfortable in their new home. We never had a feeding problem with either whale, and were so pleased with their progress that we decided to move the Pacific white-sided dolphins the very next week.

PACIFIC WHITE-SIDED DOLPHINS

With all the delays, problems, and setbacks we had faced, we were prepared for anything to happen when it came time to transport the dolphins. Fortunately, the dolphin transport was the smoothest and least troublesome of all. Some would say, however, that we took extraordinary steps to prepare the animals for this transport. We had just the opposite concern about transporting the dolphins than we had with the belugas. Pacific white-sided dolphins, or lags (short for their scientific genus *Lagenorhynchus*), have a reputation for being very hyperactive and nervous animals. We had real concerns that such active animals might not readily sit still for a long transport. Previous transport experience with Pacific white-sided dolphins had us putting on our thinking caps trying to prevent any potential problems. The Pacific white-sided dolphin certainly has a different temperament than the bottlenose dolphin.

Training had progressed well for the lags. Gating was right on schedule, husbandry training was progressing quickly, and the lags were so creative they were constantly offering new aerial behaviors. They seemed to be such quick learners that we were certain we could condition them to accept the various features of a transport. We basically wanted to desensitize them to all the stimuli associated with transport, prior to exposing them to the uncertain aspects of arriving at an unfamiliar facility. Their attitude during quarterly physicals indicated that putting them in a stretcher every three months was not sufficient to get them comfortable with the process. Besides, physical often meant a lot of poking and prodding, and we wanted to make the idea of being in a stretcher and transport carrier easy and uneventful.

Stretcher training was not feasible in Santa Cruz, so we decided to approximate the transport process and desensitize the animals to the stretcher in small increments. Fifteen months before actually transporting the dolphins, we began placing the dolphins in a stretcher every month. We used that opportunity to get regular weights on each animal, but otherwise simply desensitized them to being in a stretcher for short periods of time, five to ten minutes at the outset. We slowly increased the amount of time they were in a stretcher and by the sixth month we were placing the animals into a transport carrier as well.

Once this became a monthly procedure, the animals seemed to realize that it would not be long before they were reunited with the other dolphins in their familiar surroundings. We felt this was a major milestone, during a physical exam a nervous dolphin could quickly be returned to the pool, but once airborne we would be committed to finishing the flight. What started as a nervous jittery procedure for several of the dolphins became a calm and comfortable process. A feed or play session would follow the animals' reintroduction to the pool.

Three months prior to transport we increased the sessions to twice a month. We also increased the activity level around the carrier and simulated every possible phase of transport. We even placed the animals in their carrier onto the back of a truck and drove them around the lab just as though we were really making the move. We also varied the length of time we had them out of the water, that way they did not anticipate each session as being longer than the one before. One month before the transport, each animal had experienced sessions in the transport carrier lasting over an hour, and had been on drives of over 20 minutes long. By the time we actually moved the lags they were experienced travelers, and had been exposed to as many of the sensations associated with an actual transport as we were capable of recreating.

Water-to-water time for the actual transport was right at 12 hours. All four dolphins rode comfortably and there was no need for any sedatives or other special medical attention. Within an hour of being introduced to their new home, all four animals came to station and participated in a very good session. Just as with the belugas, we recreated as much of what they were used to in Santa Cruz as we could. Our approach may seem a bit extreme, but we wanted to make sure all potentially adverse stimuli had been desensitized, and in the end we feel that all our precautions proved beneficial.

CONCLUSION

As we look back on the various desensitization techniques we used with each of the animals groups, we are very happy with our results. We realize that each training situation is different, and we may find that the next time we transport we may need to try another approach. The one factor that will remain constant in each of our future transports is that we will not accept potential problems as an unavoidable obstacle. Instead, we will continue to look at the concerns that face us in each situation and accept them as challenging training goals that can be accomplished. After all, it's a process we have all learned to use in training new and inventive husbandry behaviors. Each time a veterinarian suggests a new test or procedure, we examine ways to teach the animal to cooperate in that process. The same methods can be applied to most situations involving our animals. For each of our transports we examined the potential problems and possible causes for those problems. We then made every feasible attempt to desensitize the animals to what we considered to be the probable source of that problem. In the end, we feel we were successful. The real winners, of course, are the animals that have adapted so well to their new home in Chicago.

Marine Mammals: Public Display and Research

The following paper is a well thought out and researched summary of the definition and application of desensitization in a training context. It was published in 1998, appearing in Volume 3, Number 1 of IMATA's journal. I recommend this article because it looks at desensitization from a technical and scientific point of view while still applying it to every day training.

A Review of the Psychological Principles and Training Techniques Associated with Desensitization

by Jenifer Hurley and Nicole Holmes
Long Marine Laboratory
University of California at Santa Cruz

ABSTRACT

Habituation is defined classically as "the relatively persistent waning of a response as a result of repeated stimulation which is not followed by any kind of reinforcement" (Thorpe, 1956). In the authors' opinion the desensitization process is an integral part of many aspects of an animal training regime involving the incorporation of both habituation and counter-conditioning practices. It is necessary for preparing an animal to accept novel stimulus, to operate in a novel environment, and to interact with apparent confidence and consistency in captivity (Flaherty, 1985; Goldblatt, 1993). A literature search on the topic is summarized and used to elaborate on conventional animal training desensitization practices.

INTRODUCTION

Diving physiology research conducted at Long Marine Laboratory necessitated the training of California sea lions *(Zalophus californianus)* to become extensively desensitized to both equipment and unfamiliar environments (Hurley, 1996). The animals had to cooperate under a wide variety of complex scenarios. To monitor heart rate, each of the sea lions wore a harness equipped with extensive wiring and electrodes. Oxygen consumption studies required the sea lions to dive to a submerged target and subsequently surface in a PVC cage covered by a plastic dome, where their sight and hearing was significantly limited. The research further required the sea lions to be subjected to the many different stimuli associated with open ocean release training, including riding in cages of both boats and trucks, and coping with a populated and erratic environment. In order to accomplish these goals and to better understand the desensitization process, we reviewed material on habituation theory from the psychological literature in an attempt to integrate this with what we already knew of animal training desensitization practices. This review of the psychology of desensitization lead to the development of a generalized desensitization model, which we believe enabled us to successfully train the sea lions to comfortably and confidently perform all of the required research tasks.

BACKGROUND THEORY AND JARGON

The word habituation appears to have first been defined in the psychological literature by J. Donald Harris (1943). At that time, habituation was becoming increasingly recognized as important to the analysis of learning. There were many terms circulating to describe the decrease in magnitude of an unlearned response: acclimatization, extinction, inhibition, accommodation, and stimulatory activation. Harris chose the work habituation to describe instances of decrement in the magnitude of unlearned responses that occur in whole organisms and were due to repetitive stimulation. Harris distinguished this process from other types of response decrement which occur as a result of receptor adaptation, loss of the effector's ability to respond, or any of the various types of inhibition.

Richard F. Thompson and William Alden Spencer (1966) specify that habituation can usually be distinguished from other types of response decrement because it is reversible. They discuss the following common characteristics that may consequently serve as a detailed operational definition of habituation (the authors have interjected relevant examples for clarification). Given a particular stimulus that elicits a response, repeated application of that stimulus result in a decreased response. For example, the feel of a harness to a sea lion will initially cause a reaction but will subside with repeated exposures. If the stimulus is subsequently withheld, the response tends to recover over time (spontaneous recover). If the sea lion has previously been trained to accept a harness placed on its body, and the behavior is not reviewed for considerable period, the animal may initially balk at the sight or feel of the reintroduced harness. If a response is habituated and allowed to recover repeatedly, future habituatio of that response becomes more rapid (potentiation of habituation). For the reintroduced harness, the time and training necessary to return to the desensitized state will be much shorter than the original training time taken to desensitize it. Other factors being equal, the greater the frequency of exposure (stimulation), the more rapid and more pronounced is the habituation. The more times a sea lion is exposed to a harness, the sooner it will become desensitized. In other words, it a trainer works with the harness five times a week versus only once a week the sea lion will become desensitized to the harness at a much faster rate. Additionally, the weaker the stimulus, the more rapid and more pronounced is habituation. Strong or aversive stimuli may yield no significant habituation. If the harness is uncomfortably constricting, causing breathing difficulty, or is associated with manipulative punishment, it will be more difficult to habituate the animal sufficiently to promote its cooperation. Additional habtuation training after the response has disappeared or reached a stable habituated level will result in a slower recovery of the original response. This indicates maintenance level training and periodic review is useful in promoting continued desensitization. Habituation of response to a given stimulus also exhibits generalization to other similar stimuli. For example, if a sea lion is desensitized to carrying an electrocardiogram (EKG) monitor on its back, the transition to wearing a camera or other objects will be much smoother. Additionally, animals with long histories of desensitization to a variety of different stimuli will generally be easier to desensitize to any novel stimulus. Presentation of another very different stimulus frequently results in recovery of the habituated response (dishabituation). If a sea lion is confronted with a crowd of people and has not previously been desensitized to crowds, it is likely that the sea lion will be wary enough of the crowd to refuse to allow its harness to be ut on, even if the harness was previously desensitized.

In general, it is recognized that the process of habituation serves an important role in the adaptation of an animal to its environment. W.H. Thorpe (1956) defined habituation as "the relatively persistent waning of a response as a result of repeated stimulation which is not followed by any kind of reinforcement." Habituation is further characterized by being specific to a particular stimulus. This is significant in that it recognizes the habituation process as being driven, predominantly, by the stimulus rather than any resultant reward or benefit. Flaherty (1985) describes habituation as "a form of learning in that it represents a relatively permanent change in behavior that is the result of the experience of the individual and not due to fatigue." Similarly, Konrad Lorenz (1981) describes habituation as a physiological mechanism whose adaptive value prevents fatigue. The ability to habituate to new stimuli associated with environmental changes is critical to the fundamental needs of the animal to minimize energy waste.

Counter-conditioning is the process where normal defense reactions elicited by an aversive stimulus, such as a shock, are modified by association with a positive reinforcer (Pearce & Dickinson, 1975). Systemic desensitization developed by Joseph Wolpe in the 1950's is a common toll in behavior therapy and is based on counter-conditioning phenomena. Wolpe administered an inescapable shock to food-deprived cats. The conditioned fear was then overcome by feeding the animals and approximating them into the chamber where the fear had been conditioned (Dickson, Mellgren, Fountain, & Dyck, 1977). In a training situation, an animal can be conditioned to accept a needle (aversive stimulus) for routine blood sampling by associating it with a positive reinforcer (food).

The term habituation is used by psychologists to describe what animal trainers refer to as desensitization (Flaherty, 1985). It is appropriate, from a training perspective, to include both habituation and counter-conditioning under the broad category of desensitization. Additionally, the authors distinguish the passive experiential nature of habituation from the more active reinforcement process of counter-conditioning as passive and active desensitization, respectively.

Sensory adaptation is often misused as a synonym for habituation. Lorenz (1981) demonstrated the distinction. Turkeys were habituated to a tome, and then subjected to a sound having the same pitch and duration but lowered amplitude. The turkeys reacted as if it were a new stimulus by exhibiting a resurgence of the pre-habituated response. If the habituation response were localized in the sensory organ, or related to any sort of fatigue, the diminished intensity of stimulation could never have resulted in the observed resurgence of response. As a result of this and other experiments, habituation must clearly be categorized as a type of learning and not merely a physiological condition.

The process of habituation is preceded by an introductory period in which an animal first considers the value of a stimulus (Flaherty, 1985). The "novelty effect" describes a characteristic set of mammalian responses to the introduction of a novel stimulus and is an important part of the "fight-or-flight" response in mammals. It is loosely defined as the innate fear provoked response associated with exposure to a novel stimulus. Flaherty described the novelty affect with the following set of responses: animals will respond initially with an orienting response, accompanied by a variety of behavioral and physiological changes including change in heart rate, skin resistance, respiration, constriction of peripheral blood vessels, muscle tone, and electrical activity of the cerebral cortex, as well as arousal and suppression of appetitive behaviors.

An individual's environmental context and unique perception of a stimulus significantly influence the resulting desensitization response (Bolyard & Rowland, 1996). For example, a mother with a pup, or a sleeping animal will exhibit an exacerbated startle response when exposed suddenly to new stimuli. Additionally, motivational states in general will significantly affect the response to stimuli and the associated process of desensitization. This is not particularly surprising since motivational states generally effect all learning processes (Bolyard & Rowland, 1996).

The opposite of desensitization is called sensitization. Sensitization is defined as "the enhancement of a response solicited by a stimulus with repeated presentations of that stimulus" (Flaherty, 1985). Remarkable, sensitization is the condition described by the novelty effect. In this sense, sensitization universally precedes habituation. In the beginning stages of exposure to a new stimulus, there is a delicate stage where an animal can become increasingly sensitized instead of desensitized. The resulting effect is primarily based on the initial stimulus strength (Flaherty, 1985). For instance, a weak stimulus introduced slowly will not invoke a strong sensitization and will thus be more easily desensitized. However, if the amplitude or strength of the stimulus is too great, one can create a sensitizing effect which will color the relationship the animal has to the stimulus for a considerable time to follow. Therefore, it is extremely important to keep in mind the possible sensitizing effect from the intensity of a stimulus, especially upon initial exposure. All stimuli will eventually habituate over time; however, there will be a lot more work involved to desensitize an animal that is nitially sensitized.

As stated earlier, dishabituation can occur when a new stimulus, usually intense or noxious, is presented just prior to the presentation of a stimulus to which the animal has already been habituated. The new stimulus negates the previously habituated response by causing its own novelty effect and sensitization response. The conditions under which the initial response was habituated are no longer the same, therefore, the habituation is lost. This process has an adaptive value. When an animal becomes habituated to a stimulus it is in a vulnerable state. The occurrence of a new, strong stimulus could indicate danger, promoting the animal to return to its original state of awareness (Flaherty, 1985). Therefore, a constant or similar environment may be important in the maintenance of desensitization. For this reason the authors suggest an animal should first be desensitized to a stimulus in one context and then, as needed, it can be desensitized in different environments, being careful to expect some context shifts.

Context shift describes the loss of a learned response when the animal is shifted from one environment to another (Richardson, Ricco, & McKennery, 1988). In the case of desensitization, a stimulus that is familiar under one context when shifted to a new situation may lose its desensitized nature and instead elicit a resurgence of response. For example, a bridge whistle sounded in an oceanarium will elicit no response from the habituated surrounding human co-workers. However, out of contest in an automobile, the sudden blowing of a whistle will cause a novelty reaction in those same people.

Psychologists make a distinction between long-term and short-term habituation (Flaherty, 1985). This may be important in training because the length of retention of learning is affected by the frequency of exposure to a stimulus. The time between exposures to a stimulus is called the inter-stimulus-interval (ISI) and is related to the length of retention. If the ISI is short, the frequency of exposure to the stimulus is increased. This allows an increase rate of habituation. However, the length of retention of that habituation will be shorter. If the ISI is longer there is less total exposure to the stimulus per unit time, and the habituation will be slower. However, the long-term retention will be increased. Flaherty suggests that these two types of habituation may be related to differences in short-term and long-term memory in humans.

Harris (1943) found that habituation of responses varies among different species. In reviewing data from all phyla, he found no single mechanisms of habituation. In fact, he felt that there were probably several mechanisms accounting for habituation, "throughout so extreme a range of organisms and under such widely varied experimental conditions any single explanatory principle would have to be general to be satisfactory." Hinde (1970) also suggested that the mechanisms underlying habituation differ considerably among phyla. He proposed the dual process theory which describes habituation involving two processes, one decremental (haabituation) and one incremental (sensitization), which are assumed to develop independently in the central nervous system and interact to yield the final behavioral outcome (Groves & Thompson, 1970). Each presentation of a stimulus is hypothesized to both have a tendency to sensitize the animal and at the same time lead to an increment in habituation. The end behavior represents the outcome of the two opposing processes. Kandel, Schwartz, and Jessel's (1991) work with the sea snail, *Aplysia californica*, lends some support to the dual process theory. However, more research is still needed to determine conclusively the mechanisms of habituation.

Based on drive state theory, the authors propose that an animal's perceptions can be placed on a motivation continuum that has at the extreme left a punishing value and at the extreme right a reinforcing value, and in the middle a stimulus with no perceived value to the animal. In this context, the process of desensitization is that which moves a stimulus from the extremes of the continuum inward until the stimulus holds a neutral value to the animal. However, in animal training, a right shift towards reinforcement is generally the objective and can be accomplished either through habituation followed by classical conditioning, or more efficiently by using counter-conditioning throughout. The left shift is important to be aware of as it describes the satiation of a previously reinforcing stimulus. This is a common problem with overexposure to conditioned secondary reinforcers at oceanariums. For example, a toy which is left too long in an enclosure frequently ceases to provide entertainment because the animal has become desensitized to it (Glodblatt, 1993).

PRACTICAL APPLICATION

Only some of the theory presented here is practically helpful to animal trainers. ISI theory may help in deciding on the spacing of training sessions relative to what your schedule allows. If the objective is lasting desensitization, theory suggests the best method is to spread out the training over a greater period of time. On the other hand, if the need is only short-term desensitization because, for instance, there is a camera crew coming in three days and the animal is never likely to see another camera in its life, the best option is to decrease the time between training sessions. Repeating many desensitization sessions close together should increase the rate of desensitization. This strategy may decrease the long-term retention, but since the goal is short-term, retention is not particularly important. If the goal is to desensitize an animal to a harness that it will wear its whole life, then an expedited rate of desensitization can be sacrificed in favor of the long-term retention which is best affordd by increasing the time between sessions.

Trainers also need to be concerned with context shift (Turner et al., 1991). Here we believe it is important to make a distinction between a constant and a changing environment. The addition of a single novel stimulus into a constant environment is different than adding multiple novel stimuli. Adding multiple stimuli at one time can create a changed environment and allows for the potential problems of context shift. It is important to recognize that multiple stimuli also represent an increased strength of stimulus which may create a sensitizing effect on first exposure. We feel it is preferable to hold the environment reasonably constant and desensitize a minimal amount of stimuli at a time, increasing the stimuli as the animal allows. However, as previously discussed, an animal with a good history of desensitization will not require such delicate approximations. We have expressed the most conservative view of an inexperienced animal in order to explore the most difficult case scenario.

The authors have devised a generalized desensitization model for our practical use in daily desensitization training. It can be applied with modification to various situations. First, we have differentiated between two types of desensitization training sessions called passive and active. Active desensitization sessions involve the use of counterconditioning techniques. In active desensitization we use reinforcement (usually food) paired with the stimulus (analogous to classical conditioning) to speed up the desensitization process. In passive desensitization (habituation), an animal is merely exposed to a stimulus over time following the careful process outlined in the generalized model. When using active desensitization it is important to be aware of the possibility of conditioning your stimulus as a secondary reinforcer. In most cases, this is likely to be an advantage. However, if neutrality is desired or food or other reinforcement is not available, then passive desensitization is the best method. We find our volunteer staff time is well spent in these passive desensitization sessions and the additional interactive time for the animals is an added bonus.

After having chosen passive or active desensitization it is important to analyze the component variables of the stimulus. Most stimuli have many component parts that would be ideally desensitized singularly. We attempt to considered all of the various sensory components of a stimulus in order avoid the sensitizing affect of stimulus strength.

Although this might seem like extreme measures, we have found with some timid animals it is necessary in order to avoid sensitization. For example, we believed we had desensitized our sea lion to sight, spray, and sound of WD40r, which was needed to clean the electrode patched on her back. However, we had neglected the component variable of smell, which greatly offended her and unfortunately resulted in delaying our data collection.

In order to avoid sensitizing the animal, we feel it is best to expose it to the stimulus from a greater distance initially and then progressively closer as it appears more confident. We also consider the safe zones of the animal; for marine mammals, it is generally best to start out with the stimulus on land before infringing on the "comfort area" (in this case, the water) and risking a sensitizing experience.

Finally, we strongly suggest carefully reading the animal's response when deciding to progress to the next step, whether in increasing the number of variables or the proximity of the stimulus. It is best to have a baseline response of the animal reacting to a trainer to compare the reactions seen when the animal is being exposed to the stimulus. This will help differentiate signs of distress. A few of the behavioral manifestations of distress often seen that an animal might exhibit are: wide eyes, increased/decreased respiration, increased stereotypical behavior, increased/decreased surface time, moving to other side of pool, or swimming frantically (Goldblatt, 1993). Hopefully, if you are proceeding with caution, few if any of these signs will be noted. However, if you should forget to desensitize a sensory component of the stimulus, we have found it is best to remove the threatening object from the proximity of the animal and to start again in a slower fashion after a rest period. After having desensitized each variable separately, you can begin combining variabls progressing toward a completely desensitized stimulus.

HARNESS TRAINING EXAMPLE

In order to better explore the generalized model we offer the following specific example from our program: training a sea lion to wear a harness. To begin this process, the trainer first decides whether to use active or passive desensitization or both. We decided to begin with passive desensitization, using our volunteer time to expose the sea lion to the bright read nylon webbing that was to be used to construct the harness. The stimulus (red nylon webbing) was broken down into three variables: sight, movement, and touch. The volunteers first watched the animal while standing in plain sight to get a baseline of the animals behavior while not being exposed to any new stimulus. The red nylon webbing was introduced by holding it in view and slowly walking around the outside of the enclosure a good distance from the animal. During this process the animal's behavior was continually assessed to evaluate for any signs of distress, such as avoidance of the area near the person holding the stimulus, decreased surface time, wide eyes, or fast swimming. When no apparent reaction was seen from the animal and it appeared to be in the same behavioral state as the baseline, the person holding the nylon webbing moved closer and closer to the enclosure until they could stand and walk closely around the fence. After the animal was desensitized to the sight again at a distance waving the nylon around, followed by moving closer to the enclosure as no reaction was seen from the sea lion (the number of sessions it takes to move the stimulus from a distance to proximate to the enclosure depends on the individual animal's desensitization history and on the strength of the stimulus presented).

When it appeared the sea lion had been passively desensitized to the sight and movement of the nylon webbing, we began the active desensitization process. Using food reinforcement, a trainer introduced the red nylon webbing inside of the enclosure, first at a distance then moving to holding the stimulus right next to the animal. In each step the animal was fed for being attentive and calm and showing no signs of distress. At any sign of distress, the trainer removed the webbing until the animal seemed comfortable and then slowly moved forward again. The process was then repeated adding the variable of movement.

The next variable to be desensitized in the process of harness training was the feel of the nylon webbing on the animal. This was begun by asking it to target on the webbing and reinforcing this behavior. The animal was asked to target on the stimulus until it repeated the behavior consistently with no signs of distress.

The next step was to slowly and lightly touch the animal on the side of the neck with the webbing, an area where it could easily observe the process. We maintained the sea lion on a stationary nose target during this training. Once the animal was comfortable with this level of touching, the trainer moved to touching the animal all over its body with the stimulus. We did this for increasing periods of time until the animal apparently ignored the webbing resting on its body.

After the sea lion was comfortable with the feel of the nylon webbing on her body, we began to use it to construct the harness. First, a head piece was constructed to slip over the head, complete with a breakaway velcro attachment in case of unexpected sensitization. The sea lion was trained to target while the piece was slipped over the head, a process that was made much easier because the animal was already desensitized to the fell and sight of the nylon webbing. The process of removing and replacing the neck piece was repeated followed by significant reinforcement (counter-conditioning) until the animal showed no response. After the sea lion was comfortable wearing the head piece while moving on land and in the water. When these behaviors were performed with apparent confidence, the trainer moved on to repeating the process adding the side of the body pieces to the harness.

Once the animal was wearing the harness comfortably in its enclosure and performing all its regular behaviors we began putting on the harness in different contexts, such as new areas of the enclosure and in completely different enclosures, until finally the sea lion would wear its harness under any scenario.

CONCLUSION

The authors feel that an understanding of desensitization is critical for animal trainers. Animals in show environments and those involved in scientific research should be adequately desensitized to their environment. A thorough understanding of habituation and counter-conditioning learning may aid trainers in addressing their animals' desensitization needs. Desensitization is the process by which an animal may learn to be comfortable and confident in any situation, which is a primary benefit of any animal training program.

LITERATURE CITED

Bolyard, K.J. & Rowland, W.J. (1996). Context-dependent response to red coloration in stickle back. Animal Behavior, 52: 923-927.

Dickson, A.L., Mellgren, R.J., Fountain, A., & Dyck, D. (1977). Wolpe's reciprocal inhabilitation principle: An animal analogue. Psychological Reports, 40: 395-401.

Flaherty, C.F. (1985). **Animal Learning and Cognition: Habituation and Sensitization.** New York: Knopf.

Goldblatt, A. (1993). Behavioral needs of captive marine mammals. Aquatic Mammals, 19(3): 149-157.

Groves, P.M. & Thompson, R.F. (1970). Habituation: A dual-process theory. Psychological Review, 77: 419-450.

Harris, J.D. (1943). Habituatory responses decrement in the intact organism. Psychological Bulletin, 40: 385-422.

Hinde, R.A. (1970). **Animal Behavior: A Synthesis of Ethology and Comparative Psychology.** New York: McGraw-Hill.

Hurley, J.A. (1996). Metabolic rate and heart rate during trained dives in adult California sea lions. Unpublished doctoral thesis, University of California at Santa Cruz.

Kandel, E.R., Schwartz, J.H., & Jessel, T.M. (1991). **Principles of Neural Science.** New York: Elsevier Science Publishing Co.

Lorenz, K.Z. (1981). **The Foundations of Ethology.** New York: Springer-Verlag New York, Inc.

Pearce, J.M. & Dickinson, A. (1975). Pavlovian counter-conditioning: Changing the suppressive properties of shock by association with food. Journal of Experimental Psychology: Animal Behavior Processes, 104(2): 170-177.

Richardons, R., Riccio, D.C., & McKennery, M. (1988). Stimulus attributes of reactivated memory: Alleviation of ontogentic forgetting in rats is contest shift. Developmental Psychobiology, 21(2): 135-143.

Thompson, R.F., & Spencer, W.A. (1966). Habituation: A model phenomenon for the study of neuronal substrates of behavior. Psychological Review, 73: 16-43.

Thorpe, W.H. (1956). **Learning and Instinct in Animals. London: Methuen>**

Turner, T.N., Stafford, S.G., McHugh, M.B., Surovik, L, Delgross, D., & Fad, O. (1991). The effects of context shift in killer whales (*Orcinus orca*). In S. Allen (Ed.), Proceedings of the 19th Annual Conference of the International Marine Animal Trainers Association (pp. 99-106).

This article by Gary Wilkes is not included in the collection of newspaper articles featured in *A Behavior Sampler*. This article first appeared in *Dog Fancy* magazine and is now available, along with many other excellent articles at Gary's web-site, see chapter 14, "The Professional Trainer." Here Gary explores the differences between two important concepts that, although different, are intricately related.

Generalization and Discrimination: Fraternal Twins

By Gary Wilkes

Somewhere, deep within the bowels of my computer is a nifty little pinball game. It is a tribute to the software designers, who have created a marvelous simulation of the real thing. Two of the keys on the keyboard activate the flippers, and two more act to "nudge" the table. The first time I played the game, I discovered something interesting. Instead of hitting the keys to make the machine "wiggle," I was actually bumping the whole keyboard. My longtime responses from "real" pinball games had leaked over into my computer simulation. In scientific terms, I had "generalized" a behavior from one situation to another. Fixing this problem requires that I "discriminate" between real pinball machines and fake ones. While we humans rarely examine this process, it may surprise you to know that your dog is an expert at both generalization and discrimination and could probably "teach us a thing or two."

While all animals have the capacity to acquire knowledge, they must also know where, when and how to use it. If a dog sits on a cactus, he will not benefit from the experience unless he possesses two mental abilities – discrimination and generalization. Simply put, discrimination is the ability to decide that two events or things are unrelated. Generalization is the ability to see a relationship between things. So, to avoid cactus, a dog must able to discriminate between cactus and non-prickly objects and be able to generalize that all cactus should be avoided.

In your home, these twin abilities are regularly displayed. If a dog races madly to the door at the sound of the bell, but does not react to the sound of a doorbell on a television program, he has correctly "discriminated" between the two. The dog has decided that some aspect of the real doorbell is unique, and not shared with the TV bell. If the dog responds to the doorbell AND the sound of a doorbell on the television, he has "generalized" the sameness between the two bells.

Another example of these dual behavioral principles occurs when you take your very obedient dog to a new location. The same dog who can sit, lie down, roll over, fetch and speak will become a distracted fool the instant he sets foot in a park. The dog has correctly discriminated that the park is different than your home, but has failed to generalize the commands associated with his obedience behaviors. This process of assuming that the park is unique, and failing to realize that it should be considered the "same" as your living room is the simplest form of this problem. The solution is to gradually introduce the dog to new locations, while continuing training on the behaviors that work at home.

While deciding "sameness" or "uniqueness" is often a simple association, it may also be a complex blend of the two. Many dogs learn to dislike people who wear uniforms. This reaction requires that the animal make both a subtle and complex discrimination AND a generalization. First the dog must learn to discriminate between people who wear uniforms, and people who do not. While we take for granted that uniforms differ from regular clothing, dogs must learn which components represent a uniform, and which things do not. This is not as easy as it seems. In reality, most uniforms are not really uniform. Animal Control officers and police wear badges – the meter reader does not. The UPS guy wears shorts. The letter carrier may not. At each step in the process, the animal analyzes which things are common to uniforms (generalization), and which things are not (discrimination).

Ultimately, the dog will learn to associate name plates, badges, hats with badges and funny shaped things hanging from a belt as signs of a uniform. If any of those cues are present, the dog may then generalize his behavior. If a man with a badge on his hat sprays the dog with pepper spray, heaven help the next bottled water delivery man who has a logo on his cap. The dog doesn't know that the first man was an animal control officer or that the second man is delivering water – he just knows that hats with badges are "intruders." If the dog's owner wears a hat and badge, the dog may make an even more complex discrimination – all guys with hats and badges are evil, except "dad."

While these specific discriminations are easy for us to understand, discrimination and generalization can also link sequential "chains of events." Many dogs come to discriminate the veterinary hospital as a place where "pain" happens. At first, the dog is happy to get in the car and visit the new and exciting location. Soon the dog starts to generalize the sights, sounds, smells and sensations of the examination room with unpleasant treatment. The dog will start to identify everything that is unique to veterinary visits and link the sequence of events that "cause" the examination room. Soon, the dog is reluctant to get in the car, go into the waiting room, or approach people who wear veterinary uniforms.

Understanding discrimination and generalization can help you appreciate the dynamic nature of your dog's behavior. Learning to better control your dog's ability to learn can help create good performance and modify unacceptable behavior. Here are a few tips for utilizing this knowledge with your dog.

- Make sure you train your dog in several places and different times of day -- gradually introduce changes and distractions.
- To help your dog make a discrimination, make two situations obviously different, just like an old western movie – the good guys where the white hats, and the bad guys wear the black hats. If you want your dog to bark at suspicious strangers, but not bark at regular visitors, have your "pretend" burglars wear funny hats, carry umbrellas, or walk unusually. Gradually remove the hats, and umbrellas, and make generally furtive movements the key to deciding if someone is a threat.
- If you want your dog to generalize quickly, be willing to drop your standards in the new location/situation. If Fido can sit at home, but is distracted at the park, simply try to reinforce him for responding to his name. Once he will listen to his name, re-teach "sit" in exactly the same way he originally learned the behavior. Once he starts to "sit," even in the park, repeat the process in the next location, or try a different behavior. If the behavior fails, drop your standards and refresh his memory.
- To successfully learn a generalized discrimination, it takes practice. Most people fail to repeat the situation enough times to give Fido the needed experience. Repetitions that end with different consequences can help the dog learn faster. If the sound of the real doorbell leads to a dog biscuit, and the TV bell leads to a five minute "time out," Fido will quickly discriminate between the two.

ABA - S.I.G.
Association for Behavior Analysis
Animal Special Interest Group Newsletter

The concept of husbandry training is certainly not new in marine mammal circles, but it is not as widespread among most dog and cat trainers. The Association for Behavior Analysis' Special Interest Group on Animal Training devoted their June 1996 newsletter to the subject of husbandry. Below are four articles from the newsletter focusing on: general husbandry and desensitization, an overview of marine mammal husbandry at Sea World, a look at husbandry training of horses and dogs, and the husbandry training of cats. Each of the authors takes a different approach to handling the subject.

Husbandry Training

by S. Grey Stafford
Positive Innovations

Whether you work with dogs, horses, or killer whales, the foundation for successful husbandry training is desensitization. Desensitization is a continuous process by which new and potentially frightening (and often uncomfortable) conditions are slowly introduced to an animal. Such introductions are paired with positive reinforcement.

However, the key to developing a calm, confident animal is to be aware of what behavior is actually being reinforced at any point before, during, and especially after the new stimuli have been presented. This is the most important part of the process, because it is here that many trainers accidentally teach their animals to be even more afraid of new situations than when they began training! This occurs because as fallible human trainers, we often react to our animal's initial reaction. Unfortunately, the animal's initial reaction to something new or frightening is usually to run away, or at the least, to tighten its muscles. This is absolutely *not* the time to reinforce the animal in any way. Any acknowledgment of this behavior by the trainer (even calling the animal's name) may reinforce the startled behavior and cause it to occur more frequently in the future.

No matter what husbandry behavior you want to train, remember, and move slowly. Unless you have a medical emergency, there's absolutely no need to rush things. Begin by planning your approximations. In other words, make an educated guess at how far you can proceed at each session before your animal will flee whatever it is you are attempting to introduce. Each individual animal will have a different "starting point" based upon its past learning experience.

For example, if an animal has previously been forced to have its nails clipped, then you probably need to spend a lot of reinforcement on the animal just for approaching the clippers. Other animals may allow you to begin by clicking the clippers in the air near them. In either case, try to prevent the animal from failing during the session by taking your time and by not pushing the animal too far, too fast. You should not expect to clip a single nail during the first few sessions. When you do go for an actual clipping, clip only one nail, reinforce and end your session. Don't get greedy! Ten successful one-nail-clipped-at-a-time sessions are much better that one long session mixed with failure.

So what should we be looking for in order to reinforce the animal in the presence of a scary stimulus? The answer is simple: anything calm. I reinforce animals for relaxed posture, no vocalizations, eye contact and even breathing! The idea is to teach the animal ultimately to ignore things in the environment, all the while teaching it to remain attentive to the trainer. If the animal reacts in an undesired manner – do nothing. Wait for the animal to restore its attention to you before you proceed further (while you are waiting, ask yourself if you moved too fast). Do not proceed to the nest approximation, or level of difficulty, until the animal is relaxed.

A few last notes about reinforcement: plan your reinforcement to match the behavior you want. Calm behavior should receive calm reinforcement. Make sure that you time your reinforcement so that the animal is reinforced only for approaching the new stimulus. If you put the clippers, syringe or brush away, don't provide any more reinforcement; your taking the stimulus away is the same as the animal running from it.

Desensitization training is so valuable because it not only teaches animals how to respond appropriately to common situation but also to unforeseen disasters.

Sea World's Husbandry Training Program: Update

by C. Thad Lacinak, Michael R. Scaruzzi, David L. Force, & Mark B. McHugh
Sea World Inc.

Training marine mammals for husbandry procedures provides a tool for the management of these animals in a zoological environment. These procedures allow the trainers and veterinary staff to closely examine and to collect a variety of biological samples without undue stress to the animal. Several species of cetacea and pinnipedia have been reliably conditioned on numerous husbandry behaviors at Sea World. For example; through desensitization and approximation training, unrestrained blood and urine samples, ultrasound examinations, and oral husbandry procedures are performed on a routine basis. These husbandry procedures provide current information on the animals' health as well as assist in the long-term management of marine mammals.

Veterinary examinations and the collection of biological samples are of vital importance for physiology research and monitoring the health of animals in a zoological environment. In some instances, these examinations and collections have required physical restraint or anesthesia in order to safely perform the procedures. This process could be stressful to the animal and could result in injury to the animal and the handlers. At Sea World, we have used operant conditioning techniques with positive reinforcement to teach several species of cetacea, pinnipedia, and mustelids to allow complete body examinations and biological sampling without physical restraint. This paper gives an overview of a variety of trained husbandry behaviors with marine mammals and other species of animals.

TOUCH ACCEPTANCE

The animals are first conditioned to accept different types of touch from the trainers. Teaching the animals to calmly accept physical contact will allow trainers and veterinarians to perform routine examinations and to help identify inconsistencies. Sudden withdrawal by the animal in response to touch may indicate a sensitive area or a potential problem. The acceptance of touch is the foundation upon which trust between the trainer and the animal begins, and from which all other husbandry procedures are conditioned.

The process of conditioning touch acceptance simply consists of touching the animal and rewarding him for not moving away. These steps should begin in an area of the facility with a strong reinforcement history, such as a normal feeding area, to help relax the animal. We have found the use of respondent conditioning to be most practical and to serve our goals best during this phase of the training; by pairing touch from the handler directly with primary reinforcers, the contact itself becomes rewarding. Later this contact can be used to both calm and relax the animal, and as a reinforcer of bridged behaviors. One touch is paired with a primary reinforcer such as food, shaping is employed. Through successive approximations of rewarding a relaxed response to the handler's touch, the animal will begin to allow taction of all parts of its body. Following this schedule, the animal can be taught to present certain body parts to the trainer by reinforcing movement of that body part toward the trainer when touched.

HUSBANDRY PROCEDURES

Once the animals have been desensitized to physical contact, we can begin placing a measuring tape along their body. This proves beneficial in a number of ways including estimation of an animal's weight, since we currently use a formula to estimate weight from measurements that include of the maximum length and girth. We have conditioned our cetaceans to accept 15 different anatomical measurements. Measurements are taken every two weeks, providing growth rate information that would be unattainable outside a zoological environment.

Desensitizing the animals to the measuring tape or any inanimate object is performed by bridging stationary behavior (not flinching) when the animal is touched by the object. Any movement away from the tape is ignored while reinforcement follows a calm and relaxed response. The training process not only allows us to collect data on the animals, but also teaches the animals to accept a variety of tactile reinforcers other than just the trainer's touch. The animal also learns to become dependent on the bridge stimulus, a stimulus emitted by and therefore associated with the trainer. This dependence is beneficial to both trainer and animal in the future.

Monitoring an animal's weight is an important aspect of any management program. To achieve an absolute reading of weight, our cetaceans are taught a sideways slideout behavior onto a stationary, waterproof scale. Another method requires swimming the animals into a stretcher and lifting them out of the water. The known weight of the stretcher is then subtracted from the total. This process is made positive, and possible, by feeding and rubbing the animal during all phases of the procedure. The animal will soon learn to swim calmly into and out of the stretcher.

Pinnipeds and otters can be weighed frequently by simply walking them into a stationary scale and teaching them to remain motionless while the weight is read. Birds are conditioned to either walk or fly to the scale and stand motionless until they hear the bridging stimulus.

MEDICAL SAMPLING AND MEDICATING

Tactile stimulation is used in teaching our cetaceans to take a breath. Allowing us to visually examine the upper respiratory tract and to collect material for microbiological and cytological studies during the animal's exhalation. The discriminative stimulus we use is a touch from both heels of the trainer's hands alongside the blowhole. Initially in training, the animal will respond to the touch by emitting several different behaviors. Yet by bridging and rewarding only when a breath is taken, adjunct and superstitious behaviors are soon extinguished and the animal learns to associate the discriminative stimulus of a touch near the blowhole with taking a breath.

The same type of training paradigm is used to condition sea lions to accept eye drops by opening their eyes in response to the verbal stimulus "open". Once again, the reward is paired only with the behavior of opening their eyes in response to the verbal stimulus. As training progresses, the sea lions are conditioned to keep their eyes held open until the bridge is sounded. Even a procedure such as eye drops, can become routine when the desired response is positively reinforced.

Animals at Sea World have also been conditioned to accept stomach tubes. Conditioning is achieved by rewarding the animal for swallowing when the tube is placed against the back of its throat. Though conditioning is achieved in steps, the animal ultimately learns a swallowing repertoire and the behavior can be maintained with reinforcement given at the end of the procedure. Acceptance of stomach tubes can be helpful should an endoscopic examination be required.

Desensitization and habituation are used to condition animals to accept the presence of uncommon objects next to the pools. In this way, we can easily perform procedures such as x-rays and ultrasound. The x-rays provide a diagnostic tool for observing some skeletal and dental structures. Routine sonograms on pregnant females provide useful information on fetal development, viability, and positioning.

DENTAL HUSBANDRY

A mouth-open behavior is conditioned by teaching the animal to open its mouth in response to a light touch to the rostrum and the lower jaw. The animal must maintain contact with the trainer's hands while allowing examination of the teeth, gums, and tongue.

The mouth-open husbandry procedure has proven very successful. In fact, our dental examination and x-ray program with the killer whales has been expanded to include several benign procedures to actually rehabilitate pulp cavity infections through voluntary presentation by the animal. Several published natural history notes on killer whales have shown that this species exhibits dental problems which include tooth wear and fractures of the teeth. With this in mind, with additional training our husbandry procedures have been utilized as the basis for therapeutic dental procedures. For instance, when an exposed pulp cavity in a killer whale resulted in dental infection, we were able to address the problem without resorting to general anesthesia or restraint. Through successive approximations the animal has allowed tool desensitization, which in turn has allowed us to use brushes, files, picks and other instruments directly on the affected tooth. The animal has remained stationed with mouth open while tolerating tooth filing, flushing and ultimately even drilling of the pulp cavity to establish drainage.

THE SIDEWAYS SLIDEOUT TO FACILITATE MEDICAL SAMPLING

A sideways slideout behavior from the whales and dolphins, taught again through successive approximations and bridging with positive reinforcement, allows us to collect four types of samples. A tactile stimulus to the genital area is a signal for the animal to urinate. The sample is collected in a specimen cup for urinalysis. Urine samples can also be collected from Asian otters and Pacific walruses. These samples can be utilized for urinalysis and monitored for levels of hormone metabolites which are useful in diagnosis of pregnancy. Anal and vaginal sample are cleanly collected from the sideways slideout position. This behavior also allows us to collect a milk sample from our lactating females, a procedure which has provided important baseline information on the composition of the milk of six female killer whales and has allowed us to monitor the components throughout lactation. Milk samples have also been collected from a female walrus through operant conditioning and positive reinforcement.

Blood samples from the cetaceans are drawn from the ventral surface of the fluke. By desensitizing the animals to many forms of contact in this area, we are able to withdraw a small sample for analysis. Movement of the needle in the vein caused by movement of the syringe to the animal's fluke is minimized during the procedure by including a length of tubing between the needle and syringe. The same conditioning procedure has been used to teach walruses and California sea lions to allow blood sampling from a gluteal or flipper vein.

Teaching the procedures to our younger animals is expedited through mimicry of the adults' interactions. Positive interactions are begun as early as one month of age. We condition these type behaviors with all species of animals and at a variety of ages.

MOBILITY & STIMULUS COMPLEXITY

Transportation of sea lions within the park can be accomplished through cart-ride training. The sea lions are first taught to target to the trainer's palm, and then, through successive approximations of the evoked target behavior, are taught to climb into the carts and come up to the handler's palm as he or she sits at the front of the cart. Once at this level, the sea lions are rewarded for staying in the cart for short periods first stationary and then in motion. The ride is then gradually lengthened.

Cart-ride training not only insures stress-free transportation for the animal, but also provides the sea lions with stimulus complexity, a process which teaches the animals to be comfortable in a variety of different environments other than the facility in which they live. Through cart-ride training, the sea lions can be transported to animal science laboratories for routine animal husbandry procedures. Some transports, however, will require the use of the enclosed and secure husbandry unit. In order to expedite the transport process, the animals are trained to enter the unit and allow the door to be closed. These same techniques are used to condition similar procedures with walruses and otters. It is important to note that the majority of the times that the animal is asked to enter the unit and the door is closed, the unit is not moved and the animal is asked the exit. Entering the husbandry unit has now become part of the animal's daily activities so there will be no hesitation from the animal when a transport is planned.

CONCLUSION

A variety of husbandry procedures have been successfully conditioned with several species of marine mammals (otters and birds) at Sea World. Successful husbandry procedures are important products of a diverse behavioral enrichment program. These procedures reduce stress and teach the animals to calmly accept routine examinations by creating a rewarding interaction. The cooperation of the animals during husbandry procedures reduces the chance of injury to the animals and the handlers. Although each step necessary to train these behaviors could not possibly be discussed within the context of this paper, we believe that similar procedures can be trained with a variety of marine and terrestrial animals to assist in the successful management of these animals in zoological environments.

Our training methods at Sea World embody the most advanced principles available for the care of our animals and culminates in the world's most successful killer whale breeding program. The training received by our adults has given us an opportunity to interact with their young in a way never thought possible. No one could have imagined that a first time killer whale mother would learn to allow man in the water with her newborn. This type of interaction has enabled us to collect invaluable data about killer whale calf development and behavior. It has also a survival rate in newborn killer whales that surpasses the estimated 43% neonate mortality rate in the wild (Olesiuk, Bigg, & Ellis, 1988). Our mission is to continue to collect information about these magnificent creatures only available through close contact and strong, positive relationships.

Husbandry Training of Horses and Dogs

by Fran Teuscher

I will describe training of horses and dogs that is useful for the following: giving injections, obtaining blood samples, applying ointments, brushing and mat removing, mane trimming, nail clipping, hoof trimming and shoeing, applying bandages, udder or sheath cleaning, hosing down, and so on.

REINFORCERS

Establish a two syllable word as a secondary reinforcer (this is related to the article by Grace McDonald in last May's issue of the Trainers Forum Newsletter, see below). I use "Good girl," and Good boy," and I *never* say those words when *not* meant as a secondary reinforcer. (When you use those words in everyday conversation, just say "g.g" and "g.b." Soon all of your friends will know the code!) Use that secondary reinforcer as a signal to tell the animal "this is right" rather than "this is the end of the exercise."

With that secondary reinforcer, teach the horse "down" (put your head down when I touch your ears and/or say "down"), "up" (pick your hoof up), "hold still" (stay where you are; keep the same position until released). Teach the dog to "stay", "stand", "sit", 'up' (lift your paw). (All of the above-mentioned words commands are just suggestions; use whatever words you are most comfortable with.) Gradually lengthen the amount of time the animal remains quiet when told to, or keeps leg lifted up for you, or keeps its head down in one position.

If the animal is clicker trained, you may use the clicker to signal the end of the command, or you may use a "release" word for the same purpose ("okay", or "let's go", preceded by "good girl" or "good boy"). The release work itself then becomes the secondary reinforcer; the primary reinforcer is freedom. Alternatively, you may use food as the primary reinforcer, to signal the end of the exercise.

Teach "no" or "eh" or "wrong" (such as Gary Wilke's "wrong"), to let the animal know when it is doing an unreinforceable behavior.

As mentioned in the Grace McDonald article, use gradations of the secondary reinforcer. This is very important for husbandry training. For example: your mare lifts her foot for you; you say "good girl." She keeps it lifted, not moving an inch even though flies are all over her; you say "Goooooood giiiiiirrrll!!, followed by the primary reinforcer.

Make sure the "good girl" *precedes* your letting go of the foot. Also, make sure you let go of the foot while the horse is *not* fighting you. If it starts fighting you, say "wrong" (or whatever word you are using), while you keep holding on to the foot. Then, as soon as the horse quits struggling, say "good girl" and *then* let go of the foot.

A colt or filly can quickly be shaped in this way to allow handling of its feet, without fear.

DESENSITIZATION

Once all of the above points have been acquired, start handling more difficult areas. If a mare does not want her udder touched or cleaned, use regular desensitization techniques along with the secondary reinforcer. Touch closer and closer to the area, reinforce "hold still" and/or absence of kicking and squealing. Move very gradually. Soon, the resistant attitude with ears back, attempts to bite, squealing and kicking, will be replaced by an expectant, ear up, "Where's my primary reinforcer?" attitude, whenever you start handling the animal.

Since most husbandry tasks require either the need to have an animal stand still, and/or be desensitized to certain tasks or objects, the same principles are applied and carried over from one task to the other, as the animal "learns to learn".

TIPS

The gradation of the secondary reinforcer comes in especially handy for painful procedures. The contingency develops, the longer the animal remains quiet, the better the reinforcer will be. If you increase the graduation of your secondary reinforcer ("Gooooood booooooooyyy!!" i.e., your reinforcer which does *not* mean "End of exercise" quite yet), this will "mesmerize" the animal into waiting for a nice primary reinforcer (such as a large, sweet apple). The animal will remain calm and often *not* react to the pain (hopefully this won't be needed too often!)

This method works best with a familiar handler, who is consistent in his/her commands and reinforcements. However, if an unfamiliar handler has to hold the animal for the vet, or do other specific handling of the animal, the desensitization and lack of fear will still pay off.

Husbandry Training of Cats

by Jonathan Krueger

I have trained my cats to tolerate and even cooperate with a variety of procedures necessary or desirable for their care. It's been a training investment that has shown excellent returns. In this article, I will present what I've done, how I did it, and what the payoff has been for me and my cats. I'll also explore alternative a little. Finally, I'll look as some possible future training.

The five areas I've worked on are: weighing my cats, giving pills, giving hairball products, applying topical solutions, and clipping claws.

WEIGHT

A change in weight can signal a health problem. Regular, accurate weight measurements can detect a problem, often earlier that it would be noticed otherwise. Early detection allows early treatment, clearly a good thing. Also, a record of stable weight gives assurance that the animal is healthy.

So, how to weigh the cat? The usual advice, repeated by most cat books, is to weigh yourself on a bathroom scale with and without the cat and subtract. However, most bathroom scales are accurate only within a pound or two. A one pound change could certainly go undetected. For a 100 pound human, that's fine; it's accuracy within 1%. For a 10 pound cat, however, that's only accurate within 10%. That's like missing a 10 pound change on the human, noticing it only when the gain or loss approached 20 pounds!

Following this arithmetic, to get accuracy within 2%, you have to get the cat's weight within a quarter pound. This rules out most bathroom scales. Kitchen scales have the accuracy, but they usually have a small, shaky platform. Cats are known for avoiding unstable surfaces. Veterinarian scales solve the problem handily: they're accurate, reliable, and have a large, stable platform. They also cost hundreds of dollars.

I solved the problem with a combination of gadgets and training. The gadget was a modified kitchen scale. I gage it a larger platform by attaching two pieces of plywood, mounted as a "sandwich" surrounding the original platform. This makes large, fairly stable platform, although still prone to tipping over. In part because it was still tippy, training was also required.

The training uses baiting and shaping. I put a food treat on the platform, placed about where the cat's head is when weighing, to center the cat on the platform. I put the cat on the platform. I hold onto the cat, and don't attempt to get its weight yet. I let it eat the food, then take it off the platform. After a few trails, the cat readily eats the food. Next, I stop holding the cat after placing it on the platform. The contingency is, jumping off the platform is an unreinforced trail. However, as long as the cat stays on the platform, I continue to place more food treats there. So the other contingency is, jumping off terminates food delivery. Finally, I introduce, and gradually increase a time delay between each food delivery. This shapes crouching quietly on the platform, "waiting for food." When the delay has been shaped up to a few seconds, I can get the cat's weight: just read it during the delay. After weighing, I take the cat off the platform. Merely terminating food delivery might lead to extinction.

Over time, stereotypy has developed, in both my behavior and the cat's. The whole procedure has become very smooth. Most times I get the weight after the first food delivery. So the sequence is, place the cat on the scale, place a food pellet on the scale, get the weight after the first food delivery. So the sequence is, place the cat on the scale, place a food pellet on the scale, get the weight, remove the cat. An unintended but harmless effect of this training history is that the cat would otherwise remain on the platform for quite some time.

These days, when my cats hear the sounds of the scale, they come running. One of them has spontaneously started jumping on the scale. Indeed I could have trained all of them to do this, but that seems diminishing returns. The scale, after all, is still tippy, so I'd have to train them to jump a certain way. Precision jumping could be trained, but the effort would be large, and the returns small. Finally, it would risk tipping over the scale, scaring the cat, and blowing all the training so far. Similar considerations apply to training the cat to jump off the scale after weighing; it seems a poor investment.

The investment I have made has had excellent returns. The cat approaches the scale at weight time, sits still on the platform, even though it's shaky, and waits quietly. As a result, I can readily get accurate weights with an affordable scale.

GIVING PILLS

The most common way people pill cats is restraint and force. They follow the usual cat book advice: Hold the cat, force its mouth open, push the pill down its throat, and hold the mouth closed, maybe hold the nose in the air, then perhaps stroke its throat to induce swallowing.

Or they try to; many give up – "I just can't give Fred pills!" That means that when Fred really needs pills, absolutely has to have them, they go to the vet. Other times, Fred simply gets by without medication that might have been useful medically, if it would have to be given in pill form. Other times, it's just not reliable; sometimes the owner get the pill down the cat, sometimes not. Then medications whose effect depends on maintaining a certain blood level don't work as well.

Even when the owner succeeds, develops reliable restraint and force procedures, the process is usually aversive for both cat and owner. This is not only unpleasant, it creates practical problems. Aversive means avoidance; the cat runs away when he sees the pill. Even pill bottle sounds become discriminative stimuli; they predict arrival of an aversive stimulus. The contingency is discriminated avoidance; the cat avoids the aversive stimulus by running away when he hears the pill bottle.

My cats run to me when they hear the pill bottle. They have a long history of getting a food treat after the pill is swallowed.

Now, I still use some force: I open the cat's mouth and push the pill down its throat. And skill on my part still counts: the further down the center of mouth I push the pill, the quicker it gets swallowed. However, in contrast to the pure force method, I don't have to try to hide the sounds of the pill bottle, chase down the cat, hold it as it tries to get away, open its mouth, and risk a bite. As a result of training, the cat comes to me. I readily open its mouth and pop the pill in; the cat promptly swallows the pill; I give the food treat. And as a concomitant but useful result, it's easier for me to aim the pill down the center of the mouth.

Of course, this didn't work the first time I gave the cat the pill. Like many investments, this training didn't begin paying off until it had been in practice for a while. In the beginning, I still had to use a fair amount of restraint. Over time that has dwindled to almost nothing. And I see few of the related problem behaviors that owners complain about.

Cats are known to hold pills in their mouths and spit them out later. When restraint and force are used, the owner releases the cat when he thinks the pill has been swallowed. The contingency is, the cat escapes restraint by looking like it's swallowed the pill. The cat may learn to give a pretty good show. Then the owner gets to (try to) chase down the cat again and start over. And the more it happens, the more times the cat has been negatively reinforced to give the show. To prevent or fix this, it becomes critical to release the cat only after the pill has been swallowed.

With husbandry training, this is less critical. You do try to give the food treat only after the pill is swallowed, thus reinforcing swallowing the pill, not giving the show. But when you miss occasionally, the penalty is small. You've accidentally reinforced an undesired behavior. The cat is still there; you give it the pill again, make sure it's down, then give it another food treat. You've now reinforced the desired behavior. Over repeated trails, another contingency develops: the sooner the pill goes down, the sooner the food treat arrives. Finally, a handy physiological fact is in your favor: it's hard for the cat to eat the food treat without swallowing the pill.

The sound of the food treat container quickly moves far from a neutral stimulus. It's a powerful effect; the food can emit a barely audible pop, and cats start to arrive. I found it useful to transfer stimulus control from food sounds to pill bottle sounds. I arranged for pill sounds to precede food sounds. The other way around, little stimulus control would have been transferred. This way, pill sounds predict food sounds. Stimulus control is transferred from food sounds to pill sounds. Over repeated trials, the pill sounds come to cause the cats to arrive.

Considering how simple this training is, it's surprising the gyrations that owners go through to try to get pills into cats. Behavioral analysis of the most common ones is interesting.

The well known "hide it in the food" method suffers from the equally well known "cat ate all around the pill" behavior, or "cat ate nothing." Pills often taste bad to the cat; eating them instead of swallowing them whole probably makes them more aversive. The cat might be expected to learn to avoid them, and avoid food that's been manipulated in ways that in the past have predicted hidden food. The upshot is, this trick may work the first or second time, but is less likely to work the more you use it. The food tastes good, the pill tastes bad, and they usually have distinctly different shapes, colors, and feels. If the goal was to get the cat to learn to eat around a foreign object in its food, you could hardly design a better training situation that this.

A similar approach is to hide the pill by pushing it inside a moist cat treat. This has similar problems. If the cat chews the treat, or even licks it on the way down, it will probably be trained to avoid the treat. Indeed, success over the long term with this method depends on the cat *not* learning, which in turn depends on keeping the aversive stimulus (taste of the pill) from the cat. Keeping the cat from tasting what it's eating is difficult, especially over time.

Another well known method is to crush the pill to powder, or get the medication in suspension or solution, and mix it into the food. This works if the taste is not aversive, or not too aversive and the cat is food deprived. However, you must get the cat to eat all the food, for proper dosing. I've found that for a medication thought to be neutral tasting, mixed with highly preferred foods, 24 hours of food deprivation can be necessary to ensure the cat will eat all the food. And for the owner, being around cats approaching 24 hours of deprivation is not fun. Finally, some medication tastes are strong; it may not be possible to mask the taste or overcome the aversion with any reasonable amount of deprivation. Thus this method works, but not always, and not very well.

Yet another method is to coat the pill with something slippery and/or good tasting, such as butter or tuna juice. I've never seen the pill turned into a positive reinforcer; it may be rendered less aversive or neutral. The coating may stimulate salivation (a classical instance of classical conditioning). However, food treats following the pill, preceded by the usual food arrival cues before the pill, might set up the same classical conditioning. Then there are practical problems: the pill can smear, shred, dissolve, stick to your finger, or all of the above, all at once.

Two other approaches involve gadgets. One is basically a pill syringe. You load it with the pill, open the cat's mouth, aim the syringe, and push the plunger. It does help put the pill dead center and all the way back. Its chief appeal, however, is probably to owners who are afraid they'll get bit when they put their fingers in the cat's mouth. This is therefore a gadget for force, not a training aid. Neither the cat nor the owner learns much. The appearance or sound of the syringe is yet another stimulus the cat may learn to avoid. And it may lead to other sorts of bites or scratches – a general problem with gadgets for force.

The other gadget is an empty gelatin capsule. You grind up the pill and stuff it in the capsule. The capsule is said to slide down the cat's throat more easily than the pill. I've never tried it, but it has potential for making the pill less aversive, particularly for large pills or those that have to be divided, leaving rough edges. It won't do anything for making the restraint less aversive. I wouldn't expect use of either gadget to lead to the cat coming to you for the pill. However, the capsule might be used in conjunction with husbandry training, to render some pills less aversive.

Thus a brief survey of the alternatives to training reveals a number of manipulations. Some of them involve considerable effort. Some depend on "stealth", they don't always work. Others are simply glorified restraint and force. None of them get better results than training, and most aren't as good. In general, husbandry training provides a simpler, more effective, less stressful approach.

Another interesting question is, why is food always the reinforcer here? Food is a handy reinforcer, but there are other choices, and sometimes better ones. I happened to hit a problem specific to food reinforcers early in the game. I was using a food treat to reinforce swallowing a pill that was an antibiotic. The very next time, I found that the treat was no longer a reinforcer, but a different tasting treat was. I had hit the Garcia effect. This is a phenomenon of one-shot operant learning specific to certain pairs of stimuli: the animal develops a taste aversion to a formerly neutral taste that precedes nausea. The problem is, many medications, including antibiotics, have side effects that include nausea. The solution is, use a non-food reinforcer. I immediately switched to a social reinforcer, petting the cat and giving it attention after it swallowed the pill. This worked fine. Social reinforcers in general have much to be said for them: they're readily available, they don't satiate, and they're fun to give. A specific advantage here, however, is they don't hit the Garcia effect. They work well for husbandry training.

Finally, given that this training takes time, perhaps it should be invested in before the cat gets sick. That way it would be in place when you need it. My cats have all needed enough pills and soon enough that the training was soon accomplished! But some cats are very healthy for most of their lives. It might make sense to train them first with empty capsules. This combines husbandry training and preventive medicine.

HAIRBALLS

While grooming, cats ingest fur, which is basically indigestible. It's expelled in one of two ways: the cat vomits up the hairball, or it's passed in the feces. A number of commercial products are available to cause the hairball to pass. They're all basically petroleum jelly with flavoring to make them palatable to cats. Petroleum jelly itself works just fine, and some cats will eat it if offered. On the whole, however, more cats will eat the commercial product more readily. Thus the first training approach is simply to use the more palatable form. If the cat will lick it off your finger, problem solved.

If not, the usual advice is to smear the product on the cat's paw. The cat then licks it off, ingesting the product. This seems like a clever application of built-in behavior common to all cats (grooming). It would appear to render irrelevant questions of palatability. The cat has to lick it off, so what does it matter how it tastes? However, any owner who has tried this can tell you about side effects: the cat flicks its paw, spraying petroleum jelly around the house.

The solution is to rub the product well into the cat's fur. This works fairly well, but is aversive to the animals. Avoidance behavior can develop, including the animal running away when it sees the tube, hears it being opened, or smells it. One solution is, still use the more palatable form. It won't make it nonaversive, but it may make it less aversive. The cat will run away less. It may also be the case that the aversiveness lies in rubbing the product in the fur, not in the taste, even when the cat won't eat it if offered. If this is the case, given the more palatable form, the cat may be more likely to lick it off than flick it off.

A positive reinforcer following the application of the product would probably help too. A food reinforcer might be bad here, as the manufacturer warns against giving the product with food. I have no idea if this is really dangerous to the cat; it may just cause the food to pass too, thus wasting some nutrition. But it's another example of how non-food reinforcers can offer advantages. I have found that social reinforcers following applications have reduced avoidance.

I still have to deal with a certain level of avoidance, however. So I keep cues hidden; I'm trying to prevent learning here. So I use different places and occasions to apply the product. I avoid approaching the cat in a distinctive way. I open the tube in another room. I wait a minute or two after I open it before applying the product.

APPLYING TOPICAL SOLUTIONS

I've had to apply skin creams, anti-fungal ointments, antibiotic solutions, and eye drops of various sorts. Most of this is just plain inherently aversive, over and above the aversiveness of any restraint used. So training has had a limited role here.

There is a way to reduce aversiveness of topical solutions, however, at least for cats: warm it to body temperature. Room temperature solutions are aversive to cats when applied to their skin, eyes or ears. So I put the tube or bottle in my pocket an hour or two before it's applied. This brings it pretty close to cat temperature. That makes it less aversive for my cats. When I don't have time for this, sometimes I can microwave the solution for 10 to 20 seconds. That's possible if the container isn't metal and the medication isn't affected by quick heating; both are usually the case.

I have also trained a "release word". I hold the cat while applying the solution. When I'm done, I say "OK", then release the cat. Since the release word is given just before termination of restraint, it becomes a discriminative stimulus for opportunity for escape. Struggling is not reinforced by escape until the release word has been given. Or, to put it another way, the cat is on a multiple schedule in which the second component is discriminated by the release word. The effect has been some reduction in struggling.

The main contingency, however, is one that I

avoid establishing: payoff for struggling. I make sure that struggling does not delay or terminate application of the solution. Thus struggling is not negatively reinforced by avoidance or escape.

Finally, as with hairballs, I prevent giving avoidance cues. I open the tube or bottle in another room. I wait a few minutes after opening before applying it. If I'm using the microwave to warm it, I wait a few minutes after the microwave stops before applying it.

CLIPPING CLAWS

This is fun example of interactions between behavior and care. Training enables you to clip the cat's claws. Keeping them clipped reduces the amount of scratching the cat does. It also makes it easier to handle the cat, and in particular to give the cat a bath when necessary.

Some cats need little training here. As long as you don't cut into the quick, you can easily restrain the cat, clip its claws, and release it.

Other cats tolerate little touching of their feet. A great deal or restraint would be needed to clip their claws if no training were used. One of my cats was like this. Before I'd owned him, he had lived on the streets for a while. At the point I became his owner, if you even touched his feet, he'd bite you. Indeed, he'd usually bite if touched anywhere that his head and shoulders.

My first goal was simply to get him to tolerate touch and inspection. I aimed at extinction of respondent conditioning (touch in the past had presumably been paired with aversive stimuli; I now removed the pairing) and establishment of new operant behavior (alternative acceptable behaviors). This was accomplished by gradual increase in the amount of touch, while at the same time establishing new contingencies.

The contingencies included time outs for aggression (snapping or biting resulted in a five minute time out), and food treats for tolerating touch (letting me inspect one of his feet resulted in a food treat). After a few weeks, the touch itself became a positive reinforcer. I gradually moved from the head and shoulders to the rest of his body.

After a few more weeks, I could clip an individual claw. Cooperation was again reinforced with a food treat. Gradually, criterion was raised to letting me clip two claws, then a whole paw, then two paws, and so on. Here too, food reinforcers were eventually phased out in favor of social reinforcers.

After about a year, I could clip the claws on all four paws. It is interesting to note that my former problem child is now easier than most cats to clip.

FUTURES

I'd like to train my cats to accept brushing their teeth. I plan gradual increases here. First I'll start brushing just the canines briefly and gently. Then I'll spend more time brushing, and gradually brush more firmly. Then I'll move to teeth further back in the mouth. Finally, I should be able to brush all the teeth effectively. I'm hoping the meat flavored toothpaste will make this more palatable.

I can take my cats' temperatures, but it's essentially all restraint. Husbandry training that would make it easier seems possible and desirable.

I'd also like to take my cats' respiration and heart rates. Naturally, these increase if you stress the animal while taking them; measurement artifacts thus become inevitable. I am looking at ways to get the measurements with negligible stress on the cat.

VOL 17, NO 3, 1992. As more trainers recognize the advantages of training husbandry behaviors, new and more detailed questions about techniques and behavior maintenance arise. Husbandry behaviors are a critical component to a good training program. The spread of husbandry training can be directly attributed to IMATA and its annual conference and quarterly magazine. Here, five experienced trainers offer responses to this multi-faceted question.

How to Maintain Voluntary Blood Sampling with Dolphins

QUESTION: 1) Our dolphins have been trained to relax in a perfect position for taking blood, but they always seem to get tense when the needle is actually inserted and we fear they may not remain in position long enough for blood to actually be drawn. How can this be avoided?

2) Does your facility allow only the veterinarian to take blood, or are animal care staff allowed to take blood in some cases?

3) Does your facility have a preference between butterfly needles or regular needles?

ANSWER 1: 1) It sounds like you have, in fact, inserted the needle but because the animal tenses up you take it out right away. No matter how well the behavior is trained, there is a possibility that the animal may not hold after the needle is inserted. You can increase your chances for success, however, by applying the following guidelines: Establish your expectations of the animal during the training before you ever use a needle. The animal should know that it needs to remain in position-no matter what-until the bridge. Practice duration of the presentation so the animal will hold steady for at least one minute (plenty of time to draw blood). During training, regardless of whatever you use to simulate the needle, only "stick" the animal once per set-up so that it will relax after the stick. When you first stick an animal in training, you may want to bridge immediately, reinforcing the animal for accepting the stick. The next step is to lengthen the time the animal is expected to hold after the stick. By the time you are ready to use a needle, the animal should be conditioned to set-up, feel a stick of a sharp object, and then hold for up to a minute. The animal should also know that if it pulls away at anytime before the bridge the behavior will be repeated.

Your next step is to put your training to the test and try to take blood. It's not unusual for animals to look tense when the needle is inserted; that doesn't mean that they are going to pull away. We have one dolphin who has been giving blood for over four years and during that procedure her eyes still look twice as big as normal, yet she holds well. If an animal does pull away, it needs to know that it is wrong, and the behavior should be repeated. As with any behavior, use common sense and your best judgement when dealing with problems should they occur. One additional suggestion, when you insert the needle, put it in at what would be your maximum depth. The animal is more likely to hold if you need to pull the needle out slightly than if you are too shallow and have to push it in further.

2) We feel that it is extremely important at our facility for members of the training staff to be experienced at taking blood. The veterinarian cannot be at any facility 24-hours a day, seven days a week. We have had several occasions where we needed to get a blood sample when the veterinarian wasn't available. We have also found that when an animal isn't feeling well and it's important to get blood, that they may refuse to set-up or give blood with the veterinarian present. They may only cooperate with the trainers they are most comfortable with. What is important is not who takes the blood, but to get the blood when you need it with as little stress as possible to the animal. The veterinarian should train each person and strict guidelines should be set. We have found that limiting the number of people is important, but it is necessary to have experienced people from both the veterinary and the training staff.

3) My personal preference is for the butterfly set-up. We used a needle on a syringe for a couple of years and then the butterfly set-up (21 gauge 3/4") for more than two years. We have had many occasions where we probably wouldn't have gotten blood if it weren't for the advantages of the butterfly.

Debra Marrin-Cooney,
MarineWorld Africa USA

ANSWER 2: 1) Although the animal may tense up at the initial insertion, once the needle is in they will usually relax. To minimize or avoid tensing as much as possible, the animal must be desensitized to the initial poke. This, of course, can be done by successively approximating the needle with a fingernail or snap of a rubber band. When the animal is accepting this well, have the blood-taker there to actually insert the needle into the fluke, with furthering your training program as the goal rather than actually drawing a blood sample. You will also strengthen the behavior by varying the amount of time that you ask the animal to remain stationary for the presentation. Sometimes it helps to rub the fluke down while bleeding thus giving the animal tactile stimulation other than just the poke of the needle. Try to have one or two additional persons with you during training sessions as much as possible to simulate the presence of the vet. Remember that even the most cooperative of dolphins has a bad day from time to time. If you find that you have an animal that just doesn't seem to be taking you seriously, you may want to feed him out early one day in preparation for your work the next.

2) Since we have a consulting veterinarian at our facility, the curator does most of the blood drawing from cetaceans. If there is an unusual circumstance, or if the vet is at the park on one of his routine visits, he will do the honors. Drawing blood from pinnipeds is usually done by the vet.

3) We use regular needles for drawing blood, primarily because that is what we're familiar with. There certainly do seem to be some real advantages to a butterfly, however, especially with fluke presentations or squirmy animals. From a training perspective it doesn't seem that it would make much difference.

Training Staff
Sea Life Park

ANSWER 3: 1) Here at Brookfield Zoo, we desensitize our dolphins as much as possible by using our fingernails, probes, etc., to get them ready for a stick. When actually inserting a needle, we do so very slowly so that we don't startle the animal. If the animal gets tense, we wait for them to relax before proceeding. In the beginning stages, just do a needle stick without drawing blood, to make the needle stick more positive. We have also found that once the needle is fully inserted, our dolphins seem to relax while the blood is being drawn.

2) At Brookfield Zoo, trainers are allowed to draw blood samples from the dolphins. This was done only after trainers attended "classes" in blood drawing presented by our veterinarian. We have found it to be more convenient for both departments, since it frees up training time and we don't have to work around a vet's schedule. It is important for trainers and the vet staff to communicate closely so that the proper tests are done on each blood sample taken.

3) At our facility, both regular and butterfly needles are used. The type of needle used is the choice of the person actually taking the blood sample. Some prefer a regular needle, as they have a better feel for when the needle is actually in the blood vessel; others prefer the butterfly needle, as it allows for animal movement without the needle becoming dislodged.

Seven Seas Training Staff
Brookfield Zoo

ANSWER 4: 1) When training and maintaining voluntary fluke presents for blood samples with cetaceans, conditioning the relaxed ventral-up position is the first step, but only a fraction of the complete behavior. The animal needs to be desensitized to unfamiliar and sometimes uncomfortable stimuli and remain still and in position. We begin introducing this portion of the behavior after the animal is holding in the ventral-up position comfortably while having their flukes held, touched, and rubbed. During this time we are also increasing the duration of the behavior. We then begin introducing novel stimuli to the fluke area by applying pressure on and around the vein with a finer, capped syringe or blunt end of a pen or pencil. We may also tap, slap, or rap on the flukes and bridge the animal for remaining still and relaxed. One very effective method for approximating the needle stick is using a rubber band snapped lightly at first, then adding a bit of a sting. If the animal accepts this while calmly waiting for the bridge, then you are very close to obtaining a successful blood sample. If you have an exceptionally sensitive animal you may even consider approximating the size of the needle. Start with a 25-gauge needle; if the animal holds for this, you could use a 22-gauge next time, then a 20-gauge, and finally a 19 T.W. (thin wall). We reinforce the animals very well (using a variety of reinforcements) for both successful approximations and successful sticks. 'Successful" means maintaining a relaxed position until the bridge or completion of the behavior. We never continue to hold the flukes if the animal is struggling or attempting to move away. Once trained, be careful not to associate the bridge with withdrawing the needle. Hold the behavior longer once the needle is removed.

2) The fluke presentation should be asked for routinely (even daily) to maintain a very high reinforcement history. We have found that periodic approximations (once a week or even every other week) with the veterinarian (or the person who normally takes the blood) will do much to maintain and strengthen the behavior. It is beneficial to have the vet bring all the normal paraphernalia he would have when obtaining blood to the approximation sessions also. The animals are aware of the different sets of stimuli surrounding "real" vs. approximation-so make them as similar as possible. On our trained show animals, only veterinarians or management level animal care personnel draw blood samples.

3) Some of the smaller and more flighty cetaceans seem to benefit by using a butterfly needle. Their flukes are more likely to shake a bit which makes it hard to keep a syringe in place. With our Commerson's dolphins we often use a butterfly needle which allows for some movement without injuring the fluke.
Julie Scardina-Ludwig,
Sea World of California

ANSWER 5: 1) We tried a variety of needle desensitization techniques with our dolphins, such as gentle snaps with a rubber band and finger pressure. While these might have been helpful early on, our best success came from doing what we called "quick sticks." At a variety of depths we would gently and quickly insert and remove the needle. Gradually we would increase the insertion time from a split second to several minutes, depending on how stable the dolphin was during that session. We noticed that the dolphins would occasionally wiggle a bit when the needle was first inserted, but usually calmed right down. If they didn't calm down immediately, we would end the trial. It is important to take the needle out before the animal gets "antsy," so that you can reinforce the stable position. If the stick is quick enough, the animals rarely wiggle, allowing you to reinforce stable positioning. Sometimes we would just pierce the skin, at other times we would go in as much as 1/4". We never did more than one "quick stick" in a session.

Once the dolphin tolerates a quick stick reliably, vary how long you hold the needle in place from session to session. If the dolphin thinks that it will be a long process each time, the behavior is more likely to break down. Although we set the animals up in blood position at least One session per day, we never did a stick more than twice week.

Whether we were planning to insert the needle, we always had all the necessary equipment present for the animals to see. Once the animals are reliably stable for samples, it is still a good idea to continue practice set-ups as a part of you regular husbandry training.
Training Staff
New England Aquarium

Marine Mammals: Public Display and Research

In 1992 the following paper won the award for Outstanding Trained Behavior at the 20th Annual IMATA Conference held in the Bahamas. This article appears in *Marine Mammals: Public Display and Research*, Vol. 2, No. 1, 1996. The steps taken to create a training program for the sea otters at the John G. Shedd Aquarium is described in detail. Although sea otters had been trained to do a few behaviors for many years in Japan, no U.S. facility had tried to extensively train their otters. The success of this program has prompted other facilities to begin training otters as well.

Initiation of a Sea Otter Training Program

by Ken Ramirez, Meg Hudson, and Lisa Takaki
John G. Shedd Aquarium

ABSTRACT

Since 1990, the John G. Shedd Aquarium has housed five Alaskan sea otters (*Enhydra lutris*). All five otters were orphaned, rehabilitated pups that were brought to the aquarium in 1989 and 1990. During their rehabilitation, the otters became accustomed to human attention, which was helpful in their early handling. As the otters grew, there was concern over the possibility of increased aggression in older animals. This paper focuses on the transition to formalized training with our sea otters. Through the utilization of standard training techniques we have had some excellent results, particularly with husbandry behaviors. Sea otters presented the training staff with unique training challenges. We will describe the various steps taken to implement a formal training program, as well as examine mistakes that should be avoided in initiating such a program. Ultimately, we hope to point out the advantages we've seen by introducing our otters to formalized training.

INTRODUCTION

The John G. Shedd Aquarium's Marine Mammal Department was created to provide care to the various marine mammals and birds housed in our new Oceanarium. Opened in April 1991, the Oceanarium houses beluga whales, Pacific white-sided dolphins, harbor seals, penguins, and Alaskan sea otters. Due to the obvious needs of the different animal groups, the aquarium created positions within the Marine Mammal Department called Animal Care Specialists. Their jobs include diet preparation, water quality, veterinary care, exhibit maintenance, basic husbandry, and training. Particular emphasis is placed on training, since the aquarium considers this to be a critical component of proper animal care for all animals, including sea otters.

The purposes of this paper are: 1) to address our success and failures for those new facilities that might express an interest in displaying sea otters, 2) to document our techniques on sea otter training, and 3) to discuss the benefits derived from training otters. In addition, we will address concerns of those who may be skeptical about creating a training program for otters.

HISTORY

To understand the direction we have taken with our otter training program, it is probably important to first review the history of our otters. All five of the sea otters were orphaned as pups. Four of them were rescued from the *Exxon Valdez* oil spill in the spring of 1989, and the fifth otter was orphaned one year later. The four pups from the oil spill were in the Alaskan rehabilitation center for over six months before the U.S. Fish and Wildlife Service asked the Shedd Aquarium to house them. Each animal had a variety of medical concerns that required special care, diet, handling, and medication.

The animals were brought to the aquarium over a year-and-a-half before the completion of their habitat; therefore, a special temporary facility was set up in one of the original aquarium galleries. At that time we began to learn about the otter's curious nature and destructive capabilities. These included unscrewing nuts tightened by machine, scaling vertical walls, and moving boulders five times their weight. This information eventually proved helpful in designing their new habitat.

While waiting for construction to be completed, we concentrated on desensitizing the otters for the eventual move to the Oceanarium (Ramirez, 1991). Because the otters were desensitized to tactile interaction, we carried them by hand to their new exhibit. Throughout the first two years, we found their tractability to be very helpful. Most of the otters had a problematic medical history. We were able to intubate medication, handle them for close-up exams, and take regular weights. But we were also conscious of the potential dangers handling might cause as they grew older. Early in our program we began more formal training which would lead to more protected contact.

FORMAL TRAINING

Before beginning formal training, we assumed that standard operant conditioning techniques would be used. But first we wanted to get a feel for an otter's attention span, as well as their likes and dislikes. We experimented with various reinforcers, bridging techniques, gating methods, and taught name recognition. After almost two years, including training experimentation, finishing the rehabilitation process, and getting settled into the Oceanarium, we were finally ready to begin formal training. We relied heavily on information about river otter training, as well as general conditioning techniques. We quickly found sea otters to be unique in many respects. Their early handling history made it difficult at first to move away from a totally hands-on approach. Instead, we had to slowly approximate the animals to less frequent handling.

Adult sea otters have a history of aggression, especially males. Consequently, we wanted to move away from unprotected contact before experiencing any problems. At the same time, we did not want to deprive the animals of a type of contact they seem to enjoy. Today, we still allow unprotected contact on a limited basis. However, no staff member is required to carry an otter unprotected. Formal training was designed to move toward controlled contact. As formal training started, we found the otters innate curiosity to be helpful in speeding up their learning process.

EARLY CONDITIONING

The first major step toward formal training was to organize our feeding methods by establishing a stationing order. Within less than one week, the animals learned to station for feedings in positions relative to one another (i.e.: animal "A" would always station to the left of animal "B," and "B" to the left of "C," etcetera). This technique allowed us to move animals from pool to pool and still maintain an order; each animal had a reference point. While reinforcing an otter for stationing, the animals would swim away from station to eat if offered large or shelled food items. Consequently, a key to early stationing success was the use of small, but frequent, reinforcers.

Another important step was to introduce a conditioned stimulus (bridging stimulus). We selected a verbal bridge and paired delivery of the various reinforcers with the word "GOOD." It took several months for the otters to fully understand the meaning of the bridge. Although the bridging stimulus eventually proved very important, we had no trouble beginning and progressing with other training goals prior to the conditioned stimulus being firmly established.

The next step was to introduce targeting. Targets had to be made out of a durable material so that the otters would not destroy them. Due to the otters' natural curiosity, their early tendency was to pull the target out of our hands and use it as a new toy. They quickly learned that targeting was followed by reinforcement. Because of our experience in training cetaceans and pinnipeds, our natural inclination was to expect them to target with their nose. However, a sea otters' natural instinct seems to be to bat it with their paw. We accepted either nose or paw targeting initially.

Within a month, all five otters were keenly focused on our targets. We used both hand and buoy targets. A closed hand was preferable to an open hand, since extended thumbs and fingers are too tempting for an otter. We increased the amount of time they would stay stationary on a target, which we called extended targeting. Interestingly, that was one of our more difficult, yet important, basic behaviors. Getting a sea otter to stay still for more that a couple of seconds is a major accomplishment. We introduced "target-following" on the water surface, underwater, and onto land. That eventually led to teaching basic A-to-B behaviors. The most important function of targeting for sea otters is keeping their busy paws occupied while husbandry work is being conducted.

TACTILE INTERACTION

A major goal of our training program was to facilitate husbandry and medical work. Once targeting was firmly established, we began controlled tactile interaction. Buoy targeting was implemented to keep the otters' paws and mouths occupied, and allow us to move from the original free-form tactile interaction to a controlled tactile interaction. Because one can never be sure when, where, or how a veterinarian will want to examine an animal, we decided to desensitize each otter to every imaginable form of tactile contact.

We first touched areas farthest from the mouth and paws and only reinforced if the otter maintained contact with a target. We slowly approximated from brief touches, to extended touches, rubs then holds. We used the same slow approximations on their flippers, paws, pockets, and tail. After many months of tactile work, we began working around the head. We wanted each otter to be comfortable with being touched on or around the nose, neck, ears, eyes, and mouth. It is important to note that each otter progressed at a different rate. At no time is a trainer required to touch an animal if they are at all uncomfortable or fearful that the otter might bite. Both the otter and trainer should be totally relaxed and comfortable with the process. For safety reasons, we always insist that targeting be maintained while any type of tactile work is done.

ADDITIONAL HUSBANDRY

There are a number of other important husbandry behaviors that are not as dependent on tactile contact. One of our goals was to eliminate tactile interaction if ever necessary; we look at alternatives to methods we had used when our otters were pups. Instead of carrying otters by hand to move them or for weighing, we used targeting as one way of moving an animal from place to place. Additionally, training an animal to go into a kennel proved beneficial in a number of situations, including moving an animal, temporary separation, or weighing.

Administration of medication and vitamins can be difficult with sea otters. Because of their manner of eating, you can't hide pills in their food.

C.J. Casson,, in 1990, reported on the Seattle Aquarium's use of "ice muffins" to hide medication in frozen ice cubes. We, too, have used something similar in the form of krill cubes. But we also continued and extended a behavior used when the otters were pups and taking formula. We continually reinforce our otters for taking fluid, squid, or cut-up fish out of a syringe. We have experimented with various mixtures so that the animals are used to various tastes. This, then, allows us to add vitamins or medication to the syringe if needed.

Formal training also made gating and separation much easier. We had managed to gain some behavioral control over the otters and, thus, could now manage them more successfully. A simple task of moving from one area to another went from chaos, as in the early days, to some semblance of order and predictability today.

VARIETY

One challenge has been keeping the otter's attention. They are easily distracted by new things, so we found we had to desensitize them to anything and everything new. Although easily distracted by new things, we have found it important to constantly provide them with variety. One way of doing that is to conduct our training and play sessions in different locations-on exhibit, in reserve pools, or even in hallways.

We found it important to provide the otters with a variety of toys. If we didn't they found and made their own. It is also beneficial to provide them a variety of special sessions, play times, or unique reinforcers. Sea otters love shell fish; giving them mussels, clams, and crabs is important for their diet and they also provide variety. Hiding these items under a bucket, or a pile of snow, makes the otter look and search for their food, which is a natural foraging behavior.

Training sessions never consist of just husbandry training. We constantly use our imagination to create games or fun behaviors for the otters. Spins, catches, retrievals, porpoising, and vocals are just some of the behaviors we have started training.

PRACTICAL USES

For us, the most gratifying part of our sea otter training program is the practical uses we've already seen. Obvious things like gating, weighing, and moving otters are very beneficial. But we've also seen benefits in some unexpected, or at least unplanned, ways.

The formula, or syringe behavior, proved very beneficial earlier this year when an otter swallowed a portion of a surgical glove. Our veterinarian felt that it was important to try to get the animal to vomit the object up. We put Syrup of Ipecac in a squid formula and give it to the otter via a syringe. She got the complete dose and the medicine had the desired effect. Although it was not designed for this, the behavior proved beneficial. One adverse side effect did occur, it caused the animal to dislike the syringe for months afterwards.

External treatment of various parts of the otters' body became another practical benefit derived from training. A number of cuts, bruises, or tender areas have been much easier to examine since the otters allow us to handle them. As an example, we were able to treat a cut on the youngest otter's paw. Last year, we had the need to examine the teeth of one of our female otters after she got a metal cap stuck on a molar. She now allows total mouth, gum, and tooth exams. We have even been able to administer eye ointment to one of our biggest otters after she developed an unusual opacity in her right eye.

Even fun behaviors, like retrievals, have been helpful. Retrievals, we feel, have cut down on the otters' desire to steal props or water-quality bottles. At least if they do steal them, they are willing to bring them back instead of keeping them for a week.

FUTURE

We are still concentrating on many of the husbandry behaviors. A major, but difficult, goal with sea otters is voluntary blood sampling. Their veins are difficult to find and they seem more sensitive to pain that other marine mammals, which compounds the challenge for us. We are approaching venipuncture slowly, and experimenting with several different methods of positioning the body.

We have also started exploring the possibilities of training for research projects, particularly non-invasive projects such as cognition work and taction related sensory projects. As our otters mature, there is the potential for breeding. The possibilities of monitoring pregnancy and birth with a trained sea otter could prove exciting.

CONCLUSION

There are many future possibilities since our sea otter training program is still in its infancy, but the practical benefits are already very evident to us. Basic training and conditioning techniques have certainly proven effective with sea otters, but their attention span and curiosity make them a continual challenge. Their strength and dexterity add to the challenge of providing adequate and safe housing. When working with sea otters it is important to remember that aggression does increase with age; we found that to be particularly true with our male. But we also discovered that training helps keep that aggression under control. The training program has certainly made handling and day-to-day care easier, and has paid off in a number of medical situations.

Within this profession, we have always maintained that training is a critical part of good animal care. There have been numerous papers written and discussions held examining the benefits to training and behavioral enrichment. Training certainly provides mental stimulation for the animals, it encourages physical exercise, and it promotes cooperative behavior, which includes husbandry behaviors. But if we truly believe that this is good for the animals, why do so many zoos and aquariums only train animals that are going to be a show or presentation? Manpower is often the problem. Sometimes it just isn't financially feasible to put too much energy into training display animals. This ultimately sends mixed messages to the public and to our critics, because we don't always practice what we preach. One of our next big challenges in the animal care field is to show more people, management, the public, and fellow keepers and trainers the benefits of training. Virtually everyone in a marine mammal program has seen the benefits of training the animals under their care. If it's good for a whale, dolphin, or sea lion, why not a penguin, seal, or otter?

ACKNOWLEDGEMENTS

The authors of this paper would like to acknowledge the incredible support of the entire marine mammal staff. The team approach to training this group of otters and the ideas that came from the entire staff have contributed to the success of our otter program. Particular thanks to Jim Robinett, Denise Dale, Pete Davey, Faith Dunham, Greg Dye, Jennifer Foskit, William Harshaw, Donnarose Janosek-Christakis, Kris Landin, Bryan Mathie, Laura Monaco, Manny Onate, and Mark Ryan.

LITERATURE CITED

Casson, C.J. (1990). Administering oral medications to sea otters, *Enhydra lutris*. In N. Hecker (Ed.), Proceedings of the 18th annual conference of the International Marine Animal Trainers Association (pp.12-19).

Ramirez, K. (1991). Using desensitization techniques to prepare animals for transport. In S. Allen (Ed.), Proceedings of the 19th annual conference of the International Marine Animal Trainers Association (pp. 142-148).

Conference Proceedings

1987 IMATA Conference, New Orleans, Louisiana, USA. Accurate weights on dolphins and whales are an important part of good husbandry. Stretcher training provides one way to get weights easily with cetaceans. Unfortunately, the set-up and placement of equipment for this type of training can make this behavior unrealistic in some facilities.

Stretcher Training for Handling Whales and Dolphins

by Debra Skaar
SeaCo, Inc.

ABSTRACT

In an attempt to increase efficiency of routine weighing of three beluga whales, each whale was trained to swim into a stretcher, initially held in place, submerged, and secured by the side of the pen. The animal was trained, using approximations to swim over the stretcher and station on a target. The stretcher was gradually lifted until the animal was resting on it. The stretcher and animal could then be positioned for lifting by a crane. This has proven to be a very convenient way of weighing the whales, it involves the help of only a few people, and it takes less time than previously used techniques. By having the whales swim into the stretcher and position there, other types of clinical studies could be conducted. This technique seems generally applicable to other small odontocetes.

OBJECTIVE

Marine mammals at the Naval Ocean Systems Center in San Diego are housed in floating pens. Each pen, consisting of a net enclosure, is surrounded by a three-foot-wide wooden walkway. Weighing or moving an animal has traditionally required hoisting the net to create a small, shallow area in which to restrain and move the animal onto a stretcher. Although the procedure was straightforward, it was time consuming, required several people to raise and secure the net, and was difficult with larger animals because of their greater bulk. To minimize these difficulties it was decided to train the animals to voluntarily swim into the stretcher for weighing.

EQUIPMENT

The stretcher for the whales is 11 ft. long and 4.5 ft. wide and supported by two aluminum poles. The stretcher is composed of herculon mesh with two-inch nylon webbing for reinforcement of the seams. Holes are provided in the bed of the stretcher to accommodate the pectoral flippers. The dolphin stretcher is made of the same material as the whale stretcher but measures 9 ft. x 3.5 ft.

Initially the stretcher is suspended between

two wooden poles (10 ft. x 4 in. x 4 in.) from the side of the pen. One end of each pole is secured to the deck of the pen using a clamp while the other end extends over the water. An eye screw is attached to the extended end of each pole and a metal hook is secured midway along the length of each pole adjacent to the side of the pen. A line is attached to each end of both stretcher poles using metal hooks. To support the stretcher from the wood poles, the stretcher lines nearest the edge of the pen are secured to the mid-length hooks of the wooden poles while the lines on the far side of the stretcher are placed through the eye screws at the end of the wooden poles and secured with quick release knots. Should any problem arise, the knots can be quickly untied to permit the far side of the stretcher to fall into the water and release the animal.

CONDITIONING TECHNIQUE

In the early phases of training, the stretcher is submerged approximately 6 ft. underwater. The animal is stationed to the right of the stretcher and is guided by approximation over the stretcher while remaining stationed on the target. Swimming forward out of the stretcher is permissible in the early stages as it is important for the animal to recognize that it can get out of the stretcher by moving forward rather than by backing out or rolling over the side.

Once the animal is comfortable swimming into the stretcher and stationing on the target, the behavior of swimming into and out of the stretcher can be brought under stimulus control. The animal is stationed at the left end of the stretcher. The conditioned stimulus or signal for swimming into the stretcher consists of tapping the animal on the rostrum using the right hand and then extending the right hand straight out to the right-hand side. The trainer should place the target at the right end of the stretcher and bridge and reinforce when the animal swims to the target and stations there. The animal can then be guided into the stretcher. Once the animal responds to the conditioned stimulus, the trainer can eliminate the target at the end of the stretcher and instead place the target in the stretcher for the animal to station on. The animal remains in the stretcher until the signal is given to swim out. This is simply a tap on the water at the front of the stretcher. Once this is brought under stimulus control, the stretcher can be raised using incremental approximations until the poles of the stretcher are at the surface of the water with a slight depression in the bed of the stretcher for the animal to swim into.

When the animal has been conditioned to enter the Stretcher at its surface position, the wooden poles can be replaced by four assistants, each holding one of the lines attached to the ends of the stretcher poles while the animal swims onto the stretcher. During the final stage of training the animal is lifted out of the water (using a crane unless the four people are extremely strong), weighed or moved, placed back into the water and signaled to swim out.

RESULTS

The finished product is actually a chain of behaviors. The original stationing point is to the left side of the stretcher next to the trainer. The signal is given for the animal to swim into the stretcher and station on a target or the trainer's hand. The animal remains in the stretcher until signaled to swim out and return to the original stationing position for reinforcement. To reach this point however, the animal is heavily reinforced while in the stretcher during the initial approximations. A variable magnitude of reinforcement may be used to maintain this behavior.

DISCUSSION

Marine mammal care begins with preventive maintenance. As we all know, once an animal shows symptoms of a problem, that problem or disease is usually in its advanced stages. Periodic physicals which include blood samples, blowhole cultures, weights, and measurements need to be maintained for early detection of a possible problem. Conditioning animals to behaviorally accept routine examinations is easier on both the animals and the trainers and decreases the time spent for these examinations.

Weighing the animal is an important part of preventive maintenance and to be efficient, the animals should be conditioned to swim into a stretcher. The technique I have discussed has worked well at the Naval Ocean Systems Center. By conditioning our animals to swim into a stretcher, we can accomplish weighing with fewer people and in less time than with previously used techniques. I feel this procedure would also be beneficial to oceanariums which house their animals in open water or natural settings. Oceanariums in which the animals are in a large tank where it is not feasible to lower the water level for routine examinations or in settings in which there are many animals housed together may also find this technique useful.

VOL 24, NO 1, 1999. The following article was presented as a paper at the 25th Annual IMATA Conference in Baltimore, Maryland, USA, in November of 1997. As trainers we are often presented with difficult training dilemmas, particularly when we must teach an animal to cooperate with a potentially uncomfortable procedure. The use of positive reinforcement has revolutionized our ability to train some very difficult behaviors. However, from time to time we are faced with important medical procedures that the animal finds uncomfortable, and consequently we are challenged with finding a way to make those procedures positive. As children (or even adults) we might recall the fear of a visit to the dentist or a dislike of the taste of an important medication. Our parents insisted that we cooperate, and if they were wise, they followed our eventual cooperation with something positive, leading to better cooperation on our part at future occasions. What? Your parents didn't do that? The point is that sometimes gaining initial cooperation in difficult procedures requires the use of advanced techniques such as negative reinforcers as described in chapter 9, "Advanced Techniques & Concepts." Skilled trainers can use these techniques at appropriate times with great success while still maintaining a positive attitude and relationship with the animal. Here is an example of just such a case at the Brookfield Zoo.

Passive Restraint Training in *Tursiops truncatus*

by Rita Stacey, Doug Messinger, Greg Dye, Wendy Komar, Jennifer McGee, Cheryl Mika, Shawn Peek, Janet Sustman, Tim Sullivan, and Jackie Weiner
Chicago Zoological Society, Brookfield Zoo

A medical condition and prescribed long-term treatment of a seven year old female *Tursiops truncatus* housed at the Seven Seas marine mammal complex at Brookfield Zoo prompted the staff to look at alternative methods to train cooperative medical behaviors. The behaviors trained included consistent gating into a medical pool and passive restraint for daily intramuscular injections.

Over the post decade, we as professional animal trainers have made tremendous strides in improving the care we give to our animals through our training programs. It is not at all uncommon today to see cetaceans and pinnipeds in zoos and aquariums around the world enthusiastically participating in their own health care through voluntary blood sampling and ultrasound exams. In fact, as we have gotten so good at anticipating our animals needs that few medical procedures pose themselves as large obstacles.

Earlier this year at Brookfield Zoo's Seven Seas, we were faced with a challenging training situation. Akea, a seven-year old female Atlantic bottlenose dolphin, developed a respiratory medical condition that required a daily intramuscular injection for several months. The treatment of Amikacin was to begin immediately, leaving us no time to condition Akea for a voluntary injection behavior through normal positively reinforced approximations. The administration of the medication was time sensitive and had to be given at the same time every day. Delaying or missing an injection was not an option.

Initially, we began the procedure by having Akea gate into a medical pool where water tight gates could be installed, allowing us to lower the water to waist level so that we could restrain her to safely administer the medication. The 30-second procedure proved to be very labor intensive, usually requiring eight people to be on hand and lasted about an hour. The effects of the procedure were felt immediately. We had to reduce the number of training sessions spent with other animals, as well as break downs in some of Akea's behaviors, especially her gating. After the first three days, Akea began refusing to gate into the, medical pool at the first session of the day when the procedure was to take place. Yet, her gating remained strong during sessions later in the day. It was obvious that the requirements of the treatment were beyond Akea's threshold to continue to cooperate voluntarily, thus preventing us from maintaining this behavior with positive reinforcers alone.

After much discussion, we realized that we had two options. We could continue to catch and physically restrain Akea for the next several months or teach her to participate in a behavior we called passive restraint. Passive can be defined as, "inactive, while acted upon" and "receptive to outside influences" while restraint is defined as, "to hold back from action!" This technique has been used at other facilities and with stranded animals with success, but we had not trained it in recent history at Seven Seas. The finished behavior, as we pictured it, would require Akea to gate into the medical pool and allow two trainers to passively restrain her in the shallow area of the pool. A third person would give the injection as a fourth person would positively reinforce Akea throughout the entire procedure. In other words, we would train Akea to cooperate under stimulus control with an aversive procedure. The second option was very appealing not only because it would greatly reduce the time staff needed, but it could increase Akea's comfort level during the procedure.

It is important to note that we have trained several behaviors that require our animals to endure some discomfort. All of our dolphins are trained for voluntary blood sampling, and due to Akea's health concerns, we have taken blood from her voluntarily every three weeks for over a year. Our adult male dolphin, Nemo, has been conditioned for an intramuscular injection of Lupron once a month for the last two and a half years. Nemo positions himself next to the pool wall and allows a three-inch needle to be inserted intramuscularly. We also maintain monthly blood sampling with Nemo to monitor the level of testosterone in his blood. The obvious difference we found with these behaviors and Akea's injections were the number of repetitions that could be done in between each procedure to keep the behaviors positive. With this in mind, we put together our training plan for the passive restraint,

This would require the staff to train the behavior while actually carrying out the prescribed treatment. We began by reacquainting ourselves with operant tools not commonly used at Seven Seas. It was important that the staff realize that we would not be able to condition this behavior fully using only positive reinforcers, and the challenge would be to balance the reinforcement using a minimum number of negative reinforcers. Preuiqe implementation of both positive and negative reinforcers would be needed to condition the passive restraint. The staff identified seven components necessary to train the behavior. The components along with their time line and setbacks are as follows:

Component 1- Basic Restraint

In the handling of any animal, it is critical that the animal never learn that it has any option during the restraint but to cooperate. This would provide the foundation in establishing the passive restraint training. This is an important first step in the training for any animal if restraint becomes necessary. We were aware that the reinforcement of just one escape would be strong enough to persist throughout her life. The procedure with Akea would never begin with out an adequate number of staff members to properly restrain her. The staff handling her also understood that once the animal was restrained, that the animal was never allowed to remove itself from the restraint. Akea quickly learned that resistance provided no reinforcement and would passively submit to the procedure.

Component 2 – Positive Reinforcement

Positive Reinforcement is the addition of a stimulus to the animal's environment that increases the frequency of the behavior it follows. From the beginning, we knew that positive reinforcers alone would not be enough to train this behavior, but we made every attempt to make them available to Akea throughout the procedure. This would begin the process of changing the balance of the type of reinforcement controlling the behavior. We anticipated that as Akea became familiar and accepting of the procedure, we would be able, to use positive reinforcement to maintain the behavior. After two weeks of training, she accepted positive reinforcers through the procedure.

Component 3 - A Companion Animal

From the beginning of the procedure, a companion animal was housed with Akea. Initially, we would ask Akca to gate away from her pool mate into the medical pool for the procedure. However, once we began training the passive restraint, we decided not to separate her from the companion animal in an attempt to reestablish good gating at this session. Besides having food reinforcement, the companion animal also serves to positively reinforce the gating behavior. Although, if at any time Akea refused to gate into the medical pool, a net forming a movable wall would be placed into the holding pool and would serve as an aversive stimulus, a stimulus which increases the probability of response upon its removal. Once she swam into the medical pool, the net was removed thus, negatively reinforcing the gating behavior. Negative reinforcement can be defined as the removal of a stimulus, which increases the frequency of the behavior that it follows. Immediate response to the gating S^D was positively reinforced heavily. During the procedure, the companion animal's trainer is needed to assist in the passive restraint, therefore leaving the animal swimming about. He has proved himself not a problem and usually remains swimming in the deeper area of the pool. After two weeks, Akea's gating was consistent.

Component 4 - Reduce Time

In order to help Akea become more accepting of the procedure, we had to make the entire process as short as possible. This meant we had to approximate the water level to its full depth. Installation of water tight gates and draining the pool were the biggest addition of time to the procedure, removing them meant Akea was in and out in just a couple of minutes. Within five days, use of the water tight gates were eliminated and we were working with Akea at full depth.

Component 5 - Passive Restraint

In order for the staff to successfully restrain Akea, she needed to be in the shallow area of the medical pool where the water is at waist level. We began approximating this portion of the behavior using a hand target to guide her next to a trainer who would initiate the passive restraint. As long as Akea continued to participate in the session, she was positively reinforced, but if she refused, a small net would be used to guide Akea into the shallow area. Once she was restrained the net was removed and the procedure continued. This step took a couple of weeks to train and on occasion we still need simply the presence of the net.

Component 6 - Fade Aversive Stimuli

As Akea made progress with the behavior, we made every attempt to fade the use of aversive stimuli. We were careful not to let the introduction of the aversive stimuli become the S^D for the different behaviors. As stated earlier, we made certain to offer positive reinforcement as often as we could throughout her learning. After only a, few weeks, all but the occasional presence of the net near the medical pool were faded. This phase of the training has proved to be the most difficult. As a side note, we were concerned that the use of aversive stimuli might cause further breakdown of behavior outside of this session. We are pleased to report that throughout the entire period where aversive stimuli were needed, Akea maintained a positive attitude and continued to interact with trainers during water work, husbandry behaviors, general sessions, and even play sessions in the medical pool.

Component 7 - Minimize Staff

As Akea's participation in the passive restraint behavior increased, we then started to fade the number of staff on hand. We were always sure to have enough people present to safely maintain the restraint should it be required, but after the first week, we began working towards our goal of four people: two for the passive restraint, one to positively reinforce, and one trainer to give the injection. We would fade the number of staff to a minimum number to effectively maintain the behavior. In approximately one week, we were able to carry out the procedure with only four people.

The passive restraint training began seven weeks ago. Currently, Akea's gating behavior and positioning of her body for the passive restraint are being maintained almost entirely with positive reinforcement. The procedure that initially required eight people and took an hour has been reduced to four people in the water for five minutes.

All of us at Seven Seas are pleased with the progress made with Akea in this procedure. We recognize that we are not the first facility to use this procedure, but it is our hope that by sharing our training plan that others will benefit from both our setbacks and successes we had.

LITERATURE CITED

Messinger, D., G. Dye, W. Komar, J. McGee, C. Mika, S. Peek, R. Stacey, J. Sustman, T. Sullivan, and J. Weiner, (1997). *Animal training manual*. Brookfield Zoo.

Reynolds, G.F., (1975). *A Primer of Operant Conditioning*. Glenview, IL: Scott Foresome & Co.

In Press. The following paper was first presented at the 25th Annual IMATA Conference in Baltimore, Maryland, USA in 1997. This article takes a unique look at husbandry behavior training. If an animal is not yet trained to voluntarily cooperate in medical procedures, does that mean training options are out of the question? Of course, not! Trainers have often taught animals to enter squeeze cages or to move into medical pools to facilitate a difficult medical procedure. In this case, good basic training steps are used to make sedation of an animal easier.

Extended Separation and Targeting of North American River Otters (*Lontra canadensis*) for Sedation Purposes

by Chip Harshaw
Virginia Marine Science Museum

Every facility with a behavioral training program has certain unique variables, which require special considerations. Careful planning can lead to a more effective means of care for the animal collection, while at the same time providing the staff with a safe working environment.

In October of 1995, the Virginia Marine Science Museum underwent a $36 million dollar expansion. This growth included a large North American river otter exhibit, a new pinniped habitat featuring harbor seals, a half-acre aviary, as well as a marsh pavilion featuring animals of the salt marsh. These exhibits, along with a 300,000 gallon (1.1 million liter) shark display, a 70,000 gallon (266,000 liter) sea turtle habitat, a 300 seat IMAX 3-D theater, and a nature trail with various live animal exhibits. With these additions, the facility increased from nine to 45 acres.

Prior to my arrival at the museum, two river otters had been acquired in July of 1995 from a local wildlife rehabilitator and were being maintained at a temporary holding location awaiting the completion of their permanent facilities. These two animals had no behavioral training experience, nor did the Animal Care Staff assigned to work with them.

It was after my arrival that our new department decided to devise a behavioral training program, which was to involve all of our existing and future mammal collections. This was done primarily to enable a more effective process of husbandry as well as providing a source of behavioral enrichment.

The first medical examinations on our otters conducted during the relocation to their permanent holding facilities proved to be a complicated and difficult procedure. The museum did not have a squeeze cage, and thus we were left with few choices in carrying out this process. Our only option was to shift the otters into a smaller kennel that was attached to their temporary enclosure. After doing this, a pole syringe was used to sedate them. Due to the otters' continuous movement and/or huddling together, this process was difficult and posed some risk to them. To complicate matters even further it was necessary to have both animals sedated in this smaller shift kennel before we could safely remove them to begin the physicals. This meant we had to act quickly before the sedative would begin to lose its effect on the animals.

After finishing these first examinations, I began to think of ways we might be able to sedate the otters in a more controlled fashion. Our first two otters had already learned solid targeting behaviors. They had also learned to work at separate locations within their temporary enclosure for fairly lengthy periods of time. I felt we might be able to apply these basic behaviors to the design of our new holding facility and ultimately sedate the otters more effectively.

Upon completing our collection of five male

otters, introducing them together, and moving them into their permanent holding area, we began devising our plan.

To gain a clearer picture of the training process that took place, it is important to understand the design of our holding facility. This area is made up with two four foot by three foot (1.2 meters by 0.9 meters) and four three foot by three foot (0.9 meters by 0.9 meters) kennels constructed of chain link fencing. Each of these kennels can be interconnected or isolated from each other and a 1,500-gallon (5,700-liter) pool with clear lexan guillotine doors. Initially we used plexiglass, but quickly learned that the otters could shatter those doors with little effort. When completed, this design gave us what we felt to be the most options when moving animals around and providing separate enclosures if necessary.

The plan to train this behavior centered around our program of protected contact and the two to three feedings that the otters are given each day. It is during these feeds that we normally conduct training sessions. The idea behind this particular training was to get all five otters acclimated to being physically separated from each other in individual kennels for up to an hour. To further complicate this behavior, we had to do this in a way that would limit the otters' food intake. This was done to simulate the conditions we felt necessary to successfully conduct the physical examinations on all five otters, since sedation is usually safest on an empty stomach.

To accomplish this goal, we decided to incorporate what we call mini sessions into our feeding and training regime. These types of sessions allow us to start and stop working with the otters repeatedly during a training period. Each mini session may last only one or two minutes with small amounts of food given. The otters have learned that the duration between these mini sessions is typically not very long, and after getting acclimated to this, they have become comfortable with the process.

During mini sessions we utilize a variety of targeting techniques which include one method we have termed extended targeting. This type of target work requires the otters to lock onto a target for a fairly lengthy period of time.

When the time came to actually sedate the otters, extended periods of targeting were critical to the success of this behavior. By having the animals lock onto their targets in either a stationary position or by following the targets around the kennel system, we were able to keep them busy, reduce food intake, and control the pace of the examinations.

Our training began by teaching each of the five otters to begin sessions in a specific order within one kennel per animal. To assist this, we have incorporated the use of shapes into our training. Each shape represents an individual animal. When first called to station to begin a session, the otters must first find their shape and target on it. We utilize both these shapes and buoy targets during sessions to hold the animals in place and/or to move them around. These objects must be held up against the chain link fence in order for the otters to make contact with them on their nose. Over time we were able to teach them to station and work within these kennels and remain on target while we slowly began to close the lexan connection doors. This was difficult to do at first because the otters were not accustomed to being separated.

At first, the sound of a guillotine door sliding closed had an instant effect on the otters closest to its location causing them to immediately leave their target and investigate the noise and movement. This investigation would at times cause some of the otters to sit inside of the door area preventing any further door movement. On occasion, more than one otter would leave their stationing areas and pass through several kennels in order to see what the distraction was.

Later, as training progressed, the otters began to accept the connection door being partially closed before they might leave the target and force the door back open. On occasion they would run into adjoining kennels where they might remain for some time before returning to station. The fact that the separation doors are clear seemed to help the otters' progress during this stage of training due to the fact that they could still see each other. With successive approximation the otters eventually allowed us to conduct entire training sessions with each connection door closed. They also allowed us to hold several back-to-back mini sessions during separation. Occasionally, these combined mini sessions would last as long as 30 to 45 minutes. Between mini sessions the animals remained separated and typically very calm. This aspect of training was an important part of our process to sedate the otters.

Full physical examinations on our otters involve sedation, pit-tag identification, various inoculations, blood sampling from the jugular vein, fecal samples, and weighing the animal if necessary. Our otters are trained to stand on a scale while on target in order to be weighed. This is helpful when trying to expedite a physical examination in a situation such as ours. This allows us to eliminate one aspect of the examination that adds time to the process. These combined examinations can take as long as 10 to 15 minutes per animal after sedation if everything goes smoothly.

The plan to accomplish the examinations involves separating each otter into individual kennels and then sedate one animal per mini session while it is being held on a target. We utilize a pole syringe administer the anesthesia. Once an otter is sedated, the mini session can be ended so that the physical examination may be conducted. Upon completion of each examination, the still anesthetized otter is then placed back into its holding kennel. Another mini session then begins in order to repeat the process of sedation on a different animal.

One of our concerns while conducting this process is giving the otters too much or too little food during the mini sessions. Their high metabolic rates enable us to give them full diets the evening before examinations, but in the morning they are hungry and ready to eat again. During the sedation process it is important not to withhold too much food to prevent hypoglycemia. At the same time, too much food poses some risks while being under anesthesia. Because of this, we choose to use Telazole as the sedative. It acts quickly to sedate the animal, but also enables the otter to recover in an expedient manner.

The mini sessions during sedation are kept brief, perhaps lasting only one or two minutes while at the same time utilizing fairly long periods of extended targeting. This type of targeting can last as long as 30 seconds between reinforcements. In doing this, we can keep the otters that have yet to be sedated busy, and also control food intake. To help make these sessions as positive as possible we also incorporate secondary reinforcers to supplement the primary food reinforcements given. These secondary reinforcements are in the form of both enthusiastic verbal praise and clapping.

Another concern is the potential reaction the other otters could have when one is sedated and then removed from the kennel for the exam, or returned to it after the exam. Due to their close proximity to each other they might react negatively to seeing and/or hearing this process occur. The plan to assist in this matter, if necessary, is to keep the otters occupied by either conducting a mini session, or to simply remain in front of them at their kennel locations during times of potential distraction. For example, another mini session could begin once the examination of a sedated otter has been completed. As the otter is being placed back into its kennel to recover, the other animals can be in the midst of a mini session, being held on target to keep them occupied.

After having become accustomed to separation we began to introduce them to the pole syringe. Otters are very inquisitive animals, thus desensitizing them to the syringe took some time. We started this process by placing the syringe pole in close proximity to the otters while they were on target so that it could be easily seen. At first they would break contact with the target to get a better look. Once they lost interest in its presence, we began to slide it through the chain link holes, inside of the kennels next to the otters. The training sessions could at this point be conducted with the pole syringe inside of the kennels. This quickly progressed to rattling the pole around the kennel structure while moving it closer to the hindquarters of the otters. Although they would occasionally leave station to look at the pole syringe, they would quickly return. In a short period of time we were able to touch the otters lightly on the gluteal muscle while they remained stationary and focused on to the target.

When first touched on the injection site of their hindquarters, some of the otters moved away from the syringe, but still maintained contact with the target. This posed a slight problem in that we could not access the most optimum site of sedation to effectively proceed with our training. To correct this, we utilized the target to reposition the otters. Well-timed bridging enabled us to shape the proper posture of the otters so that we could continue to progress in making the injection of the sedative an easier process. Once this was accomplished, not only would the otters remain in position during the contact, but as the pressure of the injection pole was increased, some of them would lean into the pole to maintain their positioning. Throughout this work we continued to use a variable schedule of reinforcements.

After approximately three months of consistent work the time for the physicals was at hand and the otters appeared ready for the actual test. Of course, there were still many unanswered questions due to the fact that, up until this point, everything done had been simulated. How would the otters react to the sedation process and the penetration of the needle? Would their reactions cause the others to resist the process that we had worked so hard to accomplish?

On the day of the physicals we chose to sedate the otters in a specific order. It was decided to begin with individuals that had shown a tendency to be wary and more easily distracted. Each of the otters we worked with has fairly distinct personalities, thus the calmest and most patient animals would be last during the process.

We soon discovered the effectiveness of the past several months of work. With one trainer assigned per animal the session began and the otters were quickly and calmly separated. We started with the wariest animal first. At the moment of injection while holding his position on target, he jumped, turned to look at the pole syringe, but immediately went back to the target. He was quickly reinforced with secondary reinforcers and a few pieces of food after which time the first of several mini sessions was ended. We waited a few minutes for the otter to be completely anesthetized before he was removed from his kennel. Just before this removal, the other trainers restarted another mini session to occupy the remaining animals while the sedated otter was taken out of his kennel for the examination. We felt that by having the other otters follow the target in a direction that was away from the otter undergoing the sedation process helped to keep them from being distracted. As hoped, each examination went very smoothly and took approximately ten minutes to complete. Just prior to returning sedated otters to their kennels, mini sessions were started to keep the remaining animals busy and to keep the process going.

Each of the otters acted very relaxed during the entire process, which took just under one hour to complete. The mini sessions kept the animals busy, and the use of extended targeting along with secondary reinforcers reduced their food intake. This enabled us to accomplish our goal in a positive way. The process went better than expected and surprised our veterinarian who had never been exposed to this type of cooperative training.

The examinations were completed by 11:00 and the otters were back out on exhibit for public viewing by 14:00 once they had fully recovered. This was significant due to the fact that we had planned to have the exhibit closed for the entire day not knowing how smoothly the physicals would proceed. That evening, the animals were back into their holding area where a simple feeding took place.

The following day we decided to simulate the events of the previous days physicals to see how the otters would respond. To our surprise, each of the otters allowed us to separate them with no resistance and conduct several mini sessions that included touching them gently with the pole syringe.

Only one of the otters showed any hesitancy with the syringe, but after a few minutes of work, he ignored it and remained on target while we touched him.

Although full physical examinations on the otters as described are usually conducted only once a year, we do periodically work this behavior to maintain it for future use. We continue to work on extended targeting to increase its duration and for other behaviors, and also utilize mini sessions as a regular part of our training. As our training program grows, many of the things done under anesthesia may eventually be accomplished entirely through voluntarily trained cooperation. In the meantime, however, just because a procedure cannot be done on a complete voluntary basis does not mean an animal cannot be taught to cooperate with parts of the procedure. We have been pleased with our early success in this area.

UPDATE

Since the presentation of this paper at the 1997 IMATA Conference, the Virginia Marine Science Museum has conducted three yearly physical examinations with our collection of otters utilizing this technique. In one separate instance we used the technique on an individual animal to treat a mouth infection. Although we have on each occasion made some changes in our strategies during the process, the concept remains basically the same.

Some of the changes include eliminating the need to distract the other otters through mini-sessions while an animal is being sedated. In other words, once the otters are separated from each other only two of us were necessary to sedate each animal. The other animals tended to lay down and relax in their kennels until it was their turn. This is an improvement in the process, because we do not have to continually distract them with additional food and behaviors during the examinations. Also, fewer trainers are needed which allows more room to work and causes less distraction during the process.

In February of 1999 we sedated our five otters for their annual examination and planned to neuter each of them. The entire process, including surgery, took approximately two hours. The otters were out on exhibit the following morning behaving normally as if nothing had happened. The process of using the pole syringe has become a standard procedure that we have been able to maintain and utilize on a regular basis.

VOL 23, NO 4, 1998. A version of this paper was first presented at the 23rd Annual IMATA Conference in Las Vegas. The work described was awarded the Outstanding Trained Behavior for 1995. As a member of the audience at that conference, I was truly impressed with the calmness and length of time that the animals willingly participated in the procedure. It is another example of the seemingly endless types of behaviors that can be trained using good operant conditioning techniques.

Voluntary Cystoscopy -Training and Mutual Dedication

by Rosana de Sousa and Geraldine Lacave
Zoomarine, Portugal

INTRODUCTION

One of eight *Tursiops truncatus* residing at Zoomarine, Portugal is a female dolphin named Colby, who has been at the facility since 1980. Immediately after arrival, Colby established strong bonds with her trainers and the other animals, proving to be a very affable and interested dolphin. She demonstrated high motivation during shows and training sessions. Nevertheless, Colby systematically presented signs of health disturbance, which were untraceable by the medical team.

In 1992, we began to notice Colby's first consistent clinical signs. The trainers observed that Colby's coloration was becoming progressively paler and, with the help of photographs, this was made clear to the medical staff. Additionally, Colby's blood samples showed a high white blood cell (WBC) count which was a strong indicator of an infection, and a low red blood cell (RBC) count, which was an indication of anemia.

Zoomarine's strong commitment to the training and use of medical behaviors for preventative medicine had proven to be useful in the past, and this situation would be no exception. Unfortunately, the parameters obtained through regular analysis of Colby's blood, feces, gastric fluid, and blowhole exudate did not reveal enough information to make a reliable diagnosis.

It was clear that initial medications relieved the symptoms temporarily, but would only control the problem for a short period of time. Colby developed a history of frequent repeated relapses. The staff was able to predict a relapse within days of its onset. Colby's food intake would drop to very low levels. She would show a tendency to isolate herself from the group and would initiate stereotypical swimming patterns that would last for long periods of time unless a member of the animal care staff would interrupt it.

Even during these relapse periods, Colby would cooperate with the staff never refusing to participate in training sessions or shows. Her motivation was not associated with food, her main interest being the interaction with the trainers. However, the staff limited her activity level, both in and out of shows, and any behavior involving considerable physical effort was discontinued.

It was decided that an ultrasound examination should be performed. The equipment, using a 5 MI-1z probe, was supplied by a private clinic in Lisbon, located 200 miles (320 kilometers) from the facility. Although Colby was removed from the water to guarantee accuracy of data for the first exam on 14 April 1992, the ultrasound did not show anything abnormal and no diagnosis was made. No other examination was conducted that year as neither the equipment nor the technician was available. Until the second exam was conducted, Colby regularly alternated between periods of apparent welfare and periods of obvious discomfort, the later being normally associated with abnormally low RBC levels. The WBC values oscillated frequently.

The second ultrasound examination took place on 16 June 1993. This exam detected an abnormal mass in the bladder. A tumor was suspected. Our consulting veterinarian for two decades, Dr. Jay Sweeney, suggested that a urine sample be collected for bacteriological culture. He also suggested attempting to collect the sample directly from the bladder to avoid any contamination. At that time, we consulted several references on the subject

(Bossart and Dierauf 1990; Sweeney, 1990).

The third ultrasound examination was conducted on 09 September 1993. The mass that appeared to be a tumor presented no changes. As agreed, a urine sample was collected for culture. The sample was very dark and turbid, providing evidence that there was blood being lost through the urine and pointing to the probable cause of Colby's regular anemia. The urine culture revealed a urinary infection. At this time, one of the members of the medical team suggested we might want to begin flushing the bladder with physiological water to ease the effects of the infection.

Although the flushing of the bladder was conducted as quickly as possible, removing Colby from the water invariably meant that it was difficult to avoid some discomfort. We believe this created change in the animal's behavior in relation to both the other dolphins and the trainers. Her participation during shows and training sessions was still reliable, but her motivation dropped in subsequent days.

A fourth examination was performed on 08 February 1994, utilizing Zoomarine's own ultrasound machine equipped with a 3.5 N1Hz probe. Nothing resembling a bladder tumor was apparent. At that time a second urine sample was collected and the bladder was flushed with Lotagen (metacresol sulfonate), an antiseptic. An endoscopy was also performed, but nothing unusual was detected.

Once the procedure was concluded, a meeting was held involving all members of the animal care team. At this meeting, it was suggested that bladder disinfection take place on a monthly basis in an attempt to control the infection locally. The idea of removing Colby from the water to undergo the procedure every month was difficult for the trainers to accept. However having no other option, the trainers decided to find the best way to eliminate, as much as possible, the negative effects the procedure could bring to Colby. We decided to train Colby to participate voluntarily in these procedures.

The aim of this paper is to describe how Colby was trained to allow the collection of a voluntary urine sample and, later on, a voluntary cystoscopy. The basic steps of the training process are described, as well as her medical condition during that period.

TRAINING PROCESS

The training sessions began on 18 February 1994. For the first two days, Colby was trained alone in a back stage pool. On the third day she was reintroduced to the group.

Step #1 – Position - The first step was simple: she was asked to position herself laterally, near the trainer, who was sitting on the pool wall, with legs in the water. Once Colby seemed confident with that, she was asked to lie in an inverted horizontal position, after which she would rotate thus allowing us to rest her flukes on our lap. With the basic position defined, the next step was the systematic desensitization of the genital area to manipulation. While Colby positioned herself as described, we would touch her near the genital slit. Gradually, Colby allowed us to manipulate the genitals with no restriction whatsoever. This way, we finally gained access to the urethra.

At this stage it was obvious that the procedure would involve more than one person, so a second trainer was introduced. The addition of the second person meant that the dolphin's general position had to change. Now the trainers would sit one meter (3 feet) apart on the pool wall with their legs in the water. Colby would then wait for the S^D to position herself laterally to the trainers. In this position, the trainers' feet and legs supported Colby, thus allowing her to relax while the trainers would manipulate her. She rapidly understood that she did not have to make any effort to sustain herself at the surface; to breathe she would only need to make a small head movement. The fact that she could easily leave increased her confidence and allowed us to gradually increase the amount of time she spent in position. After only a few days, Colby would hold and allow manipulation for periods of over five minutes.

Step #2 – Direct Manipulation - The next step involved drying and disinfecting the interior of the genital slit. The procedure was difficult with only one trainer manipulating the area. Therefore, Colby was conditioned to allow the presence of a third person that would dry and disinfect the vulva, introduce the catheter, and collect the urine, while the trainer supporting Colby would keep the genital slit open. We were careful to rotate trainers frequently between the three positions so that Colby would allow different people to manipulate her, including the veterinarians for exams or sampling.

Step #3 – Collection - On 01 March 1994, only 12 days after the onset of training, Colby allowed us to collect voluntary urine for the first time. On the same day, we were also able to flush the bladder with about 400 ml (12 ozs) of Lotagen. Colby never showed any signs of discomfort and her behavior was rated as 100%.

During the first weeks, we proceeded to remove the disinfectant about 20 minutes after its introduction. Just a short time later, however, we decided to allow Colby to naturally expel it, thus reducing the number of catheter introductions. Once the behavior was established, it was decided that it would be used on a monthly basis, Colby's condition was still not cured, but we had found a way to minimize some of the symptoms.

Step #4 – Cystoscopy - The idea of performing a cystoscopy, where a slender tubular instrument is used for manually examining and treating the interior of the bladder, came a few months later. This procedure would be fundamental in obtaining a final diagnosis.

Colby's case was brought to the attention of the most renowned human urologist in Portugal, Dr. Reis Santos. Dr. Santos found the challenge of treating urinary problems in dolphins a unique and original situation and agreed to assist us. After some lessons regarding marine mammals and female dolphin anatomy in particular, he agreed to conduct the cystoscopy in January of 1995.

Knowing that the cystoscopy would require desensitizing Colby to additional people, equipment, and general noise, she was conditioned to accept the presence of several people during urine collections. Additionally, we placed several boxes and wires where the medical station would be, thus simulating all the equipment to be used. The noise that could be expected, such as people talking, several devices working, cameras, and flashes were equally reproduced. In the mean time, the mass we thought to be a tumor was no longer visible during any of the subsequent ultrasound examinations.

The cystoscopy was scheduled for 03 February 1995. When the time arrived, everyone was ready but naturally anxious. Colby had spent the night in a backstage pool with a 27-year-old female dolphin, Cher, to avoid any difficulties in separation, and to save time, prior to the procedure.

A few minutes before starting the cystoscopy, we realized the probe had a slightly bigger girth than the catheter Colby had been trained to accept. This could jeopardize the entire procedure. To avoid any problems, a small dose of local anesthesia was administered to the urethra and the cystoscopy was initiated shortly thereafter.

The procedure took approximately 20 minutes to complete. During the entire time, Colby remained calm and immobile, without any signs of being uncomfortable with the procedure, the noise, or the number of people involved. She only began to be impatient a few minutes before the procedure was complete, but she never showed any desire to leave position. The cystoscopy went along normally, allowing us enough time to carefully observe the interior of the bladder and to collect a biopsy.

While Colby was being observed, Cher was kept in the same pool, side by side with her. Cher was calm and created no disturbance to the procedure or the technicians. At no time did she interfere with our work. Cher sometimes approached the group, observing the operations and touching Colby as if to make sure everything was all right. We strongly believe her presence helped Colby relax even further.

RESULTS

The cystoscopy did not reveal the existence of a tumor, any other kind of body, or any known etiology. The entrance of the fight ureter was much wider than the entrance of the left one. The biopsy results also did not reveal anything that could lead to a final and accurate diagnosis.

Since we knew of no other dolphin that had ever been observed in such a manner, we were lacking the "normals" often collected from a control animal. For this reason, we decided to train another female so that the results could be compared. Cher was chosen as the control animal to learn the voluntary cystoscopy.

Some differences between the two females were obvious at the entrance of the urethra. A fold of skin had to be moved aside to allow the introduction of the catheter to Cher. Nevertheless, the methodology was identical to the one used on Colby. With one ten-minute session each day, Cher was ready for the procedure in one month.

The second cystoscopy for Colby, and the first for Cher, was scheduled for 04 April 1995. A few days before the procedure, a urine sample was collected from both females. Colby's urine had a high RBC level and showed signs of an infection. Cher did not reveal any abnormal signs. As previously, both females were kept in a backstage pool prior to the procedure.

During both cystoscopies the females were

calm and very cooperative. Cher had some slight contractions upon the introduction of the local analgesic, but did not show any intention of leaving the position. The bladders of both females were found to be different. As expected, no ureter entrance was found on Cher, and the inner lining of her bladder appeared smooth. On the other hand, we were again able to see the entrance of Colby's right ureter and the inner lining of the bladder appeared rough. Urinary reflux was confirmed as the final diagnosis.

DISCUSSION

Urinary reflux is a problem encountered in humans and other species. The reflux occurs when urine returns through the ureters towards the kidneys. This causes irritation of the tissues, which can lead to ulcerations and secondary, recurrent infections and blood loss. The latest treatment in humans includes the implantation of a silicone valve at the exit of the ureter, preventing the return of the urine.

The training of voluntary urine sample collection and cystoscopy were the basis for control of this medical problem with Colby. The immediate and constant access to urine and blood samples allowed us to better monitor Colby's health problem, which insures early treatment of infections, as they occur. Since these early treatments have begun, Colby no longer suffers from periods of food refusal or periods of depressed activity levels. Her general clinical situation has improved considerably. Blood loss has decreased and, inherently, the anemia occurs less frequently and is of reduced duration.

Besides the medical aspects, there are additional advantages to having these behaviors performed on a voluntary basis. As with most husbandry behaviors, it simply eliminates the need to remove the animal from the water. Along with comfort to the animal, voluntary procedures do not disturb the trusting relationship built between each animal and their trainer. In fact, we felt the training of these voluntary procedures actually strengthened it.

AFTERWARD

On 01 October 1996, Colby delivered her first calf, a healthy female named Lua. Although Colby had attended several births from various mothers, we were nervous about her delivery. Not only because Colby was a first-time mother, but also because the urinary reflux problem had not yet been resolved. However, Colby proved to be a careful and dedicated mother.

Several months following the birth, Colby continues to suffer from periods of anemia. However, now that the onset of the condition can be monitored with voluntary urine sampling, no acute infections or elevated WBC levels have been recorded. Urine samples continue to be collected periodically to continue monitoring the situation and to maintain the behavior. Less than two weeks after delivery, Colby allowed us to collect another sample. We were thus able to monitor her clinical condition even at this delicate time.

In the next few months, as her calf becomes more independent, we will be able to conduct the surgical procedure that will correct the urinary reflux problem. The valve that would normally have closed the ureter will be reconstructed and implanted. We look forward to the opportunity to share the results of this experimental surgery with MATA members at an up-coming conference.

If everything goes as expected, four years following our initial suspicions, Colby's medical situation will be considerably improved. In the meantime, she gave us a memorable lesson on how a healthy relationship between trainers and animals, based on trust and mutual dedication, can determine the physical condition of the animals and considerably improve their welfare. This, of course, is one of the most important tasks of any trainer.

BIBLIOGRAPHY

Bossart, G.D. and L.A. Dierauf (1990). Marine Mammal Clinical Laboratory Medicine in Leslie A. Dierauf (Ed.) CRC Handbook of Marine Mammal Medicine: Health, Disease, and Rehabilitation. CRC Press, Boca Raton, pp. 1-52.

Lacave, Geraldine (Ed.) Report on Diagnostic and Therapeutic Methods in Marine Mammals in Proceedings of the Third Marine Mammal Health Care Workshop. December 4-5, 1993, Duisburg, Germany.

Sweeney, Jay (1990). Marine Mammal Behavioral Diagnostics in Leslie A. Dierauf (Ed.) CRC Handbook of Marine Mammal Medicine: Health, Disease, and Rehabilitation. CRC Press, Boca Raton, pp. 735.

Conference Proceedings

1984 IMATA Conference, Long Beach, California, USA. Once it became apparent that we could teach our animals to cooperate in almost any husbandry behavior needed, new breakthroughs were seen every year. This paper describes some of the earliest training of urine sampling, breath sampling, and mammary presentation in cetaceans. It was at this conference that the Behavior of the Year award was one by the staff at Marineland of the Pacific for their training of stomach tube insertion with bottlenose dolphins and killer whales. Much of this husbandry training was all still new as recently as 1984.

The Conditioning of Various Animal Husbandry Behaviors with Killer Whales

by Bud Krames
Sea World of San Diego

ABSTRACT

The conditioning of a killer whale to present the tall flukes for blood sample collection was a major breakthrough in maintaining good healthy animals in a training environment. Further data could be gathered by taking urine or breath samples, usually when the animals were removed from the water, or by chance collection. Animal behaviorists at Sea World have successfully conditioned three killer whales to produce urine samples on a conditioned stimulus. The purpose of this paper is to demonstrate the steps taken in conditioning this behavior, and to highlight the possible benefits. Also included will be a look at two other husbandry behaviors, breath samples and the presentation of the mammaries.

INTRODUCTION

Within the past few years It has become apparent that there is a great need for a strong connection between animal behaviorist and animal husbandry. No longer can an animal behaviorist concern himself with only conditioning research behaviors or show behaviors with his animals. The health and care of the animals is of primary concern and therefore any behavior that can aid in the monitoring of this health will prove invaluable. Animal husbandry behaviors have been experimented with in nearly every marine mammal facility with almost every species of marine mammal. This paper will describe the conditioning of three such behaviors with killer whales at Sea World.

URINE SAMPLE

The blood sample taken from fluke presentation has proven to be a valuable source of information in aiding in the care of the animals, however, blood cannot, and should not be taken on a daily basis as simply a means of observing a healthy animal. With continual insertion of needles into the fluke, damage could possibly occur to the skin tissue and blood vessel along with an increased difficulty in keeping the behaviors positive. However, urine is produced continually, and collection of a sample can be as valuable as blood, and at the same time less traumatic to the animal.

With a sample taken on a regular basis, the laboratory can begin by conducting a standard urinanalysis. By studying the pH of the urine, an infection of the kidney or bladder can be noticed early. Specific gravity of the urine can also be compared with that of blood serum. Abnormal kidneys produce urine of the same concentration as blood whereas normal kidneys produce either a more diluted or more concentrated sample. The sample can then be studied under microscope to observe bacteria in the bladder or kidneys, along with the study of any sperm cells or bladder cells present. Probably the most important use of urine is to study the sexual hormones of the killer whales. By testing for testosterone in the males, estrogen and progesterone in the females, it can be determined whether the animal is reproductively active. With several samples, the levels of estrogen and progesterone can be plotted to determine when the whale will most likely ovulate. Finally, the urine can help to determine if the whale is pregnan. It can then be seen that there are at least three advantages to the use of a urine sample: 1) the collection is less traumatic than the collection of blood, 2) the laboratory can be assured of samples on a regular basis, and 3) the time needed to analyze the sample is somewhat less than that of blood. The following is a short description of the steps taken in conditioning the three killer whales to supply urine samples on a regular daily basis.

In 1982, during standard fluke presentation, it was noted that the large male would urinate at the same time he would present his fluke. This was relatively consistent and it was decided to attempt to collect a sample. Since presenting the fluke created a situation where the genitals were submerged the first step was to modify the body position in order to raise the genitals above the water. Slight contact on the mid-section would be the discriminator between fluke presentation and genital presentation. At this point it was crucial to be very selective in reinforcing to assure the whale was pairing urination with the stimulus. Often times, urinating was reinforced even though the genitals were below the water and the presentation was unacceptable. However, to reinforce a good presentation without urination would soon extinguish the behavior. Due in part to this fact, as well as the movement of the water in the pool, urine was collected daily, but the samples would not always be pure and saltwater free. At this point it was decided to modify the presentation and move it to another location in the facility.

Work on the behavior was begun with the two smaller animals, both females. As with the male, the fluke presentation was adapted to a genital presentation. Neither female urinated as a regular part of the fluke present, therefore, the time taken to condition urination on command was slightly longer. Upon slight contact with the genitals any movement or muscle motion was reinforced. The animal's attention was taken away from the flukes and directed toward this movement. With this increased concentration, naturally some urine was voided. With magnitude reinforcement when urination did occur, the behavior soon became quite reliable, but as with the male, a pure sample could not be assured. To collect a guaranteed pure sample, the whale would have to be out of the water.

The simplest and least traumatic means of accomplishing this would be to train them to beach themselves on their sides. Since the slideout, or beaching behavior, was already conditioned, it was a relatively easy matte to have them perform it on their side, with the ventral side towards the trainer. Once the slideout was conditioned, attention could then be centered on the genitals, and the two behaviors paired together. Urination in this position became quite consistent, but as before, a good presentation without urine could not be reinforced. To avoid frustration when the animal did not urinate, methods were experimented with to increase the possibility of collecting a sample. The most reliable was to take an animal that had not urinated and have it perform a few high-energy behaviors followed by a second presentation. If a sample was still not collected, the best step would be to withdraw and work the behavior at a later time. At this point it was found that collection was most reliable if taken every day, and at a consistent point in the daily schedule. With a regular sample, the laboratory staff could then set up standard tests and monitor the whales' health much closer than with a blood sample taken once a month.

BREATH SAMPLE

The urine presentation as well as the fluke presentation for blood sampling can be considered as behaviors to aid in preventive medicine. These behaviors are worked and performed on a regular basis which tends to increase their reliability even in the case of an animal that is ill and incapable of much activity. The data collected from blood and urine is helpful whether the animal is healthy or not. Other data can be collected from fecal samples, gastric fluid samples, and mucus samples. Mucus samples can be collected without the use of tubes and therefore the shaping of a breath sample can be easily conditioned.

The animal is positioned parallel to the work platform, dorsal side up. By making soft contact with the area around the blowhole, slight movement of the blowhole is immediately noticed. By reinforcing this movement the animal begins to concentrate on this region. Experimentation by the whale develops into exhalation. The use of a collection pad or plate, held a few inches above the blowhole will collect any mucus or particles exhaled. The benefit of conditioning an animal to exhale under stimulus control is to avoid having the veterinary staff wait for an exhalation and then relying on a chance collection, or an impure sample.

At the present time, the collection of a breath sample appears to be valuable only when the animal is ill or suffering some respiratory problems. Very little mucus is exhaled when an animal is healthy, however the breath itself may be useful to the researcher.

MAMMARY PRESENTATION

Within the past year to year-and-a-half, breeding activity between the killer whales at Sea World of San Diego has increased considerably. At the onset of this activity, it was felt there could eventually be a need to help in the nursing behavior of any young produced. This feeling was based on other species' response to nursing of first born ("young mother" syndrome) along with documentation of Marineland's killer whale, Corky, and her attempts at nursing her calf. This information has been very valuable in developing the following program of conditioning the presentation of the mammary slits.

The first step taken was to condition the animal to position herself along the training platform, or side of the pool. By targeting the dorsal fin to rest on the platform, the ventral side was in the proper position for contact to be made with the mammaries. This behavior became very reliable and positive for the killer whale to perform. However, after giving birth we must assume the mother will neither station herself at the platform, nor respond to any traditional training techniques for sometime. The mother may even discontinue eating as she works at guiding and protecting her calf. With this thought in mind, the conditioning of the presentation was moved to random locations throughout the system, and the trainer worked from within the water rather than the side of the pool.

At this point a second note was made of the behavior of Corky's fourth calf. Within the first few hours of birth, the calf began nuzzling the side of Corky's head and mouth in attempt to begin nursing. Corky allowed the calf to explore, but never presented her mammaries, and the calf concentrated on the head region in an effort to nurse. When Corky eventually rolled and presented her mammaries, the calf had more or less conditioned itself to target on her mouth.

To hopefully avoid the delay in the mother presenting herself, a program was begun to imitate the nuzzling of a calf. Initially, the trainer's hands proved to be the most easily managed target available. The trainer would enter the water and position alongside the whale's head. With closed fists, he would then begin a soft bumping or prodding motion and at the same time move his body towards the genital area. After a few approximations, the trainer would then remain stationary and reinforce only movement of the whale to the trainer's touch, as well as insisting on a complete stop when the hands made contact with the mammaries. In order to prevent the whale from performing this behavior only when the trainer was present, a number of different stimuli were used to initiate the presentation. These stimuli include the trainer's feet or head; targets and rubber balls, and eventually even other whales and or dolphins in the facility. This behavior is performed several times a day, in various locations and during play sessions, exercise sessions, and even public presentations. The thought behind the large number of approximations is to make the mammary presentation almost second nature, and the likelihood of its occurrence upon any contact with the body much more predictable.

This form of presentation is developed to aid the mother and calf during the first few days following birth, when the trainer may or may not have much influence on the situation. The presentations along the side of the pool should continue to be worked and instituted when behavioral control is regained. Also, the large number of sessions with the trainer in the water with the whale may allow this control to be regained at an earlier stage than if the trainer remains on the side of the pool. The use of other animals as imitations for the calf may also make for a stronger social group and therefore aid the new mother in her nursing behavior. Once again, it is not suggested that this is the only method of conditioning a mother to allow nursing. Every possible behavior or situation having to do with nursing should be worked on a regular basis to insure the survival of a newborn calf.

CONCLUSION

Although the subjects of this paper are killer whales, the behavior mentioned here should not be considered for killer whales exclusively. To simply say a dolphin should be seined up to obtain a blood or urine sample or a sea lion should be placed in a squeeze cage for sample collection, is not the answer. Continual experiments in this form of behavior should be investigated to enable data to be collected easily and reliably.

FOOTNOTE

[1] Desmond, Tim and Rutherford, Scott, Corky's Fourth Calf, Proceedings of the International Marine Animal Trainers Association Conference, October 25-29, 1982.

Conference Proceedings

1996 IMATA Conference, Gold Coast, Australia. Even carefully trained behaviors can be put to the ultimate test when multiple husbandry behaviors must be conducted all at once. While most trainers would agree that nothing is impossible if you apply the proper techniques, the lack of careful planning can cause the simplest behaviors to deteriorate. This paper focuses on six husbandry behaviors: blood sampling, girth measurements, urine sampling, ultra-sound exams, milk collection, and stomach tube insertion. Each of the medical behaviors was being performed or trained simultaneously and this paper details the important points related to training each of these behaviors.

Husbandry Behaviors for the Care and Treatment of a Pregnant Dolphin with Kidney Stones

by Ken Ramirez
John G. Shedd Aquarium

ABSTRACT

In September of 1994 the John G. Shedd Aquarium discovered that one of its Pacific white-sided dolphins (*Lagenorhynchus obliquidens*) was pregnant. Ultrasound examinations also revealed that she had a fairly high concentration of renal calculi (kidney stones). Although neither condition seemed to affect the other, the care and treatment of this dolphin necessitated the training of multiple husbandry behaviors. The steps used in training the variety of husbandry behaviors as well as some of the setbacks encountered will be discussed. The mother delivered a stillborn calf in the summer of 1995, her cooperation in several husbandry behaviors allowed the staff to closely monitor the development of the fetus. Following the birth, an intensive effort was begun to treat the kidney stones. The treatment program, while still underway, is showing signs of progress.

INTRODUCTION

In 1996, the John G. Shedd Aquarium, in Chicago, celebrated the fifth anniversary of the opening of its marine mammal habitat. Since the opening, the young population of animals have been involved in basic training for husbandry, research and public presentations. In 1994, one of the female Pacific white-sided dolphins (*Lagenorhynchus obliquidens*) was determined to be pregnant. At the same time, the presence of renal calculi (kidney stones) were seen during ultrasound exams. The two years that followed these discoveries will be discussed in this paper.

We will only touch on some of the medical details involved in the pregnancy and treatment of the kidney stones. The principle focus will be the steps used to train six basic husbandry behaviors critical to the dolphin's care and treatment, with emphasis on the successes and pitfalls that were encountered along the way. Most of the behaviors are not unique; however, the use of all the behaviors simultaneously and with such frequency should prove interesting to most trainers.

PREGNANCY & BIRTH

The pregnancy was detected at the end of the summer of 1994 during routine blood sampling and ultrasound examinations. Although husbandry training was a normal part of the animal care program at the Aquarium, the pregnancy required more frequent sampling than normal. Throughout the pregnancy the dolphin appeared to be in good health and the fetus seemed to develop normally.

We eventually paired the pregnant dolphin with two other females in a habitat that provided good viewing opportunity, easy trainer access, and plenty of space. We monitored the pregnancy by taking girth measurements daily, blood sampling weekly, and performing ultrasound exams every two weeks. Additionally, we worked on breast pump desensitization regularly.

The birth occurred on July 16, 1995. Unfortunately, the calf was stillborn. Although the calf showed some movement after it was born, it never made it to the surface for it's first breath of air. Afterwards, the mother returned to normal quickly and engaged in normal interactions, including allowing us to collect milk samples.

KIDNEY STONES

Although kidney stones were first discovered at the start of pregnancy, we did not make any attempts to treat them until after the birth. We had not seen any evidence that the stones were causing her any discomfort and they did not pose an immediate health threat. We did begin focusing a bit more on voluntary urine sampling as a way to characterize the renal calculi.

Several weeks after the birth, the female began exhibiting signs that she was experiencing some level of discomfort. She was noticed breaching on her ventral side and rubbing her genital region repeatedly. Neither of these behaviors was normal for this particular dolphin. At the same time, we began to see blood in her urine.

Our training suddenly focused almost entirely on urine sampling. Our veterinarian needed to get regular samples and if we could not get them voluntarily we would have to drop the water level and use a urinary catheter. Within several weeks we were able to get the behavior on cue. This lasted approximately 4 weeks, then we promptly lost the behavior. The details of the training will be discussed shortly.

Several medications were considered to try to raise the pH of her urine, which we hoped would make the formation of new stones less likely. We utilized human medical specialists to help determine the type of stones, which was important in determining the correct treatment. We also relied heavily on the veterinary expertise from around the marine mammal community.

Medical wisdom indicated that we needed to increase her fluid intake to help facilitate the passage of stones. The training staff began the daunting task of trying to inject water into every fish she consumed. Not only was the volume of water injected negligible, but the time needed to inject a few cc into each fish was enormous. It was at that point that we realized that the stomach tube behavior, normally used for gastric sampling, could be modified and used for water supplementation. We are currently using the tubing behavior to administer 4 liters of water each day. We have also adjusted the dolphin's diet to include a smaller concentration of protein rich fish at any one feed. We continue to monitor the kidney stones through regular ultrasound exams. In time we hope to see either a reduction in the number of stones or a decrease in their size. The process may take many years, but lack of blood in her urine and improvement in her behavior are very promising signs.

TRAINING

During the treatments, the dolphin remained in public presentations for 50% of the training, and was removed from presentations when training became more intense. We will focus on each behavior and examine the crucial steps involved, one at a time.

Blood Sampling - The training of voluntary blood sampling has always been a focal point for all our animals. The female dolphin was already comfortable with this particular behavior prior to pregnancy. However, to monitor the pregnancy, as well as her health while treating for kidney stones, the frequency of blood sampling had to be increased. During pregnancy we were taking blood samples weekly, and occasionally more often than that. A few of the key factors that helped keep this behavior consistent and solid throughout this period included the following steps:

1. Use of volunteers - The use of extra staff or volunteers on as many sessions as possible every day was, and continues to be, an important key to successful blood sampling. These extra individuals can touch and poke at the tail, bring the medical box out onto sessions, and generally desensitize the animal to most of the aspects of an actual blood draw.

2. Dolphin positioning - Most cetaceans are trained for venipuncture by holding the animal in a ventral up position for easy access to the ventral side of the tail. However we discovered that the rigid bodies of Pacific white-sided dolphins make it difficult for them to turn up for a breath if the blood sampling procedure takes too long. Their comfort level seemed to increase if we held them on their side, with their tail against our arms for support, which makes it easy for them to take a breath if needed.

3. One stick rule - We also advocate a "one-stick rule" that we believe to be critical to successful blood sampling, particularly when samples are going to be drawn frequently. This policy does not allow us to stick an animal more than once in any session. This rule applies no matter what the reasoning for the failed attempt or how critical the sample. This helps prevent a break down in trust and a breakdown in the behavior.

Ultrasound - It was decided that we would monitor the growth of the fetus every two weeks during pregnancy, through ultrasound. We took thoracic measurements, monitored the heartbeat, and collected valuable data throughout the pregnancy. We have continued to use ultrasound imaging to monitor the kidney stones as well. Although the ultrasound positioning was a solid behavior prior to pregnancy, the use of actual ultrasound equipment and the frequency of its use was dramatically increased. We also invited ultrasound and pediatric specialists to help in our monitoring, the equipment they would bring was always different, requiring extra desensitization steps:

1. Use of volunteers - We have found that with all husbandry behaviors, the use of extra people on a session is an excellent desensitization step.

2. Vary location - Sometimes we found that certain equipment, due its size or power source needs, could only be brought to certain areas. It was important to constantly desensitize the animals to various habitats and locations for ultrasound work.

3. Feet support - Due to the length of some ultrasound exams, we found it very helpful to desensitize the animals to allowing our feet in the water. We were able to use our feet to support the animal's body during lengthy exams. This position seems to be more comfortable for both the dolphin and the trainer.

4. Equipment - It was often impossible to have the actual equipment available for training sessions. We decided to use as many different objects for training purposes as possible so that the animals would be comfortable when the real equipment was brought in. The real equipment was seldom as bizarre as the unique creations that we would develop for desensitization sessions.

Girth - Although we had trained our animals to accept a measuring tape for basic girth measurements, we did not routinely take multiple morphometric measurements, particularly not concentrated around the genital area. This seemingly simple husbandry behavior was one of the more problematic at first. Eventually, the dolphin accepted daily girth measurements without a problem. However, we believe that our lack of focus on this behavior, due to our perception that it would be easy, led to sloppy approximations and poor desensitization techniques. We took too much for granted and had focused all our energy on blood sampling and ultrasound exams.

The basic behavior, truly simple in every respect, had humbled us. We realized that we hadn't put a good desensitization plan in place, we had just jumped ahead to the finished behavior. The female dolphin would not cooperate when the measuring tape touched anywhere near her genital area. When we finally recognized that we had never actually desensitized and approximated the measuring tape as we do all other behaviors, we kicked ourselves several times. Then, we regressed, and trained the behavior properly, one step at a time.

Breast Pump - The breast pump behavior was a big unknown for us. We carefully desensitized every step, but would not know if it would work until the dolphin was actually lactating. We were concerned that despite our careful training, she might respond very differently when we were pumping actual milk and she was trying to care for a new calf. The day after the stillbirth she allowed us to collect milk. The important steps in the process were as follows:

1. Ventral up position - Holding an animal in a ventral up position is a standard husbandry position for all our animals. It was important that the dolphin be very comfortable in this position before introducing the breast pump.

2. Genital area tactile - The next step was to desensitize the animal to various types of genital area tactile, light touch, pressure, and rubbing.

3. Suction cups - We then desensitized our animals to having suction cups placed over the genital area. This was particularly important while we were locating and designing our actual breast pump.

4. The real cup - Once we had the actual breast pump, we desensitized her to having the cup placed over her mammary slits. We used the same type of manual human breast pump used by the Navy. We re-formed the circular human cup into an oval to fit comfortably on our dolphins.

5. Suction - After the dolphin was very comfortable with the cup placement, we attached the rest of the device and slowly approximated the sensation of actual suction.

6. Collection - After the birth, we collected samples twice daily for three days. Some of the milk was sent to various labs for analysis, and the remainder has been stored for future analysis.

Urine Sampling - This is the one behavior that has eluded us for years. We have opportunistically tried to capture urination on all our animals since the inception of our training program. We have been unsuccessful, until this particular case. We were encouraged by Eric Bogden's paper in 1994, which showed the Sea World staff simply patiently waiting until an animal urinated. Our success at getting this behavior is more due to sheer luck than any secret training techniques:

1. Medical condition - The combination of her pregnancy and kidney problem seemed to cause her to urinate more frequently, consequently it was easier to capture.

2. Bladder pressure - We also found that by pressing gently but firmly in the region of her bladder, it would cause her to urinate.

3. On cue - Through good bridging, we managed to pair the urination with a tapping of the genital region, and she began urinating on S^D fairly consistently. We could get urination on cue 2 or 3 times each day.

4. Behavioral breakdown - After 4 weeks the behavior broke down. Just as quickly as we acquired the behavior, we lost it and have been unable to get urine reliably since.

5. Why were we successful at the start? There may be several explanations:

   a. It could be sheer luck.

   b. More realistically it may have been the combination of medical conditions that led to more frequent urination that was followed by opportunistic bridging and reinforcement.

   c. The pressure on the bladder may have been helpful, particularly during some ultra sound sessions when we could tell if the bladder was full and use that to our advantage to ask for urination at the appropriate time.

   d. Finally, it may also have been the intense focus we had on trying to capture the behavior. It was our primary goal for several weeks.

6. Why did we lose the behavior so quickly? We have two theories:

   a. At the time that we successfully captured the behavior, her urine was bloody and she seemed to be experiencing some level of discomfort. It is reasonable to assume that urination was painful, consequently that may have led to the breakdown of the behavior.

   b. Another possibility is that our strict training policy of allowing only assigned trainers to work new behaviors, may have backfired in this case. This policy, important in maintaining consistency while training new behaviors, may not have been advisable under the circumstances. Our hypothesis is as follows: If an animal learns to urinate reliably on cue, the animal may eventually learn to withhold urinating until a session, so that they have urine to offer. If this occurs, what happens if staff training the behavior are not able to work the behavior for many days in a row, especially after the behavior has just been shaped? Holding the urine may become uncomfortable and consequently would not be reinforcing. This is seen in pet dogs that are taught not to urinate until they are taken for a walk. If the opportunity to urinate on cue is not offered or reinforced, the dog will quit waiting until its owner comes home. We failed to ask for the behavior for several days just before the breakdown. Had we reassigned the behavior and continued to reinforce it daily, the behavior may have continued to strengthen and we might still be getting voluntary urine samples today. Back to the drawing board!

Stomach Tube - Teaching animals to accept a tube for gastric sampling was another normal husbandry behavior for our animals. The new twist in this case was that we didn't want to extract fluids, we wanted to add fluids. We needed to condition our female dolphin to accept a tube 3 to 6 times each day. In addition, we needed her to be comfortable with large volumes of water being poured into her stomach. We moved slowly, taking several different types of approximations simultaneously:

1. Frequency - We gradually moved from inserting a tube once each week to once each day. Eventually we approximated to multiple tubings every day.

2. Timing - It was also important to approximate from brief tubings to allowing the tube to remain inserted for up to 45 seconds. At first we were uncertain how much water would be needed or how long it would take to get the water through a funnel, down the tube and into the stomach.

3. General desensitization - Another important step was to bring a tube out for every session, without inserting it every time. We would use the tube as an extension of our hand for mouth exams. The stomach tube became a standard prop that the dolphin would see at almost every single session.

4. Tube size - We also found that the length of standard stomach tubes was too unwieldy for these sessions. We shortened the tube considerably, and marked it so that we knew exactly how far to insert it without pushing against the stomach wall. We also moved to a smaller diameter tube. This marginally slowed down the time it took for the water to pass through the tube, but it seemed to be more comfortable for the dolphin.

5. Water - Initially we introduced only very small amounts of water into the tube, less than 50 cc. The water was lukewarm, very close to the temperature of gastric fluids. We slowly increased the quantity of water added. As the fluid total increased we carefully monitored food intake for the day and observed for post-session regurgitation, which was never seen. Once we were convinced that she was handling the water well for several days, we would increase the volume of water again.

6. Current treatment - She now receives her full dosage daily, which is one liter four times each day. We will continue this treatment along with a modified diet for as long as we continue to see progress.

CONCLUSION

We have been pleased with the dolphin's remarkable acceptance of so many husbandry behaviors. In some cases she was having as many as seven husbandry behaviors performed in a single day, tubing alone occurs four times each day. Each of the husbandry behaviors has met with great success. Even experienced trainers are often amazed at the power of good operant conditioning techniques, and even more amazed at how it has transformed our ability to provide better care for our animals. This paper is a testament to the fact that no matter how difficult or complex the training task, success is limited only by our imagination, our technical training skills, and the relationships we develop with each of our animals.

ACKNOWLEDGEMENTS

The author would like to acknowledge the hard work of the entire marine mammal staff at the John G. Shedd Aquarium. The constant request for more samples and more desensitization steps were always met with enthusiasm. The trainers involved in the training and care throughout the two years described include Kirstin Anderson, Jennifer Bazen, Maura Burns, Pete Davey, Stephanie Dill, Greg Dye, Thomas Glen, Chip Harshaw, Meg Hudson, Kris Landin, Joe Lombardi, Laura Monaco, Rob Mortensen, Maris Muzzy, Manny Onate, Kelli Rasmussen, Mark Ryan, Mark Shurilla, Stacy Starns, Lisa Takaki, Margo Thomas and Don Tremel. A special thank you must also go to Jim Robinett, who as Curator of Marine Mammals at the time supported all the unusual training protocols we put into place. Finally, an extra special thanks goes to Dr. Jefferey Boehm, the veterinarian in charge throughout the process described. Dr. Boehm's understanding of training, patience in waiting for behaviors to develop, and constant communication of his needs madeit possible to accomplish so many things.

Trainer's Forum

VOL 15, NO 2, 1990. This is a common question and topic of discussion at many IMATA Conferences. Killer whales have been trained for urine collection at many facilities with relative ease, yet the same success has not been repeated with other cetacean species. Is this a case of not putting as much effort into dolphin urine collection? Or, are their other obstacles that we have yet to learn about? The quest for an answer continues.

Training Dolphins for Voluntary Urine Sampling

QUESTION: Does anyone have any suggestions on training voluntary urine samples with dolphins? It's the one husbandry behavior we're most confused about.

ANSWER 1: Our killer whales and dolphins are all trained to beach on their sides onto a slide out area. The whales usually automatically urinate (probably due to the pressure on their bladder because of their weight). After a short period of time, they realized what we wanted and now seem to consciously attempt to urinate when we put a cup against their genitals. We have not, however, had such luck with our dolphins. Since it seems like this behavior has to be "captured," we are now just working on lengthening the time that the dolphins are beached in the hopes that they will urinate. We are anxious to hear if anyone has had luck with this behavior, too!
Training Staff
Marine World-Africa USA

ANSWER 2: Here at the Whale & Dolphin Stadium, Sea World of Florida, we have trained voluntary urine samples with two female *Pseudorca crassidens*. Initially, they were trained to slide out laterally with their genital area away from the pool towards the trainer. This is the manner in which killer whales have been taught. We reinforce them for being calm so they could feel comfortable enough to urinate. One of the Pseudorca's would urinate frequently as she was sliding back into the pool. Ibis was reinforced. However, neither of them would urinate while stationary in lateral slide outs.

These approximations were done consistently every day at the same time for several days. We found that one individual would urinate when sliding into the pool more frequently around 10:30 am, than any other trials throughout the day.

Since we were having little success with the lateral slide outs, we decided to try normal slide outs on our stage. Our stage is 3 to 4 inches above water, which allowed us to stop the animals just before their uro-genital area was on the cement. This way their uro-genital area was out of the water and we were able to get a specimen cup under them.

This procedure was repeated each day around 10:30 am. The first time the animal urinated we reinforced. Every trial after that we had one trainer slide out the animal while a second trainer touched them next to the urogenital area. They were reinforced for urinating and allowing us to touch them. Thus, we paired urination with the touch, so they could understand the reinforcement was for the urination not just the slide out. Both of the Pseudorcas are tactile desensitized and used to the trainers manipulating various body parts for veterinary procedures.

This behavior was maintained daily at 10:30 in the morning for three weeks, and every other day there after. Since we use slide outs in our show, we took them out of the show during the conditioning process.

Eventually, they were put back into shows but on stage we maintained urination with the slide out , with one trainer always looking to make sure the animal has urinated. Our Pseudorca's also slide out in either side of stage in a 2-inch deep shallow area, but here we do not require urination.

We feel that the anatomy of the Pseudorca and Tursiops is such that by sliding out on their ventral

side may put some pressure on the bladder. When we collect a urine sample (bi-monthly), we place the cup under but not touching the uro-genital area and allow the urine to flow directly into the cup. We have more success collecting this way instead of trying to spread the urogenital folds; which may contaminate the sample. This is just one way to train the behavior that worked for us, we are sure it's not the only successful conditioning process.
Dan Blasko
Sea World of Florida

Marine Mammals: Public Display and Research

In 1993 the authors of this paper won the award for Outstanding Husbandry and Research Advancement at the 21st annual IMATA conference held in Hawaii. The behavior of voluntary collection of milk samples was presented by Tricia Kamolnick in 1992 and was runner-up for the same award she and her co-authors would win the next year. The award recognized the work described in this paper combined with a lactation study that resulted from the use of this technique. The results of the study are not the focus of this paper, but the methods used for conditioning voluntary milk collection are described. Many facilities are now able to collect milk samples from their cetaceans, but much of the pioneer work in this area was done by the navy and the trainers at SAIC. This paper appears in Vol.1, NO. 1, 1994 of *Marine Mammals Public Display and Research*.

Conditioning a Bottlenose Dolphin (*Tursiops truncatus*) for Milk Collection

by Tricia Kamoinick, Michelle Reddy, Don Miller and Christine Curry
SAIC, Maritime Services Division
and
Sam Ridgway
NCCOSC RDT&E Div 5107B

ABSTRACT

A serial milk study for bottlenose dolphins is underway and requires milk samples to be collected on a regular basis throughout the lactation period. Dolphins were conditioned to present ventrally for this procedure. Samples were collected twice a day, when possible, to allow for the collection of a fasting and a non-fasting sample. Milk samples were then stored at -70°C until sent for analysis. Milk collection can be used to monitor milk for nutritional value, transfer of medications, and health assessment.

METHODS

A serial milk study was initiated for a bottlenose dolphin (*Tursiops truncatus*) to determine the constituents of the milk at various times during the lactation period. This would require the collection of milk samples on a regular basis as soon after parturition as possible and continuing throughout the lactation period until weaning. The criteria was that the milk would be collected before any fish was consumed in the morning and at the last feeding of the day, two to four days each week. The procedure was to have no negative effect on the cow and calf interaction, which meant that the cow and calf had to appear calm during the training and collecting procedure. Collecting procedures had to be efficient and reliable and milk samples had to be uncontaminated by seawater. Once the samples were obtained they were stored at -70*C in 4 ml plastic vials for future analysis.

We first considered the known requirements for milking other species. For example, milking a bovine cow is a delicate operation and not as easy as some might think. It often takes a special touch to get the cow to cooperate with the procedure. The hands must be warm and the touch gentle or the cow can become agitated which will prevent the letdown of milk. Most of us were without past experience in the fine art of milking and. considering dolphin anatomy, we were at a considerable disadvantage. However, with careful planning, always keeping in mind to minimize the frustration level -trainers' included, we set about developing a training procedure.

The dolphin's mammary glands are flattened elongated organs lying beneath the ventral abdominal skin. The retracted nipples are set in elongated recesses on each side of the midline genital slit anterior to the anus and appear on the exterior as two small slits. Nursing begins by the calf approaching the cow from behind or from the side and drawing the nipple into its mouth between the tongue and palate. There is some evidence that the "milk let-down" is sudden and that much milk is ejected in a short time (Slijper, 1962). During several years of observation and monitoring the nursing behaviors of many calves we have noticed a pre-nursing behavior. The calf usually approaches the cow, as if it is going to nurse but will pass back and forth underneath the cow rubbing up against the mammary glands, sometimes bumping the mammary with its forehead. After several passes, the calf surfaces for a breath then approaches the slit to nurse. If the nursing appears unsuccessful, the calf repeats the rubbing and bumping of the mammary gland.

Understanding the process of nursing was the first step. Next we needed to develop a device that would come close to imitating the procedure. The first device we tried was a human breast pump that consisted of a hard plastic cylinder with a suction bulb attached. The hard plastic did not conform to the dolphin mammary area sufficiently to produce a vacuum; the only thing we were able to collect with this device was sea water.

The next device used was another off-the-shelf human breast pump. It was made of hard plastic and consisted of a small cylinder within a larger cylinder. Once a seal was established, the larger cylinder was pulled away from the smaller cylinder and a vacuum was created, yielding a milk sample. This device worked well with one of the animals; however, once again the hard plastic did not allow for a good seal without considerable effort by the trainers to adjust the seal.

The third model consisted of a hand operated vacuum pump, collecting tube, and an oral nasal respirator mask. The soft silicon rubber respirator mask was modified by trimming the base until it conformed to the dolphin's body. It was then bordered with narrow rubber tubing held in place by silicon sealant. The respirator mask material was pliable enough to provide a good seal and thick enough not to collapse when a vacuum was created.

While we experimented with the first two pumps, we began the training process with Slooper, a 13-year-old dolphin that had been born at the Naval Ocean Systems Center (NOSC) in San Diego, California in June 1979. She had given birth to her first calf, Ariel, on 20 July, 1991. Slooper had been conditioned for many medical behaviors prior to her pregnancy, as is our practice. During her pregnancy, she was also conditioned to position herself ventrally alongside the deck of her enclosure to allow for a sonogram. This position was a good start for milk collection. In early October we felt that training Slooper for milk collection could proceed without creating any negative impact on either Slooper or the calf. Trainers began conditioning Slooper to hold station at the side of the pen for brief moments and to remain calm while her calf swam in a tight circle behind her.

Once Slooper stationed calmly, a trainer signaled her to present ventrally alongside the pen. Slooper was conditioned to allow a second trainer to support the peduncle, just enough to keep the mammary slit area out of the water. The duration of this behavior was extended as sessions continued. The next step was to begin massaging the mammary glands to simulate pre-nursing behaviors. This procedure was followed by rinsing the slit with distilled water and placing the breast pump (whichever model we were testing at the time) over one slit. At this point stimulation of the area by creating a vacuum brought the teat out of the slit and a small amount of milk was released. It is important to mention that if Slooper had still been pregnant we would not have proceeded with the behavior up to the stimulation of the mammary area. In mammals that have been well studied such as cattle and humans, stimulation of the mammary gland excites a part of the brain called the hypothalamus, which incites the pituitary gland to produce pitocin. Pitocin is a natural hormone that causes contraction of the muscles in the mammary gland forcing milk into the cistern above the nipple for easy suckling. Under certain conditions pitocin can also produce uterine contractions. As a precaution, we decided to avoid stimulating the mammary gland of pregnant dolphins.

Once the correct pump was developed, training Slooper to letdown the milk when she felt the pump's suction was almost immediate and milk collection went smoothly. On occasions the calf would interfere with the process by rubbing against Slooper, or worse, breaching right next to her, getting trainers wet and contaminating the sample. Sometimes she would imitate the ventral position, right next to her mother. After Slooper and Ariel were introduced to other animals in another enclosure, Ariel began to find other things to occupy her time, such as chasing birds or fish, or playing with her toys. The other animals never interfered with milk collection, which takes only a few minutes for each session, and we never observed any negative effect on either Slooper or Ariel.

As other animals became pregnant, they were also trained for the milking procedure. This will allow us to compare samples between animals. Each dam and calf pair have shown different levels of temperament and patience during the training and collection of the samples. At all times, the trainer stays acutely aware of the mood of the animal and will step back in order to pre-empt any negative situation. Sometimes a dam will break station to attend to her calf, then return.

Many milk samples have been collected to date. Studies have already begun which will help us to understand the lactation needs of bottlenose dolphins. As a medical behavior, milk collection can be used to monitor milk for nutritional value, secretion of medications and health assessment.

ACKNOWLEDGEMENTS

We thank Lauryn Crosthwaite for presenting this paper at the 1992 IMATA conference, and along with Janet Hendrickson, for helping with training and milk collection. Chris Cesinat for her clinical help, and Mark Beeler Mark Todd, Malou Mantrop, and Sherry Peterfor their patient support and assistance.

LITERATURE CITED

Slijper, ET (1962). Whales. Basic Books: New York.

Trainer's Forum

VOL 18, No 1, 1993. As technology and advances in human medicine grow, so too do the options open to our animals. Veterinarians and trainers are becoming increasingly creative in applying new technology to animal care programs. Training animals to accept new machines or instruments is done through the process of desensitization. Note that all three responses use words like "calm," "relaxed," "quiet," and "comfortable." These concepts are all key elements to any husbandry behavior.

Training a Sea Lion for an Ultrasound Exam

QUESTION: We would like to train our female California sea lion to accept an ultrasound machine to determine pregnancy. She is eleven - years old, trained, and tactile, however she is somewhat high strung. If anyone has trained sea lions to accept ultrasounds, we would be very interested in learning both the procedure and the positive and negative aspects of this husbandry behavior. Any information would be greatly appreciated.

ANSWER 1: I personally have not trained a sea lion specifically to accept an ultrasound exam, but I do have experience with dolphins and we are currently training our walrus. Accepting an ultrasound is a relatively straightforward behavior. Ideally in the finished product your animal will lie still and allow the ultrasound technician to slide the ultrasound wand across the body. To get this ideal product there are many approximation steps that you must make.

The first step is to get her to lie out calmly and allow you to touch her with your hands. It will be helpful for her to lie on her belly, back, and side. This will allow you access to a variety of ultrasound views. You will also want to get her desensitized to a pseudo-ultrasound wand. Because you said she was high strung, you may want to start introductions of new props or objects in an area where she feels very comfortable and unthreatened. Many sea lions feel very comfortable in the water. You may allow her to station in the water and allow her to investigate the wand and eventually let you touch her with it on her face and front flippers.

Once you feel she is comfortable with the wand touching her in the water, bring her out of the water and work toward her allowing you to touch her with the wand while she is lying out. Eventually work her up to allowing the wand to pass over different parts of her body with a variety of different pressures. We, in the later part of training, use a hand-held vibrating toothbrush covered in plastic to simulate a wand. The toothbrush seemed to vibrate much more than the real ultrasound wand. All of our animals had parts of their bodies that seemed more sensitive to the touch and these took a little more time to train (stick the vibrating toothbrush in your arm pit and you might jump, too).

Besides the equipment that touches the animal, there is the machine with a cord connecting it to the wand, gel squirted on skin, and the ultrasound technician. We used a cardboard box and cord for the machine. We started presenting the box in sessions unrelated to ultrasound, then worked the box in closer, and eventually worked lie-outs next to the box. Finally, we attached the wand to the fake box. You can buy some K-Y jelly and get her used to the sensation and sounds related to it being squirted on her skin. Getting animals used to a second trainer and an ultrasound technician can be tricky. It would be nice to get her very comfortable with a second person and have that second person be the ultrasound technician. Many times it is not possible to have the technician or real equipment there for training. Do your best to get her used to another person's touch and their movement of the ultrasound wand. Keep the sessions positive and try not to push animals beyond their limits. This is a rule that is sometimes hard, especially if your ultrasound technician is flying cross-country and is only there for a day. It is better to try short positive sessions than have one long disaster.

Trust is very important to establish with your sea lion, especially since you know that she has a tendency to get upset. Never surprise her with a new sensation or object in her lie-out position. Always introduce these novel experiences while she is sitting up or even stationing in the water. Make sure you take the time to keep her comfort level high. It is helpful, too, to be very familiar with the ultrasound equipment. You may want to discuss the specifics of the procedures with the ultrasound technician, such as how long the animal will need to lie out, where they will concentrate their motions, how much pressure they will put on the wand. You may want to experience an ultrasound for yourself. Answers to these questions will help avoid surprises during sessions.

In turn, you need to clearly communicate with the technician that you are responsible for the animal and have some needs, too. Let him know what you think the animal is capable of and what your goals are before the sessions. Also let him know that all your plans are subject to change as soon as the session begins. Unlike the ultrasound machine, the sea lion may not cooperate every time (although I have seen some uncooperative ultrasound machines!). Good luck with your sea lion.
Many Sevenich
Brookfield Zoo

ANSWER 2: At the John G. Shedd Aquarium we do not house sea lions, but many of our staff have worked with sea lions and we are currently training ultrasound with our harbor seals. As with most husbandry behaviors, two key elements are a tactile animal and a calm animal. The first step in preparing an animal for ultrasound exams is usually to teach the animal to accept being touched all over its body, especially in the abdominal region. Meanwhile, the animal should get used to being properly positioned for the actual exam. Depending on your veterinarian or ultrasound technician, you may find several positions necessary to facilitate the exam (proper position will also differ depending on what you are trying to see or diagnose with the ultrasound). The most common position for ultrasound is with the sea lion lying on its back or side allowing easy access to the entire upper and lower abdomen. It is very important that while in this position the animal remains calm and relaxed. As it becomes more relaxed with the position, you can begin increasing the amount of tactile stimulation used on the animal. Ultimately, you may want to increase time in that position to 10 minutes or more; ultrasound technicians often need time to find what they are looking for and mark it on their screen. Remember that during the entire desensitization process you should reinforce the sea lion for being calm and relaxed.

Once the sea lion has learned to lie in the proper position calmly for several minutes while accepting being touched, the next step is to start introducing the actual ultrasound equipment. If this is not available to you, simulating the various elements (transducer, monitor, cord, ultrasound gel, and the technician) is not difficult.

The animal should get used to the transducer touching its body; at first it is wise to touch the animal's body with an object that it is familiar with, then progress to an object that resembles the transducer. Most transducers vibrate and make a humming noise-, if the actual transducer is not available for training you may want to use a hand or back massager to desensitize the animal to that feeling.

Finally, it is usually beneficial to desensitize the animal to all of the other gadgets and activity that usually accompanies an exam. Often, a well-trained behavior will fall apart when it's time for the actual exam due to unforeseen equipment or people being present. It is always helpful if the trainer can discuss the entire process with the veterinarian, see the equipment, and discuss the number of people that will be present. Knowing this information, and using it to prepare your animal for the actual exam, should help assure that the animal will cooperate with the entire process.
Marine Mammal Staff
John G. Shedd Aquarium

ANSWER 3: Before introducing the ultrasound machine, it is important to condition your female to lie on her side in a relaxed position. Reinforcing her for lying calmly and taking easy, full breaths, and for relaxing her flippers will allow you to have access to her abdomen. You should be able to increase the amount of time that she is in this position from a few moments to six or seven minutes in relatively few sessions. Some ultrasound equipment can emit a humming sound as well as a slight vibration and it would be normal for her to react to these differences initially. You can lessen the reaction by desensitizing her to the ultrasound "wand" without the unit being on or by using a small hand massager to duplicate the sensation. The key is to reinforce her for relaxing for longer periods of time.

NOTE: There are many other advantages to ultrasound besides just determining pregnancy, including checking internal orgoans, looking for tumors, or even locating hard-to-find blood vessels for blood sampling.
Vic Charfauros
San Diego Zoo

Conference Proceedings

1986 IMATA Conference, Vancouver, Canada. This paper reports the first known successful voluntary semen collection from a dolphin. Today's emphasis on breeding programs has placed added importance on learning more about semen collection and artificial insemination. Trainers are constantly being challenged with new tasks to advance the care and understanding of these animals.

Training Atlantic Bottlenose Dolphins (*Tursiops truncatus*) for Artificial Insemination

by Karl V. Keller
Naval Ocean Systems Center

ABSTRACT

Training dolphins (*Tursiops truncatus*) for artificial insemination as part of a breeding program was accomplished at the Naval Ocean Systems Center Hawaii Laboratory. The training of a male dolphin resulted in presentation of an erect penis for routine semen collection and fluke presentation for blood sampling. The training steps for the female dolphin resulted in acceptance of a 15-minute stranding period for artificial insemination and fluke presentation for blood collection.

INTRODUCTION

The Naval Ocean Systems Center, Hawaii Laboratory, for the past ten years has maintained a breeding program for Atlantic bottlenose dolphins. Both male and female dolphins are trained for blood collection from the fluke bleeding. In addition, male dolphins are trained for semen collection, while females are trained for artificial insemination. All test animals were housed in floating pens with the dimensions of 20'x 20'and have a depth of 12 feet. All behaviors are trained using operant conditioning and fish reward.

FLUKE BLEEDING

Both male and female dolphins were trained to present their flukes for blood sampling to measure the seasonal fluctuations of testosterone and progesterone levels. Fluke bleeding is difficult to train because it requires the animal to remain motionless during a venipuncture.

Initial training began with basic handling of the animal in the water. While it stationed near the side of the pen, we reinforced the animal for allowing us to manipulate its fluke. In time, we paired manipulation of this area with a simple hand cue (S^D). After we established stimulus control, we gradually raised the fluke from the water and placed it on the pen deck while the animal remained in a lateral recumbency. With the fluke resting on a pad on the deck, we gradually increased manipulation of the fluke to simulate the actual bleeding procedure. Throughout most of the training a second person sat next to the trainer and eventually served as an assistant during the blood collection. Once good stimulus control was established, we held the fluke about four minutes for actual blood collection. Initial blood sampling was short, lasting about one to two minutes, and gradually was increased over several days to the desired time interval. A consistent body position for fluke bleeding was an important aspect of this behavior.

Having the animal on its side and parallel to the pen with its ventral surface facing the pen deck is the best position for bleeding. If the animal's head is farther away from the pen deck, the animal twists, resulting in more fluke movement. With its ventral surface parallel to the pen deck, the animal appears to be more comfortable and is able to observe the trainers. Because the animal can breathe easily in this position, the holding time can be long. The dolphin can be bled from either the dorsal or ventral side by changing the angle of the fluke.

To maintain the behavior over time, we conducted practice sessions that imitated the actual bleeding process except for no venipuncture. It was helpful to vary the length of holding the fluke so the animal does not anticipate the end of the behavior. We ended the fluke-holding behavior when the animal was quiet and relaxed.

SEMEN COLLECTION

Because this procedure has not been performed on dolphins, we developed a new process of training. The steps in training consisted of: correct body position, penis erection, and semen collection. It took about forty-nine days to train this behavior in two captive males.

Initially, the animal was trained to station in a horizontal position with its ventrum at the water surface (animal on its back). The subject's position near the pen deck allowed the trainer easy access to the genital slit area. After the proper body orientation was under stimulus control, we started the next phase of training.

The initiation of penis erection was difficult to convey to the animal. The training sessions were about twenty minutes per day. Preliminary steps started with manipulation of the genital slit opening and exposure of the penis tip. Once the exposure of the penis tip was consistent, this behavior was reinforced about every other response. Partial erections were reinforced immediately.

After penis erection was controlled, the subject's position with respect to the pen deck was shaped to allow the trainer easy access to the genital slit area.

The final stage in the training of this behavior dealt with the collection of the ejaculate. The samples were collected in glass test tubes with an attached clear plastic sleeve. The clear plastic sleeve was slipped over the tip of the penis. The trainer applied slight pressure and massage and funneled the ejaculate into the collection tube.

ARTIFICIAL INSEMINATION

The process of artificial insemination (AI) has been used with many species of terrestrial mammals, i.e. horses, cows, dogs, (Gomes, 1977; Watson, 1978). At NOSC, these are the first attempts to use AI procedures with *Tursiops truncatus*. The female bottlenose dolphin has a unique reproductive system, including a psuedocervix. The psuedocervix is composed of muscular folding of the vaginal wall. In *T. truncatus* there are at least two of these folds and there can be as many as 6-12 in certain balenopterids (Harrison, 1969). This pseudocervix is within the spermathecal recess and the site for sperm deposition during copulation. In the AI process, semen collected from a male dolphin was placed in the spermathecal process with the aid of a fiber-optic laryngoscope.

Female dolphins were conditioned to handling using simulated AI procedures. The dolphins were caught using a stranding device. The animal was placed in a fleece-lined stretcher with openings for the flippers and a slit for the genital area. The animal was placed on a foam rubber-padded pen deck in a lateral recumbency. After fifteen minutes of occasional manipulation of genital area, the animal was returned to the floating pen and rewarded.

During the actual AI procedure, we used a speculum and a fiber-optic laryngoscope to locate the mouth of the pseudocervix and direct the laryngoscope tip into the spermatheca recess. Three cc of semen were deposited in the spermathecal recess using the laryngoscope air port.

DISCUSSION

We describe basic training techniques for breeding of Atlantic bottlenose dolphins using AI. Both male and female dolphins voluntarily submitted to blood collection via flu bleeding. Male dolphins were trained for semen collection, while females were trained submit for AI procedures.

Similar breeding programs on other species of small cetaceans could decrease our reliance on acquiring these mammals from the wild. A marine mammal sperm bank could ensure genetic variability and preserve gene pools of endangered species.

REFERENCES

Gomes, W.R., 1977. In: Reproduction in Domestic Animals (H.H. Cole and P.Y. Cupps eds.), pp. 259-260. Academic Press, New York.

Watson, P.F., 1978. *In:* Artificial Breeding of Non-Domestic Animals (P.F. Watson, ed.), pp. 97-285. The Zoological Society of London, Academic Press, London, England.

Harrison, R.J., 1969. *In:* The Biology of Marine Mammals (H.T. Andersen, ed.), pp 270-275. Academic Press, New York.

Trainer's Forum

Vol. 22, No. 4, 1997. Although the question in this *Trainer's Forum* article is not specifically about husbandry behaviors, most of the answers refer to and concentrate on husbandry. Since so much focus is usually given to cetaceans, it is nice to see articles on husbandry with other species.

Training Phocids: A Focus on Husbandry Behaviors

QUESTION: What types of behaviors do people train with phocids?

ANSWER 1: The basic phocid routine would probably include a roll-over, a low hurdle or hoop jump, and a flipper wave; a little variety act in a sea lion show. Fortunately you don't have to be committed to these few common behaviors. Some of the most novel training has come from trainers who didn't know what the animals were supposed to do. Observe your animals, their movement, how they manipulate objects, their vocalizations. If you can present phocids underwater you will have a great opportunity to develop some special behaviors but there are potential new stage behaviors as well. Your animals and facility will determine some limits but try anything that seems even remotely possible. Phocids are capable of many show and husbandry behaviors and we have just begun to find out what is possible.
Jim Alexander
St. Louis Zoo

ANSWER 2: At the North Carolina Zoo, our Pinniped Training Program includes numerous husbandry behaviors. Our two harbor seals (*Phoca vitulina*) seem to excel at these behaviors so we have taken advantage of their enthusiasm. The following is a list of behaviors completed or in training and why we are training it.
- TOOTHBRUSH: Seals allow their teeth to be brushed. Our next step is to add the toothpaste. Along these same lines, we are also working on desensitizing them to

tartar removal equipment.
- EYE DROPS: Seals allow drops to be placed in eyes.
- STETHOSCOPE: Seal rolls over and allows trainer or vet to listen to heart beat or other internal sounds.
- OPEN NOSTRIL: Seal opens nostril on cue. Purpose is to eventually be able to get a scraping or swab sample if needed.
- URINE COLLECTION: To allow easy access to sample if needed.
- Q-TIP IN EAR: To allow easy access to sample if needed.
- GATING: To allow easy transfer from exhibit to holding.
- SCALE: Allow ability to consistently weigh seals.
- RETRIEVAL: Trained to retrieve various objects from pool. This is a challenge for visually impaired seals, but they CAN do it!
- LAYOUTS: Our seals are trained to layout in various positions. The seal can be vertical or parallel to trainer, in or ventral or dorsal side up. These behaviors are great for body inspections or ultrasound work. One of our seals actually allows us to insert a Q-tip into his anus.
- VOLUNTARY BLOOD DRAW: We have successfully collected blood from the lower back of one of our seals.
- VOLUNTARY BIOPSY: We have successfully collected a punch biopsy.
- VET PRESENCE: We are continually desensitizing all of our pinnipeds to the presence of a veterinarian. This has proved extremely beneficial and less stressful to the animals. Our seals allow the vets to poke and prod and even do behaviors with them.
- HAUL OUT: All of our pinnipeds are trained to haul out at various stations around the exhibit. This is extremely helpful in obtaining a good visual of their entire body.
- BRIDGE: We chose to whistle train our seals. Any type of bridge can be used; for example, clicker, touch, or verbal.
- A TO B: Train seal to go from one target to another or one trainer to another.
- FUN STUFF: Backflip, stick out tongue, spin, wave, fast swim, high jump.

And the list goes on and on and on. Train what you want and behaviors the animal can succeed at. Have fun and be creative!
Marine Mammal Staff
North Carolina Zoo

Answer 3: I was once told when training, you are only limited by the animal's physical and mental capabilities and your own imagination. Phocids can be trained to do many of the same behaviors that cetaceans and pinnipeds are trained to do. You may have to use a little creativity in how you train them, but it can be done. At the Aquarium we focus on husbandry training with our seals. Behaviors like mouth opens, teeth brushing, weigh ins, lay outs, voluntary blood draws, and lots of tactile are great behaviors that assist in medical care for phocids. We also train what we call "fun" behaviors for exercise and variety. They include spins, bow jumps, vocals, flipper waves, and fetches to name a few. We are also in the process of teaching shape recognition and window work with our phocids. Sending them to the under water windows to perform behaviors is a great way for the public to get a closer look and gain a deeper appreciation for these animals.

Phocids are great training candidates. With a little creativity, a good imagination and lots of consistency, who knows, you may be able to teach the next award winning behavior!

Good luck and good training.
Cinthia Alia-Marion
Oregon Coast Aquarium

ANSWER 4: At the Virginia Marine Science Museum in Virginia Beach we have a new 60,000 gallon seal habitat that was completed and animals placed in it at the end of last August. Our staff is also relatively new to behavioral training. This might be a similar situation to that of the aquarium who wrote to you asking what types of behaviors to train.

Shifting animals on exhibit in the morning and off exhibit after we close has been a primary concern of ours due to the proximity of our habitat to the public. This is being accomplished through target training. We feel this is important to possibly avoid ever having to physically remove the animals, for example during a storm.

Obviously, target training opens up both the trainer and animal to a variety of behavioral opportunities. While on target, we concentrate on a variety of husbandry behaviors such as, nail clipping, tactile, weighing, blood sampling. Of the five male harbor seals that we have, three have allowed us to take an unrestrained blood sample, the other two have allowed us to insert a needle into the spine. All of our seals allow open mouth behaviors both in and out of the water.

We are beginning some water work with one of our seals. He is worked in the water while the trainer stands on a ledge that is about three and a half feet deep. She is currently working on tactile in the water so that she can manipulate the seal into various positions while it lays calmly on the surface. This could be an interesting aspect of a public demonstration.

Scanning has also played an interesting role in our new training program. Scanning is a technique of training in which one can capture a behavior as it occurs and then transfer it to an S^D. We have done this successfully in capturing the vocalizing of one of our seals and teaching it to respond on an S^D.

Another interesting behavior that we are beginning to work on is having the animals quiet station in the water with their chin resting on the open palm of the trainers hand. The criteria is that the animals must be very relaxed, and its rear end must be up at the surface of the water, and its body must be perpendicular to the ledge where the trainer is working. When the animals are in this position we will eventually work towards flipping the animal ventral side up, doing inverted open mouth behaviors, and manipulating the animal to being parallel to the ledge.

Flipper waving and pec slapping on the body are a couple of other behavior we are currently working on. We hope this helps.

Chip Harshaw
Virginia Marine Science Museum

VOL 20, NO 1, 1995. We are always preaching to zookeepers about the benefits of operant conditioning, yet in non-show situations many marine mammal trainers forget the strong effects operant techniques have on all animals we care for. David Schofield from the National Aquarium in Baltimore demonstrates that even when caring for stranded animals, operant conditioning can prove very beneficial.

The Use of Operant Conditioning Techniques to Facilitate the Management of Stranded Marine Mammals under Veterinary Care

by T. David Schofield
National Aquarium in Baltimore

INTRODUCTION

Over the past eleven years, the Husbandry Department of the National Aquarium in Baltimore (NAIB) has maintained a variety of marine mammals in its collection. Species have included California sea lions (*Zalophus californianus*), harbor seals (*Phoca vitulina concolor*), grey seals (*Halichoerus grypus*), beluga whales (*Delphinapterus leucas*), Atlantic bottlenose dolphins (*Tursiops truncatus gilli*). The interaction of the training staff with collection animals is of a level to stimulate the animals mentally and physically within an enriching environment. Operant conditioning techniques are utilized to both train and maintain show behaviors, as well as medical behaviors.

Over the past two-and-one-half years, the NAIB has conducted a marine animal rescue program (MARP). This program is permitted through a Letter of Authorization from the U.S. National Marine Fisheries Service (NMFS) and provides that the NAIB is responsible for the areas of Delaware, Maryland, and Virginia, although the MARP has accepted animals from various rescue facilities throughout the northeast coast of the United States. The MARP at the NAIB responds to approximately 10-20 live strandings per year. This small number of animals, coupled with a state-of-the-art quarantine hospital area and an extremely dedicated medical staff and a well-trained volunteer staff, allows for intense care and observation of these compromised marine animals.

The interactions of MARP staff with stranded animals is at a much different echelon than that of the interactions with collection marine mammals. When dealing with compromised animals the goal is a "hands-off" approach so as not to inadvertently condition the animals. Assuming a successful rescue and rehabilitation, the ultimate goal is the animal's release. Some rehabilitation circumstances are inherently of an intrusive nature: therefore, certain techniques of operant conditioning are implemented to:

1. Reduce the excitement accompanying the performance of certain medical procedures.
2. Provide the stranded animal an environment containing diverse sensory stimulation facilitating a normal level of behavioral activity.
3. Avoid the development of dependence upon humans.

BASIC CONCEPTS

Animals are shaped by their ontogenetic history, which is defined as the behavior of a specific individual created by its own experience with the environment. During these experiences, animals are positively and negatively reinforced by natural reinforcers. A natural reinforcer is a reinforcer whose strength is to be found in the everyday or natural environment. Examples of natural reinforcers may be feeding, nursing, and mating for all marine mammals. In the case of most cetacean and some pinniped species, tactile stimulation with other members of the social group is also a natural reinforcer. The effectiveness of a natural reinforcer is maintained by its presence in everyday circumstances. Animals may be negatively reinforced, which will yield avoidance behavior; avoidance behavior being any behavior which postpones the appearance of an aversive stimulus. An aversive stimulus will alter operant behavior through emotion and/or anxiety. Naturally occuring situations which may be aversive to an animal and will therefore elicit an avoidance response include, but are not limited to, fight or flight scenarios, lack of food, and competition for mates or feeding areas.

After understanding these basic concepts, it was the goal of the MARP staff to provide rehabilitation candidates with the most positive and the least negative setting; positive in the form of a stimulating environment, least negative by keeping meidcal and feeding procedures to the shortest length of time possible and keeping distraction to a minimum.

The following are three case examples of how basic principles of operant conditioning were implemented to facilitate the management of stranded marine mammals under veterinary care at the NAIB.

CASE I

HISTORY

On 07 July 1994, a male neonate longfin pilot whale (*Globicephala melaena*), approximately six to eight months old, stranded on the beach in the area of Chincoteague, Virginia. The animal was transported to the NAIB emaciated and dehydrated. The first order of medical care was to rehydrate the animal, which involved the administration of fluid via an oral gastric feeding tube. For clarity and simplification, this feeding procedure will be referred to in the remainder of this text as "AFP" (assisted feeding procedure). For this procedure, the quarantine pool level had to be lowered to a shallow depth, at which time the whale was placed on a large bed of foam. Although many precautions were taken, this ordeal proved to be distressful for the animal and dangerous for the MARP staff. The dilemma arose on how to provide this whale with at least four AFPs per day with minimal negative consequences to all involved. The facts were that pilot whales are considered highly social animals and, after researching the role of a neonate pilot whale in its natural social structure, it was theorized that this whale was of the age (evident by morphometrics and fetal folds) where it had probably been receiving near constant tactile stimulation from its mother as well as other members of its social group.

CONDITIONING OF FEEDING BEHAVIORS

The decision was made to start offering short periods of tactile stimulation to the animal just prior to and following the AFPs while the water level was low. The whale was only approached and provided with tactile stimulation when it appeared calm. Over a short period of time, the animal responded well to tactile stimulation along the left and right lateral flanks. During these interactions of tactile stimulation it was discovered that if the attendant place his hand near the proximity of the whale's mouth, the whale would exhibit vigorous suckling behavior, cupping its tongue around the attendant's finger. The next conditioning step was to approximate the water level upward by inch increments, only if the whale remained calm during the previous AFP. The approximation of the water level was by no means a continually successful process – in several instances there were setbacks; water levels had to be dropped to a prior step. Over a four-week period, the water level was approximate to a depth of seven feet. Restraint and the use of tactile stimulation varied in each circumstance. At its most successful stage, the number of personnel needed to perform an AFP dropped from a minimum of seven, with four attendants in direct contact with the whale, to three attendants, with one person in minimal contact with the whale.

The deeper water provided a more natural setting for the whale and, since the whale readily accepted the AFP at the high water level, the presumed negative precursor of a descending water level prior to a procedure was eliminated, making the environment more positive. It should be noted that the staff's perception of the whale's calmness during the AFPs may not have been totally attributable to the tactile stimulation. Over time, the administration of fluids, the ultimately nutrient gruels, probably provided the whale with relative comfort through the perception of satiation, as nursing is a primary reinforcer.

ENRICHING THE ENVIRONMENT

Given the fact that the whale was responding so well to the tactile stimulation, a decision was made to provide the whale with interactions extraneous to the AFPs. First, it was felt that this would provide mental and physical stimulation between feedings; second, it was felt that physical stimulation should not be paired only with feedings.

AVOIDING OR EXTINGUISHING SUPERSTITIOUS BEHAVIOR

Another situation that arose with this case was the incessant "bumping" behavior exhibited by the whale, as it would bump its melon against the wall in various areas of the pool. It was theorized that there might be two explanations for this behavior: 1) the whale may have been reacting to the physical boundaries of the pool, or 2) the bumping behavior was in response to hunger. As it was medically and visually obvious that the whale was underweight, it was theorized that the animal was exhibiting the bumping behavior to elicit nursing. Reeves and Leatherwood (1990) state that "It is suggested that there is some relationship between bumping and suckling. It is possible that bumping marks the onset of the calf's initiation of suckling bouts, indicating to the mother its need to feed and allowing the mother time to ready herself and present. Bumping may stimulate the 'let down' of milk from the areolae into an empty gland...." The bumping behavior is a reinforcing stimuli.

When working with different species of wild animals, it is important to understand the different idiosyncratic behavior characteristics peculiar to an individual or group, such as flipper waving or scratching in seals or bumping behavior in neonate cetaceans. Understanding idiosyncratic behavior in individuals prevents the inadvertent reinforcement of an undesirable behavior. Behavior that results from accidental reinforcement occurring coincidentally with undesired behavior is call superstitious behavior.

There was some concern that the bumping behavior could quickly be conditioned if the whale was provided with reinforcement with high frequency while exhibiting this behavior. It was for this reason that the decision was made to keep some feeding and interaction times variable. Attendants were instructed to feed the whale only when it was not exhibiting bumping behavior. It was the staff's goal to reinforce the whale with feeding and tactile interaction when it was exhibiting natural behavior and not a recurring pattern of behavior. Consistency by staff, and a 15-pound weight gain in three weeks, saw the bumping frequency decrease.

CONDITIONING THE ACCEPTANCE OF OTHER FOOD TYPES

Calculations of the whale's daily kilocalorie squid and gruel intake provided figures still too low for good growth. It was decided to try to offer the whale other fish of higher kilocaloric value. The whale was offered Columbia River smelt (CRS). Initially, the whale would take these fish into its mouth and then "spit" them right back out. It was thought that this reaction may have been because the whale did not recognize the CRS as food fish due to it different shape, texture, and consistency.

To encourage the whale to feed on other varieties of fish, processes of desensitization were implemented. Desensitization is the extinction of a perceived emotional behavior. This process reduces or eliminated an avoidance behavior by decreasing responses to the environmental stimuli that elicit the particular responses.

The desensitization process proceeded as follows: at the time CRS was introduced, the whale was consistently eating squid, but would eat only one squid at a time. Therefore, it was not possible to "hide" an individual CRS in a handful of squid, a common technique when switching feed fish in collection animals. When the whale was consistently eating individual squid during the feeding session, attempts were made to introduce the CRS quickly followed by squid. It was thought the immediacy of the squid being fed following the CRS would act to reinforce the whale for swallowing the CRS. This worked in some feedings.

Another method that was employed was to place the CRS in the sheath of the squid. Here, staff thought the whale would be desensitized to the shape and consistency of the CRS, while the texture would be masked by the familiar texture of the squid.

Through these different methods, the whale slowly over time became desensitized to the CRS, as well as capelin, which allowed us to introduce higher kilocalorie amounts to the whale on a daily basis.

SUMMARY

The above mentioned techniques were implemented to provide the pilot whale with an enriching environment, to extinguish superstitious behavior, and to reinforce nutritional variety.

CASE II

HISTORY

In late December of 1992, a sub-adult male harbor seal (*Phoca vitulina concolor*) was transported to the NAIB for rehabilitation. Several radiographs revealed that the seal had 21 pieces of buckshot lodged in its face. An ophthalmic exam further revealed that the seal had a 90% vision loss due to scarring the retina by the shot. The vision loss, which is frequently accompanied by a hypersensitivity to environmental stimuli, coupled with the fact that the animal was underweight and very hungry, was assumed to explain the animal's nervous and jerky behavior. On several occasions the animal had been observed biting its own flipper.

This seal posed problems for the animal care staff because the animal's behavior was unusually unpredictable. To prevent injury to the animal and/or the staff, it was decided to condition the seal to eat at a specific location. It was thought that targeting the animal to eat at a specific location at a specific time would lend some predictability for the animal and thereby decrease some of the nervous behavior.

AVOIDING OR EXTINGUISHING SUPERSTITIOUS BEHAVIOR

Over time the predictability did seem to calm the animal, but a new situation arose – the seal began to display a superstitious behavior of scratching the wall just prior to feeding time (scratching or rubbing can cause flipper and nail irritations that can lead to infections). This behavior was extinguished by changing the animal's feeding location and eventually making the feeding time more variable.

SUMMARY

By using some conditioning techniques with this seal we were able to make the animal more manageable. Unfortunately, this animal was deemed non-releasable because of chronic bouts of seizuring and, although the animal gained over 80 pounds, due to an increase in the frequency and severity of the seizures, euthanasia was the only option to relieve the seal of its suffering. A CAT Scan revealed that the animal had a bond fragment from the skull in the left temporal lobe of the brain.

CASE III

HISTORY

In April of 1993, the MARP team rescued a yearling harbor seal (*P. v. concolor*) from a beach in Ocean City, Maryland. After the animal was stabilized with fluids, gruel, and an aggressive medical regime, it was offered herring, capelin, and squid.

VARIETY AND CHANGE

With the seal showing improved health, the decision was made to move to a larger pool. In this larger pool the seal had the ability to exhibit more natural behavior. To compliment the increased natural behaviors, variety and change were provided to the seal to minimize any inadvertent conditioning that could occur:
1. Feeding times and areas were variable.
2. Amounts and types of fish fed at any one feeding were variable.
3. Objects were placed in the water to provide a changing environment. Objects were designed to be visually stimulating and to provide a physical change, prompting the animal to alter its swimming pattern thereby avoiding any stereotypical swimming.

SUMMARY

Variety created a more stimulating environment.

CONCLUSION

The aforementioned goals of the National Aquarium in Baltimore's Marine Animal Rescue Program are to rehabilitate and release stranded animals. While in a rehabilitation setting, MARP's aim is to provide animals with a stimulating and as near as possible distress-free environment. The goal of this is to continue to learn about different species may require in a rehabilitation situation to facilitate a successful release. The staff will continue to observe and record behavior closely, and to discuss those observations while avoiding the pitfalls associated with anthropomorphic interpretation of the behavior of the animals. The experiences gained from these three cases will be utilized to facilitate the rehabilitation of animals under our care.

LITERATIRE CITED

Reeves, R.R. and S. Leatherwood (1990). **The Bottlenose Dolphin.** San Diego: Academic Press, Inc..

Social Animals   7
Working with More than One

With few exceptions, wild animals are social creatures. Their social structure, dominance, sexual behavior, and other interactions will have a dramatic effect on training. These social activities are reinforcing to the animals in a variety of ways; consequently, an understanding of social interactions is critical to any training program. Because of the important role social activity plays in the life of an animal, a trainer should not attempt to compete with it. In other words, there will be times when dealing with dominance or sexual activity will be far more important to an animal than participating in a training session. The reinforcing value of a sexual encounter may be more powerful than anything we offer in a session. Similarly, the impact of being chased and bitten by an aggressive animal may be of more immediate concern to the animal than interacting with the trainer. Being aware of these conditions, knowing how to detect them, and learning how to work with them are the focus of this chapter.

One-on-One Training

Ideal Situation

Perhaps the best training situation is having the luxury to work one-on-one with your animal. By allowing you to focus all your attention on a single animal, training can progress quickly. Many pet owners are able to train one-on-one. In zoological institutions, however, animals often live in communities and seldom are there enough staff members for every animal to work with its own trainer at every session.

Community Groups

One-on-one training can still occur with animals in large groups or at facilities with a limited staff.

Spatial separation – If there are at least two staff members working with an animal group, the animals can be moved to separate locations within the same enclosure or habitat. One trainer can give individual attention to one animal, while the other trainer takes care of feeding or playing with all the others. The animal getting the individual attention can be rotated from session to session, giving all the animals one-on-one attention. Of course, that will require good stationing and solid training basics from all the animals involved.

Physical separation – If the animals are trained to gate and to separate from one another, each animal can be removed from the group and worked individually. I once worked with more than 200 birds in a facility with only one other trainer. Even when one of us had the day off, we accomplished a great deal of training by removing one bird at a time from their community enclosure. We were able to train individual birds by themselves or train smaller, more manageable groups of birds away from the larger community. For cetaceans, too, that kind of training is possible, but it requires good gate and separation training, discussed below.

When One-on-One Fails

Even though working an individual alone seems like the perfect training situation, there can be pitfalls. Separating an animal from the group (spatially or physically) may be difficult when intense social activity is taking place within the group. Even if an animal separates well, being away from the group can sometimes make it nervous. Every animal and every situation is different. The better you know your animals, and the more aware you are of their social interactions, the better prepared you will be to handle these situations.

Dealing with Changing Social Situations

As described in the introduction to this chapter, social activity is important in the lives of these animals – and social structure is in a constant state of flux. When animals become socially aggressive, the first response of many trainers is to try to intervene. However, social activity is a natural part of every animal's behavior. So, how do we strike a balance between the management needs of our animal care program and the behavioral needs of our animals? In 1991 Gail Laule and Tim Desmond addressed that issue in *Meeting Behavioral Objectives while Maintaining Healthy Social Behavior and Dominance - A Delicate Balance*, which can be found on page 220.

Gating and Separation Training

In chapter 6, "Husbandry," we discussed the advantages of training animals to gate. Gating and separation are important cooperative behaviors that help us to meet training, medical, maintenance, and social needs. This topic could easily have been discussed under husbandry or several other sections, but the issue seems to become most important when there are social concerns. I often feel that gating and separation are overlooked or taken for granted by young trainers who may never have tried to train these challenging behaviors. Because of the importance of the subject I have included four relevant articles, two from Sea World and one each from the National Aquarium in Baltimore and the Point Defiance Zoo and Aquarium:

- *Animal Separation as a Trained Behavior* (Trupo and Blasko, 1985), page 225.
- *Conditioning and Maintaining Separations with Pinnipeds in a Multiple Animal Environment* (Force and Bellows, 1991), page 228.
- *Conditioning Voluntary Separations with Beluga Whales* (Aibel, 1993), page 231.
- *Teaching an Old Polar Bear Program New Tricks* (Belting et. al., 1998), page 235.

What if Separation is not Possible?

For a number of reasons separation may not always be possible. Separation training may not be finished, your extra enclosures may be occupied, or worst of all, you may have no other enclosure! Whatever the case, the result is the same: you must work through the situation. Options available will depend on the species, the habitat, and the size of the staff. At Brookfield Zoo, the original dolphin habitat was a single community pool with no separation facilities. *The Training of Dolphins in a Community Tank* (Clarke and Brill, 1985), on page 238, explains how the Brookfield staff dealt with such a difficult situation.

Group Training

Whether or not you can separate your animals may not always matter. Many times it is desirable to work them as a group. However, group training can present some unique challenges.

Stationing
We have already discussed the importance of stationing. However,

when dealing with a group of animals, the decision must be made as to where and how each will station.

Location specific – One option is to train each animal to station at a specific location, regardless of how many people or animals are working. Single trainers working a huge colony of sea lions can effectively work the entire group by teaching each animal to station on a specific rock or pool ledge. This creates a manageable group.

Position specific – Another effective method is to teach each animal to station in a specific order relative to each other. Animal No. 1 on the far left, animal No. 2 next, No. 3 next, and No. 4 on the far right. Once the animals learn where they are to station relative to the other animals in the group, you can conduct your training session anywhere and at the start of the session the animals will move into their respective positions.

"Name" targets – A third option is to teach the animals to recognize a target that is specific to them. It can be a specially shaped target, a uniquely striped or spotted plaque, or a cut-out shape. The only requirement is that it be unique to that animal. At the start of a training session these targets can be placed at whatever location you choose. The animals will go to their targets, and the session can begin.

Animal choice – Some facilities will allow an animal to choose its station; the trainer will then move to that location. By most standards that would seem to give up a certain amount of control, but in some situations giving the animal a choice may be a higher priority.

Animal shuffle – If there's a better name for this method, I can't find it. In any event it is not uncommon for trainers to start a session by allowing the animals to go where they want, then to send, move, or rearrange the animals until they are positioned where the trainer wants them. This can be an effective method, in that it allows the flexibility of the "name" target method without the use targets.

Fairness

Any time you work more than one animal at the same time, it is important that you treat each animal equally and fairly. Too much attention given to one animal, or unequal reinforcement among the group, is a sure way to cause problems. It's not that the animals understand the word *fair*, but when one animal receives reinforcement while another does not, a competitive situation arises. The animal cannot be made to understand that this piece of food "belongs" to another animal. Animals in the wild compete for their food, and those that refuse to compete may die. The concept of teaching animals to take turns can be shaped, but it's difficult: the idea of waiting or sharing must be well-reinforced or the behavior will be lost. By taking the time to treat and reinforce animals equally, you can eliminate, or at least reduce, the potential problems. It is important to remember that an animal that waits patiently while another animal performs a behavior should be reinforced equally for waiting. Waiting, though less strenuous physically, is equally important – and for some animals more difficult. The trainer who is not fair invites aggression. More about dealing with this concept will be discussed in chapter 10, "Aggression."

Bridging in a Group

Working in a habitat with multiple animals presents some shaping concerns, especially when it comes to bridging.

Avoiding confusion - If several animals are being worked at the same time, how do you bridge one animal without causing other animals in the habitat to respond to the bridge as if it were meant for them? The article, *Training Only One Animal when Others Are Present* (T. Forum, 1994), on page 241, offers several responses to that question, as does *Multiple Bridges: Avoiding the Confusion* (T. Forum, 1999), on page 244.

Unison behaviors - When animals are worked in tandem, we usually look at the group and bridge the entire group for a well-executed behavior. But what happens if some of the animals are doing the behavior correctly but others are not? How do you bridge? The methods for dealing with that problem make use of concepts that will be addressed in chapter 9, "Advanced Techniques and Concepts." However, some responses to the question appear in *Working Tandem (or Group) Behaviors: When to Bridge* (T. Forum, 1996), on page 246.

Introducing New Animals to the Group

Sometimes the only options open to a facility are to introduce new animals directly into a social group without any preparation or training. When this happens, maintaining any semblance of order is unlikely. You will often have to allow the animals time to get used to each other. Normally, however, there are many steps that can be taken to introduce new animals safely into a group. Whether you are introducing a different species or animals of the same species the techniques are very similar. Several suggestions and techniques are discussed in two separate articles, one on cetaceans, the other on pinnipeds. *Mixing Different Cetacean Species for the First Time* (T. Forum, 1992), on page 248; and *Pinniped Co-Habitation: Seals, Sea Lions, and Others* (T. Forum, 1996), on page 253.

Conference Proceedings

1991 IMATA Conference, Vallejo, California, USA. Often, when a trainer sees aggression and dominance displayed among animals under their care, there is reason for concern. Discussion will sometimes turn to separation of animals and behavioral solutions to resolve the problem. But dominance and aggression are an integral part of an animal's normal behavioral repertoire. So how do we as trainers decide when there is too much aggression? How do we balance the needs of the social group with our need to provide good care? Gail Laule and Tim Desmond search for that delicate balance in the following paper.

Meeting Behavioral Objectives while Maintaining Healthy Social Behavior and Dominance – A Delicate Balance

by Gail Laule and Tim Desmond
Active Environments Inc.

Working with social animals offers unique challenges to animal trainers. By doing the right thing, such as housing them in groups, and providing opportunities for work and play interactions with other animals, we find ourselves referees in the resultant social problems. This is not a situation caused by captivity. It is a normal part of living socially in the animal kingdom. The stakes in the wild, in fact, are very high. Being pressured by the dominant animal and pushed to the outside of the group doesn't just mean you miss your cue for the high bow. It means you now are the most likely target for predators. While captivity protects animals from some lethal consequences, it does create other complications. For instance, animals do not get to pick their own social group, they can't escape from the bullies, youngsters can't leave their mothers when they normally would in the wild, and natural bonding based on conditions like sex and age similarities, may not be possible. Although we may not be able to change the circumstances themselves, as trainers we have the tools, and the obligation, to address the resultant social problems.

During our time at Marineland, dealing with social problems and dominance was an integral part of our training protocol. Over the years we developed a very active interventionist approach to those issues. As Tim and I branched out into behavioral consulting with a variety of animals in zoos and aquariums, socialization issues continued to be central to the problems we were called in to address. So much so, that some very interesting patterns began to emerge. Those patterns, and our strategies for dealing with them, are the subject of this paper.

Marineland was my teacher as well my classroom. It was there I first learned the value of socialization training. My lessons began working sea lions in teams of two. When working an individual sea lion my attention was undivided and I simply trained new behavior, worked old behavior, and interacted one on one. However, working two sea lions changed the game completely. Now attention was divided between training new behavior with one animal while reinforcing the other animal for doing something else, or for doing nothing at all. In fact, reinforcing cooperation, one animal allowing the other animal to eat and work, was essential to being able to accomplish anything else. It's really training on multiple levels. It's reinforcing the animal for: sitting on his seat, doing absolutely nothing, and allowing the other animal to get food and attention; and not making any kind of aggressive move, not trying to steal food, and not interfering with the other animal's work. The value of one trainer and two or more animals is that every training session is an opportunity to reinforce cooperation and reduce competition and aggressive behavior between the animals. When we focused on that, the result was a dramatic reduction in breakdowns due to fighting during the breeding season.

Dolphins normally live and work in larger groups, so the opportunity, and the need, to mediate social issues are even greater. Two situations with the Marineland dolphins stand out most in my mind. The first was the effort we put into socially rehabilitating a very submissive park-born dolphin named Pepe. Unable to successfully integrate into a show community of seven animals, he subsequently developed a number of nonadaptive behaviors. Through a concerted effort including cooperative training, husbandry training, tactile work, and strengthening of the human-animal bond he was successfully integrated into another social group and his problem behaviors reduced or eliminated (Laule, 1984). To me, Pepe was an important lesson in how vulnerable an animal can be to negative social situations and how sensitive and responsive intervention can make a difference.

The other situation involved two subdominant males, Skipper and Dawn, also living in the Dolphin Arena. It was obvious they were strongly bonded, but I had no idea how strong, until Dawn died. Within four months, Skipper died as well. I can honestly say I have never experienced an animal giving up like Skipper did. At the time I compared it to an elderly human couple, where one person's death is shortly followed by the other's. it was seven years later that I learned of Randy Wells' long-term study of the wild dolphin population of Sarasota, Florida.

Wells has now documented the strong bonds formed by adult male bottlenose dolphins in pairs or trios that endure for years. That was consistent with Skipper and Dawn's relationship and also that of the two dominant males in the group, Flipper and Semo, who ruled the show community in near perfect harmony for over ten years. Wells also reports, "The importance of strong bonds to some adult males has been indicated in several cases where individuals have been followed through time. In three cases, when one member of a pair died, the surviving males formed a close bond with another male" (Wells, 1991). In hind-sight I wish we could have found another compatible male for Skipper. In the present, I believe this is one piece of critical information to utilize in creating healthy social groups and keeping them stable.

By far my most important teacher, and the animal that has left the most lasting impression on me, was Orky. He and Corky, adult breeding killer whales, lived together in a woefully inadequate facility, without holding or medpools. Everyone at Marineland would have given their last dime to help build the type of facility Orky and Corky deserved. In reality, however, they had their small world, each other, and us. Working with the whales was like working with a married couple. In fact, I considered writing them up as a case study for my Marriage and Family Counseling class. They had their roles, dominant male and subdominant female, and all the diversity and subtlety of behavior those labels fail to reflect. In fact, it was Orky who taught me that being dominant is not just a type of behavior, a position in a pecking order, it is an integral part of who that animal is. And you never want to take that away from him.

So, at the risk of sounding anthropomorphic, we made a deal with Orky. In theory, the conditions were: we need to be able to give Corky food, attention, playtime, new training, and showtime activities; we need Orky to allow Corky to have those things, and to work in the shows; and we need all these things most of the time. In return, we would offer Orky attention and play (which he could choose to accept or decline), new training challenges (which history has shown were important to him), and the flexibility not to cooperate some of the time.

In practice, we reinforced Orky for allowing Corky to receive those essentials. If showtime arrived and Corky was reluctant to work, we made our best guess as to whether it was due to her rebellion or his coercion, and reinforced or took time outs accordingly. We then assessed the animals' reactions to determine if we had guessed right or wrong, and then adjusted if necessary. We required a high yet reasonable level of behavioral performance from both animals. We frequently gave second chances. If Orky was really fired up about something we gave him the freedom to be that way, if possible. Our most rigid requirement was around shows, and even there we had the authority to cancel the shows whenever necessary.

We made our share of mistakes, and things didn't always run smoothly. But the lessons I learned from Orky and Corky have served me well with everything from gorillas to elephants. And for that I am forever grateful.

With a strong base in marine mammal training, we moved on to consulting activities and found most of our work with terrestrials, and primarily primates. The interesting thing is that no matter how diverse each job sounded on first report – an introduction, maternal incompetence, or lack of breeding behavior, ultimately the roots of the problem, and strategies we chose, revolved around social issues.

The best documented project to date was the work we did at the Los Angeles Zoo with a group of drill baboons (Desmond, 1987). The central concern was that despite the presence of sexually mature animals, who had reproduced in the past, no breeding had occurred for over seven years. This was of particular concern since this species is extremely endangered and breeding of captive drills has been successful in only a small number of groups.

Observational studies of the drills conducted by the Research Department for 1½ years prior to the project showed very little affiliative behavior or positive social interactions between group members. Our strategies, therefore, focused on enhancing socialization and reproduction. We approached it much like we had with sea lions, dolphins, and killer whales. Feeding pairs were established where animals were fed side-by-side, the dominant animal being reinforced heavily for allowing the subdominant animal to eat. In the case of Sam and Nadine, the pair that had previously produced offspring, past observations had shown that Nadine's aggressiveness toward Sam often ended any mating attempts. So they were not only reinforced for eating together, but for also touching each other, and particularly Nadine for allowing Sam to touch her. Eventually she was turning and presenting to him as he placed both hands on her, approximating the mating position.

This project was important because the process and results were documented, The Los Angeles Zoo Research Department continued observations of the drills during the project, outside of training sessions, and after the project ended. The results showed dramatic increases in every category of social interaction by the end of the project, and beyond that time, while non-social behavior decreased. In addition, aggressive behavior, although increasing on an absolute level, dropped from 34% to 25% of total social interaction (Cox, 1987).

One gorilla project relevant to this discussion began as a request from the Columbus Zoo to help with two female gorillas that had histories of deficiencies in maternal behavior. Neither had successfully raised their infants and one, Lulu, was currently pregnant. Therefore, we concentrated on her.

After talking to the keepers, curators, and veterinarians, viewing video tape records of her and her infant, and reading her animal profile and history, we formed an hypotheses. We felt that Lulu's problem was not her lack of maternal skills, or her desire to utilize them, but her discomfort with the other gorillas that interfered with her application of those skills. So our recommendations, and the game plan we implemented, was socialization training.

Lulu had recently been moved to her present group, so we reinforced initially for proximity to other animals, at times as much as six to eight feet away. We particularly focused on the silverback in the group since she had a history of not getting along with any dominant male. There were also a couple juveniles in the group that she had shown some interest in, so we reinforced that relationship whenever possible. Keepers continued the training for the four remaining months of her pregnancy. She eventually gave birth, and is currently successfully raising her infant.

We can't claim that the training solved all of Lulu's problems, and training alone rarely does. But the keepers report that she is more relaxed in the group, and with the keepers themselves. They were even able to condition her to allow them to supplementally feed her offspring. That is an important change since she did not trust people around her baby after her last one was taken from her.

One final example with primates involves chimpanzees. We currently have a long-term contract with a NIH funded chimpanzee breeding colony associated with the University of Texas. M.D. Anderson Cancer Center in Bastrop, Texas. Our job is to introduce and integrate positive reinforcement techniques into the management of the chimpanzees, numbering approximately 142. It is the most ambitious and comprehensive project of its kind that I am aware of. The Director of the facility, Dr. Michael Keeling, created a new position of trainer, and my job for the past nine months has been to train that individual and to implement training projects with the chimps. Our focus has been on husbandry and veterinary behaviors, daily maintenance behaviors, and enrichment activities. As in every other case discussed here, socialization issues and dominance have been at the heart of much of our work.

A primary example of the application of this training is Pug. His face, and his personality, match his name. He is the dominant male in a group of eight animals, and there was consensus among the staff in reporting his overly-aggressive, dominant behavior toward other members of his group. This was particularly true at feeding time. These animals live in one of eight big corrals, and feeding is done from the wall around the compound. That means you are throwing food from about 20 feet above the animals. It was in this circumstance that we initiated training of cooperative feeding.

We began by teaching Pug to sit, and reinforcing him for remaining seated throughout the entire feed. Initially, every time another animal got a piece of food, so did Pug. This worked pretty well, but the difficulty was in creating some kind of consequence for his non-compliance. Because of our distance from him, he could sit and receive one reward, chase someone and take their food, then go back and sit down again, and there wasn't much we could do about it. So verbal commands became critical. We talked to him when he was sitting still, telling him good as the apple went flying by to the animal behind him. A sharp "Pug No!" as he got up to chase someone began to stop him in mid-chase, particularly when he was rewarded immediately for sitting down again. Total breakdowns were responded to by going downstairs to the inside holding area and feeding from there. That could be tricky, because of the too close quarters, but it could be effective if you managed to get food to the others and not to him. Over time our efforts paid off.

Documentation of results included before and after video, and subjective observations from a variety of staff members attesting to the change in Pug's behavior. Most promising is data from an ongoing aggression study that may reveal significant changes in group dynamics. In any event, it is now a joy to feed the group and watch Pug sitting there like a little angel as everyone receives and consumes their equal portion. His reinforcements for cooperation are consistent but can be as little as one special treat at the end of a feed. A variety of training is being conducted with the group, and every opportunity to reinforce cooperation among all group members is utilized.

Leaving the realm of primates, there is one last experience that is relevant to this discussion, and it focuses on Chico. Chico is a very large, very aggressive, very dangerous African bull elephant. He had not been touched for over ten years, with any necessary handling being conducted remotely. He was one subject in a pilot program conducted in the San Diego Wild Animal Park. The purpose was to develop an alternate method of elephant handling that was safe for the trainers, achieved all the necessary husbandry behaviors, and utilized only positive reinforcement techniques. Our solution is a system we call "protected-contact". Briefly, trainers work from shielded positions, using targets to manipulate the animal's movement, reinforcing with praise, tactile, and carrots and apples (Desmond, 1991).

The reason this training is important here, is in the way we responded to Chico's aggressiveness. We accepted from the very beginning, that Chico is a dominant bull like Orky, that is who and what he is. We also recognized that we were introducing him to a whole new ball game. We expected some resistance, and we got it. However, because we always worked from a protected-contact position, we allowed him full freedom to express his disapproval, frustration, and dominance. Within that context, it was amazing how quickly it diminished. At first he took opportunities to swat or grab the target. He registered disapproval by charging at us. We let him make his point, gave him time to cool off, then offered him the chance to work some more. Rarely did he turn us down. We also consistently reinforced his cooperation. Approaching the target calmly, gently touching it, lifting feet without kicking, all these responses were heavily rewarded.

As a result, Chico, recognized as the most dangerous animal at the Park, has been the star of the program. He seems to enjoy the sessions, often making rumbling sounds, verbalizing his pleasure. He has amazing endurance, working for over an hour on several occasions. He also responds to the attention and tactile we can now safely offer him. He lines up against the gate and allows us to rub and scratch him, occasionally adjusting his position so eye contact is possible through the holes we've added. He voluntarily cooperates with invasive procedures such as blood sampling from his ear, and recently allowed us to apply medication to a very sore eye several times a day. We've also found it a challenge to keep him mentally and physically active by introducing new behaviors into his repertoire. Keepers in the area seem surprised and impressed at the change in his behavior.

It's important to note that Chico is still as dangerous, and as dominant, as ever. The training process has given him the opportunity to respond and interact on an entirely different level, without changing who he is. Both Chico, and ourselves, have benefited from the experience.

In conclusion, let me return to my opening statement. Working with social animals offers unique challenges to animal trainers. Socialization and dominance-related issues will always be a part of their lives, and the source of many of our training problems. However, as trainers we have the tools, and the obligation, to address these issues. In some cases that will mean adjusting our behavioral goals in order to accommodate a dominant personality and achieve a healthy social balance. Our goal should be no less than creating and maintaining as natural of a social grouping as is possible, within the constraints of captivity. Here are just a few suggestions.

Structure training sessions to include one trainer, multiple animal situations. Then take advantage of those sessions to reinforce cooperation and non-aggressive behavior between animals whenever possible.

Take a look at the growing amount of research on marine mammals in the wild. There's some valuable information there. Information that wasn't available even ten years ago. To understand their social behavior in the wild, can help in our efforts to establish and protect strong, healthy social units in captivity.

Be pro-active. When dominant behavior becomes a problem, address it behaviorally. Utilize training strategies to problem-solve solutions. Shape and reinforce cooperation. Our goal is to create social units that all animals can thrive in – the dominant and the subdominant. Don's settle for separating animals, unless it is absolutely necessary. As Koehler (1931) said, "The single individual is often merely an abstract concept. A chimpanzee kept on its own in captivity is not a chimpanzee at all." That statement is true of more than just monkeys. If separating animals is the answer, someone, or everyone, loses.

Consider the impact of moving animals between social units. Transporting animals from one pool to another, or one continent to another, has become a relatively safe procedure. But what are the social and psychological consequences of moving animals from one social grouping to another? Undoubtedly it puts pressure and stress on the relocated animals, as well as on the effected social groupings that have lost or gained a new animal or animals. What is the price they pay? It is time to ask that question and look hard for the answer.

Finally, allow dominant animals to be dominant. Reinforce cooperative behavior, enhance affiliative behavior, mitigate the negative consequences of dominance, but don't take it away from them. Just like Orky, Pug, and Chico, it's who they are. And we wouldn't want them any other way.

REFERENCES

Cox, Cathleen R. "Social Behavior and Reproductive Status of Drills (Mandrillus leucophaeus)." The Proceedings of the 1987 American Association of Zoological Parks and Aquariums (AAZPA) Annual Conference, Portland, Oregon.

Desmond, Tim. "Surrogate Training with a Pregnant Orca." Proceedings of the 1985 IMATA Annual Conference, Orlando, Florida.

Desmond, Tim; Laule, Gail; McNary, Jennie. "Training to Enhance Socialization and Reproduction in Drills. "Proceedings of the 1987 AAZPA Annual Conference, Portland, OR.

Desmond, Tim; Laule, Gail. "Protected Contact Elephant Training." Proceedings of the 1991 AAZPA Annual Conference, San Diego, CA.

Herman, Louis M. (Ed.) Cetacean Behavior, New York: Wiley & Sons, 1980.

Koehler, W. "The Mentality of Apes." In Hediger, H., Wild Animals in Captivity, New York: Dover Publications Inc., 1964: p. 168.

Laule, Gail. "Behavioral and Husbandry Intervention in the Case of a Hybrid Tursiops sp." Proceedings of the 1984 IMATA Annual Conference, Los Angeles, California.

Laule, Gail: Desmond, Tim. "Use of Positive Behavioral Techniques in Primates for Husbandry and Handling." Proceedings of the 1990 American Association of Zoo Veterinarians Annual Meeting, South Padre Is., Texas.

Wells, Randall S.. "The Role of Long-Term Study in Understanding the Social Structure of a Bottlenose Dolphin Community." In Pryor, Karen and Norris, Kenneth S. (Ed.), Dolphin Societies, Berkeley: University of California Press, 1991: pp. 199 – 225.

1985 IMATA Conference, Orlando, Florida, USA. Training animals to separate and gate from one enclosure to another is a basic cooperative behavior needed in the management of any animal. It is a relatively simple concept, but often the care and attention to training it as a specific behavior is sometimes overlooked. In this paper, Sea World describes their process for training separations with several species of animals.

Animal Separation as a Trained Behavior

by Racie Trupo and Daniel E. Blasko
Sea World of Florida

ABSTRACT

Zoological and aquatic facilities across the country employ various techniques to separate animals from their living areas. At Sea World animal separation is a trained behavior in which the stimulus for the animal(s) to separate is simultaneously the stimulus for the other animals in the group to go or stay at a designated area of the pool (targct) until the trainer terminates the behavior. Both separating and targeting animals are reinforced. To minimize individual interactions from interfering with this behavior, separation is trained as a "team" behavior, in which reinforcement is only provided if all the animals separate or remain targeting as asked.

New animals are conditioned to target and remain targeting while the pool gate is open and closed. Simultaneously, they are taught to separate by touching a trainer's hand or fist. Separation is maintained through separation training sessions and unpredictability in the type of reinforcements given to the targeting and separating animals. Reinforcements such as playtimes, social and training sessions, and shows are provided for separating and targeting animals so that both behaviors are equally reinforced.

INTRODUCTION

Zoological and aquatic facilities employ various techniques to separate animals from their living area. At Sea World, animal separation is a trained behavior in which a previously conditioned stimulus for one or more animals to separate is simultaneously a stimulus for the other animals in the pool to go or stay in a designated area (target area) of the pool.

The primary reason necessitating animal separation is animal husbandry. Both the physical and mental health of the animals must be maintained individually. The ability to give individual attention allows for veterinary exams, exercise and special medical care. Similarly, the separation behavior permits cohabitation. Since the cetaceans, pinnipeds and mustidea are social animals, living in groups is important to their total development.

The individual training of one or more animals in a social group, as well as the ability to work animals together that are different species or unrelated social groups, is also made possible by the separation behavior. This type of versatility enables flexibility in shows. Young animals can be approximated into a show by learning a small show segment. Likewise, interchanging animals to participate in different show sequences provided diversity in the animals' performance, which is important in maintaining mental stimulation.

The separation behavior that is discussed in this paper is trained with all species of animals as Sea World: cetaceans (whales and dolphins), pinnipeds (sea lions and walruses) and mustidea (otters). Although the techniques may vary slightly between species, the basic principles of the behavior are applied to all animals.

TRAINING THE SEPARATION BEHAVIOR WITH A NAÏVE ANIMAL

The separation behavior consists of two different behaviors for which there is a single stimulus:

1) the separation of the animal from one environment to another; 2) The targeting of the non-separated animals to another trainer or to a preconditioned area of the environment. Both components of behavior are simultaneously trained.

Conditioning the animal to understand the target area or to touch the trainer's hand with its nose (or rostrum) are the first approximations taken in training the animal to target and separate, respectively.

The close proximity of the animal to the trainer during hand touching (targeting) is essential in developing a trusting relationship, which must precede any attempts at behavioral conditioning. Targeting is worked in the water, as well as on land (pinnipeds, otters). The separation stimulus for pinnipeds and otters is the animal's name, which is generalized with the presentation of the trainer's hand, whereas physical contact with the animal paired with a whistle is the stimulus for cetaceans to remain with the trainer (i.e. to separate from the group).

The target area can be a specific object or a generalized area of the animals' environment. A float or another trainer (cetaceans), a rock (otters), or the swimming area (pinnipeds) are a few examples of the target areas that have been implemented at Sea World.

Targeting is conditioned initially by feeding the animals at the target site so they generalize the area with reinforcement. The animals are then reinforced for targeting while paying attention to the trainers and when the stimulus for another animal to separate is given. The stimulus for this behavior is the verbal signal "target" or "in the water" (pinnipeds) or a hand signal, such as a point (cetaceans). The stimulus to target or separate is first given in the proximity of the target area, and gradually the trainer is approximated out of the animal's pool or to the area where the separations will occur. Through generalization, the targeting stimulus is eventually faded and the separation stimulus becomes the single stimulus for the separation behavior.

Environmental desensitization is an integral part of training the separation behavior with naïve animals, especially to the movement of the pool gate. The animals are conditioned to hold at or on the target while the gate is rattled and unlatched, and when the trainer moves back and forth through the gate. Similarly, when the animal first learns to separate out of it's environment, the gate is left open until the animal becomes more comfortable with the surroundings outside of its pool.

REINFORCEMENT

Both the separating and targeting animals are reinforced for the separation behavior. The contingency of reinforcement includes an immediate response to the stimulus so that the latency period between the presentation of the stimulus and the performance of the behaviors remains constant. Likewise, the topography of targeting and separating must meet the criteria ascribed for the behavior.

TEAM BEHAVIOR

The interaction of social animals with their fellow inhabitants often has a paramount influence on training. To condition the animals to work together and minimize individual animal interactions, such as dominance, from interfering with another animals' response to the stimulus, the separation behavior is conditioned as a "team behavior"; that is, all the animals in a group must perform the behavior correctly for any of the animals to be reinforced. Exceptions to the team behavior are not frequently made, but when they are it is usually during the training, rather than the maintenance stages of the separation behavior.

TRAINING THE SEPARATION BEHAVIOR WITH MORE THAN ONE ANIMAL

The optimal situation for training the separation behavior is to have one trainer per animal for each session. Since this is often impossible, the naïve animals are usually trained individually or in pairs. Once they understand the basic concepts of separating and targeting, other animals are approximated into the pool for their continued training.

When two or more animals are trained simultaneously, a second trainer is introduced into the session. The first trainer, positioned where the separation occurs, controls the session by separating particular animals and terminating the behavior. The second trainer, positioned near the target area, reinforces the targeting animals. A two-trainer separation is advantageous because it enables immediacy of reinforcement of both groups of animals and it encourages the non − separated animals to focus their attention at the target site. Gradually, the second trainer can be faded to the first trainer and then out of the pool, one trainer can reinforce both groups of animals.

Consistent and immediate reinforcement of all the animals is crucial in training any team behavior, especially in the early stages when the animal's attention span is often limited. To ensure that the young animals are reinforced, the more dominant animals are conditioned to receive their reinforcement after the young animals are in a different area of the pool.

MAINTAINING THE SEPARATION BEHAVIOR

Once the separation behavior is trained, maintaining it is a continuous process. Along with the separations that occur daily, separation sessions are frequently conducted in which one or more animals are randomly separated at a time. During pinniped and otter sessions, the trainer may also call a name that does not correspond to any of the animals in the pool to see if the animals are responding to their stimulus to separate. Two-trainer sessions are periodically conducted with the cetaceans in which one trainer separates various animals while the other trainer receives the targeting animals inside the pool or through a separation gate in an adjacent pool. The latter separation is referred to as a reverse separation because the targeting animals are the ones that are separated from the pool.

The primary means of maintaining the separation behavior is through unpredictability. This is achieved with a variable ratio with reinforcement variety schedule of reinforcement (VRRV) in which a variety of reinforcers are provided at intermittent intervals so that the type of reinforcement, as well as the time at which it occurs is unpredictable to the animal. This schedule of reinforcement has been observed to be far more effective in maintaining behavior than a continuous schedule of reinforcement.

A variety of reinforcers is essential in maintaining the effectiveness of reinforcement. It has been proven that if an organism's interaction with its environment causes a change in the environment, and if that organism is reinforced, then the frequency of the operant behaviors increases. The trainer must provide change in the environment through reinforcement to maintain behavior. A reinforcer that is continuously used becomes predictable and causes less change in the animals' environment in a period of time; thus, its reinforcement potential decreases. Even a primary reinforcer, such as food, loses some of its ability to reinforce when its presentation is predictable.

At Sea World, the separation behavior is maintained by providing various reinforcers for the separating and targeting animals include tactile, toys, playtimes, social and training sessions and show sequences. Sessions and other reinforcers are given inside, as well as outside the pool so that both groups of animals are equally reinforced. Similarly, a targeting animal may be separated out for a session after the separation of another animal. Therefore, the type of reinforcement and the time it will occur is unpredictable to the animal, and the animal's interest is maintained.

Unpredictability of session length is also an important factor in maintaining the separation behavior. Avoidance behaviors which can occur when an animal is taken back to its living area can be prevented if the session is not always terminated in the animal's pool. Incorporating the separation into the session eliminates the animal's anticipation of the end of the session. For instance, sometimes the animal is brought back to the pool in the middle of a session and then separated out in a short period of time to continue the session, or to receive a different reinforcement, such as playtime. Alternately, the animal is reinforced for going back to its pool so that an imbalance is not created between its habitat and the outside environment.

By providing unpredictable change in the animals' environment through altered patterns of separation and continuously changing reinforcement, motivation increases and the separation behavior is maintained.

SUMMARY

Depending on the facilities available, there are many ways in which an animal can be separated from its living area. At Sea World, separation of one or more animals is achieved by simultaneously training the non-separated animals to engage in a behavior incompatible with separation (targeting). Through reinforcement complexity (variable ratio with reinforcement variety), an unpredictable environment for the animal is created, which increases motivation and maintenance of the separation behavior.

An efficient method of separation provides limitless possibilities for the individual as well as group and interspecies conditioning. The individual attention given to an animal for purposes of training is important in their learning process and in establishing a working relationship. Separation also enables the trainer to provide mental stimulation by diversifying the animal's daily activities.

Thus, at Sea World, the separation behavior is an important factor in behavioral conditioning and in maintaining the physical and mental health of our animals.

REFERENCES
Brill, R. and Barry J., "RIR in use at Brookfield Zoo - Random Interrupted Reinforcement Redefined in Perspective". Annual proceeding of IMATA, 1981, pp.49-63.

Conference Proceedings

1991 IMATA Conference, Vallejo, California, USA. This paper served as a follow up and update to the paper presented by Sea World on a similar topic in 1985. There are some differences in approach that make both papers worthwhile reading.

Conditioning and Maintaining Separations with Pinnipeds in a Multiple Animal Environment

by David L. Force and Christopher Bellows
Sea World of Texas

ABSTRACT

For husbandry and conditioning purposes, it is essential that trainers and caretakers at zoological parks be able to concentrate on individual animals. In a multiple animal environment, an individual must be removed from the area to avoid distraction from the other cohabitors. Positive operant conditioning was used to successfully train animal(s) separation under these conditions.

Pinnipeds were trained on a separation behavior which allows trainers to remove one individual from the other animals. The animals discussed in this paper include 14 male California Sea Lions (*Zalophus californianus*) ages 1 to 14 years, and 4 Pacific Walrus (*Odobenus rosmarus*) 2 male, 2 female ages 4 yrs, to 23 yrs. Through approximation training, each animal is assigned a specific target area within the pool enclosure. The animals are conditioned to remain at these positions unless provided with a stimulus to approach the trainer. This method has resulted in the increase of the desired behavior (controlled separation) and a decrease in the undesired behavior (refusal or aggression).

INTRODUCTION

Animal separations have been a part of the animal training community since anyone had more than one animal. The need to move one or more animals from enclosure A to area B while retaining animal(s) in the original holding area, is a behavior which has probably caused the most problems for trainers while at the same time, has been the behavior probably taken most for granted. Many papers, articles and deliberations have revolved around this one behavior and solutions to control problems have been debated at many IMATA conferences. The intent of this paper is to discuss the method used to condition and maintain the separation behavior at Sea World of Texas, where there are a number of pinnipeds with varying experience levels. This method was implemented to decrease the competition for food amongst the animals in the holding pool, which leads to aggression and subsequent avoidance of the separation behavior.

METHOD

Assuming that a naïve animal understands the basics of a conditioned reinforcer or "bridge", and assuming that the animal has been conditioned to his name, the concept of multiple animal separation begins with a "stay" behavior. Each animal is individually conditioned to "stay" or remain in a fixed position. This usually begins outside the holding pools. The criteria for this behavior consists of the animal's front flippers remaining motionless. He is allowed to move his head and neck, look around the surrounding environment, or just relax. The trainer reinforces the animal for remaining in the stay regardless of what is occurring in the environment. The trainer should walk around the area, make noises, talk to other trainers and eventually have other animals brought into the area while the subject animal is reinforced for maintaining his "stay" position. All of this occurs with successive approximations as the environment becomes more and more complex. During the conditioning of the "stay", if the animal does break from his position, he is returned to his original location; not given another stimulus at his new position. This assists with the assimilation of the original correct response and avoids teaching a "stop and go" behavior.

Once the "stay" concept has been conditioned, it is then taught to the animal at a particular location on the deck around the perimeter of his holding pool. Previous discussion with the trainers in the area, designates a particular location for each of the animals in the holding pool. These locations (determined by the training staff) are believed to be the most successful for the group. Taken into consideration are compatibility, size, social structure, etc. The stay behavior is initiated with the verbal stimulus: "deck". The trainer positions the animal at its designated location and through successive approximation, gradually moves himself further away from the animal's "deck" position as he delivers the verbal stimulus. (in essence, an A to B behavior starting at point B and moving further away from it.) this method serves to avoid having to introduce a second trainer to assist in the control of the animals. This lends itself to being similar to the final product, where only one trainer is utilized for the separation behavior. During the conditioning process, the trainer gives the stimulus from various locations within the enclosure. The animal is reinforced for responding to "deck" when positioning himself out of the water at the predetermined and conditioned location of the pool, remaining there regardless of what distractions occur in the environment.

Another benefit of having only one trainer involved is the administration of fish when food is selected as the reinforcement. "Tossing" food to the animal will be a necessity when other animals are in the holding area. The animal is reinforced for ignoring any distraction, eventually including the tossing of food to any other animal(s) in the holding pool.

This process continues with each animal in the holding pool. Once each animal is conditioned to his location individually, a second animal is brought into the holding pool for both to respond to the same verbal stimulus. Both animals will locate themselves at their conditioned positions and will be reinforced for the correct response. As a result of previous conditioning, when food is selected as the reinforcement, a competitive situation does not exist in the holding pool and the precursors to aggression are avoided. This cooperative attitude lends itself to the success of the entire training system, as more animals are included. It is important to note that as the number of animals is increased, the separation training is not always conducted in a set progression. In other words, we don't start with animal A and then add B, followed by C etc. Every combination is worked first with two of the three animals. This allows for stimulus control under increasingly complex conditions. It also addresses the changes that occur when the numbers of animals in the holding pools vary for any reason. Thus, animals A and B are trained together as are B and C, and A and C. following this same pattern, additional animals are added to the system. Once the concept is conditioned, the addition of animals is quite simple. Progress occurs rapidly, but it is essential that all steps be taken.

One of the advantages to the conditioning and implementation of this system is that a naïve animal can be added to the holding pool community without causing the loss of the separation behavior. Because the animals have been conditioned to ignore any other distractions in the environment while on the deck, any animal(s) that may be swimming in the pool will not disrupt the behavior. This allows the trainer to reinforce those animals emitting the correct response while not bringing attention to those animals remaining in the pool either through choice or naivete.

The separation itself consists of calling the animal intended to be separated from the group by his name. That verbal stimulus results in the signature animal coming t the trainer, while the others remain at their "deck" position. The signature animal can then be sent back to the deck or sent out the gate to a receiving trainer. Sometimes one animal is called out and then brought back into the holding area and a second animal is separated to begin a training session outside the holding area. All combinations are a part of the training process avoiding any predictability regarding which animal might be leaving the holding area. This is a critical step and must not be avoided. Predictability leads to a breakdown in any behavior.

Over a period of time our animals were taught to pair the "deck" stimulus with the sound of the gate opening. Now, whenever a trainer enters one of the holding pools, the animals will accept the sound of the opening gate as the stimulus to go to their deck positions. After the separation is completed, the trainer gives the verbal "O.K." as the conditioned reinforcer (bridging stimulus). At that point, the animals are free to re-enter the water or remain on the deck if they so choose.

The "deck" behavior is preliminary to any animal(s) leaving or coming into the holding area. Only one animal is called over to the trainer at a time. If two sea lions are going to be removed from the group, it is conducted individually. This has proven to be more reliable than trying to call two over at once. Individual separation also lends itself to being unpredictable. The animals cannot anticipate when the behavior is completed or if a second or third animal will be separated.

We utilize the same training method and concept for our four walrus as we do with the fourteen sea lions. Whereas the sea lions are positioned around the perimeter of the pool on the deck, the walrus will position themselves in a corner of the pool with a flipper on the deck or upon the skimmer drain, dependent upon their designated locus of control. The separation behavior is just as consistent with the walrus. At our Texas park, the three holding pools at the Sea Lion, Walrus, and Otter Stadium are of the same design. Therefore, the separation is maintained regardless of which of the three pools the animals are located. We also maintain the separation with combinations of walrus and sea lions if that particular mix is in any of the pools. We have found that this method of separation has resulted in the increase of the desired separation behavior and a decrease in avoidance or aggression.

SUMMARY

The separation behavior has been conducted in many different ways at many facilities. Sea World has used a number of ways over the years based upon trainer and/or animal experience, numbers of animals, training methods, facility design, etc. The intent of this paper is not only to explain how the particular system works at our Texas park, but also to point out that we made adjustments to some of the methods we had previously used. Methods of training have been evolving for years and they will continue to do so.

We all agree that some of the behaviors that animals performed twenty years ago are now "archaic" and have no part in what we do today. At what point do we take a second look at what we are doing? Do we wait for a calendar to indicate that it is time to make a change? Or even worse, do we rely upon public opinion to provide the impetus for self-evaluation. Our responsibility is to be willing to admit that there might be a better way. We must continuously monitor our own methods and practices and continue to better ourselves for our animals' welfare. Once we abandon the process of becoming better, we have resigned ourselves to becoming worse.

SOUNDINGS VOL 18, NO 4, 1993. I guess I have always felt that you can't have too much information about gating and animal separation. Here is a description of the procedures and protocols used by the National Aquarium in Baltimore at the time of the opening of their marine mammal pavilion.

Conditioning Voluntary Separations with Beluga Whales

by Steven M. Aibel
National Aquarium in Baltimore

At the end of Pier 3, in Baltimore's Inner Harbor, sits the National Aquarium in Baltimore (NAIB). Opened in August 1981, it has been home to a variety of cetaceans and pinnipeds. In 1990, the aquarium expanded its marine mammal program with the addition of the forty million-dollar Marine Mammal Pavilion newly constructed on the neighboring Pier 4. The 1.3 million-gallon facility was built as a new home for the aquarium's beluga whales (*Delphinapterus leucas*) and bottlenose dolphins (*Tursiops truncatus*). Prior to taking up residency in the new Pier 4 facility, two of the aquarium's three female beluga whales went through behavioral conditioning approximations to prepare them for multiple pool separations in this new, larger environment.

Voluntary separations are the foundation for maintaining whales in a multiple pool complex. Separations include any behavior, or set of behaviors, that asks a whale to move from one point to another point. Many times this involves swimming through a canal to another pool. The benefits of teaching these behaviors are numerous, and include improved husbandry techniques, variability within social groupings, increased individual attention during training sessions, and variety during shows. Separation behaviors can be conditioned and maintained successfully in many different ways. This paper details the approximations taken to condition voluntary separations with the whales at the National Aquarium in Baltimore.

PIER 3 FACILITY

Prior to the opening of the Marine Mammal Pavilion, two of the National Aquarium's beluga whales lived in the Pier 3 facility in Baltimore, while the third whale lived temporarily at the New York Aquarium. Initial conditioning approximations for the separation behavior began with the two whales in Baltimore. They lived in a single, indoor, 250,000-gallon pool, which was seven feet deep with a nineteen-foot deep dive area. Overhangs around the perimeter of the Pier 3 pool allowed the whales to swim beneath ledges, and a raft was positioned in the pool from which the whales and trainers could interact. Diagram 1 shows an architectural schematic of the whale pool.

In this single pool environment the whales did

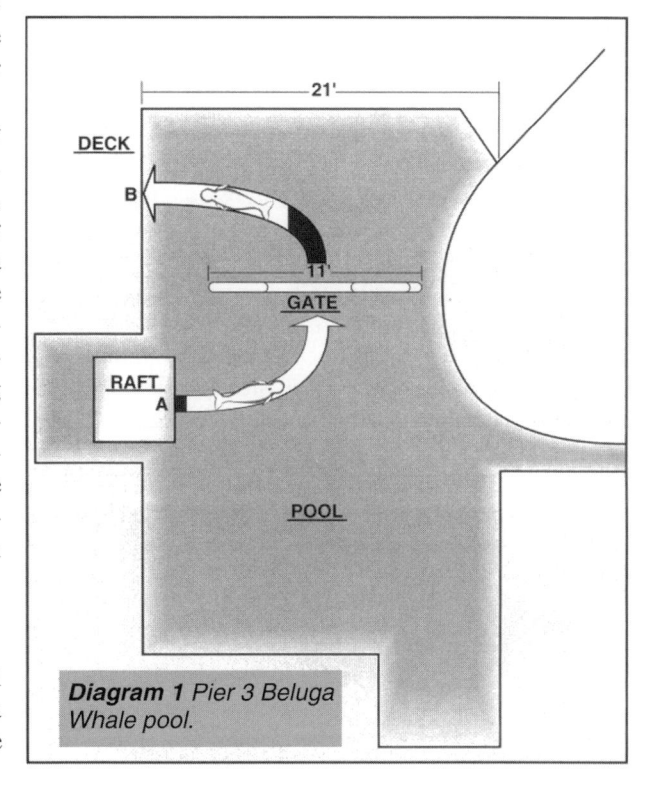

Diagram 1 Pier 3 Beluga Whale pool.

Chapter 7 - Social Animals   231

not learn conditioned behaviors normally associated with a multiple pool facility, such as separating away from one another, or swimming through a canal to another pool. Since the new facility was to be significantly larger and feature a multiple pool design, separating from pool to pool would become a new part in the daily routine. Furthermore, the whales would be expected to take part in daily public shows. The whales would be featured in the first portion of the show and then separated into one of the back pools to allow Atlantic bottlenose dolphins to finish the show. Thus, conditioning the separation behavior was to become a very important part of the daily lives of these three beluga whales.

CONDITIONING THE SEPARATION BEHAVIOR

Conditioning separations began with two of the whales in the Pier 3 facility six months before the planned move to the new pavilion. The objective was to condition the foundations of the separation behavior prior to the move to the new facility on Pier 4. The behaviors to be conditioned included "A-Bs" and swimming through a simulated canal. Initially the whales were taught to transfer control from one trainer to another in response to a new discriminative stimulus (S^D). This stimulus, a point, was a hand gesture. This was initially conditioned with two trainers next to one another and corresponded to a change in control from one trainer to another. Gradually the trainers moved farther apart. As the distance between trainers increased, a slap upon the surface of the water was often added to provide a secondary stimulus and locality. Criteria for a correct response required a whale to swim from one trainer (A) to another trainer (B) upon presentation of the new discriminative stimulus. This behavior, called an "A-B", was learned reliably by both whales within one week. Both primary and secondary reinforcers were given in response to correct behavior. The idea was to make the "A-B" a positive behavior that led to a wide variety of reinforcers. Waterwork, playtimes, and other previously conditioned reinforcers were all used in response to a correct "A-B" trial, thus increasing the frequency of the separation behavior.

As the whales progressed with the "A-B" approximations, the training staff began to desensitize them to a portable gate apparatus. This gate was designed to provide a barrier through which the whales could pass. The gate was constructed of a PVC piping frame covered with opaque tennis court type wind screening. Buoys were fastened to the top of the gate to provide flotation, while the bottom was

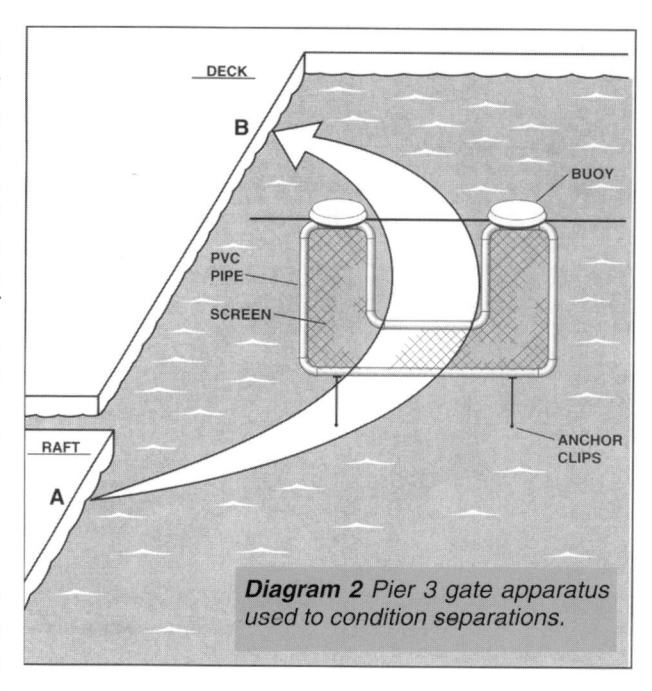

Diagram 2 Pier 3 gate apparatus used to condition separations.

attached to the pool floor by metal anchor clips. This design kept the gate upright in the water. Diagram 2 is a schematic of the portable gate used in the Pier 3 beluga pool.

"A-B" training sessions continued with the gate placed on the raft in view of the whales. Most of the time the gate was held upright on the raft. The gate was also moved to different locations on the raft during the A-B approximations. This was done to desensitize the whales to the presence of the gate apparatus. At this point no noticeable change was observed in the behavior of the whales. The next step was to desensitize them to the presence of the gate in the water. The whales were asked to remain at the raft while the gate was placed into, or removed from, the water. Initial reactions consisted of both whales breaking from control and swimming over to the gate. In most sessions, the whales quickly returned to the trainers and continued uninterrupted throughout the rest of the session. A correct response occurred when the whales remained at the raft while the gate was placed into or removed from the water. The whales were taught to ignore the gate by asking them for incompatible behaviors while the gate was beng moved. These incompatible behaviors were varied and the gate was removed from the pool at different times in each session. The whales were considered completely desensitized after ten sessions during which they remained at control when the gate was put into place or removed from the water.

The training staff then conditioned the whales to swim to a "B" position on the far side of the pool (see diagram 2). Once the whales were conditioned to station at the "B" position, the gate was placed into the pool and the whales were asked to swim through it to the same "B" position. To prevent the whales from swimming around or under the gate, a target was placed just in front of it. Reinforcement was given for swimming to the target. This allowed the staff to slowly approximate the whales through the gate and establish a positive reinforcement history for the behavior. Once through the gate, the whales were trained by successive approximation to move over to the "B" position. The target was slowly faded from the behavior as successful approximations accumulated. The whales showed no hesitation in passing through the gate structure. Reinforcement was given for responding to the discriminative stimulus by swimming through the gate and stationing calmly at the "B" position. Reinforcement was not given for swimming around or under the gate. Once established, the behavior was worked periodically while the whales awaited transfer to their new facility.

PIER 4 FACILITY

The new whale facility featured a 1.3 million-gallon, multiple pool design. Diagram 3 is a schematic of the Pier 4 facility. In addition to acclimating to a new environment, a third whale was added to the existing social structure. All three whales acclimated together in one of the back pools. Once the whales were eating a stable diet, the training staff began to open gates between pools. This allowed the whales to explore the new facility on their own. The whales swam between the pools eagerly, and quickly learned to follow the trainers through the canals under stimulus control during the training session. Actual gates were then placed into the canals and the training staff began to desensitize the whales to the opening and closing of the gates. Reinforcement was given when the whales stationed calmly while a gate was opened or closed.

When the whales were asked to swim through a canal under stimulus control, certain parameters were agreed upon and always followed. These parameters helped to maintain a consistent set of rules for the trainers to follow when the whales performed the separation behavior. These parameters established for separations at the National Aquarium in Baltimore are listed below.

PARAMETERS FOR SEPARATIONS

- The whales are always at control with a trainer while gates are opening or closing.
- The discriminative stimulus for the separation behavior is not paired with the opening or closing of a gate.
- Gates are not closed to block the path of a whale that does not remain at station when a gate opens. Reinforcement is given to the whales that remain at control.
- Upon presentation of the separation S^D, the whales are asked to swim through the gate and station with a trainer in the new pool.

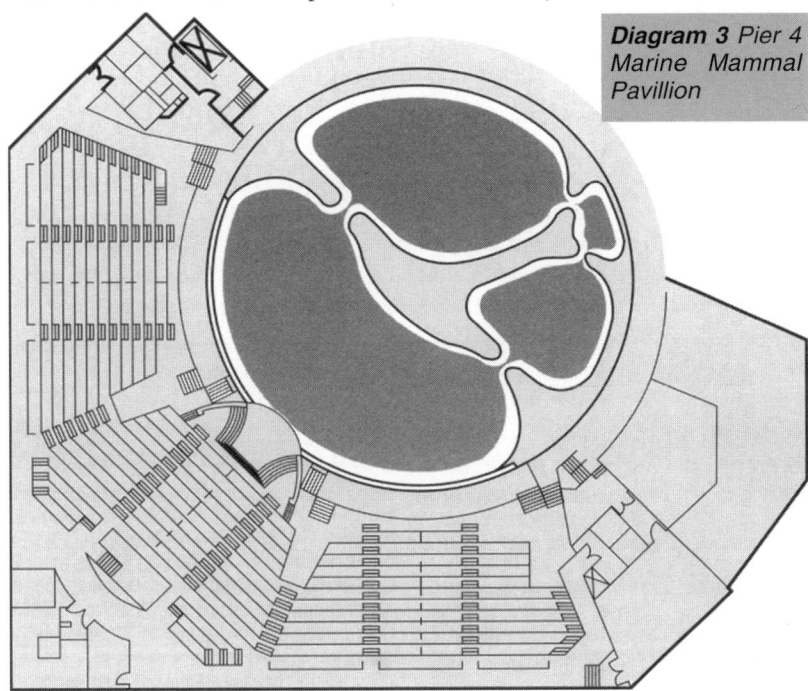

Diagram 3 Pier 4 Marine Mammal Pavillion

These parameters helped to establish separations as a very dependable aspect of the whales' behavioral repertoire and provided certain benefits to both the trainers and whales. First, the whales were reinforced for remaining at station when the gates were opened or closed. This provided an easy reinforcement opportunity for the animals, while desensitizing them to an environmental change (the opening or closing of the gate). Also, an open gate did not become an environmental stimulus for swimming through a canal to another pool. Sessions often continued with the gate opening or closing throughout. At times, a single whale would separate through the canal alone. Other times the whales would go in pairs or as a group of three. Sometimes the gates opened and the whales were not asked to separate. Once again, this helped to lessen the predictability of the separation behavior. Finally, if a whale left from station through an open gate, the gate was never closed to block the path of the animal that had left from control; thus offering the least possible change in response to an incorrect behavior.

Ideally, the NAIB staff would have liked to use a single strategy in response to every incorrect separation response. The staff did not want to provide any environmental changes when incorrect responses occurred during a separation. Unfortunately this was not a practical solution for the complex environment in which our whales lived. During the training process, certain patterns developed which resulted in the development of a four strategy model for dealing with incorrect responses during a separation behavior. Application of a particular strategy was dependent upon the environmental situation from which a particular whale broke from control. The strategies are listed below.

FOUR STRATEGIES USED
FOR AN INCORRECT SEPARATION

1. The animals performing the behavior correctly are reinforced and the gate is left open. The session is ended.
2. The whales performing correctly are reinforced and the separation behavior continues. The whales are separated into the pool with the whale that had left control and the gate is closed. The whales that performed the separation correctly are reinforced and the session is ended.
3. The gate is closed and the whales performing correctly are reinforced.
4. The session continues with the whales performing correct behavior.

The need for a four-strategy model developed because of the different scenarios under which incorrect separation responses occurred. For example, strategy 1,2, or 3 would not be practical during a show. For this reason, strategy 4 was developed. It is important to note that the usage of multiple strategies if implemented incorrectly, does have the potential to reinforce incorrect separations by providing different responses to an incorrect behavior. Since whales often left from control under different environmental conditions, the NAIB staff developed separate strategies for the different circumstances under which our whales broke from control. To avoid accidentally reinforcing incorrect responses, there was a consistent response implemented for each circumstance from which a whale could break from control. These strategies helped to keep separations as a very strong behavior in a complex environment.

CONCLUSION

Conditioning beluga whales to separate between pools in a new environment creates certain benefits for the whales and the training staff. This method is but one of many different ways to condition successful separations with cetaceans. Using this method provided certain advantages in addition to successful separations for the whales at the NAIB. Most importantly, a positive reinforcement history was established for this new behavior. Separating between pools became a means toward variable positive reinforcement as opposed to the end result of transferring to a new pool. Interactions rarely ended once the whales swam through the gate. Playtimes, toys, and other previously established reinforcers were all used in response to successful separations.

This method also provided a means for preliminary conditioning of separations in an environment where there are no gates. On Pier 3, the beluga whales were able to learn the fundamental aspects of successful separations. Conditioning "A-Bs," the switching of control, and passing through a simulated gate benefited the whales once they were transported to Pier 4. The components of successful separations were already a part of two of the whales' behavioral repertoires.

Establishing a positive reinforcement history for the separation behavior also resulted in benefits for training and show situations. Strong separations allowed the training staff to use one, two, or three whales for shows as well as training sessions. The ability to separate one whale away from the group was especially helpful in working with younger whales, whales low in the social order, or when training new behaviors. Reinforcement was given to the whale that had separated away from the group, as well as to the whales that remained at station. This method took a little longer than other separation methods, but the advantages were certainly worth the additional time. With separations a reliable behavior in each of the whales' behavioral repertoire, the training staff was able to devote more time to enriching the lives of this beluga whale population.

VOL 23, NO 2, 1998. The following article was a multiple award winner at the 25th Annual IMATA Conference in Baltimore, Maryland, USA. The paper won the Best Trained Behavior and People's Choice awards for 1997 as well as the Best First Time Presenter award for Traci Belting. It is too bad that the humorous video that accompanied this presentation could not accompany the article. Once again, gating (and other behaviors) is discussed here, but this time the emphasis is on polar bears. This paper demonstrates that the same techniques can be applied to almost any animal and used to help in the management of aquatic or terrestrial animals in free or protected contact training.

Teaching an Old Polar Bear Program New Tricks

by Traci Belting, Jean Joseph, Mike Messersmith and Lisa Nordone
Point Defiance Zoo and Aquarium

INTRODUCTION

The Arctic Tundra exhibits at the Point Defiance Zoo and Aquarium provide visitors with the opportunity to view elusive animals such as Arctic fox, musk oxen, and a variety of waterfowl. The centerpiece of this Arctic experience is the Polar Bear Habitat. Rather than the classic bear grotto design where visitors view the animals from above, this exhibit was one of the first to bring the visitor into the exhibit at a bear's eye view. Built in 1982, the polar bear complex received the Exhibit Excellence Award for the American Zoo and Aquarium Association.

The main habitat includes an eleven foot deep (3.3 meters), 90,000 gallon (342,000 liter) pool, wide dry beaches, raised islands, and a large moving stream. Water for the habitat is filtered sea water pumped from the adjacent Puget Sound. The front of the exhibit is rimmed with viewing windows and the remainder of the exhibit is secured with a dry mote and a double ring of hot wire. The habitat offers the bears a variety of substrates, including large climbing rocks and pebbly beaches. A portion of one raised island contains built in planters for growing grasses, herbs, and other food enrichment. Large gravel pits provide the bears with the opportunity to dig, roll, and rest. The stream flows directly into the pool where underwater viewing gives zoo visitors an "up-close" experience.

The off-exhibit holding areas were designed with human safety as a priority. Although all the shift doors are manually operated, they can only be accessed from the security of a second level above the bear dens. The original holding areas include four indoor rooms (two with maternity dens attached) and one outdoor unit.

Movement of the bears between the holding areas and the main habitat was achieved by using food placement on either side of the guillotine gates which separated the two areas. The opening of a gate served as the stimulus for the bears to shift. While this method seemed to work under normal circumstances, it became problematic if the bears weren't hungry or were in any way distracted. The dominance hierarchy of the bears determined which bear shifted through the door first and this "shift order" needed to be taken into consideration when trying to separate individual bears. In 1995, the zoo's bear collection consisted of a 17-year-old female and a 28-year-old male.

THE MOTIVATION FOR A CHANGE

In May, 1996, staff reorganization at the zoo included combining the Rocky Shores and Tundra areas into one new work unit. The five full-time staff would manage the Tundra exhibits described above and all of the Rocky Shores exhibits including walrus, belugas, harbor seals, sea otters, puffins, and penguins. To make a long story short, we now have marine mammal trainers taking care of polar bears. The only remaining veteran staff member was the current Tundra keeper who had been working at the zoo for 24 years and had spent a majority of that time working with the bears.

In October 1995 we had received an approximately 10-month-old orphaned female cub from Barrow, Alaska. She was housed in an empty sea lion holding facility consisting of two enclosed holding pools, which was located adjacent to polar bear holding. This sea lion holding area was built in 1994 by the National Marine Fisheries Service funded through the Washington Department of Fish and Wildlife. Several large bull California sea lions were feasting on Steelhead trout at the Ballard locks in Washington State and the holding pools were built as a part of a three year pilot project to temporarily house the sea lions during the Steelhead run.

By December 1996 the female cub was 400 pounds and the decision was made to transfer her to the polar bear holding area in preparation for her introduction to our adult bears. But wait, the New Year brought with it the news that we would soon be receiving two male yearling cubs from Canada. We needed a plan!

THE BEAR HABI-TRAIL

The thought of managing five bears of various ages in our current facility sent shivers through the spines of our staff. We brainstormed how we might be able to expand our bear holding capacity by connecting the sea lion holding area to the existing polar bear holding. We needed to be able to rotate bears, in various combinations, between the five rooms in the original bear holding area, the modified sea lion holding pool area, and the main habitat. What resulted with the resources and time available was a nightmarish series of chain-link hallways and gates we dubbed the "bear habitrail."

Chain-link walls were erected across the center keeper access area of the indoor holding area to provide a corridor to move bears from one side to the other. This was important since only one side of the building would have access to the holding pool area. A long chute was built to serve as a hallway to connect the holding pools to the outdoor unit of the original bear holding area. Sturdy rolling gates between the two holding pools as well as at either end of the newly constructed chute.

LET THE TRAINING BEGIN

The expanded holding facility now contained 12 main shift gates. If a bear didn't shift properly, the whole system would be gridlocked and movement of other bears would be impossible. We could no longer afford to allow bears to randomly walk through a doorway when a gate opened. We needed to train the bears!

In March, 1997 the two male cubs arrived from Canada and we began our formal bear training. We had already begun some protected contact training with the two-year-old while she was housed in the holding pool area, and the two young males were ripe for training. The adults would be the challenge. The now 19-year-old female and 30-year-old male were used to responding to gate movements, not trainers. We proceeded with training all the bears in the same manner:

- We began hand feeding the bears through the fence, selectively reinforcing calm responses. To maintain a safe distance between the bear's mouth and the fence (and to avoid accidental ingestion of a trainer's hand) we used whole fish and large meatballs of Nebraska Brand Feline Diet.

- A verbal "good" and visual point were conditioned as a bridging stimulus. These can be used simultaneously or one at a time at the trainer's discretion.

- Habituating the bears to gates opening and closing was achieved by using successive approximations of gate movements, only reinforcing the bears if they remained at station.

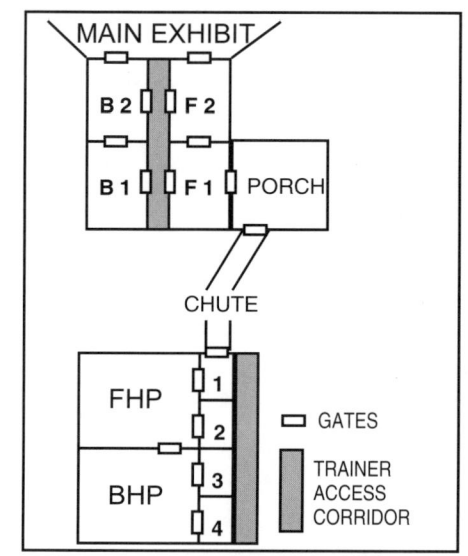

Habi-trail - Polar bear holding areas, and collection flexibility, were increased by the creation of a "bear habi-trail."

To our surprise, the adults responded as quickly to the training as the youngsters. The initial station training was actually easier to establish because the adults' actions were slower and more deliberate as compared to the excited movements of the juveniles.

In order to establish a criteria for holding station while a gate was opened, the bears could watch the gates as they moved but they had to remain in a seated position. One bear actually figures out the criteria and would attempt to scoot along on its rear end in anticipation of movement through a gate! The movements of the 30-year-old male appeared slow and labored when rising from a seated position, so it was decided he would be exempt from the "sit" criteria at station.

We opened and closed gates at unpredictable times, sometimes shifting a bear through the gate, sometimes not. Because we have a small staff and a large collection of animals in our care, we could only dedicate one to two 15-minute sessions a day to bear training. Variety was the key to solidifying the gate desensitization and shifting.

Because of the complexity of the physical facility, many of the movements of the bears require them to shift from one area to another out of sight of their trainer. We initially trained a basic follow using the words "Let's go" as a discriminative stimulus (S^D). Eventually "Let's go" would initiate the movement of a bear through a gate even if they couldn't see a trainer on the other side. Since most rooms in the holding facility have more than one gate which could be opened at one time, the "Let's go" S^D became directional, with the bear moving in the direction of the trainer's first few steps. In the case of shifting a bear onto the main habitat, the trainer's direction is initially towards the habitat to initiate the bear's movement through the gate, then the trainer reverses direction to exit the holding building, runs around the outside of the building and along the perimeter of the exhibit to reestablish contact with the bear.

WORKING WITH THE BEAR'S DOMINANCE STRUCTURE, NOT AGAINST IT

Even though we had initially planned to introduce the two-year-old female to the adult bears, once the two young males arrived we were able to observe the interactions of all the bears as they watched, listened to, and smelled each other through the various fences. We evaluated the intensity of the vocalizations, posturing, and other interactions between all the bears. Based on the behavior we observed, we decided to introduce the young female to the yearling males, instead of to the adults.

Despite the fact the female was a year older and outweighed each of the males by more than 200 pounds (90 kilograms), at the time of introduction. She immediately took a submissive role. Between the two yearling males there was an obvious dominant animal as well. Rather than rigidly controlling this natural social hierarchy, we incorporated it into the training plan. Stationing order was determined by the bears, with the most dominant animal positioning closet to keeper access. Once the order was established, we only reinforced the group when they were in the correct order, being careful to selectively reinforce the most dominant animal for allowing the others to station. Once at station, each bear could be moved in any order by a separate trainer to any area of the main habitat or holding area. The young female was reluctant to pass by a more dominant male and rather than force the issue, we ask her to hold station while the male(s) moved past her instead. This decreased the likelihood of unnecessary aggression between animals and still achieves our goal of separating individual bears in any order from the rest of the group.

CONCLUSION

In the seven months since we began this project, we have successfully trained all five bears to move through the entire complex under stimulus control. In addition to being able to safely rotate our two groups of bears between the main habitat and the holding areas, we have seen other benefits as well. Our 30-year old male would routinely lose his appetite and was losing weight with age. Now that we are delivering food as a reinforcer during training sessions, his average daily intake has increased and his activity level has improved. Even when our adult female shows no interest in food because of seasonal appetite fluctuations, controlled shifts are still possible since she responds well to secondary reinforcers. Establishing behavioral criteria and observing the bears responses gives us one more tool in evaluating their overall health.

This training program is in its infancy and future goals include expanding the training of husbandry behaviors to allow for routine exams and weights without the need for anesthesia. We know many of you have extensive experience with protected contact training and we welcome any tips and training ideas you have to offer.

1979 IMATA Conference, San Diego, California, USA. Training a group of animals without any means of separating them creates unique challenges for a trainer. Nevertheless, the Brookfield Zoo successfully accomplished this feat for over 25 years before building a new dolphin facility. This paper describes the trials and tribulations of this very successful program.

The Training of Dolphins (*Tursiops truncatus*) in a Community Tank

by James J. Clarke and Randy Brill
Chicago Zoological Society, Brookfield Zoo

ABSTRACT

Brookfield Zoo opened its Seven Seas Panorama exhibit in 1961, a daring experiment in the maintenance of marine mammals, dolphins in particular. The complex was designed without the benefits of the mass of present-day knowledge regarding dolphins and represented the first attempt at maintaining these animals in a completely inland environment. By contemporary standards, the complex today suffers from several disadvantages. Because we are lacking a readily available means of physically separating animals, the group of five dolphins are completely trained and perform in a community situation. This paper discusses some of the advantages and disadvantages of this particular situation and explores its effects on newly acquired animals as well as veteran performers.

TRAINING DOLPHINS IN A COMMUNITY TANK

In the late 1950s, the practice of housing marine mammals in a geographic location more than a few miles from the seacoast where natural ocean water is not readily available was unheard of. The task of transporting this type of animal over long distances by plane to such a facility was one that never before required consideration. To provide an awareness of life in the oceans to the people of the Midwest, the Chicago Zoological Society ventured to overcome these barriers, along with many others. Hence, the creation of the world's first inland dolphinarium, the Seven Seas Panorama, came to be. After 2 ½ years of planning and construction, the Seven Seas Panorama was opened in 1961. The exhibit was very well received and, in fact, it was not uncommon back then to see long lines forming around the outside of the building just to pass through the downstairs hallway for a glimpse of the dolphins as they swam past underwater viewing windows. Today, just as back then, the Seven Seas exhibit is still highly rated by Brookfield Zoo visitors and is also home to Olga, the walrus, the most expensive and popular animal in the zoo. However, the facility today lacks many modern conveniences. Perhaps the most prominent disadvantage is the absence of a readily available means of physically separating animals. Therefore, the group of five Atlantic bottlenose dolphins is completely trained and performs in a community situation. Through the years, however, trainers at Seven Seas have modified their training techniques and have created a show-style that seems unique to our situation.

To create a clearer understanding, perhaps a brief description of our setup is in order. The tank is oval in shape with a length of 100 feet (30.5m) and a width of 25 feet (7.6m). The bottom of the pool is shaped in such a way that the greatest depth of 16 feet (4.9m) occurs in the center of the pool and gradually slopes up to a depth of 6 feet (1.8m) on each end. At this point the 6 foot (1.8m) depth is consistent from the top of each slope to the end of the tank creating two decks, one on each end of the pool. Each deck forms a semi-circle with a radius of 12 ½ feet (3.8m). The decks may be sectioned off by means of a portable net rigging designed especially for this purpose. Should the need arise these portable net barriers are the only means we have of separating animals. Due to the fact that these portable pen-nets cut down the size of the show area, they are used only temporarily and for two basic reasons. The second reason involves the acquisition of a new animal or animals. A new group member will spend up to three months behind the pen-net depending upon how long it takes the animal to become target trained and to station (i.e. holding a position indicated by the trainer). Holding an animal at a station is a very vital part of our show.

Because we lack some type of adjacent separating facility, we are left with the only alternative of having all five animals working every show. An average show at Seven Seas runs 25 to 30 minutes in length. Ideally, the show moves along at a non-stop pace with the animals performing up to 20 to 25 different behaviors. Having each animal contribute equally to the show enables us to employ a reward system in which each animal will receive its proper quantity of food for each performance. In the case of newer, less experienced animals, repeating behaviors, such as simple back floating or unison leaps, as a more experienced animal performs a more difficult behavior, is common. This is done often throughout the show to keep the new performer busy and out of the way. The show is not choreographed and does not follow a rigid story line. In other words, what the animals do is not dependent upon the spoken script. On the other hand, the narration follows what the animals are doing. This gives the trainer the freedom to change the sequence of behavior at any time if he feels it is appropriate. This technique is commonly used in a case where an animal is supposed to do a hoop jump, for example. If, at a particular point in the show, the animal decides to go off into the end of the tank, avoiding its scheduled behavior, the trainer then has the option of passing by the hoop jumps and moving on to a behavior in which that particular animal is not involved. As soon as the animal decides to return to the feed area, which is almost always the case, the trainer can go back and pick up the hoop jump sequence whenever he is ready. Sometimes a trainer will change the order of a show routine for no other reason than to keep the attention level of the animals higher, creating a situation where they do not know for sure what is coming next.

It is our ultimate goal to create a show situation in which all animals are conditioned to perform every behavior in the show. This would be an aid in the case of a particular animal not wanting to perform for some reason. As far as the animals are concerned, they are in a situation where they do not know what they will be asked to do next. At the present, we are at a point where every behavior can be performed by two and in some cases three animals.

It is of great importance that when two or more animals are conditioned to respond to the same signal they know which one of them will be rewarded for performing the behavior. This is accomplished by designating which animal you want to do the behavior. The animals have been intentionally conditioned to recognize that such indications as eye contact or a pointing gesture from the trainer precedes a signal that will be given that particular animal. The others know to station by the feeding area during the behavior. The animals stationing are rewarded for staying, and, if the behavior is adequately performed, that animal is also rewarded for performing.

The five performers at Seven Seas range in age from approximately 23 years down to about three years. The oldest animal has been performing here for over 11 years, and the two newcomers have been performing for four short months. Hence a wide range of age, dominance order and experience exists. The advantage is that learning by imitation is quite common, especially on simple behaviors such as back floating, flipper waving and tail slapping. One big disadvantage that has existed on occasion has been the presence of a large, overbearing, dominant animal. Trying to keep tabs on five animals and passing out rewards provides an easy opportunity for fish stealing. We have found this problem to occur heavily during the mating seasons and at times have gotten to the point where a subordinate animal will actually spit out food as a more dominant animal approaches. The most effective way we have found to deal with this problem is to simply not give the aggressive animal an opportunity to steal fish. Occasionally it means holding back a reward from a less dominant animal for a satisfactory behavior until the threat is absent. Within a few days of unsuccessful attempts to steal fish, the problem subsides until next mating season.

One extreme case of a dominance problem occurred a few years back. This involved an approximately 32-year-old dolphin named Vicki who was one of the original animals shipped up to Brookfield in 1961. Vicki was dominant from the first day until she died. For a period of over a month Vicki chased the four other dolphins up to the end of the tank as soon as a trainer and food were present. Not knowing what was causing Vicki to behave this way made the problem difficult to deal with. It got to the point where another trainer would take Vicki down to the opposite end of the tank to play with her and feed her during the shows. This worked out fine for a couple of days. When this was no longer effective, the only other alternative we had was to install the pen-net and separate her at the beginning of each day and release her after the last show. This was done for a period of two days. It was obvious Vicki was not at all happy behind the net, and she still had a threatening power over the others even though she was denied physical contact. Luckily, the problem ironed itself out. With a long-term problem such as this, a holding facility would have come in handy. On the other hand, it would also have provided a means of actually avoiding the problem rather than dealing with it.

The pros and cons of a holding facility are most obvious during training sessions. Since shows are presented every day of the year, the animals are in training at the same time they are still performing. Show schedules and times vary throughout the year. In the spring and summer, four and five shows a day allow us to accommodate larger crowds. In the fall and winter two shows are presented during the week and three on weekends. This provides other feedings to be utilized for training. Just as all five animals work together in the show, all five are also trained at the same time and in the same tank. Each session is timed and runs for a maximum of twenty minutes. At the beginning of each session the animals are sent to specific areas of the tank where they will be working with a particular trainer. All five dolphins know that when a training session begins, they will only be fed in their designated area and by the trainer working with them. For various reasons, however, an animal might wander off to a different area even though it knows it will not be fed there. The trainer there can either ignore the animal until it returns to its proper place or if the animal is creating problems the trainer can point the animal in the general direction of where it should be and the animal usually responds. Each of the animals has learned that they may be sectioned off in any combination or in any area of the pool. This allows us to train two or more animals the same behavior simultaneously.

Some disadvantages to training in our situation are obvious. One major disadvantage involves the fact that there is only one deep section in the pool. If we would like to train two behaviors which require deep water, we either have to divide the training session or wait until one behavior is completed before we begin working on the other. One common disadvantage becomes obvious when one animal works exceptionally well. If the animal has been fed-out before the allotted 20 minutes are up, it will usually begin to wander into another section. This usually results in some problem. To avoid this we try to adjust our activity in order to use up as much of the 20 minutes as possible. On the other hand, there are those times when an animal is not putting forth enough effort during a training session. This rarely occurs with a younger animal, but in the case of an older, more dominant animal it usually results in the animal harassing the others. This is the primary reason the sessions are timed. We rely on the animals learning that there is only a limited period when the food is available.

There can be advantages to training in this type of situation. Because the animals are trained in the show tank, they are also readily available to perform. A new behavior requiring a prop such as a hoop or hurdle can be shaped using the specific prop that will eventually be used during the show. Finally, and along these same lines, a new behavior is shaped in the same area of the pool it will ultimately be performed, hence the transition of a behavior from training to show should in theory be easier.

From an economic standpoint a system for shifting animals, which we lack, would be beneficial in allowing us to hold more shows during the busy season without overworking the animals. This could be accomplished by dividing the group up and alternating them for performances. On a busy summer day the animals are asked to do five shows at most. On these days twice as many shows would easily sell out, but again the lack of the required facilities here prevent this possibility.

The final aspect in maintaining these animals which should be included involves the medical treatments. Twice yearly all five dolphins are given routine physicals. An ill animal in need of medication which cannot be administered orally is caught and treated. In either case, facilities do not allow us to work on the animal in the pool without draining two-thirds of the water. Hence it must be taken out of the tank entirely. The process involves at least 10 people and sometimes requires shows to be cancelled for the entire day.

Either or both pen-nets must be installed in the ends of the pool, and the animals are herded there by use of a large drag-net. Divers are positioned at various points on the drag-net to pull it across the pool. Excess divers are on hand in the event an animal should become tangled in the drag-net. Once the desired animal(s) is isolated behind the pen-net, the water level in the tank is dropped about three feet. If shows are to be run on that day, they have to be done with a lower than normal water level. A crew is sent in with a small net to capture the animal and properly position it in a work stretcher. The animal is then pulled out of the tank and onto foam rubber mats which lie on the floor adjacent to the pool. The work area here is very cramped and crowded. Our goal, however, is to complete all needed procedures and to get the animal back into the pool as soon as possible.

Since its beginning the Seven Seas facility has undergone one major renovation. Because of its high popularity among zoo visitors, plans are now in the embryonic stages for either another major renovation and expansion or possibly an entirely new exhibit. By employing the techniques presently used at Seven Seas in modern facility, perhaps we will be able to offer even more diversity in the display of our animals as well as in the methods used for their training.

Trainer's Forum

VOL 19, NO 1, 1994. Whether you have the ability to separate animals, training with more than one animal in the habitat is often necessary. How to progress with one animal and not affect others is a common concern. In addition, the use of the bridging stimulus in those situations can pose a unique challenge for trainers. Few trainers have the luxury of working one-on-one with an animal in every session. Consequently, learning to work with multiple animals is an important skill. The next *Trainer's Forum* article discusses the same subject further.

Training Only One Animal When Others Are Present

Note: The question in this Trainer's Forum has been pulled from the archives – we thought it would be appropriate to find past questions that still apply to today's training.

QUESTION: *(From the Summer of 1983)* How do you let one animal in a pool with several others know that you are training it and it alone, and how does that animal know that it should pay attention to a bridge?

ANSWER 1: Training a dolphin along with several others in the same tank is not necessarily a difficult task if the required situation is carefully conditioned and steps are taken to avoid confusion on the part of the animals. Here at Brookfield Zoo's Seven Seas Panorama, we work with five Atlantic bottlenose dolphins in one large community tank. In an effort to answer your question, let me describe our methods.

Although it is convenient to be able to work an individual animal alone in a training pool, that situation may not always be available. Our animals are made accustomed to the practice of being sent, either alone or with any combination of tank mates, to different parts of the pool with different trainers. Each animal can then be worked, or held out of the way, from any point in or around the tank allowing the trainer to achieve a one-on-one situation with an animal while other trainers and animals are working in other locations.

There are several problems associated with training in this manner. First of all, there is the possibility that one animal will respond to a bridge coming from a trainer other than the one it is working with. That's the problem I think you're indicating in the second part of your question. One possible cure for that is to have the trainers take turns during a training session so that only one animal is being worked at a time while the others are just held and kept "busy" by another trainer or trainers. Or, as in our case, it may be found that the animals can apparently learn, over time, to distinguish where, or with which trainer, the sound of the bridge originates and respond accordingly.

Another problem occurs with an animal leaving a designated area and imposing on another. This usually happens when an animal knows that it is finished with its training for that session or when it is having difficulty understanding what it is expected to do. Setting a time limit for the session and having the trainers cooperate so that all are done at the same time will help ease the first condition. The second condition is a little harder since the animal is, obviously frustrated, but can be alleviated by providing as much encouragement as possible. One way is to insert familiar behaviors in with the new ones. That way, the reinforcement keeps coming even though the animal may be experiencing difficulty, and that encourages it to stay and work things out. Teamwork and organization, among the trainers are the keys to training animals in a group. If the trainers know what they will be doing with each animal, and where they will be doing it, before the session begins, the animals will have a much easier time unerstanding what's expected of them.

Despite the inconveniences, there are some advantages to training in a situation like ours. Quite often a behavior can be trained in an exact location in the pool in which it will be performed during a show, eliminating the need for a transition from a training pool to a show pool. Additionally, the animal becomes accustomed to performing a new behavior in the presence of its tank mates right from the beginning. And, finally, one animal can experience a number of changes including trainers and pool locations in the course of one training session making the process a lot more full for all involved.

1983 Training Staff
Brookfield Zoo

ANSWER 2: Here at the John G. Shedd Aquarium we have dealt with the situation of training several animals in one habitat in a number of different ways. Certainly the preferred method of handling new training is to work with the animal alone, but sometimes that is neither practical nor feasible. Our next option is usually to try scheduling enough trainers so that each animal can have individual attention. If we have the luxury of one trainer per animal, each animal can be worked at a different location and much of the confusion is avoided. Finally, in situations where separation was not possible, and having one trainer per animal was not practical either, we have found the need to be creative when it came to one person training multiple animals simultaneously.

The first step was to get all the animals involved comfortable with working side-by-side. In most cases this was never a problem. However, with some animals, working side-by-side takes time to condition. Once animals are eating comfortably side-by-side, it is then important to reinforce every animal for stationing patiently and allowing another animal to do a behavior. Only after these two concepts were understood did we proceed with trying to train an animal while another was stationing.

As it became necessary to do extensive training, we taught the animals to target on a buoy at their station. They were to remain at their respective buoys until bridged. Thus, when it was time to train a new behavior with one animal, the other animals would be asked to target on their buoys first; then work could begin with the animal being taught the new behavior. As each successive step was bridged with the new behavior, the animals at their targets would be bridged as well and all animals reinforced. Obviously this was a lengthy process, and whenever possible we used additional trainers to work with the animals not being trained.

It was equally important not to spend all our

focused training time on one animal. We found that by spreading the training time around to each animal, they seemed more patient and accepting of this process. As the animals gained experience with this procedure we were able to approximate their targets further away from station which allowed plenty of training room for the focus animal. Again, the key was to adequately reinforce the animals who went to their respective buoys and not give attention only to the individual being trained on the new behavior.

Once a behavior is trained and on an S^D, we were able to get away from the use of targets. Each animal is taught that when being worked in association with other animals, all S^Ds will be preceded with a tap on the melon or rostrum. The tap is used as an indicator to the animal that the S^D that follows is intended for him or her. If the animal is not tapped on the rostrum prior to the presentation of the S^D, they are to ignore the S^D and remain at station. After the desired animal completes the requested behavior, all animals are reinforced.

The final part of the question concerned alleviating confusion about a bridging stimulus when more than one animal is being worked. There are a number of things we do to try to avoid confusing the animal. The most important is to communicate to everyone working when critical training steps are about to take place. This helps avoid inadvertent bridging of a behavior by someone else. We have also reduced confusion by establishing more than one bridging stimulus. We use the audible whistle, as well as a visual sharp point at the animal, or two firm taps on the animal's body. We have found that when training husbandry or other close-up tactile behaviors, that the tactile bridge is very effective and it does not interrupt work being done by other trainers and animals. Likewise, the visual bridge has been very helpful for behaviors that involve eye contact between trainer an animal. Visual bridges are very useful in many situations when physical contact is not possible and audible bridging might confuse another animal. We have used all three types of bridges with both species of cetaceans here at the Shedd Aquarium, and have found them quite helpful in avoiding the type of confusion you describe.

We hope these ideas help anyone encountering these challenges. Good luck!

1993 Training Staff
John G. Shedd Aquarium

VOL 24, NO 1, 1999. There have been numerous *Trainer's Forum* articles focusing on bridging techniques. This important tool requires precision and its importance cannot be overstated. Here are four suggestions for reducing confusion when animals mistake another animal's bridge for their own.

Multiple Bridges: Avoiding the Confusion

QUESTION: The dolphins at our facility frequently confuse their bridge with bridges from trainers in different areas of the facility. How can we resolve this?

ANSWER 1: There are several approaches to minimizing an animal's confusion when other trainers are bridging in different areas. With husbandry behaviors, we rely heavily on communication between trainers. For example, if a trainer is asking a dolphin to lay out for a blood sample, he or she will request the other trainer in the area to hold off on bridging a behavior until the sample is completed. This type of information should be communicated before the session begins and during the session. Two or more trainers in different areas can rotate bridging throughout a session.

A different approach could be used with high-energy behaviors. Depending on the acoustics of the facility, the animals can be trained to respond to the bridge coming from their respective trainers. This may be accomplished by reinforcing the animal that has returned to its trainer's location after it has been bridged. Meanwhile, the dolphin that has returned to its trainer after hearing another trainer's bridge would receive an LRS. By being consistent with the LRS, the animals that are in different areas are trained to respond only to the bridge coming from their trainer's location.

Training Staff
The Dolphin Experience

ANSWER 2: The bridge is a powerful, conditioned reinforcer that allows the trainer to provide information to the dolphin, indicating when they perform a behavior correctly. Bridge confusion is a potentially frustrating situation for trainer and dolphin alike. The communication pathway has broken down, and the animal has been told they were participating in the correct behavior at an undesired time. This situation can have detrimental effects on trained behaviors (early termination of behavior, reinforcement of sub-par criteria or incorrect behavior) and on behaviors in training (reinforcing undesired approximations, creating superstitious behavior). To maintain effective communication between the trainer and dolphin, this problem should be minimized.

A variety of bridges, or conditioned reinforcers, provides the trainer with increased flexibility in communication. Whistles, clickers, body taps, water slaps, points, and many other signals can be effective conditioned reinforcers. These conditioned reinforcers reach the animal through audition, vision, or touch. Different communication routes (different bridges) can be used in different situations to reduce the chance of bridge confusion. For behaviors where the trainer is working in close proximity to the animal, a tactile bridge can be used to reinforce. If the behavior requires the animals to look at you, use a visual bridge (point). Other animals around the pool do not sense the bridge, and therefore cannot respond to it. This technique relies on trainer awareness and communication.

Trainer communication can begin in advance of the session by identifying behaviors sensitive to "background" bridges (conditioned reinforcers not intended for a particular animal). While these behaviors are occurring, trainers avoid the use of conditioned reinforcers that may influence the behavior. For example, during blood collection at our facility we refrain from using the auditory bridge until this behavior is complete. This ensures the animal will not respond to a background bridge and terminate the behavior early. Communication between trainers can continue during the session. If an animal performs a behavior below criteria or incorrectly, other trainers in the area can be alerted to avoid bridging this behavior. General awareness of other animals' behavior by all trainers when using the bridge will assist in minimizing bridge confusion.

At the Dolphin Lagoon, our reaction to an animal responding to a background bridge is situation-specific. If the trainers are near one another, or if the dolphins are participating in a group behavior, they are reinforced as usual if performing the behavior to criteria. We believe that dolphins can localize the sound source around the pool if the separation between trainers is large or obvious. When other trainers are across the pool, or if we are working in close quarters with an animal, we give an LRS if an animal responds to a background bridge. In this situation, the animal is given a least reinforcing stimulus for poor attention or focus. Effective use of the LRS and selective reinforcement of attentive behavior can aid an animal in discrimination between their own and other bridges.

Another possible solution is the use of individual animal bridges. Each dolphin is assigned a unique tone, or bridge, to respond to. This solution becomes complicated as the number of animals increase, and if the animals do not always have individual trainers. A situation where this may work is with two animals. Each one is assigned a unique tone, but will also respond to a general bridge when worked together.

Training Staff
Edmonton Dolphin Lagoon

ANSWER 3: We have also had confusion with bridging in the past. One way that we try to prevent this is with good communication between trainers. For example, if one trainer is about to ask for a high-energy behavior, they simply ask the other trainers to "hold their bridge," in which case the other trainers respond by asking their animal for a small behavior or give tactile. We try to prevent the mistake before it occurs. However, we still have occasional problems with mistaking bridges. When that happens, we ask the animal to repeat the behavior.

Another idea would be to condition a different tone for each individual trainer, although here, we simply use communication between the staff to lessen the confusion.

Training Staff
Gulf World Marine Park

ANSWER 4: I recently worked with two dolphins that had their own individual bridge when working separately (a silver dog whistle for the female and a black plastic dog whistle for the male) and the same bridge when they worked together (the black plastic whistle). This seemed to cause some confusion. Our sessions always varied from one trainer, two dolphins to two trainers and two dolphins with trainers being next to each other or on opposite sides of the pool. Sometimes the female dolphin had to respond to one type of whistle for a bridge but in other situations she was to know another type of whistle for a bridge; and it was inevitable that someone would forget the correct whistle. In addition to these problems, the dolphins were confusing each other's bridge in spite of the whistle, the location, or the behavior. Generally speaking, dolphins are usually able to discriminate the direction (or trainer) from which a whistle came. I decided the first step was to have both animals on the same bridge regardless of whether they were working together or not.

We began all of our training sessions and/or shows with the trainers and the dolphins side by side. Trainer A would send their dolphin out for a behavior while Trainer B held their dolphin at station. When Trainer A bridged, their animal would return to station and receive a primary reinforcement. Trainer B could also reinforce their animal for remaining stationed. Then we would do the same situation with Trainer B sending their animal out for a behavior. We started close to each other then gradually moved farther apart. This may have taken a little longer but was worth it in the end.

Communication was very important during all stages of training. From time to time, there was still the occasional confusion. This can be extremely frustrating when trying to train a new behavior or working sensitive husbandry behaviors. This is a time when communication is vital. Before any sessions, the trainers would discuss their individual plans for that particular session. We used the basic idea of "taking turns" in order to eliminate any confusion for the animals during these crucial times. And as much as we should be paying attention to our animals (and them to us), it is necessary for trainers to be aware of other trainers and other animals.

I noticed quite an improvement in the dolphin's overall behavior and their criteria once they learned this. Good luck!

Suzanne Smith

Trainer's Forum

There is frequently the need or desire to train animals to work in unison. But what do you do if one animal is performing a behavior correctly and one is not? Should you bridge? This complex question must be answered every day by trainers in show situations. Depending on the experience of the trainer and the animals, the situation can be handled in a variety of ways. There are three answers to this question below.

Working Tandem or Group Behaviors: When to Bridge

QUESTION: If you send two animals on a team behavior and one performs the behavior correctly but the other does not, do you bridge? At our facility we allow the animals to terminate the behavior on their own, reinforce the animal who did the behavior correctly, and deliver a neutral response to the animal that did not. I know some facilities recall, some bridge, and some do not reinforce either animal. How does your facility do it?

ANSWER 1: When tandem behaviors are not performed to criteria by an individual animal, our trainers utilize one of two responses.

First, if the behavior reaches its point of termination within a reasonably short period of time and/or the behavior is a relatively low energy behavior, we often choose to allow the behavior to terminate on its own. As long as we are certain that the animal performing the behavior correctly did not cause the other animal to perform incorrectly (through social interaction, displaced aggression, etc.), then the trainer has the option of providing a primary or secondary reinforcer to the animal doing the behavior correctly. The animal that performed incorrectly will receive a neutral response. If there is a question of dominance or aggression interference, there is no bridge; we wait for the behavior to terminate and all animals receive a neutral response.

If the behavioral response does not fall into the first category, so that it continues for a long period of time and/or is a high energy behavior, then we have the option of utilizing a recall. Upon hearing the recall, the animals will terminate the performance of the behavior and return to the trainer. Because we believe a recall can be reinforced, and because we utilize a variable schedule of reinforcement, the trainer now has the option to provide primary reinforcement to the correct animal. We often give the animals a second chance to perform the behavior correctly, which can be reinforcing in itself by providing the animal the opportunity to succeed. If the behavior fails to be performed correctly, we give a neutral response the incorrect behavior and move on.

Because we use a variable schedule of reinforcement, where primary reinforcement does not always follow a bridge, we do not bridge the animal when only one is performing a tandem behavior correctly.

Chicago Zoological Society
Dolphin Connection

ANSWER 2: When two animals are together for the first time, or have been separated for a relatively long period of time, it is imperative to make the proper approximations to show the animals what you are looking for in "team behaviors." In the very beginning, you might start with two trainers working concurrent behaviors in close proximity. Trainers approximate the animals closer together until one trainer is able to work both animals.

If the concept of team behaviors is to be established and one animal in the team does not perform the correct behavior, do not bridge, for this would reinforce both animals. If your facility uses a recall, it would be advisable in this situation. Otherwise, let the animals terminate the behavior.

The trainer's evaluation of the situation determines if there will be any form of reinforcement,

VRRV, or food. The animal that responded correctly can be reinforced only if there is no chance of displacement or dominant behavior. Although there may not be any physical signs of displacement, it still may be occurring. If the dominant animal in a team has responded incorrectly, the subordinate is reinforced only if it can be done without stimulating aggression from the other animal. If the subordinate animal in the team has responded incorrectly, be sure the dominant animal did not cause the incorrect response before reinforcing. If there is any doubt, then neither animal is reinforced, a LRS is given, and the animals are asked for another team behavior. Remember the key to shaping team behaviors isn't who does or does not get reinforced, VRRV'd, recalled, or LRS'd, but in taking the appropriate approximation necessary to communicate to the animals the criteria in working together, or as a "team."

Animal Care Staff
Mirage Dolphin Environment

ANSWER 3: At Mystic Marinelife Aquarium, during a team behavior, if one animal performs the correct behavior and another does not, we bridge, reinforce the animal(s) that gave the correct response, and give a LRS (least reinforcing stimulus) to the animal(s) which did not, and then move on. This is also our standard protocol for training animals individually.

For aesthetics during our public presentations, we have eliminated the bridge when possible. For example with a self-terminating behavior, we do not bridge. In a self-terminating team behavior (e.g.: a hurdle jump) we don't bridge, but reinforce the animal that gave the correct response, LRS the other, and move on.

These protocols have proven quite effective for us and we wish you luck with any approach you take.

Training Staff
Mystic Marinelife Aquarium

Trainer's Forum

VOL 17, NO 1, 1992. There are four detailed answers provided to this particular question. The need to mix different species usually revolves around a show need or an animal management need. Keep in mind that many of the methods described below could also be used to introduce animals of the same species together for the first time. Although there are similarities in the answers provided, you will notice that complex training plans such as these also demonstrate differences and contradictions in the way different trainers approach problems.

Mixing Different Cetacean Species for the First Time

QUESTION: Our facility houses several species of cetacea which have never been mixed. We would like them to share the same pool for public presentations. We would like suggestions on how to begin.

ANSWER 1: A period of introduction will need to be done before you can expect to have your different species cooperating with your training system in a public presentation. This introduction can be accomplished in a number of ways and depends totally on the trainer's ability to assess each individual animal's personality and interaction history with its enclosure mates. Depending on your physical layout, it would be advantageous to work the animals proposed to be housed together in adjoining enclosures with the ability to see and hear each other both above and below the water line. By maintaining good positive control, and approximating the animals closer and closer, you accomplish two things:

1. You are maintaining your positive working relationship with your animal while exposing them to another animal's presence.
2. You are desensitizing your animal to the proximity of the second animal (This is important because you are communicating to your animal that being close to a new animal is a positive situation and does not have to be an aggressive-defensive interaction).

Eventually, and only after numerous sessions during which there are no discernible dominance displays between the animals, you can begin to open up the boundaries between the animals and continue to have each animal reinforced for cooperation. Adequate escape routes and the largest swimming area possible will allow the animals to feel less confined and hopefully less in need of defending themselves.

It would also be advantageous for each animal to have its own trainer for these sessions so they can have the maximum attention from a trainer. The trainers can switch animals back and forth to avoid possible discrimination problems and to duplicate any possible contingency. Eventually, both animals will be controlled by one trainer (by fading the second trainer) and you can increase the number of types of animals in this fashion.

It should be noted that introductions of dominant animals with submissive animals can reinforce that dominance, and it is sometimes desirable to introduce the dominant animal to the group after other members of the pod are comfortable with the newcomers.

This systematic desensitization is more desirable than just opening gates and seeing where you are after the dust settles.

Vic Charfauros
San Diego Zoo

ANSWER 2: We prefer that any animals that are asked to work together be able to live together. Our reasons are the following:

- Any time cetaceans in the same overall system cannot be intermingled, the effective living space and social opportunities for all the animals are reduced.

- If animals refuse to gate prior to the release of incompatible animals into the same pool, the trainers must stop any presentation for safety reasons.

That's not to say that there aren't good reasons (breeding, health, etc.) to separate groups of animals. We just think that whenever possible an active program to mix the animals should be conducted. So, our approach would be to introduce the animals to each other in the following way (making some broad assumptions about facilities and ignoring some species specific problems).

Before you start introduction, make sure that all the animals have all the basic control behaviors and are solid gaters.

Allow the two groups, or smaller sub-groups, of animals to have visual contact through a mesh gate. Reinforce the animals for the presence of the other animals by conducting station training or other easy training activities in areas near the barrier. If possible, conduct joint sessions where the trainer moves back and forth between pools, so that the animals get the concept that the training activity involves both groups of animals and both areas. Reinforce heavily for animals remaining at station while others perform behaviors. In fact, we would say more reinforcement should be given in these sessions to the animals that are not working.

Next, release the two groups into the same area together. A better alternative may be to take those animals from each group that seem the most receptive to intermingling and mix them first. Make sure that there are several other pools for the animals to escape to –with gates left open and someone at the ready on the gate. How you proceed from this point depends on how the animals react.

If everything is calm, let things go for a few minutes. Then, you might try bridging and feeding all the animals. Try to get them all to station, but feed them wherever they show up. Your primary goal is to reward all of the animals in the tank as close to the same time as possible. Then, release the animals again. Depending on how long the animals are left together, which we recommend be at least several hours, repeat this several times.

If aggression occurs and the animal attempts to flee into a holding pool, let it go. Don't force it back out. Close the gate only if needed to protect the animal. If things calm down, go back to the basic strategy—to reward all of the animals in the tank as close to the same time as possible.

Finally, work up to getting all the animals in the pool together. Reinforce them for stationing closer and closer together, and holding station. Remember, reinforce animals that are holding station as much or more than animals that are working. Reward dominant animals heavily while they allow other animals to station, eat, and work. Dominant animals will get more time, food, and attention in these sessions. Just make sure that they get it for cooperation.

Gating the animals will be a tricky part of this process. What you do will be driven by the context of the situation, and your normal policies on gating. Our only comment in this regard is to try to be as flexible as possible in gating the animals, and try to avoid any highly stressful attempts to net them in—if at all possible.

Tim Desmond and Gail Laule
Active Environments

ANSWER 3: When mixing animals of different species or introducing animals of like species, the basic tenet is to take it slow and easy. It's best if the animals are able to view each other through closed gates at their own leisure. It may take some time for the possible posturing and vocalizing to subside, but it's beneficial for the animals to become aware of, and calm with the knowledge of, each other's presence without too much trainer interference initially. No possibility of physical contact is allowed until they accept each other with no undue stress or excitement.

The second step would be to work with each group on opposite sides of a closed gate until they are working side-by-side. An animal of each group may even learn to share a target held at the gate bars or mesh.

Our cetaceans can be rotated through our four –pool system without having to cross paths. We take advantage of that by allowing each different group to explore, work, and play in the other's resting pool while the original group is absent. As well as sharing pools in an absentee manner, both groups play with the same toys and their trainers intermix to play with the same types of games and have tactile sessions with all the cetaceans. This allows all the animals and people to be relaxed with each other and, to a greater extent, gives trainers more confidence in deciding how and when tension levels may need to be alleviated when animals are mixed.

The situation can be made easier by not mixing all the animals at one time. Choose the more stable and amiable animals of each group (those most likely to respond to trainers in all circumstances) to intermingle first. You may not want to mix the sexes at first, or at all, depending on the make-up of the groups. Leave the dominant males of breeding age out of first meetings.

A neutral pool may be chosen for the "meeting site" or use the pool most familiar to the more reticent group of cetaceans. Try to do the actual physical introduction during a regular training session. One group is stationed poolside while the second group is gated into the same pool and brought to a different station. The cetaceans are kept busy performing small behaviors that keep them close to their station. Momentary lapses of attention and breaks from station are ignored. The animals are encouraged and well rewarded for sticking by their trainers. At least one gate is left open so if animals feel they need to leave the area they may.

The trainers are anchors for the animals. The situation may proceed calmly or not, but the trainers supply the stability. There should be large groups or any unfamiliar people standing around. The cetaceans should be stationed quietly without splashing, water-slapping, yelling, or running around. These antics don't appear to bother our *Tursiops* much, but do unnerve our *Pseudorca* greatly.

The first few meetings should be brief and under trainer control. Eventually, midway through the session, the animals are given an "all done" signal and allowed to visit freely for several minutes before being recalled to continue the session and gate out of the pool. A good idea may be to gate back and forth a varied number of times before finally closing the gate between the two species. Slowly, new animals can be incorporated into the sessions along with acclimated animals. During free time, trainers remain poolside to watch for aggressive precursors.

In time it is possible to simply open gates between pools and allow the animals to mix at will. Adding toys to the pools may allow for constructive interaction, alleviate tension, and simply give a different focus of attention.

For mixed species presentations, the group that is more reticent, or of smaller number, has access to the performance area first. After the first group is stationed, the second group is gated into the area and the animals start to work immediately. In time, one group followed by the other are gated to the performance area and allowed to mix for 15-30 minutes before a demonstration begins.

The process may take a few weeks or a few months. One may have cetaceans that can never be comfortably mixed for long periods. The key is to undertake the process in a slow and careful manner. Nothing can be gained from forcing the animals together too quickly except the realization that there are no shortcuts to good behavioral management.
Allison Douglas
Indianapolis Zoo

ANSWER 4: The integration of new members into an established group of animals or the mixing of two established groups (or species) can be undertaken very successfully by keeping a few basic principles in mind. It's obvious that the answer is not as simple as just opening a gate and hoping that things fall into place. Quite often, under these free-for-all conditions, all stimulus control disappears, animals refuse to separate, and rough play or even aggression may result. This is exactly what we want to avoid.

DISPLACEMENT / AGGRESSION
(A Natural Behavior)

We must assume that animals will perceive (in most cases) a new member, or a new group of animals, to be an intruder. This intruder(s) competes for food, space, breeding rights, etc.. Consequently, the behavioral response under these conditions is to challenge the new member(s) subtly at first (through unobservable behaviors, vocalizations, etc.), then more overtly—through displacement and fighting, especially if the new member doesn't "get in line." Therefore, our primary goal for all introductions is to create a positive perception by associating reinforcement with the introduction, and any subsequent interaction involving the new member(s).

START SIMPLE

Pick your best candidate from each group for your initial introductions. These animals should give you the best chance at retaining some control throughout your first sessions. All initial introductions should, in most cases, be consistently paired with reinforcement in order to help shape a cooperative and positive response to these introductions and to avoid the rehearsal of dominance displays, territoriality, and aggression. First impressions are lasting ones, so help your animals understand that this initial introduction is positive and non-threatening. You may also want to avoid introducing (at first) a highly dominant animal to a highly subordinate animal in order to avoid the likelihood of dominance and threat gestures. Eventually, additional animals can be systematically added as the positive history is shaped.

ESTABLISH A NEUTRAL ZONE
(Territoriality)

Ethology tells us that animals established in their home range will act to protect their "turf". This normal territorial behavior, once understood, can be used to the animal's advantage. By utilizing, if possible, a neutral zone or pool that both animals are least familiar with, stimulus control can be facilitated and dominance reduced. Animals will not act to defend unfamiliar territory and the benefit will be seen in a more positive, controlled introduction. An interesting sidelight to this principle can be exercised when introducing a known subordinate. In this scenario, it may be best to move the dominant to the subordinate's pool (or "turf"). This will help defuse any home territorial display by the dominant and give the home advantage to the subordinate, thereby helping to create more social equality. Remember to reinforce only cooperative behavior and avoid accidental reinforcement of dominance or aggressive precursor behavior.

FREE TIME
(Socialization)

After shaping our initial positive history through controlled sessions, and the animals show no indication that immediate aggression is imminent, it's time to systematically approximate longer and longer breaks or free-time. Start with maybe one or two minutes at first, then build in longer and more frequent free-time periods. Eventually, long breaks of a few hours or an entire day will be possible. However, we must remember that during "free-time" is where some non-desirable behavior is more apt to occur. The social hierarchy may dictate during free-times, and aggression displacement, sexual behavior, etc., may occur and overflow into the actual session. It is imperative, then, that during initial "free-time", periodic reinforcement of cooperative behavior is instituted (this is known as Differential Reinforcement of Incompatible/ or Other Behavior –D.R.I / D.R.O.). Be careful to avoid accidental reinforcement of an undesirable behavior when sessions resume (watch your animals carefully during a break in the session).

"TO SEPARATE OR NOT SEPARATE"

The question of whether to begin separations immediately or wait until later in training is a complex issue and may depend upon your long range goal for your entire population or the limitations of your facility. It is best, however, that separation is maintained as a reliable behavior for all individual animals, and the sooner you begin, the better. You never know when a veterinary emergency requires one individual to be isolated. In many cases, separations should be initiated during the very first introduction.

TOO MUCH ATTACHMENT?

Sometimes an even more difficult situation arises when animals that are initially introduced become so attached to one another that separations seem impossible. This can occur either immediately or within a few weeks of interacting together. Although there are many intrinsic social reinforcers acting to cement this bond, our application of primary and secondary reinforcers (during acclimation and training) may compound the problem. Often we are so overjoyed that the animals have "hit it off", that we become unaware of the separation difficulty we are directly shaping. And the animals, having associated the new member(s) with so much attention, reinforcement, and socialization, are not inclined to allow separations even for a short while. As previously stated, it is probably best to initiate separations within the first introductory sessions so that a strong bond does not develop so firmly that any attempt to separate is perceived as aversive by the animals, and avoidance behavior becomes the predominant response. If complete separation is impossible, at least reinforce approximations toward separations. Under these conditions, it is also best to avoid reinforcing mostly team-based behaviors. Keep in mind that strengthening cooperation by annoying reinforcement is redundant and can actually compound the problem in this scenario, whereas working apart, and singular control (even if in the same pool), is a more logical approximation towards a successful separation. Under these conditions, the majority of the reinforcement should occur after a successful separation until the animals respond more consistently.

"BALANCING" REINFORCEMENTS

Whether we like it or not, negative reinforcement is serving to increase the frequency of behaviors as well. When animals that refuse separation, because they're completely infatuated with one another successfully avoid the separation, negative reinforcement occurs. By contrast, animals that become territorial and aggressive with one another are negatively reinforced when dominance and submission occur. Therefore, application of primary and secondary reinforcement must be precisely placed in order to avoid compounding undesired behavior.

In our first scenario, we see that an overly strong attachment is rapidly developing. And, for a variety of husbandry reasons, this pairing is not conducive to the overall benefit of the entire population. In this case, we may want to reinforce mostly (or only0 behaviors performed apart, or separation approximations. We must provide a high degree of variable reinforcement for a successful approximation. This can, and should, include immediate access to one another after the same animals have separated. There is probably little need to apply any reinforcement for this reintroduction because socializing acts as a very strong reinforcer under these conditions. Wait for the animals to show a calm, relaxed response before the reintroduction (as a reinforcer) so as not to shape separation anxiety.

Our second scenario involves the opposite problem, social aggression. Therefore, the application of the majority of variable reinforcement should occur as the animals are introduced, and throughout the session. Little or no reinforcement is initially necessary upon separation. The negatively reinforcing characteristics of displacement and avoidance (of the dominant animal) will maintain a strong separation. Applying additional reinforcers is redundant and may compound or delay cooperative behavior.

Eventually, in both scenarios, you can adjust the application of your variable reinforcers so that a normal balance exists and all animals perform and cohabitate cooperatively and happily.

POINTS TO REMEMBER

- Pair reinforcements with the appearance of the new member.
- Expect some degree of dominance (either control/ bonding or territorial/ aggressive) and avoid accidental reinforcements that compound the problem.
- Use a neutral area at first.
- Start with only two animals (one from each group) and add after a positive history is developed.
- If one animal is dominant, move him/her into the other (subordinate) animal's home pool (give the territorial advantage to the subordinate).
- If animals exhibit too much attachment, provide the majority of reinforcement after separation.
- If animals show too much uncooperativeness with one another, provide the majority of reinforcement during introduction and throughout the session. Don't reinforce too much for the separation until they begin to perceive each other as positive.
- Approximate small breaks while animals are together and use D.R.O./ D.R.I for animals that appear uncooperative with one another.
- The initial sessions must be positive to set the stage for future success and healthy animals.

Ted N. Turner
Sea World of Ohio

VOL 21, NO 2, 1996. It has been common for people to house multiple pinniped species together for many years. In fact, it is done so often that new trainers often assume that there is nothing to it. Sometimes species get along great, but as with any species it sometimes requires special planning and hard work. Here are several approaches to the situation.

Pinniped Co-Habitation: Seals, Sea Lions, & Others

QUESTION: If you have two or more species of pinnipeds, do you house them together? If so, how did you introduce the different species to each other? Did you just open a gate or did you train them to mix?

ANSWER 1: We have housed California sea lions and harbor seals together several times in different pools without any obvious problems. Both species seem to adapt to the change in their environment. The last time we mixed species did present a small problem with individual animals. We had a compatible group with two adult female sea lions and one adult female harbor seal at our show facility. Out of necessity, we moved two juvenile male sea lions into the group. With due respect to phocid fans, young sea lions are usually more active and agile than adult harbor seals. Our harbor seal continued to work and her weight remained normal, but she received increased "enrichment" from her young sea lion companions. She got a lot more exercise than when she was just with her old pool mates. She remained with all the sea lions for about six months and then was moved back to an exhibit with another female harbor seal and a much quieter life.

Our experience would suggest that you not only have to be concerned about differing species, but differing individuals as well. It was helpful that all our animals were conditioned to station for feeding and we could separate each one. Training before introduction can increase the rate of success.

Jim Alexander
St. Louis Zoo

ANSWER 2: At Mystic Marinelife Aquarium, to segregate our harbor seals during breeding, two seals were moved to a pool housing 12 California sea lions. No acclimation or desensitization of the animals was done prior to introduction. No excessive aggression between the two groups was observed and they co-habitated well, more-or-less ignoring each other. Critical to the success in mixing these species was adequate space within the exhibit for each animal to select comfortable haul out spots without displacing other animals. Following are some of the guidelines we used for feedings that you may find helpful:

1. Each species had its own feeding station area as far from the other species as possible.
2. Target training was of great assistance. Our animals were target pole trained before introduction. The use of the target pole was essential when we established feeding stations for the harbor seals. Using the target pole, stations can be established through successive approximations.
3. The California sea lions were trained to come completely out of the water and onto the beach to their stations, keeping them out of the water while the harbor seals stationed.
4. The stations for the harbor seals were established near the edge of the beach, away from the sea lions, where they had easy access to the water.

We hope you find these suggestions helpful in mixing two species of pinnipeds. They helped to keep our introduction smooth, and aggression toward animal and staff at a minimum.

Training Staff
Mystic Marinelife Aquarium

ANSWER 3: For introducing pinnipeds, there are several possible options.
1. Open door.
2. Miss Manners suggests using the formal approach: "Mr. sea lion, I would like to introduce you to Miss harbor seal."
3. Seriously, it depends on your facility. If at all possible, give each group of animals time to adjust to the primary enclosure before the introduction. Expose the two species under controlled situations where aggression can be prevented (e.g.: on the other side of a door or gate). This way they can see, smell, and hear each other but are not put at risk of aggression. Next, begin working the groups together and separating again before the end of the session. Finally, end sessions with both groups together and allow them to interact freely. it would also be helpful if smaller groups could be introduced and gradually increase the group size.

Training Department
Indianapolis Zoo

ANSWER 4: If at all possible, I would recommend keeping the animals in adjoining pools. Our facility is set up so that animals can be separated, yet in the same pool. This allows the animals to see, smell, and touch each other through an underwater barrier or gate. We allow the animals this interaction over a 24-hour period. For the next two days following, we introduce the animals into the same pool, but on opposite sides, each working with a trainer. Successive approximations were used to bring the animals closer together until they worked side-by-side but still each with their own trainer. The time spent together was increased, and free interaction was allowed if the animals chose it. Through this two or three day adjustment, the only problem we ran into was the competition over haul-out space. Our intent was to reduce the risk of aggression between animals, or between animals and trainers, and it was very successful in our case.

Suzanne Smith
ZooQuarium

Variety 8

The Spice of Life

The saying "Variety is the spice of life" was probably first coined as a remedy for people who were bored. One of the reasons that training programs are such a good thing is that training creates variety. Variety can eliminate boredom and add spice to any life. Trainers, by being creative, can provide their animals with fun and with enriching experiences. One of the jobs of the trainer is to apply the many techniques at our disposal to making our animals' interactions with us positive and rewarding. Many marine mammal facilities have very creative ways of providing new experiences for their animals. Some of those activities at the Brookfield Zoo are described in *The Trainer's Role in the Environment of the Captive Dolphin* (Brill, 1982), on page 262.

Session Structure

Within our daily training sessions we can be more creative and provide more variety for the animals (and ourselves) than many trainers realize. Even within the structured format of a show, options are usually open to trainers if only they will recognize them. It is much too easy to fall into a routine and become predictable in how we work. While this can certainly be comfortable at times, it is not challenging and usually will lead to sloppy or lazy behavior (on the part of the animals as well as trainers). A few examples of elements that can help make training sessions more interesting include:

Length
If every training session lasts 15 minutes, the end of the session can become predictable. Longer sessions and very short sessions from time to time will help improve an animal's attention span.

Location
Holding sessions in different habitats can be an especially enriching experience for the animal. When that is not possible, moving to different locations within the same habitat can create new experiences, as well. Even if you remain in one basic location, just moving a little to the right or left, changing your orientation to the animal, and not remaining static will make your sessions more interesting.

Behavior Selection
Varying the order in which behaviors are asked will keep an animal

alert and help maintain sharp stimulus discrimination. Not requiring an animal to perform every behavior in its repertoire at every session will keep behaviors sharp and maintain the animal's interest. Training new behaviors while maintaining older behaviors is also important.

Pace

Some trainers move at lightning speed while others are slow and steady. Although different animals may respond better to one pace than to another, generally it is good to vary the pace from session to session and within the session.

Companion Animals

If several animals are working in the same habitat, it can be stimulating to work them in changing groupings. This practice may be dependent on the social considerations discussed in the previous chapter. But when practical, varied groupings can be beneficial.

Trainers

While it is not advisable to vary the trainers when training a new behavior, it is helpful to have several trainers work with an animal at other times. It keeps the animal from becoming dependent on just one person. Even within a session it can be stimulating to have different trainers step in from time to time or to send animals to new locations with a new trainer.

Reinforcers

Certainly another form of creativity is the use of varied reinforcers, differing magnitude of reinforcement, secondary reinforcers, and variable reinforcement schedules. These concepts will be discussed in greater detail in the next chapter.

Caution

Before a trainer runs off to change all of these things at once, it is important to remember that some of these changes may need to be trained or the animal desensitized first. Not all animals can deal with every change. This is where knowing your animal becomes essential. It is also important to make sure that the animal understands the rules of the game, or a change can be confusing instead of enriching. This concept is discussed later in this chapter.

'I Can't Provide Variety'

In introducing new trainers to new concepts and behaviors, I like to take it slowly. Inevitably, new trainers will reach a point where they say, "I think my animal is bored! If only you'd allow me to work more behaviors, I could keep the animal interested!" While young trainers are right to think that more behavior options give them greater opportunities for variety, they are wrong if they believe that they have run out of training options. Trainers who have worked with me over the years cringe when they hear a young trainer make a statement like that because they know my response:

I pull out my calculator and show the trainer a quick mathematical calculation. Let's assume the trainer is only allowed to work with five different behaviors from the animal's repertoire, and that the trainer has the option of working at only three different locations during the session. Let's also assume that the session is so short that the trainer has time only to ask the animal for five behaviors (the same behavior five times, each of the five different allowed behaviors once each, or any combination of five). In other words, the trainer has time to ask for five behaviors, with five different behaviors to choose from, and three choices of location. Mathematically there are 759,375 combinations the trainer can use before running out of options and having to repeat a combination. It sounds incredible, but it's true! If that trainer did ten training sessions each day with the animal and never took a day off, it would take him more than 200 years to use every combination! Then I point out that the trainer has far more than five behavioral options, including longer sessions and more than three locations – and we didn't even take into account reinforcement options or any of the other methods of providing variety.

The young trainer's head is usually spinning by then. My point is simple: although greater options can provide greater variety, it is ultimately up to the trainer to plan the session and to be creative in managing the options. Only when young trainers are able to use minimal tools and options in creative ways, will I then expand the options they're allowed. Too many options too early can sometimes stifle a trainer's creativity where it counts most – in providing the variety that keeps the animal and trainers on their toes.

Session Type

In addition to varying the structure or use of a training session, there should be different kinds of sessions for the animals, as well. Most training programs are designed around specific goals – husbandry, research, educational shows, obedience, tracking, among others. But whatever the main purpose of your training program, it is helpful to try sessions that differ in some important way from your primary sessions.

Exercise Sessions
These are sessions designed to give animals a good aerobic workout. Animals whose daily training is largely sedentary will benefit most from this kind of concentrated training. Even very active animals can benefit from sessions devoted entirely to high-energy behaviors.

Play Sessions
These are less structured sessions in which the animals choose the interactivity level, and primary reinforcement is not usually used. Specific shaping goals, other than safe interactivity, are not usually set. Play sessions may include interaction with the training staff or may be an opportunity for an animal to interact with toys or other enrichment devices.

Innovative Sessions
These sessions provide an opportunity for the animal to be creative. Usually, in such sessions the trainer will reinforce a new or unique behavior initiated by the animal. Sometimes reinforcing surprise behavior is an end in itself; at other times it is the basis for starting to scan or capture a behavior. Scanning and capturing were discussed in chapter 4, "Basic Operant Conditioning."

Focus Sessions
In this type of session, a particular focus is selected (aerial behaviors, husbandry behaviors, object-related behaviors, cognitive behaviors, research behaviors, or other specific tasks), and the entire session will concentrate on that activity or project. The lack of variety in such a session can work against you if overdone. But trainers whose programs regularly allow for lots of variety find focus sessions to be a new kind of variety for the animal.

Be Creative
The end result of all this is to find new ways of making a session interesting to your animals. No one format will always work. The key is to be responsive to the needs and behavior of your animals.

Enriching the Environment

Behavioral Enrichment
The concept of enrichment has always been important, but it was only in the 1970's that Hal Markowitz began exploring the concept in detail. One of the original ideas was to give the animal some control over its environment. Terms like "environmental enrichment" and "behavioral engineering" were used to describe the concept of giving the animal choices in its selection of activities and behavior. As the idea of enrichment has become more popular and its importance more evident, animal care programs apply enrichment concepts differently. Gail Laule provides an overview of the elements that define enrichment in *What is Real Enrichment?* (1998), on page 267.

The Animal's Home
In a zoological environment, animals spend 24 hours a day in their habitats. For that reason we must look beyond daily training sessions to create variety for the animals where they live. We must also seek ways to make their environment continually interesting.

Environmental Conditions
The décor and aesthetics of an animal's habitat do more than just look nice for the public that views the animals. Efforts to make the habitat interesting to the animals might include adding rocks and plants to change the terrain, varying the temperatures, lighting, and noises, or introducing other animal species. Some enhancements are easy to provide and some take imagination, and some are beyond all practicality. However, it is important to consider all options, remembering that the environment must first and foremost be healthy and safe.

Social Structure
This subject was discussed in detail in the previous chapter. It should never be forgotten that other conspecifics – that is, animals of the same species – will provide a great deal of variety.

Habitat Configuration
If you have the ability to open gates to other enclosures, combine two or three enclosures into one, or separate one enclosure into several, you can create great variety.

Enrichment Devices
There's no end to the stimuli that can be added to an animal's

environment: toys, feeding tubes, running water – the list goes on. Enrichment has become the newest craze in animal management at many zoos and aquariums. However, sometimes we view enriching experiences and devices as an end in themselves. There are times when toys thrown into an animal habitat make *us* feel better but may be of questionable benefit to the animals. We must remember that each tool we use to provide variety has reinforcing value that can work for us or against us. Knowing how we present variety and understanding its reinforcing potential is an important part of dealing with enrichment. That concept is explored in *Training, Enrichment, and Behavior* (Lacinak et. al., 1998), on page 269.

Consistency

Throughout this chapter we have described the virtues of variety. Yet in other chapters we insist on the need for consistency when interacting with our animals. Is there a contradiction here? Not at all!

Think of training as a game, let's say basketball. It is fun to play, you can be creative in the tactics you devise, and the outcome is unpredictable. Yet despite that variety, the rules remain the same. The players and the fans have expectations that must be met. New players are sent in and taken out of the game every few minutes, the teams travel from city to city on different days, and the jerseys change color. But the size of the court, the height of the hoop, and the type of ball seldom change. There are even different games of basketball: college, professional, one on one, "horse," etc., but each game has a set of rules that are known at the start of each game. Still, the outcome is unpredictable. That is consistency with plenty of variety. For additional views on the subject, read *Consistency vs. Predictability: Is There a Difference?* (T. Forum, 1999), on page 272.

In the workplace, you certainly hope your job will be fun and provide you with variety and challenges, but you don't want the boss to change the location of the office, then dock your pay when you don't arrive on time. You want the expectations of the job clearly defined. Having to guess what you are expected to do next is not fun. In fact, that kind of variety would be stressful. Variety may be the spice of life, but unfair expectations and radical changes may be spicier than you or your animal can stomach. It is up to the trainer to find the balance.

1982 IMATA Conference, Honolulu, Hawaii, USA. When an animal's habitat is designed in a zoological setting, care is usually taken to replicate as much of the animal's natural environment as possible. However, no habitat can be identical to the animal's natural environment. Therefore, it is the role of the trainer to provide as much stimulation as possible. Today that is a common concept, but it was only beginning to be understood and explored in the 1980's.

The Trainer's Role in the Environment of the Captive Dolphin

by Randall L. Brill
Chicago Zoological Society, Brookfield Zoo

ABSTRACT

The life of the wild dolphin encompasses a wide variety of stimuli (e.g., complex social interactions, communication systems, etc.) which heavily contribute to the animal's daily experiences and to which it must learn to respond. Those stimuli exist in an undetermined quantity and a vast variety of forms. One may assume, that captivity places the dolphin in a comparatively sterile situation, devoid of natural stimuli, which has the potential of severely limiting the animal's interaction with its environment. One of the functions of trainers should be to replenish the captive environment with motivational stimuli and prevent the animal's life from becoming a boring and all too predictable experience. This discussion will consider some methods of providing captive marine mammals, particularly dolphins, with such stimuli through training technique, diet programs, varied trainer-animal interactions, and involvement in all aspects of the animal's environment.

THE TRAINER'S ROLE...

There seems to be general agreement throughout the community of those involved in working with marine mammals that most of what we presently know about these animals, specifically dolphins, is based on information gathered within the short span of the last three decades or so. In addition, it seems to be more recently, at least within the past several years, that significant studies have shown the dolphin to be a much more complex creature than any of us may have imagined. Field-workers have begun to provide an even more detailed picture of the dolphin's life in the wild due to their improved abilities to observe and correlate behavior that in the past was, for the most part, more readily and frequently observed in captivity. Through the eyes of these observers we are beginning to discover animals that are exposed to a large number of varied experiences that determine the form of their daily lives.

In discussing the structure of cetacean schools, Norris and Dohl (1980a) describe the animal's activities in six categories: food gathering, reproduction and growth, social integration and communication, learning defense, and responses to environmental cycles. At first glance, one may view those categories as very basic, all-inclusive, and quite obviously self-evident, but the simplicity quickly slips away as the authors proceed to list and describe the activities and functions involved with life in a cetacean school under each of those categories. Something that sounds as menial as food gathering takes on new dimensions as one becomes aware of the numerous strategies and learning processes involved in that single aspect of life.

Researchers such as Wells, Irvine, and Scott (1980), Pryor and Kang (1980), as well as Norris and Dohl (1980b) have provided us with insights into the social structures of cetacean groups. Their observations begin to reveal complex relationships within a group; group structures that are solid, as well as fluid, and whose memberships change according to various ecological determinants. We begin to see more clearly animals that learn, in their lifetimes, the numerous rules necessary for dealing with social interactions, as well as many other functions at varied levels of complexity.

The ability of the dolphin to deal with complexity has also been demonstrated in the laboratories and certainly enhances the evidence observed in the wild. We are all aware of at least some of the laboratory research, and it is likely that each of us could cite at least one piece of work that made use of impressive and rigidly controlled responses on the part of the animal and required a very elegant and complex conditioning procedure. Herman (1980) has recently provided data on the dolphin's cognitive abilities which certainly point toward the animal's capabilities in effectively dealing with various conditions in its environment. The beginnings of an understanding as to the strengths and weaknesses involved in memory and conceptual processes and language learning, with research and conditioning procedures that involve a good variety of stimuli with which the subjects have learned to deal, are being provided.

It seems appropriate to summarize the apparent life-style of the dolphin by quoting Norris and Dohl (1980a): "At any rate when we attempt to conceptualize how dolphin schools may function we must allow into our thinking the demonstrated complex learning abilities of the dolphins" (p.254). The evidence available just begins to scratch the surface of all that the dolphins have to teach us, but we should begin to understand that these animals experience a wide variety of stimuli which heavily contribute to their daily experiences and to which they must learn to respond. Faced with the evidence then, what kind of world does this animal experience in captivity as opposed to the wild?

We can, at the very minimum and basic levels, describe the dolphin's captive environment as a clear water, concrete and, with respect to environmental stimuli encountered in the wild, very sterile world. Of course, there will be the interactions and experiences possible with members of its own and/or other species, including human handlers, but clearly the captive environment, even at its best, must fall short of the richness of stimuli found in the world from which the dolphin comes. If we are then aware, now more than ever before, that the dolphin comes from a complex world encompassing a wide variety of stimuli, it logically follows that we, in the act of taking possession of such a creature, take on the responsibility of providing a captive environment in which we attempt, to the best of our ability, to restore the complexity and the opportunity of which the animal may otherwise be deprived. There is no doubt that this is the sincere and common intent among the aquaria and oceanaria presently housing these animals, but as our knowledge of the animal grows, so must our efforts and methods expand.

For the dolphin in an aquarium or oceanarium, the trainer represents its closest link to the world around it. Like our counterparts in research, the training of dolphins and other marine mammals has developed in a very short period of time, and it is just within the better part of the last decade that we have seen tremendous growth and transition. In light of what we have learned and will learn, the trainer faces greater responsibility today in providing a healthy environment for the animals in his or her care than in the past. The need is becoming more evident and Markowitz (1982) phrased it well in discussing the behavioral enrichment provided for captive animals in zoos: ". . . we are emphatically confronted with the proposition that other animals besides ourselves like to do things, to see things change because of their efforts, to enjoy the pride of gathering their own food or drink, and to have some control over their lives." The role of the trainer in the life of the captive dolphin cannot be limited to training. That simply will no longer suffice, if the goal is to maintain a physically and mentally healthy animal.

Not long ago, it may have been common to find dolphins brought into captivity, trained to perform a specific routine, and then required to do so day after day, year after year, without any variations other than those most incidental to spontaneous or cyclic changes in the animal's environment. That type of handling represented the state of the art and, if it persists now, represents a sad commentary on the life of the captive dolphin and the role of the trainer. What happens to a dolphin in that kind of situation may be analogous to sending a child to school and then providing the same textbooks and lessons from grade to grade without change or progression. The child's learning ability and personal development will suffer and produce noticeable problems. We have good reason to believe that similar experience for a dolphin will also inhibit its learning and development.

A trainer's role is composed of many functions, including those of providing stimuli and manipulating the environment. These two functions are vital as the trainer seeks involvement in every aspect of the animal's life. The captive environment of the dolphin should provide as much challenge, complexity, and varying conditions as possible to recreate, even if artificially, what the animal may have experienced in the wild. The trainer stands in a position to do that, to continually seek to increase the number of stimuli an animal may encounter, and to consistently manipulate and change what may otherwise prove to be a very boring and predictable life-style.

The past two years at Brookfield Zoo's Seven Seas Panorama have seen some radically positive changes made to facilitate the trainer's ability to motivate and enliven his or her charges. We cannot claim originality or credit for a good deal of what we are doing, but we can share what we feel has proven to be effective in maintaining a healthy environment for our animals and perhaps motivate a number of others to add to, alter, or possibly even replace some of the methods that may be presently employed. Although our goal is to exert some influence over every aspect of our animals' surroundings, we feel that we have become especially effective in at least the areas of training technique, diet, and trainer-animal interaction.

When we speak of training, we are really talking about using a lot of motivation. After all, when it comes to marine mammals, none of us forces our animals to do anything, we coax them into it by making available something that they are willing to work for. The training technique that we have adopted and used for the past two years is one that we feel provides a great deal of motivation for the animals, and the trainers as well, and is greatly responsible for the attitude expressed in this paper and prevalent at Seven Seas.

Random and Interrupted Reinforcement, commonly referred to as RIR (rear), has in the past been discussed at some length and, I believe, adequately defined (Brill 1983). Allow me to summarize briefly its definition. In one case, we can define as a "traditional" training method in which the dolphin is consistently cued, bridged, and rewarded with food; a repetitive and highly predictable situation that provides little motivation once the animal becomes accustomed to it. In this situation, food is the most frequently used, if not the only, form of reinforcement the dolphin will experience, a clearly limiting set of circumstances.

The method know as RIR, on the other hand, expands the experience of the animal by combining intermittent reinforcement and a variety of reinforcers in addition to food. The dolphin begins to experience a situation of change in which the moment of reinforcement and its form are manipulated by the trainer in an effort to make it unpredictable and, therefore, more interesting. In using RIR, the trainer has the means of providing a mode of reinforcement that is complex and continually changing. Redundancy on the part of the trainer, a strong dependency on food reinforcement, and anxiety due to the withholding of food reinforcement can be reduced, if not eliminated, and the trainer and training environment are consistently recycled making them a source of interest and interaction for the animals involved.

To give you a feel for how the use of RIR affects the trainer and the animal, let's try an imaginary game that will demonstrate the elements of RIR, a variety of reinforcers, and the randomization of the order of their occurrence. For the game, you would use a circle divided into five sections that represent the available options:

1. cue a behavior and bridge (meaning that you will bridge the appropriate response)
2. cue a behavior with no bridge (you will withhold the bridge)
3. food
4. conditioned reinforcer (you will give something you have established as being reinforcing)
5. be innovative (you will respond with something unusual or unexpected by the animal).

The use of a spinner attached to the center of that circle will determine the order in which those stimuli or options will occur. In other words, the spinner will do for you what a trainer experienced in the use of RIR would do.

For the moment, we'll put ourselves in the imaginary position of working with an animal in a show or training session. We begin by presenting an initial cue for some behavior and then allow the spinner to determine our successive actions. Even with these five simple options, it would not take many turns in the game to realize that each behavior cued will be followed by a somewhat unpredictable and continually changing sequence of events. Imagine then what possibilities arise when the number of options is increased, when conditioned reinforcers are established and increase in number, when the trainer finds more and new ways of being innovative. Because the trainer has more options to choose from, the animal experiences a more interesting and complex set of circumstances: the focus moves from the food bucket and broadens to include the whole environment.

With the positive results achieved in employing RIR in our training regime, we began to look for other aspects of our animals' lives to which we could introduce some variation. Food intake became the next target. Our animals were being fed a very steady diet rationed out in the same amounts divided evenly over the number of feedings day after day. When we said our dolphins were fed 16 pounds per day, we meant 16 pounds every day, no more, no less. It became difficult for us, though, to imagine that a wild dolphin would consume its food in such an exacting manner.

Osborne (1978) described a feeding schedule called the "UP-System" in which a base amount of food was established for the animal that was lower than its regular daily amount, but sufficient for maintaining the animal's minimum requirements, and distributing the difference between the regular and base totals over a period of time to produce the effect of occasional, but significant, increases over the base amount to be fed. Let's say, for example, that an animal normally consumes 20 pounds per day and a base of 14 pounds is found to be sufficient. Over a 30-day period, that would provide the difference between 600 pounds and 420 pounds, or 180 pounds of food, to be distributed in the animal's diet. The feeding schedule would then be arranged so that the animal would experience several successive days at 14 pounds, followed by a sudden increase. That schedule would then irregularly repeat itself throughout the month. With this system, the base could then be altered according to the animal's needs.

We began to employ a strategy that is similar, accomplishes the same effect, and is easier to manage in our particular situation. Rather than determining and fluctuating bases, we determined a comfortable range of daily feeding amounts; comfortable for the animals and manageable for the trainers. Daily amounts of 12 to 20 pounds have worked well for us. The dolphins are fed on the basis of 16 pounds per day, or 480 pounds over a 30 day period. Each month, one of the trainers will prepare a diet chart arbitrarily fluctuating the daily amounts within the established range, so that there is a good deal of variation from day to day throughout the month while maintaining a monthly total equal to a 16-pound daily diet. At the end of each month, the animal's food intake is summarized on a graph with one line representing the predetermined feeding schedule and the other showing the actual food intake.

Such variations in the diet not only parallel the wild situation, but are also complementary to the use of RIR. Not only can one vary the number of feedings and amounts of each in the course of a day, as well as over a month's time, but we have found that the lower daily totals motivate the trainers to rely more on forms of reinforcement other than food.

The third area of concern, trainer-animal interaction, really is a blanket term that covers just about everything that happens, but it is used here as a heading for a few specific examples. Once our staff began to feel comfortable with altering the animals' experiences on a continual basis, we began to seek out other areas which we could manipulate and make more stimulating in addition to training and forms of reinforcement. We started incorporating variety into every aspect of an animal's life that occurred to us. The orders of behaviors performed in shows are subject to change at the trainer's discretion. Each individual behavior used has been restructured or newly designed to provide the trainer with several versions of options from which to choose each time it is used, adding even greater dimension to the form of activity and variety of behavioral responses that the animals may be required to make. The trainer's position around the perimeter of the pool, whether the food containers are visible or kept out of sight, and the locations at which the animals may be asked to station or perform are all subject to change during the course of any show.

Training sessions take on the same complexion insofar as they can. Since we have to work five animals on a common pool, our training sessions appear very strange and chaotic to visitors viewing them for the first time. In one session, any combination of four trainers and given dolphins working in several different locations around the pool is possible. Animals are sent from trainer to trainer, usually for the purpose of working on a particular behavior with a particular trainer, but sometimes just for the sake of changing the scenery. It is not unusual for one animal to have worked on several new behaviors with several different trainers within the course of one 20-minute session.

Play has become an important tool in motivating our dolphins now, more so than in the past. Play sessions may occur at any time of the day, whether it be between training sessions and shows or during them, with the trainer in the water or out, and with or without toys and props. In fact, taking some time to play with the animals is probably the best way of discovering new reinforcers that we have. In play, it becomes easier to find things that the animals will enjoy interacting with.

With all of the new stimuli and methods of manipulating the environment that we have found, there came the keen awareness that what we were doing was good and healthy for the animals and the trainers. We saw, however, one glaring disadvantage in that we, not the dolphins, were determining how, when, and what things would happen. We have since turned our thoughts to finding ways that allow the dolphins to have some influence over the events in their world. Our first step in that direction is a tool that we fondly call the "menu." It is simply a board hung over the side of the pool just above the water's surface with six symbols arrange horizontally. Each of the symbols represents one of six possible rewards determined at the beginning of the project on the basis of familiarity and acceptability to the dolphins. At any time during a show or training session, the trainer may choose to give a dolphin a menu cue to which the dolphin will respond by going to the board and touching its snout to any one of the six symbols. Upon its return to the trainer, the dolphin will receive the reward indicated by its action; a rubdown with a sponge, play with a ball, rubdown by hand, play with a floating ring, food, or being squirted with water.

In the year that we have been using the menu, it has gone through a process of evolution that is not yet complete. The original board was held by hand with the symbols arranged in two rows of three. The trainer would simply present it to the animal. Since then, we have found the present method to be more effective. From an empirical standpoint, this project carries as many confounding variables as it does possibilities if one were to question the existence or establishment of true choices and preferences. But it was not designed to be a legitimate experiment. It was designed to serve as an additional stimulus for the animals and a means of allowing them to react spontaneously. In that context, it has been successful.

I have only briefly touched on and described some of the means our trainers use to combat the sterility and monotony of the captive environment for animals that we now, more strongly than in the past, recognize as requiring a complex and stimulating environment. It all represents a good deal of work and dedication, but results in a significant enhancement of the captive environment. Having been able to witness the techniques and strategies used at a number of facilities, I find a good deal of encouragement in knowing that, even though the titles and acronyms may differ, the concerns I've expressed are not unique to any one institution. We represent the present state of our art and science. It is our obligation to teach each other, as well as those who come after us, that the role of the trainer includes much more than being a performer concerned only with the show quality of our animals, and that we can never deceive ourselves into believing that, as representatives of the art and science of marine mammal training, we represent its final form.

REFERENCES

Brill, R. L. "R.I.R. in Use at the Brookfield Zoo: Random and Interrupted Reinforcement Redefined in Perspective" In Proceedings of the Annual Conference of the International Marine Animal Trainers Association, 1981, Niagara Fall, NY, edited by Jackie Barry and Randy Brill. Boston: New England Aquarium, 1983.

Herman, Louis M. "Cognitive Characteristics of Dolphins," In Cetacean Behavior: Mechanisms and Functions, edited by Louis M. Herman. New York: John Wiley & Sons, 1980, pp. 263-317.

Markowitz, Hal. Behavioral Enrichment in the Zoo. New York: Van Nostrand Reinhold Co., 1982.

Norris, Kenneth S, and Thomas P. Dohl. "The Structure and Functions of Cetaceam School." In Cetacean Behavior: Mechanisms and Functions, edited by Louis M. Herman. New York: John Wiley & Sons, 1980a, pp. 211-61.

Norris, Kenneth S., and Thomas P. Dohl. "Behavior of the Hawaiian Spinner Dolphin, Stenella longirostirs." Fish. Bull., U.S. 77 (1980b): 821-49

Osborne, Bob. "The 'Up' System." Soundings: Newsletter of the International Marine Animal Trainers Association. 3, no. 3 (1978).

Proyer, Karen, and Ingrid Kang. "Social Behavior and School Structure in Pelagic Porpoises (Stenella attenuata and S. longirostris) during Purse Seining for Tuna." Southwest Fisheries Center Administrative Report LJ-80-11C, 1980.

Wells, Randal S., A Blair Irvine, and Michael D. Scott. "The Social Ecology of Inshore Odontocetes." In Cetacean Behavior: Mechanisms and Functions, edited by Louis M. Herman. New York: John Wiley & Sons, 1980, pp.263-317.

VOL 23, NO 4, 1998. The following article was written for the column *Enriching Environments* a regularly occurring feature in *Soundings*. Gail Laule gives a very good overview of what enrichment really is, or should be. So often, trainers misunderstand the full scope of enrichment possibilities, or the purposes for enrichment. This article is a good place for young trainers to start and a good reminder for experienced trainers.

What Is Real Enrichment?

by Gail Laule
Active Environments, Inc.

As an animal behavior consultant, I spend much of my time analyzing and addressing animal behavior problems. The problems are far-reaching: the elephant that tries to kill people, the gorilla that won't raise her young, the polar bear that paces, the ostrich that won't come in at night, the lion that won't go out in the morning, the dolphin that won't socialize with other dolphins, the chimp that beats up other chimps, and so on. The tools of my trade include a combination of positive reinforcement training and environmental enrichment techniques. Early in the process, I always ask if enrichment is currently being done. The good news is that the answer these days is almost always "yes." The bad news is that "yes!" isn't necessarily the good news I thought it was. "Yes we do enrichment" can mean anything from throwing a plastic ball into the cage and leaving it there for the next three months, to scattering the same diet in the same places around the exhibit everyday, to simply housing animals socially, to the ideal scenario of planning and implementing multiple enrichment activities on a daily basis. There are some obvious differences in the impact of these diverse methods of "doing enrichment," and only a narrow range of those methods that I would call real enrichment.

Enrichment is only effective if it has a real purpose, and if it triggers real results. The literature now offers numerous papers that define enrichment, present enrichment studies, and provide innumerable enrichment ideas. The need for variety in enrichment objects is well documented. Yet, this information is rarely applied. Enrichment should be a positive, productive, interesting, challenging, and a stimulating pursuit for animals that is rooted in "natural" behavior. From a problem-solving perspective, effective enrichment should contribute to the resolution of a problem by addressing the underlying causes, and at the same time stimulating desirable behavior. A tall order, but if systematically applied, enrichment is a powerful tool for effecting change. To be successful, I suggest five steps for doing real enrichment.

1. Define the purpose.
2. Assess the situation and develop a hypothesis on why the problem exists (the underlying causes).
3. Identify strategies and methods of implementation to address those causes.
4. Schedule and implement the strategies.
5. Evaluate results and make changes if necessary, then reassess again.

To better understand this process, consider the example of a pacing bear. Why does a bear pace? There are many potential causes of an abnormal behavior like pacing, including boredom, fear or discomfort, social pressures, general or specific stressors, and lack of control over external events. Through careful analysis and some educated guessing, determine which factors seem relevant. The purpose of the enrichment is to address those factors. Next, identify the best enrichment strategies for the situation. Conquering boredom, which is almost always a factor, calls for a more diverse environment. So, enrich with different substrates, bedding, and "furniture." Increasing the amount of stimuli, overall activity, and opportunity to perform purposeful behaviors is also critical. Bears engage in object manipulation, so provide toys and novel objects. They spend much of the day in feeding behaviors, so choose enrichment that increases the time and complexity of feeding such as: feeders that are triggered by specific behaviors, objects that must be opened or disassembled to reach the food, fish and insects that must be hunted and caught, and food that requires reaching, digging, swimming, or climbing.

Use environmental enrichment to address fear or discomfort by creating sheltered or screened areas, comfortable resting spots, and transition zones between holding and exhibit. Acclimate animals to scary areas by loading those areas with environmental enhancements and enrichment items. Create visual barriers and multiple resting and eating locations to reduce social pressures. And provide more complex feeding challenges to increase the bears' overall choice and control.

Finally, implement enrichment and evaluate results. This is done best by scheduling enrichment on a daily basis, for the entire month. This provides a baseline of enrichment each day, insures variability, provides a record of what is done, allows for preparation of items ahead of time, does not make enrichment dependent on only the motivated keepers, and eliminates the chore of daily brainstorming of enrichment ideas. Those feeling creative can always add extra enrichment, which is a real bonus for the animals! Marking a "plus" or "minus" records the effectiveness of each day's enrichment. This, coupled with an appropriate record-keeping system of the target behavior, provides a simple and effective means of evaluation.

Real enrichment, I believe, is not an individual event, but a process. Whether used for problem solving, or to simply increase the behavioral opportunities of animals in zoos and aquariums, effective enrichment requires deliberate planning, implementation, and follow-up. Only then will enrichment fulfill its potential for enhancing the care and welfare of animals in human care.

VOL 23, NO 4, 1998. Enrichment was the buzz word of the 1990's, in the zoological community. Training itself is an enriching experience, but the term usually refers to how we enrich the environment when staff is not present or formal training is not taking place. Thad Lacinak of Sea World first presented a paper similar to the one below at the 1995 AZA Conference in Seattle, Washington. Many papers have been written about unique forms of enrichment and the great benefit toys and other interactive devices can have on our animals. This article takes a close look at the consequences of enrichment if not properly timed. The ideas and concepts described below look at the reinforcing properties of how and when enrichment is offered. This paper has made many people take a more critical look at their own enrichment programs.

Training, Enrichment, and Behavior

by C. Thad Lacinak, Ted N. Turner, Stan A. Kuczaj
SeaWorld Adventure Parks

We believe that the defining characteristic of environmental enrichment is that it provides positive mental and physical stimulation for the animal, but does not produce unnecessary stress. That does not mean that all changes in the environment are enriching. For example, putting an animal that is frightened of people in a petting zoo would provide more stimulation to the animal, but this increase in stimulation would probably not be a positive, enriching experience for the animal.

We recognize that enrichment, as it is commonly employed, is meant to be positive. As shown in Scenario 1 below, enrichment can be used to decrease the frequency of stereotypic behaviors, such as pacing, by reinforcing the animal when it engages in a more desirable behavior, such as swimming and playing in water.

SCENARIO 1
1. Polar bear is pacing
2. Polar bear stops pacing and jumps in water
3. Polar bear is given boomer ball while in water
4. If this sequence is repeated, the polar bear will learn to spend more time in the water and less time pacing

Staying with the example of polar bear pacing, let us examine a slightly different enrichment strategy.

SCENARIO 2
1. Polar bear is pacing
2. Polar bear is given boomer ball while pacing
3. Polar bear stops pacing and plays with ball

This scenario is problematic since pacing is a behavior that we wish to eliminate or at least reduce in frequency. Given that enrichment may be positive, the animal can associate the behavior it was producing, in this case, pacing, with a positive outcome. Consequently, the animal will be more likely to produce the pacing behavior.

If enrichment is to be used in a behavioral management program, then it is important to understand when it should or should not be used. If enrichment is presented when an animal is engaged in an undesirable behavior, the short-term effect is to cause the animal to cease the undesirable behavior. However, the cycle depicted in Scenario 2 will cause the animal to increase the overall frequency of the undesirable behavior, in this case, pacing. As illustrated in Scenario 1, using enrichment to reinforce a desirable behavior such as swimming can result in the animal swimming more and more often-As desirable behaviors increase in frequency in the animal's daily repertoire, they replace undesirable behaviors. Given that there is a finite number of opportunities for behavior in a fixed time period, as desirable behaviors increase in frequency, opportunities for undesirable behavior decrease. To help demonstrate this point, and to illustrate both advantageous and problematic manners of providing enrichment, consider the following examples:

EXAMPLE 1

Killer whales are swimming peacefully in a group formation. Trainer slaps water, which alerts whale to fact that enrichment of some form is to be provided by trainer. Trainer turns on water sprayers and whales play in spray. Whales have learned that peaceful social interactions are rewarded and that a human can provide enrichment. Consequently, whales are more likely to interact peacefully with one another and to respond to their trainer in a positive manner.

EXAMPLE 2

Bottlenose dolphins are interacting with park guests at glass. Trainer walks out on stage. Dolphins look towards trainer, who throws toys in water. Dolphins play with toys. The association of the toys with the park guests and the trainer will cause the dolphins to be more likely to interact with park guests at glass and to associate trainer with positive experience.

EXAMPLE 3

A beluga whale spyhops in front of glass and looks at park guests in public viewing area. Fish food is thrown in pool, which causes fish in pool to school at surface in a feeding frenzy. Beluga swims through school, captures and eats fish. As a result of being reinforced with the opportunity to catch live fish, the beluga will be more likely to spyhop and interact with park guests in public viewing area.

EXAMPLE 4

Whales engage in socially agonistic behavior at gate. Trainer throws enrichment device (large rope) in water and whales play with enrichment device. Because the whales were reinforced for agonistic behavior, they will be more likely to engage in such behavior.

EXAMPLE 5

Walrus is visibly distressed when another walrus leaves the pool area. Trainer gives favorite toy to walrus in an attempt to distract walrus, but walrus ignores toy. If the walrus had enjoyed the toy, the walrus would have been reinforced for agonistic behavior. This would have been unfortunate, but so is what actually occurred. The walrus did not interact with his favorite toy, which decreases the effectiveness of the toy as an enrichment device.

EXAMPLE 6

Baby Asian otters are swimming peacefully in pool. Toys are provided and otters play with toys. Otters learn to associate swimming together in pool with enrichment. Consequently, otters will be more likely to swim together in a "socially appropriate" manner, which promotes exercise and development of social skills.

These examples demonstrate that the timing of enrichment is at least as important as the particular form of enrichment that is used. In fact, if the goals of enrichment are to increase the frequency of desirable behaviors such as socially appropriate behavior and interaction with guests, and to decrease the frequency of undesirable behaviors such as pacing, then the timing of enrichment can be more important than the form of enrichment. In this sense, successful enrichment programs and successful training programs rest on the same two principles: reinforcement and timing. These are universal principles of learning, and so we should not be surprised that knowing when to provide reinforcement is an essential aspect of both training and enrichment.

Given the importance of reinforcement for enrichment and training, we would like to briefly discuss the optimal reinforcement schedule. If reinforcement is provided after a fixed number of responses, animals quickly learn to anticipate when reinforcement is most likely to occur. In such a case, reinforcement loses much of its positive characteristics because it has become predictable. For example, an animal that has learned to accurately predict a fixed ratio reinforcement schedule might begin to return to the trainer more and more slowly. If the trainer reacts by providing stronger and stronger cues to the animal in an attempt to "speed up" the animal's behaviors, the trainer runs the risk of losing stimulus control. As stimulus control is lost, the animal becomes more and more likely to ignore the trainer altogether. In such a scenario, the animal has trained the trainer.

Since we strive to train our animals rather than to have them train us, we use a variable-ratio reinforcement schedule, a schedule in which reinforcement occurs at various, unpredictable times. Sometimes reinforcement is given after a single behavior, other times reinforcement comes after a set of behaviors, and on yet other occasions reinforcement might not be given at all. A variable reinforcement schedule maintains an animal's interest and produces consistently high levels of motivation and behavior.

Although we have emphasized the role of timing in enrichment, we recognize that timing is irrelevant if the "enrichment" is not reinforcing. Recall how the walrus in Example #5 did not play with his favorite toy when it was thrown in the pool while the walrus was upset. For an enrichment program to be successful, it must vary the enrichment elements in order to keep them reinforcing and must also provide enrichment when it is most likely to achieve the specific goals of the program. Avoid making the "enrichment" a part of a boring environment.

In addition to varying both the nature and timing of the reinforcement, it is important to avoid "routines." Because a routine is a predictable aspect of the animal's environment, animals learn to respond in specific ways during these predictable times. This can lead to stereotypic behavior before, during, and after the predictable time periods. This is one reason that fixed feeding times can lead to behavior problems. For example, an animal that produces stereotypic behavior may increase the intensity of such behavior as a set feeding nears. The animal is then fed which reinforces the stereotypic behavior. In order to avoid such problems, animals should be encouraged to produce a variety of behaviors at various times throughout the day. Moreover, the pattern for each day should also be varied to further reduce the problems associated with predictable schedules.

Because the animals and their environment are dynamic rather than static, enrichment programs must also be dynamic. Enrichment elements must be varied and continually evaluated in order to maintain their positive characteristics. For example, seeding a bear's habitat may result in the bear learning to forage in that environment. Discovering food and toys is rewarding, so the bear will continue to search the environment. Seeding different enrichment elements in different locations will cause the bear to maintain or even increase the frequency of search behaviors, a desirable outcome since searching the habitat is physically and mentally stimulating, as well as entertaining to guests who observe such behavior. The animal can be reinforced for searching even if there is nothing to be found. For example, a bucket might be thrown to the bear while the bear is searching. This will reinforce the bear for searching, and provides a broader reinforcement base (i.e., the bear doesn't have to be hungry) for the search behavior. As a result, the bear will probably increase the amount of time it spends exploring its environment.

Recognizing that each species is unique and that individual members of a species may have different needs is the first step toward establishing an effective enrichment program for an individual animal or group of animals. The more accurately that desired behaviors can be identified, the more likely that the enrichment program can be designed specifically to achieve these goals. Specifying behavioral goals also provides an objective basis for evaluating the effectiveness of the enrichment program. Let's look at penguin behavior for a specific example. The desired behavior here is active feeding with only minimal effort from the trainer. This can be accomplished if the trainers reinforce activity by the penguins with fish rewards, thereby enhancing flocking behavior during the non-breeding winter low-light cycles (when most penguin species are in the open sea). By attending to both the timing of naturally occurring cycles and the timing of enrichment in the captive setting, the penguins' normal predisposition to swim and flock in search of food is easily replicated and reinforced.

Maintaining an effective program is a continuous and dynamic enterprise. Effective enrichment can result in animals interacting with the public, while ineffective enrichment can lead to inappropriate displays of aggression toward other animals and people. Like a successful training program, a successful enrichment program increases the animal's well being while enhancing the public's experience.

VOL 24, NO 3, 1999. Most trainers accept that variety is important in a training program; but so, too, is consistency. So where does predictability fall into the scheme of things? Are consistency and predictability really all that different? Yes, they are! Consistency and variety are compatible partners in a good training program. Predictability and variety, however, do not go hand in hand as one prevents the other from occurring; they are actually opposing forces.

Consistency vs. Predictability: Is There a Difference?

QUESTION: How do you know if the behavior you are asking for is consistent or if the animal is predicting it? Is there a difference between consistency and predictability? How can we be consistent without the animals predicting behavior?

ANSWER 1: Animals begin to predict the upcoming behaviors because: a) the behaviors are performed in the same sequence time and time again. b) They can predict the S^D, (body language, they take the first part of a larger S^D, etc.). The easiest way to eliminate the animals predicting what you are going to ask for before you ask it is UNPREDICTABILITY. The behaviors should be performed on cue, no matter what order they are asked. Asking for the same behaviors in the same order over and over only leads to boredom. Once the animals are bored, it isn't long before the criteria starts breaking down.

So how can we be consistent without the animals being able to predict upcoming behaviors? People talk about how we as trainers have to be consistent, and this is the key to successful training. This is so very true. Trainers have to be consistent from training session to training session. Trainers have to be consistent in the way the animals are worked (e.g. all trainers follow the same rules for criteria, bridging, S^Ds, and dealing with misbehavior). But that's where consistency should end. Once behaviors are learned and under stimulus control, trainers are taught to randomize, and use variable schedules of reinforcement. Why? This keeps the animals thinking and it keeps the animals guessing and wondering what's next instead of predicting it.

Consistency is important in training, but once the behavior is trained, variety is the key. Variety should include the amount and kind of reinforcer for each behavior, the number or repetitions of a certain behavior, the order of behaviors in a presentation, the number of training sessions, and the length of each throughout the day. The animal should never know when you are returning to start a new session. Sometimes it is one hour, sometimes it is 20 minutes, sometimes you bring one pound, and sometimes you bring four pounds.

It is common practice for some facilities to have schedules for feeds/training sessions. This is important for some places to make sure all animals get the proper training time, but if you have the chance, surprise your animals once in a while and see how well they do for you.

Timothy Hoffland
Marine Animal Productions

ANSWER 2: An animal predicting a behavior does so without waiting to receive the S^D or without focusing on the S^D. This is generally based on the repetitive context in which the behavior has occurred in the past and has been reinforced through rehearsal. It can also occur because trainers often unconsciously give off precursor moves that indicate the S^D they are about to give (such as through a slight change in posture or other preparatory moves). In this case, the precursor move actually becomes the S^D. If you cannot tell whether or not the animal is in fact predicting the behavior it would be because your context is too repetitive and not random or the cues the animal is picking up on are subtle. It depends on your priorities whether or not this is undesirable. If you are developing a chain of behaviors, for instance, the animal predicting the next behavior can help the chain to form and flow. If you are training a novel behavior it is precisely your predictability that allows the animal to grasp the new concept. Under most circumstances, however, it is a nuisance to have the animal jumping to perform a behavior without being asked. If you wish to test to see whether your animal is predicting the S^D, maintain the context but change to an S^D for a behavior not generally requested in that context and try not to perform any precursor moves which might indicate your intent. Test for discrimination between S^Ds across different contexts (body postures, position in the enclosure, items held in hands, costumes being worn, etc.). If the animal successfully responds to a randomized string of S^Ds, generally they are just consistent, well-trained animals.

Consistency in precisely giving an S^D, both as an individual trainer, and between trainers allows clear communication to the animal. A consistent trainer will be very precise in producing the S^D, but not produce any precursor moves. However, the trainer must still randomize the sequence of behaviors and contexts in order to insure that the animal is paying attention to the S^D, and not to the repetitive context.

Jennifer Hurley
Long Marine Lab, UC Santa Cruz

ANSWER 3: There was some debate in our department about exactly what you meant by your question, but the subject of predictability is one we discuss frequently. At the New York Aquarium we have found that the animals are our best gauge for telling us when we have stopped being innovative and started being predictable. In the past we sometimes found that the animals were "responding to S^Ds" before we had even presented them. Our sessions had become patterned. So for the last few years we have invested a lot of energy into avoiding predictability. The most potentially predictable session in which we work with our animals is our shows. The shows tend to follow a pattern that is logical and interesting for our audiences. As you have undoubtedly discovered this also makes them predictable to the animals. They begin to anticipate S^Ds and they stop giving the trainer their full attention. We went about remedying this situation in a number of ways. First we varied the show order considerably, which initially caused a bit of confusion for the narrators and sound booth operators. To make things easier on everyone we generalized our script so that one basic script is used, regardless of the order of behaviors. For instance, when the narrator describes how dolphins use body posturing we may ask for a tail lob in one show and a breach in the next. We use four different show orders, which makes it easier for trainers to remember what behavior comes next. This is especially important when multiple trainers are working in the show. The narrator never "sets up" behaviors before they are performed. So if the trainer thinks the animal may be about to anticipate a behavior, based on his body position, the trainer can ask for a different behavior. Within the set show order the trainer can ask for extra behaviors that the narrator doesn't need to address. We sometimes even work on a small approximation of a new behavior, if we feel we can do it quickly and successfully, without interrupting the flow of the show. This became easier to do when we slowed down the pace of the shows. The animals still perform the same amount of behaviors. We just don't send them out in as rapid fire a manner as we did in the past. The audiences seem to respond to this more relaxed pacing, which allows us to address commonly asked questions. We have also found that the S^D may become a predictability factor. We avoid stepping forward, or backward, or in any pattern prior to giving an S^D, as those body positions tend to cue the animals. We have reduced the size of our S^Ds as well. Elaborate S^Ds may look interesting to the audience but the animals tend to cue off the first part of the S^D. (We would sometimes see the animals go off performing a behavior while the trainer was still at station flailing his or her arms around). We vary the location from which the behavior is elicited, so that location does not become a factor in predicting behaviors. We also vary which animals perform behaviors. Sometimes one animal does it, sometimes two, etc.

In general, within shows and outside of shows, we vary reinforcers and our schedules of reinforcement. We try to avoid big feed-ups when we wrap up our sessions, to avoid cueing the session's end. All this variety makes communication between trainers very important, which of course means lots of discussion. Animals still predict – remember, if they didn't look for patterns we'd never get new behaviors off target and onto an S^D. But it is the trainer's job to vary the animals' sessions, their day, and their lives in general so that they will remain stimulated, healthy, and motivated to learn.

Training Staff
New York Aquarium

Advanced Techniques & Concepts

9

What is an Advanced Technique?

It is in the application of the following concepts that great differences begin to emerge between training programs. The techniques described in this section are universal among experienced trainers. It is in *how* and *when* these techniques are applied that trainers begin to differ.

The reasons for the differences are fundamental. Basic operant conditioning works wonderfully, and its concepts are easy to grasp: *reinforce desirable behavior and ignore unwanted behavior*. There is nothing difficult in that. But, what happens when behaviors break down? What if an animal does the unexpected? No two animals respond to problems or the solutions the same way, nor do any two trainers. Trainers must rely on technique and experience to solve complex behavioral problems. So what does a trainer do if he knows the technique but lacks the experience? If a technique requires experience before a trainer can apply it properly, then I define it as an advanced concept. The problem is that everyone has a different opinion about which techniques require experience, when a trainer has gained that experience, and how to determine when a technique is applied properly. I believe that if it's that complex, it must be advanced.

Easy as 1, 2, 3

The saying that something is as "easy as 1, 2, 3" can be deceptive. Training is a learned skill that requires practice to master. Simply having the tools doesn't mean you can use them well. A trainer must first learn the basic theory, practice the theory through application, learn more basics, and practice through additional application until, eventually, the trainer will have gained experience and started to learn complex concepts. It is a continuous process that never really ends. Young trainers, although capable of understanding advanced principles, are not usually skilled enough to apply them well.

My favorite analogy is the learning of math skills. A youngster may know how to count before even going to preschool, but the child is probably not ready for trigonometry or calculus. Learning math skills is a gradual process, first you learn to count, then to add and subtract, then to multiply and divide, then to apply those skills to big numbers and fractions, and eventually to algebra and higher math. To be good at math you must constantly practice. Few of us who have been out of school for several years could tackle a complex calculus or statistics problem today, even if we had learned and understood the concepts previously. It takes practice, and you can't jump from simple subtraction to algebra overnight. Trainers should take a gradual approach in learning to apply training techniques, too.

Because training seems so simple, and the basic concepts are so easy to understand, young trainers will usually understand the previous analogy, but they don't always see how it applies to training (or to them). When you read about complex math, you usually know when you are in over your head, but when you read about complex training, it makes sense on paper. So why not jump right in? I usually explain it this way: I recently read a very good book entitled *Flying a 747: A Pilot's Manual*. I read it cover-to-cover three times. I understood it and have been on 747 jetliners many times. So how many of you would allow me to be your pilot when you take your next vacation? The answer, I hope, is none of you, because I haven't practiced or gained the experience needed to pilot a huge passenger plane. Just because I have the intelligence to read about it, and even understand it, doesn't mean that I have the skills needed to fly a jumbo jet safely just from reading a book about it. Training is just as complex and requires at least as much practice.

Cautions about the Use of Advanced Concepts

Trainer as Teacher
Keep in mind that as the trainer, you are teaching the animal through the shaping of its behavior. You must be responsive to the animal and its needs. Do not move faster than an animal can. Once you have mastered many of the advanced concepts, you shouldn't use them on every animal. Young animals must absorb new concepts gradually, too. Just because one animal responds to a new schedule of reinforcement doesn't mean that every animal will, especially if the concepts weren't shaped through successive approximations.

Understanding the Theory
Once you are comfortable with the various advanced concepts described, you will learn to apply certain concepts only when needed. Sometimes training plans get out of hand and an animal fails to respond as you had hoped. You must recognize when you are in over your head. An experienced trainer will know when to back off and go

back to basics or at least back to the drawing board to revise your plan.

Black & White: Where's the Gray?

Right or Wrong
When trainers first learn basic operant conditioning, it is important that they understand the concept of black and white. A behavior is either right or it is wrong. A behavior should not be reinforced if it is "sort of right." This is not easy for some trainers to accept. Young trainers want to help their animal out, so they let the little errors slide. But, invariably, the animal simply learns incorrect behavior. By not being consistent in bridging and reinforcing we are inadvertently shaping undesirable behavior. The concept of black and white must stay with us even as we gain experience, even when we begin to recognize areas of gray.

Gray Area
Without a doubt gray areas exist, but usually they are present while behaviors are still being learned. More often, the gray areas usually present themselves when we are trying to correct problem behavior.

Behavior in training - As we shape new behavior we are constantly raising the criteria. If we want an animal to touch a target 10 feet in the air, we start by having it touch the target 6 inches above its head. Once we have trained the animal to reach the 5-foot approximation, we do not accept anything less than that height. That is *not* gray area; we have clearly defined what is right and wrong by placing the target at 5 feet. If the animal jumps 4 feet 11 inches, missing the target by barely an inch, the behavior is incorrect. You may think, "Gee, she put out such an effort, I'd like to reinforce that." *Don't!* That's a dangerous gray area. You have no way of explaining that it was reinforced for effort. Instead you will have communicated that the correct response is jumping an inch shy of the target. If, after reaching the 5-foot mark, the animal fails to jump that high for several sessions, you may need to regress to a previous standard to keep the animal from becoming frustrated. Now you're entering a gray area. You're deciding to change the rules – to redefine right and wrong – by lowering the target to say, 4 feet 6 inches. When the animal successfully touches the target at 4 feet 6, you may have lowered your height standard, but you have stuck to your criterion for reinforcement: the animal still must touch the target! This is acceptable use of the gray area concept. It takes an experienced trainer, however, to determine *when* to regress in such situations.

Solving a problem behavior - Usually when a behavior breaks down, it is for a complex series of reasons. These reasons will be discussed in detail in chapter 11, "Problem Solving." For now, it is enough to say that as you attempt to correct problem behavior through shaping desired responses, gray areas will present themselves and your choices will not be black or white. But which *shades* of gray? This situation usually occurs when the animal has begun to fall short of two or more criteria simultaneously. To resolve the problem, you must usually correct one criterion at a time. But, which criterion do you try to correct first? As one begins to improve, what happens if the second gets worse? The solution to that will depend on the animal, on which criterion you feel is the more important, and on your experience level. Several examples are included in the problem-solving chapter.

Large Staff

Gray area decisions are made all the more difficult if you're dealing with a large staff. Some decisions are very subjective. If you want an animal to move very quickly from one spot to another, but you have no way of objectively judging what's "very quickly," you will have difficulty being consistent in bridging for speed. If there are many trainers trying to maintain this behavior, the task becomes even more difficult. Judging for speed, height, distance, or form without an objective unit of measure creates gray area. It is this concept that causes controversy in sports like figure skating and gymnastics; the scores are subjective even with detailed rules in place. If the animal being trained is getting mixed signals, the behavior will decline. This is why a single individual must almost always train a new behavior.

Setting Clear Expectations

Even an experienced trainer working alone must remember the important concept of black and white. Animals need to know what is right or wrong. We communicate that information through precise bridging. When we try to make excuses for the animal or allow criteria to relax now and then, we are only confusing the animal. In return we will receive poor performance. Once we accept that an experienced trainer will occasionally make gray area judgements, we can then remind ourselves that we should still avoid them most of the time. Gary Wilkes looks at this problem when training the family dog in *Monique, the 'One Trick Poodle,'* on page 294.

Secondary Reinforcers

Early in the training process all trainers learn to use the secondary or conditioned reinforcer, called the bridging stimulus. This reinforcer is carefully conditioned, and the rules for its use are strict. Over time, additional secondary reinforcers can be conditioned. Many facilities, however, will start teaching their trainers to use secondary reinforcers relatively early. At Shedd Aquarium we are much more conservative. The definitions, applications, advantages, and steps for implementation of our methodology are described in *Secondary Reinforcers as an Indispensable Tool* (Ramirez, 1996), on page 295.

More complex uses and questions are also described and answered in articles at the end of this chapter. The article *Secondary Reinforcers for California Sea Lions* (T. Forum, 1994), is on page 300. The use of secondary or conditioned reinforcers to provide variety to our animals is discussed in the 1998 *Trainers Forum* (1998) article, *Conditioned Reinforcers vs. Environmental Enrichment Devices*, on page 302. In addition, the Pittsburgh Zoo tried using *only* secondary reinforcers for training, an experiment described in *Sole Use of Non-Food Reinforcers in Daily Training Sessions with an Amazon River Dolphin* (Burrows et. al., 1990), on page 304.

Punishment, Negative Reinforcers, and Aversive Stimuli

Varied Concepts
Each of these concepts is different. Yet the terms are often used interchangeably and incorrectly. Even some very good trainers have difficulty understanding these terms or the application of the concepts they represent. The subject gets even more confusing when you throw the public's definition and perceptions into the mix, but we'll deal with that later. First let's clarify the operant terms.

Definitions
When you start hearing apparently contradictory terms like "negative reinforcement" and "positive punishment" it is easy to see why trainers get confused. Here is where common terminology and technical terminology begin to collide. To understand the terms

below, you should read two different explanations of the terms. First look at the glossary excerpted from *The Syn Alia Series on Animal Training* (Cover and Zeligs, 1991), on page 307. Focus on definitions 1-7 and the discussion that follows those definitions. Then read the article *Operant Definitions of Reinforcement and Punishment: Getting the Jargon Right* (Kirtland, 1993), on page 312. The terms you need to fully understand are listed below. What follows each term is a simple definition in italics, then my comments or explanations.

Aversive stimulus – *This is anything an animal seeks to avoid.* It might be a net, another animal, or an alarm bell. Aversive stimuli are used as positive punishers and negative reinforcers, as explained below.

Positive – *Added to the environment.* For the purposes of this training discussion we must think of the concept of "positive" as being neither good nor bad, just something added.

Negative – *Subtracted (removed) from the environment.* Again, for purposes of this discussion, we must realize that "negative" carries no meaning of good or bad. It simply means something removed.

Reinforcer – *Something that increases the frequency of the behavior it follows.* As we have discussed throughout the manual, for a reinforcer to be effective in increasing behavior, it must be delivered immediately following the desired behavior.

Punisher – *Something that decreases the frequency of the behavior it follows.* Just like reinforcers, for a punisher to effectively decrease behavior, it must be delivered immediately following the undesirable behavior.

Positive reinforcer – *Something added to the environment that increases the frequency of the behavior it follows.* A fish given (added) to a dolphin immediately following the animal's calmly accepting a veterinary exam, increases the likelihood that the dolphin will remain calm the next time the veterinarian conducts an exam (calm behavior has been reinforced). This is probably the easiest of the concepts to understand, as it is the most widely used.

Positive punisher – *Something added to the environment that decreases the frequency of the behavior it follows.* This is probably the most common type of punishment. You see your dog in the process of urinating on your new carpet, so you yell, "No!" and swat the dog on the nose (both the word "no" and the swat were added to the environment). The dog will likely want to avoid these consequences (aversive stimuli) in the future so it will be less likely to urinate on the carpet (decrease of undesirable behavior); at least he is less likely to do so in your presence. Punishment may work, but it is a concept that can produce other problems and is generally avoided by most trainers.

Negative reinforcer – *Something removed from the environment that increases the frequency of the behavior it follows.* A horseback rider wants his horse to turn left, so he pulls the reins putting pressure (an aversive stimulus) on the right side of the horse's head, causing the animal to turn left (which removes the pressure of the reins and increases the frequency of the "left turn" behavior). This is where some trainers can get confused, because the pressure from the reins is both a positive punisher and a negative reinforcer, depending on which behavior you are talking about. Adding pressure on the horse's face positively punished the horse's "going straight" behavior; while the removal of the pressure negatively reinforced the horse's "turning left" behavior. (Most trainers would view this as a negative reinforcer because the desired behavior is turning left). Once the animal has learned the consequences of an aversive stimulus, the sharp pressure of the reins will not literally be removed in all situations – if the animal anticipates the pressure it may simply *avoid* the aversive stimulus altogether, turning at the slightest suggestion of rein pulling by the trainer. Over time, the aversive nature of the stimulus will have diminished considerably, while still retaining its effectiveness.

Negative punisher – *Something removed from the environment that decreases the frequency of the behavior it follows.* A macaw in the middle of a training session suddenly starts screeching loudly. So the trainer leaves the room, taking his bag of sunflower seeds (reinforcers) with him. The removal of the seeds is a time-out from training that the trainer hopes will reduce the occurrence of the screeching behavior. If the macaw likes the seeds and the attention from the trainer, the removal of both from the environment may very well decrease the frequency of screeching (as long as the bird associates their removal with its own screeching behavior). A drawback would arise if the bird had become tired of the seeds or no longer wanted the trainer's attention. In that case, the trainer's leaving the room would not decrease the screeching; it might, in fact, reinforce it. For negative punishment to work, the trainer must remove something the animal wants or desires – and that may not always be as clear to the trainer as one might think.

Using the Terms & Concepts in the Real World

Part of the problem with punishment is that it is seldom applied properly. The concept of punishment is poorly understood by most people, yet it is part of everyone's vocabulary. Even when some forms of punishment are used correctly they can take on a vindictive nature, affect other behavior, or create different problems. Gary Wilkes takes *A Look at Punishment* of pets, exploring some of its drawbacks, on page 314.

Real concepts that work – There is no denying that the concepts of negative reinforcement, aversive stimuli and punishment are effective tools when properly applied and understood. But they must be used sparingly and appropriately. Our behavior is reinforced and punished everyday. Here is an example: If you are driving at 85 mph in a 50 mph zone, and you suddenly see a police car on the side of the road ahead, you will likely slow down. The mere presence of the police car has changed your behavior. Because a police car has threatened you with a fine, something you want to avoid, the unexpected appearance of the police car negatively reinforced your "driving the speed limit" behavior, while at the same time positively punishing your "speeding" behavior. In other words, the police car is an aversive stimulus; slowing down to avoid getting a ticket removes the aversive stimulus (you have removed or reduced the likelihood of getting a ticket). Therefore, your proper driving behavior has increased (been reinforced negatively). The same situation can be looked at as a punisher; the presence or addition of the police car to your environment positively punished your speeding behavior, decreasing the frequency of its occurrence. The very same stimuli can be either a punisher or a reinforcer depending on the behavior you are trying to affect. If your focus is to increase the desired behavior, you are reinforcing something. If you focus on decreasing the undesirable behavior, you are punishing something. It's the "is the glass half-full or half-empty" question. I prefer to look at things optimistically and focus on the reinforcing properties if at all possible.

Reinforce rather than punish – As just described there is usually a punisher working opposite every reinforcer. The difference depends on the intent of the trainer and the goal of the animal. Some of us do well at our jobs because we enjoy it; others do well out of a fear of getting fired. The former is preferable because the employee is happier, better motivated, and working for the reinforcement derived from the activity rather than the avoidance of some possible punishment. As trainers, we should similarly motivate our animals so that they look forward to each session and find sessions positively reinforcing experiences. Punishment may be a part of every operant equation, but the trainer should always try to focus on the reinforcing aspect of each interaction.

The public's use of punishment – Punishment, as defined and applied operantly, is a difficult concept to understand because the public uses the term so differently. Most people try to punish the animal or the person rather than punishing the behavior, which is why punishment as applied by most people fails to work. Here are some examples of poorly applied (yet often used) punishment:
- You arrive at home and notice that the dog has urinated on the floor in your absence. As your dog approaches, you scold him for his actions. Because you did not catch him in the act, you have not actually punished his behavior (urinating on the floor); you have positively punished the behavior of greeting you at the door (not the behavior you wanted to decrease).
- Your daughter shows you her report card (she has received poor grades this semester), so you ground her for a week. You have used negative punishment (removed the privilege of going out), but the behavior you have punished is the behavior of showing you her report card. The next time she gets poor grades, she is likely to be more reluctant to show you the report card. The better approach would be to reinforce your daughter after she has studied hard or done her homework well.

These are just two examples of the way the public often uses punishment. In reality, they are not punishing the behavior; instead they are punishing the animal or the person. Punishment is unfortunately used vindictively (a vain attempt to "teach the animal a lesson"), which should never be the goal or objective of a good trainer. For a general look at *Why Punishment Doesn't Work* (Pryor, 1986), see the article on page 315.

A note on deprivation – Perhaps one of the concepts most frequently misunderstood by young trainers is deprivation. The use of deprivation (reducing an animal's rations, removing companion animals or depriving an animal of its favorite toy) to negatively punish behavior is mistakenly believed to be a common practice in animal training. Yet, in professional training programs, which focus on positive reinforcement, this technique is not necessary. The use of variable reinforcement schedules, secondary reinforcers and creative enrichment devices make it possible to keep animals interested and motivated without ever using deprivation. There is additional confusion because the scientific definition of deprivation is much broader than the definition most often used by trainers and the public. In reality, according to the scientific definition, deprivation is a natural occurrence. When we are hungry, we are food deprived; if we are thirsty, we are water deprived; when the sun goes down, we are light deprived. These natural occurrences are not necessarily aversive, and in those naturally occurring states they are not problematic. However, when faced with trying to rectify a behavioral problem, an inexperienced trainer may be tempted to take deprivation past its natural stage, and therein lies the problem. Trainers should avoid the use of deprivation techniques as training tools, or they may face the same drawbacks that are encountered when other forms of punishment are employed.

Avoiding the bad perceptions – Because punishment has such bad connotations to the public – and by the public's definition and use of the concept, it is bad – trainers frequently say that they never punish their animals. In the context of the common definition, this is true; we don't use punishment. The contradiction between the operant term and the common term is so extreme that it is usually best to speak about the subject using common terminology – especially, when you consider how difficult it can be even for experienced trainers to distinguish the concepts. In almost every professional training situation we are training animals for public display, or to help pet owners, or to achieve other purposes where the terminology will baffle onlookers who lack the expertise to fully grasp operant concepts. It is for that reason that trainers make the generalized statement, "We only use positive reinforcement with our animals; no punishment is ever used." That statement conveys the proper message and intent of our training programs. The semantic distinctions and discussions can be saved for the psychologists and the experienced trainers.

Summary
In reality, our focus as trainers should be to look for ways to positively reinforce behavior. However, the concepts of aversive stimuli, punishers, and negative reinforcers are real and should be thoroughly understood by the experienced trainer. The most impor-

tant concepts to keep in mind are:
- Behavior is reinforced or punished, *not* the animal.
- The focus is on achieving desired behavior rather than on eliminating undesired behavior; this keeps the focus on reinforcement rather than punishment.
- Technical operant definitions of punishment are different from the common definitions. But most trainers use common terms because few people understand the technical operant definitions and their uses.

Schedules of Reinforcement

Looking at it Simply

After that complicated discussion about punishment, let's try to simplify this discussion, even though schedules of reinforcement can be made to seem even more confusing and controversial. Very simply put, there are two ways of applying reinforcers – on a continuous (consistent) schedule or a variable (intermittent) schedule. These techniques have been used in operant labs to study how animals learn. A fairly thorough and readable summary of the basic concepts is described in *Definition Drift* (Van der Toorn, in press), on page 318.

It's an Alphabet Soup

As trainers began to implement creative schedules of reinforcement to provide variety for their animals, new terms and acronyms were developed. The more you read, the more acronyms you will find; it can boggle even the most experienced trainer's mind. Perhaps it would be helpful to separate the original operant terms from those that were created to describe the application of the original concepts to specific training situations.

Original terms – Psychologists and behavior analysts have a number of basic terms that they use in describing reinforcement, and usually each term has an acronym. These terms include continuous reinforcement (CRF) and four types of intermittent reinforcement: fixed-interval (FI), fixed-ratio (FR), variable-interval (VI), and variable-ratio (VR). These terms are defined and described by Van der Toorn, as referenced above, on page 318, and by Beeler and Sullivan, in chapter 4, on page 80. Most marine mammal trainers, however, do not use these abbreviations or all of the terms. This is probably because some reinforcement schedules are very specific and better suited to studying and analyzing learning in a laboratory setting. Animal trainers tend to combine these concepts, which is why they created new terms not in the operant textbooks.

Marine mammal variations – Most training programs used a continuous schedule of reinforcement. But as marine mammal trainers began to explore the operant literature, the value of intermittent schedules of reinforcement seemed obvious, but a way was needed to make the technical approach more accessible to trainers in their day to day interactions with animals. Trainers at Sea World first coined the terms RIR and VRRV that would become popular with marine mammal trainers in the 1970's and 1980's. Today, most trainers have reverted to using the original term, they are all Variable Schedules of Reinforcement. Although not widely used today, the following terms are common in many articles on training.

- RIR – Random and Interrupted Reinforcement was defined by Sea World and for a time embraced by the training community. As more trainers began to implement and fine-tune the concept, the technique was brought more in line with the original operant definitions and renamed Reinforcers delivered Intermittently in a Randomized order (still RIR). Although many variations of the concept developed, one of the clearest descriptions of the importance of this technique was provided in 1981 by Randy Brill in *RIR in use at the Brookfield Zoo, Random and Interrupted Reinforcement Redefined in Perspective*, on page 320.
- VRRV – It was inevitable that RIR would be deemed not quite representative of the best ways to provide a variable schedule to our animals. The next incarnation was Variable Ratio with Reinforcement Variety (VRRV), and that concept, too, was redefined several times as trainers searched for a way to make the original operant concepts more usable in the real training environment of a marine mammal facility. RIR and VRRV were important steps in the transition from continuous schedules of reinforcement to the variable schedules most commonly in use today.

Other terms – As you learn more about training, the "alphabet soup" of reinforcement acronyms will continue to grow. I have tried to limit their use to those terms you are likely to find most often (and most useful). Other terms such as LRS (chapter 4), DRI, and DRO (chapter 10) are discussed elsewhere.

Implementing a Variable Schedule

Just as there are many types of variable schedules, there are just as many ways to put those schedules into effect, depending on the animals to be trained and the staff. Making the transition from a continuous schedule to a variable schedule is not always easy. In 1996 Paul Komanski described how one facility made the transition in *Changing from a Fixed-Ratio Schedule to a Variable Schedule*, on page 330. At Shedd Aquarium we gradually approximate our staff and animals from a consistent to an intermittent schedule of reinforcement. To understand the implementation of a variable schedule, you must first fully understand the use of secondary reinforcers described earlier in this chapter. Then, just like the use of secondary reinforcement, each new trainer and naïve animal must be approximated from a continuous schedule to a variable schedule. The approximations I recommend for implementing a variable schedule are as follows:

1. Each new trainer (and new animal) must begin with a continuous and fixed schedule of primary reinforcement. Variety is still provided through the application of these steps:
   - Behavior selection is not fixed; and multiple staff members work each animal.
   - Duration of behaviors will vary (number of jumps, length of a fluke present, etc.).
   - Vary the type and quantity of primary reinforcement offered.
2. Begin to condition and establish secondary reinforcers. See article on page 295 (Ramirez, 1996).
3. Use of secondaries as the only reinforcer is approximated using these steps:
   - Use for simple, easy behaviors first.
   - Incorporate into reinforcement schedule with more complex behaviors.
   - Use while training new behaviors.
4. The use of other behaviors (those not previously conditioned as secondaries, but well-established) as reinforcers is generally the final step to fully integrating a trainer or an animal into a variable reinforcement schedule.

How Long Does it Take?

The implementation of any plan will vary with the animal, the trainer, and the situation. A trainer with a great deal of experience, working alone with an experienced animal can begin utilizing variable schedules of reinforcement within days or weeks. An inexperienced trainer, working with a naïve animal, as part of a large staff, may take many months to several years to establish a full variable schedule. It is important to point out that even the youngest trainers, working on a consistent schedule of reinforcement, can still provide animals with a great deal of variety.

Variety is the Goal

The point to these schedules is variety. In a never-ending quest to challenge our animals and to find better shaping techniques, we will constantly invent new or revised methods of applying our techniques. We must be careful not to let a "new" method overshadow the many proven techniques at our disposal. Often when a new concept is introduced, trainers will look at it as a magical cure for all training ills. There's no such thing. In many cases the search for a solution reverts to knowing and understanding our animals needs. Experienced trainers recognize the pitfalls and drawbacks of the tools at hand. The wise trainer will choose the technique that is appropriate to each situation. For an alternative look at RIR and variable schedules that tries to put it all in perspective, see *RIR A New Schedule of Reinforcement or a Method of Training Trainers* (Desmond, 1983), on page 335.

Recall, Delta, and "No"

Different Concepts

Here again are a series of terms that trainers misinterpret or mistakenly use interchangeably. Their similarity lies only in the fact that they can be used in similar situations *sometimes*. The meanings of the three terms, however, are quite different.

Recall

This is the most commonly used of the three techniques. A recall is simply a signal that indicates to the animal that it should return to station. A discussion of this term and its confusion with another is found in *Understanding the Use of Recall vs. Delta Signals* (T. Forum, 1990), on page 339. The use of a recall is also discussed in the chapters on aggression, problem solving, and complex training. Although the concept of the recall is fairly clear – a stimulus is presented indicating that the animal should return to station – young trainers will confuse the recall with a delta or a bridging stimulus. Depending on the situation, the bridge and the delta will often bring the animal back to station, just like a recall. The intent of the message to the animal, however, is very different with each stimulus: recall means "return to station," bridge means "good," and delta means "wrong" or "warning." We certainly would never use those meanings interchangeably when speaking to each other, why would we want to confuse our animals by using them interchangeably when we train? For additional discussion of the question, read *How is a Recall Trained and Used?* (T. Forum, in press), on page 341.

Delta

Perhaps the least used of the three techniques, the delta is defined as a signal to warn an animal that an aversive stimulus is about to be presented. The article referenced under "Recall" discusses the delta in some detail. An example of the delta in use in a fairly complex training scenario is presented in *Microcomputer Assisted Training of a Bottlenose Dolphin* (Kamolnick et. al., 1985), on page 344.

The "No" Signal

This is a variation of the delta, although it is more flexible and need not indicate warning of an aversive stimulus (though it can). Just as a secondary reinforcer is a means of communicating "yes" or "good" to an animal, a "no" signal can be thought of as a secondary (or conditioned) punisher. "No" signals, when used correctly, can shape behavior by providing guidance to the animal and decrease undesirable behavior. Its effective use is analogous to the "hot and cold" game played by children: A child is looking for an item, and someone indicates whether the child is "hot" (getting close to the item, the bridge), or "cold" (nowhere near the item, the "no"). Pet owners often teach their animals the concept of the word "no," but since this is more often a warning to stop a behavior "or else," it would technically be a delta. The problem with a "no" signal is its potential for overuse, which would decrease its effectiveness. Psychologists often recommend that parents say no to their children less frequently and suggest that they instead offer alternatives to an unwanted behavior. However, once the word "no" has been added to the vocabulary, it flows from a parent's mouth all too easily. I frequently discourage young trainers from ever conditioning a "no" signal, because if there is not a signal for "no" it cannot be overused. However I have seen skilled trainers use the "no" or "wrong" signal very effectively. As with any tool, if properly understood and used, it can be worth keeping in the toolbox. Karen Pryor describes some good examples of the uses of a conditioned aversive stimulus (DOG, pp. 18-20).

Effective Tools

All of the techniques described can be extremely effective tools in the training process. But the potential for misuse with adverse effects on the animals is serious. Therefore, I believe in reserving these techniques, especially the delta and the "no," for only the most experienced trainers.

Chained Behaviors

This is an advanced concept in which completion of one behavior cues the start of the next, and each subsequent behavior reinforces the previous behavior. Animals that work in films are often trained to perform behaviors in a chain, so that one behavior naturally follows another without the need for additional cues or reinforcers. Karen Pryor describes the concept well (*DOG*, pp. 85-90). Another description of how behaviors are chained can be found in *Chaining Behaviors Together* (T. Forum, 1998), on page 348. Chained behaviors can create difficult challenges if a behavior in the chain starts to break down, dealing with that problem is discussed in the previously cited article as well as in *Fixing a Problem Behavior in the Middle of a Chain* (T. Forum, 1984), on page 352.

Technical Chains

In the technical chain, the trainer gives no cues or reinforcers other than the S^D to start the chain, and sometimes a bridge at the end of the chain. All other cues and reinforcers are the behaviors within the chain itself. The simplest of chains is the series of leaps, or porpoising behaviors, that many dolphins are trained to do. A dolphin will leap in the air and continue to jump until it is bridged. The completion of each leap cues the dolphin to jump again. Dogs in agility competitions are often trained to complete a long series of maneuvers, one after another; the completion of one task cues the next and the thrill of moving to that next task reinforces the previously completed behavior.

Common Chains

It seems that every concept is modified or adapted by someone. You may frequently read about behavior chains in which the trainer bridges after each correct response in the chain. Sometimes you may hear about chains in which the trainer gives S^Ds to the animal to cue certain behaviors within the chain. These are not true chains, even though many trainers call them chains. Use of the term chain is based loosely on the idea that behaviors are being linked together without benefit of primary reinforcement after each. In reality, the "common chain" is often a creative use of a variable reinforcement schedule. Nevertheless, trainers should be familiar with common chains as well as technical chains.

"Continue" Signal

Some trainers have developed a special signal to indicate to an animal that it is doing well, but that the behavior is not yet complete. The purpose of the signal is to provide encouragement without bringing the animal back to station. Karen Pryor refers to this as the "keep going" cue (*DOG*, pp. 17-18). This cue is especially helpful for behaviors of long duration. For example, if an animal is being asked to remain still for a particularly long voluntary medical procedure, the trainer may periodically rub or pat the animal on its side. In many cases, the rub or the pat is a secondary reinforcer that reassures the animal that you haven't forgotten to bridge. Many trainers use this technique without conditioning it specifically as a "continue" signal. In fact, experienced trainers, who use a widely variable schedule of reinforcement, probably convey many signals that encourage their animals to continue without bringing them back to station for primary reinforcement. Cetacean water work, behavior chains, and lengthy husbandry sessions are examples of times when trainers may put this technique to good use. Some trainers, who want to have the maximum number of tools at their disposal, will condition a variety of bridging and other specific informational stimuli. Any signal that specifically indicates to an animal that it has done well but shouldn't stop or return to station would be a "continue" or "keep going" signal.

Combination Behaviors

The concept of combining two or more cues to form a new (or combined) behavior is different from the concept of chaining behaviors together. Combining behaviors is a technique sometimes used in various cognition projects. However, sometimes trainers have used this concept simply to provide variety for the animals or to create new and unique behaviors. Although I am aware of many facilities that combine cues, there is relatively little written about the training that goes into such endeavors. *Training Combination Behaviors with Bottlenose Dolphins* (Losch, 1998) is included here, on page 354.

End of Session Signal

This is not an advanced concept so much as a controversial topic (which, by my definition, makes it advanced) among marine mammal trainers. Experienced trainers frequently debate the merits and drawbacks of signaling to the animals that a session is complete. Over the years I have used both systems and am now a firm believer in not using such a signal. My reasoning and that of three other trainers (with views split two and two on either side), are described in *Using an End of Session Signal: Yes or No?* (T. Forum, 1995), on page 358.

Other Advanced Concepts

There are many other important advanced concepts, but their discussion seemed more appropriate in other chapters. The chapters with additional advanced concepts include: 7, "Social Animals"; 10, "Aggression"; 11, "Problem Solving"; and 12, "Complex Training."

A Behavior Sampler by Gary Wilkes

An all too common problem for many trainers is not sticking to the criteria originally set for a behavior. Laziness on the part of the trainer or excuses that the animal was "tired," "cute," "scared," etc. will often cause trainers to reinforce incorrect or sloppy behavior. Ultimately, not viewing behavior as black or white (right or wrong) will cause the behavior to break down and will do a disservice to the animal.

Monique, the "One Trick Poodle"

by Gary Wilkes

Monique, the Poodle, knows how to sit. She sits when you ask her to sit and when you don't ask her to sit. She will also sit when you ask her to lie down and when you ask her to speak. When you ask her to come, she will run slightly out of your reach and then sit - just far enough away so that you cannot grab her. Though this behavior may not appear intelligent, Monique is actually a very bright dog.

Before you can appreciate Monique's intelligence, you must realize that she behaves this way, not because she is stupid, but because this behavior "works." Whenever she is asked to do anything, she stands a good chance of being rewarded by performing her favorite behavior - sitting. This pattern is the result of a long standing family tradition. Her owners are convinced that Monique is cute, no matter what she does. When they ask her to sit or lie down, they never really pay attention to whether she performs the desired behavior or not. They laugh and cuddle her and joke that she is "brain dead." This lackadaisical attitude has taught Monique an important rule for living with her human companions - when in doubt, sit.

Many pets have adapted to their surroundings exactly as Monique has. If they are not required to perform precisely, they don't. If they are expected to perform behaviors without being taught how to do them correctly, they eventually quit trying and fall back on behaviors that have succeeded in the past. Trainers who decry the stupidity of such animals are missing a major rule of training - animals do not intentionally fail. Most often their failures can be directly linked to poor training or improper reinforcement.

Avoiding this problem starts with realizing that only a tiny percentage of dogs are truly "brain dead." The vast majority are capable of better performance than they usually offer. They simply need to know that there is a benefit that comes from precise performance. If you can find something your pet is willing to work for, such as treats, toys, or affection, you can find out your pet's true potential.

A good place to start is with the behavior "sit." Almost every adult dog knows a version of this behavior. Get a handful of treats and call your dog. Ask Fido to "sit" and count to two. If Fido does not drop his buns to the floor within two seconds, turn your back on him and walk a few feet away.

A few repetitions of this and Fido is momentarily puzzled. In the past, all he had to do was lazily sit after the third or fourth command and he still had a good chance for a reward. Fido smiles at this thought. This is something he can really understand. His wild ancestors never had two or three chances to slowly chase a rabbit. He may be a domesticated dog, but he knows about instantaneous reaction to cats, letter carriers and joggers. Fido wakes from his fog and sits quickly on the next repetition. You congratulate him with verbal praise and give him a treat. Move to a new location and try it again. Begin to raise your standards for any behavior that Fido knows how to perform. If he is inattentive, walk away and ignore him for a few seconds.

Expanding this exercise to other areas of Fido's life is simple. Start asking him to perform a behavior before you pet him. Ask him to sit or lie down before you give him a meal. If the behavior is not done well, turn away and ignore him for awhile.

This simple process of expecting a dog to "work for a living" is the first step toward getting better performance from your pet. If you reinforce a dog for sitting when you asked for "down," or repeat commands many times, you are teaching poor behavior. Teaching Monique and Fido that they can get affection and treats in exchange for minimal performance will undercut any control you may currently have. Your new approach to training will develop responsive and enthusiastic performances. Your pet will also gain a reward far bigger than a food treat - an occupation.

The following paper was first presented at the 1994 IMATA Conference in Tacoma, Washington. This article appears in Volume 2, Number 1, 1996 of *Marine Mammals: Public Display and Research*, it takes a close look at how and why secondary reinforcers are effective. It explains in detail the John G. Shedd Aquarium's philosophy for applying these techniques properly.

Secondary Reinforcers as an Indispensable Tool: The Effectiveness of Non-Food Reinforcers

by Ken Ramirez
John G. Shedd Aquarium

ABSTRACT

The term "secondary reinforcement" is defined in various ways by different behaviorists. The use of secondary reinforcement is even more varied in its applications from facility to facility. This paper identifies some of the differing definitions of secondary reinforcement and possible reasons for confusion among trainers. These reinforcers play an important role in good animal care, as demonstrated by an examination of the application of non-food reinforcement in various situations.

INTRODUCTION

Secondary reinforcers are effective and important elements of a good training program. However, even within our own profession trainers use quite a variety of different terms when referring to secondary reinforcement. The extent and methods of implementing secondary reinforcement also varies greatly from one facility to another. To resolve this confusion we 1) attempt to find a consistent definition for secondary reinforcement, 2) explain one of several methods for introducing secondary reinforcers to new animals and trainers, and 3) discuss and demonstrate the importance of their use.

DEFINITIONS

Originally, we thought that most trainers understood secondary reinforcement. But a review of the literature and an informal survey of trainers indicated that terminology differs greatly from facility to facility. The following list includes 12 of over 25 terms found in the training literature that were used to refer to this subject (IMATA, 1971-1994):

GROUP 1
- secondary reinforcer
- conditioned reinforcer
- alternative reinforcer
- trained reinforcer
- non-food reinforcer
- non-appetitive reinforcer

GROUP 2
- tactile reinforcer
- bridging stimulus

GROUP 3
- varied reinforcer
- planned reinforcer
- organized reinforcer
- natural reinforcer

Note that these are terms found in papers of various levels of scientific credibility. This list is only intended to show the wide variety of terms used, not to indicate their accuracy. Their inclusion here means that they were used in the context of what the behavioral literature would call a secondary or conditioned reinforcer. They are grouped in three categories; the first group contains terms that might be accepted as somewhat synonymous with a secondary reinforcer. Group number two are examples of secondary reinforcers, not synonyms. The final group contains meaningful terms that are either related to secondary reinforcement or taken from a non-behavioral discipline. With so many terms, it is understandable that some people might be confused.

We must define the terms being used before proceeding. A definition of reinforcement:

A reinforcer is an event or stimulus which follows a desired response and increases the frequency and probability of the occurrence of that response (Reynolds, 1975).

In operant conditioning, we usually refer to two basic types of reinforcers; the first is a primary reinforcer:

A reinforcer whose effectiveness does not depend on the animal's past experience with it, food and water are examples of primary reinforcers (Kelleher, 1966: Brill, 1981).

The other basic type of reinforcer is called a secondary reinforcer and is also referred to as a conditioned reinforcer because it is:

A reinforcer whose effectiveness is determined by the conditions under which the animal has experienced it in the past (Kelleher, 1966: Brill, 1981).

On the basis of these definitions, this paper will refer to secondary or conditioned reinforcement. Each time trainers from different facilities begin to discuss training concepts, terms should be defined first. Often, trainers have difficulty discussing training concepts because their terminology is so different. The need for all marine mammal trainers to adopt a common language continues to be a concern and a goal that we are hopefully all trying to achieve.

IMPLEMENTATION

Before formally introducing secondary reinforcers to an animal, it is helpful to understand the natural history of that animal. Learning how it lives and interacts with its counterparts in the wild can help determine the types of reinforcers an animal might accept. If past experience of the animal has already conditioned certain types of reinforcers, it might be helpful to put those to good use. Macaws, for example, are often seen preening each other and, thus, are often very accepting, after some conditioning, of trainers scratching under their feathers. Most birds of prey, on the other hand, tend to be self-preeners and consequently not as readily accepting of tactile reinforcement. After noting that wild chimpanzees sometimes tickled themselves, trainers teaching sign language to chimps found tickling to be one of their most effective reinforces, (Gardner, 1969). Beluga whales are regularly observed in the wild rubbing their bodies along shallow river bottoms (Norris, 1994), which may explain why belugas tend to be one of the most tactile cetaceans in an aquarium environment.

A common mistake made by young trainers is in assuming that since an animal seems to respond well to a given stimulus, that same stimulus will automatically be reinforcing if offered in a training situation. In other words, just because a beluga seems to seek out rough surfaces to scratch its skin does not mean that the animal will seek out, desire, or find the same thing reinforcing when offered by a trainer. However, armed with the knowledge that belugas regularly engage in skin scratching behavior, a trainer could condition the animal to accept scratching from a brush or the trainer's hand. In time, the animal may actually seek this type of tactile attention from the trainer. The scratching, therefore, has been conditioned as a reinforcer.

This process of learning the animal's likes and dislikes, is part of developing a relationship. Each trainer must develop individual relationships with each animal. An experienced trainer, for example, may condition tongue scratching as an effective secondary reinforcer with an individual dolphin. The animal has learned to accept, and perhaps even enjoy, this tactile reinforcement during a session. A young trainer, having watched this exchange, decides to offer the same dolphin a tongue scratch at a later session. Much to the new trainer's surprise, the dolphin clamps down on the unsuspecting newcomer's hand. It can happen often, yet young trainers are usually very surprised when it happens to them. Every secondary reinforcer, particularly when first being introduce, must be established by each individual trainer. Once it has been used by enough trainers, it may become so well-conditioned that a dolphin may be accepting of it from anyone who offers it. But unless trainers take the time to develop the relationship themselves, they can never be certain.

This concept is usually best understood by a young trainer when given a human example:

> I happened to have noticed that after work one day, a trainer's wife met him in the office. As she approached him, she thanked him for some errand he had helped her run earlier, then she caressed his shoulder and kissed him on the neck. His face lit up and his rather solemn mood changed immediately. I thought to myself, now there's a woman who knows how to use reinforcement. Two days later, I noticed that the same trainer had done an exceptional job of cleaning one of the animal areas. As he was leaving the well-cleaned area, I decided to offer him that seemingly effective reinforcer. But just as I was about to kiss him, he nearly punched my lights out! Why? Because I don't have the same relationship with that trainer as he has with his wife.

While our relationship with the animals is certainly different, that story clearly illustrates that just because something is reinforcing in one context does not mean it will be reinforcing in every context.

The steps to conditioning a secondary reinforcer are really quite simple. The reinforcer to be taught should be paired with a primary reinforcer. This is the same procedure used when establishing a bridging stimulus during the early stages of training. Whether one uses a whistle, an underwater tone, a clicker, the work "good," or a flashing light, they are all secondary or conditioned reinforcers. These stimuli mean nothing the first time they are experienced by an animal, but after constant pairing with a primary reinforcer, most trainers have witnessed the powerful effect of the bridging stimulus. The training of other secondary reinforcers can have the same effect.

At the John G. Shedd Aquarium, we methodically introduce secondary reinforcers. During play sessions, in which food is not used, trainers are encouraged to be creative and learn what each animal seems to enjoy. That information is then used to help determine what secondary reinforcers should be conditioned next. The new stimuli (which is not yet conditioned as a reinforcer) is treated like a new behavior in training. Once the new stimuli has been paired regularly with a primary reinforcer, the new reinforcer is then used only sparingly following easy or simple behaviors. In time, each trainer will take the next step at their own pace, using secondary reinforcers on more difficult and complex behaviors. Eventually, as a trainer becomes more experienced, he or she will begin introducing new reinforcers which have not yet been conditioned. This is a step reserved for experienced trainers who have worked with an experienced animal for some time.

The use of secondary reinforcers is treated as an advanced concept at the aquarium. A new trainer must first demonstrate a thorough knowledge of the species, the individual animal's training history, a knowledge of all it's behavioral criteria, and a thorough understanding of basic operant conditioning principles. We teach these concepts to new trainers much the way we train our animals, or the way we teach each other in school, through approximation. If you are teaching someone to read, you don't start with **War and Peace**, you begin by teaching the ABCs. Later, you read "see Spot run," and gradually move on to more difficult and complex material. We introduce concepts like secondary reinforcement the same way.

There are many other good ways of introducing secondary reinforcers, but for a staff as large as ours and a collection as diverse as ours, we have found this approach to be effective. It allows the training supervisor a system to monitor each trainer's and each animal's progress. This system assures consistency among staff, allows experienced trainers the freedom to explore, and gives the animals the opportunity to be constantly challenged and stimulated.

Below are three case studies that I believe demonstrate how critical secondary reinforcers can be to a good husbandry program.

CASE STUDY #1 (Pacific white-sided dolphin)

The first example occurred during the summer of 1994 when a female Pacific white-sided dolphin (*Lagenorhynchus obliquidens*) began exhibiting a decreased appetite. She seemed mildly lethargic and, although not interested in eating, she willingly offered behaviors asked of her. Two activities that seemed to interest her most during this period were following us around the habitat and accepting taction. Although very cooperative for most behaviors, we could not reliably get her to eat. Our veterinarian prescribed an antibiotic regime that required fairly precise timing of medication. Since we could not be sure she would be hungry when it was time for medication (she often was not), we made medication-time into a game. We would run, then pet her, then run and pet her gain, then ask her to open her mouth, put a medicated fish into her mouth, then run, then pet her. In all the excitement she would swallow the fish. As time went on, we began using secondary reinforcers to reinforce her for swallowing the fish. Although it took several weeks before she began eating reliably again, she never missed her medication. Our ability to successfuly treat this dolphin was due primarily to her playful nature and strong ties to secondary reinforcers.

CASE STUDY #2 (Beluga whale)

The temperament of beluga whales (*Delphinapterus leucas*) is very different from most other cetaceans. One of our oldest female belugas used to have an unusual reaction to changes in her environment. Less than a year after opening our new Oceanarium, we provided habitat space for a sister institution to house their false killer whales (*Pseudorca crassidens*) at our facility. The day these whales arrived, the female beluga decided to stop eating. Although we realized that this might be a reaction to the arrival of the new animals, we did not want to take any chances. The veterinarian insisted that we get a blood sample. Although she had been trained for voluntary blood sampling, conventional wisdom told us that an animal that was not eating might not cooperate for a voluntary exam. However, we found that despite the fact that she would spit out every fish offered, she readily cooperated with every behavior asked of her. Our belugas have always been very taction-oriented, and the use of melon rubs, tongue scratches, and body massages were reinforcers that had been easily conditioned. This proved to be extremely beneficial during the week that followed the arrival of the false killer whales. The female beluga participated in every session that week, spitting out every fish offered but accepting every tactile reinforcer. Most important, during that week she allowed usto take three voluntary blood samples, which fortunately confirmed that she was not ill. Had we not already established the use of secondary reinforcers, we would not have formed that kind of relationship with the whale and could never have taken blood samples in that manner.

CASE STUDY #3 (Rough-toothed dolphin)

Early in 1994 I had the opportunity to work with a group of rough-toothed dolphins (*Steno bredanensis*) in a natural lagoon facility in French Polynesia. These dolphins were native to the islands and were to be part of a new interactive program being developed by Dolphin Quest. One of the most unique attributes displayed by each of these animals was that they would solicit tactile interaction by rubbing against our hands and feet even before they began eating regularly. Within one week, each dolphin in the group had developed an interest in seeking tactile interaction from the animal care staff.

Meanwhile, as we began feeding the dolphins, we found that they used a feeding technique that they also exhibited in the wild. They would rigorously slap the fish on the water's surface until they had removed the head. Next they would swallow the head, then slowly work on swallowing the rest of the body. At that rate, a feeding session could last for over an hour. We tried feeding fish without heads, but they still removed the top portion of the fish's body before eating. We tried offering cut fish, but they wouldn't eat that. We knew that with time, we could condition them to eat smaller fish and to swallow more quickly. But, until then, using fish as a reinforcrer meant more than five minutes between each interaction.

As we worked with their feeding behavior, we continued to conduct play sessions. Within several days we began to establish a very positive relationship with each animal. Their response to taction was so strong that we began to shape behaviors using solely tactile reinforcement. We taught them to work in shallow water for body exams, girth measurements, and voluntary mild restraint. All were shaped using rubbing, petting, and body massages as reinforcers. Sessions were also conducted at dockside proving that gating, tail presentation, mouth open, and breaches could all be shaped using exclusively tactile forms of reinforcement. These behaviors were all established with animals that had been in human care for less than six weeks.

We assumed that taction must play an important role in the life of this species in the wild. Even with that pre-existing condition, we had to gain the animals' trust and develop a relationship with each animal. The first several weeks were critical in conditioning the animals to accept physical contact from us, which ultimately became a very strong secondary reinforcer.

CONCLUSION

Secondary reinforcement is not a new tool, yet it is not consistently used and certainly not uniformly defined by many of us in the marine mammal training profession. Training is a technology based on scientifically proven behavioral principles. As our profession expands, new trainers must combine scientific knowledge, operant terminology, and the years of experience gathered at our collective facilities to continue to improve the lives of the animals under our care. Secondary reinforcers, when properly used and carefully implemented, are not only powerful reinforcers, they are one of many indispensable tools which help to make our animals' lives so much better.

Most experienced trainers could probably share many more examples of the effective use of secondary reinforcers. For those who still do not believe in the use of anything but food as a reinforcer, I hope this paper has presented some of the advantages to using conditioned reinforcers. For the trainer who wants to use secondary reinforcers but gets baffled by the sometimes erratic nature of their effectiveness, perhaps I have suggested some paths which may lead you to better incorporating those reinforcers. And finally, for the majority of you who have probably used secondary reinforcers in more effective and creative ways than I can even imagine, I hope this paper has, at the very least, provided some interesting examples of secondary reinforcement in action.

ACKNOWLEDGEMENTS

I would like to acknowledge those who have helped make this paper possible. I alone must accept responsibility for any errors or unusual perspectives. But, I am indebted to those whom I have had the good fortune to work with the various case studies described. In particular, I would like to thank the marine mammal staff of the John G. Shedd Aquarium and the staff of Dolphin Quest French Polynesia and Hawaii for their support.

LITERATURE CITED

Brill, R.L. (1981). R.I.R in use at the Brookfield Zoo: Random and interrupted reinforcement redefined in perspective. In J. Barry & R.L. Brill (Eds.), Proceeding of the 9th annual conference of the International Marine Animal Trainers Association (pp.49-58).

Gardner, R.A. & Gardner, B.T. (1969). Teaching sign language to a chimpanzee. Science 165:664-672.

IMATA. (1971-1991). (Various Eds.), Proceedings of the annual conference of the International Marine Animal Trainers Association.

IMATA. (1976-1994). (Various Eds.), Soundings.

Kelleher, R.T. (1966). Chaining and conditioned reinforcement. In W.K. Honig (Ed.), **Operant behavior: Areas of research and application** (pp. 160-212). New York: Appleton-Century-Crofts.

Norris, K.S. (1994). Beluga: White whale of the North. National Geographic 185 (6): 2-30.

Reynolds, G.S. (1975). **A primer of operant conditioning** (Rev. Ed.). Glenview, Illinois: Scott Foresman and Co.

Trainer's Forum

VOL 19, NO 2, 1994. When training techniques are found to be successful with one species, there naturally follows a question as to how to apply the same techniques to new species. Sometimes there is very little difference, while with some animals the differences can be enormous. Often it is a matter of knowing as much about the species in question as possible, as well as understanding the individual characteristics of the specific animal being trained. Here is a look at the use of secondary reinforcers with California sea lions.

Secondary Reinforcers for California Sea Lions

QUESTION: Our training staff would like to learn more about using alternative reinforcers other than food (e.g.: toys, scratching, etc.) with California sea lions. We are also interested in knowing whether using a bridge during a play session (when no food is present) will undermine the effect of the bridge during regular sessions.

ANSWER 1: Secondary reinforcers can be very effective with all pinnipeds, especially California sea lions. Like most new situations with animals, it is probably most effective to train secondary reinforcers just as you would any new behavior. Secondaries are often based on something we as trainers perceive to be positive for the animal, but there is no way we can be sure of that. Assuming that a secondary is already positive can lead to undesirable behaviors and even aggression. So by initially always pairing the new secondaries with primaries, you can desensitize the animal to those secondaries and assure that they end up as positive reinforcers, regardless of whether the animal is already favorably predisposed towards them.

When starting out with new secondaries, keep in mind that all animals are individuals and may like or dislike different stimuli. Secondary reinforcers are also part of a relationship developed between a trainer and an animal, so different trainers can make the same secondary appear differently to the animal each time. This is all the more reason to train secondary reinforcers consistently before trying them in a variable schedule of reinforcement. Desensitize the animals slowly, watching for signals such as backing away, tensing up, avoiding tactile interaction, or ignoring a toy. Once you feel that the animal is positively reinforced by a secondary reinforcer, it is a good idea to strengthen the reinforcer for a period of time before assuming that it is ready to be used on its own. Periodic strengthening with primary reinforcers is a good idea, no matter how long the animals have been conditioned to the secondaries. Be flexible, some animals will never like secondaries, which kind of defeats the purpose. Some commonly used secondary reinforcers are verbal praise, ice, tactile interaction, toys, and water spray. You'll find that sea lions are responsive to all sorts of new stimuli.

We can't think of a single good reason for using a bridge during the play session (although as one committee member put it, "the world probably won't explode"). Without a connection to a reinforcer, however, the bridge can be diluted over very little time. There is also a very good chance (especially with bucket conscious sea lions) that the bridge won't solicit the desired response anyway. Depending on how your facility defines a "play session," the use of a bridge will turn it into a training session and the animal may not consider it play at all (and at this point, sea lions tend to wonder where that bucket is and why there is no reinforcement for the bridge – a good formula for irritating those 750 pound bulls!).

This also brings up a point regarding verbal bridges. If the word "good" is utilized as a bridge, and new trainers or volunteers are participating in play and using "good" frequently (as in "good girl," etc.), they may be inadvertently extinguishing that bridge.

Animal Tech. Training Advisory Committee
IMATA

ANSWER 2: The training staff at Sea World of Australia works with eight species of pinnipeds. Our trainers have effectively used alternative reinforcers such as tactile interaction, toys, play sessions, social interaction, chained behaviors, and innovative training sessions. The trainers have found two elements key in the use of secondary (or alternative) reinforcers:

1. Some species of pinnipeds are naturally more receptive to alternative reinforcers than other species.

2. Some individuals will be more receptive, even within the same species.

Pinnipeds of the genus *Arctocephalus* seem to be naturally more receptive than other species with regard to tactile reinforcement. It appears that fur seals spend significantly more time grooming, and perhaps this is why they seem to enjoy and respond to tactile interaction more than California sea lions. Also, certain species of fur seals react differently than others; the New Zealand fur seal *(Arctocephalus forsteri)* is more responsive that the Australian fur seal *(A. doriferus)*. Australian sea lions (and other pinnipeds of the *Neophoca* genus) also respond well to tactile reinforcement.

Toys have been successfully used, in varying degrees, as reinforcements with a number of species. Access to the toys is limited, however, in order to prevent boredom in a specific toy and to maintain its interest value. Age, species, and individuals may again factor in the success of this form of reinforcement. Australian sea lions are extremely receptive to toys, even when fully mature. In fact, they seem more inquisitive of their environment compared to other species of pinnipeds. We find that the California sea lion responds more to toys during adolescence. Favorite toys have been used as reinforcements for gating and separation procedures. One particularly successful toy that we use here at Sea World is a PVC pipe attached to a rope that is hung from the roof of the exhibit. An adolescent female California sea lion derived much enjoyment from swinging the pipe back and forth over the pool.

Social interaction with other species of pinnipeds and cetaceans has also been a successful reinforcer. This can, however, sometimes produce a negative effect in that the participants may like the experience so much that they may refuse to leave each other's company.

Favorite activities have also been used on occasion. One classic example of this is the use of a motorized inflatable boat with our cetacean collection. Sea World of Australia's cetaceans have been reinforced for gating into another lagoon by enjoying a vigorous session of bow-riding with the boat. In fact, sometimes the cetaceans can hardly wait to be gated into the lagoon with the boat, presumably hoping for some bow-riding.

It has been Sea World of Australia's experience that the use of a bridging stimulus does not undermine its effectiveness during regular sessions. Our trainers have "floated" back and forth between play and structured training sessions and on occasion, desired behavior was exhibited and bridged during play and/or innovative sessions. These sessions were often achieved with minimal use of primary reinforcers.

Marine Mammal Training Staff
Sea World of Australia

Trainer's Forum

VOL 23, NO 3, 1998. Because many tools and techniques used in training are similar and interelated, it is understandable that trainers might get confused. This question may seem simple at first, but upon further examination the question is much more thought provoking than it may seem.

Conditioned Reinforcers vs. Environmental Enrichment Devices

QUESTION: Please explain the difference between a conditioned reinforcer and an environmental enrichment device.

ANSWER 1: The main difference between a conditioned reinforcer and an environmental enrichment device lies in training. Secondary reinforcers are trained to be a good thing. Compare it to how reinforcing money is to humans. Basically, it's just a piece of paper, but it represents 'treats', be it a house, a toy, or a burger at your favorite fast food chain. When training or conditioning a secondary, the item (ice cubes, tactile, squirt of water on tongue) is initially followed by the primary reinforcer (fish). Over time the animal associates the secondary with fish and thus the secondary itself becomes positive to us! It's always nice if an animal responds well to, for example, tactile interaction, but keep in mind that virtually anything can be trained as a secondary, as long as it is initially, and then intermittently, followed by the primary reinforcer. Secondary reinforcers are vital to a solid training program. They keep training interesting through variety!

Environmental enrichment devices (EED's) differ in that they are not used as reinforcers per se. At the Minnesota Zoo they are used outside of training sessions to make the exhibit an interesting place to be for the animals. This doesn't mean EED's can't involve fish. Live fish release and fish frozen into blocks can be used to stimulate the environment, however they are not formally conditioned. Floating mats, bubble rings, water jets, and various toys are used to stimulate the environment, not to reinforce correct responses to S^Ds as secondaries are.

Both secondary reinforcers and EED's provide unique opportunities to stimulate the animals in our care. Be creative and have fun!
Dolphin Training Staff
Minnesota Zoo

ANSWER 2: A square is always a rectangle, but a rectangle is not always a square. In other words, a conditioned reinforcer is always an environmental enrichment device, but an environmental enrichment device is not always a conditioned reinforcer. Sometimes an environmental enrichment devise is intrinsically reinforcing.
Michael Osborn
Sea Life Park Hawaii

ANSWER 3: At first glance, the answer to this question may seem very straightforward, conditioned reinforcers and environmental enrichment devices are very different concepts. But upon further examination, it is clear that the two concepts overlap in a number of ways. The more thought you give it, the more confusing it can be and the more they seem to be the same. The difference between the two can be looked at in various ways and is influenced by the following factors: semantics (definition), trainer intent (how are the concepts being used?), reinforcement history (what is the animal's experience with the toy or device?), and context (when are they being used?).

At the Shedd Aquarium we use a variety of conditioned reinforcers ranging from our bridging stimulus (whistle, clicker, saying "good", etc.) to secondary reinforcers (clapping, rubbing, spraying water, etc.). These reinforcers have all acquired reinforcing value by being paired with a primary reinforcer. We use conditioned reinforcers during training sessions to indicate to an animal that it has performed a specific behavior correctly and to give us additional reinforcement options. We believe that training sessions are a vital part to an enrichment program, consequently one might argue that a bridging stimulus and a secondary reinforcer are environmental enrichment devices. While this is probably true, most people refer to enrichment devices in a different context.

Environmental enrichment for most animal care programs takes on many forms. Often people refer to enrichment as toys given to the animals for free-form play or devices designed to allow the animals to manipulate their environment (feeding tubes, levers that control lights or bubbles, etc.). However, enrichment programs also include providing habitat options, variety in social structure, play sessions, formal training sessions, and much more. Usually when we refer to an environmental enrichment device specifically, we are indicating a toy or device given to an animal outside of a formal training session. Although the enrichment device may not have been purposely conditioned as a reinforcer, all forms of enrichment usually have some reinforcing value. Therefore, it is important to take great care when giving an enrichment device to an animal, so that you do not inadvertently reinforce any undesirable behaviors.

There are many examples of how one item can be used as a conditioned reinforcer in one instance and an environmental enrichment device in another. We might condition our animals to accept a wide variety of secondary reinforcers, such as water sprayed from a hose. During a training session or presentation we could then use the hose as a reinforcer following a behavior, this would be an example of the spray hose being used as a conditioned reinforcer. Later in the day we might hook the hose up over the pool surface so that it constantly provides a spray, allowing our animals to interact with it when and if they choose. This last example is an instance when the spray hose is being used as an environment enrichment device. The fact that it may have been conditioned as a reinforcer as well, is not the issue. The spray hose might serve as an area for one animal to play and be an area another animal chooses to avoid; yet in both cases it adds to the environment, providing variety and choices for the animals.

Your question provided our staff with an opportunity for a very stimulating discussion. We hope our answer clarifies the differences as we see them rather than confuses the issue.

Lisa Takaki
John G. Shedd Aquarium

Conference Proceedings 1990 Chicago, Illinois, USA. Secondary reinforcers are generally considered only one part of a reinforcement schedule. However, at the Pittsburgh Zoo a river dolphin was trained for more than one year using only secondary reinforcers. Although this presented some problems, it was their attempt at solving a poor response to more traditional training methods.

Sole Use of Non-Food Reinforcers in Daily Training Sessions with an Amazon River Dolphin, *Inia Geoffrensis*

by Annie Burrows, Sandi Schreib and Tim Smith
Pittsburgh Zoo

ABSTRACT

From December of 1989 to January of 1991 exclusive use of non-food reinforcers was made during daily training sessions with a single, older, male Amazon River dolphin, *Inia geoffrensis.* Feeding sessions were separate from training sessions. Exclusively using non-food reinforcers during training sessions gave more flexibility In both length and frequency of training sessions and gave an alternative when undesirable developments had appeared in the dolphin's behavior during training sessions.

INTRODUCTION

The Pittsburgh Zoo's dolphin training program exclusively used non-food reinforcers during every training session from December of 1989 to January of 1991. The dolphin, a solitary male 23-year-old Amazon River dolphin, *Inia geoffrensis,* received his food in separate feeding sessions that occurred approximately 30 minutes prior to each training session. During training sessions, all reinforcement was non-food in nature.

WHY ONLY NON-FOOD REINFORCERS

There were three factors that prompted the try of exclusive use of non-food reinforcers. First, the dolphin's response rate and success rate had gradually gone down to less than 50%. This typically took the form of repeatedly substituting one behavior for the one asked for or not responding at all. Second, the dolphin began to manipulate the trainers with food games. He had conditioned them to offer food almost every time he opened his mouth, and then often refused the fish offered or chewed it up and spit it out. Or, he ate his fish only after the trainer squeaked on the glass walls of the tank, splashed the water, then pretended to leave. Third, incidences of serious aggression (i.e., biting and snapping) were increasing.

GOALS

All three of these factors appeared to be attempts at manipulating and controlling the trainers and the session to an unacceptable degree. In an effort to solve these problems and regain reasonable control over the sessions, the trainers began using only non-food reinforcers. They hoped that this would eliminate the often frustrating food games. Also, by concentrating on reinforcing the dolphin with new, varied, and unexpected items, it was hoped to decrease his (and the trainers') boredom, increase the dolphin's motivation, and get correct response rates back up to his previous 90 and above percentage. Equally, the trainers hoped to decrease the dolphin's frustration and aggression.

METHODS

The first concern was to find non-food reinforcers that the dolphin liked on that particular day. This was done during the feeding sessions. These were about 30 minutes before the actual training session and lasted between 10 and 15 minutes. In these sessions the dolphin ate his entire allotment of food for the day [about 2.2 Kg. (5 lbs.) of live trout, between 10 and 14 individual fish]. Play activities were also incorporated into the feeding sessions, such as brushing, splashing, etc. These feeding sessions not only served the purpose of feeding but helped to identify what kinds of non-food reinforcers the dolphin might like during that particular day's training session.

After feeding and playing with the dolphin briefly, the trainers left the exhibit and came back to begin the training session 30 minutes later. The training session proceeded as usual, except there were no food reinforcers.

The first days of this program were sometimes confusing and frustrating for both the dolphin and the trainers. The dolphin was still opening his mouth for a fish after each bridge but, since food was not available, the trainers had to concentrate on giving interesting and desirable non-food reinforcement. The dolphin had conditioned all of us to give a fish most of the time he opened his mouth and he initially had a hard time accepting anything else as a reinforcement. The trainers also had a difficult time in becoming creative again after relying heavily on the fish bucket for so long.

Gradually, though, the trainers got better at watching for the dolphin's responses to the reinforcement offerings on a particular day and coming up with new, weird and desirable reinforcers for him. It became fun to try and come up with the weirdest reinforcer that the dolphin would like, such as playing tug-of-war with a rubber stingray or making sounds against the glass walls with a rough "doodlebug" brush (Figure 1).

The dolphin also became more open-minded about accepting non-food items as reinforcers. Although both food and non-food reinforcers had always been used in the past, the dolphin had not attended as well to non-food reinforcements recently. His responses to non-food reinforcers had to be carefully observed to learn which ones were acceptable at all. He clearly demonstrated if they were acceptable (by continuing to attend or participating) or not acceptable (by swimming away or showing signs of frustration, such as tail slaps). When the dolphin made it apparent that the reinforcement offered was unacceptable, usually something else was tried.

For the most part, the dolphin's preference for reinforcers varied (and still does) from day to day, but occasionally he liked one or two of them for days or weeks at a time. The reinforcers that he has favored over extended periods of time include brushing (Figure 2), trainers making bubbles, trainers squeaking on a bucket, the sound of maracas shaking underwater (he's from Latin America) and chasing the trainer's whistle across the surface of the water.

RESULTS

Since instituting this program the Pittsburgh Zoo has fulfilled all of the goals that were set for the use of only non-food reinforcers. The dolphin treated food as food and not a game. He stopped the game of opening his mouth for a fish and then closing it when offered one, or chewing it up and spitting it out. When he opened his mouth in feeding sessions, the dolphin got a fish and usually ate it. When he did not want any more, he did not open his mouth when we offered one. During training, the dolphin still occasionally opened his mouth after a bridge, but since there were no fish available, he usually did not continue.

Most pleasing is the fact that the animal did not get aggressive as a result of not getting food during training. Aggression, in fact decreased. This may, of course, be due to factors other than the new program used, but it is significant to note that it did not increase.

The dolphin's response and correct response rates also improved. The dolphin responded almost 100% of the time and was correct at least 85% of the time (on the basis of success sheets). New

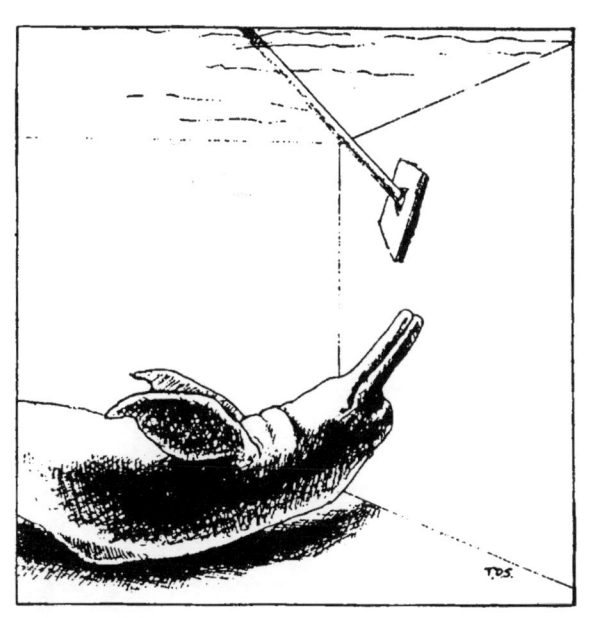

Figure 1 One of the dolphin's favorite reinforcers. As the trainer rubs the "doodlebug" across the glass wall the dolphin turns upside-down attends, following the motion of the brush with his head. (Artwork by Tim D. Smith).

behaviors also worked successfully under this program. As with aggression, the better response and correct response rates may have been due to factors other than the exclusive use of non-food reinforcers. Again, it is important to note that his response and correct response rates did not go down when fish were not used.

A large part of the success in meeting these goals may have been due to the fact that the trainers were having a great deal of fun coming up with things that the dolphin liked as a reinforcer. While it was exhausting and frustrating at times, it let them be as creative as possible and this certainly must have come through to the dolphin.

In the past, when the dolphin had the trainers conditioned to use food as the overwhelming majority of reinforcements, the number of sessions that could be done per day were fairly limited, as was the length of them, based on the fact that there was a limit of only 10-14 fish per day to feed him. In the past trainers cut up the fish into pieces to try to have more for reinforcers, but the dolphin usually would not accept this. By not relying on fish, trainers were able to do more sessions per day, lengthen individual sessions and provide reinforcers that the dolphin liked.

CONCLUSION AND FUTURE APPLICATIONS

The sole use of non-food reinforcers allowed a successful alternative for when performance, the dolphin's control over the trainers, feeding, and aggression became a problem. This type of reinforcement program also expanded the number and types of reinforcers the dolphin would accept (previously limited due to his obsession with fish reinforcers).

The public also benefits from this type of reinforcement. Through the sheer variety of reinforcers to which the dolphin responds, they get to see that dolphins have likes, dislikes and moods. Food may be perceived by visitors as a bribe. Also, it is hard to argue with animals working for play reinforcers and not out of hunger or desire for food.

In January of 1991, trainers began using fish as a reinforcer again. This was started for the same reason trainers had started using only non-food reinforcement: the absence of fish made it a novelty, strengthening its reinforcement value. If performance levels drop again, if feeding becomes a game again, if aggression escalates outside of rut or if the dolphin's control over the trainers becomes unreasonable again, there is an option in training that would allow the elimination of these problems.

ACKNOWLEDGEMENTS

We wish to thank the keepers, laborers, security guards, docents, the Curator of the Aqua Zoo, and all of the Zoo's administration who have cared and supported our work with "The Dolphin". Thanks especially to the entire training staff who make it all possible: Connie Fedunok, Lisa George, Karen Kello, and Sandy Moeslin.

Figure 2 Another of the dolphin's favorite reinforcers. He typically likes to turn upside-down while his belly and flippers are vigorously brushed.

(Artwork by Tim D. Smith)

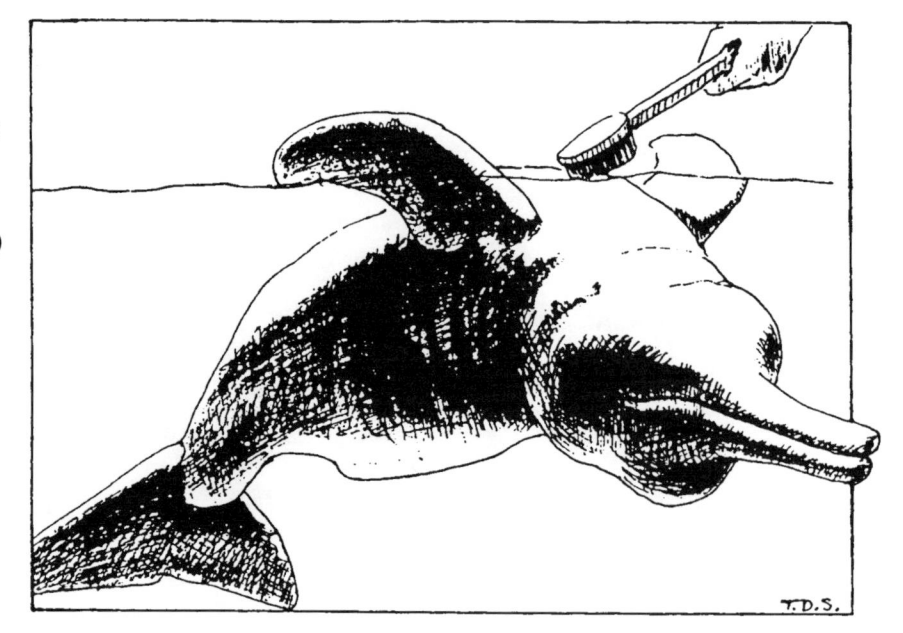

Conference Proceedings

1991 IMATA Conference, Vallejo, California, USA. This glossary is an excerpt from a presentation called "The Syn Alia Series on Anima Training." This is a unique glossary of terms because it includes commentary and examples that help to explain the concepts more clearly. An attempt is made by the authors to group the terms by manner of application: consequences the trainer delivers, information the animal receives, responses the animal offers, and learning process and strategies. It is not unusual for individual facilities and programs to write their own glossaries because it allows them to explain training to their staff in a way that makes the most sense for their program. The structure, order, and commentary of this glossary are examples of organizing information to fit a specific program's needs. I include it because it describes technical definitions, while including everyday examples. For the most up to date glossary, please see chapter 14.

Excerpt from
The Syn Alia Series on Animal Training

Compiled by Kayce Cover
Presented by Jennifer Zeligs

The following terms are grouped (loosely) according to purpose:

CONSEQUENCES
THE TRAINER DELIVERS

1. REINFORCER: Increases the frequency of the behavior it immediately follows.

2. PUNISHER: Decreases the frequency of the behavior it immediately follows.

3. POSITIVE: Add to the environment.

4. NEGATIVE: Take from the environment.

5. POSITIVE REINFORCER: Frequency of the behavior increased by the addition of something the animal desires, immediately after the behavior.

6. NEGATIVE REINFORCER: Frequency of the behavior is increased by the subtraction of something the animal doesn't like, as an immediate result of the behavior. *Not a punisher.*
    Example: Mother with crying baby; Mother picks up baby; It stops crying; The baby was positively reinforced for crying; The mother was negatively reinforced when the baby quit crying.

7. Punishers can be positive or negative also.
    Discussion: Below is a table of example punishers and reinforcers to help clarify how punishers and reinforcers, both negative and positive, are related to one another.

	POSITIVE	NEGATIVE
PUNISHER	a slap	loss of priviledge
REINFORCER	a food treat	removal of disliked food

The examples listed are neither always punishers nor reinforcers - it depends on the perception of the individual animal and *where the added stimulus is relative to the behavior under consideration.* Remember that the same stimulus, such as a "bee stinging" can be either a punisher or a negative reinforcer depending on whether it was administered in response to a behavior.
    Examples: The bear stole honey and the bee stung it; the bear was punished for stealing honey.

Or, the bear killed the bee and removed the stinging sensation; the bear was negatively reinforced for killing the bee.

The above example illustrates how important it is to be precise when applying reinforcers and punishers to behaviors. Behaviors occur in a steady stream. As trainers, we decide which point in the steady stream we want to increase or intensify. We use a tool such as a bridge to pinpoint the exact instant on the behavior continuum, for the animal's understanding.

As seen above, not only can a single stimulus be either a reinforcer or a punisher, it can serve two different functions in the same application. It can be the punisher for the behavior it follows and the stimulus which, when removed, becomes the negative reinforcer for the behavior that immediately follows it.

Analogously, the positive reinforcer for one behavior can be the negative punisher in another case. The animal does a behavior - it gets to play with a ball. The animal disregards a cue, the ball is taken away.

When speaking of reinforcers and punishers, refer to the behavior - not to the animal (or its "character"). In other words, the behavior is punished (or decreased), the dog is not. The behavior is reinforced - not rewarded. The animal can be rewarded - although it may be hard for the trainer to know when the animal feels rewarded. It is easier to see if the frequency of a behavior increases than to make a subjective judgment of the animal's state of mind.

8. PRIMARY: A quality that an animal responds to innately in a certain way, without any conditioning from a human. A primary reinforcer might be food, sex, water, sleep, etc. A primary punisher might be the deprivation of any of the above, fear, pain, etc.

9. SECONDARY: A quality that an animal responds to because it's perception has been conditioned. A secondary reinforcer is something that initially had no significance to an animal and then became desired by the animal because of its association with other desired, primary reinforcers, in training this is often food. Once a secondary reinforcer is established it can be very strong, just as strong as primary reinforcers in animals that are in normal drive state (not deprived of anything) and are not driven by hormone surges at the time.

Explanation: There can be both primary and secondary punishers. A bridge is a secondary reinforcer and a "no" or negate, is a secondary punisher in many training systems.

10. TIME OUT: The cessation of stimulus or response from the trainer for some interval of time. In essence, the animal receives no cues from the trainer, but also can not influence the trainer to produce a consequence such as food or praise until the "time out" or "TO" has passed.

11. SCHEDULE OF REINFORCEMENT: The type, amount and frequency of the reinforcement that will be given when a task is completed. There are generally considered to be three basic schedules (relative to frequency):

A. CONTINUOUS: One reinforcer for one task, or a set amount of reinforcers for one task, every task gets paid the same. Often still preferred for work with birds, but is usually considered dangerous to use with many animals because it sets up a rigid expectation, a right to payment as it were. When the time comes that the trainer has no reinforcers on hand, he may have no behavior or the animal may become frustrated, angry, and aggressive. Also this strategy sets the animal up to plan how many behaviors, and which behaviors he will do today. He can even manipulate the situation so that he does something wrong which he has to be paid to correct, earning all the reinforcers he can appreciate that day, and letting him refuse all subsequent behaviors at no loss to himself.

B. FIXED: A set amount of reinforcers for a set amount of task, for example one apple for every ten lever pecks. In some case this schedule can cause an animal to work longer and faster to get a reinforcer.

C. VARIABLE: A random amount of reinforcers are given in a random way to behaviors that are completed. This is the "jackpot" or "lotto" concept. The animal knows the chances for the huge payoff are not great but there is a chance. He will therefore often continue to work for reinforcers that he values lowly or not at all in order to stay in the running for the grand prize. In addition, this strategy is intrinsically interesting to the animal, and therefore further increases the animal's interest and response.

INFORMATION THE ANIMAL RECEIVES

12. STIMULUS: Any environmental condition that

impinges on the animal's sensory perception.

13. DISCRIMINATIVE STIMULUS: A stimulus that has a specific meaning; in animal training, usually denoting a stimulus which elicits a specific behavior, or a cue. Usually noted as S^D.

14. CONDITIONED STIMULUS: A stimulus that has a specific meaning; usually to denote the successful completion of behavioral criterion. A bridge is a conditioned stimulus. Usually denoted as S^C.

15. STRESSOR: A stimulus that requires some adaptation from the animal.
Explanation: It is recommended that stressors be considered as costs of living. Any animal has an energy/adaptability "budget" for living, just like humans make a certain amount of money. If you spend more money on medical bills one month, there is less for entertainment. All expenditures together cannot exceed the total income without severe repercussions. Likewise, if an animal is sick, it has less to invest in adapting to a new environment or strange conditions.
Stressors are valued differently by different animals. Some animals love to have physical exercise and have a higher tolerance for demands in this area than the normal animal of their type. Perhaps the same animal has a terrible time holding still for a veterinary examination, subsequently finding this "stressful." With good training the animal will become proficient at the vet examination, it will no longer require as much "adaptation" effort, and the animal will no longer perceive it as being "stressful." A second animal could be the opposite, enjoying the veterinary examination and being stressed by rigorous physical demands.

16. BRIDGE: A signal that pinpoints an instant in time for the animal in training.

17. TARGET (noun): A prop that pinpoints a critical location for an animal in training. This location may be a body contact point on the stationary animal, it may be a destination point, or it may be a place where other critical information will appear. The target can be an extended finger or fist, the end of a pole, a mark on a wall or a paper, a plaque, etc. Essentially, the trainer and the animal each extend a target contact point toward the other, meeting in the middle. Thus, the human extends a pole and the dolphin touches with a rostrum, or the human extends a finger and the primate extends a finger to touch.

18. NEUTRAL CUE: A discrete signal with no initial meaning. Its meaning is acquired through association with a primary stimulus and related reflex response.

19. CUE: A signal that will elicit a specific behavior or reflex, as a result of a learned association.

RESPONSES THE ANIMAL OFFERS

20. REFLEX: An involuntary physiological reaction to a stimulus.
Example: Drooling when food is presented.

21. OPERANT: A response to the environment (a stimulus) that the animal initiates.
Examples: Pushing a lever is an operant, so is barking, sitting down, or biting down.

22. INSTRUMENTAL BEHAVIOR: Behavior emitted by an animal in order to obtain a goal, such as a behavior that is "instrumental" in obtaining a goal. That behavior could be in response to a trainer's request (instrumental in obtaining a reinforcer from the trainer) or it could be in order to obtain any goal the animal set.
Examples: Digging a hole to get under a fence, stacking boxes to reach a banana, or waiting to get prey.

23. HABIT: A behavior that an animal routinely emits without a cue presented by a trainer. The behavior may have initially been taught by a trainer or the animal may have originated it.
Examples: A person is initially taught by his mother to brush his teeth after eating. This can become a habit that the person continues without his mother there to remind him. A person may develop certain gestures while speaking that were not specifically taught and are not part of the actual speaking process, and continue these gesture habits indefinitely. Or a person may be conditioned to eat at a specific time. He habitually eats at that time, cued by internal body conditions.

24. TARGET (verb): A "point" of behavior. The smallest unit of behavior consists of an animal's action to touch a designated spot.

25. COMPONENT: The smallest piece of a behavior after the target. A target vector, or a target with an additional quality such as motion, duration, or pressure. The basic building block of a behavior.

26. MODULE: A specific set of components, a subset of a behavior.

27. BEHAVIOR: A specific action created by an animal. For the purposes of training, an animal action defined and named by the trainer.

28. BEHAVIORAL CHAIN: A group of behaviors in a specific order forming a more complex behavior, and defined as a unit to the animal.

THE LEARNING PROCESS AND STRATEGIES

29. CONDITIONING: To create a predictable "automatic" behavioral response in an animal in response to a cue. The process of learning how signals, behaviors and consequences are related.

30. CLASSICAL or RESPONDENT CONDITIONING: Sometimes referred to as Pavlovian conditioning. Classical conditioning results in a reflex (versus a behavior) which can be elicited by a cue. A reflex is elicited by a primary stimulus.

*Examples: S*avory food elicits saliva, pain elicits rapid withdrawal, etc. In classical conditioning, a neutral cue is associated with an eliciting stimulus, and eventually becomes an eliciting stimulus. This type of conditioning does not involve any voluntary choices made by the animal, just a reflex response or reaction.

31. OPERANT CONDITIONING: To predictably elicit a specific operant, or behavior in response to a cue.

32. INSTRUMENTAL CONDITIONING: To predictably elicit a specific behavior in response to a trainees cue so that the animal may gain the reinforcement from the trainer.

33. SUCCESSIVE APPROXIMATION: The process of refining an animals behavior, or operant, from a spontaneous initial behavior to the behavior which is planned by the trainer.

34. AN APPROXIMATION: A single step in the refinement process.

35. SELECTIVE OR DIFFERENTIAL REINFORCEMENT: The process of reinforcing only those operants which are like, or increasingly like, the end-point desired behavior.

Explanation: Of all the operants the animal offers, approximations of the end-point desired behavior are selectively reinforced until the behavior is formed. This entire process is considered successive approximation. The trainer's strategy is selective or differential reinforcement. This is not usually the strategy used with bridge and target technique. This is because with a bridge and a target you start with a definite specific instruction. When the animal is successful it is given the next instruction. Each step is extremely simple, touch the target. However as the process continues the set of instructions which communicated the behavior are more complex than the first instruction set, but no less specific.

In general, in bridge and target training, if the animal is motivated it will be successful (it has all the information it needs to do so). Therefore, every response will be reinforced. The behavior goes from simple to complex, but it is always refined. In successive approximation the behavior evolves from general to specific, and the animal zeros in on the desired response by a process of elimination. In bridge and target technique the animal zeros in on the desired response by following a target.

Do not be misled to think that targeting will be a long and tedious process. Rather, the initial progress will be slow because the steps are small. As the animal and the trainer become proficient in the system, it can become almost as fast as explanations are in any language. Going back to the reading analogy; consider how much time each human invests in learning the alphabet, but in the end reading and speaking are very fast and seem simple (except in front of audiences).

36. AVOIDANCE LEARNING: The process of learning to emit a behavior in order to prevent an aversive event.

Example: Children learn to duck an oncoming ball in order to avoid being hit by it.

37. ESCAPE LEARNING: The process of learning to emit a behavior in order to escape an aversive event in progress.

Example: If a room is too hot, a person will

leave it to escape the heat. If the person or animal can predict when the room will be too hot, they can then avoid the room when it becomes hot. Thus avoidance learning can directly follow escape learning.

38. GENERALIZATION: The process of comparing events, consequences or objects which have some trait in common and recognizing that common trait. That trait can then be extrapolated into new situations, guiding the animal's response, without the animal being specifically taught about that new situation.

Example: If a child is specifically taught not to cross a street in front of an oncoming car, bus, and bicycle; then the child is likely to also wait for a motorcycle to pass. Eventually, the child conceptually groups all the vehicle traveling on a road into a set "traffic." In animal training, an animal can be taught to allow a series of specific people to touch it. Eventually, the animal will let all people pet him, even if they are strangers.

39. LEARNED HELPLESSNESS: The state of considering oneself helpless because of the failure of attempts to control a situation.

Explanation: Some animals will eventually quit trying. This is why it is important for a trainer to set the animal up to be successful, so that it will gain confidence and believe, through generalization, that since he could solve any situation presented to date, he could solve any situation that could ever be presented. Thus he will work hard to meet challenges rather than give up and passively accept consequences.

40. DISTRACTIONS: Qualitative aspects of the environment.

Examples: Things such as bells applause, audience, animals, the feeling of pressure, other animals, or flying objects.

41. PARAMETERS: Describe the amount or intensity of the distraction.

Examples: How long or how hard the pressure feeling is; how close, numerous, or loud the audience. There can be any number of distractions in an environment and there can be any number of parameters to a given distraction.

Getting the marine mammal training community to speak the same language may seem like an impossible goal. However, articles like this are aimed at helping trainers understand operant terminology. It is often argued that since we deal with the public, we should use more common verbiage. Even if this is true, understanding reinforcement and punishment are critical concepts.

Operant Definitions of Reinforcement and Punishment: Getting the Jargon Right

by John Kirtland
Marine Resources and Technology

The fundamental principle of operant conditioning is that behavior is determined by its consequences. As we know, behavior does not occur as isolated and unrelated events: the consequences that follow the actions of an organism, be they good, bad, or indifferent, will have an effect upon the frequency with which those actions are repeated in the future. In the operant setting, the manipulation of behavior is accomplished with the use of positive reinforcement, negative reinforcement, punishment, and extinction.

As marine mammal trainers we almost always assert that our animals are trained using only positive reinforcement because either (a) we naively believe this to be true or more likely because (b) we assume (and rightly so) that the average individual will misconstrue such terms as negative reinforcement and punishment unless they are provided with a laboriously lengthy and detailed explanation of operant psychology. Nevertheless, negative reinforcement and punishment are necessary and sometimes useful tools in the training of any animal (including humans), they are used routinely in our daily training programs, and they should not be an athema to our thinking.

REINFORCEMENT

By definition, **reinforcement** is the presentation of a stimulus, the result of which will increase the frequency of a desired behavior. Most of us understand that a **positive reinforcer** is something that an organism seeks to encounter—food to an animal, good grades to a student, a paycheck for the worker. Behavior that produces desirable consequences is reinforced and, thus, repeated. By offering a dolphin a fish after it presses a paddle, the likelihood of its pressing the paddle again will increase.

On the other hand, a **negative reinforcer** is any stimulus that, when removed, reduced, or prevented — increases the probability of a given response over time. For example, the seat belt buzzer in your car is a negative reinforcer: your buckling up (the desired behavior) is negatively reinforced by the termination (removal) of the annoying buzzer (an aversive stimulus). Negative reinforcement is perhaps most frequently used in dolphin training when the animal is first learning to go through a gate. A net may be presented at the end of the pool opposite the gate: the net is a negative reinforcer, something the animal seeks to avoid. The dolphin swims through the gate and is negatively reinforced by its avoidance of the net. Usually this training is combined with positive reinforcement by the delivery of a fish to the dolphin after it actually passes through the gate.

To clearly distinguish between positive and negative reinforcement, remember the following: Both positive and negative reinforcement increase the probability of the response that precedes them. Positive reinforcement increases response probability by the presentation of a positive stimulus following a response; negative reinforcement does the same in reverse — through the removal, reduction, or prevention of a negative stimulus following a response.

When training an animal it is always preferable to obtain results by reinforcing desired behavior and ignoring undesired behavior. Technically, the act of ignoring a behavior is called **operant extinction**: it is a procedure in which the delivery of a positive reinforcer is withheld. If the behavior does not produce any consequences, it will usually fade over time — in other words, it is extinguished.

PUNISHMENT

Another technique for decreasing the probability of a response is punishment. A **punisher** is any stimulus that — when it is made contingent upon a response — decreases the probability of that response over time. **Punishment** is the delivery of a punisher following a response. Touching a hot stove, for example, produces pain that punishes the preceding response so that you are less likely to touch the stove the next time. Many people confuse punishment and negative reinforcement. Although they are closely related operations, they differ in important ways. The best way to differentiate them is to think of each in terms of its effects on behavior. Punishment, by definition, always reduces the probability of a response occurring again: negative reinforcement, by definition, always increases the probability of a response recurring.

As is true of reinforcement, punishment may also be thought of as positive or negative. **Positive punishment** is the addition of an aversive stimulus—something the animal seeks to avoid—to the organism's environment following a response, thereby decreasing the frequency of that response. For example, if you catch your dog chewing up your brand new shoes, you may swat him on the nose to let him know that chewing up shoes is an unacceptable behavior. The swat across the nose is a positive punisher that will decrease the likelihood of your dog chewing up your shoes again. It should be noted, however, that the use of positive punishment is generally discouraged in the training of all animals. In training dolphins it is definitely counter-productive to use positive punishment in that if the trainer was to hit or otherwise inflict physical pain on the dolphin, the dolphin will in all probability retreat to the far side of the pool and no longer participate in any training. As should be apparent, positive punishment is an ineffective method of controlling the responses of marine mammals, it has absolutely no place in the training process and its use is not condoned by the training community.

Conversely, **negative punishment** is the removal of a positive stimulus—something the animal seeks to encounter—from an organism's environment following a response, thereby decreasing the frequency of that response. If your child stays out past curfew, for instance, you may ground him or her for a set period of time. Being grounded is a negative punishment in that it removes a positive stimulus—going out with friends—and subsequently decreases the probability that your child will stay out past curfew the next time.

Negative punishment is sometimes used in training marine mammals, most commonly in the form of what is known as a "time out." If a dolphin is misbehaving or is not responding to cues, the trainer has the option of taking the fish bucket and leaving the training station for a period of time (the time-out). The trainer and the fish are positive stimuli that the dolphin seeks to encounter; by taking a time-out following undesired behavior, the trainer has removed the positive stimuli—the fish and himself—from the animal's environment, thereby decreasing the likelihood of that undesired behavior occurring when he returns. It is important to realize that, unlike what is possible with positive punishment, there is no pain associated with negative punishment. In the training of marine mammals (and almost any other animal, for that matter), negative punishment can be an effective tool for decreasing unwanted or inappropriate behavior.

It is obvious that the focus of any marine mammal training program should be on positive reinforcement, with negative reinforcement and negative punishment techniques used rarely, only in extreme cases. Each training situation should be thoroughly thought out and the modification technique chosen should be implemented judiciously. Nevertheless, reinforcement and punishment are concepts basic to an understanding of the behavior of all animals. As such, they are essential to the development of positive training techniques and to maintaining the health and well-being of those animals in our care.

REFERENCES

Kazdin, A.E. 1984. Behavior Modification in Applied Settings. Dorsey Press. Chicago, Illinois.

Reynolds, G.S. 1968. A Primer of Operant Conditioning. Scott, Foresman, and Company. New York. New York.

Skinner, B.F. 1966. The Behavior of Organisms. Appleton-Century-Crofts, Inc., New York, New York.

Stephens, B. 1989. SeaWays Animal Behavior Notebook. Unpublished manuscript.

A Behavior Sampler by Gary Wilkes

Few people truly understand what punishment is, or understand why it seldom works. Gary takes a refreshing approach to explaining it to pet owners in clear (and still accurate) terminology.

A Look at Punishment

by Gary Wilkes

The domestication of animals started about fifteen thousand years ago. Since that time, punishment has been the primary means of controlling these created critters. Over the centuries, many people have developed an almost superstitious awe of punishment, even though it rarely accomplished the desired reaction. To understand why punishment is so popular and why it rarely works, requires a closer look.

The word "punishment" should not automatically imply thumbscrews or eye gouging. Punishment can occur even if no actual harm befalls the punished. A working definition of the term would be "the presentation of something that reduces the chance that a behavior will occur." For example, sharks can "punish" swimmers just by showing their dorsal fins. Hot rooms punish those who wear heavy clothing. Once the shark is removed, or the temperature drops, swimming and wearing heavy clothes will return to a normal rate of occurrence.

Punishment, therefore, decreases the likelihood that something will happen. To say, "I punished the dog for soiling the carpet" is inaccurate if the behavior has not decreased in its rate of occurrence. The practice of inflicting discomfort after the fact is more accurately described as retaliation or retribution, i.e., you may have inflicted pain or terror but the animal did not connect it to the behavior. By definition, when used correctly, punishment always decreases response. The problem is that punishment is rarely the best solution to a problem and is almost never practiced correctly.

The first rule of punishment is that it must be closely connected with the event that you are trying to punish. For instance, many cat owners face the problem of cats that investigate kitchen countertops. Most people wait until they see that the cat is already on the counter before they scold it. While this may terrify the cat at the moment, it will do little to decrease the likelihood that the cat will jump on the countertop tomorrow. The cat may associate you with the punishment and simply get on the counters only in your absence.

In order to decrease counter-sitting, the punishment must start at the instant the cat begins to jump on the counter, not after he has already gotten there. Here is a practical way to quickly extinguish the behavior. Go to a hardware store and get some thin, clear, hard plastic sheeting or Plexiglas. Tape the plastic sheet between the counter and the wall so that is forms a transparent slope. When Felix jumps upward, he is going to hit the angled plastic and slide off onto the floor. A few "alley oops!" and the cat will be permanently trained through safe punishment.

The second rule of punishment is to make sure that it is consistent and permanent. For instance, the dog that attacks the front door in response to the doorbell, is a common nuisance. To punish this wild and crazy behavior, simply start ringing the doorbell before you enter your own front door. As Fido races toward the door he is expecting the mailman or an unknown visitor, and is gearing up for some wild barking. Instead of a stranger, there stands his master! A few well placed "punishing" words may be enough to instantly interrupt Fido's confidence. Over a series of repetitions, the likelihood that he will race to the door decreases and the behavior will soon disappear completely. (For more resistant pups, a blast from a squirt gun may be necessary to stop such a powerful behavior.) Once the behavior is eliminated, start giving Fido a treat for remaining passive when guests arrive. This will change his motivation and help to maintain his good behavior.

While these examples of punishment are relatively straightforward, there is a caution that accompanies any use of aversive control. The behavior you punish may not be the only one affected. You may wipe out a number of desirable behaviors unintentionally or create more problems than you started with. For instance, chasing small children is a typical but objectionable canine behavior. If you are expecting a number of small bipeds at your home, you may use balloons to punish chasing behavior. First, inflate some balloons and pop them in your dog's face. Once Fido is totally appalled by the sight of balloons, simply pin one on each of the children. Fifi is not going to approach any "wee ones" as long as they wear the dreaded balloons. You have now successfully "punished" child-chasing behavior. If you think this sounds like a foolproof solution, think again. Your first concern may be that your dog may become afraid of all loud noises. Second, she may become afraid of children, and third, she may become terrified of balloon-like objects such as watermelons and cantaloupe.

Another difficulty with this type of training is that intentionally terrifying an animal is a justified stumbling block for many owners. Even though they may regularly punish and terrify the pet in anger, to do something in such a coldly calculating fashion is emotionally difficult. Ironically, it is the precisely executed punishment that is more effective and potentially more humane. Punishment may be reduced dramatically if it is used to disrupt behavior in concert with a program of positive reinforcement for correct behavior.

Despite the fact that punishment rarely accomplishes the behavior changes desired, some people retain an unrelenting belief in its effectiveness. Many pets are traumatized and ultimately ruined by failing rituals of punishment, retribution and reprisal. Before considering punishment to change your pet's behavior, ask, "Is it safe?" After punishing your pet, ask, "Did it work?" and "What was the cost?"

Karen Pryor

On Behavior

Essays & Research

Although Karen Pryor no longer works with dolphins, and hasn't for many years, she continues to have a dramatic impact on the training community. She spends much of her time working with pet owners and giving seminars on the marvel of using positive reinforcement. One of Karen's great skills is her ability to take her training knowledge and share it with the public in easy to understand terms. In this article she looks at punishment, not from a technical perspective, but from a realistic one. Her audience was parents, and this article first appeared in *Mothering* magazine in the summer of 1986.

Why Punishment Doesn't Work

by Karen Pryor

The kids are fighting, or making too much noise in the car; your toddler deliberately runs out into the street; your teenager flouts the household rules. And you have to put a stop to it. Whether the problem is dirty words, dirty clothes, or dirty tricks – in every household there are some behaviors that just cannot be tolerated. What do we do when these behaviors arise? We punish. We threaten, we coerce, we scold, we deprive. We may even strike out. When pushed hard enough, nearly every parent on the planet has felt the urge to slap and yell; and most of us have done it at least once.

Did you ever notice that it does not really work? Behavior that is punished may stop for an instant, but it will not necessarily stop forever. Nevertheless, punishment is humanity's favorite method of stopping behavior. We scold the child, beat the dog, dock the paycheck, fine the company, torture the dissident, invade the country. Yet, the child goes on whining, the dog still chases cars, the employee is tardy, the company is dishonest, the dissidents still protest, and things are not serene in Afghanistan.

And what happens when we punish someone and then they go out and do the same thing again? Do we say, "Hmm, punishment isn't working. Let's try something else?" No. We punish harder. If a little scolding or penalty does not have an effect, why not try a bigger one. If whipping doesn't convert the heretic, try thumbscrews, or the rack. The worst thing about the escalation of punishment is that there is absolutely no end to it. The search for a punishment so intense that "maybe this one will work" has preoccupied humans since history began, and probably before.

WHY PUNISHMENT DOESN'T WORK

One of the rules that psychologists have discovered about behavior is that whatever you do to change behavior must occur during the behavior, and not afterward. For example, a positive reinforcement, or pleasant consequence of an act, must be timed right in order to produce learning. Suppose you are in a hotel room and trying to turn on an unfamiliar TV. You touch all the likely-looking buttons and knobs until one of them produces a click and a picture, or at least a hum. From then on, this is the one that you will probably use. But what if each button took 15 seconds to work? You would have a difficult time figuring out which one produced the picture, and might have to continue trying them all every time you wanted to catch the news.

We can also change behavior with undesirable events, or negative reinforcement. Here to, the event must coincide with the behavior in order to produce learning. Suppose you are cooking in someone else's kitchen. The negative reinforcement of pain from the heat will quickly teach you which pan handles require a pot holder. From this experience you will develop learned behavior to protect yourself from the handles that get hot. If you could not feel the heat at the moment of contact, you would not know that you had been badly burned until later, when the blisters develop. So, without the immediate sensation of pain, you would have a hard time learning which objects on the stove are safe to touch and which ones are not.

Punishment is an unpleasant consequence of a behavior. But, like a burn that is not noticed until it blisters, it often does not coincide with the behavior closely enough to produce learning. Spanking a roaming toddler after he returns to the sidewalk may intimidate or frighten him, but he will be more likely to connect the spanking with the sidewalk than with the traffic. Even if the child understands the verbal message explaining why he or she is being punished, the desired improvement may not take place.

For example, a child who is punished for a bad report card cannot mitigate the punishment in the present. This is because people cannot change their actions of the past; one cannot do anything about a bad report card that one has already received. Furthermore, punishment teaches the child nothing about how to achieve better report cards.

The most any punisher can hope for is that the child's motivation will change, and that the child will try to alter future behavior in order to avoid punishment. That is a lot to ask, even of intelligent adults. We know that society's punishments and threats do not prevent adult misbehavior. Moreover, if a child's behavior is strongly motivated – snitching food when hungry, being part of the gang in adolescence – what the child does learn is to try to not get caught. Evasiveness increases rapidly under a punishment regime – a sad situation in a family setting, and not so great in society either.

HOW THE PUNISHER GETS REINFORCED

One reason why we keep thinking that punishment works is because sometimes the punished behavior stops, at least temporarily. *Punishment has the best chance of halting behavior if the subject understands which action is being punished, if the behavior is not well-established, and if the person can control the behavior in the first place.* (For example, punishment does not cure bedwetting.) The punishment is also more likely to be effective if it is a novel experience for the subject, a shock to which the person has not become hardened. A child who is scolded sharply the first time he or she crayons on the walls may stop defacing the house. A citizen who gets caught and fined for cheating on his income tax may not cheat again.

My parents punished me exactly twice throughout my upbringing. They scolded me once at age six for pilfering and once at age fifteen for skipping school, which caused everyone to fear I'd been abducted. The extreme rarity of the punishment experience contributed vastly to the effect. Both behaviors stopped instantly.

When a punishment effectively halts a behavior, the sequence of events can be quite reinforcing for the punisher. The punisher may tend to sally forth confidently to punish again, I have seen punishment exhibited and defended by disciplinarian school teachers, bullying athletic coaches, domineering bosses, and well-intentioned parents. Often they reenact old harsh methods despite meager successes and many disappointments. And often they tend to neither notice nor accept the good results of others around them who are not using punishment at all. The repeated use of punishment by such practitioners can produce nasty side effects in the punished ones: fear, anger, resentment, resistance, and even hate – mental states definitely *not* conducive to learning improved behavior!

ALTERNATIVES THAT WORK

One promising way to change behavior without punishment is to reinforce behavior that you do like. Sometimes this requires a lot of self-discipline. It is easy to call out "I told you not to slam the door!" every time the children come home with a bang; but it is another matter entirely to alert yourself to notice and say "thank you" when they come in quietly. Sometimes the behavior that needs reinforcing can be subtle and easily misunderstood. For example, a teen-ager who is testing the limits of family rules may really be trying to participate in family life in newly adult ways. Youngsters in this transition stage need to be responded to for making conversation, for being helpful, for the good things that they do.

All too often, parents assume that because doing chores pleasantly is expected of their children, the behavior deserves no comment or attention. Eventually the behavior may dwindle. After all, the child reasons, if I love my parents and want them to notice me, and if the only comment or attention I get is for being horrible, then this is the way I will be.

Three negative ways to change behavior, besides punishment, may occasionally be appropriate. The first, the "Shoot the Animal" method, is to get rid of the doer, temporarily or permanently. Send the child to his room if he is disrupting company; tie up the dog so that it cannot chase cars. This method stops the undesirable behavior, but it does not teach desirable alternatives. Negative reinforcement can also provide a solution. With a load of cranky, tired, noisy kids in the car, I have been known to pull off the road and park on the shoulder until everyone is quiet enough to permit me to drive safely again. Simply ignoring the misbehavior until it goes away by itself is often the easiest way to cope. Parents sometimes tend to correct every annoying little thing that their young children do, without realizing that some behavior is self-limiting and will disappear on its own.

Of more value are the ways in which you can use positive reinforcement to get rid of behaviors that you do not want. For example, you can *substitute and reinforce permissible behaviors to take their place.* One mother told me that her 18-month-old son developed the habit of splatting his hands in his food on the high chair tray when he'd finished a meal, thus sending food all over the kitchen. Naturally, this brought his mother on the run – but always too late to prevent the mess. So, she watched him carefully and soon arrived at an incompatible behavior. She taught him to throw his arms in the air and cheer when he was finished eating. This brought Mama on the run too, but with laughs and hugs instead of a cross face and a washcloth. The substitute behavior turned out to be easier on the baby, the mother, and the kitchen.

You can also *reinforce the absence of the undesirable behavior.* When I have to spend time with children who have developed bad (parent-trained) habits such as whining or teasing, I pay a lot of attention to the times when they are quiet or pleasant. This way, they tend to be quiet and pleasant more and more often.

Finally, the most fundamental method of changing behavior without punishment is to *eliminate whatever is causing the behavior in the first place.* Take, for example, the familiar disaster of the toddler having a tantrum in the supermarket. Frequently, the underlying cause of the tantrum is hunger. The child may be specifically yelling for the brightly displayed candy, but what he or she needs is food – and the sight and smell of all these edibles, now that the toddler is old enough to recognize them, is more that he or she can handle. Solution: Feed the children before you market.

The laws of how reinforcement changes behavior were worked out in psychology labs by research scientists. Applying these laws in real life, however, is a task for creative and imaginative teachers and parents. It requires imagination, thoughtfulness, self-discipline, and attention to your children. Good parenting always did, but reinforcement theory adds a few new tools to the problem-solving kit. Using reinforcement is fun, too. And, properly used, reinforcement always works; you need never revert to punishment in the hope that maybe just this once it will not backfire. Perhaps this generation of parents will really work out ways of using reinforcement to supersede the old and regrettable traditions of force and punishment – once and for all.

SOUNDINGS EXCERPT, 1996. What follows is an excerpt from an article on the changing terminology in marine mammal training. The paper was under review for possible inclusion in *Soundings* when this book first went to press. Only the section on reinforcement schedules is included, which is the conclusion of the paper. Understanding the various schedules of reinforcement is a challenge for many trainers. The definitions offered in this paper are accurate and well explained. At the conclusion, the author offers opinions about these terms and a commentary on the idea of combining different schedules of reinforcement. Experienced trainers will often find that even if they agree on terminology, they may still disagree on the application of the concept.

Excerpt from...
Definition Drift
or
Are We Monopolizing Marine Mammal Training by Changing the Definitions?

By Jaap Van der Toorn

REINFORCEMENT SCHEDULES

Basically, there are two ways of applying reinforcers.

1. After each correct response. This is called a continuous reinforcement schedule.

2. After a certain number of correct responses or after a certain time has passed. These are called intermittent reinforcement schedules. Four "flavors" of intermittent reinforcement schedules are defined.

- Fixed-ratio schedule: every N^{th} correct response is reinforced, where N is a fixed number for the session. For example, you ask Delphi to touch a target a number of times. Every 3rd time he touches the target you use the bridge (apply a secondary reinforcer) and also supply some primary reinforcement. Delphi is reinforced on a 1:3 fixed-ratio schedule.

- Fixed-interval schedule: a correct response is reinforced every N^{th} minute or second, where N is a fixed number for the session. Again, Delphi is asked to touch the target a number of times. You don't count the number of times that he touched the target, but instead you reinforce him every 15 seconds, immediately after he touches the target. When he touches the target somewhere in the 15-second interval he is not reinforced. He is now reinforced on a 15-second fixed-interval schedule. Note that in this schedule, Delphi is not asked to hold the target for 15 seconds; the duration of the response is irrelevant in this context.

- Variable-ratio schedule: every N^{th} correct response, where N varies randomly around a predetermined average number for the session. If we reinforce Delphi on a variable-ratio schedule with an average of 1:3, he gets reinforced after 3, 5, 4, 2, 3, 5, 1, 4, 2, correct responses. This yields an average of 1:3, but the actual ratio varies.

- Variable-interval schedule: a correct response is reinforced after a certain amount of time has elapsed. The interval between the availability of reinforcement varies randomly within the session around a predetermined average. If you reinforce Delphi on a variable reinforcement schedule with an average of 15 seconds, you may, for instance, reinforce a correct response after 1, 8, 21, 13, 11, 25, 5, 26, 16, seconds.

CONCLUSIONS

From the point of the animal, there is no obvious difference between variable-interval and variable-ratio schedules. Outside a more-or-less controlled laboratory type environment, interval-based schedules are often hard to use. Also, a real random distribution of reinforcement, as is needed for a real variable-ratio schedule, needs preparation and a constant monitoring. Often, trainers vary the ratio of reinforcement by "gut-feeling," which yields at best a pseudo-random distribution of reinforcement which can be predictable.

Within the marine mammal community there is also a special flavor of a variable-ratio reinforcement schedule known as **V.R.R.V or Variable-Ratio with Reinforcement Variety.** V.R.R.V. is a variable-ratio schedule as described above. It also needs use of a variety of primary reinforcers, so it relies on the use of a generalized secondary reinforcer (or bridge).

A reinforcement strategy that is often seen but that has no official name (yet) is the following: each correct response is bridged (secondary reinforcement is applied) and that is followed by primary reinforcement on a variable-ratio schedule. A variety of primary reinforcers may be involved as well. So not every bridge is followed by primary reinforcement. Since every correct response is reinforced, this is strictly speaking a continuous reinforcement schedule. You might call this **Continuous Reinforcement with Variable-Ratio Primary Reinforcement Follow-up** or C.R.V.R.P.R.F. (yes, an even longer abbreviation than the V.R.R.V. You can forget this name if you want and propose a better one as long as you remember the concept). This approach is very useful when you are still in the process of developing a behavior. In such a situation you want good control over the behavior and want to reinforce every response that meets or exceeds your criterion for the session. Once the behavior is performed reliably, you can switch to an intermittent reinforcement schedul such as V.R.R.V.

Conference Proceedings

1981 IMATA Conference, Niagara Falls, New York, USA. The current use of "variable reinforcement schedules" with marine mammals probably began with R.I.R. These techniques were new for marine mammal trainers in the late 1970s. Randy Brill writes one of the clearest explanations available about R.I.R. in this article. In later years, R.I.R. would get redefined several times, but the concepts and principles described here are still sound.

R.I.R. in Use at the Brookfield Zoo: Random and Interrupted Reinforcement Redefined in Perspective

by Randall L. Brill
Chicago Zoological Society

ABSTRACT

To reduce a dependency on food reinforcement and the aggressive tendencies resulting from its withholding after incorrect responses while working with killer whales (*Orcinus orca*), Butcher and Stephens initiated a training procedure that they named Random and Interrupted Reinforcement (R.I.R.). The procedure has been duplicated and used with success at Brookfield Zoo's Seven Seas Panorama with Atlantic bottlenose dolphins (*Tursiops truncatus*). This report explains the procedures followed to establish R.I.R.'s use in this specific situation. A definition of R.I.R. in operant terminology in contrast to the "traditional" training situation is given and the role of innovation on the trainer's part and its impact on R.I.R.'s effectiveness are considered.

RIR...IN PERSPECTIVE

The art and science of training and maintaining small cetaceans in captivity has made great advances since P.T. Barnum first exhibited a beluga whale *(Delphinapterus leucas)* and an Atlantic bottlenose dolphin (*T. truncatus*) in the early 1860's (Wyman, 1863). The increasing curiosity that developed over the years with regard to marine mammals eventually gave rise to the establishment of the first oceanariums during the post-World War II era. The construction of facilities such as Marineland of Florida and the Miami Seaquarium not only provided the animals and settings in which eager scientists got their first good look at a dolphin but, out of a newly discovered necessity, fostered a need for the development of reliable training techniques as it became apparent that these animals were willing and capable performers that easily attracted the attention of the general public.

The actual development of training techniques used with cetaceans is a story of many parts and, indeed, the many parks and oceanariums that have and do maintain these animals. The literature is scant and the bulk of what is available has been reviewed by Defran and Pryor (1980). Some of the early techniques were based on those traditionally used with circus and other performing animals while other situations found individuals from unrelated backgrounds charged with the responsibility of training dolphins and left to rely on instincts and trial and error to accomplish the task.

At about the same time that the art of training dolphins was developing, the science of operant conditioning was becoming a familiar and popular field of study (Skinner, 1938). Keller and Marian Breland, students of Skinner, recognized its applications to the training of dolphins (Breland & Breland, 1966) and techniques based in operant methodology developed quickly and became widespread among trainers. An array of styles and accomplishments came into use all bearing the underlying characteristics of operant conditioning. Though the products of training cetaceans have become increasingly complex and impressive over the years, the method used to achieve them has remained, with the exception of a few variations, unchanged and for the purpose of comparison, can be identified as "traditional".

By considering the training and performance of any given behavior, we can identify and define the operant method and terminology that we, as trainers, rely upon so heavily and of which we may be, at least some of the time, unaware.

The method traditionally used to establish new behaviors by marine mammal trainers can be identified in the operant jargon as "shaping" (Pryor, 1975). The shaping of a behavior employs the giving or withholding of reinforcement to convert a general response into a more specific response. The conversion is accomplished by following a predetermined series of steps known as "successive approximations," leading to the finished product. Once the animal learns the response required in Step 1 or the first approximation, reinforcement is withheld for that response in favor of the one required at Step 2, the second approximation, and so on; each successive approximation more closely resembling the selected behavior. For the trainer, training involves the art of selecting an effective series of approximations.

At some point in the shaping process it becomes necessary for the trainer to be able to cue the behavior. Some type of signal or "discriminative stimulus (S^D)" must be established. A response given in the presence of the appropriate S^D) will be reinforced while a response in its absence will be ignored (Ferster and Skinner, 1957). By establishing an S^D, usually a visual or audio cue, the trainer controls the occurrence of the response. For example, an animal trained to leap through a hoop will not do so until the appropriate cue or S^D is presented.

Both the shaping process and the establishment of an S^D are dependent on the effectiveness of reinforcement. In operant terminology, a "reinforcer", or what most of us commonly refer to as a reward, is an environmental event or stimulus which follows a desired response in time and increases the frequency and probability of the occurrence of that response (Reynolds, 1975). A reinforcer that an animal seeks to encounter is referred to as a "positive reinforcer" while a reinforcer an animal seeks to avoid is referred to as a "negative reinforcer"; in other words, a cube of sugar as opposed to an electric shock. In the training of cetaceans the use of positive reinforcement is the preferred and accepted standard among trainers (Pryor, 1975).

There are two types of reinforcers to be considered. A "primary" or an "unconditioned reinforcer" is a reinforcer whose effectiveness will not depend on the animal's past experience with it; food and water, for example. A "secondary" or "conditioned reinforcer," on the other hand is one whose effectiveness is determined by the conditions under which the animal has experienced it in the past. An unconditioned reinforcer will be reinforcing to most members of a particular species while a conditioned reinforcer will be reinforcing only to those members of a particular species that have been exposed to a particular conditioning process (Kelleher, 1966).

A conditioned reinforcer commonly used in training cetaceans is referred to as a "bridge" or "bridging stimulus," usually an audio cue such as a whistle or pinger. The bridge can be used to readily indicate correct responses and its effectiveness is acquired by its being paired with an unconditioned reinforcer, food, early in the training process (Pepper and Defran, 1975). Interestingly, the bridge not only provides a form of reinforcement but it also acts as an S^D that cues the animal to anticipate and orient itself for reinforcement of another form.

The times at which and the conditions under which a reinforcer will be delivered are determined by "schedules of reinforcement." While there are a good number of schedules of reinforcement that have been developed and tested there are two basic schedules that have been widely used in the training of cetaceans. A schedule of "continuous reinforcement (CRF)" determines that reinforcement will follow every correct responses. A schedule of "intermittent reinforcement" determines that some, not all, correct responses will be followed by reinforcement (Fester and Skinner, 1957).

There are a number of other terms and "tricks of the trade" that have been derived from operant psychology and put to frequent use. Their definitions and applications to the training of cetaceans have been adequately reviewed by Pryor (1975). With the few terms that have been considered and defined thus far, it is possible to construct an operational definition of a very basic training procedure which will henceforth be referred to as the "traditional" method.

Figure 1 provides an illustration of the traditional approach to the completion of one successful behavior from the trainer's point of view. To begin

TRADITIONAL

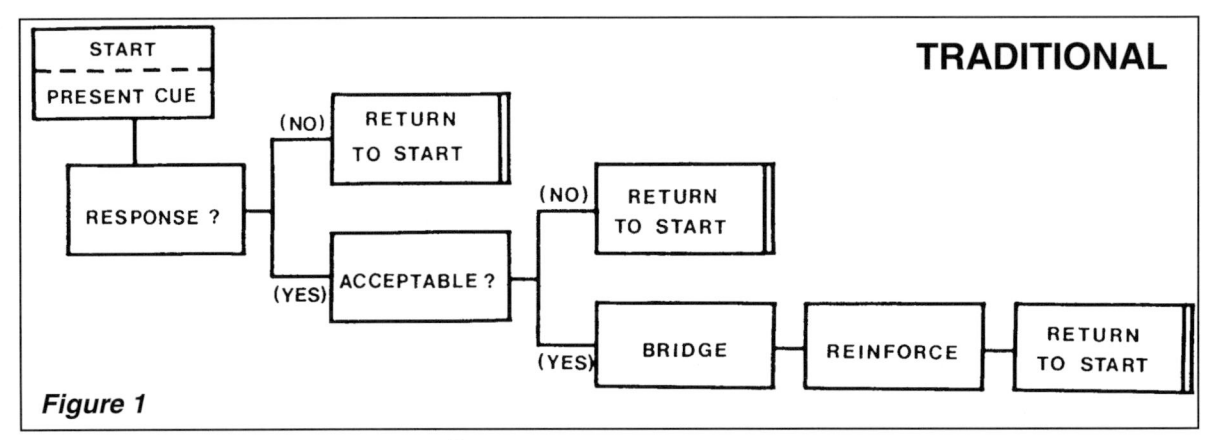

Figure 1

at "Start" the trainer presents a cue, S^D, seeking a particular response on the part of the animal. The trainer expects a response to the given cue and if there is none, a "Return to Start" is necessary.

In the traditional method, "Return to Start" represents an option of two choices in the event that the trainer's expectations are not met. The trainer may either present the same cue again, immediately giving the animal another chance to respond accordingly, or the trainer may terminate the session for some period of time; in operant terms, take a "time-out." Keep in mind that the trainer, in this method, is committed to stimulating the animal to emit a correct response and thus successfully complete the desired behavior.

If there is a response to the cue, the trainer must judge whether or not it is "Acceptable." If it is unacceptable, a "Return to Start" is in order. If the response is acceptable, a bridging stimulus is given. The bridge, a conditioned reinforcer, is followed by an unconditioned reinforcer, food, and the options of "Return to Start" are again available but in the more positive sense in that the desired behavior can be cued again or the session can be ended on a successful note.

Again, this definition serves to describe the traditional method in its simplest form without the inclusion of possible variations. It can be more simply illustrated as shown in Figure 2, and the form of reinforcement can be described in the operant terms already reviewed as the use of an unconditioned reinforcer, food, on a schedule of continuous reinforcement (CRF).

The term "reinforcement" applies to an event or stimulus when its occurrence is contingent upon a particular response, produces a learning effect and is associated with a motivational state that is relevant (Kish, 1966). The anticipation of a reinforcer on the part of the animal should provide a good deal of motivation to respond. Food, generally considered to be an unconditioned reinforcer of high strength in most organisms, especially hungry ones, has become the traditional reinforcer in the training of cetaceans and other marine mammals (Pryor, 1973). When we deal with reinforcement we are, in fact, dealing with motivation (Morse, 1966). For the trainer of cetaceans in the oceanarium where animals are subject to respond "on schedule" in show situations, effectively motivating an animal is a key factor in success as well as it is to the trainer in a laboratory situation.

We have already defined two basic schedules of reinforcement. The traditional model of training provides for food on CRF which may instinctively appear to be a very motivating situation. It is a common experience among trainers, however, that shows or training sessions held earlier in the day are more productive than those held later simply because the animals are hungrier. The opportunity to encounter food is motivational as long as a state of hunger exists. To receive it after every correct response is not necessarily a guarantee of maintaining a consistent response level either. Skinner and Morse (1958) found that making the availability of food contingent upon the operation of a running wheel by a rat actually decreased the amount of activity normally observed; play became work.

Intermittent schedules of reinforcement yield higher response levels with the Variable-Ratio (VR) producing the best effect. On a VR the number of times an animal must respond in order to receive reinforcement will vary in an irregular manner from the delivery of one reinforcement to the delivery of the next (Reynolds, 1975). For example, a VR6 is in effect if, on an average, every sixth response is reinforced.

Intermittent schedules of reinforcement have been used with impressive results in a variety of

CUE ➡ BEHAVIOR ➡ BRIDGE ➡ FOOD

Figure 2

laboratory animals including pigeons and chimpanzees (Ferster 1958, 1960). Beach and Pepper (1971, 1972) reported that dolphins responded as well to intermittent schedules as laboratory animals with VIR showing the most promise. Schusterman (1975, 1976) found that varying the amount of food reinforcement as well as schedules was effective in both dolphins and sea lions.

Forms of reinforcement other than food have been used in the training of cetaceans but not regarded as equal in effectiveness by trainers (Pryor,. 1973). Pepper and Beach (1972) alternated food with tactile reinforcement with some success until attacks from the dolphin, apparently related to manual stimulation, were experienced. Defran and Milberg (1973), however, were able to maintain a paddle pressing response in a dolphin using only tactile reinforcement; manual rubbing or a squirt of water.

Forms of innovation or creativity may be reinforcing for cetaceans. Pryor (1969) was able to shape and maintain impressive behaviors by allowing her subject to be creative and offer spontaneous responses. Pearson (1979) suggested that unpreferred behaviors offered during training may be an attempt on the dolphin's part to be innovative and should be taken advantage of by the trainer.

With the exceptions of the use of VR schedules and occasional attempts at including other forms of reinforcers in addition to food, the traditional model presented holds true for the training of cetaceans. But intermittent schedules, additional reinforcers and taking advantage of creativity and innovation on the part of the dolphin as well as the trainer seems to offer some viable alternatives.

Those three elements can be seen at work in a technique developed at Sea World as an alternative to the consistent use of food reinforcement and the traditional method. The technique as used predominantly with killer whales (*Orcinus orca*), was initially described by Butcher (1974) as a means of providing very positive motivation in the training process and was eventually named Random and Interrupted Reinforcement (R.I.R.), (Butcher, et al, 1976). Stephens (et al, 1977) reported its use with other marine mammals and contrasted its employment of innovation, individualized reinforcement and stimulus complexity with the more conventional giving and withholding of food as dictated by the traditional method. Over the past several years, R.I.R. has been developed, refined and reported as a successful standard practice in the training of small cetaceans, as well as pinnipeds, at Sea World (Butcher and Stephens, 1977; Lacinak, 1977, 1979; Scardina, 1978; Butcher, 1980). Unfortunately, there have been no reports of other oceanariums having duplicated the technique with which to compare the results reported.

Acceptance of R.I.R. by training staffs outside of Sea World has been slow if not, in fact, nonexistent. Perhaps the strongest criticisms voiced against it have been related to a lack of an explanation for the technique that could be more easily understood and validly defined in the jargon of operant psychology and the lack of supporting evidence from other oceanariums. Dealing with these two criticisms will hopefully relieve the tension surrounding the subject. The discussion that follows is based upon the experience and knowledge gained in the use o R.I.R. by the training staff of the Seven Seas Panorama at the Brookfield Zoo (Brill, 1981).

The procedure involved in R.I.R. was initially described as an "interrupted schedule of reinforcement" accomplished by presenting a secondary reinforcer (whistle) and withholding the primary reinforcer (food) on behaviors selected at random in shows and training sessions (Butcher, et al, 1976). The later reports, already cited, included the use of reinforcers in addition to food that could follow correct responses in an unordered fashion. Butcher, Stephens, and the rest argue that the more unpredictable the occurrence and form of reinforcement becomes to the animal, the higher the motivational state of the animal will be.

The term "Random and Interrupted Reinforcement" was apparently intended to convey the idea that, in opposition to the traditional use of food reinforcement on CRF, what reinforcement, if any, followed a correct response should be randomized and, in doing so, move the animal away from the predictable experience of food reinforcement. In other words, the anticipation of a food reinforcer on the part of an animal accustomed to the traditional method was being randomly interrupted. Having already considered Figure 2, Figure 3 illustrates the

Figure 3

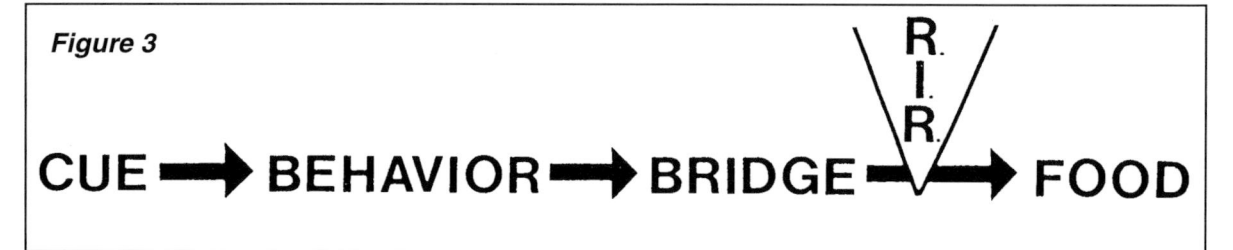

CUE ➡ BEHAVIOR ➡ BRIDGE ➡\R.I.R./➡ FOOD

idea in simple terms. By utilizing additional reinforcers and/or an absence of reinforcement, the anticipation of food is further removed. One of the beneficial effects of the method would be, of course, that a diminished anticipation of food reinforcement after a correct response may relieve the anxiety resulting from the withholding of food after an incorrect response as indicated by Stephens (et al, 1977).

It is possible to describe the method in operant terminology as the use of unconditioned and conditioned reinforcers, individually or in combinations, delivered on an intermittent schedule of reinforcement, VR, in a randomized order. To soothe any need for a more acceptable title then, let the acronym R.I.R., stand for *R*einforcers delivered *I*ntermittently in a *R*andomized order.

Figure 4 provides an illustration of R.I.R.'s use in the completion of a selected behavior from the trainer's point of view. The format and terminology used to describe the traditional method in Figure 1 appear again with one exception to be noted, "Return to Start" in Figure 4 represents several options available to the trainer: 1) cue the same behavior, 2) cue a different behavior, 3) introduce some innovation not anticipated by the animal, or 4) "time-out." Innovation will be considered again later in this discussion. We can now consider how R.I.R. differs from the traditional method.

The trainer again begins by presenting the cue or S^D for a selected behavior to which the animal should respond. Even with a failure to respond, a "Return to Start" is already providing the trainer with options to pursue. It is assumed that the option taken will be appropriate to the particular situation. It is unlikely, for instance, that a time-out would follow a correct response at this point. The same options are available if the response given is not acceptable. However, if it is, the number of options that can be taken by the trainer begin to increase dramatically in contrast to the traditional method. A "Return to Start" may be taken as opposed to the other option of giving or withholding a bridging stimulus.

Because we have indicated that a bridge functions as an S^D as well as a conditioned reinforcer, it is treated in Figure 4 as a separate component which may or may not precede the additional stimuli established as reinforcers. The successful behavior may or may not be followed by a bridge, which may or may not be followed by additional reinforcers.

The reinforcement that may follow an acceptable response is a component of R.I.R. that signals a departure from the traditional method. The reinforcement made available may be an unconditioned reinforcer (food), a conditioned reinforcer (number of types of which are available will depend upon the animal's past conditioning experience), multiples of either (variations in the amount of food and variations of quantity and form in conditioned reinforcers), or various possible combinations of both. The possibilities of variety and unpredictability, or randomness if you will, from the form and content of one reinforcement to that of the next are quite high in potential.

R.I.R. certainly provides the trainer with the opportunity to vary the time and form of reinforcement, providing the animal with an environment that is interesting and unpredictable. Variety and innovation in the delivery of reinforcement are the purpose and foundation of the method. Not only are they built into the method, their continual presence and use by the trainer is vital to its success. R.I.R. is certainly nothing less than a dramatic departure from the traditional method already defined. If worked at and used effectively, it is at least one way of creating new attitudes toward and relationships with the animals served. That has been exactly the case at the Seven Seas Panorama since the use of R.I.R. was initiated in December, 1980.

Since the opening of Brookfield Zoo's Seven Seas Panorama in 1960, trainers and dolphins (*Tursiops truncatus*) there functioned under the traditional method of training. Seven Seas came into being during a somewhat prolific period of oceanarium construction and at a time when training techniques or shaping strategies for particular behaviors were still somewhat jealously being guarded in secrecy. The first training staff set about using the shaping process in its most basic form. The training methods used at Seven Seas evolved much like the methods of other oceanariums and eventually included the use of whistles, targets and other tools borrowed from operant conditioning. The one element that went unaffected by change over the years was the use of food on a schedule of continuous reinforcement.

When this author joined the Seven Seas staff in 1975, the rules for delivering reinforcement were the same as they had been in 1960: feed the dolphin when it does something right, don't feed it when it's being uncooperative or making mistakes, even if it means cutting back on the amount of the daily diet and don't expect much response from a dolphin that's not very hungry. No one was being intentionally cruel or mistreating the animals. That just happened to be the accepted, practiced and unquestioned tradition.

Several of the members of the present Seven Seas staff have vivid memories of an animal named Vicki. Vicki was one of the original dolphins brought to Seven Seas at its opening and she lived and performed there until 1978, when her life and career finally ended at the age of 32. The last several years of Vicki's life were a trainer's nightmare for several reasons. One was that, according to the consensus of her trainers, Vicki, a product of her training environment was bored. She had learned the training game too well and was not motivated by the predictable set of events that accompanied her responses. She simply did not find the scenario very motivating and obviously got more stimulation from devising effective methods of preventing her pool mates from performing and frustrating her trainers. Vicki had effectively conditioned trainers to respond with an extremely upset stomach whenever she cornered her pool mates in one end of the tank for an undetermined length of time just as a performance was about to begin. When Vicki expired, there were mixed emotions of grief and relief.

Over the last several years, a number of progressive changes have been made by the Seven Seas staff, at least in contrast to its particular past. One of the concerns addressed has been a reaction to the lessons learned from Vicki; the adaptation of a training method or style that would prevent the inadvertent creation of a new Vicki. After consideration of the information available on R.I.R., a decision was made to test its effectiveness by putting it to use. With the commitment made, we set out to establish R.I.R.'s use, with a good deal of cooperation from its originators, by closely duplicating their initial attempts to make the transition

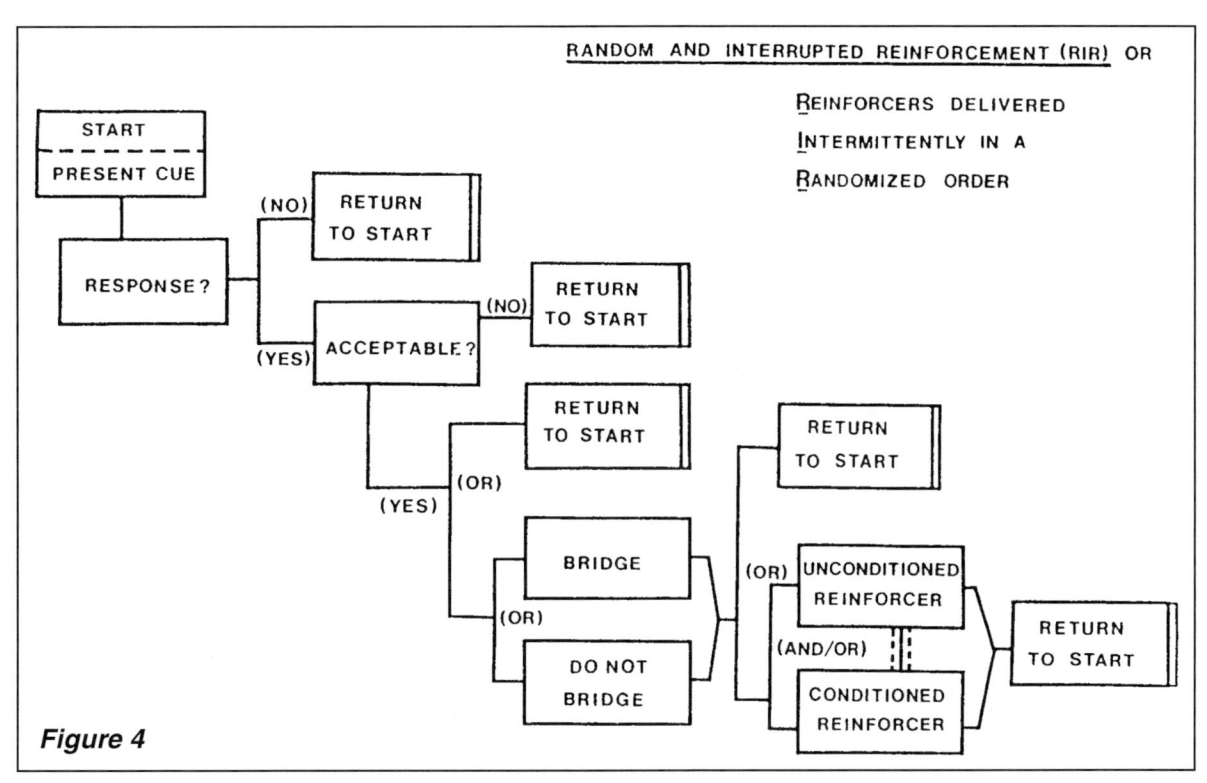

Figure 4

from the traditional method.

Our first step concerned breaking away from the CRF schedule to which both trainers and animals were accustomed. We carefully set about communicating to our dolphins that food would not necessarily follow each bridged response. In other words, we began moving away from a schedule of CRF to an intermittent schedule, VR. What occasionally followed a bridging stimulus rather than food was a cue for another behavior that was considered very easy and rudimentary (for example, a wave of a flipper, slap of the fluke or a vocalization). That behavior was then bridged and followed by food reinforcement. As the dolphins seemed to become comfortable with performing an additional behavior before being reinforced with food, the frequency of those occasions were increased as well as the number of additional behaviors that might be requested.

The second step included occasionally eliminating the bridging stimulus and gradually increasing the difficulty of the additional behaviors that might be requested after a correct response.

The transition accomplished in those two steps was followed through in training sessions as well as performances. Within n few weeks, we were reasonably sure that the dolphins had become comfortable with the new situation. Not every correct response was followed by reinforcement and one or more behaviors of varying degrees of difficulty could be cued successively without frustrating the animals by having them interpret the action as punishment or the withholding of reinforcement due to an incorrect response. In addition, we began to sense that our dolphins were, in fact, becoming more curious about what we were doing and what we might ask them to do.

The third step is the one that we have found can never be considered *finished;* seeking and establishing new stimuli as reinforcers. Once the animals were comfortable with not receiving a food reinforcer where they had previously come to expect one, other reinforcers could be delivered in addition to and eventually in place of the expected reinforcer. We began by selecting stimuli that we subjectively judged as acceptable or pleasing to the dolphins such as various forms of tactile stimulation, playing with favorite toys or props, inventing games extemporaneously and even cueing behaviors that the animals seemed to enjoy performing. Some of the stimuli we selected seemed to be readily accepted while others were initially paired with food to condition them as reinforcers.

We pooled our thoughts and communicated closely with each other in order to be consistent in our efforts. Lists of "potential reinforcers" were compiled and worked from as additional stimuli were suggested for use. Training sessions became fertile ground for discovery as the provided time for the trainers to engage their animals in a more relaxed and intimate setting. A small and growing arsenal of reinforcers was soon at the trainers' disposal. We, as well as the animals, were becoming comfortable with the use of "non-food" or conditioned reinforcers which we, like our Sea World counterparts, began to refer to as RIR's (rears).

The remaining element to be considered in establishing the use of R.I.R. cannot justifiably be considered as a step in the transition as it is and should be a prevalent ingredient throughout the entire process. It is that which Butcher (personal communication) has referred to as "consistent inconsistency," innovation. One of the objectives in our use of R.I.R. was to establish the trainer as an unpredictable and, therefore, interesting source of reinforcement. From the beginning, an effort was made to make each occasion of reinforcement somehow different from the last, whether in form or manner of delivery, even if reinforcers were being used repeatedly throughout a session. We began to occasionally follow a response with anything that had not been previously conditioned and that we felt would catch the animal by surprise. A number of those things did and still do appear to be silly, such as making faces staring eyeball to eyeball or whistling a quick tune into a dolphin's ear, but occasionally pulling such stunts clearly appeared to keep the dolphins' interest. By February 1981, we were noting some impressive results in exchange for our efforts and visitors from other areas of the Zoo were commenting on the alertness and willingness to respond that they observed in our dolphins. There were two significant measures of success that we felt were encouraging.

In beginning the transition to using R.I.R. it had been suggested that a count of the number of RIR's used on each animal in a session should be kept in order to record the progress made in increasing their frequencies. After a short time of doing so we began to feel that being so closely aware of those numbers may have been inadvertently creating a pattern that made us predictable to the dolphins. As an alternative, we designed a tally sheet (Figure 5) on which the number of food reinforcers used during a session, usually a public performance, could be tallied for each animal by an observer revealing the percentage of non-food reinforcers used as compared to the combined total of reinforcers. The tally sheet provided a method by which we were free to react spontaneously with our animals and could be occasionally spot-checked and provided with an indication of the progress being made. By February 1981, tallies were indicating that food accounted for an average of 60% of the total reinforcers delivered by a trainer during a session where it had previously represented 100% of the reinforcers.

The other indication we had of having established in the dolphins a newfound interest in the trainers was eliminating the need for the presence of food buckets during shows and training sessions. The common practice at Seven Seas had always been having the trainer stand behind a food bucket placed on the pool wall in full view. That had often led to frustrating moments resulting from the fact that the dolphins would stubbornly refuse to respond unless a bucket was in view and, furthermore, would not follow a trainer to any other location around the pool unless a bucket was also present. In the course of using R.I.R. we eliminated the buckets in favor of food containers that could be hung on the trainer's side of the tank wall, completely out of sight of the dolphins, without affecting their response and providing the trainer with the freedom to change his position at will while maintaining the dolphins' attention. That innovation was a triumph in light of the history of the Seven Seas Panorama.

What we have accomplished at the Seven Seas Panorama is to have effectively done away with the practice of using food on CRF to establishing an environment in which the animals are not only uncertain as to when they will be reinforced but are uncertain of how they will be reinforced as well. That condition has, over the months, extended into every element of our animals' environment that we can possibly affect and, in addition, has extended in varying and appropriate degrees to our pinnipeds as well. The use of R.I.R. has become the accepted practice and an attitude as well. We believe that interactions and relationships with our animals have become heightened and more meaningful. The almost military-like approach to training that existed in our facility for years is gone and has been replaced with one that is far more open to change and innovation. Members of our training staff have become uninhibited in exploring the behavioral potential of our animals.

The animals, particularly the dolphins, have reciprocated with what we identify as greater attention spans, more reliable response levels and more consistent and improved levels of food intake. The fact that the last session of the day, as a general

Date 6-8-82

REINFORCEMENT TALLY

Session S3
Trainer EK

ANGIE		NEMO		SHANA		WINDY		STORMY		ALL	
F	NF	F	NF	F	NF	F	NF	F	NF	F	NF
13	9	20	12	13	5	19	4	5	15	4	6

	tl. F	tl. NF	tl. R	%NF
ANGIE	17	15	32	46
NEMO	17	11	28	39
SHANA	24	18	54	33
WINDY	23	10	33	30
STORMY	9	21	30	70

Observer [illegible]

Figure 5

rule, is just as productive as the first is a strong indicator of those factors when compared to past experiences in our facility. In short, the results we have experienced concur, for the most part, with those reported by our Sea World counterparts. And yet, our particular interpretation of R.I.R. and the exact manner in which we employ it makes it a method that is uniquely our own as would be the case at Sea World or any other facility that chose to use the method.

We credit R.I.R.'s success to, first of all, the fact that there are several well tested theories of operant psychology effectively combined to provide a logical and quantifiable basis from which to operate. Secondly, it provides a setting for the use of innovation and continual change in the animals' environment. Finally, it encourages its users to view their animals as organisms capable of handling more complexity than they may have been given credit for in the past.

Of course it would be a gross error to view R.I.R. as the perfect solution or eliminator of all training problems. There will always be problems of one form or another. Without them our lives as trainers would provide no challenge. But while R.I.R. can never completely eliminate problems encountered in shaping and maintaining behavior, it certainly provides a larger number of alternatives that can be used to meet them than what is provided by the traditional method.

Using R.I.R. is not by any means a simple undertaking. It requires a good deal of effort on the trainer's part. As a training tool, and like any other tool, its effectiveness will depend on the abilities of an individual that uses it. Used effectively it has the potential of yielding impressive results. Misused it can lead to confusion. It is the opinion of the training staff of the Seven Seas Panorama that R.I.R. provides an effective method and that it should be given serious consideration by any training staff seeking an alternative to its present situation.

REFERENCES

Beach III, Frank A. and Pepper, Ross L. (1971). *Marine Mammal Training Procedures: The Effects of Scheduled Reinforcement in the Dolphin (Tursiops truncatus).* NUC TP 214, Naval Ocean Systems Center, San Diego, California.

----------(1972). "Operant Responding in the Bottlenosed Dolphin *(Tursiops truncatus)*", J Exper. Anal. Behav., 17, pp. 159-160.

Breland, K. and Breland, M. (1966). *Animal Behavior.* Macmillan, New York.

Brill, Randy (1981). "Dolphin Training Does a Flip", Brookfield Bison, in press.

Butcher, Dave (1974). "The Trainer as the Trainee", in *Fourth Annual Conference Proceedings of the International Marine Animal Trainers Association, 1974, Orlando, Fla.,* edited by Rusty White and Bill Scronce. Sea World of Florida, Orlando, Fla., pp. 107-115.

Butcher, David G. (1980). "Reflections on Reinforcement", in *Proceedings of the Annual Conference of the International Marine Animal Trainers Association, 1980,* Miami, Fla., edited by Jack Pearson and Jackie Barry. New England Aquarium, Boston, Mass., pp. 58-59.

Butcher, David and Stephens, Bruce (1977). "Conditioning Killer Whales to Cooperate with Man in a Water Environment", in *Proceedings of the Annual Conference of the International Marine Animal Trainers Association, 1977, Boston, Mass.,* edited by Don McSheehy and Gail Pieterson. SEACO, Inc., Kailua, Hawaii, pp. 88-91.

Butcher, Dave; Stephens, Bruce and Charfauros, Vic (1976). "R. I.R. -The Interrupted Schedule of Reinforcement", in *Proceedings of the Annual Conference of the International Marine Animal Trainers Association.* Honolulu, Hawaii. Abstracts.

Defran, R.H. and Milberg, L. (1973). "Tactile Reinforcement in the Bottlenosed Dolphin", in *Proceedings 10th Annual Conference Sonar Diving Mammals*, Palo Alto, Cal., Stanford Research Institution.

Defran, R.H. and Pryor, Karen (1980). "The Behavior and Training of Cetaceans in Captivity", in *Cetacean Behavior: Mechanisms and Functions,* edited by Louis Herman. John Wiley and Sons, New York, pp. 319-362.

Ferster, C.B. (1958). "Intermittent Reinforcement of a Complex Response in a Chimpanzee", J

Exper. Anal. Behav., 1, pp. 163-165.

Ferster, C.B. and Skinner, B.F. (1957). *Schedules of Reinforcement.* Prentice-Hall, Englewood Cliffs, New Jersey.

Kelleher, R.T. (1966). "Chaining and Conditioned Reinforcement", in *Operant Behavior: Areas of Research and Application,* edited by W.K. Honig. Appleton-Century-Crofts, New York, pp. 160-212.

Kish, G.B. "Studies of Sensory Reinforcement", in *Operant Behavior: Areas of Research and* Application, edited by W.K. Honig. Appleton-Century-Crofts, New York, pp. 109-159.

Lacinak, Thad (19,77). "Advantages of Random and Interrupted Reinforcement with Pinnipeds", in *Proceedings of the Annual Conference of the International Marine Animal Trainers Association, 1977,* Boston, Mass., edited by Don McSheehy and Gail Pieterson. SEACO, Inc., Kailua, Hawaii, pp. 34-46.

----------(1979). "Making Learning Fun", in *Proceedings of the Annual Conference of the International Marine Animal Trainers Association, 1979,* San Diego, Cal., edited by A. Earl Murchison. SEACO, Inc., Kailua, Hawaii, pp. 31-32.

Morse, W.H. (1966). "Intermittent Reinforcement," in *Operant Behavior: Areas of Research and* Application, edited by W.K. Honig. Appleton-Century-Crofts, New York, pp. 52-108.

Pearson, Jack (1979). "Innovation as a Training Tool," Soundings, 4.

Pepper, R.L. and Beach, F.A. (1972). "Preliminary Investigation of Tactile Reinforcement in the Dolphins," Cetology, 7, pp. 1-8.

Pepper, R.L. and Defran, R.H. (1975). *Dolphin Trainer's Handbook: Part l. Basic* Training. NUC TP 432. Naval Ocean Systems Center, San Diego, California.

Pryor, Karen (1973). "Behavior and Learning in Porpoises and Whales," Naturwissenschaftem, 60, pp. 412-420.

----------(1975). *Lads Before the Wind.* Harper and Row, New York.

Pryor, K.W.; Haag, R. and O'Reilly, J. (1969). "The Creative Porpoise: Training for Novel Behavior," J. Exp. Anal. Behav. 12, pp. 653-661.

Reynolds, G.S. (1975). *A Primer of Operant Conditioning,* rev. ed. Scott, Foresman and Co., Glenview, IL.

Scardina, Julie (1978). "Not Just Any Pinniped: Observations on Working with a Walrus," in *Proceedings of the Annual Conference of the International Marine Animal Trainers Association,* 1978, Redwood City, Cal., edited by Jeffrey E. Haun. SEACO, Inc., Kailua, Hawaii, pp. 24-27.

Schusterman, Ronald J. (1976). "California Sea Lion Underwater Auditory Detection and Variation of Reinforcement Schedules." J. Acoust, Soc. Am., 59, pp. 997-1000.

Schusterman, Ronald J. and Barrett, Barry (1975). "Detection of Underwater Signals by a California Sea Lion and a Bottlenose Porpoise: Variation in the Payoff Matrix," J. Acoust. Soc. Am., 57, pp. 1526-1532.

Skinner, B.F. (1938). The *Behavior of Organisms: An Experimental Analysis.* The Century Psychology Series edited by Richard M. Elliott, Appleton-Century-Crofts, New York.

Skinner, B.F. and Morse, W.H. (1958). "Fixed-Interval Reinforcement of Running in a Wheel," J. Exper. Anal. Behav., 1, pp. 163-165.

Stephens, Bruce; Butcher, Dave and Defran, R.H. (1977). "Goodbye Deprivation; Hello Innovation," in *Proceedings of the Second Conference on the Biology of Marine Mammals.* San Diego, California. Abstracts.

Wyman, J. (1863). "Description of a 'White Fish' or 'White Whale' (*Beluga borealis* Lesson*),*" Boston Journal of Natural History, 7, pp. 605-612.

Marine Mammals: Public Display and Research

In most training programs, there is little doubt that variable reinforcement schedules are far more effective than a fixed, continuous schedule. However, most trainers begin with a continuous schedule and add variety as they gain experience. So, how does an entire program switch from a continuous schedule to a variable schedule? Many facilities gradually make the transition over time. This paper describes one facility's transition and discusses the effects the transition had on their training program. Although the author is credited as working at the National Aquarium in Baltimore, his paper references work done at his previous employer, the Aquarium of Niagara Falls. This paper appears in Vol. 2, No. 1, 1996 of the journal *Marine Mammals: Public Display and Research*.

Changing from a Fixed-Ratio Schedule to a Variable Schedule

by Paul J. Komanski
National Aquarium in Baltimore

ABSTRACT

After twenty-four years of fixed-ratio schedules for the Atlantic bottlenose dolphin (*Tursiops truncatus truncatus*) collection at the Aquarium of Niagara Falls, the staff changed to a variable-ratio and reinforcement schedule. Through increased awareness of successful variable reinforcement programs used at other institutions, and these programs' positive effects upon the animals, it was decided to change the method of reinforcement being used at the Aquarium of Niagara Falls. This involved the elimination of the fixed-food reinforcement schedule and the introduction of novel reinforcers such as toys, water interactions, innovative sessions, and interactive social sessions as an integral means of reinforcement. By means of rating sessions, it was observed that the animals, under the new system had increased performance levels as well as a decline in the number of sessions in which the animals broke from stimulus control. Here at the National Aquarium in Baltimore, we are in the process of a similar change with the dolphin collection which involves an environmental enrichment program with a variety of structured sessions.

INTRODUCTION

The Aquarium of Niagara Falls (ANF) has recently taken part in the implementation of a variable reinforcement schedule. In the past, the ANF maintained a fixed continuous schedule of reinforcement, in which only correct behaviors were reinforced with food. Through increased contacts and networking, the staff gained valuable insights into techniques and methods of reinforcement being used at other facilities. As a result of this new influx of knowledge regarding reinforcement schedules, the training staff decided to implement a change in the method of reinforcement.

The dolphin collection at ANF consists of three (3) female Atlantic bottlenose dolphins (*Tursiops truncatus truncatus*) who were on a fixed-ratio schedule of 1, or a continuous schedule, meaning each correct behavior received primary reinforcement (Kazdin, 1984). The ratio number sets the number of correct behaviors before reinforcement is given. A fixed-ratio of 2 would mean that every second behavior receives reinforcement. Prior to the change of reinforcement schedules, ANF used a stimulus delta, which is an antecedent event stimulus that signals that a certain response will not be reinforced (Scarpuzzi, Lacinak, Turner, Tompkins, & Force, 1991), to stop a behavior in progress. ANF also used a conditioned aversive stimulus, which is an initially neutral event that acquires aversive properties by virtue of being paired with a signal that no reinforcement will be forthcoming (Scarpuzzi et al., 1991), following a behavior which was not meeting established criteria. As a result of continually incorrect behavior, staff leaving or walking away from the animals was also a common practice. The use of food was the only reinforcement which the animals received. Toys were used only as time fillers during interactive sessions.

METHODS

The goal of the ANF staff was to change to a variable-ratio with reinforcement variety schedule in which both primary and secondary reinforcers are provided at intermittent intervals for correct responses (Aibel, 1993). Once the decision was made by the staff to implement a change, the first step was to condition secondary reinforcers, which are events that become reinforcing through learning (Kazdin, 1984). The initial secondary reinforcers were common or known toys such as balls, hoops, and rings. The introduction of a secondary reinforcer was slow, so as not to introduce too much at once. After a correct behavior, the animal was presented with the secondary reinforcer. Upon any interaction with that reinforcer, a bridging signal was given and the animal was reinforced with fish. The animals soon began to show interest in the secondary reinforcers. With only four trainers, it was easy to communicate between the staff the effectiveness or lack of interest in the secondary reinforcers, thus increasing the use of the more effective reinforcers. Communication took place after shows, sessions, in meetings, and by entries in the staff log book.

When the animals were conditioned to the first set of secondary reinforcers, the staff began to expand reinforcement by experimenting with other types of secondary reinforcers. A light-hearted competition among the staff helped to develop new secondaries. Some of the reinforcers that increased the animals' attention were mirrors, a variety of children's toys, and musical instruments. The staff also found that providing puzzles and games as reinforcers increased the animals' attention. For example, a 25-foot pool filter hose had one end firmly attached to the stage. Rings, which the animals interacted with frequently, were placed at the other end of the hose. The animals had to remove the rings to interact with them. Puzzle-solving was time-consuming and resulted in high levels of interest from the animals. A similar game involved the use of long poles with dangling rings which also required removal by the animals. Also, by placing toy balls on the stage, the animals had to figure out a way to slide up on the stage and get the balls back into the water in order to interact with them.

As the variety of reinforcement grew, behaviors were able to be maintained using primary and/or secondary reinforcement. At staff meetings and note sessions following interactions, the success and failure of each reinforcer was discussed. Reinforcers were developed for use following an above-average presentation. One of these secondary reinforcers included the conditioning and use of an innovative session. Innovative sessions were periods of time during which the animals were allowed to elicit behavior in order to receive reinforcement. Innovative sessions gave the staff insight into the types and kinds of behaviors and responses the animals created. This allowed staff to develop ideas for future training goals.

After presentations, water play and water interaction sessions were provided in response to exceptional performances. The introduction of non-trainers for social interaction sessions was also given to the animals as a consequence of exceptional performances. With the large variety of reinforcement now available, the trainer had the option to do a non-food presentation, thus demonstrating just how effective the secondary reinforcers truly were. The ability of the trainer to be creative helped to maintain a high level of animal motivation. The staff found that by making the non-food demonstration highly variable, it became an effective change in and of itself.

The trainers continually pushed themselves to develop and maintain creative reinforcers. They developed a slogan: "we must be consistently inconsistent." All the different variabilities and reinforcers were continually developed and refined through staff discussions, as well as by the animals' response to them.

With the changeover in full swing, the staff eliminated the use of the stimulus delta and the conditioned aversive stimulus following incorrect behavior. Both brought attention to incorrect behavior and were found to increase the frequency of the incorrect behavior. Food became just another reinforcer to the animal, when in the past it was the only tool of reinforcement. Secondary reinforcers, as well as trainer creativity, became the mode of reinforcement.

Before, during, and after the changeover, the animals' performance was scored with a rating system. The animals were given a number score following each presentation, and a written description of the session was recorded. All the scores were averaged at the end of each day and a daily score was given. The rating system was designed as follows:

(5): perfect criteria, high energy, no breaks of control
(4): strong criteria, good energy, no breaks, missed a discriminative stimulus or two
(3): a good average demonstration, good criteria, average energy. no breaks
(2): breaks from control, poor criteria, low energy
(1): continuously breaking, or animal does not come to control

The use of this rating system is the basis for the data presented below. The three animals' daily scores were averaged together to arrive at a single daily average score. All averages for individual days were then averaged to arrive at the average demonstration score and average break for the given month. These numbers were then used on all graphs. Daily food intakes were averaged to obtain a monthly average for each animal. These monthly averages were used for all graphs.

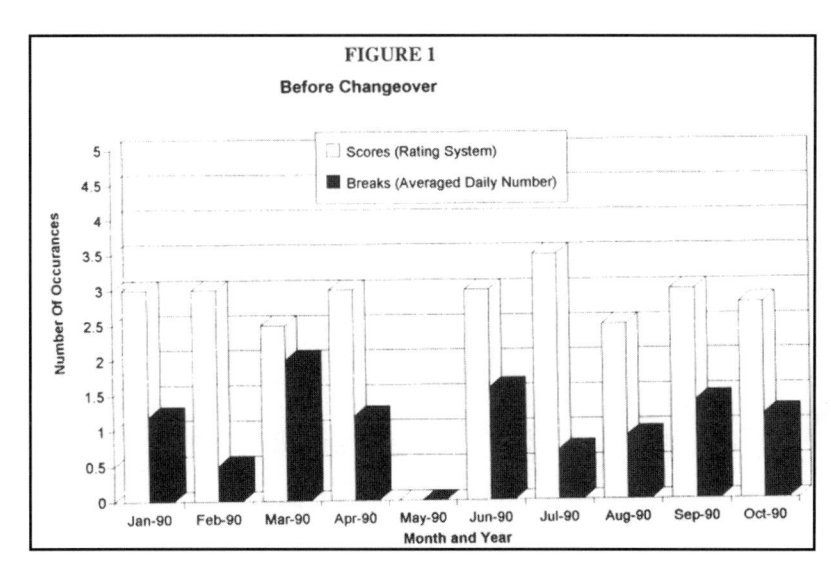

FIGURE 1
Before Changeover

RESULTS

Figure 1 shows the average daily scores for the ten months, as well the daily average breaks, before the changeover. There is no data for the month of May, because one of the animals, named Echo, gave birth during that month and no demonstrations took place. Figure 1 shows the average demonstration rating before the changeover as below 2.9. The number of breaks averaged 1.13 breaks per day.

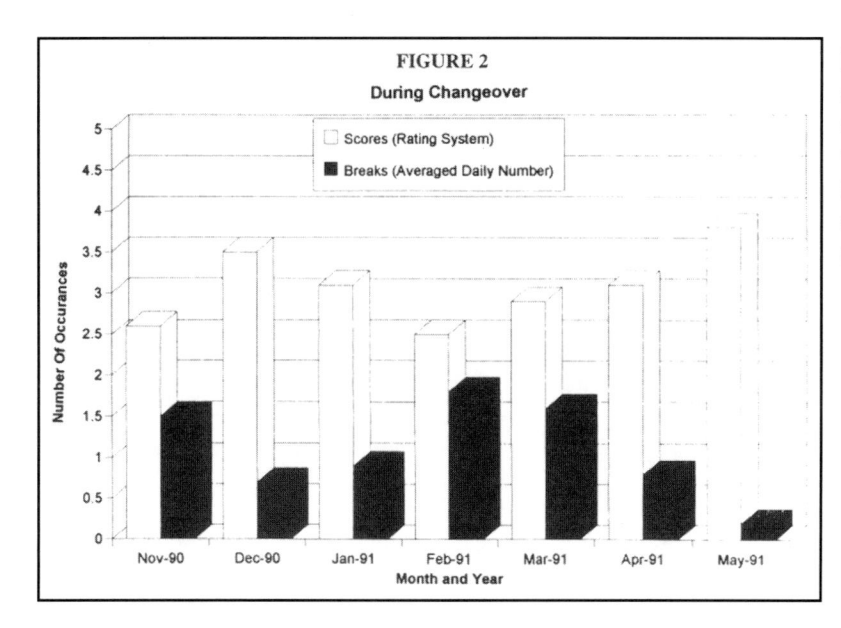

FIGURE 2
During Changeover

Figure 2 shows the average daily scores and average daily breaks during the seven months during which the changeover process took place. The daily scores averaged 3.07 per day and the breaks averaged 1.07 per day.

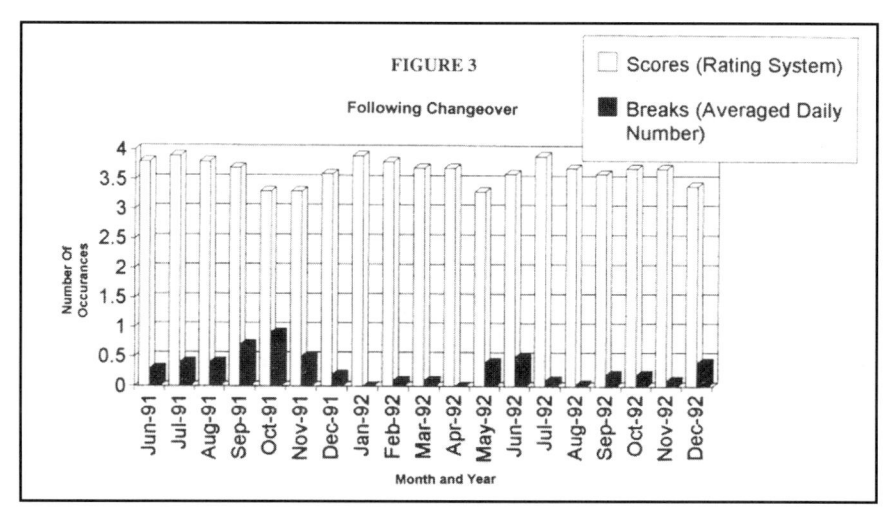

Figure 3 shows the average daily scores and average daily breaks for the nineteen months during which the variable reinforcement system was being used. The daily scores averaged 3.6, while breaks averaged 0.3 per day.

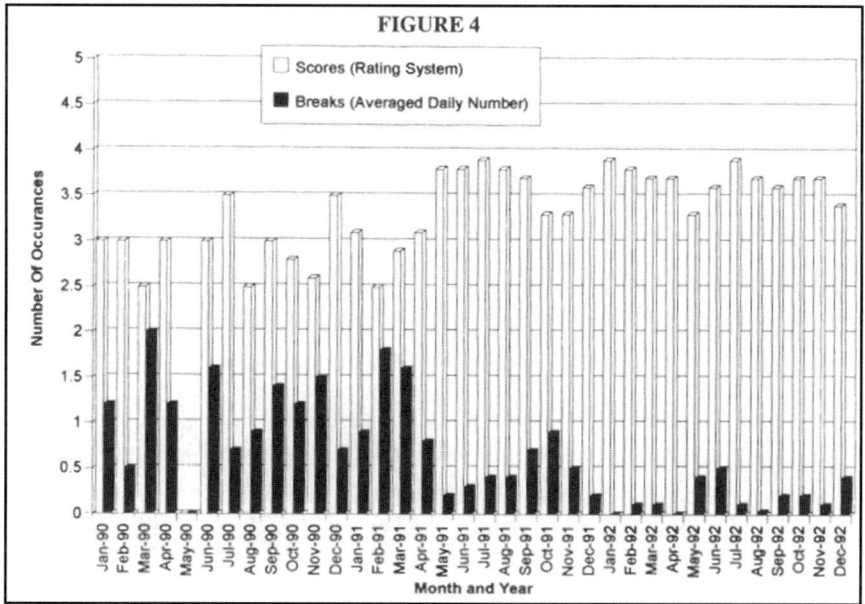

Figure 4 shows the entire three periods of average daily scores and average daily breaks.

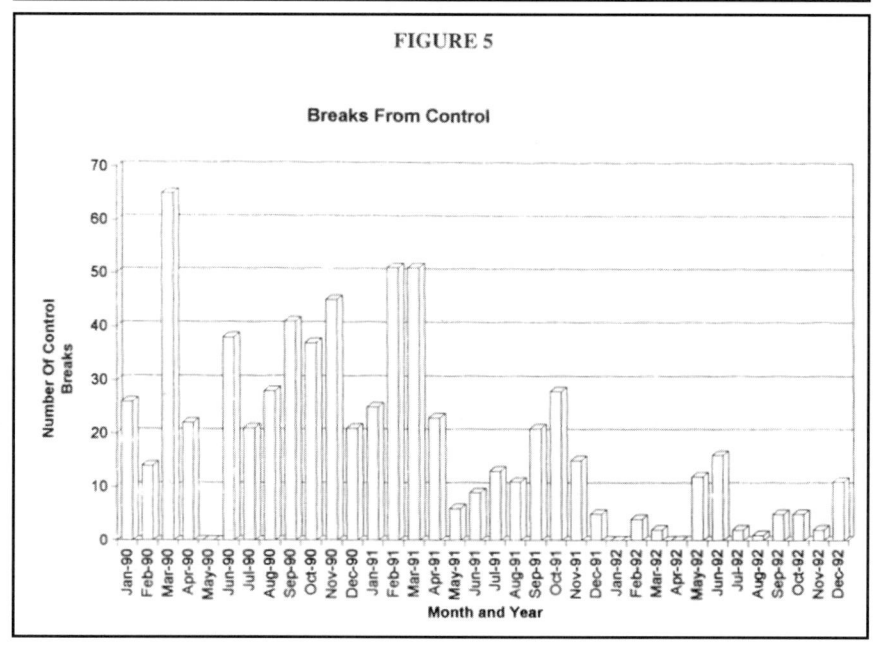

Figure 5 shows the actual number of episodes of all animal breaks during the three year period. The decreased number of breaks should be noted.

Chapter 9 - Advanced Techniques & Concepts   333

Figure 6 shows the average monthly food intakes of the three ANF animals and confirms that the increased scores were not based on increased or decreased food consumption. ANF did not do any kilocalorie analyses on feed fish. For the most part, the animals remained at constant base levels throughout the changeover process. A point to be noted is the increased food totals for Echo. They are due to Echo's nursing period with her calf and a veterinarian prescribed base increase from June 1991 to August 1991, in hopes of increasing her weight to the levels of the other animals. There is no significant increase or decrease in food consumption for any animal which had a causative effect on performance.

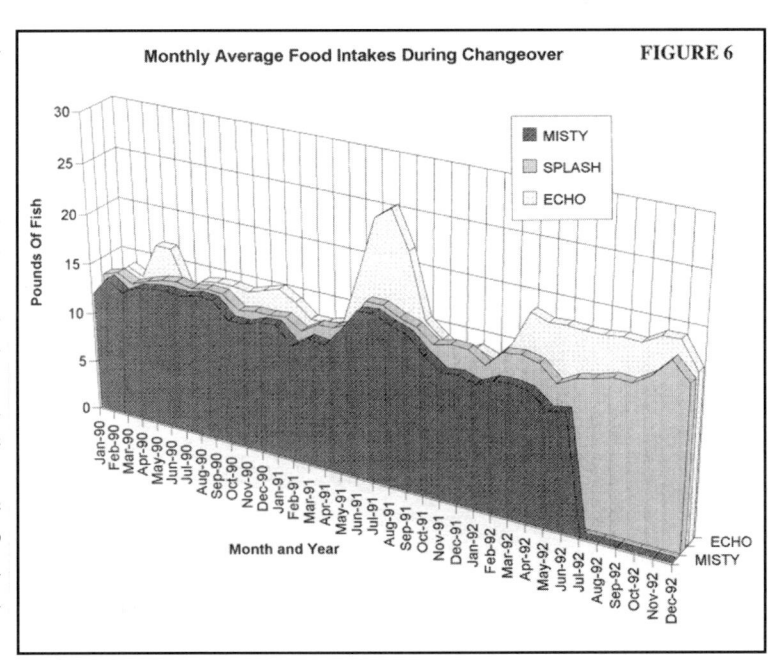

FIGURE 6 Monthly Average Food Intakes During Changeover

DISCUSSION

During the entire changeover process, the use of record keeping, the rating system, and trainer communications were the true keys to the changeover's success. Without these channels of communication it would have been impossible to judge how well the animals were progressing.

The original goal at ANF was to change the method used to reinforce its dolphin collection. During the process, the staff developed a new protocol for reinforcement. The data over a three year span of time showed that the daily show scores increased and became consistent at the higher levels. In the past, they had no consistency and were at lower levels. At the same time, the number of episodes of animals breaking from stimulus control decreased. While all this change with reinforcement was taking place, there were no significant increase or decrease in the animals' base diets that might have influenced the new variable reinforcement schedule.

It is important to note that during the changeover process, ANF-discontinued the use of the stimulus delta and the conditioned aversive stimulus following incorrect behavior. Though their elimination was not measured, the probable positive contribution their removal had on the overall improved performance on the ANF dolphins cannot be overlooked.

During the changeover it was observed that the animals had increased attention spans. The novel reinforcers and variable changes continue today. The trainers constantly push and support each other's reinforcement ideas. The new variable reinforcement schedule also made each trainer more aware of how to better reinforce and maintain an animal's behavior. The results of the successful change at ANF provide quantitative evidence that this type of change works and is beneficial. This can be used by any facility looking to make a change in reinforcement schedules.

LITERATURE CITED

Aibel, S. (1993). National Aquarium in Baltimore training manual for animal behavior. Unpublished manuscript.

Kazdin, A.E. (1984). **Behavior modification in applied settings.** Chicago: Dorsey Press.

Scarpuzzi, M.R., Lacinak, C.T., Turner, T.N., Tompkins, C.D. & Force, D.L. (1991) Decreasing the frequency of behavior through extinction: An application for the training of marine mammals. In S. Allen (Ed.), Proceedings of the 19th annual conference of the International Marine Animal Trainers Association (pp. 113-120).

Conference Proceedings

1983 IMATA Conference, Apple Valley, Minnesota, USA. Just when it looked like R.I.R was the best training tool on the block, someone came along with another perspective. Tim Desmond does not argue so much with the potential effectiveness of random schedules of reinforcement as he does with the blind faith that so many trainers began to place in R.I.R. No tool or technique is a substitute for knowing your animal and responding to its needs. Operant conditioning principles are one of the cornerstones to a good animal management program; but each new technique, whether it be the use of RIR, an LRS, a time-out, a negative reinforcer, or whatever is developed next, is but one of many tools at the trainers' disposal. Trainers should not let the excitement of one new tool cause them to throw the rest of the tools, or common sense, out the window. Some tools are only needed on special occasions, but they all serve a purpose.

R.I.R. A New Schedule of Reinforcement or a Method of Training Trainers

by Timothy J. Desmond
Marineland Amusements, Inc.

ABSTRACT

The presenter questions whether or not R.I.R. as a schedule of reinforcements is responsible for many of the successes that have been attributed to it. He wonders if those gains could have resulted from shifting away from the operant conditioning approaches of the mid '70s in which little weight was given to those factors which influence behavior besides food reward. He will suggest that R.I.R. is less significant as a schedule of reinforcement than it is as a useful methodology to sensitize trainers to their animals.

R.I.R. A Schedule of Reinforcement or a Step in the Direction of Supplementing Operant Conditioning Theory with Other Theories of Behavior When Analyzing Animal Behavior?

I think that those who developed and implemented RIR should be commended because I think they've made a valuable contribution to marine animal training. However, I do not think RIR will be remembered as a unique schedule of reinforcement. It will be remembered, I believe, as a stepping stone which helped trainers learn when operant conditioning theory is useful as an approach to controlling and modifying behavior and when it is not.

Before B.F. Skinner developed his theory of operant conditioning, animal trainers functioned in a very different fashion. There was a magical quality to it all. The secret to training a difficult trick was as closely guarded as a witch doctor's sacred incantation. Each trick had its own special formula to be followed, in order to be trained and there was little or no connection between the formula for one trick and that of another. And there was even less connection between the way two different trainers trained the same trick, unless of course one trainer taught the other how to do it. Confusing? Just imagine the confusion of the young apprentice when he was told the only way to learn how to train animals was to spend a year or so scooping last night's dinner from its enclosure in the morning.

Now, aside from the obvious janitorial drawbacks, there were some serious problems with the old way. First, it was very difficult and time consuming for the apprentice trainer to learn the experienced trainer's methods. Second, the development of new behavior was even more difficult, because each new trick was a separate entity - a separate trial and error challenge. The result was that the training process was slow and highly resistant to change and innovation.

Then B.F. Skinner developed his theory of operant conditioning, a simple, clear method of analyzing and modifying behavior. It revolutionized the training of marine mammals. The theory was simple to understand and it allowed the trainers to apply the same approach to solving any training problem. Trainers were able to train behavior much more quickly and efficiently. Novice trainers were provided with a clear structure within which to develop their skill. Finally, it allowed trainers and training supervisors to plan and account for their activities. In short, operant conditioning made training more understandable to everyone involved.

But nothing that powerful is without its negative aspects, Skinner pragmatically chose primarily food as a positive reinforcer because it's impact on behavior was the greatest. This worked fine for the development of his data, but it had an unfortunate after effect. The working trainer, having learned to rely on food to modify observable behavior, became prone to overlook or dismiss entirely the social and environmental influences on the behavior of their animals. They came to believe that problems in modifying the behavior of their animals could be solved by re-examining how the known reinforcer (food) was applied to the animal's observable behavior. This resulted in two things: 1) A lot of trainers who were subtly alienated from their animal; looking at them as response organisms instead of individual animals. 2) A lot of nagging behavioral problems that seemed unresponsive to attempts to correct them.

When trainers realized that their basic reinforcer, food, was not sufficient to meet their goals with their animals, they began to look for something else. RIR is one such attempt to find that something else. It is a formal attempt to incorporate reinforcers other than food into the training structure. Several papers have reported on improved behavior as a result of the application of RIR over the last several years. I believe there were two reasons why these successes were achieved. First, coming from the very sterile situations created by trainers over estimating the power of food as a motivator, any attention paid to other motivators of an animal would have a positive impact on its behavior. Second, and more importantly, in the process of searching for other reinforcers for their animals, these trainers became more sensitive and responsive to the overall motivational make-up of their animals.

But there are problems with RIR. First, and least significant, I do not believe that RIR is a unique schedule of reinforcement. Randy Brill, in his very clear account of his use of RIR at last year's conference, stated that his people still reinforce with food 60% of the time. Regardless of whatever procedures for application of other reinforcers, it still sounds like a variable ratio of food reinforcement to me. Cases can be made that these other "reinforcers" buffer the unrewarded responses of a variable ratio schedule or that multiple reinforcers on variable schedules are at work but I haven't encountered anything that indicates a "new" schedule of reinforcement is at work.

A more important objection, I believe, is that there are many environmental and social conditions which are of a continuing nature and hence cannot be applied to behavior as a reinforcer, but which may have a dramatic impact on behavior. For example: health problems, food quality, water quality, isolation, mistrust of trainers, threatening lights, objects, or activities in the environment, over or under activity, preferences between trainers to name a few. Also, many of the needs, which are dealt with in a RIR work setting, could also be dealt with outside of the work setting. RIR can become an obstacle to meeting those needs in the same way that operant conditioning alienated us from our animals in the first place. By constantly channeling our thinking about the needs of our animals through the RIR paradigm we begin to forget about certain reinforcers and miss opportunities to use others.

In fact, I'll even go farther than that. I'll say that at this point, that the operant conditioning paradigm itself becomes a handicap. Animals work best when they are comfortable and relaxed with their total environment, including their trainers. They are more receptive to operant conditioning techniques in this state than any other state. Getting them to and keeping them in this receptive state is not something that operant conditioning theory handles very well.

The usefulness of operant conditioning for the marine mammal trainer lies in the basic paradigm - discriminative stimulus – response - reinforcing stimulus, in its power to help his analysis and reinforcement of behavior. While there is no doubt that differences in the effectiveness of schedules of reinforcement do exist, I believe these differences are minimal when compared to the impact of social and environmental influences on behavior of highly intelligent marine mammals. For example, if I am playing the dollar slots in Vegas one might debate that I will be more strongly motivated to pull the lever if the payoffs occur on a variable ratio schedule than if they occur on a continuous schedule. However, if a 300-pound Sumo wrestler tells me to lay off "his" slot machine or he'll break my nose, I won't play at all.

In the psychological community, operant conditioning or behaviorism is one of many theories invented to explain behavior. There is continued discussion about which school of thought best explains or deals with different aspects of behavior. We, as animal trainers, have by and large been exposed to just one of these schools of thought. Why? Because operant conditioning has been the easiest to understand, and for most it is the most efficient at the modification and control of animal behavior. Operant conditioning seemed so useful and effective it never occurred to us to question the applicability of the theory as we encountered new circumstances. We just worked at applying that theory more effectively. RIR is just such an attempt. Perhaps more than anything else, RIR is telling us that we've just about exhausted all the utility operant conditioning offers us when such a complicated and convoluted expression of operant conditioning is required to solve those nagging behavioral problems.

It should be noted that we aren't the first to notice persistent contradictions to schedules of reinforcement. In 1961, two behavioral researchers, Breland and Breland, wrote an article called The Misbehavior of Organisms. They stated that "the behavior of any species cannot be adequately understood, predicted, or controlled without knowledge of its instinctive patterns, evolutionary history, and ecological niche." I agree with them and I believe it goes a step further with the animals we work with. I contend that we must also consider the immediate social dynamics at work on and the individual experience and preferences of each of the animals we work with.

When we begin to consider the effects of instinctive patterns, evolutionary history, ecological niche, social dynamics, and individual experience on behavior, I believe that operant conditioning or behavioral theory is not as useful as other theories of behavior. Wessel (1981) stated, "...cognitive accounts may fill in some of the gaps that now exist in behavioral analyses... In the absence of systematic investigations of an account of the effects of biological factors on learning, theories of stimulus control are incomplete."

He closed his article by stating, "Even in the absence of reconciliation, the present research of cognitivists and behaviorists may be viewed as complementary. In particular, cognitive research may specify important private events and biological properties that influence behavior, and behavioristic research may specify the environmental determinants of private events and of the relations between private events and overt behavior. In view of the substantial gains that follow from collaborative research, it seems worthwhile to bridge the explanatory chasm that now exists."

In essence, I believe that most of us have become entangled in a trap. We learned one theory of behavior that offers a powerful tool to analyze and modify behavior. Yet, we haven't clearly understood the weaknesses of limitations of that theory and we know little or nothing of other theories that might better explain behavior in those areas of weakness.

What then are we to do? Do all trainers have to go back and get a masters in psychology? No, although it wouldn't hurt to do some reading on other ideas about behavior. What I believe we need to do is to realize that it is okay to make guesses about the motivational state of and the social and environmental influences at work on our animals and adjust our approaches with the animals based on those guesses. Furthermore, it's unnecessary for us to reconcile those guesses with operant conditioning theory. What is necessary is to empirically test these guesses. How do we do that? Whenever we adjust our criterion for reinforcement based on a guess, pay attention to the results. Improved behavior supports the effectiveness of our guess. Non-improvement or continued deterioration tells us to guess again. Now one response is not going to give you much information. But over a longer period of time, one can develop a reasonably good idea of what things influence an animal's behavior and what things do not.

Obviously, our guess may not accurately state the true factors at work on the animal, but if our conception of those factors allows us to accurately predict behavior, that's all we need. Let's let behavioral theoreticians explain the whys. For most of us, theoretically explaining the whys of our guesses goes beyond our level of expertise. A large part of what we do is intuitive by nature. Attempts to reconcile that intuition with one school of thought or another can-restrict our options to work with our animals.

Our intuitive ability with our animals is developed or enhanced in several ways; by learning as much as possible about the behavior of the species in the wild; by close and continuing observation of the animal's behavior during controlled and uncontrolled activity; by close and continuing observation of social dynamics between animals living together; and by close monitoring of changes in the physical environment.

None of this seems earth shattering at first. But once the connection between the animal's behavior and its overall state of well being is established, a subtle shift in priorities occurs. The trainer no longer looks at the quality of behavior as his primary task; keeping the animal in a receptive positive state. Once in a receptive state, a clear and simple accurately implemented operant conditioning regimen will produce the quality. This does not relieve the trainer from the obligation to be a good behaviorist. Sloppy training not only leads to poor quality behavior, but also to less accurate a sense of the animal's need structure. However, the trainer is quicker to break off from an impasse with his animal and look elsewhere. The relationship between training and curatorial staff becomes more inter-related as trainer becomes an enhanced source of information for curators and curatorial decisions are made to help deal with behavioral problems. Some examples are in order.

At Marineland, this approach has been evolving over the past decade and has been formally pursued over the last three years. The following are examples of how our system works.

With our orcas we do a tremendous amount of subjective assessment of the social interaction between the whales before reinforcing behavior. I believe the vast majority of our whales' "misbehavior" results from their interaction with each other. Our goal is decidedly not 100% correct behavior. We deliberately tolerate a significant amount of misbehavior so as to allow the animals the social structure we believe they need to maintain their well being. Pushing too hard to eliminate such "misbehavior" resulted, we believe, in an unsatisfactory social climate. So we compromised and struck a balance between social and show behavior.

We closely monitor social behavior in our dolphin and pilot whale show area during uncontrolled periods and take that into account when reinforcing behavior, paying special attention to the impact of dominant animals on the behavior of subdominant animals and sexual behavior. It is important to note that when trainers do make such guesses about social dynamics they are cautioned to be empirical. The results of their reinforcement will tell them the accuracy of their guess.

We regularly schedule staff time and volunteer time for playing with as many of our animals as possible. But these games or attention giving sessions are never linked directly with behavior, and deliberately so. Our attention is available to the animal regardless of its behavior.

We monitor overall workload using the animal's demeanor as a guideline. We work hard to alter behavioral repertoires so that our animals work well below what we believe their maximums are.

We attempt to expose each of our animals to as wide a variety of training projects as it can tolerate. For example, only 2 of our 8 show sea lions are used in all, outside our show area and public contact activities. However, 6 of them are regularly walked to and from their show area every day. The last two, who are youngsters, are regularly walked in areas not opened to the public. Our goal is not to have all eight checked out on all forms of public contacts, although that would be nice. I believe it is stimulating, enriching activity, which keeps the animals bright, sharp, and receptive to training in general. I also believe that it has contributed greatly to the stability of their show behavior.

Finally, we do not look at that nagging behavioral problem only as something to be solved by adjusting our reinforcement of that particular behavior, (although we all know how often that is the case). Many times it is the clue through which we can identify hidden social and environmental conditions.

It is our goal to manage our show animal populations and activities in such a fashion that each show animal, except on peak attendance days, will have some part of its daily behavioral routine involved in some environmentally enriching activity. Be it a new show, husbandry, research behavior, or just playing around.

In a way, we're on the same track as RIR - get to know your animals and try to meet needs as well as you can. In that regard, RIR performs the valuable service of telling trainers to give greater consideration to the motivational state of their animals. However, I believe RIR is limited, as operant conditioning theory in general is limited in accomplishing this task. We must act outside of the behavioral setting; responding to our intuitive sense of the animal's overall set of needs to bring the animal to that receptive state in which the animal is most responsive to operant conditioning regimens. Once in that state, we use operant conditioning not only to obtain behavior but to monitor the emotional and physical state of our animals.

Trainer's Forum

VOL 15, NO 4, 1990. It is interesting how often confusion between a recall, a delta, and a "no" signal causes debate between trainers. The three answers provided are very different in their approach. Answer 1 is an accurate explanation of the benefits and applications of a recall. Answer 2, on the other hand, ignores the recall and focuses on an anecdotal explanation of the use of a delta. As the editor for *Trainer's Forum* in 1990, I chose to give myself the last word in Answer 3, where I attempt to address both. In retrospect, I might answer the question differently today, but only in style not content.

Understanding the Use of Recall vs. Delta Signals

QUESTION: We have recently had some heated discussions at our facility about the use of a recall or "delta" signal. We would appreciate hearing from others how and when you use your recall signal. As well as how, when, and if the response to the recall is reinforced. We would like to hear several opinions. Thanks.

ANSWER 1: There has been quite a bit of discussion, much of it heated, on the subject "the use of recall." Frankly, I don't understand the controversy, as the recall has always proven to be a valuable tool of training. The recall, I believe, should be conditioned in the same way that any other behavior is conditioned and, as such, certain controlling parameters need to be factored into its purpose and use. The following is a suggested game plan for recall use.

    A. Recall S^D (Form to be determined by trainer)
    B. Animal terminates present behavior
    C. Animal re-orients to the trainer – or - animal returns to the trainer
    D. Trainer responses:
        1. Reinforce acceptable response to recall S^D
        2. Reshape present behavior (fall back on approximations)
        3. Have animal go on to another behavior

In this scenario an animal is performing some type of behavior and the trainer activates the recall S^D (A). The animal terminates what he or she is doing and re-establishes contact with the trainer (B). This can be done by returning to the trainer or by re-orienting to the trainer and awaiting further instructions (C). The form of the proper response is conditioned into the parameters of the recall behavior. The trainer then has a number of behavioral options that can be used (D). These include but are not limited to:

    1. Reinforcing a positive response to the recall
    2. Reshaping the present behavior
    3. Going on to an incompatible behavior

The key to the effectiveness of a recall is in the perception of the animal. If a recall is only used when an incorrect behavior is performed (i.e. as a delta) and the consequences for doing this behavior are negative and punitive, the response of the animal to the recall can also be negative. If, on the other hand, a recall communicates to the animal that he or she is to stop one behavior and the trainer will guide them to the next behavior or task, a recall becomes just one more component of a positive training system. There has been some thought given to using the established bridge as a recall but this may cause some confusion in the animal's mind. A bridge should always mean "yes" to an animal and a recall should elicit a "pause" response from the animal, followed by guidance from the trainer. If the recall is used in this way the animal should never have to feel confusion or frustration in a training situation, because he or she will always be guided positively through any interaction with the trainer. As always, the attitude of the animal is a key component in the acceptance of any behavior, including responding to the recall. A recall can allow a trainer to more effectively shape new behaviors, move animals more easily from one location to another, and to reinforce the positive working relationship between trainer and animal.

Vic Charfauros
San Diego Zoo

ANSWER 2: The delta signal can be a very useful tool. It basically is a way of saying, "That is incorrect, return to station." This can be as important in animals as it can be with people. If someone is doing something wrong, you can say, "That is not right, try again."

In choosing a delta signal, it can be just about any signal that an animal does not normally hear. Some examples are a double blast on the whistle, tapping the fish bucket on the wall, slapping the side of the pool, or an underwater tone.

The delta can be used in certain circumstances. Say, for instance, you give the signal for a front flip and the animal starts its normal run for a buoy touch. If the delta is given immediately, the animal is told it has done something incorrect, come back to station before expending energy on the buoy touch. It may have mistaken the signal for another, possibly similar signal. If the same signal is given again and the animal responds correctly, then it may have misunderstood the first signal. If it responds in the same way, trying for the buoy touch, then there is probably a confusion of signals on either the animal's or trainer's part. The delta can be given again.

In this instance, when the animal returns to station, ask for a simple behavior that the animal will do correctly, immediately. Reinforcement can then be given. At this point, use fast and simple behaviors such as hand targets, vocals, head nods, pec waves, or any behavior you know the animal will do correctly. This way the animal is not rewarded for an incorrect response, but for returning to station when it hears the signal and responding to the request for a simple behavior.

Now if an animal is given the signal for a front flip and it does a poor front flip, the delta should not be used. The animal responded correctly, but simply performed poorly. This can be controlled through the use of selective reinforcement of better trials as opposed to the delta.

Other instances where the delta may be helpful is when an animal anticipates a signal and "jumps the gun." The delta is given, the animal returns to station. No reinforcement need be given, but the signal for the behavior is given instead. The animal responds correctly, then reinforcement can follow.

If an animal becomes frustrated in a training session and swims off, the delta can be used. When the animal returns a simple behavior can be done immediately and reinforcement follows. This brings the session back into positive terms for the animal and training can continue. By doing this you have more control over the situation and can help keep everything positive. Remember, saying no is not always a punishment, it can be a very useful training tool.

Craig LaMere
Gulf World

ANSWER 3: After reading your question about the use of a delta and recall signal, several of us began to discuss the question. Although our discussion never became heated, there were certainly some differences of opinion. Upon further examination of our discussion, we realized that our problem was semantics. We each had a different idea of what a recall or a delta signal means, therefore we had different views as to how to go about implementing them. Once we agreed on a definition, most of our thoughts on handling the situation were in agreement as well.

After speaking to a number of trainers at our facility as well as at others, I realized that many people have opposing definitions of the two terms. As long as everybody working with the same group of animals at the same facility has the same understanding of what they're doing, it probably doesn't matter what definition is used. The problems tend to arise when two trainers think they're executing procedure "X," but each of them have a different idea of what "X" means. When that happens, both trainers are positive they have done the right thing. A disagreement often follows because they keep claiming to have done "X" and each is certain that the other trainer didn't do "X." Well, in their own minds they are correct, but in reality they simply have never sat down to discuss a definition of the procedure.

I probably have not really answered the question yet. But, so often, when our staff gets into a "heated discussion" (as worded in the question) the answer we are looking for is not really the answer we need. I certainly don't know your situation, but I have often found that heated discussions arise not so much from different opinions, but from different uses in terminology. As trainers, we all come from varying backgrounds: biology, psychology, education, general science, or good old fashion experience; so it stands to reason that we all use different terms for different things. Once we agree on the meaning of the term or words, many of the problems are smoothed over. To me, that is the answer to the question, particularly since my definition of recall and delta are probably no better than anybody else's. However, since we're on the subject ...

I've always viewed a recall as being very different from a delta. Although I have seen many variations of them used by different trainers. To me, a recall is a trained behavior. You give the recall signal (whatever stimulus you have chosen), the animal returns to station (is recalled), and the animal is then reinforced just like any other behavior. Depending on the animal's reinforcement history, you may reinforce with food, tactile, toys, or even the presentation of a new cue (S^D). As I view it, a recall is just another stimulus asking the animal to exhibit a specific behavior, in this case the behavior is "return to station." This is an invaluable behavior that can be used in many training situations. It should always be a positive experience, just like any other behavior.

A delta, on the other hand, is a warning that lets the animal know that an aversive stimulus is going to he presented. For example, let's say an animal refuses to gate. Before resorting to the use of a crowder net, a signal is sounded warning the animal that it has one more chance before the net is pulled (Pepper & Defran, 1975). The warning signal in that example is technically called a delta. A slightly different example, that I have seen used: an animal continues to leave station to stare at a companion through a gate. This continues until the trainer decides to terminate the session. Before doing so, the trainer sounds the delta, warning the animal it has one more chance before the aversive stimuli is presented (i.e. ending the session). The delta, if over used or in the hands of an inexperienced trainer, has the potential of doing more damage than good. On the other hand, I have seen good trainers use a delta much as a parent uses an occasional but firm "No" with a child. Because of the possibiliry of misuse, many trainers avoid the use of the delta altogether.

I have also seen many variations of the above-described definitions. I hope my philosophical ramblings and follow up definitions have been helpful to someone. Happy training!

Ken Ramirez
John G. Shedd Aquarium

Trainer's Forum

IN PRESS, 1999. At the risk of confusing the reader, I have included the following column about the training and use of a recall. Although I firmly believe that the recall and the bridge should be distinctly different tools, several of the writers have indicated that their distinction is not as great. I have included this column because I believe that each answer offers valid points, particularly in regard to actually training a recall. In addition, it is only through the comparison of various techniques that we each grow as trainers – each of the facilities have had good success with the techniques described below. My explanation of a recall (as well as that of trainer Vic Charfauros) can be found in the *Trainer's Forum* column that precedes this one.

How is a Recall Trained and Used?

QUESTION: We are interested in knowing what other facilities use for a recall. Our animals have not been trained for a recall. How would you begin the training and what is the importance?

ANSWER 1: Your question comes at an opportune time for us, as we have recently undergone some staffing and program changes. We have existed for many years without the benefit of a recall, but as we are planning to develop a research program involving our California sea lions (1.3) and gray seals (1.2), the importance of a recall cannot be denied. One of our staff, Rebecca Singer, has experience using recalls in a research setting. She compiled the following information, which will serve as our guide for training the recall behavior.

The importance of using recalls

• Defining the meaning of the recall: Recalls can be either positive or negative. Recalls *may* become an aversive stimulus if only used with a negative connotation, for instance when the asked for behavior is done incorrectly. Avoiding aggressive behavior out of frustration (from always being "wrong") is a prime reason to practice positive recalls.

• Recalls are instrumental in research to indicate that an animal has "answered" or responded incorrectly to a question.

• If your research involves a certain apparatus that is tempting to the animal, recalls are vital to maintaining the integrity of the apparatus, as well as control of the situation. In other words, if the animal is interested in biting or playing with the apparatus in ways it was not meant to be used, a call back at the appropriate time (before the object becomes more reinforcing than the trainer and food) will reestablish the situation and keep the apparatus safe.

• When to use recalls: recalls are used to indicate that the behavior your animal is performing is incorrect OR to ask the animals to return to the trainer. Asking the animal to return to the trainer could be for the animal's safety or another person's safety in the vicinity.

What to use as a recall "signal"

• Most of the time a trainer wants to use a recall when the animal is "out of reach" and/or not looking directly at the trainer; therefore, the signal must be heard at distances. The signal must be distinct from all other signs used in the training process.

• Pick a signal/sound that carries throughout your exhibit/training area. Choose a signal that can be heard underwater and across a large exhibit area. In short terms: make sure your signal isn't absorbed by the "land" of the exhibit: rather, it carries across the exhibit.

• The sound must be distinct so the animal has the least chance of misinterpreting what the trainer wants.

Training the recall

• Determine the desired destination of the animal when the recall is given. Does the trainer want their animal to return to a specific place within the training area that is always set or does the trainer want a more flexible recall, where the animal is requested to return directly to the trainer, regardless of the trainer's position?

• If the trainer is the destination of the animal during a recall, starting with the animal a few feet away, sounding the recall and having them do a hand station, etc. will start the association between the sound and the action of returning to the trainer. The next step would be to recall when the animal is farther and farther away. Using a target pole may be more useful at greater distances. Weaning off the cue of the hand station/target pole would be the last step.

• Continuing to practice the recall in positive situations will help establish the behavior as a routine behavior for the animal.

Training Staff
National Zoo

ANSWER 2: I am a trainer at the new Dolphin Cove here at Sea World Australia with the fortune to work with a diverse and skilled team of people. Below is a summary of lengthy group discussions relating to our use of a recall.

The Oxford Dictionary states that "recall" is to:

• summon back
• signal to return
• annul, abolish or cancel.

Recall for us here is a valuable sound stimulus that enables the trainer to say "come here," however the various interpretations and applications are numerous. When using a recall it must always be maintained as a positive stimulus otherwise the tool becomes a delta.

The initial training of a recall can be as simple as the training of a bridge – recall, food, etc. Upon starting a session, the first stimulus the animals receive is the recall. In effect you are pairing food, training sessions, or any positive stimuli to the tool.

The benefits we find in using a recall, particularly in a group context, are many and varied:

• the primary A to B concept
• enables us to identify the precise moment of

incorrect behavior to those animals who aren't reinforced when they return;

• the use of recall prevents the continuation or practice of undesirable behavior;

• in the absence of an underwater cueing system the recall is an effective reinforcer when a whistle cannot be detected;

• can be used as a prompt;

• is a discreet tool that is easily implemented in a show context.

The two main recall tools used here are:

1. A stainless steel ring that is worn on a trainer's finger and when struck against a hard surface (metal, fiberglass or concrete) creates a sound stimulus;

2. A stainless steel object that when shaken creates a sound stimulus.

While an advocate to the use of recalls, we also acknowledge the disadvantages in the implementation of such a tool:

• doesn't allow the animal to think independently about where the failure occurred;

• highlights undesirable behavior;

• if used repeatedly in a delta context it could raise the possibility of aggression;

• can cause dependence in certain loud behaviors, i.e. the desensitization of the bridge in a tail lob.

If we stress one thing with the use of a recall, it is to maintain the positive value through constant maintenance everyday.

Nina Fitzgerald
Sea World Australia

ANSWER 3: We use two types of recall. The first we trained for water-work – it is a black plastic dog whistle (louder and of a different pitch then the metal dog whistles we use as normal bridges). When beginning water work, we felt that it was critical to train a recall for use in an emergency or any situation where the trainer feels uncomfortable with the seals being away from deck. Before we even started going in the water, we made sure that the recall was well established. Training the recall was relatively straight forward – the final behavior was to have all of the animals return to station from anywhere in the pool as soon as they heard the whistle. We began by having all the animals stationed at deck and blowing the recall (loud and long so there was no question that all of the animals could hear it). As the recall was being blown, we began heavily reinforcing all of the animals. The noise was a little louder then the seals were used to, so it took some of the animals a couple sessions to get desensitized to the sound. As soon as we saw a look of interest from the seals when they heard the recall, we moved on to the next step. This consisted of sending the animals on short go-outs, waiting until their attention was focused on us, blowing the recall while giving the return to station cue. As soon as the animals returned to station, they were heavily reinforced. Once this had been mastered, we then started recalling: during other behaviors, when the animal's attention was not focused on us, with a trainer in the water, etc. Beause we had to train in a group setting, the individual pace of each of the animals varied – some animals were still working on step #1, while others had progressed to step #3. At this stage, it was very important that the trainers coordinated their cues so that the recall didn't sound until everyone was ready. As the training progressed, we were able to add an element of "surprise," with one trainer choosing a "surprise" time during the session to recall. As the animals became proficient at the recall, we started to vary the reinforcement. We ALWAYS reinforce any response to the recall with primary reinforcement, however the schedule is now more variable. Good responses get more fish. We make a point of practicing recall several times a week to keep the response fresh (we have found that it is possible to practice too much – there is a point where response time starts to slow). We also have "recall" sessions where we go on deck, recall and then feed the entire bucket of fish. It is important to keep in mind when training that the recall is essentially a bridge, so which ever behavior the animal is performing when the recall sounds is going to be reinforced.

In addition to the water work recall (which effects all of the animals in the group), we have also trained an individual recall to two of our vision-impaired seals. Our seals station to plastic letters at deck, and the recall cue for these animals is to tap the letter on the deck. This recall was trained the same way as the water work recall and has worked very well. We can use the tap at the beginning of a session to let the seal know where we are in the exhibit or recall a miscue (although keeping in mind the recall is a bridge, we don't use this option too often!).

Training Staff
New Jersey State Aquarium

Conference Proceedings

1985 IMATA Conference, Orlando, Florida, USA. The training for this research project won the behavior of the year award in 1985. The uniqueness of the task was not the only reason for the award, it was also the innovative use of a delta stimulus that had the conference in a buzz. Many trainers at the conference had trouble grasping (and in some cases debated) the training concept used in this project, but there was no debating that the training had been successful. Although I seldom advocate the use of a delta, here is an excellent example of an important training tool used effectively by skilled trainers.

Microcomputer-Assisted Training of a Bottlenose Dolphin (*Tursiops truncatus*)

by Tricia Kamolnick
SEACO, Inc.

Hal Goforth & Eric Cartegena
Naval Ocean System Center

ABSTRACT

An ergometric study was conducted to determine the force production characteristics of a swimming dolphin. A microcomputer (with analog and digital capability) and a sine wave signal generator controlled the frequency of the tones given to a dolphin while it "swam" against a mounted force transducer. During each trial a hydrophone emitted one of four tones (10, 5, 3, or 1 kHz) to signal a specific performance condition. The 10 kHz tone signaled the animal to continue at present work level. The 3 kHz tone signaled the animal that he had dropped below the acceptable work level. If the force level increased to an acceptable level and the duration criterion were met, the 5 kHz pulse tone signaled a successful trial. If the force level did not increase, then the 1 kHz tone signaled failure. The microcomputer was programmed to collect analog force data (144 Hz) and determined whether or not the physical work performed satisfied a predetermined set of criteria (e.g. tail beat force and swim duration). The microcompter allowed both the animal and trainer to receive immediate feed back of the work performed and enabled the trainer to achieve a precise criteria, a consistency in stimuli, and a real-time evaluation of force production. The use of a warning tone decreased the number of failures (especially during the long swims) and reduced the stress and frustration experienced by both the animal and trainer. Microcomputers can enhance training by improving the precision and consistency in measuring, evaluating, and signaling the behavioral and physical performance of dolphins.

OBJECTIVE

A training program was developed by the authors at NOSC, San Diego, to meet criteria necessary for an ergometric study of a bottlenose dolphin (*Tursiops truncatus*) while it swam on the surface at different levels of intensity. The objective was to establish relationships between relevant physiological parameters, such as respiration rate, tail beat frequency, and relative force produced by a dolphin exercising at selected levels of muscular effort. This was a pilot project for a larger study being done for a larger project at NOSC, Hawaii, to determine the energy output of a swimming dolphin in order to calculate its hydrodynamic efficiency.

SYSTEM EQUIPMENT

A microcomputer system was designed to assist in training and collecting data. Computers provide a rapid means of collecting, analyzing, and storing data. In this study, the microcomputer functioned additionally as a behavioral and physical training device. Software was developed to collect the force data and determine if the physical work performed by a dolphin during an exercise trial satisfied a predetermined set of criteria, such as tail beat force and work duration. The force exerted by the dolphin was measured as it "swam" against a well padded, mounted load cell. Real-time force data were collected by the microcomputer at a rate of 144 samples per second. This rate allowed the computer instantly to evaluate the data and determine the specific tone produced by a variable wave form generator. The generator sent signals to an underwater transducer that projected one of four tones (1, 3, 5, 10 kHz) to the dolphin. The trainer monitored these tones throughout the trials with the aid of a headset and a hydrophone receiver. This integrated system was capable of receiving, analyzing, and storing force data while it simultaneously controlled the tones projected to the working dolphin. In effect, the microcomputer system made the critical quantitative, real-time decisions regarding work parameters necessary to condition the dolphin.

TRAINING SITE

The animal used for research, a 309 kg (680 pound), 21-year-old male bottlenose dolphin (*Tursiops truncatus*) called Ivan, was housed in a floating pen moored alongside a pier in San Diego Bay, California. The pen measured 7.6m x 7.6m (25' x 25') and was 2.4m (8') deep with a .9m-wide (3'wide) wooden walkway along each side. A small equipment shack was located on a section of floating pontoon causeway moored between the pier and the dolphin pen. The shack housed the microcomputer and other electronic equipment used for this experiment. The padded load cell was mounted on a stainless steel plate that was bolted diagonally across the corner of the pen directly in front of the equipment shack. A metal frame ran diagonally across the same corner of the load cell and was secured to the walkway. This frame served as a mount for a microphone that was suspended 45.7 cm (18 inches) above the dolphins blowhole and was used to record respiratory sounds during swim trials. To record fluke and tail movements during the testing, an underwater video camera was held in the water approximately 1m (3') from the dolphin's right side.

CONDITIONING TECHNIQUIES

The morphological characteristics of the dolphin and the aquatic environment were taken into account in developing methods of behavioral control during exercise, training, and testing. During conditioning, emphasis was placed on positive reinforcement rather than negative reinforcement. Techniques such as deprivation were specifically excluded from the conditioning program to maintain a high motivational level in the animal. Standard operant conditioning techniques were used to train Ivan to station parallel to the side of the pen close to a corner. He was then physically moved forward until his rostrum touched a padded target. The voice command "in" was paired with this action. Immediately following contact, pressure was applied to his peduncle, simulating a swimming motion. The voice command "go" was paired with this action. Within a few sessions Ivan was moved to the load cell. At this time, in order to protect Ivan's rostrum from the constant pressure, the load cell was heavily padded with 1.27 cm (1/2")neoprene and covered with a chamois cloth. Ivan was also conditioned to wear a custom-fitted rostrum glove made of .64 cm (1/4") closed-cell neoprene with nylon lining on the outside. Once Ivan stationed in front of the load cell, a pole target was gently held on the midline of his back, anterior to the dorsal fin. This was to aid in maintaining a straight alignment with the load cell, which was imperative for measuring force level readings. Ivan was then given the voice commands and immediately began a swimming motion. At first he held his breath during the entire trial. His swimming style was characterized by short bursts with erratic tail beat thrusts. Through successive approximations the work time was extended and the thrusts became more stable. once the work time was extended past 30 seconds, Ivan began to breathe regularly during the trials.

At this time, the microcomputer was integrated into the training program. It had previously been used as a data collection and storage device to provide the trainer with immediate feedback of the swimming forces via a tone emitted through a loudspeaker. However, it was difficult for the trainer to monitor, evaluate, and respond to these tones in order to bridge at the precise moment. Since the timing of the conditioned reinforcer (bridge and delta stimuli) was a critical feature of this procedure, it was decided to bypass the trainer and to provide the animal feedback directly from the microcomputer, which would be more accurate and faster in delivering the bridge and delta stimuli. Any delay in delivering either of these tones could confuse the animal and result in poor swimming styles and weak forces.

When the tones to be used as the command stimuli and conditioned reinforcers were chosen, it was necessary to consider the hearing ranges of both the dolphin and the trainer. Audiograms obtained on dolphins show a sensitivity range from about 75 Hz to about 150 kHz. Human hearing sensitivity ranges from about 20 Hz to about 20 kHz. Ivan responded to tones as low as 1 kHz, and the 10 kHz tone was well within the upper limits of the trainers hearing range.

Since a 10 kHz tone was initially heard by the trainer through the loudspeaker and the animal had already adapted to hearing it a trail, it was decided to retain this tone as a command stimulus (work tone). When it was projected into the water through the transducer, Ivan maintained a relatively smooth swimming pattern. A 5 kHz pulsing tone was introduced as a conditioned reinforcer (bridge stimulus) by pairing it with a dog whistle to which Ivan had previously been conditioned. The dog whistle was then faded out. A 1 kHz tone used as a conditioned reinforcer (delta stimulus). It was followed by a 1-to-3-minute rest period. Ivan's reaction to this tone was to increase tail beat frequency and force level dramatically for several seconds, then stop and move away from the work area.

Difficulties arose when attempts to extend the duration of the trials failed. Many times Ivan maintained force level and tail beat frequency criteria until a few seconds before the criterion time was met. For this he would receive a delta stimulus after a gallant effort, which caused frustration and hampered training progress. After the situation was evaluated, an additional command stimulus referred to as the "warning tone" was added to the program. A 3 kHz tone was used as the warning tone because it was close to the delta stimulus in frequency but was discernable from the other tones by both the dolphin and trainer. Introduction of the warning tone gave the animal the opportunity to recover his tail beat force and reach criteria without failing the trial and losing the subsequent reward. His first reaction to the warning tone was to stop swimming, possibly confusing the warning tone with the bridge stimulus. He was not rewarded however, and on subsequent trials his reaction to the warning tone was much the same as to the delta stimulus. This response brought him back to the criterion level, the warning tone went off, and the work tone came back on. He learned quickly to make the necessary adjustments and exert enough force to regain predetermined criteria. With the addition of the warning tone, rapid training progress was made. Trials became longer and more consistent in force from beginning to end. Once the required 3-minute swim was achieved reliably, the force level criterion was increased.

On several occasions, following the 3-minute trial, Ivan was stationed in an adjacent corner and given the hand signal command to present his flukes for blood collection. This completed the chain of behaviors required for final testing.

This process for developing a feedback system for the dolphin was progressive. Animal performance and attitude were constantly evaluated. After many software and hardware modifications, a reliable system was developed that provided clear responses to precise parameters. Ivan adapted with few difficulties and appeared to understand the parameters well enough to exert the least overall force level to meet the predetermined criteria.

Many factors had to be considered in developing the software program. Force produced by the tail beat would go from zero to some positive level [e.g. 159.1-kg (350 lbs)] then back to zero. Therefore, it was necessary to use a window of time to sample the data. For example, if the force level was set at 159.1 kg and the window was two seconds, any one of four tail beats reaching 159.1 kg would satisfy the criterion and reset the sampling clock. If none of the tail beats reached 159.1 kg, then a 2-second warning tone would be projected into the water, allowing the dolphin an additional four tail beats to reach the required level. Any one of these tail beats meeting or exceeding 159.1 kg level during these two seconds would stop the warning tone, activate the work tone, and reset the sampling clock. This process would continue until either the predetermined time criterion was satisfied and the dolphin received the bridge stimulus or until he failed and received the delta stimulus.

TRAINING PROGRAM AND WORK TESTS

The dolphins task was to swim continuously for three minutes against the padded load cell at a prescribed tail beat force level. To achieve this criterion, the animal was trained 1-1.5 hours, twice daily, 5-6 days a week. Daily sessions were separated by 4-5 hours. Individual exercise trials within a session lasted 30-180 seconds and were conducted on a 1:4 work-to-rest ratio. Total daily exercise time averaged 8 minutes (range: 5-16 minutes). After six months of physical and behavioral conditioning, the dolphin

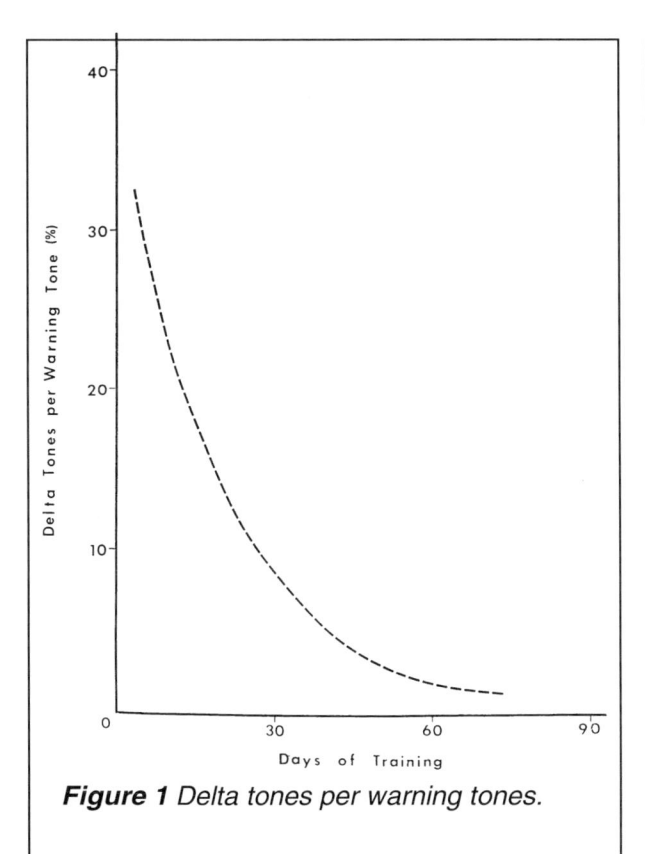

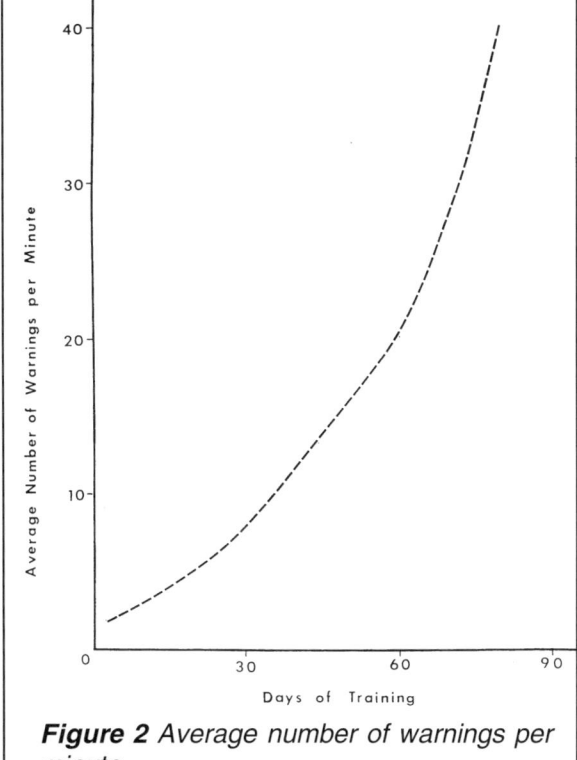

Figure 1 Delta tones per warning tones.

Figure 2 Average number of warnings per minute.

was considered to have reached testing criteria (i.e., maximum sustainable average force for 180 seconds). Some aspects of the experimental design may have been influenced this determination and therefore this force value may be considered less than the true maximum sustainable force capacity for this dolphin.

Data were collected from a total of six 3-minute work tests conducted at five different average force levels equivalent to 100, 95, 90, 65, and 57% of the maximum sustainable force. Blood glucose and lactate levels were determined from samples collected 5-10 minutes after the exercise following each of the six final work tests. These metabolites were used to evaluate the dolphin's energy metabolism at the different work levels.

In order to evaluate the dolphin's energy metabolism it was necessary to compare the metabolites at the different work levels. Therefore, blood glucose and lactate levels were determined form samples collected five to ten minutes after the exercise following each of six final work tests.

DISCUSSION

Once the final program was developed and the warning tone was introduced, the number of failures decreased dramatically. The percentage of delta tones per warning tones went from about 30% to less than 1%. Throughout this study many environmental variables were uncontrollable; for example, there were many ships moving through the Bay, helicopters and jets flying overhead, pile drivers in operation at the adjacent pier, wild sea lions cavorting freely near the training site. Although these variables were random and occurred throughout the entire training and testing period, any one of them could have had an effect on any given trial. Nevertheless, the data collected demonstrate an interesting trend. Initially, *warning tones* occurred sporadically throughout the trial, but as Ivan adapted to the tones, the number of warning tones increased dramatically. This trend led us to speculate that Ivan was using the warning tones to find the minimum force level required to meet the trial criteria. It appeared he had learned to capitalize on the warning tone by "riding" it. At this point, Ivan's style began to change. His fluke movement had become erratic, with high and low force peaks and total body movement increased. To reduce this behavior it was necessary to increase his tail beat frequency by shortening the sampling window to 1 second. This forced him to put a little more effort into the fluke movement and improve his style by decreasing upper body and head movement. Ivan's swimming style was still modified, showing a definite pattern of responses to the warning tones.

Although swimming is a natural behavior and the first one learned by dolphins, training behavior under restrictive and sometimes aversive conditions can be a difficult task. Swimming with a high degree of exertion against a fixed-position object and sustaining this effort for a duration of three minutes would have been more difficult to condition without the aid of a microcomputer. In the final phase of the study, the predetermined criteria could be raised or lowered to any level. Ivan was able to perform at maximum effort, reducing him to a 50% effort would have required weeks of trial and error. The microcomputer was a training device that allowed us to decrease his effort in only a few trials. It also enhanced the training by improving the precision and consistency in measuring, evaluating, and signaling the behavioral and physical performance of the dolphin.

ACKNOWLEDGEMENTS

A special thanks to those individuals whose help contributed to the success of this project: Bill Scronce, Clark Bowers, Milo McManus, Don Carder, Don Miller, Jim Kadane, Les Bivens, and Jeff Haun of NOSC, and the NOSC veterinary staff; Debra Skarr of SEACO, and the entire SEACO training crew.

Trainer's Forum

VOL 23, NO 3, 1998. It is fairly easy to find literature defining a behavior chain, but it is hard to find explanations of how a behavior chain is actually trained. Chains are advanced concepts, because once a behavior within the chain breaks down, it takes a skilled trainer to fix the problem. Fourteen years prior to the publication of this article, the dilemma of a behavior problem within a chain was discussed in another *Trainer's Forum* column (which follows this article).

Chaining Behaviors Together

QUESTION: How do you go about chaining behaviors together? How do you prevent confusion with a single cue once it's part of the chain?

ANSWER 1: As you are well aware, a chain of behaviors is a series of behaviors done one right after the other in a specific order. The correct completion of the preceding behavior signals the start of the next behavior in the chain. Likewise, the opportunity to do the next behavior acts as a conditioned reinforcer to the behavior it follows. This type of sequence is known as a technical chain. There are other types of chains that allow the trainer to give immediate feedback to the animal after each behavior, although some trainers call this a chain, I won't talk about them here.

Chained behaviors are often thought of as an exciting addition to public presentations, but there are many research scenarios where the chaining of behaviors is an important concept for the animal to understand. As with any training goal, I highly recommend writing out your training plan and discussing it with the other members of your training team to make sure everyone understands the route you intend to take to get to your final product.

When deciding what behaviors to chain, it's important to keep the following things in mind. First, each behavior must be under stimulus control. As I mentioned earlier, each subsequent behavior reinforces the earlier one. In this situation the conditioned stimulus not only signals the animal to the desired response but also signals the opportunity for reinforcement, thus it's a conditioned reinforcer. Second, how many behaviors do you want chained together? Remember the more behaviors you have, the more complex the actual chain becomes. This is important to keep in mind if you are working with a short time line, not to mention the time needed to maintain the behavior. Third, how is the chain going to be used? Is it going to be used in a specific setting like a research project, will it always be the show's opening behavior, or is it going to be context specific? This is important to identify for several reasons. A context specific chain will allow the animal to discriminate more easily between individual behaviors within the chain and the actual chain itself, and may not require the conditioning of a new S^D to emit the chain. A behavior chain that is going to be used randomly throughout your show with no other obvious discriminator will require you to condition a new S^D to initiate it. Fourth, what kind of reinforcement schedule do your animals currently work under? When you work with a chained sequence, your animals will need to be familiar with a variable schedule of reinforcement. Going from one behavior to the next without primary reinforcement is a foreign concept to an animal that normally works with a continuous schedule of reinforcement, where they receive a primary reinforcer for each correct response. You will want to teach this concept to your animals prior to starting your chain. Finally, how are you going to teach the "chaining" concept to your animals? To start the actual training process you need to know the specific sequence of behaviors because you will need to start with the last behavior.

When training a chain of behaviors, you work backwards. Start with the last behavior in the chain, again make sure it's under stimulus control, then introduce the next to last behavior and so on until all of the desired behaviors are in place. In this set up your animals will be going from the newest behavior in the chain, and at first the weakest, to the stronger reinforcing parts of the behavior. Anyone who has had to memorize a long literature passage for school may have had the experience of starting at the beginning of the passage and working towards the end. You end up working from your strength to your weakness which is not always a reinforcing set up, it actually can be quite frustrating. But by starting with end sections and gradually working your way towards the beginning you finish strong, it's what you know the best and that's reinforcing. With practice, the whole passage becomes well memorized. The chaining of behaviors is the same concept. Once all of the behaviors are in place, how do you maintain the criteria for each?

It will be essential that you occasionally interrupt the chain and reinforce a particular behavior with something other than the next behavior in the chain. This keeps the individual behaviors within the chain strong and hopefully problem free. To get started I would suggest randomly reinforcing the earlier components, all except the last, approximately 25% of the time. That means that one out of every four times the chain is sent, one of the earlier behaviors will be reinforced. Obviously, this means 75% of the reinforcement will occur after the last behavior. This is just a suggested ratio, your situation may dictate a lower or higher frequency of providing reinforcement earlier in the chain. Do what works best for you. Keep in mind that if more than one person is going to be working the chain of behaviors, good communication will be necessary to make sure all parts of the sequence are periodically reinforced.

The second part of your question regarding how to maintain the individual behaviors outside of the chain we have already touched on. If you have a specific context in which the chain will be used, then the animal should have little difficulty with the discrimination. However, if you use the chain randomly in different situations you may find it necessary to condition a separate S^D in order to emit the correct response. Good luck!

Greg Dye and Training Staff
Brookfield Zoo

ANSWER 2: At Theater of the Sea we define a chained behavior as linking a series of behaviors together in a fixed sequence, typically bridging and reinforcing after the chain is completed rather than bridging and reinforcing each behavior. An example of a chained behavior is the common three-part chain seen in many sea lion shows – the ball retrieval, rollover, and handstand. Another is a dolphin doing a series of bows.

When training a chain, two or more behaviors are requested in a fixed sequence. Initially, each individual behavior is requested with an S^D, bridged and reinforced. With repetition of the sequence, the order becomes conditioned.

The reinforcement of each separate behavior can eventually be eliminated and given at the completion of the chain. Next, the bridge can be eliminated for each behavior and instead be delivered at the end of the sequence. In time, it becomes unnecessary to give an S^D for each behavior in the chain. When the S^D is given for the first behavior in the chain, the others are elicited by the preceding behavior. (You can see how a trainer who performs show behaviors in a set, predictable order could inadvertently condition a chain).

At Theater of the Sea, we prefer not to use many chained behaviors. It can limit the amount of variability you have in a show. Also, criteria can be more difficult to maintain as the S^D, bridge, and reinforcement for each behavior cannot be isolated. It is a good idea to randomly bridge and reinforce the separate behaviors in the chain in order to maintain their criteria.

Sentencing involves requesting two or more behaviors simultaneously such as asking a dolphin to vocalize while doing an unwind (a.k.a. hula, dance, spin). At our facility we use a signal indicating to the animal that we are going to be requesting a sentenced behavior. When the animal sees the cue, they know to wait for more than one S^D.

When initially training the concept of sentencing, we use behaviors where the S^D for one behavior can be given while the other behavior is being performed. An example is conditioning an unwind/spit water sentence. While the animal is unwinding, we can easily give them the signal to spit water, which is to splash them. Once the animal comprehends doing two behaviors together, we introduce the sentence signal. With this cue, the animals quickly learn to wait for all the S^Ds to be given. Once the concept is learned, there are numerous options. We were able to train an inverted speed run to one dolphin in a single session by giving the sentence signal followed by the cues for the layback and speed run (a.k.a. fast swim). With sentencing, we always give the S^D for each behavior we want them to perform and then bridge and reinforce the behaviors together as a combination.
Training Staff
Theater of the Sea

ANSWER 3: There are actually two questions to be answered: one, is how to go about training a chained behavior and two, how to prevent the animal from confusing cues. I would like to start out by saying, training a chain of behaviors is clearly communicating to the animal how to emit a predictable sequence of behaviors. It can be rewarding for both the trainer and animal to combine a number of already known behaviors into a chain of behaviors. (That's if proper steps are taken to maintain clear understanding by the animal of what is being asked and the correct response is being reinforced.) In a true chain of behaviors, the completion of one behavior is the S^D (discriminative stimulus) to begin the next behavior and so on until the chain is completed. There are many methods of training any behavior and the same goes with training a chain. One of which is to start out with the final behavior and add the preceding behaviors in perspective order. To help establish stimulus control over the chain of behaviors, a distinctive S^D can be used to begin the chain. Props and other stimuli can be used to guide the animal from one behavior to the next, then faded as the learning progresses. As the behaviors are being reinforced as a chain, there is a good chance you will see interference with some of the individual behaviors. Therefore, throughout the training, the behaviors comprising the chain should be maintained on an individual basis. The accomplishment of chaining behaviors in one more way of adding variety to life.

To give an example, I would like to set up a hypothetical chain of behaviors. Remember; there are many ways to train a behavior. So kids, don't try this at home unless you're a professional. You give an S^D to a bottlenose dolphin and it emits a back flip, followed by a sighting bow, finishing with a human hurdle. When combining these individual behaviors, it is imperative that the dolphin clearly understands what you are asking, for the safety of both animal and trainer in the water.

To start training, we will choose a clap of the hands in front of the body as the S^D to begin the chain of behaviors (which will be referred to as "C" S^D). Assuming the dolphin knows all of the behaviors, the first approximation will begin with the sighting bow followed by the human hurdle. Light taps will be used at the surface of the water to help maintain the positions of the aerials during the training process. One trainer at poolside (referred to as T1) will control the session. First the "C" S^D is presented, followed by the S^D for the sighting bow. When the dolphin takes off, a light tap is used for the position of the bow. After the sighting bow is emitted, the trainer in the water gives a light tap for the human hurdle. After the human hurdle is completed, T1 uses a call back to have the dolphin return to poolside for reinforcement. Several rehearsals should be performed, making sure the dolphin does not initiate the behavior until "C" S^D and sighting bow S^D are given.

The next approximation would be adding the back flip before the sighting bow. With safety in mind, this can be done without the trainer in the water. The "C" S^D is given followed by the back flip S^D. When the dolphin takes off, a light tap is used for the position of the back flip. After the back flip is emitted, a target pole can be used to tap at the sighting bow position, leaving the target slightly under the surface so it can be used to guide the dolphin through the bow. If the dolphin emits the behavior correctly, a bridge will be used to reinforce the transition from the back flip to the sighting bow. After several successive approximations with this scenario, the target can be faded to a light tap for the sighting bow. Once the dolphin is consistent with this step, the trainer can begin to re-enter the water in a safe position to make sure the dolphin maintains accurate runs for the back flip and sighting bow. When absolutely sure runs are consistent, the trainer is positioned for the human hurdle. The "C" S^D is given followed by the back flip S^D. When the dolphin takes off, a light tap is used for the back flip position. When the back flip is emitted correctly, a light tap is used for the sighting bow. When the sighting bow is emitted correctly, the trainer in the water gives a light tap for the human hurdle. After the human hurdle is emitted correctly, T1 then uses a call back to reinforce the completion of the chain. (VERY IMPORTANT!!!! The dolphin must have a very strong history with a call back, so at any time the run is not correct, T1 can call the animal back to avoid any possible accidents! If this does occur, do not continue training with person in water at that time. Take a few steps back to make sure the dolphin is consistent with the runs for the aerials). If it is successful, continue rehearsal with this step until you can fade out the light taps – at which point the completion of one behavior is the S^D to go into the next behavior.

While building a strong reinforcement history with the chain, there may be some interference with the back flip as an individual behavior. Steps can be taken to avoid the interference by using a call back after the back flip when giving just the back flip S^D. Also using the "C" S^D just before back flip S^D, when asking for the chain behavior, along with the environmental stimulus of a person being in the water, will help discriminate between the two.

Once the chain is trained, it should be maintained by intermittently bridging various parts of the chain. One can also add to the chain by putting another behavior in front of the back flip using similar techniques, each behavior becoming strong links within the chain. Just remember that a chain is only as strong as its weakest link.

Michael Osborn
Sea Life Park Hawaii

Trainer's Forum

VOL 9, NO 4, 1984. Creating a behavioral chain is a complex task. Answer 4 gives a good textbook definition of a chain in the first paragraph. Because of the complexity of working with chains, correcting a problem in the middle can be a challenge. However, if trained carefully from the start, safeguards can be trained into the chain to make the behaviors easy to maintain. As you read the responses, please note that a chain means different things to different trainers. You may also notice the use of the terms "delta," "recall," and "no" used similarly in different answers (these terms were discussed in more detail earlier in this chapter). The use of variable reinforcement schedules is also mentioned in several responses. The complex nature of a behavior chain puts many operant principles to work at the same time.

Fixing a Problem Behavior in the Middle of a Chain

QUESTION: How do you let an animal know, in a chain behavior, what part they did wrong in a chain?

ANSWER 1: The way we let a sea lion know which part of a chain behavior was done incorrectly is by actually stopping the animal in the chain. Most behaviors in the Sea Lion Show are done on land, so it's not difficult to interrupt the sea lion in the chain. After stopping the animal we have him repeat the improperly performed portion of the chain behavior and finally complete the chain. If the problem portion of the chain is done correctly, the animal is reinforced. Other times, especially in a show situation, we may let the animal complete the chain improperly, uninterrupted, and with little or no reinforcement. After the show, we work the step of the chain that gave the animal trouble or we have the sea lion repeat the whole chain. When the problem portion is done correctly, we bridge, reinforce and finally have the animal complete the rest of the chain behavior.

With the dolphins, we sometimes use and instrument called a "recall." A recall is just the tap of a metal pipe. When the dolphin hears this tap he stops whatever he's doing (chain behavior) and returns to the trainer. When the dolphin returns, he is either reinforced and/or repeats the behavior (chain) or goes on with the show. At a later time, in a training session, we work the chain behavior or if possible the portion of the chain that was done incorrectly. When the problem step is done correctly, we bridge and/or recall and reinforce.
Bill Winhall
Marineland of the Pacific

ANSWER 2: By immediately interrupting the chain the moment the isolated undesirable behavior occurs. It is important that the precise moment is arrested by some form of "delta" in order to communicate to the animal which part was incorrect. If necessary, break up the chain to rework the particular behavior. Once it is strong, reinsert into the chain. (Added suggestion: if you haven't already been randomly reinforcing the components of the chain, once the animal is confident again, do so.)
Dierdre Ballou
San Diego Zoo

ANSWER 3: I try to stop the chain at the point the animal makes the mistake. Then I can try to get an acceptable behavior and continue the chain. This might be easier for me with sea lions that work on a stage with a moat. For the next few attempts I can stay close to the animal and "walk it" through the chain. If there is an error I can catch it quickly.
Jim Alexander
St. Louis Zoo

ANSWER 4: A chain is said to exist when one performance produces the conditions which make the next one possible. The stimulus linking the two performances serves both, as a conditioned reinforcer maintaining the topography and frequency of the first performance and acts as a stimulus for the second.

Whenever we address the problem of an animal emitting an incorrect behavior within a chain, we must first determine the cause of the problem. If the animal is just learning the chain, it is essential that each individual behavior be emitted under stimulus control. At this point, you can begin to chain the behaviors that have been selected for the sequence. In the early stages, if an animal is emitting incorrect behavior within the chain, it then becomes necessary to stop the sequence at that point. If you allow the animal to continue then, by definition, you are bridging the incorrect behavior and it will increase in frequency.

On the other hand, if an animal has been emitting a chain of behaviors for a considerable period of time and then begins to emit incorrect behaviors within the chain, another approach might be warranted. Keep in mind that if one particular behavior slowly starts to deteriorate it most likely stems from the fact that it has been "bridged" by the above definition and has therefore been conditioned as being correct. If all of a sudden incorrect behavior shows up in a chain, ignore it and do not reinforce the sequence at all. As any change in the environment is reinforcing to an animal, do not attempt to stop him as it will draw attention to the incorrect behavior and inadvertently reinforce it, resulting in its increased frequency.

It is essential in all chained sequences to periodically interrupt the chain and reinforce a particular behavior with something other than the following behavior in the chain. This keeps all the individual behaviors within the chain strong and hopefully a problem can be avoided.

Dave Force and Randy White
Sea World of Florida

ANSWER 5: If you are having trouble with one part of a chain, one alternative is to bridge each of the other parts as the animal is doing them, and when he reaches the trouble spot, hit a delta or a call-back and terminate the response. You can then isolate that one part and work on it separately. It may be helpful then to add the preceding part and the following part to the problem spot in a progression, rather than immediately going back to the entire chain response. This puts the problem spot into a larger context while continuing to strengthen it.

Gail Laule
Marineland of the Pacific

ANSWER 6: (1) Use call-back at that specific spot of error, (2) during training set start chain at that particular point of error (to bring focus to that spot) and then heavily reward for correct response, and (3) bring each individual part of chain up to the point of error and then give a loud, verbal "NO" at the specific spot of error.

Tish Flynn
Marineland of the Pacific

ANSWER 7: Consider a chain that involves a number of bows (or any aerial, but just one kind of aerial). The main points of concern tend to be the quality of each jump, the direction the animal faces, where the jump occurs, the height, and the time interval between jumps. Usually all these factors and any I have overlooked, can be controlled in each behavior of the chain by varying which jump is bridged and immediately followed by some form of reinforcement. That way each part of the chain is intermittently strengthened and improved since the bridge is more than a mere secondary reinforcer. It serves as a blatant reminder of what the desired behavior is, what to strive for, and helps to eliminate various undesirable aspects of behavior. Varying which jump is bridged allows you to troubleshoot by providing opportunities to correct slight weaknesses and wayward tendencies without having to break the chain down or to work on any part separately.

Having the freedom to use a recall at the point of weakness is most helpful if you haven't effectively used an intermittent reinforcement schedule within the chain, or if you chose not to for some reason. Besides the standard audio tone recall and tapping (or banging) of a metal rod, it is simple and effective to condition the animals to respond to visual recalls such as suddenly squatting if you normally stand when all is well, extending a target, terminating the S^D if you use a continuous signal, or reaching for or lifting the fish bucket as the animal performs the undesired behavior. At this point if would be helpful to work on that particular behavior in the part of the pool that it would be performed during the chain. Your reinforcement schedule is very important here, as it is easy to be manipulated into breaking the chain regularly and rebuilding behaviors continually out of the context of the chain. This potential problem can be avoided by varying which behavior is bridged and the length of the chain, which allows you to have control over each part of the chain. It would also be helpful to vary the starting location of the chain if possible.

When the chain behavior involves various behaviors and/or props such as hoops, hurdles, balls, platforms, people, and other animals, it is easy to drop a problem behavior out of the chain for a while, or to rearrange the sequence of the behaviors in the chain. You might find that some behaviors are not really problems if they are performed in the beginning of the chain while others are more reliable at the end. By varying which behavior ends the chain you can intermittently directly reinforce every behavior in the chain without decreasing the number of behaviors in the chain, if you are not comfortable varying the length of the chain.

In a chain where a person is the S^D or is giving a different signal for each behavior of the chain and is in close proximity to the animal, as in a water ballet, behaviors can easily and smoothly be repeated and corrected without the use of a recall or disrupting the chain. This proximity also enables the trainer to use verbal and tactile reinforcers regularly with each part of the chain, continually giving the animal feedback.

Kathy Krieger

VOL 23, NO 3, 1998. Combination behaviors can be useful in many training situations. The concept can be critical in training some cognition projects, it can be a way of providing variety to the animals, and finally it can be a way of creating new behaviors. Several facilities combine behaviors for a variety of reasons, and the techniques for training this particular task can be just as varied as the uses. The methods used to train this task at the Dolphin Research Center are described in detail in this article.

Training Combination Behaviors with Bottlenose Dolphins

by Barbara Losch
Dolphin Research Center

Training dolphins – it's the career of many people's dreams! People who are privileged enough to have a career working with marine mammals take the responsibility seriously. Trainers strive to keep the animals in their charge physically and mentally stimulated. One of the most difficult aspects of this responsibility is providing mental challenges. Almost everyone loves an occasional challenge and marine mammals are no different. They constantly amaze us with their eagerness and ability to learn new things and to solve problems. At Dolphin Research Center (DRC), we've started experimenting with training that incorporated mental and physical stimulation for both the trainer and the trainee, in this case the dolphins.

Josephine (Jo), a dolphin who joined DRC's family for retirement purposes, actually gave us the idea of combing behaviors. Jo previously worked in research projects with Dr. Ken Norris at Long Marine Lab in Santa Cruz, California. One of her trainers was Michelle Jefferies who shared with us how Jo loved to be "in charge" and had a goofy sense of humor once you got to know her. We had decided to let Jo do basically whatever she wanted (that retirement mindset we humans have). We would do medical and behavioral work with her, but pretty much had no set training plans. Jo decided she wanted no part of this boring protocol and started to train herself. Her first invention, a spit-dive, was what started DRC staff down the path of combining behaviors. Jo took two behaviors she already knew and combined them. She created a high flying dive with a spit at the height of the dive, adding a wonderful twist to two well-known behaviors. The training staff decided to run with the idea of combining behaviors.

We came up with two methods of training combination behaviors. The first idea was to teach the dolphins a "combine" signal. This brand new signal would eventually mean combine known behaviors together. The second method was to combine, or chain, two signals together to see if the dolphins would then figure out how to put behaviors together. If we trained the combinations (combos) in the latter manner, we would not need to teach them the meaning of a new signal. We decided on the second method. As it turns out, the trainers got as much mental stimulation as the dolphins, figuring out how to combine two signals together. The following is an example of how we might combine signals to request a kiss-dance combination: The signal for two dolphins kissing is placing your hands in a fist and bringing them together so they touch. Our dance signal is rotating one hand in a counter clockwise motion. Putting the two together, the signal is now two hands and fists touching, keeping the hands together and rotating the hands in a counter clockwise motion.

THE TRAINING PROCESS

As with all training, when you introduce something new to an established behavior, you should relax your expectations of that behavior. This rule holds true when combining behaviors. The criteria when performing the known behaviors would not be as high during the training process. The training staff decided to start working on spit combinations. Spitting is a very visual behavior and a signal (a splash of the hand in the water) easily performed with other signals. We attempted to train other dolphins the spit-dive that Jo invented. This initially proved more difficult than anticipated. The dolphins would take off, dive in the middle of the pool and fail to see the trainers splashing wildly back at the dock. We then decided to switch to behaviors performed closer to the dock, giving the dolphins more obvious visual clues as to our expectations of them.

At DRC we train the dolphins to look up at the trainers with both eyes above the water. We call this behavior stationing. When the dolphins see a station signal, it translates to: "look at the trainer, a signal or cue is coming." Stationing helped with combining because the dolphins watch the trainers carefully to "translate" the combination of signals. We started with some slight chaining at first. Chaining is when the dolphins do one behavior immediately followed by another. Let's go through training a tummy up-spit to give you an idea of how the training takes place.

During the spit behavior, the dolphins put water in their mouth and squirt it back out. For the tummy up behavior, the dolphins roll over and lie belly button up. To combine the two behaviors, we show the dolphins the spit signal, wait until the dolphins have a great spit, bridge and reward them for it. Immediately after the reward we station and show the spit signal again. As the dolphins start to spit, we immediately show the tummy up signal. Generally the dolphins roll over tummy up in the process stop spitting. The trainer gives them a hint by splashing on the surface to the water and bridging if the dolphins attempt to spit. A quick bridge at the moment the dolphins start to spit is the key to this portion of training. Some of the dolphins would lie on their backs, see us splashing and starting to put water in their mouth while turning upright again. We would quickly bridge that intake of water into their mouth. We repeated the above steps, delaying the bridge to see if the dolphins would stay tummy up. If they did turn upright, we would repeat the tummy up signal to encourage the end product of a tummy up-spit. With most of the dolphins, the idea of spitting while tummy up took all of about three attempts at the signal. A new twist on a behavior trained in one session. What fun for the dolphins and the trainers!

We kept it simple at first for the dolphins. We

worked on traveling tummy up-spit (the dolphins move away from the dock spitting with tummy up), spit dance (where the dolphins are sitting upright spinning around and spitting), spit-strut (the dolphins hold their heads up and move forward, spitting at the same time), and spit-razz (the dolphins make a raspberry sound and spit at the same time). Then it was time to try training behaviors performed with higher energy further away from the dock. We thought the idea of combining was now an experience we could expand on. The dolphins seemed to "get it."

We decided our first high energy behavior was going to be the spit-dive Jo invented. The training process was similar to the training of tummy up-spit. We stationed the dolphins, showed the spit signal, when the dolphins spit we bridged. We immediately stationed and showed the spit signal again. When the dolphins spit we showed the dive signal. Just like the training of the tummy-spit, the dolphins dove and forgot about the spitting process. Trainers would be splashing wildly from the dock and the dolphins were oblivious to this action. We noticed if the dolphins stopped diving (terminated the behavior) and returned to the dock as the trainer was continuing their splashing they would then start spitting again. The trainer immediately bridged for the spitting action. This may sound like unusual training however, due to the previous training experience of combining tummy and spit, we felt this helped the dolphins make the connection that the two signals went together. The dolphins tended to come back to dockquickly, especially when they notices their trainer splashing crazily. When they did the spitting action, they would tend to come up out of the water with enthusiasm and that movement was what we wanted to catch. We also started to bridge the dolphins as they were taking off for their dives. We define the take-off as the moment the dolphins leave the dock to do a behavior. The dolphins actually do a small porpoise as they are leaving the dock. At times, the dolphins would be in the middle of the spit as we were giving the dive signal. If we executed the dive signal at the right time, the dolphins would do a mini take-off and accidentally spit. A quick bridge would capture that moment. The dolphins got so excited they started watching their trainers closely and we were soon able to catch their eyes while they were diving. They still had problems spitting during the dives. They would stop diving and come back, do a high body out of the water with a spit. We had them thinking and watching. In a few sessions, it all fell into place for them. The practice of being rewarded for spitting on the take-offs and at times being rewarded for spitting at the end of the dives paid off. We had high flying spit-dives. Our signal for the spit-dive was a large clockwise circle of the right hand, (our dive signal) paired with the splashing spit signal at the bottom of the circle. After the dolphins were comfortable with the spit-dives, it was easy to then pair the spit with other high energy behaviors. The training time for other high energy behaviors was minimal, some dolphins learned in one session. We now have dolphins that do back dive-spits, spiral-spits, and flip-spits to name a few. There seemed no end to these spit combinations.

On to something new! Our next combinations were twisting combos. When doing the twist, our dolphins move their head from side to side. We again started simple. We worked on tummy up twist, twist-strut, and twist-dance. Success!! The dolphins learned these twisting combinations very quickly. We expected the same quick training success to occur with the high energy behaviors. The training was not as easy as we anticipated. The dolphins, once they left the dock, would revert back to the spitting combinations. One dolphin has such a strong preference for spitting, he would actually begin with the twist take-off and as soon as he passed the dock he would stop twisting and start spitting. We had to move more slowly with the high energy twist behaviors. During these sessions, we decided to exclude any spit behaviors. We hoped if we did not ask them to spit in any part of the training session, they would not add to the twist combos. We started slowly, working mostly on getting the dolphins to twist on the take-off for a few sessions. We then went to not bridging the take-off, waiting to see what happened when they went out to do a dive. Some of the dolphins added a spit, some dove, and some just quickly returned to the dock. In all these instances, the trainers reacted in the same way; they showed the dolphins the twist signal while they were returning to the dock and bridged if they started twisting. We progressed to alternating our bridges. Sometimes we would bridge the twisting take-offs and sometimes we would bridge the dolphins twisting after they had been diving. It is unclear if alternating was the best method, but it worked for training twist and spit combinations.

GROUP COMBINATIONS

Group behaviors are fun and exciting to watch. These incredible behaviors always captivate and awe our visitors. How could we incorporate combination behaviors involving two or more dolphins? Yes, they can all go out on a spit-dive together, but what if we were to incorporate the dolphins doing combinations where they had to have some physical contact during the behavior? At Cedar Point in Sandusky, Ohio, I worked for three summers with trainers Sheryl Young and Craig Vadja. They trained their dolphins (Striker, Cocoa, Misty, and Breeze) to do a kiss behavior. The dolphin would touch their rostrums together, simulating a kiss. Two of the dolphins also did a kissing spinning behavior where their rostrums would remain in contact and they would spin around at the same time. Here was a combination behavior where the dolphins maintained contact with each other. We decided this was going to be our next avenue with the combination game. It was fairly easy to teach two dolphins to kiss-strut, kissing-spin, and kiss-tummy up. Surprisingly enough, it was also very simple to teach kiss-speed and kiss-tummy up speeds. The dolphins would race around the pool trying to keep their rostrums together. What a lot of fun to watch! We were able to accomplish training a new repertoire of unique behaviors by applying the techniques described earlier. Pairing all the signals together was challenging at times but the trainers become adept at performing some very unique and complicated hand motions.

DRC's trainer's choice for favorite combination behavior has to be the kissing-flying forward tail walk. Not only is it difficult to say, but for this behavior the dolphins need cooperation from each other to complete it. The flying forward tail walk looks like this: the dolphins take off and come up in a tail walk, the flukes stay under water while the rest of the body is up out of the water. The dolphins maintain the tailwalk briefly, dive out of it and come back up again in the tailwalk position. They repeat this skipping action, moving very quickly around the lagoon. Picture, if you would, two dolphins flying around the lagoon in this manner and kissing at the height of each tailwalk. You now have an inkling of kissing-flying forward tailwalk looks like. The precision is amazing and the timing impeccable.

Training for the kissing-flying forward tailwalk, as you might expect, took a bit longer. We followed the successful training formula we had developed earlier, training the low energy duet kiss-combinations. Quick bridging was again the key to obtaining this behavior. The trainer would give the kiss signal. Once the dolphins had their rostrums together, the trainer would give the flying forward tailwalk signal. The two signals were somewhat similar and we believe this helped with the behavior. The kiss, as stated above, has the hands in fists meeting together, the flying forward tailwalk signal has the hands together and then quickly moved to the right with a turn of the body. Once the dolphins saw the kiss signal and were kissing, the trainer moved their hands, turned their body and generally yelled "Go!Go!Go!." At DRC we often encourage our dolphins with vocals.

You could see the dolphins thinking about this behavior. They would try and keep their rostrums together and we would reward those attempts. The logistics of keeping their rostrums together was something they had to figure out. We kept the training short and sweet, bridging for take-offs that had rostrums touching. Sometimes the trainer would quickly give the kiss signal as they came back up together after the take-off. The trainer would even travel the length of the dock, running with the dolphins to see if they would initiate the behavior again. After a few weeks the dolphins were kissing together and flying across the pool. We were also successful teaching kiss-dives, kiss-back dives and we are working on kiss-spirals. We have not yet tried training a kiss-flip but it sure would be interesting.

Well, that is how DRC trains combination behaviors. We hope other facilities give it a try and report back to us on their fun experiences. Be prepared for dolphins adding their combinations when you least expect it. That may be the most rewarding part of teaching combos. The dolphins enjoy performing them so much, they want to do them all the time. It is our philosophy that training for mental stimulation should, above all else, be fun for the dolphins. DRC's dolphins give every indication that we are achieving that goal!

Trainer's Forum

VOL 20, NO 2, 1995. Interestingly, this is not a topic discussed in many books on training, yet it is often debated in marine mammal circles. At the 1994 IMATA Conference in Tacoma, Washington at least 45 minutes was spent on this issue. This column limited the responses to four, two facilities that use an end of session signal and two that don't. There are certainly good points discussed in each answer. The final decision will usually depend on the circumstances and needs of a particular program.

Using an End of Session Signal: Yes or No?

QUESTION: Do you use an end-of-session signal? What are the benefits and drawbacks of using such a signal?

ANSWER 1: As with most training situations, the answer to this question may vary among facilities, staffs, and animals. Here at Oceana, we do not use an "official" end-of-session signal. However, we do purposely indicate to the animals (in a variety of ways) that the session or show is concluded. For example, with our dolphins, we take the bucket and leave the stage. This creates a marked difference for the animals between concluding a positive training experience and temporarily leaving for a timeout due to less desirable behavior.

The drawback of using an end-of-session signal certainly becomes more apparent when working with an animal that doesn't want the session to end, and especially if that animal has the ability to endanger the trainer. For example, with our sea lions, we like to make sure that we have food or secondary reinforcers left over for the animals once they are safely back in their enclosure. Again, the desired result is a session concluded in a positive manner for both trainer and animal.

Craig Vajda
Oceana

ANSWER 2: Although there are discrepancies as to the necessity of an end-of-session signal, we at Oceans of Fun have considerable success using such a signal.

We began using an end-of-session signal about five years ago to cue the animals that the primary reinforcer was being removed. We felt this was necessary for a couple of different reasons. The first reason dealt with our method of primary reinforcement, and the second reason dealt with our commitment to interact with the public after the presentations. During the course of public presentations, animals are intermittently reinforced at a variety of feed stations located throughout the theater. This method alleviates the need for carrying a bucket and allows the animal to focus entirely on the trainer. Because the animals are not reinforced with food at specific parts of the presentation, we feel that an end-of-session signal helps clarify (for the animals) when the session has ended. This is especially beneficial in avoiding aggression between animals when two or more are working together. After the presentations are completed, animals remain in the main pool while the public exits. This allows the public a coser look at the animals, and trainers stay around the pool area to field any questions from the visitors. An end-of-session signal indicates to the animals that although trainers are still in the pool area, the primary reinforcers have been removed. We do, however, use secondary reinforcers with positive results.

Training Staff
Oceans of Fun

ANSWER 3: At the John G. Shedd Aquarium, we do not use an end-of session S^D. This was a conscious decision that we made when we were first designing our training program. Several of us had come from facilities that regularly used a signal to indicate to our animals that the session was over. After reviewing the various problems encountered from time-to-time with an end-of-session S^D, we decided not to use one. Some facilities use an end-of-session S^D quite successfully, and in some research projects there is a need to indicate a session's completion. However, in general, we have found that avoiding the problems associated with an end-of-session signal is beneficial. Below, we have outlined the problems associated with an end-of-session S^D, and the benefits of not using one.

Problems: There are a number of problems that sometimes occur when an animal is given an end-of-session signal. Here are three very different potential problems:

AGGRESSION – When cetaceans are interacting in an aggressive manner (sexual or otherwise), a training session may temporarily interrupt the aggression. But when the session is over, an end-of-session signal could be perceived as an S^D to start being aggressive again. The aggressor will use it as a cue to begin chasing a sub-dominant animal. In addition, if the trainer is not careful, the sub-dominant animal may start associating the aggression as being cued by the trainer. This ultimately makes a session an undesirable activity for the subdominant animal.

RUSHING THE GATE – Pinnipeds, otters, and other land animals have often been known to rush at a gate when a trainer tries to leave. This has often been described as an attempt by the animal to prevent the trainer from leaving. This seems to be provoked by the animal being able to tell when the session is over. In many cases, a formal end-of-session S^D may not even be in use, simply leaving the enclosure is the signal. Either way, the effect is the same: an indication that the session is over has caused undesirable behavior in the animal. This problem is often corrected in one of several ways:
- changing the way a trainer exits the enclosure
- continuing to feed over or through the fence once the trainer has exited
- returning to the exhibit often, so that the animal is never certain when the session is actually over

In each case the solution stems from the avoidance of any signal (intentional or not) indicating an end of the session.

MISUSE – Perhaps one of the biggest problems with an end-of-session S^D is the ease with which it can be misused by a novice trainer. An end-of-session S^D can be misused in an emotional situation in which the trainer becomes frustrated with the lack of progress by an animal. At the height of frustration, an inexperienced trainer can be tempted to simply use an end-of-session S^D and walk away. The S^D becomes an indicator which precedes a time out and, thus, begins to take on negative connotations. Admittedly, any training concept has the potential for misuse, and that in itself should not condemn the end-of-session S^D. Certainly experienced trainers with an understanding of this negative potential can avoid its misuse. But if not carefully monitored, an end-of-session S^D in the hands of an inexperienced or overly emotional trainer could have very negative effects on an animal.

Benefits (of not using an end-of-session S^D):

VARIETY – One of the strongest reinforcers for our animals tends to be variety. Variety can take many forms, whether that be in the types of sessions, length of sessions, quantity and type of reinforcers, creative use of behaviors in a session, et cetera. Use of an end-of-session S^D puts a sudden end to the training session by indicating to the animals that you are done. Since we try to mix training sessions with play sessions, food reinforcers with tactile and other reinforcers, we don't want the animal to anticipate that a session is complete. We have found that animals may stay around to play, or that we may want to add something to the session at the last minute, and these options come more easily when there is no indicator formally ending the session. This type of creativity seems to hold an animal's attention longer and opens additional options to the trainer.

REDUCED PROBLEMS – Although we have witnessed many trainers using an end-of-session S^D effectively, we have chosen not to use an end-of-session signal to reduce many of the problems encountered when using one. The potential problems associated with an end-of session S^D seem to outweigh any positive effects of its use.

Conclusion: At the John G. Shedd Aquarium, we are strong advocates of not using an end-of-session signal . But we also believe that if something ain't broke....don't fix it! In other words, if someone is successfully using an end-of-session S^D, you may create more problems by attempting to discontinue its use. However, if you do use some indicator that your session is complete, and you've experienced any of the problems outlined above, you may want to consider whether the end-of-session S^D contributes to the problem. Finally, we seriously doubt that the use or non-use of such an S^D is the secret to a great training program, but it certainly makes for an interesting discussion. Happy training!

Ken Ramirez
John G. Shedd Aquarium

ANSWER 4: At all of the Sea World Parks, we do not use an end-of-session signal. Since our behavior program is based on variability and unpredictability, the application of a signal that is consistently paired with non-reinforcement as an end to a session is not necessary or useful for our program.

Having talked with many trainers from a myriad of institutions, I have heard and seen varying examples of both successes and failures using this technique. However, the application of an end-of-session signal has become quite confusing for most; therefore, it is helpful to define this technique as a learning element before we go further.

The common theory for the end-of-session signal is to communicate a break or stop in interaction by the trainer. This, it is suggested, lets the animal know that reinforcement will no longer be given and that the animal is "free" to do what it "wants." It can easily be argued that, in fact, "a stimulus consistently associated with the absence of reinforcement may become aversive" (Azrin & Holz, 1966) This signal or stimulus is commonly referred to as a "Stimulus Delta." Chance (1994) describes the two types of antecedent stimuli this way: "An S^D indicates that responding will be reinforced, while an S-delta indicates that responding will either not be reinforced or will be punished" (p. 194). Kazdin (1989) defines S-delta as "a stimulus whose presence has been associated with non-reinforcement" (p. 44). His glossary provides further clarification of S-delta as 'an antecedent event or stimulus that signal that a certain response will not be reinforced."

What does all of this mean? Simply put, when we use a signal that indicates that a session (and reinforcement) is over, we are applying an S-delta. This stimulus can become aversive, and can create behavior problems. Practically speaking, problems such as a sea lion blocking a trainer from leaving an enclosure, dolphins that keep you from exiting pools, animals that end sessions prematurely, social displacement, aggression, or resumption of a stereotypic pattern can all result when an end-of-session signal is used.

In some scenarios these problems never manifest, and in these cases, the end-of-session signal is, in fact, a cue to engage in other reinforcing activities. Therefore, the stimulus is really an S^D and signals more reinforcement.

It can be argued that all animals eventually recognize signals that precede the end-of-session, and if a predictable pattern develops they certainly can! We teach our folks to avoid this by being aware of their own behavior lest they encounter some of the potentially dangerous problems described above, but more importantly, we teach them to understand that interaction with the animals is a dynamic, ever-changing, and positive experience that occurs at unpredictable places and times during the day or night, even immediately <u>after</u> a session "appears" to be over. This, we feel, provides the safest and most interesting environment for trainers, guests, and animals.

Literature Cited

Azrin, N.H. and W.C. Holz (1966). Punishment. In W.K. Honig (ed.), Operant Behavior: Areas of Research and Application (pp. 380-447). Appleton-Century-Crofts: New York.

Chance, P. (1994). Learining and Behavior (3rd Ed.) (p. 194). Brooks/Cole: Pacific Grove, California.

Kazdin, A.E. (1989). Behavior Modification in Applied Settings (4th ed.) (p. 44). Brooks/Cole: Pacific Grove, California.

Ted Turner
Sea World of Ohio

Aggression 10

A Natural Phenomenon

When discussing aggression, we must keep in mind that it is part of an animal's natural repertoire. Aggression is a way of dealing with fear, nervousness, and dominance. Sexual activity, illness, or the desire to protect the young can prompt aggression. Understanding the causes of and reasons for aggression are the first steps toward working with it. Changes in the social dynamics of a group of animals can play a large part in creating aggressive scenarios. It is important that a trainer understand the importance of social groupings as discussed in chapter 7, "Social Animals." But aggression can develop for many different reasons. To deal with aggression, the trainer should recognize the various but distinct factors motivating aggression. To start, recognize that causes of aggression generally fall into one or a combination of three categories:

- **Reactive** – This describes a situation in which the animal has no choice but to defend itself. A reactive response does not have to be learned or to be part of the animal's normal disposition. All creatures will become aggressive if forced into it.
- **Innate** – Many animals may become aggressive due to pre-programmed, or innate, responses. Often, for example, hormonal changes will cause an animal to respond with aggressive behavior.
- **Learned** – Many types of aggression are learned. Trainers inadvertently shape some aggression, but animals also regularly learn aggression from each other.

Dealing with Aggression Operantly

Remain Calm

When trainers must deal with aggression in their animals, panic can cloud the thinking of a normally sharp trainer. The dangerous aspect of aggression can cause trainers to become emotional in their decision-making. When that occurs, sound operant training principles are often forgotten. So trainers should take the time to understand the principles that affect aggression before a problem rises up to challenge them. Many techniques can be effective in managing aggressive situations. Knowing them and keeping a cool head will get you started on the right track.

Operant Principles

Applying operant principles to solve aggression problems is not easy. However, the basic operant principles at work are quite simple:

- **Success is reinforcing** – If an animal succeeds in intimidating another animal, the aggressive animal is reinforced and will likely look for more opportunities to assert its dominance.
- **Failure is aversive** – An animal that is defeated in an encounter is more likely to avoid contact with the other animal in the future.

Once trainers understand these simple facts, it can help them assess an aggressive situation and recognize why it can escalate so quickly. Even if these facts are understood, however, solutions to aggression problems can be difficult to find. Included in this chapter are two articles on dealing with aggression. The first deals with aggression in marine mammals, *Aggression: Exploring the Causes and Possible Reduction Techniques* (Turner and Tompkins, 1990), on page 366; the second looks at *Aggression Mediation in Pet Dogs* (Sobie, 1995), on page 374.

Turner's Rules on Dealing with Aggression

I have always considered Ted Turner of Sea World to be one of the best sources of information on dealing with aggression. He has written extensively on the subject, and his combination of practical experience and technical knowledge make him a respected source on many training subjects. This chapter is short, not because aggression is not important, but because Ted and his colleague Chuck Tompkins on page 366 do such a fine job of exploring the topic in depth. Their article is well-researched and is an important source for all marine mammal trainers. It explores the causes of aggression (social, hormonal, shaped, and schedule-induced), describes a number of examples, lists some "rules" of aggression, and suggests methods for reducing aggression. Turner and Tompkins' five-point list on how to reduce aggression is worth knowing by heart:

1. **Understand the scenarios** – We must know and understand the kinds of situations in which aggression is most likely to occur.

2. **Recognize precursors** – Most animals give signals before becoming aggressive. It is important that we know our animals and understand those precursors. Turner and Tompkins give many examples of precursors in cetaceans and pinnipeds.

3. **Use DRO and DRI** – These forms of "alternate response" training are highly effective in dealing with aggression and other behavioral problems. These two concepts – Differential Reinforcement of Other behavior and Differential Reinforcement of Incompatible behavior – as well as other techniques for solving behavioral difficulties are discussed in detail in chapter 11, "Problem Solving."

4. **Stop before it starts** – If you are in the middle of a session, and can detect signs of aggression, end the session or change training plans. Don't attempt to work through it.

5. **Keep records** – As mentioned many times in this manual, good record keeping is a key to tracking trends and monitoring changes.

When to Intercede

Trainer Directed

Aggression takes on many forms but generally it falls into two categories: aggression toward people or aggression toward other animals. (Obviously, if aggression is threatening the safety of a trainer or guest, immediate intervention is critical). Applying the principles described in this chapter is often a complex process, which must be mastered. If aggression is directed at a trainer while working in an animal's environment, several approaches may succeed in solving the problem, as described in *Dealing with Cetacean Aggression Towards Swimmers* (T. Forum, 1994), on page 378, and in *Handling Escalating Dolphin Aggression: A Complex Problem* (T. Forum, 1998), on page 379. If there is no short-term solution, removing the trainer from the animal's environment may be necessary, at least temporarily. Protected-contact training was developed as a safety-first response to potentially aggressive animals. A discussion of protected contact training with elephants can be found in chapter 12, "Complex Training."

Animal Directed

When aggression is aimed at another member of the group, how, when, and if to intercede is not always as clear. As discussed in the article *Meeting Behavioral Objectives while Maintaining Healthy Social Behavior and Dominance* (Laule, 1991), on page 220 of chapter 7, social dominance is not only natural but also necessary.

However, you can't allow one animal to seriously injure another just because it is natural. Handling aggression of that seriousness can be managed in a number of ways, as described in *Dealing with Aggression in a Community Pool* (T. Forum, 1990), on page 386.

Putting Aggression on Cue

Jaw Pop Study

One of the techniques used to get rid of unwanted behavior is to put it on cue. Then, once the behavior is trained, never give the cue (DOG, pp. 124-131). This technique, although useful with some behaviors, was not developed with aggression in mind. At Shedd Aquarium we trained two of our Pacific white-sided to dolphins to "jaw pop" (a forceful clapping of the jaws) on cue. Although we were not trying to reduce aggression or jaw popping, that is precisely the effect that cued jaw popping had. Dr. Ted Cranford at the University of California, Santa Cruz was trying to characterize the jaw popping sound in cetaceans. He noticed that our white-sided dolphins often jaw popped at the two bottlenose dolphins that lived on the other side of a net gate. Cranford asked if we could train them to jaw pop on cue, while stationing on a target underwater (where the whole procedure could be recorded). Since jaw popping is considered a threatening or aggressive act, I felt that teaching our animals to jaw pop on cue would be like reinforcing two kids for arguing. I discussed the possible ramifications of this training with many colleagues, and we finally consented to try the experiment with two of our dolphins. The dolphins learned the behavior well, and we collected some valuable data. We were fascinated that the jaw popping, though not completely extinguished, did decrease considerably.

Protection Dogs

An example of deliberately shaping aggressive behavior can be found in the training of protection dogs. The concept of putting aggressive-like acts under stimulus control is not commonly used by most trainers. But it is a part of training protection dogs, as explained in *Positive Reinforcement Techniques for Training Controlled Aggression in Schutzhund and Protection Dogs* (Kirkpatrick-Sanchez, 1995), on page 388.

Aggression is a topic that every trainer must eventually face. It is, after all, a natural part of an animal's behavioral repertoire. Ted Turner and Chuck Tompkins of Sea World have explored the topic in quite a bit of detail. This article is a very good reference and provides one of the most comprehensive looks at dealing with marine mammal aggression in operant terms. The paper was first presented at the 1989 IMATA Conference held in Amsterdam.

Aggression: Exploring the Causes and Possible Reduction Techniques

by Ted N. Turner[1] and Chuck Tompkins[2]
[1]Sea World of Ohio, [2]Sea World of Florida

ABSTRACT

Understanding the pre-conditions of aggressive behavior in marine mammals is vital to the health and well being of our animals, trainers, and handlers. Certain precursive behaviors are frequently exhibited and certain behavioral contingencies may develop during the course of a training session that may lead to actual aggression. This paper will explore early warning "signs," common training errors, and scenarios leading to aggression, and reduction techniques utilizing operant conditioning, specifically DRI (Differential Reinforcement of Incompatible Behavior).

INTRODUCTION

It can most probably be stated that virtually everyone who has observed animals for any length of time has seen some type of agnostic or aggressive behavior. Aggression is quite common within the social dynamics of any group of animals, whether it be a subtle threat gesture or a more obvious attack response. That is not to say that its origin can be explained in simple terms, or that the aggressive act be analyzed or relegated strictly by the observable events. On the contrary, the complexities governing aggression are intricate and not easily identifiable, however, a significant amount of empirical evidence exists that suggests aggression can be predicted, controlled, and reduced But for all of the literature that does exist on the subject, little has focused on marine mammals.

The control of aggression is an important issue for us as animal behaviorists. Not only do our animals risk injury, but so do we, especially if we try to intervene. Quite often during intervention, aggression may actually be escalated. Intervention during an aggressive response usually takes place in the form of aversive or positive stimuli (whether we recognize it or not), and usually serves only to increase the frequency and or intensity of aggression, through accidental reinforcement. Often trainers will allow the animals to "work out their differences." However, mounting evidence suggests that aggression as a cathartic tool will only serve to escalate problems (Huntingford & Turner, 1988). In other words, the "get it out of their systems" philosophy will actually increase the frequency of fighting (Johnson, 1972). During this free for all, a social hierarchy may eventually develop and behavior should stabilize as a dominance-subordination relationship develops (Scott, 1975), but the risk of injury does not make this a recommended form of fight reduction. How, then, do we attempt to control or reduce aggression without exacerbating it? We must first understand the causes.

CAUSES OF AGGRESSION

As ethologist Konrad Lorenz stated "...aggression is part of an animal's normal behavioral repertoire enabling it to cope with its environment." A synopsis of the physiological process shows that the external stimuli travel to the brain via the peripheral nervous system where stimulation of the hypothalamus causes activation of the autonomic nervous system. This system then stimulates the endocrine glands which, in turn, produces adrenaline. The process prepares the body for aggression or escape (activation syndrome) and at this point certain observable behaviors become evident. A careful observer can recognize these precursors as "preemptory" aggressive behaviors and take steps to avoid the inevitable outcome. Marine mammal species have their own precursive behaviors, many of which we will identify in a later section. For now, (if I may oversimplify) let us just say that the causes of aggression are influenced by physiology and include hormonal factors, endocrine involvement, and biochemical fluctuations. From this point on, we will focus on the external factors that dictate aggressive behavior.

SOCIAL AGGRESSION

Much of what is learned by an animal is governed by the social group. As the organism develops, punishers and reinforcers derived from the group or environment shape what is learned and, subsequently, exhibited by the animal. Experimenters have found that many learned, social aggressive responses come from three main sources: the mother, competition from littermates, and "play" with prey (Wolgen, 1982). From this learning situation, a more involved repertoire of predatory behaviors develop and are rehearsed. Film footage of killer whales supports this theory in relation to marine mammals. Often we see the adults incapacitate prey and allow juveniles the opportunity to mimic and rehearse aggressive and predatory responses. Much of this behavior is credited to observational learning.

Albert Bandura, the social psychologist, was highly publicized in his theory that aggression can be learned or influenced by watching others. Much of what we see in our training situations support this. An aggressive environment provides the opportunity for animals to learn and rehearse aggressive behaviors, thereby increasing the likelihood of aggression. We see the application of this process in the social dynamics of bottlenose dolphins. Johnson and Norris (1986) suggest in their observations that the social dynamics of dolphins consists of a dominance hierarchy based on threat behavior whereby an alpha male usually dictates social status and breeding access. This dominant animal usually controls the group by initially aggressing towards these members that have not yet learned some of the social nuances. Eventually, through punishing consequences (instrumental learning) the aggression behavior fades into an aggression precursor (S^D) - a head nod, fluke slap, or other subtle threat display, and becomes the only necessary signalment needed to control the group. This learning process eventually stabilizes (social learning) until only periodic fighting takes place. If, however, a new member is added or subtracted, the social dynamics change, thus increasing the frequency of threat displays and fighting, until the

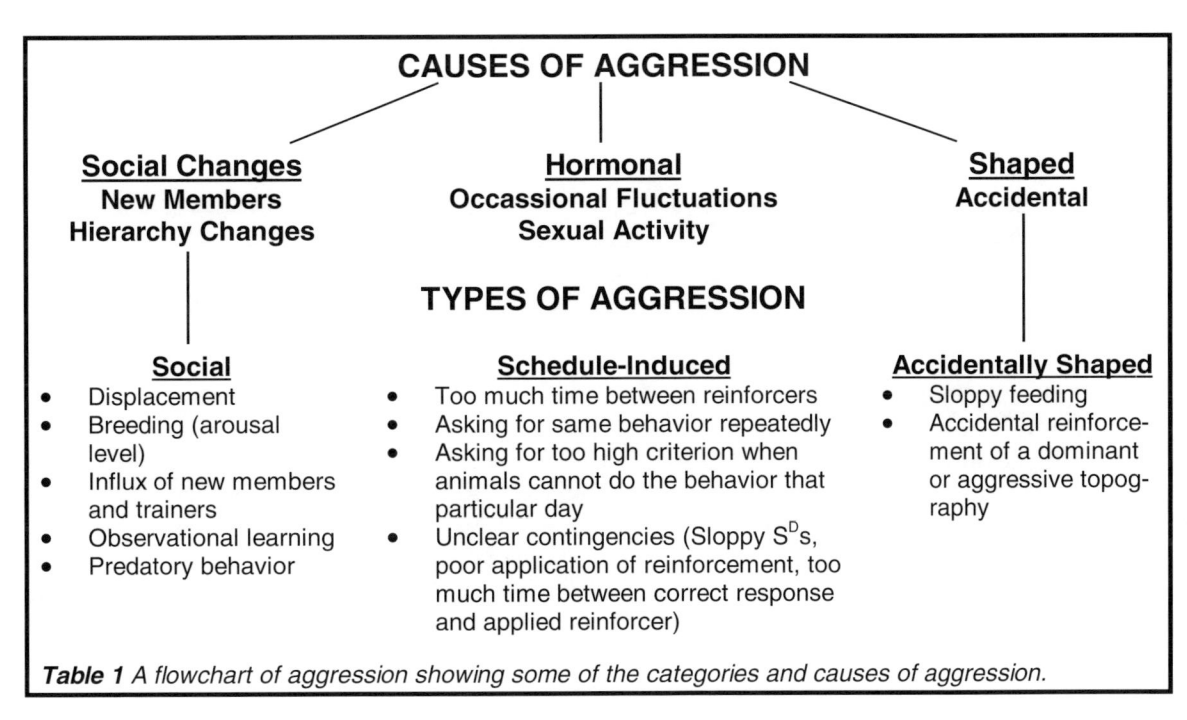

CAUSES OF AGGRESSION

Social Changes	**Hormonal**	**Shaped**
New Members	Occassional Fluctuations	Accidental
Hierarchy Changes	Sexual Activity	

TYPES OF AGGRESSION

Social	**Schedule-Induced**	**Accidentally Shaped**
• Displacement	• Too much time between reinforcers	• Sloppy feeding
• Breeding (arousal level)	• Asking for same behavior repeatedly	• Accidental reinforcement of a dominant or aggressive topography
• Influx of new members and trainers	• Asking for too high criterion when animals cannot do the behavior that particular day	
• Observational learning	• Unclear contingencies (Sloppy S^Ds, poor application of reinforcement, too much time between correct response and applied reinforcer)	
• Predatory behavior		

Table 1 A flowchart of aggression showing some of the categories and causes of aggression.

new member finds his subservient niche or the dominant animal is replaced (Goodall, 1986). Obviously, many other factors influence the evolution of social aggression, however, most social fighting, threat gestures, and predatory behaviors are shaped and learned through the social environment. Much of what then manifests in a training situation has its roots in the observational learning affect or vicarious processes (Kazdin, 1984) of the social group.

Let us now take a look at a training scenario that may further clarify an example of a type of social aggression.

A group of sea lions have recently been transported to your facility from two zoos. Initially, all is quiet and the animals seem highly compatible. Within three days, fighting begins to occur with increasing frequency. Eventually, fighting decreases and the area becomes stable with only a few, periodic outbreaks of aggression.

This is a normal course of events and is usually brought about by the following reasons:

1. Establishing alpha position
2. Establishing prime territory
3. Acquisition of sleeping space
4. Acquisition of breeding rights
5. Acquisition of food, and as training progresses
6. Acquisition of attention (reinforcement from trainers)

Now we take this a step further, and we find that two of these sea lions have started doing presentations in the show arena.

As the two sea lions perform, the dominant animal begins to displace the sub-dominant animal by barking and moving toward the other animal. The sub-dominant animal runs off; the dominant animal remains and continues with the presentation.

In the analysis, we find that the dominant animal is positively reinforced by being allowed to continue, and negatively reinforced by the removal of the sub-dominant animal. At the same time, the sub-dominant animal is negatively reinforced by escaping from the possible aggression. As we know, reinforcement, by definition (whether positive reinforcement or negative reinforcement) will serve to increase the behavior which preceded it. Consequently, the same thing happens the next show.

This next scenario represents a combination of social hierarchy and accidental reinforcement in the shaping of displacement and, ultimately, overt aggression.

A trainer begins to feed a young dolphin while, at the same time feeding an adult dolphin. As the trainer feeds the young animal, an occasional fish misses and lands in the water. The adult quickly turns his head and eats the fish. Over the next few days the adult begins to grab the younger dolphin's food and starts to snap at the younger animal. By the next week the adult is chasing the youngster away and quickly turning back towards the trainer, he is ready for his next meal.

If reinforcement is delivered at this point it might be advisable to shoot the trainer, although another alternative could be substituted. Both of these scenarios are examples of social aggression with accidental reinforcement adding to the problem. By taking these precautions both situations could have been avoided:

1. Look for warning signs (precursors)
2. Divert attention (redirect energy)
3. Reinforce any behavior other than an aggressive one (D.R.O. & D.R.I.)
4. Feed more carefully

These will be explained at length in a later section.

SCHEDULE-INDUCED AGGRESSION

During the use of partial reinforcement schedules, including FR/FI and VR/VI, interim behavior referred to as schedule induced behavior can develop (Houston, 1986). This can also manifest itself into aggression and is known as schedule induced aggression (Staddon, 1977). Schedule-induced aggression can be seen as a build-up of frustration caused by the use of a partial reinforcement schedule. The problem is then compounded when, during the presence of this conditioned emotional frustration, reinforcement occurs. The animal quickly learns that "being frustrated" is part of the contingency for reinforcement (Houston, 1986). Accidental shaping of aggression begins once again. A clearer understanding of schedule-induced aggression can be seen in the following scenario:

> A false killer whale is asked for a bow by giving a hand signal. The response is incorrect and no reinforcement is delivered. The signal is given again, and again an incorrect response is exhibited. The S^D is given a third time and immediately the animal begins to swim off, vocalizing loudly.

Another example might proceed as follows:

> Two killer whales are being asked for a pec wave. One does it the other does not. The correct whale receives the reinforcement. The other animal does not. The same two are asked for a squirt. Again, the first whale responds correctly, the other does not. The squirt S^D is repeated and this time the second whale chases the first whale then ignores the trainer.

In the preceding scenarios, two types of schedule-induced behavior are observed, frustration/avoidance and displaced aggression/avoidance. As you can see, many principles are at work controlling subsequent responses, and learning, for the good or bad, is still taking place. The first example might be handled by "shifting gears" and utilizing a decrease procedure known as DRO (Differential Reinforcement of Other Behavior) (Kazdin, 1984). In this particular situation, the false killer whale may be performing a "vocal" response only, under the control of the "bow" S^D. The "vocal" may be also performed under a number of S^Ds, giving the impression that the animal is mentally "stuck." Continuing to give the animal S^Ds with no reinforcement and assuming that he is "playing games" is a mistake that can lead to aggression or, at the very least, a negative learning history. DRO is "the delivery of a reinforcer after any response except the target ("vocal") response" (Kazdin,1984). This procedure will decrease the "vocal" and increase another response. In human behavior modification programs, DRO is used very effectively in eliminating hitting by children, (through non-reinforcement) and increases cooperative behaviors by reinforcing any cooperative response. Once again, DRO provides reinforcement for not engaging in a behavior. This behavior can be used when a group of dolphins, known to be aggressive with one another, are seen not engaging in aggressive activity. Instead they are resting, swimming, or exploring their facility. These behaviors should be reinforced periodically (and more often, initially) to help in controlling social aggression. Our next example shows one killer whale exhibiting schedule-induced aggression towards a sub-dominant. Here we see displaced aggression brought upon by a schedule-induced aggression scenario. In this example, it is advisable to once again "shift gears" and move on to a different behavior. If the pattern continues for the next S^D, it is advisable to terminate the session by calmly walking away for a few minutes. "Working through" the situation often does not work and allowing the chance for one animal to injure another is not worth the benefits of obtaining a desired response at this point.

DRI

One of the most effective ways of controlling aggression is through the use of DRI (Differential Reinforcement of Incompatible Behavior) (Kazdin, 1984). This is a very proactive method of address-

---

"RULES" OF AGGRESSION

1. Animals that have the opoportunity to aggress will do so more often (Johnson, 1972).

2. Use of punishment or aversive control will cause aggression (Kazdin, 1984).

3. Aggression can be shaped by accidental reinforcement [also deliberately, example: attack dogs] (Skinner, 1963).

4. Animals <u>may</u> initially respond more favorably to a consistent environment (condition radical changes slowly and positively).

5. An animal that is food deprived will aggress more readily (Staddon, 1977).

6. Most all animals have some degree of aggressive repetoire (Konrad Lorenz).

Table 2 Universal "rules" of aggression. These rules will usually apply across all species.

ing aggressive behaviors. DRI reinforces behaviors that directly compete with aggressive behaviors. The effect is to increase the frequency of the incompatible behavior (e.g. attention or control position) and to decrease the frequency of the desired response (e.g. biting or snapping). For example:

A sea lion begins to bark and attempts to displace another. Instead of letting the animals fight, the trainer asks the animal to lie down on his stomach. The animal does so, is rewarded, and the show continues without incident.

Ideally, the trainer may have an inclination that this may occur and may recognize the behavioral nuances leading up to the barking. If an incompatible behavior S^D is given at this point, there is a higher likelihood of averting aggression. In other words, the early recognition and application of DRI is the most effective means of controlling aggression. Once the animals begin the process of aggression; the more difficult it is to divert their attention. The best offense is early recognition. DRI is related closely to Alternate Response Training (Kazdin, 1984).

WARNING SIGNS

As mentioned above, understanding what takes place just prior to aggression, and taking action at this point, is where injuries can be prevented. The following is a list of aggressive precursors that may indicate impending aggression. Animals, like people, usually give plenty of warning signs before they become violent. These precursors include:

CETACEANS
1. Head bobbing
2. Unusual vocalizations
3. Fluke or pec slapping
4. Short/rapid explosive breaths
5. Mouth open
6. Jaw popping
7. Ignoring signals
8. Unsolicited squirting
9. Deliberate, slow movement (predatory topography)
10. Spitting food
11. "Exploratory" mouthing
12. Avoidance
13. Blocking of other animals
14. Sinking under surface of water
15. Blowing bubbles
16. Tight back or body
17. Jerky movement
18. Eyes opened extremely wide
19. Any abnormal behavior (sliding out)

PINNIPEDS
1. Neck pulled back / eyes open wide
2. Avoidance
3. Lunging
4. Barking
5. Head swinging
6. Blocking other animals
7. Prolonged eye contact
8. Exploratory mouthing
9. Charging
10. Unusual vocalizing (walrus "whistling")
11. Sudden change of expression
12. Cautious or stand-offish
13. Any abnormal behavior

This list is probably far from complete and may not cover all of the behavioral idiosyncrasies specific to all marine mammal species, however, awareness of these warning signs is a must for trainers and keepers who wish to operate a safe environment for animals and people.

A NOTE ON PUNISHMENT AND AVERSIVE CONTROL

It is hoped that by now most of us have learned enough from the literature to understand that punishment or forced aversive control will cause a variety of negative manifestations including aggression (Staddon, 1977; Kazdin, 1984; Ferster and Culbertson, 1982; Houston, 1986), and although it may immediately reduce or eliminate the above list of behaviors or undesired responses, the animals will soon learn to aggress by masking these warning signs, thereby avoiding punishment. This is an extremely dangerous situation, for to lose the "warning signs" is to invite disaster. It also decimates the "trust" that you have developed with your animals. Remember that attempted aggression or numerous incorrect responses by the animal should not be considered a personal assault against the trainer. Animals, like us, have good and bad days and forced control or punishment will only increase the number of bad days. Nothing will replace the benefits of utilizing patience, tolerance, and positive interaction with your animals.

DANGEROUS SITUATIONS

Knowing the precursors is a start in controlling aggression, but experience has taught many of us that there are specific contingencies and situations that increase the risk of aggression. Knowing these will allow us to either avoid the situation or use DRI during the early warning signs when we must place ourselves into a possible aggressive scenario. Again, I have covered some, but certainly not all, of the possibilities and it is hoped that this paper might generate discussion that may provide more helpful information. These situations are as follows:

1. Poor separations
2. Numerous incorrect responses to S^Ds
3. Feeding only one animal in a group
4. Animals not receiving reinforcement after several trials
5. A change in reinforcement contingencies
6. Low intensity, criteria, or motivation seen in training situations
7. Attempting to disrupt courtship or sexual activity
8. Social aggression "overflowing" into session
9. Putting animal in a position vulnerable to attack by others (putting sea lion in a pool with a dominant sea lion)
10. Animals pushed too far or hard causing frustration
11. Use of aversive control
12. Medical treatment that may cause discomfort
13. Utilizing behavioral extinction [Extinction Burst (Kazdin, 1984)]
14. Animals that are startled
15. Animals that are sick or injured

A NOTE ON EXTINCTION

When extinguishing a behavior that has a previous reinforcement history, a degree of frustration can sometimes build to the point of overt aggression. This is especially true during the final phase of extinction known as extinction burst. Obviously non-reinforcement of a previously reinforced behavior is aversive and leads to the same side effects we see in punishment (Kazdin, 1984). Extinction burst, is an increase in intensity and/or frequency of a behavior, as a function of frustration, just before a major reduction in the target response. It is advisable to avoid aggression by slowly (over a period of months if necessary) extinguishing a response, especially with a known aggressive animal. This can be done by giving the S^D with no reinforcement maybe once or twice a day. Don't attempt to extinguish a behavior in one session. Anticipate extinction burst and ensure that the behavior is not accidentally reinforced otherwise the animal may learn that frustration is part of the response.

THRESHOLD TRAINING

A killer whale is trained to jump "bow" in three positions. One of the trainers decides that six jumps would be more impressive and suggests that the animal could use more exercise anyway. All agree that from now on only six bows will be accepted. The S^D is given, the whale quits after the third bow as usual. Being a perceptive group of trainers, they decide that the animal needs help and a secondary S^D is given in the fourth position. The animal quits after the fourth position. The trainers suggest that the animal is "playing games," remove the secondary S^D, and decide to give the signal once again. They volunteer the newest trainer. This brave soul once again gives the S^D, the animal flies out of the water at our newest comrade, jaw popping and vocalizing as he approaches. All trainers are later found in the shower cleaning out their shorts.

REDUCING AGGRESSION

1. **Understanding situations** where aggression can usually occur.
2. **Understanding precursors,** warning signs that may predict aggression.
3. **DRI/DRO/DRL,** alternate response training, provide alternative to aggression, train reaction, use desensitization.
4. **Terminate before it occurs,** don't attempt to "work them through it," shift gears or walk away!
5. **Keep records** so trainers can learn from own mistakes.

Table 3 Reducing or eliminating aggression.

Increasing thresholds should be approximated slowly, utilizing secondary S^Ds at the point just before the animal terminates. This will provide a "reminder" to the animal and avoid frustration response.

MORE SCENARIOS AND SOLUTIONS

Having a quiet, interactive swim with a favorite dolphin, the animal begins to mouth your arm.

This could be the initial phase of schedule-induced frustration, activated by too long of a latency between reinforcements. A control behavior of any type (DRI), should divert the animal's attention and provide a reinforcement contingency for an appropriate response. This trainer should anticipate the animal's control deficit and in the future use DRI before the mouthing occurs and slowly increase the animal's control threshold by giving a secondary S^D before the animal terminates the initial response. Be careful not to allow the animal an opportunity to mouth consistently, or soon it will be the animal giving the signal (aggressively) for reinforcement (accidental shaping). You may want to ignore it the first time, anticipate mouthing the second time and use DRI before it occurs.

A male walrus is very interested in a female walrus for the first time today. You come to work after your first day off and decide to train the male walrus in a water-work session. During the session you suddenly feel the sensation of an object about to make contact with the backside of your neoprene suit. You exit the water quickly praying that you don't win the AAZPA Bean Award for the first born human-walrus hybrid.

Assume that poor response is a given during periods of sexual activity. You must also assume that attempting to remove the male from the female might be perceived as aversive. Aggression soon follows. Instead, provide high magnitude reinforcement. If you must work with the animal, avoid all water work or buy a very thick wet suit.

SUMMARY

No longer can we assume that aggression spontaneously erupts from nowhere, nor can we hope that it goes away by itself. Instead, we must exchange information in forums such as this so as to provide a safer environment for the animals we all care so much about, and the people who care for them. And, we must approach these aggressive behaviors delicately but directly, with a solid foundation of principles and a keen awareness of the possibilities by:

1. Knowing the scenarios
2. Knowing the precursors
3. Utilization of DRI

Finally, we must continue to teach others what we all have learned - each animal is an individual and nothing replaces patience.

ACKNOWLEDGMENTS

We would like to acknowledge a few patient individuals without whose patience we would not have been able to procrastinate so effectively: Cindi Sheppeck on her complete attention to ensuring timely preparation, Fawn Bryan for enabling our panic to motivate her towards a massive literature search the result of which has cost her overdue library fines, Stan Searles whose subtle prodding and occasional anecdote provided relief, and Harvey Barnett for interjecting creative energy, organization, and technical expertise.

REFERENCES

Ferster, C.B., & Culbertson, SA (1982). Behavior Principles (3rd ed.). Englewood, NJ: Prentice Hall.

Goodall, J. (1986). The Chimpanzees of Gombe. Cambridge, MA: Belknap Press.

Houston, J.P. (1986). Fundamentals of Learning and Memory (3rd ed.). New York: Harcourt-Brace.

Huntingford, F., & Turner A. (1988, August). Aggression: A Biological Imperative? New Scientist, pp. 44-47.

Johnson, C.M., & Norris, K.S. (1986). Delphinid Social Organization and Social Behavior. In R.J. Schusterman, J.A. Thomas, & F.G. Wood (eds.), Dolphin Cognition and Behavior: A Comparative Approach (pp. 335-346). Hillsdale, NJ: Lawrence Carlbaum.

Kazdin, A.C. (1984). Behavior Modification in Applied Settings (3rd ed.). Homewood, IL: The Dorsey Press.

Reynolds, G.S., Catania, A.C., & Skinner, B.F. (1963). Conditioned and Unconditioned Aggression in Pigeons. Journal of the Experimental Analysis of Behavior, 6(1), 73-74.

Scott, J.P. (1972). Animal Behavior (2nd ed.). Chicago, IL: The University of Chicago Press.

Scott, J.P. (1975). Aggression (2nd ed.). Chicago, IL: The University of Chicago Press.

Staddon, J.E.R. (1977). Schedule-induced Behavior. In W.K. Honig & J.E.R. Staddon (eds.), Handbook of Operant Behavior (pp. 125-152). Englewood Cliffs, NJ: Prentice Hall.

Vander Zanden, J.W. (1985). Human Development (3rd ed.). New York: Random House.

Wolgen, D.L. (1982). Motivation, Activation, and Behavioral integration. In R.L. Isaacson & N.E. Spears (eds.), The Expression of Knowledge: Neurobehavioral Transformations into Action (pp. 243-290). New York: Plenum Press.

ABA - S.I.G.
Association for Behavior Analysis
Animal Special Interest Group Newsletter

It is rare to find an article that looks at dog training from a technical operant perspective. The audiences for most pet articles are not experienced trainers skilled in operant techniques. Here, Jennifer Sobie, editor for the ABA - S.I.G. newsletter writes in the December 1995 issue about solving a biting problem with a pet dog. She takes a very analytical look at how to find the causes and solutions to the problem.

Aggression Mediation in Pet Dogs

by Jennifer Sobie

Aggression in pet dogs is far more common than most people realize. However, with mediation techniques based on the principles of behavior analysis, it is also very treatable.

There are two facets to effective mediation of a dog's biting problem: the prompts to biting, and the consequence of biting. Both must be examined and understood to find the motivation behind the problem. Either or both must be changed to solve the problem. Mediation helps the owner and family to do this.

AGGRESSION

Biting is a behavior, just like sitting. As with other behaviors, its causes may lie in its consequences or its antecedents.

In some cases of aggression in dogs, the behavior is operant. The dog learns to bite because biting is effective for him. Biting has been reinforced in the past. Contingencies may still exist which reinforce biting and maintain the behavior.

In other cases, the behavior is respondent. In the past, certain stimuli had been paired with aversive events for the dog. The dog comes to respond to those stimuli with emotion accompanied by agonistic display.

In yet other dogs, biting is an adjunct behavior that accompanies an inherited behavior specific to certain breeds. An example is biting that accompanies herding behavior in collie type dogs. In these dogs, usually certain events create prompting situations.

AGGRESSION MEDIATION

Aggression mediation works to change the contingencies behind the behavior, and to change the reaction of the dog to certain prompts.

Much of aggression mediation deals with consequence. The consequences of the biting must be changed. This is often the most difficult aspect of aggression mediation for owners to accomplish. That's because, contrary to popular opinion, successful aggression mediation does not rely on force or intimidation. In changing the consequence of biting, success depends on removing the reward found in biting, and not in attempting to positively punish the behavior.

Positive punishment attempts seldom if ever work in established aggression problems. Instead, they usually aggravate the problem, either through negative reinforcement (biting terminates the aversive stimulus), or through respondent conditioning (the aversive stimulus is paired with biting).

Far more effective is negative punishment. However, it can be difficult for owners to change their habits, particularly those that include reacting in anger or with force.

Aggression mediation also looks at the situations that prompt the dog's biting response. By discovering and controlling these situations, and by changing the dog's reaction to certain prompts, biting can be controlled.

Biting specific to certain breeds may also be analyzed in terms of prompting situations. By learning about the dog's breed characteristics, discovering circumstances that key into breed specific responses, and changing the set-up of these situations, trouble can be avoided.

BEGINNING THE MEDIATION PROCESS

It can be very difficult for families to carry out certain aspects of effective aggression mediation in their pet dogs. So the very first step in any program is to canvas the interpersonal dynamics of the family.

Considerations:
- Are there children in the home? Children and their friends increase the risk of housing a dog with a known behavioral pattern of aggressive or agonistic display. Also, children living in the home must be included in the mediation program or the program will not succeed.
- Do the primary caregivers of the family have the time and conviction to commit to the dog and a comprehensive aggression mediation program? If the people most responsible for the care of the dog and household are uncertain of their ability to commit to the program, it is unlikely that the program will succeed.
- Are the people afraid of their dog? If a situation has gotten to the point where a family is afraid of their dog, this fear will make each person's reactions to the dog very difficult for them to control.
- Is the family experiencing a major emotional upset such as divorce or a severe illness? Unusual and emotionally charged circumstances both affect the dog's behavior and make it difficult for families to commit to training.

SAMPLING AND BREAKDOWN OF BEHAVIORS

The next step is to convince the family to stop looking at the dog and his aggressive displays as a package deal. They must stop viewing the dog and his aggression as a whole. Instead, they must break the dog's aggression down into behaviors.

Viewing the aggressive displays as distinct behaviors serves two purposes. First, it helps to avoid labeling of the dog as "bad." Labeling interferes with the owners' ability to control their responses to the dog's behaviors. Second, and most important, in any situation where the dog has built himself a variably scheduled repertoire of agonistic displays, mediation can't be accomplished if it is not done behavior by behavior.

Some specific behaviors that can be included as agonistic are:
- growling to control another's behavior in any situation; this includes guarding of possessions, growling to warn people not to get too close, growling to get you to stop doing something, etc.; it does not include growling during games such as tug-of-war
- intolerance of certain family members
- preoccupation with one family member
- theft of the children's toys
- preoccupation with the children's toys
- theft of food directly from children or adults
- drinking out of the kitchen sink
- intolerance of being petted on the head
- intolerance of being restrained; stiff body posture when held
- noticeable agitation in unfamiliar environments
- indulgence of escape behaviors, such as hiding under tables
- obvious and intense emotional change in reaction to specific events or people
- exaggerated alert responses to house guests or passers-by
- physical greeting displays; forceful, full-body jumping, or the pressing of the chest against any part of the newcomer
- standing above family members and watching, as at the top of stairs or on furniture
- direct unflinching and unquestioning eye contact

DEFINING THE CONTINGENCIES

Once you have identified the target behaviors, you can go ahead with your mediation program. The next step is to establish the parts of the existing contingencies that comprise the agonistic behaviors. You can then change the behavior by changing the dog's response to the prompting stimulus, changing the consequence of that response, or becoming aware of those prompting stimuli that should simply be avoided (as in breed specific biting).

A helpful recipe for analyzing and defining a target behavior's contingency is:

BEHAVIOR - Define your target behavior. Define specifically what behaviors you must work to eliminate.

ANTECEDENT - Identify the circumstances establishing or surrounding the behavior When is the dog most likely to perform the undesired behavior? Can you eliminate those circumstances? Identify specific prompts to the behavior. What sights, sounds or actions are most likely to set the behavior in motion?

CONSEQUENCES - Identify the reward. Why is the dog doing what he's doing? What happens after the dog bites? What things or events are reinforcers?

As with many behavioral interventions, in aggression mediation usually the only way to identify the antecedent and reinforcement to certain agonistic behaviors is to keep a chart that records the occurrence of the target behaviors. This chart lists the behavior, the events leading to the behavior, and the owner's and any other involved organisms' immediate responses to the behavior.

It can be helpful to families charting agonistic behavior in their dog to provide them with a list of common antecedents to and reinforcers of aggression. This helps them find prompts and consequences that they might otherwise overlook. Here are some things that prompt biting:
- threatening situations such as physical punishment
- restraint, as produced by a tie-out chain, tight leash, or being held
- presence of food
- presence of possessions
- any interpretation of a challenge to authority
- sight of feared person, animal or event
- fast or sudden movement
- entrance of a non-family member into the house
- the exit of a non-family member from the house
- movement of a non-family member within the house
- reaching gestures toward the dog
- approach of anyone toward a favored family member physical contact, such as petting pain

And here are some things that reinforce agonistic behavior:
- attention from owners
- retreat of intruder
- emotional display
- approach of another dog

The next step is analysis of these charts. If the records suggest that consequence is not controlling the dog's response to the prompting stimuli, respondent conditioning is indicated. This works to reduce the ability of a prompt to evoke aggression by pairing it with neutral, non-aversive stimuli. A sample recipe for respondent conditioning:

ANTECEDENT - Identify the circumstances prompting the behavior. When is the dog most likely to perform the undesired behavior? Can you eliminate those circumstances?

HANDLER RESPONSE - Upon sight of the antecedent, give non-contingent attention. Present owner directed distractions to the dog regardless of his behavior.

If the records suggest that consequence is controlling the dog's aggression, operant conditioning is indicated. This works to remove existing contingencies, extinguish the behavior, and/ or establish new contingencies. A sample recipe for operant conditioning:

ESTABLISHING OPERATIONS - Change the establishing operations. If agonistic behavior is socially motivated, work outside of actual confrontations is also needed.

BEHAVIOR - Allow the dog to attempt undesired behavior. (This is behavior modification, as opposed to behavior management. Behavior management tries to block the dog from attempting the behavior on a given occasion. Behavior modification uses each occasion as a training opportunity).

CONSEQUENCE - Ignore the behavior. Provide no reinforcement. Reward alternative behavior. Reinforce anything that is not agonistic.

Another sample recipe (dealing entirely with consequence):

CONSEQUENCE - Remove the reward. Make the behavior non-productive for the dog. Break old contingencies: make sure not to allow reinforcers that have been identified as maintaining the behavior.

Make the act unpleasant. Punish the behavior.

Reward alternative behavior. Reinforce anything that is not agonistic.

Repeat all steps. Be prepared to immediately repeat all steps until the dog stops trying the behavior.

Follow through. Reinforce desired behavior when you see it in place of the old behavior.

SOCIALLY MOTIVATED AGGRESSION

A certain number of dogs attack their own families. In these cases, it is not uncommon for the root of the problem to be one of social dynamics. In the vast majority of cases, a dog that has developed problem behaviors in one family would not have developed these same behaviors in a different family. It has to do with how the dog interacts with his family, what the dog wants and needs, and how the family interacts with the dog. Dogs who perceive themselves as in authority are those that learn how to use aggressive displays to discourage others from usurping their social positions.

To effectively deal with aggression in dogs under these circumstances, it is best to avoid the confrontation of an agonistic display, and work instead to eliminate the motivation behind the behaviors. To do this, the owners must assert themselves as effective leaders, taking the job from the dog and building a reliance upon them in its place.

How this is done is terribly important.

NO MORE FREEBIES

The technique is deceptively simple. A family can teach their over-insolent dog that he's not quite the high ranking official he thought he was simply by keeping the things he wants and needs from him until he acknowledges a family member and does something for that person. He should be made to sit and 'wait' until he's told he can actually take or have whatever it is he needs.

If a family can integrate this concept into the day-to-day care of their dog, they will subtly but dramatically change the dynamics of their relationship with that dog. Every time they feed the dog, give him treats, let him out, give him a toy, play a game with him or, with a very arrogant beast, every time they bestow upon him the gift of their affection and attention, he will be reminded that the people in his family control his environment.

By keeping each of these things out of his reach until he sits for one of the family and waits on that person's signal to take, he'll learn that people are important and to be indulged. He'll learn that he must work through them, as opposed to over them.

This serves three purposes in aggression mediation. First, it changes the dog's perception of his authority as opposed to - the authority of - family members around him, which means that he will not be so prone to claiming and defending articles he finds. Secondly, it teaches the dog to be reliant on family members - that it is in his best interest to be compliant. And third, in changing authority position, you change roles and duties; the dog is no longer responsible for the decision of who or what is allowed to come in contact with the family.

CONTROL YOURSELF

Making the dog wait isn't the end of the story, however. More important is how he's made to wait. The dog must control himself, as opposed to being physically controlled by the owner. He must learn that he gains things through his family members, not that he is kept from things by them. He can only learn this by taking the initiative himself to keep still with no guidance or interference from the owner. Instead of physically controlling the dog, the owners should control access to those things the dog wants, removing them each time the dog moves before he's been told he's able, until he teaches himself to keep still.

TEACHING THE "WAIT"

Grab a dog food bowl, a handful of kibble, and the dog. Let the dog know that you have kibble with you, and then put the food in the bowl and set it on a chair or counter or anywhere else handy to you. Place the dog into a sit. (If the dog bites when handled, either guide him into a sit with a bit of food above him, or do a stand and "wait"). Once he's sitting, switch hands on his collar or chest so that your most dexterous hand is free to control the food bowl. Next, pick up the bowl. Tell the dog to "Wait," let go of his collar or chest and put the bowl on the floor about two feet in front of the dog. When he gets up, don't tell him "No" or reach for him. Instead, pick up the bowl. Quickly. Your control of the bowl is your ultimate control of the dog. Then, without talking to the dog or scowling, put him back in the sit and start over. Say "wait," let go of the dog, and put down the bowl. Don't take your hand from the bowl; you must keep it there so you're ready to snatch it up if he moves.

You'll probably have to do this "pick up the bowl and start over" thing five or more times. But, with each consecutive repetition, you'll notice a change in the dog's behavior. He might get up faster at first (extinction burst), he might lie down (trying a new behavior), he might begin to wait up until the instant you take your hand off from the bowl, or he might leave. If he leaves, let him go he'll get hungry sooner or later - but, as for his other attempts, you simply need to keep repeating the lesson until he sits while your hand is off him and off the dog food bowl. Then, the moment this happens, say "Go!" and nod toward the bowl to help the dog figure out that he can have the food now. You might have to repeat "Go" more than once.

Trainer's Forum

VOL 19, NO 1, 1994. Water interactions with our animals can be an enriching experience for everyone involved. However, as soon as the trainer puts themselves in the animals' environment, there is the potential for aggression. Even play behavior by a large animal can be dangerous for the trainer. Safety has always been a topic of great interest to trainers working in a free contact environment with large animals. Below are answers from two facilities that responded to the same question, seven years apart. Training concerns remain similar over time, because only on occasion do new techniques emerge in the training world. Usually it is in the application of those techniques that creative trainers find new avenues to respond to their animals.

Dealing with Cetacean Aggression towards Swimmers

QUESTION (From the Spring 1986 issue): We are presently training a 2-year-old *Tursiops truncatus* in the same tank with its mother. It knows about 20 behaviors. We are now concentrating on water behaviors and both animals usually have a good attitude toward swimmers. Occasionally, the calf has a temper tantrum and can be very aggressive. At the moment, whenever the calf exhibits aggression, the swimmer does not react, but leaves the water soon after. We'd appreciate help from those more experienced at training water behaviors.

ANSWER 1: In addition to play sessions in the water, conduct a water session with a trainer (or trainers) controlling dolphins from the side of the pool. Another trainer then enters the water (you may even want to approximate the amount of body you put in the water at first), initially staying near the side of the pool. Work the dolphin on a variety of behaviors, occasionally reinforcing the animal as it moves past the trainer in the water on its way to perform a behavior. Since the attraction to the trainer will be very great, you can't prevent the dolphin from investigating. So send the animal to the swimmer on command, and reinforce it on its return. In other words, the trainer becomes a prop to be retrieved or ignored.

As control near the side increases, the swimmer-trainer can begin to increase his movements around the pool. Additional people in the water will also be helpful. At this point, the trainer in the water can begin feeding and working the animal, always keeping the A-B and B-A (moving between trainer in the water and trainer on the deck) stimulus strong. Eventually the activities will require no initiation by the dolphins.

In play sessions, I believe an immediate response to aggression should be instituted. Leave the water and the entire area at once. No delay and no variations.
1986 Training Staff
Marineland of the Pacific

ANSWER 2: Aggressive response and behavior can be controlled and/or reduced with basic operant conditioning. During water interaction, it is important to remain aware of conditions or situations that could result in an aggressive response. Early recognition of events that may lead to aggressive behavior allows implementation of two techniques that we have found to be successful in reducing the behavior. Differential Reinforcement of Other Behavior (DRO) and Differential Reinforcement of Incompatible Behavior (DRI) are ways to reinforce a response or behavior that competes with the aggressive response. The topic of aggression and the use of these training techniques is covered in *Aggression: Exploring the Causes and Possible Reduction Techniques* (Soundings, Spring 1990, vol. 15, no. 2).

In addition to understanding basic behavioral principles with regard to aggression, the National

Aquarium in Baltimore has certain guidelines we follow before water work begins with our marine mammals. First, the animals are conditioned to respond to a stage call stimulus. We use a slap on the deck or an electronic tone. The animals are reinforced for returning to the stage upon receiving this stimulus. Once the animals establish a positive learning history with the stage call, a program of water desensitization is started. This program approximates a trainer into the water, while reinforcing the animal for remaining calm. A second trainer on deck is the one actually working the animal. Once the animal goes through its behavioral repertoire without worrying about the swimming trainer, then the animal can be sent to, or transferred to, that trainer for water work. Conditioning a "stage call" and desensitizing the presence of trainers in the water sets up a basic foundation for safe and positive water work. Approximating a trainer into the water slowly, while steadily reinforcing the animals for staying calm, will hopefully override any neutral or aversive stimuli. With consistency, water work can become a positive interaction for marine mammals and a source of new, variable types of reinforcement.

1993 Training Staff
National Aquarium in Baltimore

NOTE: This *Trainer's Forum* question has been pulled from the Soundings archives. We thought it would be appropriate to find some "nostalgic" questions from past issues that still apply to today's training.

VOL 23, NO 2, 1998. When aggression becomes a problem, trainers are often perplexed as to how to go about solving the problem. The question posed below is one of the most complex ever presented to *Trainer's Forum*. Because the question offers quite a bit of background information, it makes the answer more involved than simply solving the question, "how can we reduce aggression?" Each respondent approaches the answer in a slightly different way. You may recognize many of the techniques described by Turner earlier in this chapter interwoven into answer 1. In the second answer I worked with my staff at the Shedd Aquarium to focus on the history of the particular problem presented before providing a suggested solution. Answer 3 focuses on the general operant principles that affect aggression. All the facilities that responded work frequently in the water with their animals, the final three responses (3 - 5) are from those facilities that conduct interactive programs with the public.

Handling Escalating Dolphin Aggression: A Complex Problem

QUESTION: We have two very large bottlenose dolphins, both born at our facility, nine and 13-years-old, and both of which show aggression during water work.

Water shows were attempted when these animals were very young, with the swimmer as a prop only. As with most animals, the time came when they began to explore the swimmer by mouthing the swimmer's feet, hands, legs, arms, and even breach near them. Unfortunately, the situation was not addressed at that time, instead water work was abandoned altogether. Other aggression was noted when trainers accidentally fell in. Today the situation has worsened to the point of trainers actually pulled into the water aggressively, and the dolphins do not respond to the control trainer on deck at the side of the pool.

A year ago, a foreign object-desensitizing project was started to cure the animals of ingesting foreign objects. The animals were taught to stay at station no matter what was thrown in the water. The next step taken was to introduce a life-size dummy, dressed in a wetsuit, intending to teach the animals to perform normally without touching the doll. Six potentially aggressive animals were trained this way, but three males are still very aggressive toward the doll. There are no noticeable precursors to the aggression and using a least reinforcing stimulus (LRS) would mean leaving a dolphin being aggressive to a trainer for a 2-3 second lapse. We have tried many approaches to dealing with this problem. All we want to do is to be able to get in or fall in the water without major aggression. We would appreciate any suggestions.

ANSWER 1: What you may want to consider is a water-work desensitization plan. This desensitization will do two things: it will teach the animals to ignore trainers in the water and it will give the animals other appropriate and reinforceable behaviors to do that are incompatible with any aggressive behavior. In the first approximations of water desensitization, you would train a "call back" to the station area that you are already using. Continuing with your object desensitization will also enhance your animals' call back, which will stay reliable when trainers begin slipping into the pool. The call back signal should be trained so well, that a reliable response can be obtained in many different scenarios, under a variety of environmental conditions, at many different times during the day. Reinforcement application for this behavior should remain very high as to increase the number of correct responses.

The approximations would begin with a trainer sitting at the edge of the pool with their feet only in the water. Proceed as you feel comfortable, with the trainer increasing the amount of body they place in the water. As the station and water desensitization behaviors gain reinforcement, you can then increase the amount of activity that the water work trainer will do. This activity may eventually include basic water work behaviors. This desensitization plan should also be used with dolphins that you are currently able to do water work with. It will help you to strengthen the water work foundation with all animals using the same approximations.

We would also strongly recommend that you discontinue the use of the wet-suited dummy. This is only allowing the dolphins to rehearse aggression after leaving the trainer and the station area. We can not stop the animals from leaving, but we can do things that will prevent the animals from increasing their aggressive tendencies towards a person (or in this case, the likeness of a person).

Although aggression may seem to be mysterious and appear without warning, there are actually many ongoing factors that escalate towards aggression. When dealing with aggression in general there are many points that you want to consider. These are some ideas that may help.

Understand the situation. Look at when and where aggression can occur. If there are areas where trainers accidentally fall in or are more likely to be pulled in, do not work the animals from this area.

Look for precursors. These will be warning signs that may predict aggression. They will start out almost invisible but will escalate. If the animals are not interested in the trainer, or are fast swimming and physically active with one another, this is not the time for any water interaction.

Use DRO, DRI and DRL. Differential Reinforcement of Other, Incompatible, and Lower intensity behaviors will be crucial when dealing with aggression. Give the animals other behaviors to focus on. Work the things that will keep them calm and more interested in the trainer at station rather than the trainer in the pool.

End the session before aggression occurs. Do not work the animals through it. Change the course of the session or end it and come back later. Make the sessions short and positive. Teach the animals to succeed in the session before the aggression occurs, and their perception will eventually change from frustration to excitement.

Make a behavior plan for the aggression. Communicate to all trainers what the plan for water desensitization is going to be. It should be documented so future trainers can learn from prior successes and/or mistakes. Look for places when and where aggressive patterns have happened in the past. If it is at a specific location in the area, let others know to work the animals away from that area. If it is a certain time of the day, again communicate to others to choose a different water work time for now.

This information can be used in many different situations with a wide variety of animals. We hope this is helpful in your area. Good Luck.

Training Staff
Sea World of Ohio

ANSWER 2: What a fascinating question and unique set of circumstances! If you approach the situation as if you were training a new group of animals, it may allow you to take a fresh approach. Sometimes it is too easy to get bogged down trying to get rid of unwanted behavior rather than focusing on obtaining the desired behavior. The truth of the matter is that the difference in perspective can change your whole approach to dealing with your animals. If you work toward teaching the animals to have a positive interaction with swimmers in the water, you are focussing on the positive rather than the negative. It is still important to keep in mind the animal's history and have a complete knowledge of what has been done in the past, but do not let those factors stop you from approaching the situation as a new training task.

Before starting over, let's examine some of the animals' training history. Obviously you have tried many approaches, and it might be helpful to consider what worked and what did not. Here are some initial thoughts about the original questions and scenario as described:

Mouthing – Your comment that "most animals" will explore the swimmer by mouthing their feet, hands, legs, and arms does not have to be the case. If you are interacting with the animals while under stimulus control, the timing of your bridge and other reinforcers can strengthen positive interactions and extinguish any attempts at mouthing. Trainers should not accept mouthing as an inevitable situation.

Control Trainer – If an animal is not responding to the control trainer on land, that is usually an indication that the aggressive interaction with the swimmer is more reinforcing than being at station. This may be caused by any number of things, including a lack of a strong reinforcement history at station, lack of sufficient variety (in reinforcement schedules or behavior selection), or lack of a strongly established or well-maintained recall signal.

Life-size Doll – The use of the doll was a fascinating experiment, but there may have been several problems with that approach. The first problem lies in the assumption that an animal would not be able to distinguish a doll from a real person, which may be an unrealistic assumption. Secondly, even if you successfully train the dolphins to associate the doll with the swimmer, the first time they interact with either the responses will be so different that you would be unable to control the reinforcing value of the interaction.

LRS – It was unclear whether you had tried the use of an LRS during aggression or were simply commenting that it was an inappropriate tool in that situation. Because an LRS in meant to minimize changes in the animal's environment to prevent reinforcing undesirable behavior, a true LRS as described by Scarpuzzi (1991) can't be utilized. The very nature of aggression provides many changes in the animal's environment and is one of the reasons that aggression is so reinforcing for an animal.

Training the dolphins in your situation to ignore swimmers in the water may be an eventual goal, but it may not be the easiest way to start eliminating aggression. The aggression seems so strongly reinforced (albeit unintentionally so) that a more realistic goal may be to focus on changing how the dolphins interact with swimmers rather that eliminating the interaction. The key would be to make positive interactions with swimmers far more reinforcing and fun for the dolphins than aggressive interactions.

The first step might be to examine your training program overall. Are training sessions fun and varied? Aggression can be a result of boredom, and sessions or shows that always have the animals doing the exact same thing with no variety. This can cause animals to search for other things to keep them occupied (like aggression). Does your reinforcement schedule keep your animal motivated? It is important to make sure that your reinforcements are big enough, varied enough, and interesting enough to keep an animal's interest. Otherwise, frustration can result and this can be another cause of aggression. Finally, have you looked at the whole enrichment picture? Training sessions are one of the most critical forms of enrichment, but training is only a small part of the animals' day and we must always be conscious of how they spend their time outside of training sessions. Play sessions, social interactions, habitat changes, toys, environmental conditions, public access, and so much more have an effect on our animals. If the whole enrichment picture is stagnant, frustrating, or unhealthy it can lead to aggression. For purposes of this discussion, it will be assumed that these items have been considered and are not a factor.

The next step might be to desensitize the animal to having the trainer's feet dangling in the water during a session. By sitting at poolside, feet and legs hanging in the water, the trainer is not totally exposed to a potentially aggressive dolphin. From this position, basic behaviors can be worked and a strong reinforcement history can be established. If you are truly concerned that your dolphins may bite your feet in this position, wear thick protective steel-toed boots that will keep you from being injured. With time, the lack of response to any biting will hopefully decrease the reinforcing value of this activity; meanwhile dolphins that ignore the feet in the water will be well reinforced. Eventually you could have the animal A to B to another trainer who is also dangling his or her feet in the water. Once the animals are doing this well, you can move to the next step.

Perhaps one of the most critical steps is to approximate the trainer in the B position into the water. The goal is to make going to the person in the water a positive and reinforcing experience. The key, of course, is to make it positive and reinforcing on your terms. It is critical that you have developed a strong and positive relationship with each of the animals before committing to this step, this will be the result of a good reinforcement history. If your knowledge of the animal's past still worries you, there are a number of safety precautions that can be taken. Wear protective clothing to minimize injury should an animal bite. Work at the pools edge and if possible start in a shallow or protected part of the habitat, this prevents the animal from being able to pick up great speed or come at you from behind.

Slowly you will be able to approximate yourself out into the pool and increase the variety of interactions with the dolphin. It should be emphasized that you are working to create a new relationship. The past problems went on for a long time, so you must work slowly and build on each step gradually. Every animal will respond to training differently, so be prepared to adapt your plan to each animal. Once the animals have learned to interact with swimmers positively, it will be easier to teach them to also ignore a swimmer during a session. It is important that an animal learn to remain at station unless asked to go interact with the swimmer. This can be accomplished through making sure that being at station is as strong a behavior as any other behavior and by making sure that your sessions are never predictable.

Eventually, it is possible that your animals will learn to interact positively with swimmers while not under stimulus control. However, since your animals have had such a long history of aggression, this goal may not be realistic in the immediate future and you may find it safest to only enter the water while the animals are at station. Success will depend on a well thought out plan, a consistent approach by the entire staff, and the establishment of a good reinforcement history.

There are always obstacles and pitfalls that can side track a good training plan. Anticipating or predicting all of them would be impossible. There are two that come to mind immediately that should probably be discussed.

Swimming in the interim. While water desensitization and training is taking place, it is important not to allow the animals the opportunity to engage in the old aggressive activity. While this may seem obvious, situations may arise that require you to send a swimmer or diver into the water for maintenance, cleaning, or retrieval of an object. You should gate the animals out of the habitat before entering the water. Although time consuming, failure to do this will give the aggressive animals the opportunity to be aggressive and continue the undesired behavior. Even if this only happens on occasion it will work against all the careful positive training you are trying to accomplish.

Recall signals. Although you do not mention a recall signal in your question, you do mention that your animals did not respond to a control trainer on land. If you are going to use a recall, which in many cases can be quite useful, it is imperative that it be well established. A recall is a behavior like any other, it should be a signal that calls an animal back to station, and should be reinforced as you might other behaviors in the animal's repertoire. If a recall is used only when an animal does something wrong, the signal takes on a new meaning and may serve to frustrate and anger an animal when used. This of course, is the last thing you want a recall to do if you plan to use it in an aggressive situation. If you want to use a recall, train it separately from your water desensitization training, and don't allow it to become associated with aggression. Make sure your recall is used frequently in positive situations. In aggressive situations the effective use of a recall usually requires an experienced trainer to apply it properly. We would recommend not using a recall at all during any of your early water work training, particularly due to the animals' history or you may simply exacerbate the problem. When used properly, the recall can be a very effective tool; however, when used incorrectly it can create enormous problems. Ultimately, each facility must determine whether the recall is the right tool for their program and their staff.

There is no doubt that your problem is complex, but it is not impossible to solve. There are many approaches to handling your situation; this is just one suggestion. Hopefully, you will find some of the suggestions useful and at the very least some of the discussion thought provoking. Good luck!

Training Staff
John G. Shedd Aquarium

ANSWER 3: There are a number of factors to consider with the aggression problem that you are experiencing with your dolphins. It is unfortunate that the situation with the animals was not addressed when it initially started occurring, however the following are techniques that we use at The Dolphin Connection to decrease the frequency and intensity of undesirable behavior.

The thing to remember is that there are reinforcers controlling the aggression. It is important to try to determine what the reinforcers are and learn how to remove them from the animal's environment. Drawing attention to and attempting to apply many approaches to deal with this behavioral problem may have actually reinforced the behavior, thereby increasing the frequency of the aggression.

Psychologists have found that animals that have the opportunity to aggress will do so more often. Therefore, removing the opportunity for the animal to aggress may help identify the causes of the problem and allow you to develop a protocol to eventually reduce the possibility of aggression in your scenario. An effective way we handle these problems is to involve animal care staff in listing the influences that affect the behavior. These could include environmental factors, social components, reinforcers, and reinforcement schedules. We never allow ourselves to project what the animal may be thinking as this is impossible for us to know. However, an experienced trainer may be able to apply past knowledge of an individual animal's behavioral history to narrow the choices when problem solving. With this information defined, we can easily identify the most effective plan of action to correct the problem.

An effective way to insure that undesirable behavior is not reinforced is to provide the least reinforcing stimulus (LRS) following the emitted undesirable behavior. For example, if an animal is given a flip S^D (with an established criteria of one and a half rotations), but emits only one rotation, the trainer does not bridge, and when the animal returns to station, the trainer, by utilization of the LRS, does not reinforce the low criteria of the behavior. Trainers reacting to the animal in any way, especially by changes in their body position or attitude (e.g. stomping feet, rolling eyes), may be effectively reinforcing undesirable behavior. The LRS should not be applied as the aggression is occurring, but rather as a consequence of the undesired behavior. (For more information on the use and application of a LRS, we recommend: "Decreasing the Frequency of Behavior Through Extinction: An Application for the Training of Marine Mammals" in IMATA Proceedings, 1991).

Generally speaking, there are several causes of aggression, including social changes, hormonal fluctuations, and aberrant behavior that is shaped through accidental reinforcement. The aggression problem that you are experiencing seems to have been heightened by accidental reinforcement. One of the most effective ways of controlling aggression is through the use of DRI (Differential Reinforcement of Incompatible Behavior). DRI reinforces behaviors that are incompatible with the aberrant ones. Applied use of DRI will lead to the increase in frequency of the incompatible behavior and decrease the frequency of the aggressive response. For example: A sea lion is being trained for a voluntary blood-draw from its rear flippers. During a training session, the sea lion stretches it's head back and attempts to bite the trainer. During later approximations, the trainer makes being reinforced for the husbandry behavior contingent upon holding it's muzzle on a target, which is incompatible with the biting behavior. The trainer is then able to train the behavior without any other aggressive response.

Another application that may help reduce the frequency of aggression is the use of DRO (Differential Reinforcement of Other Behavior). Essentially DRO involves reinforcing any behavior except for the one that is undesirable. For example: A beluga whale consistently vocalizes when at station. The trainer decides to apply DRO to decrease the frequency of the vocals and reinforces the whale for any behavior other than that of vocalizing. Over time, the whale vocalizes less frequently and the undesired behavior is extinguished. (For more detailed information on the causes and handling of aggression, we recommend: "Aggression: Exploring the Causes and Possible Reduction Techniques", IMATA **Soundings**, Spring 1990).

If faced with a problem similar to yours, we would consistently apply all of the techniques mentioned above to decrease the frequency of the aggressive responses. We would also start from "square one" in an attempt to establish positive interactions between animals and trainers again by developing a long range training plan. One of the first goals of the training plan, besides applying the aforementioned techniques, is to determine the precursors to the aggression. Even though trainers may not see obvious precursors, there are most likely some pre-aggression behaviors that are being missed. These could be as subtle as the animal avoiding eye contact, sinking under the surface of the water, or even just ignoring a hand signal. Using DRI/DRO upon the onset of the precursor to the aggression can help to positively refocus the animal's attention before the aggression actually occurs.

Also, it seems the animals need to be desensitized to swimmers in the water. The desensitization process would have to start with a very solid stationing or targeting behavior that the animal must hold as the swimmer is introduced to the environment. We might start with animals being held at control and a swimmer sitting pool-side near the trainer. The animal is reinforced for not responding to the swimmer. The next step would be for the swimmer to put their feet in the water and to continue to reinforce calm responses from the animal. Obviously, the approximations would continue until the trainer was in the water and was completely ignored by the animal. If undesirable responses occur during the training approximations, utilization of the LRS, DRI, and DRO will help reduce undesirable behavior.

We have found that the consistent application of these techniques has minimized the frequency of aggression in our animal collection.

Training Staff
The Dolphin Connection

ANSWER 4: All of our dolphins are involved in interactive programs with the public, therefore, recognizing and extinguishing aggressive behavior is a top priority for our training staff. Based on the information provided in the question, our best advice would be to begin at the beginning: in other words, treat water work or in-water interaction as a brand new behavior. We recommend that the animals be worked on a 1:1 trainer/animal ratio. If it is possible to have only one animal in the pool area at a time, that would be ideal; otherwise individual stations should be established around the pool area with the 1:1 ratio maintained during all training sessions.

All initial in-water desensitization should be done by the primary trainer. The desense could be accomplished with the progression of feet in water, legs in water, then standing in shallow water. If the pool does not have a shallow area, a small underwater platform at mid-thigh level could be constructed. During this phase, primary reinforcement should be used heavily. If other reinforcers are established, they should be incorporated as the desensitization progresses. The next step would be to establish a secondary trainer who is out of the water as a positive into the sessions using A to B's, differential feeding techniques, etcetera, and then progressing to in-water desensitization similar to what was done with the primary trainer.

As the water work progresses, we suggest the use of behaviors that have a history of high reinforcement with a particular animal, thus making it less likely for the animal to display aggressive tendencies while performing that behavior. For water work, it is usually better to use interactive behaviors (e.g. foot-pushed, dorsal tows, pec tows) that require the animal to work with the trainer instead of behaviors where the trainer serves only as a prop (i.e. hurdles).

In conjunction with the water work training, a recall (such as a pinger or underwater screamer) should be well established. This recall should be made highly reinforcing so that the animal responds whenever it is used. Remember that the recall should **always** be reinforced if performed properly and should not be over-used. Once established, the recall can serve as a valuable safety tool should aggression occur.

As always, communication among staff members is vital when dealing with any training problems. All trainers that are involved with these particular animals should be aware of training progression and should adhere to established protocol.

Training Staff
Dolphin Encounters

ANSWER 5: Anytime you have a situation that is going the wrong direction and is becoming consistently worse, you need to eliminate the scenarios and opportunities in which the undesirable behaviors take place. With the example of the male dolphins being aggressive (mouthing, fluking, breaching, etcetera) with trainers in the water and progressing to the point of pulling trainers into the water, the best approach may be to stop water interaction with the animals involved for a period of time. Do not allow them the opportunity to continue their undesirable behavior. You want to be able to interact on your terms, not theirs. Once you've eliminated opportunities for the animals to be aggressive, it's time to establish a game plan towards your goal of "being able to get in or fall in the water without major aggression."

Eliminate the water work portion of the aggressive animals and arrange training periods. Plan to maximize these training periods with heavy primary reinforcement (food) so you can magnitude positive steps and progress. We have had success increasing the diets of animals within the limit of behavior regression or shutdown. The disadvantage is that you lose some criteria, however the advantage is you have a more relaxed animal. Work the animals that have the problem of being aggressive individually to avoid distractions and undesirable "feeding" off each other. The goal of these training sessions is to strengthen the trainer/dolphin relationship and develop a successful approximation towards positive interaction. The initial goal is for trainers to avoid getting into the water so the animal doesn't have the opportunity to be aggressive. Create a fun training session with toys and creativity. Implement controlled tactile and contact. Ideas include sonogram line-ups (animal floating on its side) or establishing trainer to trainer A to B's. The animal can touch a target as you approximate to a trainer's hand. That can be approximated to a trainer's foot in the water and eventually a surfboard or inflatable boat. If all is progressing well, you could approximate to a trainer floating with a life jacket on, which is easier to work from the water. The key is you are establishing the correct, non-aggressive, behavior and approximating the trainer back into the water. It will be a slow process and it is vital that trainers reinforce "proper" behavior by not reinforcing any behavior related to aggression. Another important key is that you will be re-establishing trainer control.

As with many of these questions, there are no short answers or absolutes. We would be happy to exchange ideas and share previous experiences relating to this topic if interested. Good Luck!

Training Staff
Dolphin Quest Bermuda

VOL 15, NO 2, 1990. Although community pools, without the ability to separate animals, are rare these days, there is always the possibility that separation will not be an option. All three answers to the question below are very practical. Notice the subtle differences in technique and terminology. Answer 2 uses very good operant terms in suggesting a solution (note: Ted Turner's more comprehensive paper on dealing with aggression is included on page 366). The other two answers use similar principles, each described in a different way.

Dealing with Aggression in a Community Pool

QUESTION: During mating season, our oldest male dolphin gets very aggressive toward the other dolphins in the group. We do not have the ability to separate this animal. Has anyone ever found a successful method of handling this problem, or reducing it? Any ideas are welcome.

ANSWER 1: The information you have supplied about your animals and facility is very limited. We don't know much about your male's behavior and we may interpret very aggressive behavior very differently from you. It would also be helpful if we knew more about the size of your facility, the total number of animals, and the number of shows and/or training sessions you do each day. We can offer some general information that may be helpful in cutting down or eliminating some aggression.

There are two different types of situations you'll need to work around - show and/or training sessions, and the animals' free time. Whether you work the old male alone or as part of the group, the trainer should be in control during those times. The trainer must know the animals well and be very observant. The trainer may be able to recognize early warning signs, which may precede aggressive behavior. In that case, staying one step ahead of the animal, the trainer may ask for behaviors that can separate the animals or divert their attention. What is even more important is recognizing overt and subtle acts of aggression and not reinforcing them. If the aggression on your male's part prevents others from participating in sessions, a good rule of thumb may be no one works until all are present. Try to keep your sessions very positive. Work behaviors that the male enjoys. Avoid behaviors he dislikes, don't give him a reason to leave or get mad since it may add to your aggression problem.

The other situation you're faced with is the animals' free times. Since you aren't in control during these times, we suggest finding toys and activities that will give your male something to do. If your animals are left for long periods with nothing to keep them occupied, you'll probably see an increase in the aggression. Take into consideration the time you can have a person(s) there interacting with the animals and what kind of toys the animal likes.

Your problem is more complex than can be solved fully by people who don't know as much of your animals' background as you. We hope we've been helpful. If you want to call and discuss it, feel free. Good luck.

Training Staff
Marine World-Africa USA

ANSWER 2: Certainly aggression, like any behavior can be reduced and even eliminated by the utilization of well documented and proven behavioral principles. Although social aggression, aggravated by hormonal fluctuations and sexual activity is a tough problem, it is not insurmountable. The most important aspect of controlling any type of aggression is by applying behavioral techniques <u>before</u> you see overt aggression or fighting. Very often trainers attempt to modify the fighting <u>after</u> the damage has already been done, and quite frankly, the correction is futile. In some cases, the well-intentioned trainer may even <u>increase</u> the frequency, intensity, or duration of the behavior through accidental reinforcement. During training sessions, aggression can be controlled effectively by understanding the warning signs that lead to aggression. These precursors include, head nods, jaw popping, vocalizations, fluke slaps, and even more subtle "threats" recognized by experienced trainers. Upon the earliest recognition of these aggressive precursors, a principle known as D.R.I. (Differential Reinforcement of Incompatible Behavior) can be used to prevent the precursive behavior from escalating into outright aggression and possible injury. D.R.I. directly competes with the aggressive precursor by training a behavior that is incompatible with fighting. For example, if your alpha male consistently jaw pops at the sub-dominant members before he becomes aggressive, a hand signal for a "heads up" behavior or a targeting behavior will decrease the aggressive behavior. This will provide him reinforcement for not fighting under conditions where he normally would. Eventually, he may learn that the conditions that normally cause him to aggress may instead provide reinforcement for remaining calm and in control.

Your other problem will be the reduction of aggression during non-training. This can be done by utilizing D.R.O. (Differential Reinforcement of Other Behavior). D.R.O. reinforces any response other than aggression. The effect of a D.R.O. schedule is to decrease the target (unreinforced) response. This principle can be used when a group of dolphins, known to be aggressive with one another, are observed not engaging in aggressive activity. Instead they are resting, swimming, playing, or exploring their facility. Reinforcement (often, at first, and then intermittently) will increase cooperative interaction and decrease social aggression. By using all of these principles, you should be able to significantly reduce aggression. Remember:

1. Know the precursors (early detection is your best defense)
2. Use D.R.I. (before aggression actually takes place)
3. Use D.R.O. (any "cooperation" between animals should be reinforced)

Ted Turner
Sea World of Ohio

ANSWER 3: We have found it very important and quite successful to address aggression and social problems behaviorally. If an animal is displaying aggressive behavior towards other animals this usually triggers a variety of problems. Besides the potential of physical injury, the social structure is negatively impacted, and training sessions and shows can be disrupted as the sub-dominant animals become less willing to work or cooperate with the trainer in the presence of the dominant animal. Often times the situation is muddied by the fact that the dominant animal is working perfectly, while everyone else is refusing to work. Or maybe the dominant animal is less subtle and nobody is working at all.

In situations like this, our strategy is to reinforce the dominant animal for peacefully cooperating with the other animals, rather than intimidating them. This can be accomplished in a number of ways. One suggestion is to work the dominant animal with one other animal at a time. (For purposes of simplicity and clarity, I'll call the dominant animal A and the sub-dominant animal B). in this paired session, A is very specifically reinforced for cooperation - allowing B to work and eat. Depending on how intimidated B is, start small. Ask B to do a very simple and short behavior, duration is important, a head shake or stationary pec wave, something you feel reasonably sure B will do. Then bridge and pay both animals. A has done nothing but allow B to work and eat, and that's all you want.

Be careful when you feed B that A doesn't try to steal it. I would also suggest a ratio of 1 to 2. For every 1 fish that B gets, A gets 2 fish. Precise bridging is also critical. A second bridge, as B gets his fish, helps A understand why he's getting paid too. If A should interfere with a behavior or a reinforcer, give them a short time out (10 seconds) then try again.

Shows are also important times to reinforce cooperation. If several animals do a tandem behavior, you might reinforce A each time another animal gets paid, or feed them all carefully, then bonus him. Throughout your day, in any activity where it is possible, reinforce cooperation. Initially I would suggest using a food reward, since it is usually the most powerful reinforcer. Down the line, other reinforcers are fine, as long as they're positive for the animals, and especially for A. The important point is that it is very clear what A is being reinforced for: cooperation, non-aggression, allowing other animals to work, eat, socialize, play, and so on.

Gail Laule
Active Environments Inc.

ABA - S.I.G.
Association for Behavior Analysis
Animal Special Interest Group Newsletter

The following article appeared in the December 1995 newsletter of ABA - S.I.G. It describes the training of protection dogs using positive reinforcement. Many people have a misperception about "attack dogs" or "guard dogs," but most people have never seen well-trained protection dogs who can work and interact with anyone unleashed and unmuzzled! For these dogs, biting, growling, or attacking is under stimulus control and they will only exhibit the behavior when specifically asked. Sharon Kirkpatrick-Sanchez trains protection dogs, and her love for the animals is evident here as she describes some of her techniques.

Positive Reinforcement Techniques for Training Controlled Aggression in Schutzhund and Protection Dogs.

by Sharon Kirkpatrick-Sanchez

This article is not about pets showing inappropriate aggression. It is about developing a dog who is meant to show aggression and bite people when instructed. It is about well socialized animals who are safe in a crowd, safe around children, and have wonderful discrimination skills on what human aggression looks like.

Protection dogs have a bad reputation with the public because people don't understand them. Now, dogs whose biting is controlled by reinforcers or discriminative stimuli not specified by the handler/owner are a menace, and at times a danger. However, there is a place for dogs who are trained to respond with aggression in specific situations to a specific set of cues. The police, armed forces, and certain individuals want or have a need for such animals.

In a different vein, some owners are disappointed when told they shouldn't depend on their pet dog with no previous training to bite if someone breaks into their home. The dog may, but you shouldn't count on it. Raging and growling from behind a fence, at the front door, or at the end of the leash comes easy. Ability to do a true physical confrontation with a person is rare, and requires training.

DEFINITIONS

Schutzhund ("protection dog") originated as a breed temperament test for German Shepherd Dogs in Europe. In the U.S. it was first seen as a competition sport, and is now also becoming a breed temperament test.

"Protection dog" can mean just a dog trained to bite or threaten under certain circumstances, e.g. any stranger within his territory. It can also refer to a dog meant to be with a certain person or family, and who will be in public. In this article, "protection dog" means a dog that will be a good citizen in public, around strangers, and who will not threaten when there is no threat, unless called for by the handler. Fear biters are not acceptable.

SELECTING A DOG

STARTING WITH A PUPPY - Some of the behavior desired here is inherited. Select a puppy that displays high prey behaviors: retrieving, chasing moving objects, and carrying objects in its mouth. Look for a puppy whose parents have developed good protection behavior. Early training also has an effect. Dogs socialized to not bite as puppies often will not do so as adults.

STARTING WITH AN OLDER DOG - Have

a qualified trainer of schutzhund or protection dogs test the responses of the dog when stressed or threatened. Have your tester check the untrained defensive behavior of the dog, but without backing the dog down (making the dog avoid the tester).

TRAINING THE DOG

Make the dog responsive to you. Do behavior shaping of beginning obedience. Use food, toys, or whatever is reinforcing to the dog. Make yourself into a powerful conditioned reinforcer, so the dog will offer you behaviors in order to obtain reinforcers. Refer to seminars such as those offered by Karen Pryor and Gary Wilkes.

OBEDIENCE TRAINING

Schutzhund Obedience Training - In Drive by Sheila Booth and Gottfried Dildei describes the obedience required for schutzhund trials and how to train it. It is not written in behavioral terminology, but the techniques are operant and based on positive reinforcement.

DISCRIMINATION OF AGGRESSION AND SOCIALIZATION

A protection dog should not be afraid of people, especially when people are just acting normally. Does the dog show fear threat behaviors of growling, raised hackles, and barking when no threat behaviors are shown by the person being threatened? We consider this a temperament flaw or bad socialization. Many novices think this is wonderful when their dog rages at strangers for no reason. They think they have a wonderful protection dog. However, this is fear based aggression and *not* useful for protection or police dogs who may be sent off leash for 100 yards to physically stop a man. Fear biters who try to make strangers go away will not pursue a man at a distance to stop him from getting away. We do intense socialization with dogs who show some fear or unnecessary aggression, and reinforce appropriate social responses.

If a dog doesn't make progress quickly, it is probably not a good candidate. It may bite for reasons such as fear biting, not the stimulus control we train. Some "guard dog" trainers will intentionally train fear biting. Schutzhund and police dog trainers don't. Fear biting is not a useful behavior. The chances of an inappropriate bite are much higher. A fear biter bites in response to his own discriminative stimuli (whatever he fears or tries to avoid), and not the cues the owner has taught.

Protection dogs are taught to discriminate who is showing aggression: staring at the dog, the equipment worn, body stance/frontal body posture, yelling, arm waving, whatever else is chosen as discriminative stimuli. At first we watch for small amounts of aggression as correct responses: frozen face, ears up or forward, stiffening of the dog's body posture, tail up, barking, or moving forward toward the person showing aggression. Training begins at 30 to 50 feet from the dog to prevent the dog from showing avoidance behaviors. If the dog backs up, we have made an error, because we have elicited an avoidance response instead of forward aggression. When that happens, the helper backs up and starts again at a greater distance.

The reinforcer for these tiny aggressive responses is given by the helper (the man showing aggression), not by the handler. When the dog shows even a little aggression, the helper slinks or runs away from the dog, and the dog has "won" the little confrontation. The aggression is slowly shaped, raising the criteria on what level of aggressive response the dog must show before the helper runs away.

Other people around during training periods are not to show aggression to the dog. Only a trained helper may do that, since she is the one responsible for shaping the aggression in the dog. The owner may praise the dog gently at first that the dog is correct in his response, but we have been shown time and again that the dog responds more to the behavior of the helper running away than to the praise of the owner.

BITEWORK

Encourage tug-of-war as a wonderful game. This is the beginning of bitework. Little obedience work is done at this stage. The dog is taught it always wins. Duration, strength of bite, calmness of bite are all shaped if the dog doesn't do it naturally (without training).

Trainers use two operant classes of biting: prey (hunting) and defense. Prey is chasing moving objects, killing, shaking, full mouth bites. The end reinforcer of this natural chain used to be food and killing the prey (positively reinforced biting). Defense is defending self/handler/territory from intruders. The reinforcer is described as chasing the bad guy away (negatively reinforced aggression-as a consequence of the dog's aggression, the bad guy is withdrawn), or winning a confrontation (positively reinforced aggression). Dogs whose biting is only negatively reinforced are called fear biters.

The two response classes of biting are combined when actually teaching the dog to bite. The dog has learned to recognize aggression from a human, and knows how to bite at tug-of-war. The helper begins to combine his movements into some threat toward the dog, run laterally or away from the dog elicit chasing, and gives the opportunity for the dog to bite while running or backing away from the dog. He may turn and face the dog as the dog reaches for the bite, as this is an aggressive response.

Stress relief is also the helper's responsibility if he sees signs of stress in the dog, such as growling and raised hackles. The helper will turn his head away from the dog to remove eye contact (which is a threat). He may actually gently pet the dog with his free hand while the dog is biting. The dog is taught to hold on until the helper gives up the sleeve to the dog, or until told to let go. Dogs taught in this way, with stress relief as part of the training, almost never growl or raise their hackles. Instead, they tend to wag their tails with excitement/arousal during protection work. They do not give the appearance of the growling, hackling, lunging, control beast that many picture as an "attack dog."

OBEDIENCE FOR THE BITE

A dog who bites must have excellent obedience both on and off leash so unauthorized bites do not occur. So, after basic obedience and basic biting are learned, obedience during protection is trained. In this stage the bite itself is the reinforcer. This is because the dog will not respond to the food or toy reinforcers used to train regular obedience.

State dependent learning is at work here. The level of arousal is so high that the class of effective reinforcers changes. Also, the Premack principle applies here: high frequency behaviors are used to reinforce low frequency behaviors. Biting is the high frequency response to the aggression cues which have been trained. The dog is allowed to do a large class of natural behaviors (chasing, biting, dominance displays) which are reinforced when they occur in response to the trained discriminative stimuli.

So, although it may sound strange at first, the reinforcer for correct obedience in protection is allowing the dog to bite. The dog learns to respond very quickly to instructions from the owner in order to earn the reinforcer.

OTHER PRACTICAL CONSIDERATIONS

During schutzhund, protection and police work, or a judged schutzhund trial, the dog commonly works off leash. If bitework training is done with all negative reinforcement and/or punishment (leash "corrections"), it results in the dog frequently failing to respond to instructions off leash. The leash becomes a discriminative stimulus, discriminating which set of contingencies is in effect on a multiple schedule. Off leash, the dog's performance becomes unreliable.

Thus it's better to limit negative reinforcers and punishers to when really needed. An example is when the dog has the ability to reinforce himself by biting if the correct setting event is present, but the cue to bite has not been given by the owner. This could happen when the dog is closer to the helper than to the owner, and may take an unauthorized bite if the owner is out of reach.

In summary: personal protection dogs must be safe in public. A dog that bites due to poor stimulus control will have to wear a muzzle in public. A dog wearing a muzzle is not very useful if you are assaulted. A dog trained to bite as a reinforced response with tight stimulus control is a sound, social animal who is an asset to his owner. This is the kind of dog people make comments about to schutzhund trainers such as "Wow, I never knew a dog could be trained to do that," or "I wish I had a dog like that," or (my personal favorite) "how much does a dog like that cost?" The answer is, "He is my friend and protector, and he is priceless."

Problem Solving 11

Planning

Behavioral problems will develop from time to time. It happens to the best trainers and the best animals: an animal develops a bad habit; a behavior begins to break down; you run into training road blocks; the animal seems to have forgotten what it has learned – these are not uncommon problems. But the solutions, at times, seem so complex that trainers don't always know where to begin. The key to successfully working through a problem is planning – careful planning. A few basic steps, which will be described in detail throughout this chapter, are summarized here:

Identify the Problem
This is a straightforward step: acknowledge and recognize there's a problem; only then can you set out to correct it.

Determine the Cause
This requires time and is usually not easy to do. There will be times when you never determine what caused a breakdown of behavior, but that doesn't mean you can't solve the problem. To start, objectives must be clearly articulated and records carefully analyzed. Anyone on the staff who might be able to offer valuable ideas should be brought into the discussion. The cause of the problem usually will lie in one of eight areas, all of which will be discussed shortly.

Implement the Plan
Once you have determined a course of action, implement it with great care. Problem behaviors are not easily resolved, especially if they are long-standing problems. Frequently a breakdown in behavior may involve multiple problems. If you succeed in solving the obvious problem, you may have removed one layer only to find another problem lurking below. You must be patient in searching for a solution.

Constant Monitoring
Once a problem behavior is corrected, it is important to evaluate the immediate success of the plan and to monitor the results over time. It is easy for animals to revert to a bad habit or return to the problem behavior if their behavior is not closely watched.

Determining the Cause

Finding the cause of a behavioral problem is easier said than done. The underlying reasons for problem behaviors are not readily apparent. Trainers should be prepared to accept that the cause may never be definitely determined. Still, it is helpful to remember that behavioral problems usually lie in one of eight areas. Using the eight areas as a checklist can help the trainer find clues to the problem. At the very least, such a list may help to rule out a few possibilities. I was first introduced to this kind of checklist years ago by Gail Laule and Tim Desmond of Active Environments. I have found the technique very helpful. Problem solving in this manner is like being a detective, and trainers who thrive on a challenge will find the exercise fun. Other trainers will find it frustrating. Keep in mind that animals want to succeed, I don't believe that animals make mistakes on purpose. Therefore, the problem invariably will fall into one of these eight areas: environmental, social, psychological, physical, trainer, session use, regression, or desensitization.

Environmental

Changes in the animal's environment will often cause an animal to behave unusually. Some changes are not immediately evident, but if the behavior of all the animals is similarly disrupted, something in the environment could be the problem. Environmental changes also can affect individual animals without affecting the group. When considering environmental conditions, note that the potential problems may lie in some less than obvious places:

- **Weather** – In an outdoor environment, hot sun, strong wind, snow, or a driving rain can cause animals to behave differently than usual. Even in indoor facilities, sunlight, temperature, humidity and barometric pressure can be factors affecting behavior.
- **Facility changes** – Any physical changes in the habitat or its structure are suspect. Ladders propped up in an unusual place, nearby construction that creates noise or vibrations, or a malfunctioning filter are examples of potential facility changes that can affect an animal's performance.
- **Prop changes** – Surprisingly small things can throw an animal off course. A new prop that is slightly larger or smaller than the original, a broken object, or even a change in the trainers' uniforms may cause problems.
- **Public activity** – Sometimes the activity of people around an animal's habitat will distract an animal or cause its behavior to break down. An unusually noisy group of kids or a strobe

flash from a camera in an underwater viewing window are examples of public activity that might affect behavior.

Social

We have discussed this subject in some detail in previous chapters. It is a major influence on every animal's behavior and can directly cause any number of problems.

- **Dominance/submissiveness** – Being at either end of the social ladder can be a very stressful part of an animal's life. It will often be the cause of problems even if there are no overt signs of aggression.
- **Aggression** – This topic was discussed in detail in the previous chapter.
- **Competition** – Various social activities can create competition among animals. Trainers can be the cause of such competitiveness during training sessions; see the discussion on "fairness" in chapter 7, "Social Animals."
- **Sexual activity** – The sexual urges and drives of an animal are very strong and often will be at the root of behavioral problems.

Psychological

These problems can be more difficult to pinpoint, but they are often the result of inadvertently shaped behavior or poor training technique. Psychological problems may grow out of trainer-related causes discussed later, but when such a problem becomes ingrained in the animal's repertoire of trained behaviors, correcting it may take time.

- **Boredom** – Lack of variety over long periods can create big problems. Short-term boredom should be easier to solve but is still a serious concern. See chapter 8, "Variety," for a more detailed discussion of the subject.
- **Neurotic or aberrant behavior** – Such behaviors by definition arise from no apparent organic disease or injury and involve symptoms such as insecurity, anxiety, depression, and irrational fears. Although we may not know that an animal is experiencing these specific symptoms, the roots of these problems usually lie in one or two areas: social interactions or trainer interactions. Careful behavioral observations can be helpful; see the discussion and articles related to ethograms in chapter 5, "Non-Formal Interactions." In rare instances genetic abnormalities or health problems can cause aberrant behavior.
- **Superstitious behavior** – See the discussion in chapter 4, "Basic Operant Conditioning."

Physical
There may be physical limitations causing a behavioral problem.
- **Health** – An important question to ask when witnessing a behavioral breakdown throughout an individual's performance is "Could the animal be sick?" If the breakdown seems tied only to certain types of behaviors such as aerial behaviors or mouth behaviors, then the animal may be suffering from some type of specific injury.
- **Body capabilities** – Is the behavior something the animal is physically capable of doing? Is it too strenuous for that particular animal?

Trainer
Asking yourself, "Am I the problem?" should be one of your first considerations.
- **Skill level** – Is the task being trained over your head? Are you trying to use a technique that you haven't quite mastered?
- **Basics** – Are your S^Ds correct and precise? Are you bridging accurately? Are your reinforcements appropriate? Even experienced trainers will sometimes find that they must revisit some of these basic concepts to discover the cause of a behavioral breakdown.
- **Emotion** – The mood of a trainer can have an unbelievable impact on the quality of a session and the accuracy of decisions, as discussed in chapter 3, "The Human Element."

Session Use
The way in which the trainer uses a session will often affect an animal and can cause problem behaviors. These are some of the important considerations:
- **Planning** – Planning is an important part of a successful session and prevention of problems, especially if several trainers are working in a session.
- **Number of sessions** – Too many sessions may create boredom; too few sessions may cause satiation in an animal by feeding too much at once.
- **Frequency of sessions** – Sometimes if sessions are too close together, the animal has not had the social time needed, or it may still be full from a previous session.
- **Pacing** – Are you moving too slowly or too fast for the animal, or are the approximations in your training moving at a comfortable pace?

Regression

When training a new behavior, regression is a normal part of the learning curve. Sometimes the animal just needs to take a few steps back. However, you should be careful that the animal does not regress permanently or continue regressing, this would be a symptom of another problem. But it is helpful to keep in mind that natural regression occurs in the learning of all new tasks, and is not necessarily indicative of a breakdown.

Desensitization

An animal can never be desensitized to every distraction or new stimuli; consequently, desensitization is a continuing process. Understanding that no animal is ever "completely desensitized" will help trainers recognize that desensitization takes place every day with each animal under our care.

Implementing the Plan

Once you have determined the cause and selected a method of working through a problem, it's time to get started. It is helpful to continue a methodical approach throughout the process. The San Diego Zoo and Wild Animal Park use a staff behaviorist to work through behavioral problems at both locations. Their methods for analyzing a problem and implementing a plan are described in detail in *Animal Behavioral Management at the San Diego Zoo and Wild Animal Park* (Priest, 1991), on page 400. Gary Priest's descriptions are detailed, and he focuses on solving a number of problems.

Untraining Undesirable Behavior

If you are lucky, you will identify the cause of a behavioral problem and find that it is easily remedied. Moving a ladder, getting a new whistle, restructuring your session, or some other fairly superficial solution may be the only "fix" the behavioral problem needs. However, even if the cause is determined and removed or corrected, other behavioral problems may have been created. Then you must buckle down and pull out your bag of training tools. Karen Pryor lists eight methods of getting rid of unwanted behavior in chapter 4 of *Don't Shoot the Dog* (DOG, pp. 98-147). Her explanations of these eight methods are a must-read for all trainers, here is a summary of the basic techniques she describes:

"Shoot the Animal"
Of course, Karen does not mean that literally, but the idea behind it – get rid of the problem by getting rid of the animal – inspired her book title, *Don't Shoot the Dog*. When pet owners send their animals to the pound because they can no longer tolerate certain behavior, this is what "shooting the dog" whimsically implies. If a zoological facility has a problem animal, perhaps it will send the animal to a willing facility or stop training the animal altogether. This practice may not change the animal's unwanted behavior, but it does allow the trainer to avoid an untenable situation. It's not the operant alternative of choice, but it is sometimes a trainer's last resort.

Punishment
Although punishment can get rid of some behaviors, it can also lead to other problems. This topic is discussed in detail in chapter 9, "Advanced Techniques and Concepts." The use of punishment usually means that a trainer is focusing on getting rid of an unwanted behavior rather than trying to shape desirable behavior. Focusing on the desired goal, as we've emphasized, is a more productive approach.

Negative Reinforcement
The use of negative reinforcement is the preferable flip side to punishment, because it focuses attention on the desired results. This can be an effective technique in some very difficult situations. For a more complete discussion of the use of negative reinforcers, again consult chapter 9.

Extinction
This operant concept suggests that if you ignore unwanted behavior, it will go away. By not calling undue attention to an undesirable behavior, you are not accidentally reinforcing it. This is part of the theory behind the use of an LRS (least reinforcing stimulus) when dealing with an incorrect response (see chapter 4, "Basic Operant Conditioning"). Extinction can be effective when dealing with small problems such as a single incorrect response, but when you're faced with more complex problems, extinction can take a long time to have any effect. It is still wise to ignore unwanted behavior even as you're applying other techniques, because that ensures that you are not inadvertently reinforcing the undesirable behavior.

Training an Incompatible Behavior (DRI)

Operantly this is known as DRI, or Differential Reinforcement of Incompatible behavior. It means training the animal to do something that it cannot do at the same time as the unwanted behavior. If two dolphins, for example, are constantly displacing each other at station during a session, teaching them to target on a buoy fixed at the side of the pool while at station is incompatible with the shoving and posturing that occurs during displacement. Stationing on the target must then be well reinforced, which is an example of DRI. Other examples of the use of this technique and the use of DRO can be found in *Aggression: Exploring the Causes and Possible Reduction Techniques* (Turner and Tompkins, 1990), on page 366 in chapter 10, and in *Training, Enrichment, and Behavior* (Lacinak et. al., 1998), on page 269 in chapter 8.

Put the Behavior on Cue

Once a behavior is put on cue, you theoretically have some control over when the behavior is offered. At Shedd Aquarium, you'll recall, our beluga whales took to "spitting" mouthfuls of water at passersby. We believed the reactions of people hit by the water were enough to reinforce the behavior. Ignoring the behavior helped solve the problem, but what helped more was to *train* the belugas to spit on cue. Since behaviors of this kind can be self-reinforcing, the animals may still spit without prompting from time to time, but this was minimized by our cueing the animal to spit every so often.

Shape the Absence of the Behavior (DRO)

Operantly this technique is known as DRO, or Differential Reinforcement of Other behavior. This is similar to DRI, except that reinforcement of "other" behavior is not always "incompatible" behavior. Instead you are simply reinforcing the absence of the unwanted behavior. If a group of dolphins is being aggressive toward one another, you may want to wait to start a session or wait to give an enrichment device until you see all the animals swimming peaceably together. The absence of the aggression, which is what you want, prompts you to reinforce the animals in some manner.

Change the Motivation

If you know what is causing the behavioral problem and can change or remove the motivating factors, you will often solve the problem. If a dolphin is constantly leaving station to socialize with a dolphin watching on the other side of the gate, for example, the motivation for leaving may be the distraction of the other dolphin's presence. If you occupy the other dolphin in a training session at the same time as you train the first dolphin, you might eliminate the problem. As long as trainers can identify the suspected motivator as the precise cause of the unwanted behavior, the technique can work. However, trainers frequently look at intangible motivators that can lead them to making anthropomorphic decisions or assumptions. The dangers of that kind of decision-making are discussed in chapter 3, "The Human Element."

Complex Problems

Sometimes behavioral problems have multiple causes, or the first problem creates a new problem, and several solutions and remedies are needed to get rid of both. Since each problem is unique, choosing from an array of possible solutions requires a solid understanding of the principles involved in each. Learning how other people solved a complex problem can also be helpful. There are several articles located in the next chapter that describe some examples of problem solving techniques being used effectively. Additional articles in this chapter include:

- Dealing with an animal requiring multiple S^Ds is explored in *What You Teach is What You Get* (Wilkes), on page 408.
- Handling a sea lion that is nervous about leaving its home is the subject of *Teaching Pinnipeds to Work in Public Areas* (T. Forum, 1989), on page 409.
- When a medical problem becomes behavioral is discussed by Gary Wilkes in *How the Mind and Body Build New Behaviors*, on page 411.
- Dealing with a fish stealing sea lion is the problem in *The Case of the Fish Stealing Sea Lion* (T. Forum, 1993), on page 412.
- Correcting unwanted chewing in dogs is the subject of Gary Wilkes' article *Sinking Your Teeth into Destructive Chewing*, on page 414.
- *Training a Blind Sea Lion* (T. Forum, 1990), can be found on page 415.
- Perhaps one way to look at problem solving is to think in terms of regaining "behavioral control," but, what does that mean? That's the subject of *Have You Lost Control?* (T. Forum, 1999), on page 418.

Conference Proceedings

1991 IMATA Conference, Vallejo, California, USA. One of the first zoos to hire a trainer to oversee behavioral needs of an entire collection was the San Diego Zoo. Where did they find a behavior specialist with the right qualifications? You guessed it, in the marine mammal field. Gary Priest has done some very innovative work with animals ranging from snakes to cheetahs. Here he presents a few problem solving case studies.

Animal Behavior Management at the San Diego Zoo and Wild Animal Park

by Gary M. Priest
Zoological Society of San Diego

There are many needs that require the behavioral management of captive animals. For zoological institutions, the primary needs include:

- routine maintenance
- facilitating veterinary care
- research
- environmental and behavioral enrichment
- and most important, keeper safety

Some animals, by virtue of their evolution, natural history, and ability to learn, are well suited to a program of behavior management that employs operant conditioning. This paper will focus on these animals. There exists, however, a need to safely manage the behavior of every species requiring keeper contact, including those with which operant techniques are less effective, such as reptiles.

Reptile keepers occasionally have the need to safely handle and manage venomous snakes. A knowledge of the particular animal's natural history and physical capabilities aid in developing safe animal behavior management policies. To avoid exposure to predators, most snakes prefer confined spaces. Therefore, a keeper that needs to handle a snake can provide a length of clear plexiglass pipe for the animal, which will naturally seek the security of a confined space. If the pipe is large enough in diameter for the animal to crawl into partially, but too small in diameter to allow the snake to double back, the animal can be handled safely. No behavior modification is necessary. The animal's natural behavior is used to suit the keepers need to examine and handle a potentially lethal animal. Thus, a technique is developed that will accommodate both the husbandry need and the animal's natural inclination.

PROBLEM SOLVING METHODOLOGY

In San Diego, we have found that problem solving techniques originally developed by industrial psychologists for humans also work well with animals. We routinely employ a methodology for solving animal behavior management problems that uses a simple five-step formula. The formula can be identified in the above example of the reptile keeper and venomous snake:

1. PROBLEM IDENTIFICATION/ NEED (To care for venomous snakes).
2. IDENTIFY BROAD OBJECTIVES/ PLAN SPECIFIC GOALS (To safely handle venomous snakes).
3. DATA COLLECTION (Knowledge of the animal's physical and mental capabilities and its genetic predisposition).
4. METHOD SELECTION (Plexiglass was chosen for visibility, availability, etc.)
5. EVALUATION (Can we improve on the technique? Keepers establish which size plexiglass pipe is appropriate for each snake).

Behavioral problems are not usually difficult to identify. It is normally much more difficult to visualize broad objectives. To identify the objective, it is helpful to ask, "What will it look like when the problem is corrected?" Frequently, solving a behavioral problem is accomplished by simply eliminating the cause. In problem solving, establishing goal(s) is critical to success. The goal(s) should be to eliminate the cause of the problem or, if this is not possible, to control it and modify its impact. The specific goals must be compatible with broad objectives. Data collection is another essential component; the actual cause of the problem is often identified in this phase, and may provide clues to a solution. The method simply determines how the goal will be accomplished and which tools will be used. Finally, careful evaluation of all these steps will provide a refined technology for future applications, a mechanism for tracking progress, and standardization.

DATA COLLECTION

The process of assessing an animal's potential for a behavior-management program that features operant conditioning begins by asking many questions about the subject specie's natural history (Priest, 1991 A):

- How does the species exploit and interact with its environment?
- What are the species' typical postures when relaxed, excited, agitated, or aggressive?

The assessment narrows as a species profile begins to emerge. The focus shifts to the specific animal and its individual behavior, characteristics, and idiosyncrasies:

- Does the particular animal have any physical limitations? Limiting factors could include age, sexual state, size, agility, health, and sensory loss.

METHOD SELECTION

A variety of reinforcement strategies (tools) may be used in accomplishing behavior management paradigms with captive animals. The following case studies will present three common tools used to shape behavioral solutions or to correct behavioral problems. These tools are: operant conditioning, systematic desensitization, and randomized automated feeding schedules. Although different reinforcement strategies are used in each of the following case studies the same methodology for problem solving has been employed in each case.

CASE STUDY #1:
Routine Animal Management

It is always preferable for an animal to raise its own offspring. For a variety of reasons, sometimes this is not possible and intervention is necessary. Margarita, a Celebes macaque (*Macaca nigra*), had not had an easy first delivery. The baby lodged breech in the birth canal and had to be delivered by emergency caesarian section. Margarita survived the ordeal, but her baby did not. Two years later, Margarita again became pregnant. The 22-week pregnancy went smoothly, but, because of her previous difficulty with a vaginal delivery, a caesarian section was indicated. A hysterectomy was necessary and was performed during the delivery. With help, Margarita gave birth to a strong and healthy baby female.

The macaque was the consummate mother. Even though she was recovering from her own major surgery, she tended to every need of her infant, named Tamboo. Margarita would tirelessly examine, caress, suckle, coo, and lip-smack to her helpless infant daughter. But the zoo's veterinarians became concerned when they discovered that despite Margarita's exemplary maternal care, Tamboo was losing weight. It was soon discovered that Tamboo had spent many frustrating hours attempting to draw milk from her mother's mammary glands. Possibly as a result of the hysterectomy, Margarita was not lactating a sufficient quantity of milk to support Tamboo. Drug therapy proved futile, and intervention would be required if the baby was to survive.

NEED/PROBLEM IDENTIFICATION

Infant primates raised by the mother learn important social skills. Margarita was a good mother, and so it was advantageous to allow her to continue to manage her baby. The problem was that every time the baby required feeding, it was necessary to anesthetize Margarita so the baby could be pried from her arms. Margarita was paying a heavy price. The stress associated with the administration of the anesthetic (accomplished via the veterinary squeeze cage), the recovery from her major surgery, and, most of all, the anxiety of being routinely separated from her infant was just too much to ask of her. Veterinarians were considering permanently pulling the infant to raise it in the zoo's neonate hospital facility.

OBJECTIVES/GOALS

Discussing the problem, keepers and veterinarians posed an interesting question, "Could Margarita be trained to give us her baby?" That idea was rejected as unattainable, but it lead to another question, "Could we train Margarita to hold her baby in place for us while we fed the baby, long distance?" We felt this might be accomplished through a program of operant conditioning.

METHOD SELECTION

A paradigm was designed so that each step would progress logically toward accomplishing our objective, Margarita first learned to associate the bridging stimulus (a clicker sounded just prior to the delivery of a reinforcement) with a food reward. Once she understood the reinforcement system, we could reward her for being relaxed and comfortable in the restricted space of a veterinary squeeze cage. This was an important step for two reasons. First, macaques can host the Herpes B virus with no ill effect, but an accidental scratch from a macaque with the virus has proven fatal to humans. Restricting the space in which this animal could maneuver was an important safety factor. Second, until she learned to trust us and our intentions toward her baby, we know that she would instinctively shield her baby from us, which would make it impossible to get the nipple to the infant. The restricted space, made possible by a cage designed with a collapsible wall, would not allow her to easily turn her back toward us. She soon learned that a relaxed attitude was reinforced, and the collapsible wall was eliminated from use by approximations until, finally, she had access to the entire cage. Margarita was a quick study. Within the course of a single day, she preferred to be at the front of the cage, where she could be easily rewarded for her cooperation.

The final step required Margarita to become familiar with the device that hospital keepers devised to get formula to the Infant. The device was constructed using a long piece of surgical tubing with a nipple on one end and a syringe on the other. A wire coat hanger was fixed to the nipple and wrapped around the rubber tube so that we could maneuver the nipple in place. Once Margarita was desensitized to the nipple, rod, and syringe apparatus (later replaced by an Even-flo disposable nurser bottle) and realized that these objects would not hurt her or her baby, little Tamboo had to do her part. Fortunately, Tamboo had an incredible suckling response and would latch on to virtually anything that even remotely resembled her mother's milkless nipples.

By using the common language of operant conditioning and a plan of carefully orchestrated steps, we experienced the thrill of participating in the ultimate storybook ending. Margarita successfully raised her daughter with minimal human intervention.

CASE STUDY #2:
Special Veterinary Care
A Diabetic Drill at the San Diego Zoo

Of the 200 living species of primates currently recognized, about one in every seven are endangered. The drill is an endangered species of baboon with restricted and decreasing numbers. In July of 1989, Loon, our male drill (*Mandrillus leucodhaeus*) one of only 19 drills in the country, was diagnosed with diabetes. Like human diabetics, Loon required daily insulin injections. A veterinary squeeze cage immobilized the intractable animal so that insulin could be administered daily.

NEED/PROBLEM IDENTIFICATION

Loon is a wild, 60-pound baboon with three-inch-long canine teeth. It was not surprising that the stress produced in the animal by daily injections resulted in the increased exhibition of aggressive, abnormal, and neurotic behaviors (Priest, 1991 B). It became obvious that the stressful procedure was not an acceptable long-term solution, because the procedure being used to save Loon's life was also making his life intolerable. Euthanasia would certainly be considered a humane option.

OBJECTIVES/GOALS

Voluntary venipuncture is regularly accomplished with trained marine mammal (Cornell, 1983; Schroeder, 1990), as well as with laboratory macaques (Vertein, 1989). Our objective was to save Loon's life and reduce stress levels imposed on him by his required treatment. The goals in this experimental behavior modification program were to train the animal to voluntarily accept daily insulin injections for a food reward and if possible, train him to allow us to take periodic blood and urine samples for routine analysis.

DATA COLLECTION

The project presented several unique challenges. Although Loon had been stabilized, he was not healthy by normal standards. Loon's medical history of being poked, prodded, squeezed, and tested had left him a very dangerous animal, and safety was an important consideration. We required a strategy that would incorporate behavior that was incompatible with aggression directed toward the trainer. In addition, diet is critical to diabetics, and, a behavior modification plan using operant conditioning would depend on a food reward. As a final challenge, Loon would have to receive all his food, every day, whether he chose to work for it or not.

METHOD SELECTION

The animal's medical condition dictated our training priorities. First, Loon was conditioned to accept his insulin injections, for without them, he would slip into diabetic shock and would soon die. We began by using the squeeze cage to immobilize him for injections and pairing the event with a food reward. Loon quickly learned to quietly accept his shot for the food treat that would follow. Soon, Loon was presenting his backside in anticipation of the injection. Gradually, the use of restraint was diminished and finally eliminated. Observations of the overall improvement in the animal's behavior caused us to conclude that this technique had proved useful in reducing the stress load imposed on the animal by the trauma of daily restraint.

For blood withdrawals, Loon was trained to reach into a stainless steel tube, the exact length of his extended arm, and grasp a steel rod positioned crosswise at the end of the tube. This would expose the vessels on his forearm for venipuncture. The idea was that as long as the drill was grasping the rod, he could not easily grab a trainer. Holding the rod was incompatible with any aggression directed toward the trainer. Thus, rod holding was reinforced, the probabilities were increased that the rod-holding behavior would be consistently more rewarding to the animal than non-compliance. So, in a positive and rewarding environment, the animal's behavior was shaped to comply with the specific needs of captive-animal management.

After a few days of training, Loon was rod grasping and holding position until the bridging stimulus sounded to signal the termination of the behavior and the presentation of a food reward. Through an ellipse cut in the tube, Loon was reinforced for allowing touch on his shaved forearm while he continued to grasp the rod at the end of the tube. This was especially rewarding to Loon because by nature, baboons enjoy this social contact with conspecifics. As training progressed, different textured objects were dragged over the bare skin of Loon's forearm. This procedure desensitized him to a variety of tactile stimuli and simultaneously provided an occasion to reward him for continuing to grasp the rod. Within a few weeks, Loon was voluntarily allowing the veterinarians to draw blood from his forearm. The technique has also proved safe. Loon has never injured a trainer or veterinarian during any procedure. In fact, Loon has tolerated six consecutive failed attempts to draw blood from the vessels in his forearm, without once withdrawing from the tube and rod.

Because vessels on Loon's arm became scarred, Loon was later trained to offer the vessels on the ventral side of both of his legs for venipuncture. Now, venipuncture sites are rotated to help reduce damage to any single vessel site. Loon has voluntarily accepted his daily insulin injections and blood withdrawals for over two years and has rarely required restraint.

CASE STUDY #3:
Research
Cheetah Breeding Project at the
Wild Animal Park

At the Wild Animal Park in 1985, Senior Animal Trainer Terri Paterson was responsible for caring for a young male cheetah named Pesach. As the hand-reared cheetah matured, Terri noticed the animal engaging in sexually oriented play behavior with a variety of inanimate objects. She discussed her observations of the cheetah behavior with Center for Reproduction of Endangered Species (CRES) reproductive physiologist Dr. Barbara Durrant and research supervisor Susan Millard. Together the group developed a plan to capitalize on the opportunity the animal was presenting. Their objective was to eliminate the stress associated with sedation and electroejaculation for semen collection, and to increase opportunity for collection. The original strategy was to attempt to train the cheetah to mount a phantom or dummy. This proved unsuccessful even though estrous urine was splashed over the phantom as an enticement. In response to the failure, Dr. Durrant set to work to design an artificial vagina for the cheetah similar o the kind used with domestic livestock. Ultimately, it was this device, manipulated by a handler that proved successful.

DATA COLLECTION

With cats, breeding can be violent. Although it is not yet known if cheetahs are induced ovulators, most felids are. Most cats begin to ovulate only after the first copulation of the new cycle. During copulation, the male normally holds the female in place by biting her at the nape of the neck. The male's behavior is likely a defense mechanism for the female cheetah always terminates copulation by violently turning on him to break the neck bite. It is believed that because the female cheetah prefers a solitary existence in the wild, aggression following mating may serve to eject the male from her territory. In light of their sexual genetic predispositions, collecting semen has the potential to be very dangerous, no matter how well disposed the cat might be.

METHOD SELECTION

Again, a paradigm incompatible with aggression was developed. Similar to the example of the snake in the plexiglass tube, in this paradigm, trainers Terri Peterson and Cheryl Nix used a food reward of cubed jack cheese to train the cheetah to enter a narrow crate. Once in the crate, the cheetah could not turn around, it could only back out. This gives the trainer ample time to move out of the way if the cat should terminate the collection procedure. If the cat becomes aggressive, the collection is terminated. While in the crate, semen from the cheetah could be safely collected. As an interesting side note, the behavior quickly became intrinsically reinforcing.

Dr. Durrant and Susan Millard have expanded on the initial program of collecting from a hand-reared cheetah. The researchers now regularly collect from mother reared cheetahs, as well. They have discovered, however, that to a large extent, their success depends on the temperament of the individual animal. By constantly evaluating the program, the group found that it is safer for the people doing the actual collecting not to interact with the animals for purposes other than collection. This helps prevent the cheetah from bonding sexually with a keeper that is responsible for its daily care. It also serves as a good discriminator, helping the animal avoid confusion as to the purpose of an individual's presence. To date, samples from a total of five male cheetahs have been collected on a regular basis.

CASE STUDY #4:
Environmental and Behavioral Enrichment with Alaskan Brown Bears

This experimental program is currently being developed. The study features the process of integration that is often necessary to develop objectives and behavioral solutions that meet the needs of everyone involved.

NEED/PROBLEM IDENTIFICATION

Nearly 15 years ago, the San Diego Zoo abolished the practice of allowing visitors to feed exhibit animals. The last vestige of this tradition came to an end in 1991 when the zoo bus drivers were told to stop feeding biscuits to bears on their tours. The bears were not happy about this turn of events and the bus drivers were unanimous in their agreement that this form of interaction was the high point on their tours for visitors. However, animal care managers felt at least as strongly that it was their responsibility to determine the exact quantity and quality of food items fed to exhibit animals. The action taken was necessary to insure the health of the animals and to present a consistent message to our visitors regarding the care of our living collection.

Every year, over 1,500,000 people enjoy bus tours at the San Diego Zoo. An average of between 25 and 30 tours are conducted every day of the year, with the busiest days doubling the figure. Because more than 40 percent of our guests elect to purchase tickets for a bus tour, it remains one of our most effective tools to educate the public about our collection and our organization's purpose. Bus tours also generate nearly $3,000,000 in annual revenue.

OBJECTIVES/GOALS

In this case, the objective was clear. We needed to develop a solution that could meet the psychological needs of the animals, the need of the keeper to determine diets, and our corporate need to enhance the visitor experience. Several goals were identified. Through several meetings, all parties independently agreed that it was important to insure that our animals received the best possible care. All agreed on the importance of preventing stereotypic, neurotic, or destructive behaviors by providing the bears with opportunities for the expression of natural behaviors. Further, all agreed on the need to enhance outdated, second-generation, bear exhibits by developing an exhibit that was a closer approximation of nature.

DATA COLLECTION

At its essence, nature is variety and change. Inexpensive, off-the-shelf technology now exists that can be adopted to provide an almost endless variety of behavioral opportunities for exhibit animals. Randomized bear exhibits (Markowitz, 1982) would enhance the bus tours, and provide the keeper with control over diets, but, most importantly, they would provide an environment more conducive to better animal health. Significant positive change in animal physique has been reported for animals living in a behaviorally active environment (Schmidt & Markowitz, 1977; Markowitz, Schmidt, & Moody, 1978). It has also been well documented that given a choice, animals will typically work to obtain food even when the same food is available free of effort (NurInger, 1969; Stevens, 1978).

METHOD SELECTION

By providing opportunities for natural foraging behavior, animals could fill activity vacuums that are sometimes the result of confinement in relatively sterile environments. In an activity rich environment, there is little room left in an animal's behavioral repertoire for aberrant behaviors.

The randomization of our bear environments will be accomplished by timers set by keepers specific to the requirements of each species in each exhibit. Each exhibit will have three or four types of mechanisms paying out different food types (ie. honey, sunflower seeds, grapes, apples) in different ways, (i.e. dripping, scattering, rolling, blowing, and dumping). This simple equipment, consisting of gravity-fed food dispensers with solenoids, will be used to randomize the bears' world.

Opportunities for the bears to catch live fish dropped into their pools, snatch grapes as they roll down hill, or stalk live crickets will be provided by the equipment. These events will be triggered remotely by the bus drivers (enhancing the visitor experience) but controlled by the keepers (facilitating animal care). Dispensers will be loaded for the entire day each morning.

Each exhibit will be programmed for one event every 15 minutes, for a maximum number of four events per hour. If the opportunity for one event occurs every 15 minutes, four times per hour, with six exhibits, the possibility for 24 events would occur every hour. Even on our busiest days, when 70 bus tours may be required to meet visitor demand, nearly one event every two minutes would be available somewhere on the bear string. On our busiest days, this rate would provide behavioral opportunity without tiring or satiating the bears.

In agreement with the Bear Behavior Management Plan, drivers will reinforce only those behaviors that have been identified as species-typical. Some potential behaviors for reinforcement include vocalizations, locomotion, swimming, digging, chewing, shredding. Aggressive or anthropomorphic behaviors will not be reinforced.

Markowitz noted that one great benefit of giving animals increased behavioral opportunities is that they will discover unique ways to use them. As a result, this project should continue to be dynamic and exciting indefinitely. Inspiration and imagination will be required to keep ahead of the bears as they learn to exploit their random and stimulating surroundings.

CASE STUDY #5:
Keeper Safety
"Protected Contact" Elephant Management at the San Diego Wild Animal Park

Elephants are intelligent, social, and potentially lethal animals. In the U.S., during the last 15 years, 15 keepers have been killed by elephants (Lehnhardt, 1991). Maintaining healthy elephants in captivity requires that keepers have total access to the animal. For 3,000 years, elephant handlers accomplished this by exercising social dominance through occasional physical discipline. This control system was patterned after the wild elephant's own social behavior and hierarchical society. In India, where traditional control methods evolved, a mahout (Hindi word for elephant handler) is often associated with an elephant for a lifetime. The keeper's dominance is established early on in the relationship, and the need for physical dominance decreases as the social bonds develop between trainer and animal. Unfortunately, this control system also requires 100% compliance from the animal 100% of the time. There is no room for deviation, nor can the keeper safely allow any breakdown in control, as this can lead to catastrophic results.

Although hundreds of elephant keepers have been killed as a result of the failures of this system, it has remained largely unchallenged and unchanged. No alternative has existed. The system was carried into this century and to zoos by many fine circus trainers. Now, several fundamental societal shifts are causing us to rethink the traditional elephant management system.

NEED/PROBLEM IDENTIFICATION

Today's society is increasingly mobile. As a result, employment behavior has changed. We can no longer expect elephant keepers to remain with a single animal for a lifetime or, for that matter, even for a few years. By trying to maintain the old system in this new environment, relationships continue to grow less secure. Under these circumstances, challenges by elephants, and the need to use physical discipline to maintain control, will become more frequent. Zoological institutions have helped link animals with the environmental crisis. This new awareness has very naturally created a heightened sensibility toward animals. The traditional method of elephant management may come to be regarded by the public as offensive and inhumane.

OBJECTIVES/GOALS

The objective of the "protected contact" system is to develop a non-aversive method that uses operant conditioning for managing elephant husbandry behaviors. This method does not rely on physical or social dominance to control behavior. Instead, behavioral paradigms have been developed that allow the animal a choice between cooperation and a reward for desired behavior or breaking contact. Cooperation is completely voluntary. A "time out" or loss of opportunity to earn a reward punishes aggression or lack of attention.

METHOD SELECTION

All "protected contact" behaviors are designed to allow the contact necessary for husbandry while being simultaneously incompatible with aggression toward the handler. This system provides many benefits:

- there is no catastrophic consequence if the animal chooses to deviate from the training program
- aggression is held in check
- the system allows the keeper to maintain important husbandry behaviors on aggressive animals and bulls in must with little risk of injury
- by using the common currency of a food reward, new keepers can quickly become as reinforcing to the animal as established keepers
- this system provides new keepers with time to establish a "protected" working relationship with an animal long before (if ever) being exposed to the animal in the traditional "Free Contact" system
- the system presents an opportunity to reinforce positive social interactions between animals in a herd and to control movement from point A to point B remotely, without the need of exposing a keeper to risk of Injury.

Times change, and organizations, like organisms, must be responsive to environmental changes or suffer consequences imposed on them from without. Each of us in the profession has embarked on an exciting voyage that today, as never before, has the sole purpose of preserving as much of the planet's biological diversity as possible for future generations to appreciate and enjoy. On this voyage, we have seen many changes in the way we exhibit and care for our animals. We have already journeyed far, but have, just now, come to a place where we have the tools to care for our animals' psychological as well as physical well being. We are now about to enter an exciting era in the care, management, and exhibition of captive exotic animals. New opportunities exist for anyone willing to accept the challenges that change and technology present.

REFERENCES

Cornell, L. (1983). Hematology and Clinical Chemistry Values in the Killer Whale (*Orcinus orca*). Journal of Wildlife Diseases V. 19 #3, pp. 259-264.

Lehnhardt, J. (1991). Elephant Handling-A Problem of Risk Management and Resource Allocation. Proceedings of the National AAZPA [American Association of Zoologica Parks and Aquariums] Conference, San Diego, Calif. AAZPA, Wheeling, W. Virginia. (in Press).

Markowitz, H. (1982). Behavioral Enrichment In the Zoo. New York: Van Nostrand Reinhold.

Markowitz, H., Schmidt, M.J., and Moody, A. (1978). Behavioral engineering and animal health in the zoo. International Zoo Yearbook, 18:190-194.

Neuringer, A. (1969). Animals respond for food in the presence of free food. Science 166:339-341.

Priest, G. M. (1991). The Use of Operant Conditioning in Training Husbandry Behavior., with Captive Exotic Animals. Proceedings of the National AAZK [American Association of Zoo Keepers] Conference 16: 94-108, 1990.

Priest, G. M. (1991). The Psychology of Animal Care, Part 11: Protecting Primates. Zoonooz. February 1991.

Schmidt, M.J. and Markowitz, H. (1977). Behavioral engineering as an aid in the maintenance of healthy zoo animals. Journal of the American Veterinary Medical Association. 171 (9): 966-969.

Schroeder, P., and Keller, K. (1990). Artificial Insemination in the Bottlenose Dolphin. pp. 488. [In] Leatherwood, S. & Reeves, R. (Eds.), The Bottlenose Dolphin. San Diego: Academic Press.

Stevens, V.J. (1978). Basic operant research in the zoo. In Markowitz H. and Stevens, V.J. (Eds.) The Behavior of Captive Wild Animals. Chicago: Nelson Hall: pp. 209-246.

Vertein, R. and Reinhardt, V. (1989). Training female rhesus monkeys to cooperate during in-home cage venipuncture. Laboratory Primate Newsletter, 28, 1-3.

A Behavior Sampler by Gary Wilkes

Repeating an S^D when an animal fails to respond on the first cue is a mistake made by many trainers. In so doing, we unknowingly create behavioral problems, which makes it all the more difficult to correct later.

What You Teach is What You Get

by Gary Wilkes

Biff is a smart dog. He has learned how to please his master, Jim, perfectly. Every time he hears a command, he dutifully ignores it for 30 seconds. After waiting patiently, Jim gives the command again and this time it's louder. Biff ignores the second command as well. By the time Jim gives the third command, he is screaming so loudly that he is in danger of shattering crystal. That's when Biff finally obeys the command.

Repeatedly yelling commands is probably the most common training error. If Biff does not respond instantly to a cue, he hears Jim say it again. This repeating of signals means that Biff can safely ignore the first few requests and still get treats and affection. Before criticizing Jim, it may help to know how this behavior developed.

Humans are capable of conceptual thought and the ability to communicate through speech. The assumption that these two abilities are connected is often unjustified. We often say things because we have been reinforced for saying particular words in similar situations - not because it is intelligent to do so.

Several years ago, my wife and I were visiting a drive-thru wild animal park near Seattle. A female elk tried to stick her head into our car - a small convertible sports car. The animal's huge head squeezed between the window and the cloth top. I automatically shouted "No!" My wife burst into laughter. The elk continued her assault. I yelled "No!" even louder. The elk finally pulled her head from the window when I moved the car gently forward. My shouts had no effect on the elk, yet I had yelled again without thinking. The reason for this reaction is simple but not obvious. I repeated myself, not because I "knew" it would affect the elk, but because it had worked to stop other animals in the past.

When we speak, we assume that our words will be understood. If a person does not respond to our speech, we assume that he has not heard us and we automatically repeat the phrase. If this second attempt succeeds, we will continue to repeat in similar situations. As long as everyone speaks your language, repeating yourself will succeed. What if the person is a foreigner and does not speak English? If you say a word louder, or twice, you will fail to communicate unless the listener already knows the word. That's where Jim made his mistake - Biff doesn't speak English.

In the early stages of teaching Biff to lie down, Jim followed tradition and chanted "Down-down-down" as he forced Biff to the ground. Jim was not aware that he was saying the word several times on each repetition of the behavior. Biff automatically connected all three repetitions of the command into one signal. As Biff learned the behavior, he sometimes miscounted and lay down on the first or second repetition of the cue. Jim believed that Biff "knew" now to lie down because of these responses. Biff thought of them as mistakes. Soon Biff and Jim developed a consistent pattern. Jim would command "Down" and wait a few seconds. Biff thought "OK, one down and two to go!" Biff would hold his position perfectly, waiting for the next signal. Jim would get frustrated that Biff was still sitting. He would say the command again, "Down!" - this time still a little louder. Biff would think, "There is number two. One more to go!" and hold his position. Finally Jim would scream the command with exasperated force. "DOWN!!!" Biff would obediently lie down. He was secure in the knowledge that he had performed the behavior exactly as his master had taught him.

In nature, wild canines survive by using their acute senses to their fullest potential. They must respond instantly to the first indication of a tasty rabbit or a hungry cougar. To take full advantage of your pet's potential, remember, say it once and say it softly. It's a no-no to say it twice-twice.

VOL 14, NO 4, 1989. Teaching animals to move into new areas or to trust new things can be a challenge. However, it is usually just a matter of using good desensitization techniques. The methods described below are useful for moving into a public area or for moving into any new place.

Teaching Pinnipeds to Work in Public Areas

QUESTION: We have been working to desensitize several sea lions to work in the public area. So far we have been very successful with the exception of one 14-year-old male. After about three minutes he becomes very nervous and if he is not taken home quickly he starts to search frantically for a way home. We have followed the same steps we utilized for our other sea lions but the results are not the same. We have become discouraged and are wondering if he is an impossible case. Does anyone have any thoughts?

ANSWER 1: Pinnipeds, unlike cetaceans, can be adept at performing in places distant and unrelated to the areas where they are normally housed. The development of this capability often becomes a desirable goal to the trainer, but to the animal the removal of the security of "home" can cause fear and apprehension. Therefore, the trainer's goal is to create a positive atmosphere for the animal in a place other than "home." To do this, we use several steps. The first step is to build a trusting relationship with the animal. Once achieved, the animal is reassured simply by the trainer's presence. The second step involves the use of a stationing object in the animal's "home," in our situation, a seat. The seat is a positive position where the animal is trained, fed and secure. Although these first two steps are simplistic, they are the building blocks to the desired goal and ones that are often overlooked. From here we progress to walking the animal from "home" to a seat positioned outside of the enclosure. Our most important aim in these beginning stages is to always allow the animal free access to "home." Do not close gates behind you! Although the animals may leave stationing position to return "home," a common mistake is to deny the animal access to the enclosure during the initial desensitization to the new environment. This only compounds the problem, making a panic situation worse. When the animal is satisfied in the knowledge that he can return to "home" whenever threatened by sea-lion-eating monsters such as dried leaves, vacuum hoses, and garbage cans, he builds confidence in this new environment as well. As time progresses and the animal's confidence builds his need to return "home" is extinguished and gates may be closed behind him. Using this method, we have found an animal can be desensitized to almost any situation or area by simply moving the stationing prop.
Doug Messinger and Cheryl Snyder
Entertainment Plus

ANSWER 2: I try to keep my sea lions busy by frequently asking for simple behaviors; i.e. raising a flipper, "talking," etc. Variety in when he goes out, the route you take, and how long he's out may also help. Both techniques may keep him distracted around the magical three-minute mark. He's probably not an "impossible case" but working in the public area may not be his forte. I've had some sea lions that were steady as rocks and some that are a thrill a second.
Jim Alexander
St. Louis Zoo

ANSWER 3: Perhaps the best approach would be to let the sea lion take his home with him when investigating a new area. By training the animal to ride on a cart or in a roll cage, you can easily desensitize an animal to new areas while always being able to offer the security of a home on wheels close by. When and if an animal feels nervous or uncomfortable he will always have the ability to run back to his cart for a few positive and secure moments. Later on, as his motor home becomes more and more comfortable the animal will have the opportunity to view more and more areas safely from the wagon or whatever you choose to use. Always remember to reinforce the animal anytime he returns to his cart rather than running back home. Certainly the most important idea here is to help the animal learn that many places can provide security and be as reinforcing as home. A special bench or picnic table (even a duck pond) can serve as a secondary work station, and if kept positive enough a sea lion will usually choose to run to the closest area of comfort and security when nervous. Good luck, aloha!

Christian Harris
Dolphin Quest

A Behavior Sampler by Gary Wilkes

When a behavior breaks down, finding the cause may not always lead to an easy solution to the problem. Correcting unwanted behavior may require a multi-tiered approach, particularly if the original problem has led to more complex problems.

How the Mind and Body Build New Behaviors

by Gary Wilkes

Fluffy had a bladder infection. She first noticed it while using her litter box. The act of eliminating had gradually become painful. Fluffy didn't know about bacteria and infections. She thought the pain was caused by the box.

To remedy her discomfort, Fluffy started to experiment. She could not stop eliminating, but she could try new locations. Her first goal was to find a surface that felt like fresh dirt. She raked her paws across a variety of surfaces until she felt the same resistance she got from her cat litter.

Fluffy's first target was the carpet in the dining room. It was as far from the box as she could get. The tight nap of the carpet gave the same sensation to her paws as her litter. She sniffed to see if the spot was clean and then eliminated. Fluffy got a rude surprise - it still hurt.

The second location she tried was the bed in the guest bedroom. The ribbed comforter had the proper feeling as she pulled her claws across it. The surface moved a little bit as she pulled at it, just like litter. Fluffy eliminated on the comforter. She was again frustrated in her attempts. Her infection was still causing pain.

After several weeks, Fluffy's owner started to smell a peculiar odor in the house. The inescapable conclusion was that Fluffy was wetting the carpet.

A quick trip to the vet confirmed the suspicion. Her owner was relieved to know that Fluffy's behavior was caused by a physical problem. Everything would get back to normal once the medication did its job.

After her visit to the vet, Fluffy used the box again. Antibiotics take a few days to start working, so the return to the box was painful. Fluffy was further convinced that the box caused the pain. She continued her quest to find a painless place to eliminate.

As the medication started to take effect, Fluffy's discomfort decreased. This confirmed that she could reduce the pain by avoiding the box. By this point, Fluffy was one step away from never using the box again.

To get Fluffy back on track, several things must happen. First, she must be prevented from having more accidents in the house. Second, she must be forced to use her box, and third, she must be reinforced for correct elimination.

The easiest way to prevent more accidents is to confine her to a room with a slick floor. Fluffy has an instinctive preference for surfaces that can be moved around. A concrete or tile floor is less likely to stimulate elimination than carpet. Fluffy is going to spend a few days in the laundry room.

The slick surface leaves Fluffy with only one suitable area to eliminate - her box. The first time she is forced to use it she will anticipate the pain that she experienced before. She may try to avoid urinating as long as she can. When she finally eliminates she will be pleasantly surprised - no more pain. If her owner is smart, Fluffy will spend about a week in the laundry room. Whenever her owner hears her using the box, Fluffy is going to receive lots of praise and food treats. She is going to learn that using the box is a pleasant experience.

It is obvious that pain and discomfort from an illness can change the behavior of a normally perfect pet. It is important to remember that relieving the physical cause of the problem may not automatically correct the behavior. Getting Fluffy to return to the box will require a combination of medical and behavior solutions.

Trainer's Forum

VOL 18, NO 1, 1993. Correcting a problem behavior that is self-reinforcing can be one of the biggest challenges for a trainer. The question at hand is very common with sea lions, but as all four respondents note, it can be corrected. The most common mistake made by trainers in this situation is that they get angry, insisting that their animal "knows better." This is not a good (nor likely very accurate) way to approach solving the problem.

The Case of the Fish Stealing Sea Lion!

QUESTION: As trainers, we have recently been confronted with a challenging situation. One of our California sea lions began stealing fish from our feeding buckets during training sessions. This particular animal is older and well trained, which creates even more questions for us. The interesting thing about her behavior is that the bucket diving doesn't occur under the same circumstances every time. We have tried various methods to correct her behavior but do not feel she understands. We would like to correct this behavior before it becomes a habit and would appreciate any advice or shared experience from trainers who have handled similar situations in the past.

ANSWER 1: It is unclear from your question whether the feeding buckets in use are stationary, carried by handle, or are worn by the trainer. Different types of feeding buckets would require different strategies, so let's discuss some of these strategies.

Handled or Stationary Buckets: It would be a simple matter to design a lid that would be functional for the trainer while eliminating the possibility that the animal would gain access to the fish. After the animal was unsuccessful a number of times, it should become less reinforcing for her to dive for the buckets.

Worn by the Trainer: This situation poses a different set of problems as the trainer can be in jeopardy if the animal chooses to dive the fish bucket while it's worn by the trainer. If the animal is really intent on getting food out of the bucket, the trainer could be viewed as "in the way" and could accidentally be bitten in the process.

Bucket diving has, more often than not, been a symptom of a larger problem. If the animal is confused, unsure, or otherwise finds that what the trainer is doing is not reinforcing, she can try to terminate this situation by using bucket diving as a displacement behavior. By moving slowly and deliberately, and by reinforcing behaviors which are incompatible with bucket diving, such as heeling on target or keeping their head in a position away from the bucket - it should be a simple matter of reconditioning.

Vic Charfauros
San Diego Zoo

ANSWER 2: There are several ways to try to stop problems with sea lions stealing fish from buckets. It can be a difficult problem to extinguish because every time they steal a fish they are reinforced.

One possibility is to make buckets less attractive. A sea lion may view a bucket as a fancy, wrapped container that probably has something good inside. Empty buckets won't be very reinforcing, they're just another prop. If the animal comes in frequent contact with empty buckets, the bucket itself won't be an attractive stimulus. Training the sea lion to "dive" into an empty bucket may also make buckets less desirable.

Perhaps the easiest way to solve the problem is to remove the bucket. Have your fish placed in several areas, perhaps in different types of containers, where the sea lions can't see or reach them. For the sea lion, the reinforcers will appear magically from a variety of sources. A bonus is that the animal should pay more attention to you. You're the source of reinforcement and not the defender of the bucket.

Jim Alexander & Jackie Ott
St. Louis Zoo

ANSWER 3: Unfortunately I have had much experience with animals that steal from buckets: sea lions, walrus, and even dolphins. Each time serves as a learning experience and entertainment for anyone watching.

I am not sure what methods you have tried to correct the behavior, or what your particular situation is, but here are a variety of ideas that we have tried that may help.

The first and best (in my opinion), is to take away the stealing opportunity by using a hip bucket (with a lid, if you are short like me) or by keeping the fish in out-of-reach stations around the exhibit. This is based on the premise that if there is no bucket, she can't steal from it. Of course, if you go back to using buckets later, the stealing behavior may again rear it's ugly head. In this case you may want to do some work with empty buckets and reinforce her when she ignores them. Eventually, you will want to put fish in the bucket. Use short, very positive sessions, reinforcing her when she ignores the bucket. Then increase the length of the session and the amount of food in the bucket gradually. You will have to make sure that you maintain the behavior of ignoring the bucket and make sure that you do not inadvertently reinforce her focusing on the bucket. Consistency between trainers is very important. Many times new trainers may not be able to tell when the animal is displaying behavior that could eventually lead to stealing. On the other hand, experienced people may be too relaxed and may not pay close attention.

You mentioned that this is an older, well--trained animal. You may try jazzing up the sessions by changing the behavior order, reinforcement schedule, or add new training. These changes in the sessions may get her to focus more on the trainer than on the bucket. We have also slightly raised the diet of some of our animals, which seemed to remove the stealing problem.

You said that you wanted to correct the behavior before it is a habit. I am pretty sure that at this point, if she has stolen the bucket a few times, she is just waiting for that opportunity at each session. I hope that one or more of these ideas have been helpful.

Here are a few more important points to keep in mind:
1. Keep in mind the philosophy "trick me once, shame on you; trick me twice, shame on me." Make it the trainers' responsibility to not provide stealing opportunities.
2. Make sure all trainers are consistent in how they work with the animal. Decide as a group what to do to prevent stealing and what to do if stealing occurs. If a steal does occur, I would collect any fish (and pride) I had left and leave, watching the sea lion carefully (during the excitement they can get aggressive).
3. Do not tempt the sea lion if you think that she may go for a steal. Make a new approximation only when she is ready. Always set her up to succeed. And never, ever make the mistake of thinking that you are quicker than she is! Mutual dives for the bucket can make the process into a game that you will almost always lose.

Good luck.
Marty Sevenich
Brookfield Zoo

ANSWER 4: Perhaps the most difficult thing about dealing with a sea lion that steals from your bucket is that the behavior is self-reinforcing. The answer to your problem may be difficult to determine without knowing your situation or work environment. The easiest answer is to move the bucket out of your animal's reach. This may be easier said than done, depending on your situation. However, too often trainers try so hard to "teach the animal not to steal fish" rather than simply removing the temptation. An easily accessible bucket of fish will always be tempting to a sea lion, no matter how well-trained she is. Once she has been reinforced by stealing fish, it will be difficult to break her of the habit of trying again unless you can keep her from being reinforced for a long period of time. Several ways of keeping the bucket inaccessible or out of reach are:
1. Keeping the bucket high enough that only the trainer can get to it.
2. The use of lids that prevent the animal from getting fish if they do happen to try.
3. The use of side pouches that the trainer can wear around the waist with openings too small for an animal's head.
4. The use of various feeding stations in which buckets or containers are hidden and the animal is not aware of their location.

There are likely other methods that could work as well, depending on your training situation. You should find that once the pattern of being reinforced for diving for the bucket is broken, the animal will attempt to steal fish less and less frequently. Good luck.
Marine Mammal Staff
John G. Shedd Aquarium

A Behavior Sampler by Gary Wilkes

Solving tough behavioral problems requires taking an objective look at the big picture. Sometimes trainers are too close to the problem to recognize when they have made a training error. The problem becomes even worse if the trainer takes the wrong type of corrective action. This article also demonstrates the dangers of anthropomorphizing.

Sinking Your Teeth into Destructive Chewing

by Gary Wilkes

Joann came home from work today expecting to see her dog, Butch, eagerly waiting to greet her. Instead, Butch was cowering under a table trying to blend in with the carpet. Joann did not have to look very far to see that Butch had chewed up the TV remote control - again!

A common belief of pet owners is that their animal knows right from wrong. Since Butch "looked guilty," he obviously knew that chewing up the remote control was wrong.

Joann is convinced that Butch chews things out of spite. He always seems to pick items of special importance to Joann - but of little importance to himself.

It is understandable that she might feel this way. It certainly appears as if Butch is selecting items that are guaranteed to make his owner unhappy. But is he really choosing things based on his knowledge of what Joann finds valuable?

To start with, Butch was a very "mouthy" puppy. When his permanent teeth came in, he chewed everything he could reach. At first, Joann used an old tennis shoe to keep Butch occupied. Butch soon graduated to Joann's $75 aerobic shoes. Next, Joann used some flat rawhide chips that Butch loved to gnaw on. One day, as she slipped her shoes off and took a nap, Butch finished his rawhide chip and looked for a likely substitute. Joann's $60 leather pumps made a perfect appetizer.

Frustrated by Butch's destruction, Joann started leaving him in the backyard. Butch liked it at first, but that old desire to chew came back very quickly. Butch looked for a suitable surface for dental demolition. The drip irrigation system was the perfect answer. The black plastic had the same texture of softened rawhide. It offered just the right amount of resistance to give him a challenge.

Hours later, Joann came home from work and saw the damage. Butch approached her happily with wagging tail and slobbering tongue. Joann went nuts. She ranted and raved and scared Butch to death. She threw her purse at him - and missed. Butch hid under a lawn chair. After a while, Joann brought Butch in and apologized to him. Butch didn't understand any of it, but he was happy that the violence was over. The days that followed led to more destruction. After each incident, Joann got angrier and more violent. Butch tried to surrender by rolling on his back and cowering. He had no way of knowing why she was angry. Whenever she came home he would wait cautiously to see if she was angry about something.

Joann decided that Butch just wasn't paying attention. She started taking him over to any object that he had destroyed and scolding him. Butch learned immediately to avoid the object - when Joann was present. Later, when she was gone, he would investigate the object. He discovered that the things were never associated with punishment unless Joann was there. When he actually chewed the object, he always made sure that Joann was not around. If he had chewed one of these objects during the day, he would then be completely terrified when Joann entered the room after work. He did not know that it was the destruction that was bad, he merely knew that being in the same room at the same time with a chewed object and Joann was a bad idea. This look of fear is what Joann decided was guilt. Joann's attempt to connect the punishment with the destruction was futile. She thought that holding the object to his nose and punishing him would make him "realize" that chewing was bad. While this type of training didn't work, some of her other efforts were more effective.

By providing him with an old sneaker and rawhide chips she gave him a taste for shoes and leather. The plastic of the drip system was remarkably like the remote control. Rather than teaching him to avoid chewing, she inadvertently taught him what objects to look for.

Dogs are simple animals. In nature, they may dig, chew, and bark with no ill consequences. The concept of monetary or sentimental value is completely beyond them. Their lives move from moment to moment with no thought of the future. Punishing a dog, hours later, will only teach fear and confusion - and looking "guilty."

Assuming that your pet is trying to make you angry is generally a mistake. Blaming the pet for the destruction will make you even angrier but will not correct the behavior. The first step in changing your pet's behavior is to change your own.

Trainer's Forum

Pinnipeds are known to have occasional eye problems. As animals get older, many species of animals must deal with failing vision. There is no reason to give up on the relationship already established with these animals. New relationships can be formed and new training can begin even when an animal is blind from the start. Often it is an animal with a disability or a medical concern that can benefit most from a good training program.

Training a Blind Sea Lion

QUESTION: I would be extremely grateful to anyone who can give me advice or tips on the training of a blind California sea lion for just a few basic behaviors. I understand that signals will have to be touch, but apart from that I am somewhat lost. Thank you for your help.

ANSWER: Several years ago we worked together at another facility, and had the opportunity to work with a blind sea lion, his name was Jones. He was a very large animal who had performed in shows for many years. As he got older he began to develop cataract and other eye problems that led to a gradual loss of sight. At one point, we considered surgery, but due to his advanced age it was decided that surgery was probably unwise. Over the years we continued to work with him and allowed him to continue his participation in daily shows. In a way, as his ability to see diminished, Mother Nature took care of approximating him gradually from visual cues to vocal and tactile cues.

As soon as we realized he was losing his ability to see our hand signals well, we began combining them with either a tactile or a vocal stimulus. Finally, once his eyesight was gone, the transition had already been made. Our situation may not directly relate to the question asked, since it appears you want to just get started training an already blind animal. However, we did continue to work with Jones even after he had lost his sight, and hopefully some of our experiences might prove helpful.

Seat position - Prior to going blind, Jones had already learned a solid stationing behavior. In his case, it was a sea lion "seat." Being at his seat became even more important when he lost his sight. He needed a secure place where he was comfortable when we were not in direct contact with him. Since he could not see, if we moved to pick up a dropped fish or get a prop or feed another animal, he needed to know that he was not being abandoned. Thus, a firmly established seating or stationing behavior allowed us to work with Jones without having to be right next to him every single second. He learned that he was to stay at station until given further instructions. This important behavior served two functions:

1. It allowed us to maintain behavioral control at all times.
2. It gave him something to do when we were not directly interacting with him.

Name recognition - Another factor we considered to be a key in working with Jones, was getting him to respond to his name. We worked him in the presence of several other sea lions, so he became very accustomed to lots of activity and noise. So, whenever we wanted to work with him, feed him, or interact with him in any way, we would say his name loudly. By conditioning him to hearing his name prior to any type of interaction he was never surprised or frightened by anything we did. While this may seem silly at first, you might be surprised how frightened a blind animal could become when you simply touch them (since he can't see, he has no idea what you are about to do). We said his name prior to feeding him a fish, prior to touching him, and prior to initiating a new behavior.

Moving the animal - There was always the need to walk Jones from one area to another, either a different enclosure, a new pool, or to a training area. Most of our sighted animals would simply follow us wherever we went and could avoid obstacles along the way. To facilitate this with Jones, we taught him to rest his snout in our cupped hand and move around slowly at first. He followed the cupped hand as he would a target. As he and the trainers became more comfortable with this procedure, we were able to move around faster and faster. He eventually progressed to a point where we could move anywhere, at any speed, with one arm extended down behind our back, Jones would simply follow. We, of course, had to be more conscious of areas we walked through, to insure that there was nothing that might cause injury to the sea lion. A sighted animal will slow down as they approach an object or a wall, but Jones was following us faithfully. His trust was in our hands, literally! if we cut around a corner too quickly or swerved by an object too closely the animal's flippers could easily have been injured. By being aware of these problems we were able to make walking from place to place an easy procedure.

Feeding - Since Jones was part of a larger social group, we wanted to feed him at the same time as the other animals in his pool. At the same time, we wanted to avoid allowing the other animals to take advantage of Jones and steal his fish. We accomplished this by asking each animal to assume a particular position in the pool and only feeding them when in that position. Jones, also in the pool, had to be within an arm's length away so we could place the fish directly above his mouth. By evenly disbursing the fish between the animals we had the time to make sure Jones got his entire diet. We did need to be careful not to drop too much of Jones' fish into the water or he would try to find it and inevitably lose the fish to another animal. However, by setting up feeds in a controlled manner, we never experienced any real problems. And, as with everything else, the more we did it the easier it became. Another factor we had to watch for when feeding, particularly during a session, was accidental biting by Jones. When approaching his mouth he can't tell if that's a fish or a finger, until it's too late. To alleviate that problem we always fed him from above his head. We would tap the top or back of his head, he would lean his head back, and we would drop the fish in. By never approaching him with fish straight on, he was never confused when we wanted to use our hand as a target or do a mouth exam. In the long run we think it saved him from confusion and saved us from too many Band-Aids.

Molding - Whenever we wanted to train new behaviors with Jones, almost all behaviors had to be molded. In other words, if we wanted him to lift his flipper we would lift his flipper for him, bridge, then reinforce. Very quickly he understood, and we only needed to touch his flipper to get him to lift it. If we wanted the behavior on a vocal rather than tactile cue we simply used the vocal cue at the same time we were shaping the behavior, and in time, the vocal was all that was needed. As mentioned earlier, many of his behaviors were trained while he could still see, but we did train new behaviors through the molding process and we managed to maintain most of his repertoire as well. Since husbandry behaviors are primarily tactile, those tended to be very easy behaviors to maintain.

Complex behavior - Once Jones had lost his sight, we did not try to train any complex behavioral sequences. We did however, try to maintain quite a variety of his original behaviors. We found that as long as we didn't "rearrange the furniture" he got around fine. Anytime we needed to change prop or seat placement, he had to be walked through the area slowly until he was familiar with the new arrangement. Surprisingly, anyone who didn't know he was blind, usually couldn't tell. Once comfortable with an area, he utilized his space very well.

Limitations - We found it very beneficial to Jones and to ourselves not to look at his blindness as a limitation. By continually treating him like any other sea lion, with simply a different behavioral repertoire, he never lost his place in the social hierarchy. Prior to losing his sight, Jones was the dominant animal in the group. Even after being blind for a number of years, Jones successfully fought off challenges by younger males. We also found some benefits. Since he could not see, new surroundings, strange people, or other similar disturbances never bothered him. As long as we were nearby, he had learned to trust us completely, consequently he would follow us anywhere.

Certainly, there are differences in our respective circumstances, but we hope this information will be of some help to you and your animal. We felt that Jones was able to lead a normal and healthy life, and that his training program contributed to his well being. We would be very interested in hearing about your results and would be happy to answer any further questions that you may have. Good luck.

Ken Ramirez
John G. Shedd Aquarium
and
Cheryl Messinger
National Aquarium in Baltimore

IN PRESS, 1999. When searching for a solution to a behavioral problem, we are usually looking for a way to re-establish order or regain behavioral control. When sessions go awry and animals are uncooperative, we frequently feel that we have lost control. The truth is that we never really had control. Training is successful because the trainer and the animal are working cooperatively together. It is that cooperative effort that most trainers are looking for when they refer to behavioral control.

Have You Lost Control?

QUESTION: What is behavioral control? How do you maintain it? If you lose behavioral control due to sexual behavior or inexperience, what are the steps to regain it?

ANSWER 1: Perhaps behavioral management is a more appropriate term to use than behavioral control. Through a variety of training techniques, we are able to establish a type of dialogue with animals that allows us to nurture certain types of interaction and request the performance of selected behavior patterns. However, regardless of our reinforcement techniques, there are times that other things are more reinforcing than what we have to offer. So, we never actually have behavioral control over an animal. Nevertheless, in an effort to address the question, we defined behavioral control as successfully maintaining /redirecting an animal's attention when the animal responds inappropriately to a specific conditioned stimuli as well as having a 90% correct response rate to a conditioned stimulus. We have found that the most effective way to accomplish this level of "control" is to attend to the animal's physical and emotional state and to synchronize the behavioral program with the animal's cycles and idiosyncrasies. This enables the trainer to anticipate an animal's readiness and receptivity to various programs in an effort to determine which animal is the best "fit" for a particular training and/or presentation program. Awareness and consideration of the animal's state of being helps the trainer to develop a success oriented program that literally avoids confrontations and "tests of will" between trainer and animal.

Consideration for the animal's physical or emotional state helps the trainer understand why an animal responds inappropriately at times. In certain circumstances it seems that "behavioral control" is best maintained by NOT asking the animal to perform certain behaviors. For example, when our males start increasing their weight as they go into rut, they tend to refuse to do flipper stands. We are not sure why they refuse, but it is likely that after gaining 200 pounds it is more difficult or uncomfortable for them do flipper stands. Likewise, when our sea lions are molting they become somewhat lethargic and tend to refuse high-energy behaviors such as galloping and aerial behaviors. Since these changes in response are predictable, we alter our presentations to accommodate the animal's state, and in effect maintain "control." From past experience we know that although the animals tend to refuse to perform certain behaviors during molt, once molt passes they will readily resume a consistent response without any remedial training. So there is no reason to insist on these behaviors or waste time re-training them when the animal is not in a receptive mode.

Another descriptive example is when during rut one of our sea lions tends to get a bit pushy and frequently tests our limits. He particularly likes to push past the trainer as the pen gate opens. Other times of year he is totally cooperative and is no problem. We address this in a variety of ways. Sometimes we will do sessions that do not require opening the gate. Other times he is more cooperative when asked to station in the water as the gate opens, rather than at target on the deck. However, if we have to access the pen and it is clear he is going to challenge us, we open the gate, giving him plenty of room to barrel past us, ignoring him as he goes by. When he is not challenged at the threshold, he generally hesitates briefly and returns to his pen assuming a more peaceful and cooperative demeanor overall. Perhaps he realized that he was about to engage in "much ado about nothing!" Sometimes you can maintain more "control" by being less controlling.

Some folks think that the animal is controlling the trainer when a behavior is refused and thus temporarily dropped from a program. The animals have many reasons for refusing to respond to the trainer's direction. They do not refuse to do something just to be contrary. When an animal responds inappropriately to a conditioned stimulus, the trainer may be able to effectively redirect the animal's attention so that it does not become an issue. If an animal is simply confused, then additional training sessions, a change in training technique, or a different reinforcement schedule may help to increase the probability that the animal will readily respond appropriately to the stimuli presented.

There are times that a trainer cannot effectively influence an animal's behavior. Examples are when there is an aggressive response to a newborn or newly introduced companion, reaction to new exhibits, to changes in their exhibit, or when behavior is driven by the sex drive or subtle social interactions that we do not fully understand or recognize. In some cases training can prepare the animals by employing habituation techniques and conditioning guidelines for response using models, as has been done to encourage inexperienced mothers to nurse their young. However, a trainer cannot totally control interactions between animals and their reactions to changes in environment.

Training Staff
New England Aquarium

ANSWER 2: Quite simply, behavioral control is being able to keep the animals under control by maintaining discipline while at a station and overcoming any possible distraction by the animals.

We maintain behavioral control by conducting small discipline training sessions with the animals. If we lose control due to sexual behavior, the animals will usually come back to the control station once they have "finished." If the animals do not come back to the control station, we just let them complete what they are doing. Who are we to interrupt their "games" at a crucial time like that? I firmly believe that if the animals are involved in sexual interactions, it probably means that they are happy and enjoying their "sexual time." It may take a few days for them to get over this period.

As far as inexperience leading to the problem, carefully train your staff and prepare them for these situations is the best solution for maintaining behavioral control.

Daniel Juarez
Marineland Mallorca

ANSWER 3: Concerning behavioral modification programs involving animals, behavioral control consists of two major components: general mannerisms and stimulus control.

We monitor general mannerisms at all times when interacting with an animal. Such mannerisms include, but are not limited to, overall focus attention, energy level, aggression, precursors to aggression, and displacement with other animals involved. Any interactive session allows the opportunity for the animal to learn what is acceptable or not. Even during playtimes the animal learns what it can or can't "get away with." If an animal's mannerisms are not desirable for a planned session (e.g. calm is good for husbandry behavior, hyperactive is not), progress is unlikely. To maintain the desired mannerisms we utilize intermittent reinforcement both during informal and formal interactions.

Stimulus control is the ability to elicit a particular response upon cue. In simple terms, when an animal is given a signal to do a behavior, it does it. Most stimulus control programs, including ours at Mystic, include three main elements: an antecedent stimulus (signal cue), a behavioral response, and a contingent consequence (acknowledgment of the response). If any one of these three elements are absent from an interaction, stimulus control cannot be established and/or will break down.

To give the animal a fair chance for a correct behavioral response, we keep the antecedent stimulus (a discriminative stimulus, or S^D) consistent. All staff must present the stimulus in the same way. Whether this stimulus is presented through verbal, visual, tactile, or other means, it must be clearly interpreted by the animal. A stimulus that is presented in an unclear manner is comparable to a boss slurring instructions from the other room; the outcome may or may not be as desired.

The behavioral response itself must be carefully monitored. Not only does the proper behavior need to occur; it must be performed at the proper criteria level if it is to be adequately maintained.

Again, to maintain clear communication, any criteria must be monitored consistently by all individuals that present a stimulus.

Some form of consequence must follow every elicited response. The consequence communicates to the animal whether or not their response was performed at an acceptable criteria level. It has been found that when given an option of receiving nothing versus receiving something of desire, an animal will choose the item it desires. As basic as this last statement is, it is the very guideline to providing an effective consequence. Accepting that we cannot know everything an animal will find to be positive (e.g. abused dogs crawl to the abuser soliciting more attention), it seems that the aspect of offering nothing is more effective than even punishment when an improper response is emitted. With this in mind, we apply a known positive reinforcer when their behavior is acceptable, while we use a least reinforcing stimulus (LRS) in the form of a 3-second neutral response when their behavior is unacceptable.

If any of these three elements of stimulus control are omitted, behavioral control may be lost. It may also be lost for other reasons. It can best be regained by breaking the completed behavior into stages of development (approximations), training the animal through these approximations, and eventually reestablishing the criteria level.

If the general mannerisms of behavioral control have broken down, the cause for the breakdown must be analyzed. When an animal seems sexually distracted, we have found several methods that are helpful in regaining control. Often it is easier to work with this animal when it is separated from other animals and slowly reintroducing them together under controlled sessions. By observing the animal before sessions we can time our interactions to when sexual activity is at a low. Providing intermittent reinforcement at times when the animal is not behaving sexually (differential reinforcement of other behavior or DRO) is effective in decreasing the amount of sexual activity (especially when those giving the DRO are present).

If a trainer's lack of experience causes a breakdown in general control, we explain to the trainer what the criteria is for general mannerisms. Basic issues such as sitting still, not playing with food, following closely, and quick responses to first stimuli are common examples. Once the trainer has an understanding of what is acceptable behavior and how to maintain it through intermittent reinforcement, the animal that is "out of control" needs to be reconditioned.

One approach would be to first get the animal to focus its attention on the trainer. Early sessions should be kept short and the time duration gradually increased. Random behaviors may be elicited with a focus on those that keep the animal's attention tight on the trainer. If the animal does display undesired mannerisms, the LRS should be applied beginning when the animal is again focused on the trainer. If regaining focus takes longer time than deemed acceptable at this stage, the trainer may choose to temporarily leave the scenario (a time-out) in order to avoid accidentally reinforcing any undesired mannerisms. Hopefully, reinforcement of consistent attention or focus by the animal combined with neutral response to undesired mannerisms will strengthen overall behavioral control.

These techniques have proven effective for us and we hope that they are helpful to you as well. Good luck!

Training Staff
Mystic Aquarium

Complex Training & Modern Applications

12

Putting all the Theory Together

There is no magic answer as to how to put all animal training theory and techniques together effectively. The components are fairly straightforward, but it takes time to master anything as complex as animal training.

Get to Know the Animal
You can never learn too much about each of the animals you train. The relationships you build with them are an intangible but important element of effective training.

Expand Your Knowledge
Learn the theory and understand it intimately. As you gain experience, revisit the literature, where the theories will take on new meaning. Undiscovered nuances appear as your base of experience grows. Watch other trainers, whether they are less or more experienced than you and whether or not they are working similar animals; every training session can be a learning opportunity. Ask questions of other trainers, share information, and join professional training organizations, described in chapter 13, "The Professional Trainer."

Practice and Gain Experience
No matter how much you read, no matter how much theory you know, there is no substitute for experience. There is no shortcut to gaining experience. Many trainers get to a point in their careers where they think they know more than they do. If that happens, be prepared to be humbled. Every animal, every facility, and every trainer has the potential to teach you something new. Learn from it and grow with it. This chapter is intended to provide you with interesting training stories and articles that can help you learn from the experiences of others.

Interactive Programs

Interactive programs are a rapidly growing, complex use of animal training. They are different because they place trainers, animals, and visitors into the same environment. Interactive training is not really new. Zoos have been offering camel rides and elephant rides for years, and many marine mammal programs include petting pools or opportunities for visitors to meet the animals up close during shows. But the newer programs take interaction a step further by allowing visitors to experience the animals up close for extended periods of time. In the late 1980's, when such programs were just getting started, "swim-with-a-dolphin" programs created some controversy. But innovative programs, developed by experienced trainers, proved that these programs could be safe for the guests and animals, as well as an incredible educational experience for visitors. Many new interactive programs are developing, and the literature about them will certainly be more readily available in the years ahead. The articles included in this chapter provide a good introduction to these programs.

- Getting a new interactive program started at the Dolphin Connection is described in *The Initiation of a Dolphin Interactive Program* (Messinger & Messinger, 1998), on page 428.
- Handling inappropriate behavior was the subject of chapter 11, "Problem Solving." But the article *Interactive Programs: Protocols and Managing Inappropriate Behavior* (T. Forum, 1996), on page 432, seems more appropriate in this chapter.

Protected Contact Training

The use of protected contact training is neither a new concept nor a particularly advanced one. However, in the zoological community, as training has become more common and the dangers of training some animals have become more evident, protected contact training has become increasingly important. In some circles, it has even become controversial. Many traditional elephant trainers, for example, have been reluctant to switch from free contact to protected contact training. Many examples of protected contact training are scattered throughout this manual; the articles in this chapter, however, will focus on the evolution of protected contact with elephants.

- Management concerns that have led to an increase in protected contact training, are discussed in the abstract to *Elephant Handling – A problem of Risk Management and Resource Allocation* (Lehnhardt, 1991), on page 436.
- An introduction to protected contact is described in *Pro-*

tected Contact Elephant Training (Desmond and Laule, 1991), on page 437.
- Application of protected contact with an isolated elephant is the subject of *"C" is for Cindy: A Case History* (Miller, et. al., 1993), on page 444.
- *The Politics of Protected Contact* (Desmond and Laule, 1993), on page 447 discusses some of the misconceptions and reasons for controversy surrounding protected contact.
- A good overview of a protected contact program after several years of experience with the system is described in *Managing Multiple Elephants Using Protected Contact at San Diego's Wild Animal Park* (Priest et. al., 1998), on page 453.

Other Zoo Applications

This manual has tried to focus on training as a technique applicable to any setting. However, the focus has been on marine mammals. Zoo settings naturally provide excellent examples of unique applications, further evidence that operant conditioning techniques are applicable in any animal training situation. Additional resources about zoo animals will be listed in the next chapter. The following articles are in this chapter:

- Karen Pryor was involved in trying to introduce operant conditioning to zoos many years ago. She describes some of these efforts in her 1981 article *The Rhino Likes Violets*, on page 459.
- IMATA's usual focus is on cetaceans and pinnipeds, but the organization's members are also involved with many other species as discussed in *Polar Bears and Warthogs: Training in the Zoo* (T. Forum, 1997), on page 463.
- The attention of the media is often drawn to high profile zoo animals as described in *Maternal Feelings Prevail as Gorilla Rescues Tot at Zoo* (Bils & Singer, 1996), on page 464.

Research Training

Only a handful of trainers are equally comfortable designing a research protocol and implementing a training plan. Most trainers rely on outside investigators to help design a research project. But this doesn't exempt the trainer from learning how a research project works. The better a trainer understands a research project, the more likely he or she is to save training time and to avoid training that invalidates the research. An in-depth discussion of various research paradigms is beyond the scope of this manual, but I have selected articles that either describe a specific research training principle or introduce a concept that has not been presented elsewhere in the manual. Research can be an important component to a public display program, even if research is not the focus. Trainers who work entirely in a research setting will find that articles in this chapter barely scratch the surface of research possibilities and training. However all trainers, should find the challenges of these complex training situations interesting.

- **Research in a show** – Training research behaviors for use in a show is not uncommon. One of the most common research behaviors used in public demonstrations is the subject of the article *Training Echolocation Discrimination in a Show* (T. Forum, 1990), on page 466.
- **Go, no-go paradigm** – The Training and use of a "go, no-go" paradigm is common in many types of research projects. Two articles that describe training animals with this paradigm are *Training a False Killer Whale for an Underwater Audiogram* (Chun et. al., 1986), on page 468 and *Conditioning a Pacific Bottlenose Dolphin and a California Sea Lion in a Taste Experiment* (Hall and Richards, 1982), on page 473.
- **Matching to sample** – The concept of "matching to sample" is another frequently used paradigm in research projects. The use of this concept is part of the article *Echolocation Matching for Shape, Material, and Internal Structure* (Xitco, 1990), on page 475.
- **Two-choice paradigm** – The "two-choice" paradigm is sometimes confused with the "go, no-go" paradigm. However, there are important distinctions in the training and in the interpretation of the results between the two paradigms. The "two-choice" paradigm is used in the research training described in *The Manatee Mind: Discrimination Training for Sensory Perception Testing of West Indian Manatees* (Gerstein, 1994), on page 484.
- **Cognition Training** – Few areas of research capture the imagination of the public and trainers alike as does cognition research. Designing a good cognition project can be a real challenge, as can training for the project. Two articles that describe this kind of work are *An Introduction to the Living Seas Dolphin Keyboard Communication System* (Xitco et. al., 1991), on page 493

and *Teaching Sea Lions that Signals Represent Objects, Object Qualities, and Behaviors* (Shusterman and Krieger, 1982), on page 499. For those interested in more information on cognitive projects, see the bibliography at the end of the manual.

- **Foreign object acceptance** – Many research projects require that animals be trained to wear, carry, or come in contact with strange and unusual objects. Although this usually requires basic desensitization techniques, research projects often require more complex desensitization as well as additional training. Two articles that provide examples of the training for acceptance of foreign objects are *Video Recording the Nasal Passage of an Echolocating Dolphin* (Marrin-Cooney, 1989), on page 501 and *Training an Atlantic Bottlenose Dolphin to Wear a Harness and Remote Underwater Camera* (Gouvin and Wood, 1988), on page 504.
- **Open ocean training** – Working in the open ocean probably deserves an entire section to itself. Many facilities, not just research facilities, work with animals in the open ocean. Certainly the forerunners in this kind of training have been the trainers and contractors working in the U.S. Navy's marine mammal program. The challenges of training in an open ocean setting are unique, and the research that can be accomplished in that setting are nothing short of incredible. One example of the research that can be carried out in an open ocean setting is described in *Conditioning Bottlenose Dolphins for Voluntary Diving Studies* (Shippee et. al., 1994), on page 507.

Training Pets and Other Domestic Animals

This manual regularly discusses dogs and other domestic animal training, especially through the eyes of Gary Wilkes in his many well-written articles. I like to use pets as examples (even for marine mammal trainers) because almost anyone can relate to a story about pet behavior. Good trainers are needed in many areas of domestic animal training, including search and rescue dogs, service animals for the disabled, and basic pet obedience. The number of animals that are put to sleep every year because pet owners are not prepared to handle the behavioral problems that can accompany pet ownership is alarming. The importance of understanding the behavior of dogs and other pets is becoming more and more evident. Consequently, a growing number of veterinary behaviorists have emerged. This new field is described in *When Fido More than Misbehaves* (Shaw, 1996) on page 515. I am only sorry that there is not room to include more articles on these subjects, but they are beyond the scope of this manual. Resources on these subjects are described in the next chapter as well as suggested reading material in the bibliography.

Conference Proceedings

1998 IMATA Conference, Albufeira, Portugal. A version of the following article was presented at the 26th annual IMATA conference. As the 1990's come to a close, interactive programs have become very popular. Several very good programs have been established, but there is relatively little literature about the training involved in this new hands-on approach to the public display of marine mammals. This is one of the first articles to explain the basic concepts behind the training and introduction of an interactive program.

The Initiation of a Dolphin Interactive Program

by Doug Messinger and Cheryl Messinger
The Dolphin Connection, Inc.

INTRODUCTION

Changing public attitudes, including heightened awareness of ecological issues, wide-spread recycling efforts, and abundant eco-tourism vacation opportunities, all point to the publics new found desire for direct involvement with the environment and the creatures that live there. Due in part to these attitudinal changes, there has been a recent increase in numbers and scope of interactive programming offered by marine parks around the country. Here, under the direct supervision of experienced, professional animal care staff, guests are permitted opportunities to come in contact with marine mammals in ways never available to them before. The interactive concept has a long and successful history in the zoological community, so there is little doubt that the educational and conservation messages guests receive in such memorable encounters will have an enormous impact on their stewardship to the natural environment.

We recognize two distinct types of encounter programming emerging from this surge of development. Although it can be simply dismissed as semantics, facility personnel tend to be very specific about the terminology utilized to identify their programs, mostly in a desire not to mislead the publics' expectations of their upcoming experience. "Swim" programs typically refer to any situation where guests are, either wholly or partially, allowed to free swim in the animals' environment. "Interactive" or "encounter" programs then, refer to those which do not allow guests to free swim, where animal interactions take place only under conditions where guests can stand or sit in the water. Regardless of the venue, guests are given the still rare opportunity to interact with dolphins, whales, sea lions, or seals under the watchful eye of an experienced trainer. A moment that will leave a lasting and unforgettable impression.

We have developed our own version of an in-water interactive program with bottlenose dolphins (*Tursiops truncatus*). In doing so, we attempted to develop a program format that allowed for maximum flexibility of trainers, variability for the animals, and safety for the guests. Our hope is that our insights will be useful for others in the field, whether developing an entirely new program or simply re-designing an existing one.

PROGRAM FORMAT

Classroom

The guests' initial contact with the dolphin's world is typically provided by an introductory classroom period. Conducted prior to the animal interaction time, its goal is to provide participants with basic knowledge that will enhance their experience. Typical topics of discussion include classification and natural history of cetacean species in general, followed by a more specific introduction to the life history of the specie they will shortly come in contact with. Once covered, some discussion of habitat destruction and conservation usually follows. For example, we focus on placing the bottlenose dolphin in context within the entire marine ecosystem and then narrow our educational scope to the importance of protecting the Florida Keys coral reef, which guests are also likely to encounter during their vacation.

It is equally important to provide the guests with an understanding of proper etiquette while interacting with a trained, but non-domesticated, animal. Details such as how to properly enter the water and approach the animal are often included here. Because the entire program will be an experiential learning opportunity for guests, it is recommended that classroom learning maintain consistency in this hands-on atmosphere. Props, displays, and sounds that guests can manipulate will assist in greater retention and interest, even during such tedious topics as anatomical information or scientific classification.

While the scope of information offered during formal classroom time could easily encompass a few hours, we feel guest anticipation of interacting with the dolphins lends itself to a shorter classroom period. For this reason we treat our entire program as a "classroom" session by offering continual learning from start to finish. This effectively enables us to keep the formal classroom period relatively short. By pacing information throughout the entire program, we address the guests' immediate desire to meet the animals while fulfilling our desire to provide a broad educational basis of information. As a further benefit, it can be argued that information offered during direct interaction with an animal can be subject to a higher rate of retention, as the benefits of activity-based methods of learning have been well documented by educators throughout the world.

Dock Time

While there is little question that program guests have a great desire to directly interact with dolphins, they often experience a period of reticence when first confronted with these large, powerful mammals face to face. For this reason we have incorporated dock time interaction at the onset of the animal-guest introduction. Time spent on the docks provides guests the opportunity to experience, from a less intimidating position, many of their dolphin "firsts": their first look at the animals up close, their first time to hear a dolphin breathe, give their first discriminative stimulus to the animal, offer their first primary and/or secondary reinforcer, and experience their first dolphin touch. We feel that dock time enables the guests to become comfortable with the sounds, movements, and size of the animals, which may otherwise be too overwhelming if experienced from in the water. It also enables the trainers an opportunity to evaluate the guests comfort level with the animals prior to their in-water encounter.

Trainers maintain variable reinforcement schedules to encourage animal participation while offering both primary and secondary reinforcers. These may be administered by the guests or by the trainers themselves. Believing that variability is key to high animal motivation levels, we have further designed this portion of the program to be non-location specific. Therefore, trainers have the opportunity to conduct dock time in the main lagoon, in a secondary lagoon, in one of two holding pens, or to divide the dock time between any of the four areas. In addition, the number of animals required to conduct dock time can be varied from one to three animals which can participate in full or in only portions of the section. All combined, this scenario provides the trainers with maximum flexibility to provide a stimulating interaction for both the dolphins and the guests.

At the conclusion of dock time, the animals are released from stimulus control for a short period. This break enables the trainers to comfortably situate guests in the water for their direct encounter while re-emphasizing the importance of proper etiquette. This also allows for the addition or exchange of animals utilized for the next portion of the program.

Shallow Water Interactions

When the time arrives to finally submerge guests in the water, many programs offer combinations of wading in from beach areas, snorkeling and/or free swimming as alternatives to meeting the dolphins. In an effort to develop as stimulating a program as possible without the use of free-swim alternatives, we have incorporated shallow water and deep water submerged platforms into our programs. Shallow water interactions can either immediately follow dock time, or can follow the deep water interactions described below. The interchangeability of these two segments allows, once again, for the all-important variability factor. However, it should be noted that we have found the shallow water area to be extremely accommodating when assisting physically challenged individuals. In fact, many of our special needs participants enjoy a lengthy and comfortable encounter from the shallow docks alone. So, if necessary, the entire program can, and has, been done from this location.

Shallow water interactions provide guests with the opportunity to sit in low level water on a shallow shelf that is designed to allow for a high amount of guest contact time with the animals. The behavioral repertoire on shallow platforms consists mostly of husbandry style behavior, for example ventral and dorsal layouts, fluke presents, ultrasound layouts, mouth opens, and blowhole presentations. The large number of behaviors to choose from gives the trainers flexibility and provides little repetition for the animals throughout the day. While maintenance of husbandry behaviors dictates variable interval bridging, the relatively long duration of these presents allows the possibility for lengthy contact time between guests and animals during this portion of the program. Interestingly, the trainers observe that animals often close their eyes and achieve seemingly complete relaxation. It is therefore no real surprise that the benefit of using these vital medical behaviors in the public arena has actually strenghened behavioral response overall.

At the conclusion of shallow water interactions, the dolphins are either released within the interactive lagoon or gated into adjoining areas for a period of free time. Trainers are also free to bring additional or different animals out for interaction at this point if so desired.

Deep Water Interactions

From a programming context, deep water interactions are interchangeable with the shallow water interaction described above. In contrast to the more sedate behaviors experienced in the shallow encounter, the deep water interaction strives to provide more action and response from the guests with the use of high energy behavior from the dolphins. Designed to show off the dolphins' natural abilities, aerials, speed swims, and tail walks are often the goal. With the guests now standing in waist deep water, this portion of the encounter also provides the perfect opportunity for squirts, lob tails, pectoral splashes, interaction with a wide variety of toys, and any other behavior that can illicit a reaction from the guests. The idea here is FUN! Again, the high number of behaviors to choose from allows for little repetition throughout the day for the animals.

As may be surmised, establishing low energy behaviors in one distinct location and high energy behaviors in another can ultimately lead to behavioral breakdown. In addition, establishing the majority of tactile interaction at one location versus another can be equally problematic. For these reasons, we offer the above information as an overview only. As with any training program, it must be ever dynamic and changing, versatile and variable, to meet the needs of the animals, the trainers, and the guests.

Back to the Classroom

Exiting the water and returning to the formal classroom can literally be a time of "debriefing" for the guests, transporting them out of the unique experience of direct contact with marine mammals and back into the everyday world. For guests, we find it is a highly emotional time and one in which they have many questions they would like answered. For trainers, it is an important time to get across your final message. We choose to thank guests for interacting with dolphins in human care and offer information on the dangers of interacting with wild dolphins and manatees.

This can also be time used to gain feedback from guests through written evaluations. The evaluations can be a valuable tool used to impart or obtain important information related to the animals, customer service, education, and/or demographics. We choose to collect information from a small cross section of our guests, including what information they knew prior to attending our program and how that information was gathered, for example via television, books, other interactive programs, etc. This information insures our educational content is as dynamic and changing as our training program, offering something new to even repeat visitors.

KEYS TO SUCCESS

1. **Provide trainers with maximum variety.**

This can include the choice of animals utilized for programs, the number of animals utilized per program, adjusting the framework, order and components of the program, choosing which behaviors are elicited, choosing the order of the behaviors elicited, and deciding the variety of secondary reinforcers to be offered. This extensive variability ultimately translates into high motivation for our animals.

Yet within a program of variety, there must also exist a framework of stability. Supervisors observe programs at random to insure trainers are displaying consistency to the animals in their hand signals, behavioral criteria expectations, and their average primary reinforcement schedule. Supervisors also determine that programs, while differing greatly, still offer participants overall consistency where educational content and animal interaction time is concerned.

2. **Establish educational content in outline form.**

When developing the educational content of our

programs, trainers receive an outline of information to be covered rather than a fully written script which must be memorized. We find the outline-only concept inspires trainers to share their personal enthusiasm and excitement about topics discussed, which is infectious to our guests. Without fear of forgetting a portion of the memorized script, the delivery of information is natural and appealing. Additionally, we find it is much easier for our staff to cater their delivery to suit any age, educational level, or area of interest without compromising the consistency of the overall product. This allows for a more personalized feel and approach to each program.

3. Keep interactive segments short.

Even though our total animal-guest interactive time averages about 25 minutes per program, this total is divided into three mini-segments, some being dock segments and others being water interaction segments. Each mini-segment is separated from the next by a short break where trainers have the opportunity to answer questions, relocate guests to a new area of the lagoon, and supply continued instruction for the next interactive event. The short break also provides the animals with the ability to interact with conspecifics or other stimulating elements within the environment. Therefore, we utilize the breaks as another means of variability and find that they assist in increased focus and motivation.

4. Establish criteria for the guests and for the animals.

Proper etiquette should be defined for all participants of an interactive program. Identifying and communicating basic safety policies and what participants should or should not do while in the water with the animals will greatly assist in eliminating problems before they happen. We have summarized our policies into a written document that all participants must read and sign prior to involvement in animal interactions. In addition, our trainers verbally review the material during the formal classroom portion of the program. This is our assurance that guests will clearly understand the safety guidelines established to make their interaction as enjoyable, and safe, as possible.

Establishing a policy of inappropriate behavior for the animals is equally as important. We have identified a baseline list of inappropriate behavior to be followed by the least reinforcing stimulus (LRS) should such behavior occur. Thorough knowledge of these "black and white" areas will help to insure that inappropriate behavior is not inadvertently reinforced by an error in trainer judgement, as any response from the trainer is potentially reinforcing. Should a precursor to inappropriate behavior be displayed, Differential Reinforcement of Incompatible behavior (DRI) and/or Differential Reinforcement of Other behavior (DRO) can be applied at the onset to immediately redirect the animal into behavior which can be reinforced. This assists in extinguishing unwanted behavior and effectively achieves a session that sets the animal up to succeed.

5. Take the time to train control behaviors.

In an effort to vary an animal's day, it is often desirable to have the flexibility to rotate animals during programs. Shifting animals during programs can provide the potential for uncontrolled behavior to develop as an animal is often distracted by guests in the water. This novelty can prove to be just reinforcing enough for latency to develop between the successful gate behavior and stationing at attention with trainers. For this reason, we have paired a control behavior with gating to increase proper behavioral response overall, and as an additional safety precaution. After giving the discriminative stimulus for gating, the completion of the behavior is dependent on holding to a fixed target located on the opposite side of the gate. When the trainer releases the behavior, the animals are under stimulus control and prepared for further instruction.

6. Beware of bridging stimulus response.

Obviously, animals should respond immediately to the bridging stimulus, in our case a dog whistle, every time it is presented. While this is desirable, it can also prove dangerous in an interactive setting. A quick animal response to the bridging stimulus, even if selectively paired down to a relatively calm response, can still sometimes correspond with hard fluke kicks or otherwise exaggerated movements by the animals. Because the animals' enthusiasm could potentially be a safety hazard for our guests, we have chained our husbandry layouts with a "release" behavior. When a layout with guests is completed to criteria and duration, the animal is pushed away from the guests where it coasts in position on the surface until reaching a safe distance. This allows the trainer to present the bridging stimulus, and the animal to respond, in an area where accidental injury is unlikely. In addition, we have also introduced a second bridging stimulus, a double tap on the animals' side, which we trained contingent on a slow and gentle response. Both bridges have been successfully incorporated into our programs.

7. Resist the urge to offer primary reinforcement underwater.

While it is easy, and sometimes convenient, to provide primary reinforcement to an animal whose face is underwater, we avoid it. The behavior being reinforced is an underwater, open mouth approach to people, exactly the type of baseline unacceptable behavior we wish to discourage. Therefore, we have established a "heads up" primary reinforcement policy with all of our animals.

CONCLUSION

We must not overlook the value of the educational experience offered to each visitor that participates in one of the many interactive programs now offered throughout the world. The great potential of interactive display is to change attitudes and values, not merely to impart facts. When direct contact is made, a personal link to the marine environment will forever remain. With thousands of dolphins being killed needlessly each year, the seas polluted, habitats destroyed and entire global ecosystems threatened, every effective educational tool must be used to influence a lasting desire to act on behalf of the environment we share with marine mammals. Interactive programs have the ability to do just that.

Trainer's Forum

VOL 21, NO 4, 1996. As interactive programs moved into the 1990's, new and varied forms of interaction were devised and more facilities began to implement programs. Inevitably questions arose about how to monitor guest interactions and what to do about inappropriate behavior on the part of the guest or the animal. Here are responses from three of the earliest such programs, Theater of the Sea, Dolphin Quest, and Dolphin Research Center.

Interactive Programs: Protocols and Managing Inappropriate Behavior

QUESTION: With your swim or interaction program, what protocols do you have in place as related to guest-animal interaction, especially with inappropriate behavior on the animals' part?

ANSWER 1: Theater of the Sea has been offering the Swim-with-the-Dolphin (SWTD) program since May of 1987. We have five female and three male *Tursiops truncatus* that participate in the program. We have had 53,000 swimmers and one incident.

At Theater of the Sea, our protocols for guest interactions are designed to prevent inappropriate behavior on both the dolphins' and humans' part. To conduct the SWTD program, we require our trainers to have at least three years experience with dolphins so that they are extremely familiar with dolphin behavior. Additionally, our trainers work with consistent teams to facilitate awareness of any deviation from normal behavior for the individual animals they handle in these programs. The dolphins who participate in the program are carefully selected for temperament and conditioned for gentle interaction.

In preparation for the swim. participants are required to take a thirty minute pre-swim, along with an orientation. Among other things, swimmers are told that if they do not follow instructions, they will be removed from the program. Additionally we require that they speak and understand English.

The SWTD program is a controlled interaction, meaning the dolphins are trained, and an experienced trainer directs any and all interaction between the human and dolphin participants. This format was recommended after a National Marine Fisheries Service (NMFS) study of swim programs indicated controlled interactions were less risky (than free or spontaneous swims) for both people and dolphins.

Two employees conduct each swim. A swim trainer handles the animals, and an observer helps look for any aberrant behavior (human or dolphin) and assists in the event of an incident. All employees must complete an instruction and evaluation before being involved in the SWTD.

Safety equipment is kept in each swim area, including a life ring, shepherd's hook, and a pinger. The pinger has two tones. One is a recall for the dolphins, who are given a minimum of three herring for responding to the toile, thus maintaining a strong response. The other is an emergency tone for swimmers, who are instructed to swim quickly to the stairs for their safety if they hear a tone. We have periodic safety meetings where mock emergencies are simulated. However the staff are not trained as lifeguards.

If we do not have the animals' full attention prior to an interaction, then we do not go ahead with the swim. During swims, content can be modified as a technique to prevent unwanted behavior. If any unwanted behavior or precursors to unwanted behavior are observed, we would remove all swimmers from the water for a time-out or to cancel the swim if necessary.

Beverley Abbitt
Theater of the Sea

ANSWER 2: When developing an interactive dolphin experience, it is necessary to design a course of action in the event an animal displays some form of inappropriate behavior toward a guest. As will be discussed later, the likelihood of aggression can be minimized through a strong training protocol and proper management plan, but in case such behavior does occur, the most important concept to remember is: guest safety is number one.

To minimize the chance of inappropriate behavior, the following practices should be followed to promote safety and maximize control during the interactive encounter:

1. Provide sufficient space for dolphins to leave the interaction.
2. At least one staff member must accompany guests in the water during all in water interactions.
3. Provide sufficient water clarity so dolphin behavior can be observed at all times.
4. Do not allow guests to grasp or hold onto any portion of a dolphin's body unless assisted by a staff member.
5. Guests participating in interactions should wear a life jacket.
6. All operations must be attended by a supervising trainer with at least three years experience directing human/dolphin interactions.
7. Operators must have a sufficient number of animals to provide a selection of participating dolphins on the basis of existing behaviors.
8. In the event of injury, operators must complete an incident reporting form assessing the cause and suggesting the action plan.

Even with these set protocols, the training staff must be prepared in the event of an injury to a human during a dolphin encounter. Should this unlikely event occur, the following source of events is suggested:

- Remove the guest from the water and provide first aid if needed
- Notify security and a supervisor
- Remove all other guests from the water
- Assess the animal situation and the cause of aggression
- Remove dolphin involved from further interactions until full evaluation complete
- Supervisor makes full written statement of event/re-training required

As stated earlier, prior to conducting an interactive experience, the training staff must have a complete understanding of what is desired behavior and what is not. Understanding aggression is a vital part of this training. All living creatures are capable of displaying some type of aggressive behavior and will do so, often in the form of a threat rather than actual physical contact. Also, all aggressive acts are in response to some stimulus and will be preceded by any number of obvious precursors. It is essential that the staff be aware of the various situations which will increase the chance of aggression, as well as the many signs which warn that aggression is imminent. It is only when a trainer fails to recognize a threat display that the danger of injury may occur if threat is followed by active aggression.

A few typical scenarios where aggression may occur include competition for food, competition for breeding, human harassment, and surprise. Although this list does not include all the possible scenarios, it highlights the obvious need for the trainer to be aware of all the variables which affect dolphin behavior each moment. In response to any of these scenarios, a dolphin may display precursors to aggression such as refusal to respond to an S^D, not meeting behavioral criteria, backing away from tainers/guests, playing with food, barking or jaw-clapping, wandering, or many other abnormal behaviors. At this point the trainer should respond in a manner to prevent a further escalation of the aggression.

By studying the above mentioned statements, a plan can be formed to reduce the chances of aggression. First and foremost, work within the social structure of the dolphins. This social structure will change constantly and must be closely monitored. Do not force animals to work together if they are uncomfortable. Avoid competition, whether for food, attention, or other animals. Reinforce cooperation between dominant and submissive animals.

Second, build a strong dolphin/trainer relationship. In the event of surprise, discmfort, or poor interaction by guests, the dolphin will generally respond to the trainer which they respect and trust. This relationship is often a stronger method of control than food or other positive reinforcers. A trainer must always accompany the guests in the water to observe behavior, watch for precursors to aggression, and be at hand in the event of any problems.

Third, the interactive program should be designed with enough flexibility for instantaneous change in the case of any sudden situations which may threaten the animals. Guests need to be gradually guided through the experience to avoid getting over-excited or fearful. Excessive enthusiasm or reluctance can possibly trigger an aggressive act; therefore, human behavior must be watched as closely as dolphin behavior.

Finally, trainers should be ready to apply differential reinforcement of incompatible behavior (DRI). By reinforcing behaviors other than aggressive ones, the dolphin's behavior is re-directed away from possible aggression toward a more positive approach.

In conclusion, if a training staff is totally aware of behavior before and during the entire interaction, then the potential for aggression is minimized. Through constant observation and communication we can keep these interactions positive.

Bud Krames
Dolphin Quest

ANSWER 3: We have several experiential education programs at the Dolphin Research Center (DRC). They include a structured dolphin swim encounter, a dockside signals session with the dolphins, and what we refer to as "docktime" or playtime on the dock. The guests do not feed the dolphins in any of these programs. Docktime is unique in that there are no trainers or food reinforcement at all in these sessions. Participants in docktime are limited to staff, volunteers, and DolphinLab participants (1 week program).

For each of these programs, the protocol begins with the education of the guest. We have workshops where a staff member teaches the guest exactly how they will be interacting with the dolphins. DRC staff give specific guidelines for the activity, teaching guests what they will and will not be doing in their session, and explaining why. For the swim encounter, we use a dolphin model to help explain things, and we include a videotape showing guests exactly how they will interact with the dolphins. Just prior to the swim, the trainer again goes over the rules and behaviors at dockside. In our experience, the more thorough the explanation (and the more times you repeat it), the fewer problems when you get the guests and the animals together.

The dolphins that are trained to participate in our structured swim program have all been selected because they are gentle and patient with people in the water. In DRC's experiential programs we have identified three areas for potential inappropriate behavior on the dolphin's part: frustration-related, sexually-related, or dolphin/dolphin dminance-related. The dolphins at DRC have learned to generalize the signals that the guests give them and we see very little confusion or frustration on their part. Our trainers direct the swim from floating docks the entire time, and if they see a dolphin confused or a person that cannot complete the behavior for whatever reason, the trainer will direct the person to swim back toward the dock. The dolphin will usually follow the guest in, offering the dorsal fin for a tow. By allowing the dolphin to offer a dorsal, they can engage in a successful behavior, earning reinforcement and getting the swimmer back to the dock. The dorsal tow is one of our strongest behaviors and the dolphins consistently offer it.

The Dolphin Encounter at DRC is structured so that there is no unsolicited interaction allowed between guests and dolphin. This means that as the person is holding on to the dock , the dolphins do not just freely swim by for unlimited rubs. A "back rub" is a behavior in our swims. Some precursors to sexual behavior are the dolphin going to the sides of the dock (where the swimmers hold on) to solicit rubs and have "dreamy" or half-closed eyes. This is avery rare occurrence at DRC. If the trainer sees this, they will pick up the pace of the session, mixing some non-swim behaviors to sharpen attention. This usually works and the swim session can be completed. There is no definite protocol because the trainer must make assessments based on the dolphins, the people, and the situation at the time.

DRC's swim sessions often involve two dolphins together at the same dock. For the most part the dolphins paired together are very compatible. They live in the same lagoon and are teamed to participate in other types of sessions in addition to the swim sessions. Before the swimmers even go into the water, the trainer works with the two dolphins doing the swim, assessing their behavior, attention, and compatibility. If there is a conflict, it is usually obvious at this time and a change is made (possibly a different pairing of dolphins) before the guests enter the water. There are rare times when we've had dominance problems during the swim. For example, a dominant dolphin will approach a sub-dominant dolphin at the dock with an open mouth or in some intimidating way. The protocol in this instance is to have the guests get out of the water and leave the dock. The swim may continue with a different pairing of dolphins or with a single dolphin.

What about inappropriate behavior on the part of the guests? This is a far more common occurrence than inappropriate behavior from the dolphins. Trainers will ask guests to leave the water if they consistently refuse to follow directions. Guests are not allowed to hop in and out of the water during a swim. DRC staff will not force frightened children to interact with the dolphins and we will not allow the parents to do so either. A trained monitor, observing every swim session, assists by reminding guests to hold onto the floating docks until it is their turn to interact with the dolphins. In the event that a trainer needs to go into the water to assist a swimmer, the monitor helps all of the guests out of the water as quickly and efficiently as possible.

During the structured Dolphin Insight session, the guests join the trainer on the floating dock to give signals and touch the dolphins. Trainers do not observe inappropriate behavior during these sessions other than the dolphins choosing not to participate or being inattentive. We handle these situations behaviorally, based on the individual circumastances and dolphins involved. Our other dockside interaction program "docktime," is always monitored by a staff member or intern trained in interpreting dolphin behavior. The DolphinLab students go onto the floating docks and offer back-rubs and attention to the dolphins in the lagoon. It is up to the dolphins to initiate the interaction, sometimes by bringing seaweed to toss back-and-forth. The docktime monitor watches behavior in the lagoon closely. If there is any sexual activity, dominance behavior, or any signs of agitation among the dolphins, the students leave the dock and do not return. If the dolphins exhibit any "mouthiness" with the students on the dock, or if they showno interest in interacting, the students leave as well.

We are very proud of all our experiential education programs at the DRC. Our dolphins interact closley with hundreds of guests each month. The guests leave with a special gift and, very often, a commitment to help preserve our environement. Because of the structure and clear expectations (both for people and dolphins) the dolphins stay excited about thc sessions. They are more consistent behaviorally in the interactive sessions than any other type of session thay participate in.

Linda S. Erb
Dolphin Research Center

This is only the abstract of John Lehnhardt's paper on elephant handling from a management's perspective. John's progressive work at the National Zoo has been very proactive in utilizing training in all areas of the zoo. He presented this paper in San Diego in September of 1991. I have included just the abstract because some of the statistics about fatalities are staggering. Here is evidence and a strong argument for a well managed training program. Please see the articles that follow which discuss protected contact training in more detail.

Elephant Handling - A Problem of Risk Management and Resource Allocation

by John Lehnhardt
National Zoological Park

ABSTRACT

Approximately 600 elephants are maintained in North America with an estimated equal number human handlers. Attention has been focused on the risks involved in managing elephants by several injuries and six elephant related human fatalities in the last 2 1/2 years. Hard data on elephant related human injuries does not exist. A questionnaire is being distributed to develop a data base on the frequency and circumstances of these incidents. Without this database to analyze, the causes of elephant related human injuries in North America cannot be fully determined. Elephant related human fatalities are better documented, with 15 occurring in the last fifteen years, or a rate of approximately 1 per 600 handlers per year. This is the highest fatality rate of any occupation documented by the U.S. Bureau of Labor Statistics and the National Safety Council. An elephant handler is three times more likely to die on the job than someone working in the next most dangerous occupation (coal mining). Adult male elephants were involved in 7 of the 15 fatalities. Since males currently comprise under 20% of the North American elephant population, the handler fatality rate is four times higher working with male elephants than it is working with female elephants. Ten fatalities occurred when the handler was out of sight of other handlers. All fifteen occurred when handlers were not separated from the elephant by a barrier. From this small data sample and analysis it would appear fatalities could be reduced by reducing handler contact with male elephants, requiring more than one handler be present when anyone is within reach of an elephant, and providing barriers (Elephant Restraint Chutes) for handling difficult elephants. On the job safety is proven to be directly effected by managerial emphasis on the problem. Managers control the resources and thus have both the ability and obligation to reduce risk in elephant management by allocating their resources toward elephant programs.

AZA Conference Proceedings

Tim Desmond and Gail Laule are both marine mammal trainers who have formed a well-respected consulting firm called Active Environments, Inc. They have been innovators in taking operant techniques used for marine mammals and applying them to various zoological settings. They have been on the forefront of the development of protected-contact techniques for elephants and have had some remarkable results. Their approach to animal behavior is very systematic and is always well documented. If you read only one paper on the introduction and application of protected contact techniques, this is the one I recommend. It was first presented in 1991 at the AZA (then called AAZPA) conference in San Diego.

Protected-Contact Elephant Training

by Tim Desmond, Gail Laule
Active Environments, Inc.

INTRODUCTION

Exhibiting elephants these days is a complex task. OSHA is taking a much more active role in mandating trainer safety issues. Animal activists, the press, and even legislators are attempting to dictate policy on elephant handling practices. The general public is exerting pressure to make methods more aesthetically pleasing. Elephants, it would seem, have entered the public domain.

All this controversy is calling into question centuries-old tradition of elephant care and management. Physical dominance and aversive methods, as necessary as they may be, are becoming less and less acceptable methods of training. Institutions are facing the dilemma of how to deal with a growing number of maturing bulls and aggressive cows residing in their facilities. Except for the crush, which most facilities do not have and which constitutes a major capital investment, there are no alternate handling methods currently available to utilize in these situations.

The San Diego Zoological Society requested Active Environments to design and conduct a pilot program to explore alternate methods of elephant handling at the San Diego Wild Animal Park in Escondido, California. The requirements of the program were that it be safe for trainers, that it include no punishment of the elephants, and that necessary husbandry behaviors be trained and conducted without the use of restraint or anesthesia. A second objective of the project was to develop preliminary functional specifications for design of facilities to support this type of elephant handling program.

Active Environments subsequently developed what is now called a protected-contact handling system which relies solely on positive reinforcement operant conditioning. It is important to emphasize, however, that it is not the use of operant conditioning that distinguishes this system from other systems of elephant training. In fact, operant conditioning, intentionally or not, is a part of every training system, including the traditional free-contact methods for elephants. What makes this system unique and new, is the <u>context</u> in which operant conditioning is being applied. In this case, the context is that there is no free-contact between trainers and elephants, there is no use of punishment or negative reinforcement, and the elephant's participation is totally voluntary. The only discipline used is a "time-out," which is simply a withdrawal of the trainer's attention from the elephant for a short period of time before resuming activity, or in extreme cases, actually ending a session and coming back later to try again. The animal is always fed its daily allotment of food.

This program differs from the confined-contact system described by the AAZPA SSP Elephant Group in two ways. First, the animal is not restrained in any way. Contact is made through a barrier that has been modified to allow physical access to the elephant while protecting the trainers from injury. However, it can be used to desensitize an elephant to a crush and to work the animal once inside. Second, protected-contact is not a remote or "hands-off" system. There is a great deal of physical contact and interaction between elephant and trainer.

We feel this physical contact and interaction is critical to maintaining the psychological well-being of the elephants. It is unfortunate that, in most cases, when elephants are transferred from a free-contact system to a confined-contact system they lose all the good things that free-contact work has to offer. An often overlooked fact is that free-contact provides a great deal of positive interaction between elephant and trainer and behavioral opportunity that contributes to an active, enhanced life for the animal. These positive elements must be maintained in the new system, in a safer form, or the result is a bored, neurotic animal. Trainers, too, benefit from the human-animal interaction, so it is important to provide trainers with continued, albeit safer, contact with the animals.

This program was conducted in two phases. Initial work involved two bull elephants, an Asian named Ranchipur, and an African named Chico. The purpose of Phase I was to develop protected-contact techniques, test their feasibility as a handling methodology, and identify preliminary facility specifications. With that accomplished, Phase II was initiated to develop components of a functional operating system of elephant handling utilizing the protected-contact techniques. We will focus on Phase II in this paper.

METHODS

When applying the principles of operant conditioning to elephants, our basic training tools consist of a silent dog whistle, which serves as a conditioned reinforcer, and a bucket of sliced apples and carrots. Our plans to shape physical movement are drawn from our experience with marine mammals, particularly killer whales, who share huge body mass and remote positioning (they're in the water, we're on land) with our elephant subjects. So our third set of training tools is an assortment of targets - fiberglass poles from 3' to 15' long, with a foam float on one end.

The use of targets to shape behavior is a proven method in the marine mammal field. The principle of using targets is that, when presented, the animal orients toward and touches the target. We start with the head target to control gross movements of the animal within the enclosure. By presenting this target the animal can be drawn from any point in an enclosure to a specific location. Other targets are then used to control the movement or position of specific parts of the elephant's body, like lining animals up parallel to the working wall, and accessing feet, hips, shoulders, ears, tusks, and so on.

When elephants have had free-contact training with a hook, the use of targets presents some interesting complications. Initially, the action of a hook is used to physically manipulate the elephant's movement by escape-avoidance. In other words, the elephant is uncomfortable when the hook touches the back of a leg, so the elephant moves the leg forward to escape or avoid the hook. The physical movement is away from the hook. Once established, the animal will respond to the hook as a cue whether or not it is used in an aversive fashion. A target works the opposite. The target touches the front of the leg, and the leg moves toward it. Although it may sound like a small point, from the elephant's perspective, it is a very big difference. Elephants that have had any extreme measures used, like hot shots, are even more wary of any object coming toward them and are naturally inclined to try to avoid it.

This is where the process of desensitization is important. In very basic terms, desensitization is a process designed to train out, or overcome, fear. By pairing positives with any action or object that elicits fear, that fearful entity slowly becomes more positive, and thus less fearful. For all its apparent simplicity, desensitization is a critical component of a good training system, requiring expert skill and timing in its application to be successful. In the training of elephants, it is an ongoing process. In the course of our training we desensitized each animal, to varying degrees, to a myriad of objects and experiences including: targets, foot trimming tools, rubber tubs, needles, alcohol swabs, new openings in gates, different people, a microphone popping, working outside of normal routines, and so on. Often, thorough desensitization must occur before you can even begin to shape a desired behavior. At times the animal's movement is completely ignored, and the process more closely resembles respondent conditioning rather than operant conditioning.

A necessary part of the training project was modification of existing facilities. The simplest approach was to modify existing gates between animal enclosures to allow protected-contact between trainers and elephants. Holes were cut in the

African bull yard gate (Chico) to allow access to his feet, ears, and eyes. These holes were fitted with doors that are kept locked except during training sessions. A bar was welded across the top of the gate to keep him from reaching over with his trunk. Later upper portions of the solid gate panels were replaced with expanded metal so he had better visual access. The Asian bull yard gate was modified in similar yet simpler fashion, with open areas for trainer access (see Figures 1 & 2). Fortunately, the San Diego Zoo and Wild Animal Park's welding crews are patient fellows, since they returned more than once to expand an existing hole or make a new one.

Although these modifications are functional, without any major redesign, our access to the animals has been limited. In most cases we only have direct access to them from one side. Consequently, we have learned to be creative in our manipulation of targets, and have benefited tremendously from the malleability and cooperation of the elephants.

The notable exception to that problem is an existing room in the Asian barn called the introduction chute. Its location, similar to a crush, is between the outside yard and the inside barn. However, two sides are solid, including the door to the outside and one side wall. The other two are open with vertical bars spaced 11 inches apart. On these open sides we added horizontal chain to prevent the animals from throwing their trunks. With complete access to the animal on two sides, it affords us a much improved training environment. However, ultimately access from three or four sides seems ideal.

A key feature of the protected-contact program is how the trainer is shielded from injury by the elephant. The physical barrier is only part of the protective strategy. The animal must be in a physical position where it cannot strike the trainer without repositioning itself. The trainer is in a position where he or she can easily move out of striking range while the animal repositions. This strategy is backed up by a buddy system in which trainers work in pairs where one focuses on the behavior to be conducted as the backup watches the animal. When working through an opening, the trainer never creates the opportunity for the animal to pin an arm by never extending the arm through a hole past mid-forearm or reaching around the corner of the opening. The arm is always in a position to be quickly withdrawn directly backward. When working on feet, the trainer positions in such a fashion that, if the animal kicks, its foot

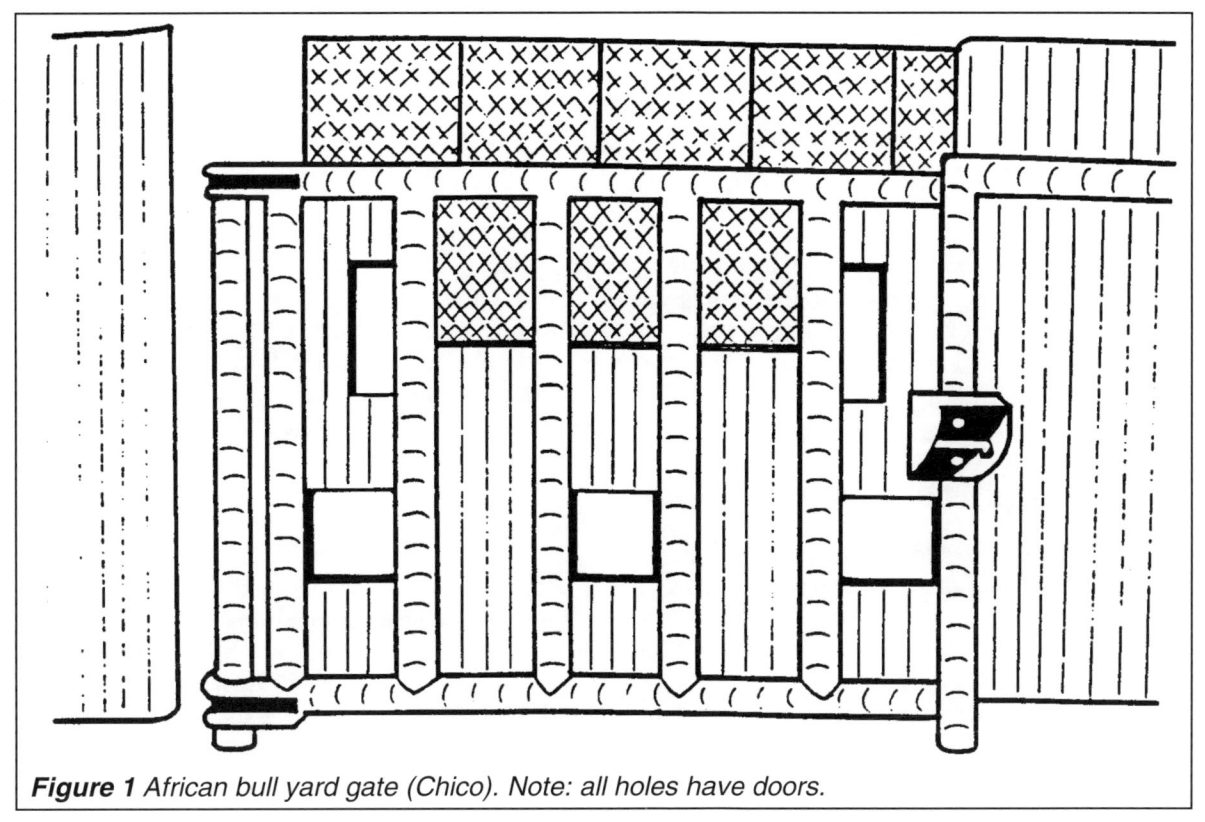

Figure 1 *African bull yard gate (Chico). Note: all holes have doors.*

will impact the edge of the opening before the trainer's body.

The current program involves four elephants -the two bulls from Phase I work, Ranchipur and Chico, and two females, an African named Sabu and an Asian named Cookie. The bulls were obvious choices since they were already in remote handling situations and were not accessible for husbandry or veterinary procedures. The females were chosen because of some handling problems within the free-contact system; not because of aggression, but because of their flighty nature or lack of cooperation in certain procedures. The following is a brief profile of the subject animals provided by San Diego Wild Animal Park.

Chico
African bull, age 26 years. Aggressive nature, considered very dangerous. Handled within a free-contact system while young but never trained on blood draw or foot trim. Not had free-contact with trainers for over 10 years.

Ranchipur
Asian bull, age 25 years. Fairly docile for a bull. Very suspicious and fearful of new things. Came from a circus where highly aversive measures, including hotshot, were used. Up until 4 years ago, trainers could do foot trims by using a female elephant as a shield. No work done since that time. Has very long tusks that require periodic anesthesia for trimming.

Cookie
Asian female, age 35 years. Functioning in free-contact system. Third ranking in the herd, she is rather flighty and is not consistent in cooperating with blood draw.

Sabu
African female, age 31 years. Functioning in free-contact system. Third ranking in the herd, she is flighty and is the only female that refuses to cooperate in routine blood draws. Very suspicious of any veterinary procedure.

Working with females currently being handled in a free-contact system raised some concerns. Could the animals discriminate between two systems which have different rules, criteria for performance, and consequences for misbehavior? Could they readily make the transition from one system to another? Most importantly, would there be any greater risk to free-contact personnel once the animals were exposed to a protected-contact system?

Trainer safety is a critical issue due to inherent differences between the two systems. In free-contact, trainer safety depends on total control requiring social dominance over the elephant. Any slip in performance by the animal, or failure to respond to a command, can be a challenge to that dominance. If so, trainer safety dictates a swift and consistent response. The trainer must make the elephant do it right, including using punishment if necessary. In a protected-contact system, participation is voluntary. There are no consequences for the animal if they do not respond, or if performance criteria is not met. Even overt aggression is either ignored or, at the most, responded to with a time-out. That is possible because none of these situations can result in risk to the trainer.

Working with the females also gave us a chance to explore the potential benefits of working with animals who were currently functioning in a free-contact system. We could utilize control commands they heard everyday like back-up, steady, and come to help manipulate gross movement. We could also take behaviors they already knew, like foot trims and convert them to the new system instead of training the behavior from scratch. Most importantly, however, working with the females was an opportunity to explore what it would take, and how difficult it would be, to convert them to a protected-contact handling system, if that became desirable in the future.

Training sessions were conducted two to four days per week, with the bulls scheduled for three sessions per day and the cows two sessions per day. The training was conducted by the authors, and Society Animal Behavior Specialist Gary Priest. Society Elephant Supervisor Alan Roocroft participated in training in Phase II and he had worked with the authors in Phase I training as well.

RESULTS
As of this writing, training has been conducted over a period of three-and-a-half months. During that time, there were a total of 47 days of training, with the number of sessions each animal participated in as follows: Cookie 72, Sabu 78, Chico 105, and Ranchipur 110. During that time, all of the animals learned the basic control behaviors, and each was conditioned to voluntarily cooperate with

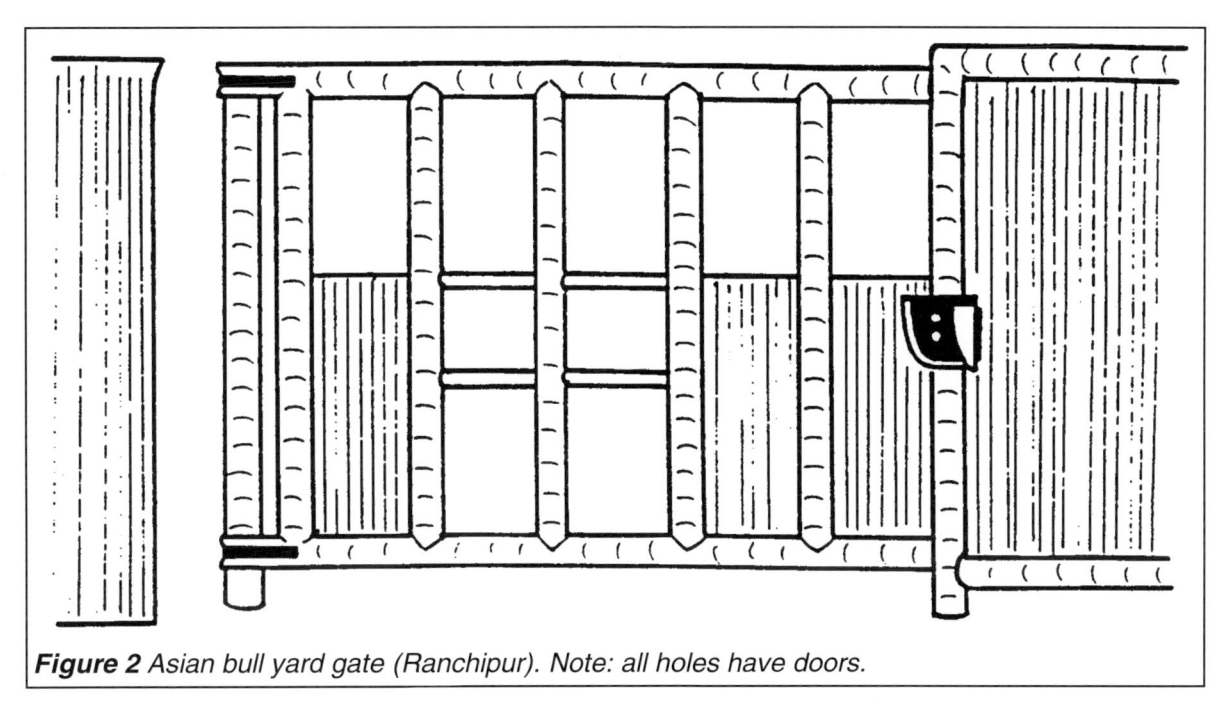

Figure 2 Asian bull yard gate (Ranchipur). Note: all holes have doors.

the husbandry behaviors to varying degrees. Chico also learned some enrichment/demonstration behaviors. Table 1 shows a list of behavioral goals, and what each animal achieved. Several factors impacted the results.

First, identifying, installing and limiting the cost and complexity of facility modifications had a significant impact on results, directly effecting progress on certain behaviors, and in some cases dictating which behaviors could or could not be worked.

Second, there was difficulty maintaining a full training schedule. Initially work was scheduled four days a week. That quickly became three days a week, and for the last month of training, we averaged two to three days a week. There is no doubt that a five to seven day a week schedule of training would tremendously accelerate progress. It is important to note, however, that even with our limited schedule, retention by all the elephants was excellent, and progress continued unabated.

Third, animal health problems impacted training. Cookie, the Asian cow, was suffering from an eye infection at the beginning of the project, which seriously impaired sight in the left eye, and slightly impaired it in the right. We initiated training with her in the bull yard, where we were positioned above her, on the wall surrounding the yard. Progress was extremely slow and her level of responsiveness minimal. After about four weeks we considered using another animal even though her eyes were getting better. However, we opted to continue with her, but moved work to ground level in close enough proximity to touch and interact with her directly. Her responsiveness and progress accelerated dramatically. She was conditioned to come inside the introductory chute in just 6 sessions. She quickly equaled, and in some cases exceeded, the level of progress of the other animals. It appeared that the close proximity, and direct contact (in a protected context) was critical to her level of performance.

There were several beneficial results that are not reflected in the behavioral list. About half-way through Phase II training, Ranchipur the Asian bull, who was in full musth throughout most of the project, developed an abscess in his right front foot, and soreness and discomfort from an overgrown nail in his left front foot. There was serious concern about his condition, and consideration was being given to anesthetizing him to deal with the situation. Voluntary cooperation with foot trims had not yet been achieved, and his apparent discomfort made him less cooperative. However, with the veterinarian's and Alan's approval, we attempted to deal with the situation behaviorally. We washed his feet down regularly, applying the force of the water stream to the infected areas; attempted training him to soak his feet in a rubber tub; and continued work on foot trims. Over a period of approximately 4 weeks, we conditioned him to tolerate progressively longer bouts of trimming and washing of his feet. Through this approach, these problems were corrected and a risky procedure avoided.

Another noteworthy result was the change in Chico's behavior. In Phase I, we encountered a moderate level of aggressive behavior from this African bull. A touch of the target was often followed by an attempt to grab or eat it. Calling him to the target included an obligatory charge somewhere along the way. When really annoyed he would lunge his front feet up onto the wall where we were working, doing his impersonation of Godzilla. Because of the protected-contact positioning, none of this aggression was dangerous to us. Consequently, our response was to ignore it, and simultaneously reinforce any gentle or non-aggressive moves made toward the target or us. Throughout Phase I, his aggressive behavior almost completely disappeared.

In Phase II work, this low level of aggression has continued. In fact, it is almost exclusively limited to situations of difficulty or confusion. Most instances of aggression occur when working on his back feet. Because of facility limitations, to present his rear feet, Chico has to rotate 180 degrees to a head target, then back up, shift his back end to his left, look back over his shoulder, and extend whichever rear foot we requested (by a second target tapping it) behind him and through the hole. It is as complicated as it sounds. With some regularity he will register his protest by butting the gate with his head before going to the first target. However, he then proceeds to work with tremendous patience and tenacity, holding his foot calmly in the hole for scrubbing or trimming.

Overall, Chico, recognized as the most dangerous elephant in the collection, has been the star of the program. He seems to enjoy the sessions, often making rumbling sounds which the staff tell us are pleasure sounds. He has amazing endurance, working for over an hour on occasion. He also responds to the attention and tactile we can now safely offer him. He lines up against the gate and allows us to rub and scratch him, occasionally adjusting his position so eye contact is possible through the ear holes. Trainers in the area seem surprised and impressed at the change in his behavior. He is the most striking example of the enriching aspects of a protected-contact training program.

Our work with the females currently being handled in a free-contact system, did not seem to have negative consequences to the animals or handlers. The elephants moved from one system to the other, responding to the different commands without confusion or disruption of normal work patterns. Most importantly, there was no evidence of increased risk to the free-contact handlers working with these two cows. However, this is still an area of concern, and must be carefully evaluated in any attempt to introduce or integrate these two systems.

One final observation on all the animals, is an overall increase in tolerance for new stimuli. While desensitizing animals to specific stimuli, which is an integral part of this training, a general increased tolerance of the unusual seems to occur simultaneously. Some of that is very deliberate on the part of the trainer, some is simply a by-product of reinforcing animals for tolerating new events. Our observations indicate that overall the elephants react less fearfully to new stimuli, and if they do, are quicker to recover and continue working.

CONCLUSIONS

A great many capabilities remain to be demonstrated before protected-contact is ready to be implemented as an operational system for handling elephants. However, this project has proven successful on several levels. In Phase I we demonstrated that protected-contact methods could be used to train desired behavior while meeting increased requirements for trainer safety. We also identified initial facility modifications needed to implement the program. Phase II demonstrated that a protected-contact program can be applied to a variety of situations and animals, and that protected-contact has the potential for development into an operational system.

Several clear benefits of a protected-contact system have emerged. Protected-contact handling methods provide an enriched behavioral environment because behavior is volunteered not demanded. Opportunities are created for positive trainer-animal interactions in a safe context while avoiding situations that are likely to induce aggression. By eliminating punishment and utilizing positive reinforcement exclusively, protected-contact addresses animal rights issues and public relations concerns, and demonstrates an obvious commitment to the welfare of the animals. Protected-contact also provides increased opportunities to reinforce cooperative or tolerant behavior to enhance socialization of individuals into groups. Finally, a variety of innovative presentations and demonstrations can be developed using protected

-contact techniques.

It appears to us that protected-contact is a system that addresses many of the tough issues facing facilities and managers exhibiting elephants today. At the very least this preliminary work indicates that the protected-contact system of elephant handling is worthy of a closer look.

ACKNOWLEDGMENTS

Active Environments would like to acknowledge and extend our thanks to Alan Roocroft for his insight, invaluable input, and commendable flexibility; to Gary Priest for his collaborative training efforts; to Larry Killmar for his logistical and operational support; to the elephant trainers at the San Diego Wild Animal Park for their assistance and interest in the program; to Doug Myers and the San Diego Zoological Society for their foresight and willingness to try something new; and to the elephants, for making us look so good.

Behavioral Objectives and Progress Report
Progress through 9-1-91

Behavior	Chico	Sabu	Cookie	Ranjipur
Whistle trained	X	X	X	X
Target trained (head)	X	X	X	X
Target trained (#2)	X	X	X	X
Left front foot up	X	X	X	X
Right front foot up	X	X	X	X
Left rear foot up	X	X	X	X
Right rear foot up	X	X	X	X
Left front foot trim	X	75%*	75%*	X
Right front foot trim	X	75%*	75%*	X
Left rear foot trim	X	75%*	75%*	25%
Right rear foot trim	X	75%*	75%*	25%
Lean-in right	X	X	X	X
Lean-in left	X	X	X	X
Trunk up	X	X	X	X
Trunk down	X	X	X	X
Retrieve object	X	--	--	--
Go through gate	X	--	X	X
Present ear right	X	X	X	X
Present ear left	X	X	X	X
Bleed from ear	X	50%	75%	50%
Anal/vaginal palpitation	--	25%	50%	--
Back up	X	75%	X	X
Steady	X	75%	X	X
Come	X	X	X	X
Enter introductory chute	--	--	X	X
Put object in bucket	X	--	--	--
A to B	X	--	--	50%
Present eye	X	25%	X	--
Tusk trim	--	25%	--	50%
Soak foot in tub (front)	--	50%	X	25%
Soak foot in tub (rear)	--	--	50%	--

X   Complete
--   Not worked
*   Complete except for actual trims which are done in free contact

Table 1 *Behavioral objectives and progress report*

AZA Conference Proceedings

The best way to judge the effectiveness of a new methodology, such as protected contact, is to have it implemented at various facilities. Many zoos began to use systems similar to those described by Desmond and Laule in 1991. Hardly an AZA conference is held without at least one or two papers on the subject. Many are case histories like this one, first presented in Omaha, Nebraska in 1993.

"C" is for Cindy: A Case History

by Gary Miller, Craig Wilcox, Sally Latores, and Bruce Upchurch
Point Defiance Zoo and Aquarium

The Elephant Management Program at Point Defiance Zoo and Aquarium (PDZA) incorporates free and protected contact systems. As with many institutions, we operate under the premise that an elephant's mental and physical stimulation are necessary and integral parts of basic elephant husbandry. Proper elephant management utilizes all possible tools available. Protected and free contact should not be thought of as exclusive of one another. It is not a question of one or the other. but rather what is right for an elephant program. They both utilize operant conditioning; they both take time to develop the skills necessary to administer them properly. We think of protected contact as a system that 1) utilizes operant conditioning techniques including target training to accomplish all the husbandry needs of the animals and 2) increases safety by placing the handler out of elephant trunk reach.

Currently at PDZA, we house two 12-year-old female African elephants *(Loxodonta arficana)*. They have been at PDZA since they were approximately one-year-old and have always been cared for in a free contact system. This program includes offering public rides and handling demonstrations. In addition, we house one female Asian elephant *(Elephas maximus);* she is 31-years-old: her name is Cindy. Many have heard about or of Cindy. Some have seen her in action. Cindy is the focus of this presentation.

Cindy spent 17 years in a sterile asphalt and cement exhibit. She did not receive any formal training, although she would offer some behaviors for treats. As she grew older and larger, she became progressively more selective about her handlers. A few she accepted; others were not tolerated, and attacked. She became a management problem. In 1982, she was transferred to the San Diego Wild Animal Park (SDWAP) in hopes that she would develop social skills and possibly even breed. This was riot to be. Her pattern of accepting few continued. At the end of the seven-year breeding loan, she was transferred to the Washington Park Zoo in Portland, Oregon. While there, she was handled in the same manner as their adult bulls. Much of this may make it sound as it she had become basically an annoyance. This is a major understatement. She had in fact become a very. very dangerous elephant. She has attacked and injured to various degrees at least 12 people.

In February 1992, Cindy returned to PDZA. She moved into a new facility complete with restraint chute, stalling options. spacious yards and pools. However, within the first month, Cindy started a familiar pattern; she became demonstrably affectionate toward a single handler and aggressive with others. A characteristic in her past was that at some point the accepted handler vanishes. We feel that this has shaken her trust in people and actually reinforced her tendency to gravitate toward a chosen few handlers. It was obvious that we needed a system where various handlers could administer care. a system that would be consistent over time and be as safe as possible for the handlers.

Because of these factors, it was decided that she would be managed in a totally protected manner. The challenge then became how do we give this animal all of the management advantages of free contact without endangering handlers. We were aware that some success had been realized with several elephants in which operant conditioning techniques were employed from behind barriers. Certainly, we had the restraint chute available

444 ANIMAL TRAINING

to us to handle her in the same way many mature bulls are cared for, but we felt there was great potential to explore and experiment with operant conditioning applied in a protected contact system.

In November 1992, we began intensive protected contact training with Cindy. The overall goal was to see just what protected contact could do for Cindy and our elephant management program and to try to determine what the limits might be. In an effort to save time, we decided to use behaviors and codes generated by Active Environments in a paper titled, "A Program for Exploring Alternate Methods for Elephant Management." Of the 33 original behaviors, we chose not to train eight behaviors because they do not fit our program needs at this time. We at PDZA have trained 13 additional behaviors, most of which are task oriented and designed to stimulate Cindy mentally and physically. As of today, we can work Cindy through 38 individual behaviors (Table A). In 10 months of work, we have completed over 500 training sessions, with a total refusal to work occurring only one time, early in the program, Each session lasts an average of 10 to 15 minutes. Each trained behavior and Cindy's responses are logged. Cindy willingly responds to four different handlers (one of which was introduced six months into the program) with little, if any, discernible variability. She definitely has her up and down days. We have been able to work her no matter what her disposition or mood for the day might be.

At this point, we would like to address Cindy's history of aggression. Prior to the program, Cindy would throw extreme and very exuberant tantrums, slamming bars, gates, or doors and rushing handlers she did not like. As the program has progressed, her aggression has decreased in frequency and intensity. Generally, we treat the aggression with a "time-out." We remove ourselves from her attention, sometimes simply leaving the periphery of the work area: other times removing ourselves from the barn totally. This has always had the desired result in her attitude; she calms down and cooperates. Just as in free contact, we establish the rules and what is expected in terms of a response. An interesting occurrence that requires further investigation is that Cindy exhibits temporal drainage similar to that witnessed in bull elephants experiencing musth. What's more, the drainage appears to be cyclical. Accompanying her drainage is usually a behavior change. She becomes more aggressive, has a shorter attention span, and is less patient. However, we are able to work her even during these periods. Sometimes she reacts slower, and we will not ask for as many behaviors. We do not pressure her, but we can still administer necessary care. It is important to note that she does each of the 38 behaviors for each handler. Any handler can work any behavior any day, any time, or train new behaviors. All in spite of the fact that she still chooses favorite people. And, most importantly, she has injured no one. Cindy now works in a program that can remain consistent despite personnel changes.

An important test for any protected contact system is its ability to meet the medical needs of the elephant without resorting to extreme measures such as chemical restraint. The behaviors Cindy has learned along with the use of a restraint chute allow us to meet all of Cindy's day-to-day medical needs short of surgery.

At the beginning, we asked the question "does protected contact work?" The answer for Cindy is YES. The reasons it works are very simple. As an institution, we have committed ourselves to acquiring all the tools necessary to making the program a success. This includes 1) an experienced staff of two handlers with more than 20 years around elephants: another with 20 years of operant conditioning experience, with a variety of animals, primarily marine mammals; and a fourth, our "rookie," has nine years of elephant experience; 2) a team approach governed by an Elephant Management Committee that includes the director, general curator, education curator, elephant manager, veterinarian, and elephant staff; 3) a clearly defined and comprehensive procedural manual: and 4) a facility designed for flexibility, safety, and proper husbandry. Everyone involved is dedicated to the program. We are all in this for the elephants. We are committed to their future, and we are convinced that Cindy is receiving more attention and training than at any time in her life. This point alone would be enough to call the program successful, but we continue to look to the future. We have plans to add an additional yard and expand our holding facilities. We feel strongly that the only limitations are with our own imagination and our own creativity. Our goal is for Cindy to keep pace with the African elephants, except, of course, for rides.

The protected contact system is very new and raises many questions. Our system is working for a single, anti-social cow. Will it work in a herd situation? Will it work when a newborn calf needs intervention? Will it be possible to make difficult introductions? What if the elephant is ill? Questions like these need to be answered.

Each institution has a different set of variables. What might be a solution to one program's difficulties might not be the right choice for another program. It is time to coordinate intense efforts as a zoological community to create care systems that give the animals quality care and create a safe working environment. As stated before, protected and free contact are simply tools. High quality, free-contact skills take time and commitment to develop; the same is true for protected contact. As elephant keepers, we are excited and encouraged by the success of this program and the future it holds for elephant management.

TABLE A: Currently trained behaviors under protected contact

The 33 behaviors in List A below along with codes used for record keeping were published in a paper by Active Environments titled "A Program for Exploring Alternate Methods for Elephant Management". List B includes those behaviors added by the elephant staff at Point Defiance Zoo & Aquarium.

LIST A:
1. Whistle conditioned
2. Head target conditioned
3. Introduction to Chute
4. Front left foot touch target
5. Front right foot touch target
6. Rear left foot touch target
7. Rear right foot touch target
8. Lean left side to barrier with head and hip on targets
9. Lean right side to barrier with head and hip on targets
10. Front left foot trim
11. Front right foot trim
12. Rear left foot trim
13. Rear right foot trim
14. Hold trunk up
15. Trunk down
16. Back up
17. Steady
18. Come to keeper (move forward)
19. Go through gate on command
20. Lie down
21. Present left ear/blood draw
22. Present right ear/blood draw
23. Retrieve an object
24. Head on tusk presentation*
25. Lateral tusk presentation*
26. Present left eye*
27. Present right eye*
28. Tolerate intra-muscular injection*
29. Vocalization*
30. Anal/Vaginal inspection*
31. Hose down
32. Soak foot*
33. Rotate 360 degrees (counter clockwise)

* Behaviors not yet trained

LIST B:
1. Stretch
2. Line-up
3. Lie down right side
4. Rotate 360 degrees (clockwise)
5. Push an object
6. Kick ball
7. Load/stack tires
8. Hold-up left front, rear right feet
9. Hold-up front right, rear left feet
10. Hold-up two feet same side
11. Tub work
12. Balance beam (includes behaviors 8,9,10 while on beam)
13. Present tail

AZA Conference Proceedings

To many trainers, protected contact training might seem like a logical way to safely interact with and care for elephants, or any other potentially dangerous animal. However, as protected contact programs were started at various zoos, detractors started voicing their opinions. Often, dissent arises from a misunderstanding of the concepts in question. Sometimes, if protected contact techniques were applied poorly or incorrectly, people could be lead to believe that a technique was bad when it may have been the application that was flawed. After Tim Desmond and Gail Laule of Active Environments published the results of their protected contact work, questions, criticisms, and confusion greeted this relatively new approach to working with elephants. To answer some of the most common concerns Tim and Gail presented the following paper at the 1993 Conference held in Omaha, Nebraska.

The Politics of Protected Contact

by Tim Desmond, Gail Laule
Active Environments, Inc.

INTRODUCTION

Protected contact is:

> "...a concept of elephant confinement that consists, principally, of eliminating tactile human contact..."

> "...the relegation of elephants to a kind of penal confinement."

> "...a return to the unhappy era of enforced isolation."

With protected contact:

> "...those relationships (human/animal) will become a robotic, remote relationship."

> "...we could wind up with a generation of unmanageable "wild" zoo elephants."

Protected contact will:

> "...reduce the quality of life for these magnificent animals."

In reading the preceding comments from a variety of newspaper, magazine, and newsletter articles, it is difficult to imagine that protected contact was developed as a positive alternative for traditional elephant handling. In addition, looking at the many forms of protected contact that have cropped up around the country, many significantly diverge from the fundamental principles of protected contact. And there really are some basic tenets upon which it was built. They have just gotten a bit distorted along the way.

The rather rocky road protected contact has traveled thus far is to be expected. Although not a new idea, it is one that, once organized into a cohesive methodology constituting the beginnings of a real system, fundamentally challenged the status quo. It is irrelevant that that was not the intention. The emotional resistance to protected contact arises from a community under siege. Ironically, the rush to protected contact by crisis-driven zoo management also threatens to undermine its structure and intent. So, in order to sort out the confusion and to address the concerns. a review of the basic tenets of protected contact from the perspective of those who developed it is in order.

1. KEEPER SAFETY

The cornerstone of a protected contact program is keeper safely. Protection comes from three elements - physical barriers, elephant positioning, and trainer positioning. When the trainer works in close proximity to the elephant, a physical barrier allowing safe access to the animal is required. Next, the elephant must be in a physical position where it cannot strike the trainer without repositioning itself, Finally, trainers must take positions which they can easily vacate if the elephant repositions. In situations where a barrier is not used, such as in yards or pens, trainers must work beyond the maximum reach of the elephant's trunk. This strategy is backed up by a buddy system in which one trainer focuses on the behavior being conducted as the backup watches the elephant.

Although the level of risk is far less than in free contact, protected contact is not a foolproof system. Safety ultimately relies on human judgement and is vulnerable to human error. It is absolutely critical that both staff and management understand the basic rules of keeper safety and adhere to them, or people can and will be hurt.

Human/Animal Interaction

The rules of protected contact that apply to keeper safety are there to allow human/animal interaction, not to prohibit it. Given the right facility modifications, it is possible to have tactile contact with virtually every inch of an elephant's body. The same positioning that allows contact for husbandry behaviors and veterinary procedures can and should be used for physical contact simply for the sake of human/animal interaction. This is not a unique concept. Keepers that work with the vast majority of zoo animals create and maintain lasting relationships with the animals, always interacting through barriers of steel, mesh, bars, fences, or moats.

Those that lament the loss of a special human/animal relationship when free contact is suspended, must acknowledge that a free contact system necessitates the handler maintaining a socially dominant position over the elephant. It is reasonable to assume that that factor impacts, and to some extent limits, the human/animal relationship. Protected contact, on the other hand, places some constraints on physical contact, but at the same time removes the barrier of sustained domination. Each system has its costs and benefits, and ultimately the extent and quality of the human/animal relationship is up to the individual humans and animals to develop and assure.

2. HANDLING METHODS THAT RELY PRIMARILY ON POSITIVE REINFORCEMENT

In a positive reinforcement system animals are reinforced with rewards they like for the desired behavioral response. Operationally, it means that we exhaust the positive alternatives before any kind of negative reinforcement is utilized. On the rare occasions when an escape-avoidance technique is necessary, such as restraining an elephant in a chute, it is kept to a minimum and balanced by positive reinforcement the vast majority of the time. Punishment is only used in a life threatening situation for person or animal. The only discipline used is a "time-out," which is simply a withdrawal of the trainer's attention from the elephant for a short period of time before resuming activity, or in extreme cases, actually ending a session and coming back later to try again. The elephant is always fed its daily allotment of food.

This training does not rely on the handler being socially dominant. Participation by the elephant is voluntary. With good trainer skills the level and consistency of elephant behavioral performance will remain high. Our records show that in 365 protected contact training sessions between four elephants, the animals chose to work 99% of the time (Laule, 1992).

Negative versus Positive Reinforcement

Good free contact trainers regularly utilize positive reinforcement in their training and handling. However, free contact as a system relies much more heavily on negative reinforcement or escape/avoidance. This is illustrated in contrasting the use of a hook and the use of a target (a pole with a soft tip which is the basic tool of protected contact) to elicit a physical movement.

Initially, the hook controls the elephant's movement by escape-avoidance. The elephant is uncomfortable when the hook touches the back of a leg, so the elephant moves the leg forward to escape or avoid the hook. The movement is away from the hook. Once trained, the elephant will respond to the hook as a cue whether or not it is used in an aversive fashion. However, if the animal does not respond appropriately, the hook is used as a negative reinforcer. A target works the opposite. The target touches or is presented in the front of the leg, and the leg moves toward it. The target is not used in an aversive way (i.e. tapping the leg harder) to elicit the response.

Some facilities currently use combinations of free contact techniques in a confined contact setting, and call it protected contact. Keepers work from shielded positions, but continue to use hooks and free contact voice commands and body language to access behaviors. It is important to understand the repercussions of such a mix. To an unknown extent, the animals are being maintained through a process that utilizes negative reinforcement and harkens back to the animal's memory of the social dominance structure. Although both the hook and the target can elicit movement, the hook has significance to the elephant that is neither necessary nor desirable in protected contact. It can create the perception that the trainer is attempting to dominate the animal when the trainer is no longer in a position to back it up. This can result in challenging and aggressive behavior by the elephant. It also denies the elephant all the benefits positive reinforcement offers. Utilizing protected contact as it was designed, relying on positive reinforcement, meets behavioral objectives while minimizing the chance of aggression.

Greater Choice and Control

In a positive reinforcement environment, animals are free to experiment with a broader range of behavioral responses because there are no negative consequences to experimentation. In fact, skilled trainers consistently reward animals not just for overt correct responses, but for more subtle and subjective actions like "problem solving" a task, offering "creative solutions," and "trying" hard.

Animals are also free to express displeasure, frustration, and aggression without negative repercussions. Because trainers are not functioning in the precarious "alpha" position, which is always vulnerable to being challenged, and because they are working from protected positions, they can ignore aggressive behavior and selectively reinforce any gentle or non-aggressive behavior that occurs. With three different bull elephants, keepers, managers, and veterinarians subjectively report dramatic reductions in aggressive behavior with the use of protected contact techniques (Desmond & Laule, 1991; Maddox, 1992; Flanagan, personal communication, 1993).

Pro-Active Techniques

Positive reinforcement training offers techniques to address behavioral issues in a pro-active manner. Through the process of desensitization, animals learn to tolerate scary or uncomfortable stimuli. This is the procedure used in training voluntary cooperation in veterinary procedures that may be physically uncomfortable, such as drawing blood. In basic terms, desensitization is a process designed to "train out," or overcome, fear. While desensitizing animals to specific stimuli, which is an integral part of protected contact training, a general increased tolerance of the unusual seems to occur simultaneously. Some of that is very deliberate on the part of the trainer, some is simply a by-product of reinforcing toleration of new events. Our observations indicate that overall the elephants react less fearfully to new stimuli and, if they do, are quicker to recover and continue working (Desmond & Laule, 1991). This is consistent with our extensive work with marine mammals (Laule, 1983) and many other animals. This may have significant implications for keeper safety. A study on elephant inflicted injuries indicated that attacks often came as a result of exposure to startling or unexpected stimuli (Bernirschke & Roocroft 1992). One group of keepers stated that in a free contact system, "...elephants, look to the keepers for security..." (E.M.A., 1992). One could argue that by actively utilizing desensitization, elephants are taught and encouraged to be independently secure, rather than dependent on human handlers for security.

3. THE ABILITY TO PROVIDE OPTIMAL CARE FOR ELEPHANTS.

The most serious concern of those contemplating the implementation of protected contact is whether it can provide optimal care for the elephants. Specific issues that are cited are: the ability to train and conduct necessary husbandry behaviors reliably; the ability to access sick or injured animals; the ability to address social issues including introductions and aggression between animals; and the ability to deal with novel situations such as accessing calves.

Training and Conducting Husbandry Behaviors

Protected contact training entails two processes: transferring existing behaviors that an elephant knows to a safer, positive reinforcement context, and training new behavior. As long as the requirements of keeper safety are adhered to, the techniques are versatile enough to be used in a variety of training settings - through a barrier, in an open yard, or in a restraint chute. In our experience, with skilled personnel and adequate facilities, all basic husbandry behaviors can be trained in a reasonable time-frame and accessed on a reliable basis. Reports on positive reinforcement training with a variety of species indicate that the reliability of animals voluntarily cooperating in husbandry and veterinary procedures is very high while the stress level is low (Reinhardt, 1990; Turkkan, 1990; Reichard & Shellabarger 1992). Reliability will not be 100%. However, realistically, no system insures 100% reliability, and the ease of accessing animals for repeated attempts makes success rates in the 80-90% range more than adequate to maintain basic health. The availability of an elephant restraint chute increases the probability of success, as long as the animal's experience in it is positive.

Accessing Sick or Injured Animals

This is an acknowledged concern in any animal management system. As discussed previously, although high reliability can be expected, there will be times when animals will not cooperate. Unfortunately, non-cooperation is more likely to occur when an animal is sick or injured. However, two factors are critical to increasing the likelihood of accessing animals in trouble: the skill level of trainers; and the functionality of the facility in providing adequate access to the animals. In our initial work at the San Diego Wild Animal Park, both bull elephants encountered health problems during the project. The Asian bull cooperated in a protracted process to treat a painful foot problem. The African bull was successfully examined by a veterinarian and treated for an eye problem requiring frequent application of medication. Both these efforts were accomplished solely through protected contact techniques (Desmond & Laule, 1991).

Addressing Social Issues and Aggression

Another area of concern is the ability to monitor and referee social problems within an elephant group in a protected contact program. In a traditional free contact system, when animals are on exhibit and free to move about, trainers physically intervene in social disputes between elephants, up to a point. However, because of the high risk to keepers, some free contact programs no longer allow keeper intervention in elephant disputes under any circumstances. Many programs still require elephants to be put on chains or separated at night to control their movement and thus eliminate the potential for life-threatening physical interactions.

In converting to a protected contact system, it is no longer possible to physically intervene to end fighting between animals. Properly designed facilities should allow for chaining animals at night, if required, while providing the opportunity to leave animals off chains as well. There is reason to believe that protected contact techniques can directly address and mitigate social problems. Utilizing a training technique we call "cooperative feeding," it is possible to enhance introductions, mitigate dominance related problems, and reduce aggression. This technique has been used successfully with a variety of marine mammals and several species of primates (Laule, 1991). Data has shown that this method can reduce aggression and increase positive social interaction between group members (Desmond et al., 1987; Cox, 1987; Bloomsmith et al, 1992). To date the same procedure has not been tried, and results have not been demonstrated, in elephants. However, with the significant results achieved thus far, it is likely that the technique is applicable to other large mammals as well. Again, the skill level of trainers and the amount and type of animal access the facility provides are critical factors in successfully dealing with social issues.

Dealing with Novel Situations

Expert and creative utilization of positive reinforcement training constitutes a powerful problem-solving process that is useful in addressing novel situations. By identifying potential problem scenarios, like accessing new-born calves, training can be designed to address those issues. For example, a protected contact system must have the ability to manage animals in a group as well as access animals on an individual basis. This is approached in several ways. First, control behaviors like "come," "go" (to a particular location), "back," and "steady," are worked and maintained in a variety of social contexts and physical locations. Second, animals are fully desensitized to every environment they may be required to work or spend time in, socially or atone. Third, active socialization training, like cooperative feeding, is conducted on a regular basis to facilitate regular movement of animals in and out of the group.

Even without 100% cooperation on the part of the elephants, with this level of control in place, there are many options available to trainers to safely access a particular animal or animals, for whatever reason. There is an established track record and a host of accomplishments resulting from trainers and keepers addressing novel problems with a variety of animals while working through barriers or without the use of restraint (Joines, 1976; Desmond, 1985).

4. ADDRESSING THE PSYCHOLOGICAL NEEDS OF ELEPHANTS.

No system for elephant management and care is adequate if it does not address the psychological needs of the animals. One of the strongest arguments for the use of positive reinforcement techniques is the enrichment value they offer. A study was conducted with four adult male chimpanzees to assess the enrichment value of positive reinforcement training (Bloomsmith, 1992). Results show that three positive changes occurred during training: reduced self-directed behavior, reduced inactivity, and increased social play. Each of these behavioral changes is typically considered to be a positive outcome of an enrichment procedure. Further, in two documented studies involving socialization training, neurotic and self-directed behaviors were also significantly reduced as a result of a positive reinforcement training program (Cox, 1987: Bloomsmith, 1992). As discussed previously, positive reinforcement is the preferred method in protected contact because it offers animals greater choices and control. These elements have been documented as important to the psychological well-being of animals (Hanson et al., 1976; Mineka et al., 1986).

On an operational basis, a protected contact system is built upon a training regimen and activity budget that addresses all the elements of good mental and physical health that a free contact system does. That includes regular training sessions that provide elephants the following benefits: a chance to work for their food; mental stimulation; increased physical activity: expanded behavioral repertoires; and human/animal interaction.

It is important to reiterate that human/animal interaction is an integral part of a protected contact program and a critical factor in addressing psychological well-being (Bayne, 1993). Behavioral and environmental enrichment are as well. In protected contact, the ability to move animals on and off exhibit easily and frequently creates maximum opportunity to: rotate enrichment devices and toys, seed exhibits and holding areas, make minor changes to the environment, add new exhibit furniture, and access animals for daily training sessions.

CONCLUSIONS

Given these four fundamental principles, protected contact has the potential to address many of the tough issues facing facilities exhibiting elephants today. However, it must be implemented in a way that meets the concerns of handlers and managers alike. The first step, therefore, is a planning process which allows full discussion of all concerns and which results in formal institutional consensus on goals, methods, and objectives of the elephant program. Next, detailed facility and other support requirements must be identified. Finally, a schedule and budget must be created which takes into account all resource requirements. Only then is the program ready to be implemented.

Once under way, it's critically important to carefully monitor and document the implementation of protected contact. It's important to learn and share with the community which techniques work and which don't. Although any system of elephant handling will vary somewhat from institution to institution it is important to standardize protected contact training protocols as much as possible from the outset. Understanding and embracing the basic principles upon which protected contact was built is the first step.

ACKNOWLEDGEMENTS

The authors wish to acknowledge and thank Dr. Joe Flanagan and the elephant staff of the Houston Zoological Gardens, Scott Maddox and the elephant staff of the Caldwell Zoo, and the San Diego Wild Animal Park for their contributions to this presentation.

REFERENCES

Benirschke, K.; Roocroft, A., Elephant-Inflicted Injuries. VERH.BER.ERKRG.ZOOTIERE 8:239-247, 1992.

Bloomsmith, M., Chimpanzee Training and Behavioral Research: A Symbiotic Relationship. AAZPA *Annual Conference Proceedings,* Toronto, 1992.

Bloomsmith, M.; Laule, G.; Thurston, R.; Alford, P., Using Training to Moderate Chimpanzee Aggression. AAZPA *Western Regional Conference Proceedings,* Dallas, 1992.

Cox, C., Increasing the Likelihood of Reproduction Among Drills. AAZPA Annual *Conference Proceedings,* Portland, 1987.

Desmond, T., Surrogate Training with a Pregnant Orcinus Orca. *International* Marine Animal *Trainers* Association Annual *Conference Proceedings, Orlando,* 1985.

Desmond, T.; Laule, G., Protected Contact Elephant Training. AAZPA *Annual Conference Proceedings:* 606-613, 1991.

Desmond, T.; Laule, G.; McNary, J., Training to Enhance Socialization and Reproduction in Drills. *AAZPA Annual Conference Proceedings:* 435-441, 1987.

Hanson, J.; Larson, M.; Snowdon, C., The Effects of Control Over High Intensity Noise on Plasma Cortisol Levels in Rhesus Monkeys. *Behavioral Biology* 16:333-340, 1976.

Joines, S., A Training Programme Designed to Induce Maternal Behaviour in a Mulliparous Female Lowland Gorilla. *International Zoo Yearbook* 185-188, 1977.

Laule, G., Training Pinnipeds to Work Without Walls. *International Marine Animal Trainers Association* Annual *Conference Proceedings,* Minneapolis, 1983.

Laule, G., Meeting Behavioral Objectives While Maintaining Healthy Social Behavior and Dominance -k Delicate Balance. IMATA *Annual Conference Proceedings,* Vallejo, 1991.

Laule, G.; Desmond, T., Addressing Psychological Well-Being: Training as Enrichment. AAZPA *Annual Conference Proceedings,* Toronto, 1992.

Maddox, S., Bull Elephant Management: A Safe Alternative. AAZpA *western & Central Regional Conference Proceedings, 1992.*

Mineka, S.; Gunnar, M.; Champoux, M., The Effects of Control in the Early Social and Emotional Development of Rhesus Monkeys. Child *Development 57:1241-1256, 1986.*

Reichard, T.; Shellabarger, W., "Training for Husbandry and Medical Purposes." AAZPA *Annual Conference Proceedings, Toronto, 1992.*

Reinhardt, V.; Cowley, D., Training Stump-tailed Monkeys *(Macaca arctoides)* to Cooperate During Inhomecage Treatment. *Laboratory Primate Newsletter 29 (4):9-10, 1990.*

Turkkan, J., New Methodology for Measuring Blood Pressure in Awake Baboons with Use of Behavioral Training Techniques. *Journal of Medicine and Primatology 19:455-466, 1990.*

SOUNDINGS VOL 23, NO 1, 1998. The following article is an update of the use of protected contact at San Diego's Wild Animal Park. It is the most recent of all the articles on protected contact included in this manual. The article provides a great overview of the use of protected contact with elephants in a facility that has used the system for quite some time and thus they are able to evaluate its effectiveness from a broader perspective.

Managing Multiple Elephants Using Protected Contact at San Diego's Wild Animal Park

by Gary Priest, Jennie Antrim, Jane Gilbert, and Valerie Hare
Zoological Society of San Diego

[*Soundings* Editor's Note: In an effort to focus the content of our magazine on a foundation of marine animal training techniques and advancements, the following article highlights how operant conditioning principles have been successfully applied to the management of elephants.]

INTRODUCTION

Elephants have proven to be exceptionally intelligent, social, and capable of learning any number of complex tasks. The husbandry behaviors normally required of elephants trained using the traditional methods are now being matched in protected contact at a number of zoological institutions (Green, Olsen, & Ruhter, 1992; Maddox, 1992; O'Sulivan, 1993; Flint, 1993; miller, Wilcox, Latores, & Upchurch, 1993; Parrott, 1993). Since December of 1992, a large group (1.5) of Asian elephants at the San Diego Wild Animal Park has been managed exclusively by protected contact methods. In July 1994, a year-long program evaluation was concluded. The evaluation of the program covered a review of the keepers' consistent ability to gain access to the animals, the animals' behavior and health, and the keepers' ability to use their new skills in order to maintain the behaviors exclusively through protected contact. As a result of this program's success, the Zoological Society of San Diego engaged in retrofitting its elephant facilities to support this style of management and is transitioning all three of its elephant facilities to protected contact management.

San Diego's elephant management plan employs a three-branched strategy to provide complete health care for its elephants. The three methods in order of priority are: (1) routine access through behavior modification and protected contact, (2) occasional access by means of a restraint chute, and (3) in rare cases, veterinary intervention through chemical restraint.

The term protected contact was coined to describe an alternative system to traditional elephant management. In this system, keepers do not enter into the enclosure with the animal. Instead, they use food reinforcement to form a cooperative relationship with the elephant and work with the animal from a shielded position outside the enclosure, no physical discipline is required to insure keeper safety or maintain behavioral control. The premise is that keepers working from positions behind protective barriers can selectively reinforce, shape, and maintain all the behaviors required for proper elephant husbandry. The pilot study proved the feasibility of this idea (Desmond & Laule, 1991).

SOCIAL TRENDS IMPACTING ZOO ELEPHANT MANAGEMENT

During the last decade, several disparate social trends converged to create an environment where changes in traditional methods of captive elephant management could be considered. The traditional methods in the new environment frequently failed to meet organizational needs.

INCREASING RISKS

Ensuring routine access to the captive elephant's feet for cleaning and regular maintenance is critically important. Yet because of their sheer size and power, elephants can be lethal (Benirschke & Roocroft, 1992). During the last several years, zoo directors and collection managers have become increasingly sensitive to an impending crisis in traditional captive elephant management. Elephants are responsible for injuring more zoo keepers in the United States than any other zoo animal. Between 1976 and 1994, 17 keepers in the United States were killed by elephants and eight of those fatalities occurred in this decade (J. Lehnhardt, personal communication, 1994). Statistics indicate that the risks associated with traditional management methods seem to be increasing. Each year, with shocking regularity, reports of keeper fatalities continue to occur. No statistics are available as to the number of near misses or elephant-inflicted injuries that have been suffered by keepers. The United States Bureau of Labor Statistics and the National Safety Council list elphant keeping just beneath coal mining as the most dangerous occupation in America. In the United States, elephant keepers are at greater risk of being killed on the job than either police officers or fire fighters (Lehnhardt, 1991).

GREATER MOBILITY OF THE LABOR FORCE

Today, employees change professions on the average of every five years n the United States. This high rate of employee turnover has impinged on the ability to safely manage elephants using the traditional free contact or "mahout" style of management. The foundation of the traditional method was based on an intimate, long-term relationship, developed early in the elephant's life. A vacuum is being created in the ranks of free contact keepers. Attrition and modern employment behavior have served to effectively short-circuit many institutions' ability to safely manage the needs of their captive elephants by using traditional methods.

ANIMAL RIGHTS

During the last two decades, society has been warned that our global biodiversity is being lost at alarming rates. Scientists have predicted that if trends continue, the earth will enter a period of species extinctions unparalleled since the age of the dinosaurs. Growing awareness of the dangers of an expanding human population coupled with the knowledge of the accelerating loss of habitat and decline of wild animal populations has helped fuel the social phenomenon known as the animal rights movement. Americans now have a greater appreciation for the uniqueness of each of the species.

As a positive result of these sensibilities, the care and treatment of all captive animals is coming under increased scrutiny at zoological institutions, from both internal sources as well as external ones.

The traditional method for managing the behavior of a captive elephant occasionally requires the use of physical discipline. The traditional method for managing the behavior of an endangered animal seems incongruous. Without respect for the potential for loss of a keeper's life due to an intractable elephant, the public's tolerance for the physical discipline of any animal is diminishing. Wild populations are in decline and it has become increasingly apparent that human intervention is necessary if elephants are to survive beyond the 21 st Century. Captive elephants play an important role in serving to marshal public support and act as ambassadors for their wild counterparts. Against this back-drop, zoo directors and curators have found themselves squarely in the center of the increasingly uncomfortable dilemma of how to continue to meet the husbandry needs of the elephants in their collections.

ADVANCES IN BEHAVIORAL SCIENCE

Concurrent with the pressures of several significant social changes has been a growing acceptance of a more positive method of training animals. Operant conditioning has proven to have wide application with a wide variety of both marine and terrestrial animals in the zoological environment (Priest, 1990; Mellen & Ellis-Joseph, 1996). Unmet needs are the engines that drive nearly all revolutions in human thought. All three of these components have played a part in changing elephant management in North America.

In 1990, in light of the many trends effecting captive elephant management, the San Diego Zoological Society questions its own purposes for managing elephants. The result of this critical self-evaluation was to galvanize the Society's resolve and commitment to dedicating the resources necessary to safely manage its elephants for the purposes of exhibition and reproduction. In a break with the past, and in view of the future, public and television appearances with elephants and elephant rides were no longer deemed appropriate, as they were not consistent with the Society's purposes of education and conservation.

BACKGROUND

In March 1991, one of the Wild Animal Park's Asian elephant keepers, operating in free contact, was accidentally stepped on and killed by an Asian elephant cow. This death galvanized the park management's resolve to continue its efforts to develop a safer method for managing elephants.

By April 1991, based on the success demonstrated in the pilot project, a second, more elaborate test was undertaken. The objective was to begin to refine the requirements for elephant training based on the application of positive reinforcement. The second test involved four animals, two bulls and an Asian and an African cow. In this extended program, animals considered by the Wild Animal Park's elephant manager and supervisor to be "worst case," owing to either their individual disposition or their tendency toward aggression, were selected for protected contact training. At the end of a six-month trial period, managers were encouraged and began to make plans to develop a facility that would allow the application of these techniques to the management of a large group of elephants (Priest,1992a ; 1992b). The entire staff of elephant keepers attended staff development classes in behavior theory and operant conditioning (Stephens, 1992).

Consistent application of technique is a critical component in behavior modification. Keepers were required to take and pass written examinations covering a variety of topics including elephant training under both free and protected contact, elephant ethology, and husbandry.

During the spring and summer of 1992, the Society invested nearly 500,000 toward developing facilities that would support the protected contact management of the herd. In December 1992, with facility modifications and keeper training complete, the park began to manage a large group of Asian elephants (1.5) exclusively by protected contact.

FACILITY MODIFICATIONS

For our Asian elephant cows, the San Diego Wild Animal Park constructed five individual barn stalls with access down a central corridor or along a back wall, designed hydraulic gates with remote capability, and installed latches that operate from outside of the elephant's enclosure. We also use panels of 2" x 2'x ¼" (5x5x0.6 cm) welded rod placed between 8 inch (20 cm) steel uprights to protect keepers in most keeper access areas. The Asian bull is housed by himself in an adjacent concrete cinder block building. We feel that this facility provides a safer work place, is functional, and provides the staff with a variety of management options. We plan a restraint chute at each of our three elephant facilities. We also redesigned over ½ mile (0.4 km) of moat line that would, for the first time, enable us to leave the cows on exhibit overnight, weather permitting. Finally, the entire show area was redesigned with two small holding areas behind stage, and steel bollards and cable configured to skirt the stage area. In this way, the elephants could perform behaviors for audiences, with keepers giving directions and reinforcements from outside the enclosure.

METHODS

In protected contact, the keeper remains outside both the enclosure and the elephant's social structure. The keeper works together with the elephant in order to form a cooperative relationship. Unlike free contact, where a keeper's life depends on the elephant's compliance, the elephant in protected contact is a voluntary participant. Keepers rely exclusively on the power of a timed or selective delivery of positive reinforcements to accomplish his/her objectives.

Protected contact is a "hands-on" system designed to maintain physical contact with captive elephants while maximizing keeper safety. The elements of protected contact management include a combination of the following: facility design, animal and keeper position relative to protective barriers, and operant conditioning techniques designed to encourage the animal to voluntarily comply with the keeper's objectives. In the protected contact system, behavior modification is accomplished through the use of positive rewards, including a wide variety of food, taction, and social reinforcers. No physical discipline or food deprivation is ever used with our elephants. The elephants receive their normal diet of sudan, or oat, hay and alfalfa. For training reinforcements, we use monkey chow, cut carrots, apples, sweet potatoes, corn-on-the-cob, and other seasonal fruits.

Reinforcement is delivered when the animal performs correctly in response to a specific signal. If the animal performs a behavior incorrectly, or in a manner below standards, it is simply given another opportunity to earn reinforcement. The elephant's behavior is modified exclusively through the skilled use of operant conditioning.

Operant conditioning is a systematic conditioning process used to modify or shape an animal's behavior toward a desired goal. In essence, operant conditioning is a universal language that an animal can understand and use to its benefits. The consistent and skillful use of this language provides information to the animal about its environment and how to go about gaining something its desires. These behavior modification techniques fall under the well-established principles of behavioral theory (Holland & Skinner, 1963; Mazur, 1990).

Through conditioning, our elephants quickly learned to pair the sound of a dog whistle with the delivery of a food reward. The whistle, in effect, serves as an I.O.U. to the elephant. The whistle provides important information that helps the animal pair its actions with a positive consequence. It also bridges the gap in time between when the animal performs a behavior and the delivery of a reward. Rewards can take a variety of forms as long as they are something that the animal desires. Operant conditioning, in the non-technical sense, is a controlled process that enables animals to naturally acquire, process, and use the information discovered about their environment. It is an adaptive learning strategy and, within the animal's genetic and physical capabilities, will work with any species.

The techniques used for moving elephants from one place to another were borrowed from marine mammal trainers. After whistle conditioning, the first behavior that the elephant is trained to perform in protected contact is to touch the bridge of its trunk to a foam target. Once the elephant has learned this behavior, we use the targets to move elephants into a desired position and then from one place to another. The elephants also learned to hold their position while other elephants in the group were given the opportunity for training sessions.

To a large degree, our training in protected contact has relied on conditioning already done in free contact. In San Diego, we have been fortunate to have many well-trained and tractable cows with which to work. As we introduced protected contact to them, it was, in many cases, simply a matter of changing the context and orientation of the training tools we used in order for the animal to understand, generalize, and comply with our wishes. The cows did take a while to learn that the target and bull hook were used very differently. With the bull hook, the cows has been conditioned to move away from the stimulus; conversely, when the target was presented, the cows were required to approach and touch it in exchange for a reward. Naturally, the cows were wary at first, but in every case, this shift was accomplished in a few hours total training, spaced over three weeks time.

Neither of our bulls has been worked in free contact for several years, yet they have been able to learn and perform the same husbandry behaviors as the cows. All captive elephants have been exposed to at least some degree of traditional training. Though it has yet to be demonstrated with a completely naïve elephant (juvenile or wild-caught), the authors are convinced that behavior modification relying exclusively on operant conditioning and positive reinforcement would prove similarly successful, although it might take longer than our experience.

ENRICHMENT

Our enrichment program was developed with several concerns in mind. First, because keepers were no longer part of the social structure of the herd, they would be unable to intervene should a fight break out between the elephants. Consequently, enrichment was used as a tool to redirect aggression to other more peaceful activities. Second, we wanted to enhance the elephants' "quality of life." And finally, we use enrichment to improve the elephants' general health by increasing their movement throughout their enclosure space.

Our Asian elephant enclosure at the Wild Animal Park has over three acres (1.2 hectares). The elephants have access to a nine foot (2.7m) deep, 100,000 gallon (378,540 L) pool. When the moats were re-designed, we also installed 53,000 square feet (1,500 square meters) of sod. Elephants are now left on exhibit overnight. In this environment we experimented with a variety of olfactory enrichments. Food treats are hidden in the exhibit regularly and a variety of extract scents (perfumes spices, oils) are deposited around the exhibit space. Interest was greatest in cinnamon, nutmeg, cloves, coriander, chili powder, paprika, and vanilla. Twice each week, keepers place browse in the exhibit. Other toys include boomer balls, logs, and tires suspended by chains from an overhang.

Training sessions and the elephant show provide the animals with problem-solving opportunities. We believe these activities to be enriching because during the evaluation year we conducted between 1,500 and 2,000 training sessions with a total of only seven refusals, with most of those coming in the early days of the program. Elephant shows have been conducted at least twice daily since 03 April 1993. To date, we have not canceled a single show due to an elephant's refusal to participate.

RESULTS

For protected contact management to be viable alternative, veterinarians must have access to the animal in order to meet its health care needs. Complete veterinary exams were conducted twice during the evaluation year. At the end of the year the veterinary team concluded that the elephants had been maintained in excellent general health. The veterinarians also reported satisfaction with their ability to gain access to the animals during the exams. Oral exams and access to the genitals are still problematic.

The following are some of the more important benefits that we have come to associate with protected contact elephant management:

- SAFETY- Through voluntary cooperation on the part of the elephant as well as trainer, and animal position relative to protective barrier, protected contact can reduce the potential for animal-related keeper injuries.

- EMPLOYEE TURNOVER – Protected contact can establish a safer training environment for new or inexperienced keepers when operating under experienced supervision.

- CONSISTENT APPLICATION OF TECHNIQUE – Consistency of technique is always a critically important issue in animal training, regardless of the species or system. According to the American Zoo and Aquarium Association (AZA) Elephant Species Survival Plan Group, the lack of consistent handling often results in unmanageable elephants. Operant conditioning establishes a clear formula and a common basis for consistency and uniformity within the elephant keeper staff.

- Operant conditioning establishes a COMMON LANGUAGE understood by both animal and keeper and provides a medium of exchange or currency between the two. The system will in short order allow a new keeper to become as reinforcing as a keeper the animals are familiar with.

- Operant conditioning is animal rights and public relations sensitive. It projects a much more consistently POSITIVE IMAGE to the public. Elephants are "free" to be elephants without human domination.

- The system provides elephants with positive rewards for VOLUNTARY COOPERATION and eliminates the need for physical discipline to establish and maintain the social dominance sometimes required to control the behavior of elephants in free contact.

Since this paper was first presented several years ago at an IMATA conference, the San Diego Zoo and Wild Animal Park have completed the reconfiguration of all three of their elephant facilities. All of their elephants are now managed by protected contact. During the same brief period, the concept of managing elephants exclusively with positive reinforcements and protected contact has gained wider acceptance in the zoological community. Many institutions across the country have made, are making, or plan on making in the near future, this same transition with their elephant programs. There have been many well documented factors that contributed to this trend. Perhaps the strongest was the need felt by many institutions to insure greater safety for their elephant keepers while maintaining the health care of their elephants.

LITERATURE CITED

Bennirschke, K. & Roocroft, A. (1992). Elephant inflicted injuries. Paper presented at the Symposium on Erkrankungen der Zoo-und Wildtiere, Spain

Desmond T. & Laule, G. (1991). Protected contact elephant training. In Proceedings of the 1991 Annual Conference of the American Association of Zoological Parks and Aquariums ((pp. 606 – 613). Wheeling, West Virginia: AAZPA.

Flint, M. (1993, Winter). Elephant safety and protection at the zoo. Reid Park Zoo, pp. 1-2.

Green, R., Olsen, T. & Ruhter, D. (1992). Elephant management at the Houston Zoo. In Proceedings of the 1992 Western Regional Conference of the Americal Association of Zoological Parks and Aquariums (pp.730 – 733). Wheeling, West Virginia: AAZPA.

Holland J. & Skinner, B.F. (1961). The Analysis of Behavior: A Program for Self Instruction. New York: McGraw-Hill.

Lehnhardt, J. (1991). Elephant handling: A problem of risk management. In Proceedings of the 1991 Annual Conference of the Americal Association of Zoological Parks and Aqquariums (pp. 569-575). Wheeling, WV: AAZPA.

Maddox, S. (1992). Bull elephant management: A safe alternative. In Proceedings of the 1992 Central Regional Conference of the American Association of Zoological Parks and Aquariums (pp. 376-382). Wheeling, WV: AAZPA.

Mazur, J. (1990). Learning and Behavior (2nd Ed.). Engleewood Cliffs, New Jersey: Prentice-Hall.

Mellen, J. & Ellis-Joseph, S. (1996). Learning and training. In S. Lumpkin and D. Kleiman (Eds.), Management of Wild Animals in Captivity (pp. 88-99). Chicago: University of Chicago Press.

Miller, G., Wilcox, C., Latores, S., & Upchurch, B. (1993). "C" is for Cindy: A case history. In Proceedings of the 1993 Annual Conference of the American Association of Zoological Parks and Aquariums (pp.32 –34). Wheeling, West Virginia: AAZPA.

O'Sullivan, T. (1993). Protected contact at the St. Louis Zoo. Paper presented at the Elephant Mangers Association Conference, Vallejo, CA.

Parrott, J. (1993). A new modified protected contact elephant management program to maximize keeper safety. In Proceedings of the 1993 Annual Conference of the American Association of Zoological Parks and Aquariums (pp.35-38). Wheeling, West Virginia: AAZPA.

Priest, G. (1990). The use of operant conditioning in training husbandry behaviors with captive exotic animals. In Proceedings of the 1990 Annual Conference of the American Association of Zoo Keepers (pp. 94-107). Topeka, Kansas: AAZK.

Priest, G. (1992a). Caring for elephants and reducing the risks. Zoonooz, LXV(2), 12-15.

Priest, G. (1992b). Elephant training: Creating contrast between two training systems. In proceedings of the 1992 Western Regional Conference of the American Association of Zoological Parks and Aquariums (pp. 369-374). Wheeling, West Virginia: AAZPA.

Stephens, B. (1992). Keeper staff development programs. In Proceedings of the 1992 Western Regional Conference of the American Association of Zoological Parks and Aquariums of (p. 375). Wheeling, West Virginia: AAZPA.

Karen Pryor

On Behavior

Essays & Research

Today, more and more zoos are recognizing the benefits of a behavior management program for their animals. Training is a good thing, yet some zoos still frown at the thought. Karen Pryor addresses the problem in this 1981 article from the April issue of *Psychology Today*. Her story is an effort to help zookeepers (and more importantly zoo managers) understand the benefits of training the animals under their care. Many of the larger zoos now have trainers overseeing the behavioral needs of the entire collection. Many of these individuals started as marine mammal trainers!

The Rhino Likes Violets

by Karen Pryor

We sat on the ground just outside the rhinoceros enclosure. Mary, an adult rhino, put her very large head through the fence, resting it on the bottom railing so that her chin overhung my lap. Since I was sitting in a patch of violets, I picked some violet leaves and fed them into her huge jaws. She took them with apparent pleasure. She seemed, too, to enjoy having me stroke her mouth and face. The heavy skin that looked like armor plating felt like suede; it seemed to be very sensitive. Mary could not see which way to turn for more leaves, even if I held them up to her eyes, but if I touched her face with the greenery she oriented easily and folded in the leaves adroitly.

Mary's ears tilted calmly and pleasantly to keep track of the whereabouts of her baby and to follow the conversation between Melanie Bond, a keeper at the National Zoological Park in Washington, D.C., and me, a visiting consultant. We had just finished a training session with the great apes, part of an experimental program at the zoo, to see if modern, nonforce behavioral modification techniques could be of use in handling zoo animals. Now, while we took a break in the spring sunshine, Melanie was playing with Mary's baby. Using violets and petting as rewards, she had just taught the baby to pick up one of its front feet on command, as horses and elephants are trained to do. The baby was quite excited at discovering such an easy way to earn Melanie's attentions, and between bouts of foot raising it gamboled clumsily about, now and then bumping heftily into its mother.

The half-hour of play reinforced for me a concept I'd long been aware of. If you have something an animal wants, you can train virtually any animal. People often don't realize how easy it is to train even difficult, dangerous animals without knocking them around. I wouldn't have dreamed of going into the rhinoceros enclosure and trying to train either animal by force, like an old-fashioned circus trainer. But obviously one could shape rhino behavior with positive reinforcements: in this case, greens and, I think, attention and diversion.

Shaping behavior with positive reinforcement is a technique described in the laws of learning first defined by B. F. Skinner and generally called operant conditioning. In the last 20 years or so, the technique has revolutionized animal training. All dolphin shows are based entirely on positive reinforcement, not aversive control. Bird shows involving free-flying birds of many species have proliferated; birds, too, cannot be trained by force (they just panic) but will work hard and learn well for food rewards. In Hollywood, shaping with positive reinforcement is called "affection training," and it has produced results that in the past would have been considered impossible: the Hartford Insurance stag is one example.

I gained my background in the applied uses of operant conditioning as the head trainer and curator of Sea Life Park, an oceanarium in Hawaii, where we trained dozens of dolphins, small whales, birds, and other creatures for both public performances and research. Positive reinforcement, properly used, could produce spectacular shows. Sometimes, though, I was even more impressed with its practical value in the everyday maintenance of our animals. For example, some whales are too large to restrain by force, so when our whales needed veterinary attention, we trained them to present their tails and allow blood samples to be taken and shots to be administered, for a reward of food and petting. (The amount and kind of reward is not important; what is important is that the animal know exactly what it has to do to get the reward.) All of our animals were trained to move from tank to tank on command; they did not have to be chased or forced. Also we used training to relieve the boredom of dolphins that were being kept in solitude; for dolphins, boredom can literally be fatal.

I had then been asked to see if the same techniques could be applied to wild animals in a zoo; thus I found myself feeding violets to the rhino. Theodore Reed, director of the National Zoo, had read a book I'd written about my porpoise-training experiences and had decided that these techniques might be useful to his keepers. He mentioned specific behavioral problems to me: the polar bears that banged on their steel doors hour after hour; the giraffes that sometimes refused to go indoors before a cold snap and had to be chased about by 10 men with sticks in a slipping, kicking, cursing, and risky rodeo; the chimp that sat in a corner all day plucking the hair out of its arms from boredom.

Reed, a veterinarian, was also worried about boredom among the keepers. He prided himself, and justifiably, I was to discover, on a staff of intelligent, capable men and women who took serious interest in the animals they cared for. But a lot of the work of animal care is grueling drudgery: feeding and cleaning, cleaning and feeding. Reed thought that, for those who took to it, ongoing training interactions might add interest to the keepers' lives as well as the animals'.

I agreed to go to work for the zoo as a consultant, teaching a group of keepers as much as I could about training techniques. Twenty-five people came to the first class: young, old, male, female, black, white. I was intrigued not only by the variety of lively faces but also by the variety of animals they had to work with: birds, reptiles, apes, elephants, mammals I'd never even heard of, such as grisons and binturongs. I explained that it would not be my job to train animals nor to solve specific problems, necessarily, but to give the keepers methods by which they could do those things. I outlined a basic technique: you let the animal discover that every time you blow a whistle, it gets a piece of food. Then you let it discover that it can make you blow the Whistle by, say, moving toward its den. Presto. You are training the animal to move into its den. Or it is training you to be reliable about whistle blowing and food giving, depending on the point of view.

Everyone had to pick an animal to practice on and a behavior to shape. I recommended choosing a lively, greedy animal. Melanie Bond, in the great ape house, had dandy subjects to start with-two juvenile orangutans. Keepers had been forbidden to play or interact with the apes, on the ground that it was dangerous, but now that rule would be relaxed so that Melanie could participate in the training class. Bela Demeter, in the reptile house, was dubious about training snakes or lizards, but I knew reptiles could be conditioned; the late reptile collector Grace Wylie had had a number of trained alligators years ago. Birds, reindeer, elephants-everyone picked good subjects. However, Art Cooper in the lion/tiger complex had fixed his heart on training his best tiger, Peela. (Actually Art and the other keepers called the tiger Ajax, but the Zoo insisted I use his official name in this article. KP)

"No, Art," the others protested. "That tiger never does anything! He just lies on the top of his hill all day. What are you going to reinforce?"

"Well, he's cool," Art explained. "He's saving his strength." Art intended to persuade this cool cat 1) to come down to the front of the exhibit, to the edge of the moat; 2) to get into the water in the moat; 3) to retrieve a floating beer keg that was sometimes put in the moat as a tiger toy (tigers like to swim, and like all other cats, they will play with moving objects); 4) to put the beer keg on the beach; and 5) to get back up on shore himself. A five-step behavior chain, and quite difficult even for a seasoned trainer, especially with a disinterested animal. I suggested doing something simpler, but Art's mind was made up.

Training is time-consuming, and some people found that they could not fit it into an already overcrowded day's work. Curators, too, sometimes objected to the keepers' frittering away valuable minutes on apparently trivial tasks. "I do not see the value," one curator huffed at me, "in training the panda to stand on its head to impress the other keepers." The value, of course, was in the process, not the product: the trainer was learning to train. What he or she chose as a practice behavior was irrelevant to me; I have found that first-time trainers make much better progress if they choose their own task rather than have one assigned to them, so I let them do what they like. But I could empathize with the practical zoo people who not only saw no point in the particular behavior (who needs a retrieving tiger, after all?) but felt that it interfered with the animals' "natural behavior" as well although, given the alien zoo environment, much of the behavior we see is not at all normal.

In a few weeks, some people had successes to demonstrate to the class. Melanie had trained Junior, one of the young orangutans, to clean up his cage and toss trash into her bucket in return, not for a food reward, but for the chance to blow on a whistle; Junior was fascinated by the whistle. Next to his cage there was a large female orangutan who seemed to me to be suffering from clinical depression. She sat slumped against the wall all day long, looking like an exhausted shopping-bag lady. Melanie, with food, taught her to play a simple Simon Says: I pat my head, you pat your head; I clap my hands, you clap your hands; I rub my stomach, you rub your stomach. To everyone's amusement, the orang discovered she could play this game with the public, especially with groups of schoolchildren. It was gratifying to see her, active and bright-eyed, clapping her hands, then rubbing her stomach, while a corridor full of hilarious children copied her.

Melanie also began playing the training game with melancholy Ham, the chimpanzee (our first U.S. chimp in outer space), now a grown male with formidable fangs. She paid him with food for various actions, and slowly, he began to participate. One morning, Melanie informed us, she was about to let Ham outdoors after having given him his breakfast. When he saw that she was going to open the outside door, he graciously rewarded her by handing her a piece of celery. He understood the game.

Grayson Harding, in the small mammals building, had trained a chinchilla to weigh itself by hopping in a basket which could then be put on a scale-a big improvement over chasing it all over the cage with a net to catch and weigh it. Bela, at the reptile house, had trained two thin green lizards about 18 inches long to take insects from the tip of a forceps. He then held the forceps higher, shaping an upward jump. By the time he showed the behavior to the class, the lizards ran to the cage door as soon as he opened it and then, eyes bulging and pink, toothy mouths agape, jumped two feet straight up to the forceps tip with a tiny ferocity that was funny to see. Bela really did have leaping lizards. He himself wasn't impressed, though I pointed out that this Olympic-effort, straight-up leap is the high point of all dolphin shows and is trained in exactly the same way.

Meanwhile, Art actually was making progress with Peela. Peela got into the spirit of things and came bounding down the hill when he caught sight of Art. He learned to get into the water and to get out. He played with the keg. Training sessions, however, took a long time, because Peela appeared to have trouble making up his mind. He could take 20 minutes to get into the water and 45 to get out again. It's a trait common to cats, as anyone knows who has ever opened a door to let an importunate house cat out and then had it stand in the doorway. Peela just did it on a bigger scale.

In the long run, Art did accomplish his behavior chain and, I am sure, acquired in the process training skills that can be applied henceforth to any animal in his care. By the end of the program, Melanie's work with the apes was generally recognized as valuable; Barbara Bingham had some partially trained reindeer and had discovered that currycombing was reinforcing to them. The giraffes now came indoors when the keepers rang an electric bell. A few keepers, and a few animals had benefited. The program had been fun for the participants, but did it have any value for the whole zoo?

Six months later, I went back to see. In the elephant house, where training sessions had previously been brief, with fixed routines, and held before opening hours, training demonstrations were now being given daily for the public. In the great ape house, morose Ham now laughed, played games, and even let himself be tickled; gorillas opened doors and tidied cages on request; the zoo had sent Melanie to night school to learn American Sign Language; she was teaching Junior.

I found that keepers were being hired specifically for their training skills. A Hollywood-trained keeper had all the bears going indoors on command for a food reward; previously, it had sometimes been necessary to chase them in with fire hoses in order to clean the yards. A new seal and sea lion exhibit, Beaver Valley, which had been under construction during my time at the zoo, was being run by an experienced trainer. On the site where I had once stood and listened to a head curator worry about how they would ever catch an individual seal for medical care since the pool was so large, I was now able to look over the completed pool and its barking inhabitants and hear a curator tell me that every animal was being trained to come out of the water on command and that he considered training to be integral to the staff's daily work.

The polar bears had also come under the care of the Beaver Valley keepers. They had noticed, I was told, that one of the bears had a broken canine tooth. This called for veterinary attention, since a broken tooth can get infected. Customarily, the bear would have had to be "knocked down," or shot with a tranquilizer gun-and with a stiff dosage, too, since you certainly do not want a polar bear to wake up while you are examining its teeth. To spare the bear this risky and potentially even fatal procedure, keeper leader Kayce Cover and her staff trained the bear to stick its nose out through a slot in the door and allow its lip to be lifted. When the behavior was shaped, they called the vet, the trainer signaled the bear, the bear poked its nose out, and the vet inspected the tooth and pronounced it healed. No trouble at all. And they did it with raisins.

That, I thought, was exactly the use of training as a zoo management tool that Dr. Reed had been hoping for. The incident had nothing to do with me or my class, directly. The keepers had learned their obviously excellent training skills from others. But their success depended on a favorable climate of opinion at the curatorial level, in which such keeper-animal interactions are not forbidden but permitted, perhaps encouraged, maybe even expected. There, I thought, our class may have broken the ice.

What about other zoos? At the New York Zoological Park - the Bronx Zoo - director William Conway and some of his curators have also been interested in operant conditioning as a zoo-management tool. They have installed some automated exhibits, such as a "honey tree" that makes bears stand to their full height and show off their long tongues to get the occasionally dispensed honey. They have also undertaken a pilot training program, hiring an experienced marine-mammal trainer, Jerry Winsett, to be trainer-at-large in the zoo for a year. Some of the behavior problems Jerry solved seemed routine to him, but they were serious to the keepers. For example, a certain gorilla took to sitting in his doorway, refusing to go in or out, when the keepers wanted to clean the cage. No amount of banana waving could coax him from that position, and with his huge strength he prevented the door from being closed. Jerry pointed out that banana waving is bribery; you are reinforcing behavior that hasn't occurred yet, and trainers know that doesn't really work. Jerry suggested ignoring the gorilla when he sat in the doorway and rewarding him when he went out by himself. Problem solved.

The Bronx Zoo has an exhibit of nocturnal creatures, "The World of Darkness," in which many small birds and mammals are displayed under a dim, or red, light going about their normal lives. It is difficult for the keepers to check on the health or even the viable presence of each specimen in the darkness. Jerry taught the keepers techniques for "shaping" animals to come to their hands. To coax a timid douroucouli (a nocturnal monkey) or galago (a tiny primate) to take food from your hand might take weeks of patience. To shape it to do so, however, by reinforcing every step closer to you with morsels of food, which at first are put in a dish or on a branch where the animal can reach them easily, is a matter of a few five-minute training sessions. Now almost every important specimen in that exhibit is shaped to take food from a keeper's hand everyday, which not only allows the keepers to count and inspect the fragile creatures but also facilitates catching animals who must be doctored or moved.

The Brookfield Zoo near Chicago has experimented extensively with automated exhibits in which animals are conditioned to show natural behavior, such as hunting, and are reinforced by food from an automatic dispenser when the behavior is performed correctly. Moral and esthetic objections are often loudly voiced in the zoo community to this "mechanizing" of the animals, but surely it is kinder to keep them active than to let them doze their lives away in hopelessness and apathy. Properly designed, automated exhibits appear to be fun for the animals. Brookfield's cougar, which was conditioned to lie on a branch until an artificial marmot (a sort of ground squirrel) stuck its head out of a hole, and then to leap on the marmot before it disappeared again, would go on playing long after the food dispenser was empty.

Humanists often view operant conditioning, or any use of Skinnerian techniques, as inhuman, monstrous, Machiavellian. Yet with captive animals it is more often the failure to use the techniques that is inhumane. Positive reinforcement training constitutes an exchange of deeds for goods in which a pleasant communion arises, a salutary sort of equality between animal and trainer. One cannot work without the other, and both must do their part. That is reinforcing in itself, for both parties. I was just as pleased, just as reinforced, by Mary the rhino's taking violets from my hand as she was pleased to eat them. The baby rhino's learning to pick up its foot so quickly was reinforcing to Melanie. Operant conditioning in zoos is not only a benign addition to animal management practices, but rewards staff and animals alike. I am sure B. F. Skinner would not be surprised to hear that; he would just wonder why it took so long.

Trainer's Forum

VOL 22, NO 4, 1997. There is no doubt that training throughout the zoological community is an increasing trend. Here are two questions, one about teaching polar bears to respond to a bridging stimulus and the other on the training of warthogs. For those of us who have spent most of our careers training, it is very exciting to see training occurring in new settings.

Polar Bears and Warthogs: Training in the Zoo

QUESTION 1: Has anyone ever clicker-trained polar bears?

ANSWER 1a: The trainers and keepers here at the San Diego Zoo have successfully bridge conditioned many of our exhibit animals using clickers, whistles, and the verbal "good." The five polar bears here at the zoo (with the exception of Bonnie, our 32-year-old deaf female) are conditioned to a clicker because all our training sessions are done up close in the den area. They all, Bonnie included, respond exceptionally well to operant conditioning and seem to enjoy their interactions with the trainers.

The stimulation provided by the training sessions has many positive results. One obvious bonus is that the den area becomes a very positive place to be for keeper and bears. Husbandry behaviors are our main focus along with a lot of attitude work. Mouth opens, weekly weights and general physical inspections are the norm. We are also working with our BRC (bear restraint device or cage). The bears are rewarded for calmly accepting the doors closing and the side walls moving toward them. This will help our team of veterinarians to inspect the bears safely without the need for anesthesia.

Other animals on exhibit that are bridge conditioned are baboons, brown bears, Transvaal lions, and giant panda.

Jennine Antrim
San Diego Zoo

ANSWER 1b: We originally clicker trained our polar bears but switched to a whistle bridge. The main reason, we switched was so we could have both of our hands free for cues, rewarding, and targeting. Also, your hands get full of meat and fish slime; who wants that stuff on their clickers? There you go! Short and sweet.

Marine Mammal Staff
North Carolina Zoo

QUESTION 2: Has anyone ever target trained warthogs?

ANSWER 2: We do not have an established training program with our warthogs, but we have used targets in training programs with pinnipeds, primates, and Malayan tapirs and babirusa.

For the tapirs and babirusa, the goals of our training included assisting with veterinary care, and to enhance our husbandry practices. These two species are part of five mammal species that we randomly rotate between four separate exhibit areas. To maximize our ability to move these animals at random intervals into and out of these areas we determined before the animals arrived at the Zoo that training would be the key.

Training started by desensitizing the tapirs and babirusa to our presence as we stood at the stall doors. Once they became curious and approached us calmly, we would give them a food reinforcer. The next step was establishing a conditioned reinforcer. We paired the food reinforcer with a whistle.

Then we began to work in with these animals. At first we had a shield available if needed, and the sessions are always conducted with two people present for safety. The target was introduced into the training to help facilitate moving animals from one place to another. This included training the tapirs to climb up onto and off of an elephant tub. This was preparing them to climb steps, which are included in the transfer chutes between our holding building and the four exhibit areas.

The training has been very successful in many ways. Not only are we able to move the animals through the exhibits, but we have been able to accomplish tasks such as lancing an abscess on a tapir's face and trimming the male babirusa's tusks. We have found that our training of these animals and many others around the zoo has proven to be a very valuable tool in our husbandry programs.

Jane Anne Franklin
Louisville Zoo

Chicago Tribune

The following article appeared on the front page of the *Chicago Tribune* on Sunday, August 18, 1996. It became an international story making the front page in Chicago again two days later and appearing on national television. It demonstrates the public's fascination with animals and the desire to attribute human qualities to the animals. The gorilla was called a "hero." In the stories that appeared after this one many experts on animal emotion were interviewed to discuss whether or not the female gorilla felt "compassion" for the boy, did she "know" he was injured, was she "consciously trying to save him?" While the story was a major PR bonanza for the zoo, it could have just as easily been a very different headline. "Boy Mauled By Vicious Ape" or "Zoo Criticized For Lack of Response In Gorilla Attack." Thankfully, the story turned out better for the zoo, the gorilla, and the boy. However, a key point that is mentioned in this article but not in any of the ones that came later, is the training the gorilla had undergone to learn good mothering skills. The fact that she brought the child to her keepers is an example of trust and relationship building in a zoo environment. Who's to really say whether she knew or acted a certain way for a certain reason? But it is certain that had her past experiences with people not been positive, her actions with the boy might have been very different.

Maternal Feelings Prevail as Gorilla Rescues Tot at Zoo

by Jeffrey Bils and Stacey Singer
Chicago Tribune

It was a case where maternal instincts paid off in gorilla-size proportions.

Zoo keepers attempting to save an endangered species had no idea that their efforts to teach a female gorilla good parenting skills would eventually lead to the quick rescue of a human toddler who tumbled 15 feet into a Brookfield Zoo exhibit Friday.

While a crowd of horrified zoo patrons cried out for help expecting the worst for the 3-year-old boy lying battered on the concrete near seven gorillas, an unlikely hero emerged.

Binti-Jua, a rare western lowland gorilla. Who has received training on how to be a good mother, appeared to act out of purely maternalistic compassion for the human child, onlookers said.

The simian Good Samaritan, with her own baby clinging to her back, lumbered over to the boy, gently scooped him up and carried him to a doorway where she placed him gingerly at the feet of waiting paramedics.

"She picked up the boy, kind of cradling him, and walked him around," said zoo spokeswoman Sondra Catzen.

"Another gorilla walked toward the boy, and she kind of turned around and walked away from the other gorillas and tried to be protective," said Carrie Stewart, a zoo visitor who witnessed the incident.

Binti's maternalistic response to the boy comes on the heels of "behavioral-enrichment training" that was intended to "teach her basically how to be a mom," Catzen said.

As a baby gorilla, Binti was rejected by her

mother and raised by humans, so trainers later worked with her using dolls in an effort to teach her the good parenting skills she had never experienced first-hand. The goal was to make sure that Binti would not reject her own offspring, according to Melinda Pruett-Jories, a curator at the zoo.

The boy appeared to suffer a head injury, but "there was no aggressive behavior toward the boy" by any of the seven gorillas in the exhibit, Pruett-Jones said.

Zoo keepers trained three fire hoses on the other gorillas in the pit to prevent them from approaching Binti and her newfound ward.

"Keepers responded quickly," she said. "The whole thing was over in 10 minutes or less."

At first it appeared the boy had been knocked unconscious by the fall, witnesses told zoo officials. But "he was alert and crying when the paramedics came and got him," Catzen said.

The boy was taken to Loyola University Medical Center in Maywood, where he was in critical condition Friday night, said hospital spokesman Michael Maggio.

Neither the zoo nor the hospital released the child's identity or hometown, and Maggio said the boy's parents did not wish to be interviewed.

This is the first time that anyone has fallen into the Brookfield Zoo gorilla pit, part of the zoo's Tropic World exhibit, in the 14 years that it has existed, Catzen said. She said zoo officials have not yet determined exactly how the child managed to fall in.

The pit is surrounded by a railing that is about 3½ feet tall, Catzen said.

"He had to climb up," she said. "I don't know if he lost his balance or what."

The boy was visiting the zoo with a group of eight other children and three adults including his mother, Catzen said. He fell into the pit at about 2:10 p.m.

Catzen said zoo officials have not yet determined whether it will be necessary to change the barrier surrounding the pit.

"It's a safe exhibit," she said. "Right now we're concerned about the child's well-being and the gorilla's well-being. Then we will look at why this happened."

The most recent similar incident at the zoo occurred two or three years ago, when a child climbed over a stone barrier and got onto the baboon island, Catzen said. That child was not injured, she said. The barrier involved in that case was different than the one involved in Friday's incident, she said.

Binti is one of 10 western lowland gorillas at Brookfield Zoo, Pruett-Jones said. The endangered species is native to Africa, and only about 35,000 remain in the world.

The female gorilla has been on loan for four years from the San Francisco Zoo as part of a breeding program, Pruett-Jones said. The ape received her motherhood training before giving birth and continues to care for her 17-month-old daughter, Koola.

Binti's reaction to the human child is not unprecedented, according to Jackie Ogden, a curator and gorilla behavioral researcher at the San Diego Zoo.

Several years ago at the Jersey Zoo, which is a British zoo on an island in the English Channel, a young boy fell into a gorilla exhibit and apparently was guarded by a dominant silverback male until help could arrive.

"This is not to say gorillas are completely harmless," Ogden said. "They are very big, strong, and have big teeth."

Ogden said she was "amazed but not surprised" by Binti's behavior, but added: "This shouldn't cause people to try jumping into gorilla habitats."

Tribune staff writer William Mullen and The Associated Press contributed to this article.

VOL 15, NO 2, 1990. One of the best uses of IMATA's *Trainer's Forum* is the straightforward question, "How do you train _____?" Here are two similar approaches to the same behavior. Answer 2 utilizes a step by step approach to "map" or "set up" the training plan. This approach to setting up a training plan is the one described in earlier chapters.

Training Echolocation Discrimination in a Show

QUESTION: We are trying to train echolocation via ring recovery to our cetaceans. Our animals are already trained to wear eye cups and retrieve rings. What we need is an outline or ideas on how to teach them to discriminate between different density rings and retrieve only one type.

ANSWER 1: At Brookfield Zoo, two of our dolphins perform a blindfolded retrieving task One animal is trained to find rings that contain sand and the other retrieves rings filled with lead shot. The rings are formed out of hollow plastic tubing and they are suspended one half meter below the surface by a length of rope attached to a plastic float.

Since your cetaceans are trained to retrieve blindfolded, you're half way there. Your next step is to condition the discrimination and combine it with the existing echolocation task.

A good way to start this type of training is to make it very easy for your animals to make a correct choice. Make the rings very different at first, then approximate them towards being identical with the exception of their density. Originally, our rings were of different lengths so that they would hang at different depths below the surface. Also, one ring was completely filled with sand while the other type was only half-filled with lead shot.

Work with each animal individually at first, presenting only the correct ring for them to retrieve. Once they get a good "feel" for their own rings, start to present the "different" ring and only reinforce the retrieval of the correct one.

When both animals successfully discriminate every time, try having them retrieve at the same time. Once they've mastered retrieving together, it will be time to start modifying the rings, making them alike except for their density. Make these approximations slowly and only when you are sure that the animals are making their choice based on the ring's density. If they're not, you'll find out soon enough and you may have to take a step back. Good Luck!

P.S. For further information contact Dr. Randy Brill, N.O.S.C., Hawaii. The current staff were mere children when this was first trained.

Seven Sea's Trainers
Brookfield Zoo

ANSWER 2: As with most behaviors, there are probably as many different ways to train this behavior as there are trainers. Among ourselves, we knew of three distinctly different ways to successfully train echolocation discrimination. We have chosen to describe the simplest. Based upon your question, we have responded with the following assumptions in mind:

1. The animal in question already knows how to wear eye cups and locate rings.
2. You want the animal to retrieve one ring of a specific density, and ignore any other.
3. And most important, the desired behavior is for show or demonstration and not specific research or data collection.

The third point is important, since some types of research or data collection may indicate a specific method of training. You may, for example, want to throw out two rings of different densities and record the number of trials before your animal can accurately discriminate between the two. But unless that method serves a particular purpose, you are likely creating a confusing situation for your animal. Thus, for the purposes of a show, we suggest a simple method that helps the animal to clearly understand the objective. Here are our suggested steps:

1. Train the animal to consistently retrieve one ring of the desired density (e.g. sand filled) using his echolocation. This should be simple since your animal is essentially doing this already.
2. Add a distinctly different shaped object to the pool (e.g. basketball or cone). This teaches the animal that other objects may be present and that they should be ignored. By selecting a distinctly different object, there is little likelihood that the animal will confuse it for a ring.
3. It is important to vary the additional objects used from session to session. This helps to ensure that the animal is not just discriminating against that particular object, but truly searching for the desired ring.
4. Eventually, introduce a large ring instead of the "other" object, this large ring should be several times larger than the ring being retrieved. How large depends on your animal's ability not to confuse it with the desired ring.
5. Slowly approximate it into a smaller and smaller ring, until it is the desired size. Once you have introduced the large ring (in step 4), make sure its density is always different from the original ring (fill it with a totally different substance).
6. Maintaining the behavior should not be a problem. To keep the task from becoming boring, we suggest increasing the number of rings and occasionally reintroduce the unusual objects (step 3). A word of caution however, too much variety, too quickly, can be confusing to the animal. Take it slow and keep the goals clear.

Depending on the training history of your particular animal, you might eliminate steps 2 and 3. We have found, however, that those additional steps seem to assure the concept of discrimination and diminishes the likelihood of the animal making wrong choices further down the line. This behavior seems to invite confusion and subsequently frustration of both the trainer and the dolphin. But by taking small, clear approximations, echolocation training doesn't have to be a major obstacle. We would enjoy hearing about your results.

Marine Mammal Staff
John G. Shedd Aquariun

Conference Proceedings

1986 IMATA Conference, Vancouver, Canada. Many research projects require the use of a go, no-go paradigm. This paper describes the training of this technique for a hearing project. Training for research projects often present new challenges due to the controls that an experiment requires to be considered scientifically valid. The interaction of researchers and trainers is made easier if the research goals and animal limitations are outlined in advance.

Training a False Killer Whale for an Underwater Audiogram

by Norman Chun[1], Kiana Pugh[2] and Jeanette Thomas[1]
[1]Naval Ocean Systems Center and [2]Sea Life Park

ABSTRACT

Over a six-month period, a male false killer whale (*Pseudorca crassidens*) at Sea Life Park in Hawaii was trained to test its underwater hearing sensitivity. This animal also was required to perform three shows daily, two training sessions per day, and learn a new show routine. For the hearing test, the animal was trained to station with its body resting on an underwater crook and attend to a set of lights which defined the listening interval. The animal's behavior was controlled by a series of tones: a 3 khz tone to send him to station, a test signal (ranging from 1 to 160 khz), a 3 khz release tone, and a 7 khz bridge tone. Each component was trained separately then combined into the final test behavior.

The procedure was a go/no-go paradigm. The animal was sent to station and when positioned properly, two underwater lights were turned on, signaling the animal to "listen." Half of the trials were control trials (no signal) in which the animal had to wait 14 seconds until the lights were turned off and a 3 khz release tone was given. During signal trials, a test tone was presented 3 seconds after the lights were turned on; if the animal heard the tone he backed out of the crook, was given a 7 khz bridge and fish reward. If the animal did not hear the tone, he was required to wait until the lights were turned off and a release tone was given. Preliminary results will be discussed.

OBJECTIVES

The objective of the project was to measure the underwater hearing sensitivity of a false killer whale between the range of the frequencies from 1khz through 160 khz. The data collected during the experiment would be used for comparisons with hearing data taken from other odontocetes. The odontecete species from which behavioral audiograms have already been obtained include: the bottlenose dolphin (Johnson, 1967), the Amazon River dolphin (Jacobs & Hall, 1972), the harbor porpoise (Anderson, 1970), the beluga whale (White, Ljungblad, Norris, & Baron, 1977), and the killer whale (Hall & Johnson, 1972). Data on the animals' hearing sensitivity are important background information for assessing echolocation abilities in each of these species.

APPROACH/ APPARATUS

A 20-year-old adult male *Pseudorca crassidens* named Ianui was used as our test subject. The hearing experiment was conducted at Whaler's Cove in Sea Life Park on the island of Oahu. The test apparatus was mounted on the side of the replica of the whaling ship "Essex" located in Whaler's Cove. The apparatus consisted of a plank supported by two vertical legs which extended 12 feet down to the bottom of the holding pool. The plank and vertical legs were lowered into and pulled out of the water using a system of blocks and tackle which could be operated either by hand or with an A.C. powered winch. The apparatus was pulled up out of the water after each training and test session to prevent the possibility of injury to the animal. When pulled out of the water, the legs folded alongside the plank for easy storage

During training and testing, the signals were

projected from an underwater hydrophone submerged 3.5 feet below the water surface. The transducer was suspended by a long pole attached to one end of the plank. Two different types of projectors were used in the experiment because of the wide range of frequencies tested. We used a J-9 transducer to project signals from 1 to 85 khz, and a NOSC-developed high-frequency transducer to project signals from 85 to 160 khz. At some frequencies, data will be taken using the J-9, and will be retaken with the high-frequency transducer to replicate the animal's performance under both conditions. This is to insure that the hearing data are reliable and actually reflect the animal's hearing threshold instead of some artifact of the projected sound characteristics of the transducers.

A curved, 2 inch diameter aluminum pipe welded between the two vertical legs of the platform served as the animal's stationing crook. The crook was located 10 feet away from the transducer at approximately the same depth as the transducer. The crook helped to insure that the animal's head and lower jaw were centered on the axis of the transducers beam pattern. If the animal's head is off the axis of the beam by as little as 5 degrees, this may result in a loss in received signal strength by as much as 6 db; therefore the geometry of the projected signal and the animal receiver is extremely important.

Another important consideration, especially when conducting an underwater hearing test in a confined space such as a pool, is the ability of controlling signal bounce of the transmitted sound. Signals from the side lobes of the transducer may be reflected at the water surface as well as of the sides of the tank, contributing to variability in the received sound level. To prevent this from occurring, underwater sound baffles were placed at strategic points on the bottom pool as well as at the water's surface. The sound baffles were fabricated of ¼ inch thick neoprene and corprene mat laminated to a ¼ inch thick aluminum plate. The corprene material is acoustically opaque and prevented the reflected signal from reaching the animal. The irregular shape of the walls of the tank and its distance from the test apparatus were great enough so that signal bounce from the side walls of the tank was not a factor in this experiment. Prior to conducting the test, the acoustic field of projected sounds around the animal's station was mapped by measuring the sound pressure level with a hydrophone. We measured the received level at the hydrophone for each of the frequencies tested, and will use these measurements to determine the animal's hearing threshold.

A function generator, amplifier, and attenuator was use to control the frequency, waveform, and amplitude of the test signals. A gating circuit was interfaced with this system to clip the initial rise-time-to-projection amplitude. The electronics equipment was located beneath the deck of the ship. The test coordinator operated the electronics from below, monitoring the equipment and selecting the amplitude of the test signal to be presented. The trainer, meanwhile, controlled the animal from the platform outside the ship using a control box and underwater hydrophone that emitted a 3 and 7 khz tone. Two-way radio headsets enabled the trainer and the test coordinator to communicate with one another.

TRAINING

Initially, we began training the animal to station with its head out of the water directly in front of the platform on hand cue. The whale was then trained to target on a float mounted on the end of a long pole. The animal was required to remain targeted on the float until it was bridged and rewarded with fish. We then extended the time that the whale was required to remain targeted on the float to 14 seconds. At first, the float was placed directly in front of the platform, then was gradually lowered to a position near the crook, about 3 ½ feet below the surface.

During this early stage in training, when the float was lowered near the crook, the whale had a difficult time maintaining the proper body position underwater. The animal was buoyed up by the air in its lungs which would force him to the surface. As he rose to the surface, he would roll over to one side of the platform, or he would try to keep his head positioned on the float by rapidly moving his pectoral fins while the rest of his body was floating at the surface. This head down positioning was awkward and obviously not acceptable for testing, so we tried to eliminate the buoyancy problem by first training the whale to exhale while targeting on the float. We did this by extending the targeting time underwater and reinforced him whenever he exhaled. When he learned to exhale it became easy for him to remain submerged, and the pectoral fin and body movement that we saw during much of the preliminary training simply disappeared. As the animal became more proficient at stationing

Figure 1

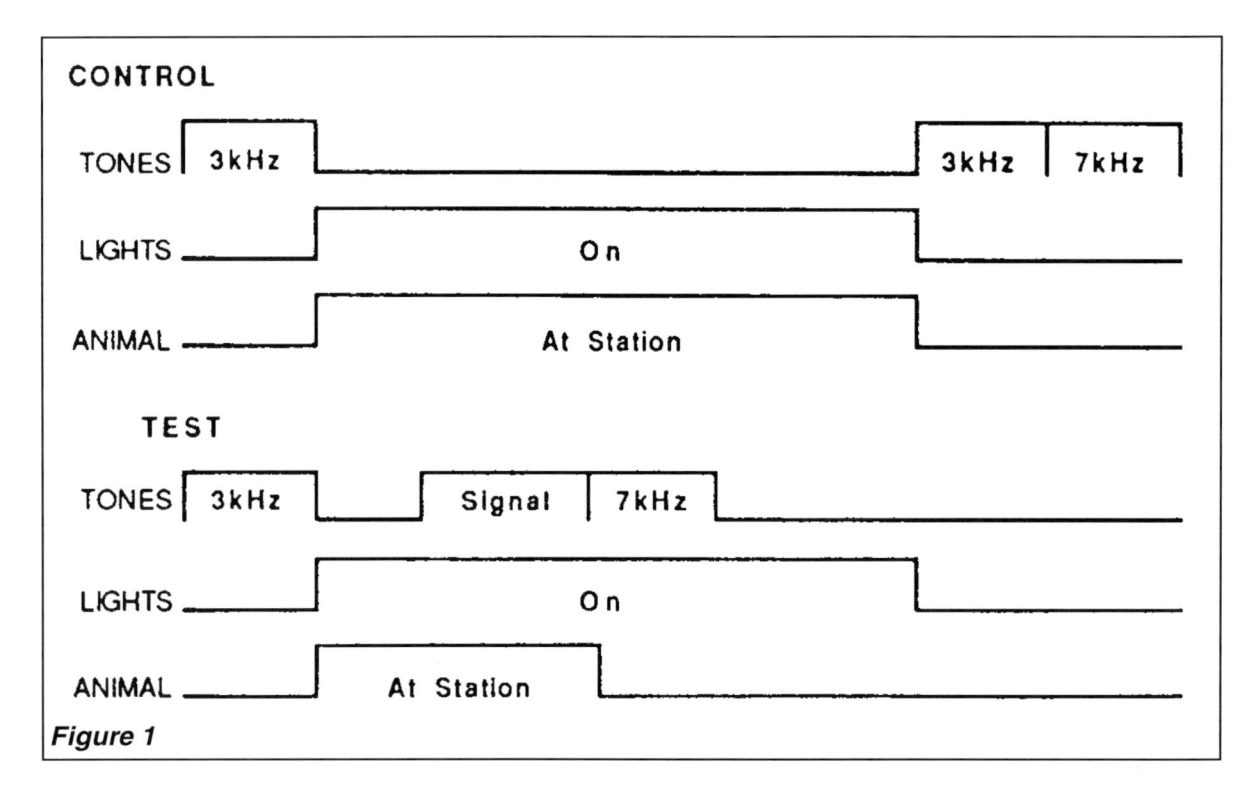

[Figure 1: Timing diagram showing CONTROL and TEST trial sequences with TONES (3kHz, Signal, 7kHz), LIGHTS (On), and ANIMAL (At Station) traces.]

underwater near the crook, a 3khz "come-to-station" tone was paired with the presentation of the float. The 3 khz tone served as a cue for the animal to exhale and also helped to mark the start of the trial. The training emphasis at this point was to transfer the targeting response to a smaller object, such as a lead weight at the end of a string, then to eliminate the object completely. By using a smaller target we could be much more precise in training the whale's head positioning, making sure that his chin was resting in the right position on the crook. When the behavior was stable, we used an even smaller weight suspended from monofilament line and gradually faded out the target completely. When the targeting-to-the-weight was eliminated, the animal simply stationed on the crook under control of the 3 khz tone.

As the animal's stationing response on the crook became more consistent, we then trained it to "release-from-station" by pairing a second 3 khz tone with presentation of fish. The animal would naturally leave the stationing crook whenever it heard the fish hit the water, and by pairing the second 3 khz tone with the presentation of fish over many trials, the tone itself would elicit the "release-from-station" behavior. This response would then be followed by a reward of fish several seconds later.

In order to facilitate listening more intently during a specified time period, we also used a set of underwater lights to delineate a listening interval. The lights were turned on when the animal was properly positioned in the crook, then turned off as the 3 khz, "release-from-station" tone was initiated. So up to this point in the training regimen, the whale would be called to station with a 3 khz tone as the lights went off. When it heard that second tone, it would back out of the crook and then receive its reward along with a 7 khz bridge. This behavioral sequence constituted a "signal – absent" or "control" trial (see Figure 1).

During a "signal-present" trial, the test tone was given 3 seconds after the start of the listening interval. Since the animal was already conditioned to back out whenever it heard the 3 khz release tone, transferring the "release-from-station" behavior to any tone that preceded it during that time interval was easily accomplished. This response procedure is called a "go/no-go" paradigm and is a common technique used in animal psychophysics, especially in signal-detection experiments. Using this procedure, the experimenter can determine what levels the animal can or cannot hear by observing whether the animal breaks from station or maintains its position for the prescribed time interval.

TESTING PROCEDURE

In the testing sequence with the false killer whale, the subject first positions itself in front of the apparatus to signify that it is ready to be tested. The trainer then calls the animal to station using the 3 khz tone. When the animal hears the tone, it exhales to become negatively buoyant, then positions itself with its head resting on the crook. When the test coordinator, looking through an underwater porthole determines that the animal is properly stationed in the crook, she turns on a set of lights directly in front of the animal to tell him to "listen." On a "signal-absent" or "control" trial, the lights remain on for 14 seconds, after which they are turned off while simultaneously turning on the 3 khz tone once more. This signals the animal to back out of the crook to receive its reward. Reinforcement of fish is then paired with a 7 khz tone. On a "signal-present" trial, the test tone remains on for two seconds. If the animal hears the test signal, it immediately backs out of the crook to receive its reward. The amplitude of the test frequency can then be varied to determine the animal's hearing threshold for each frequency tested.

We are using a descending form of the staircase method, beginning at a high amplitude, then gradually lowering the amplitude until the animal can no longer hear the signal. Figure 2 is an example of the testing procedure for 16 khz. We start off first by giving the animal three warm-ups at a very high signal level. The warm-up trials are decreased in 5 db steps. When testing begins, the signal is lowered in 2 db increments until the animal no longer hears the signal. When the animal cannot detect the signal, the source level is increased by 2 db until it detects the signal again. The transition between not detecting the signal and detecting the signal is called a "reversal," and the average of these two values is called the "reversal level." The testing continues in this up-down technique until we get 5 reversals. The amplitude of the signals are averaged across the 5 reversals for each session. If the averages of the reversals for two consecutive sessions fall within 3 db of one another we compute the average as the threshold of attenuation. This attenuation level is subtracted from the sound pressure level (SPL) that we obtained when we mapped the acoustic field at the animal's stationing position. This gives us the db level at threshold which is used to plot the points in the animal's hearing curve.

RESULTS

The data points for each of the frequencies tested can then be plotted to depict the animal's hearing sensitivity. Figure 3 depicts the preliminary data obtained for frequencies from 2 to 85 khz. In figure 3, the frequency tested is plotted on the abscissa, and the sound pressure level at threshold is plotted on the ordinate. The lower the value of the SPL, the better is the animal's hearing sensitivity. Thus, the data in Figure 3, show that the animal is most sensitive in the frequency band from 16 to 32 khz. Near the very low-frequency end of the spectrum, the animals hearing sensitivity starts to dramatically fall off around 4 khz.

So how does the false killer whale's hearing

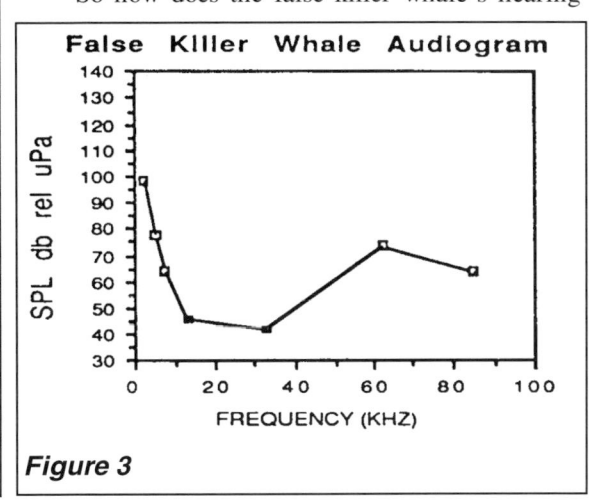

EXAMPLE OF UP/DOWN STAIRCASE METHOD			
15 kHertz 1 October 1986 Warm-up Levels: 45+ 50+ 55+			
Tests:			
Level	Response	Reversal	
56	+		
58	+		
60	–		
58	+	1	Reversal level = 59
60	–		
58	–		
56	+	2	Reversal level = 57
58	+		
60	+		
62	–		
60	+	3	Reversal level = 61
62	+		
60	+	4	Reversal level = 61
62	–		
60	–		
58	+	5	Reversal level = 59

Mean of reversals = 59.4 dB of attenuation
Received level at animal – attenuation = dB level of threshold

Figure 2

Figure 3

performance data compare with other odontocetes? The data collected thus far for the low frequencies suggest that the false killer whale is somewhat similar to the beluga whale in hearing ability. The SPL at the low frequency end of the spectrum is about 100 db re µPa for both species with the peak sensitivity centering around 30 khz. The high frequency end of the spectrum has not yet been tested and it will be interesting to see if the audiogram follows the beluga's profile for the higher frequencies as well. We anticipate obtaining the high frequency data by mid December 1986 and should be able to outline the entire hearing curve of the false killer whale at that time.

REFERENCES

Anderson, S., 1970. Auditory sensitivity of the harbour porpoise *Phocoena phocoena*, In: "Investigations on Cetacea," G. Pilleri ed., Bentell: AF., Berne.

Hall, J.D. and Johnson, C.S., 1972. Auditory thresholds of a killer whale *Orcinus orca* Linnaeus. J. Acoust. Soc. Amer. 51: 515-517.

Jacobs, D.W. and Hall, J.C., 1972. Auditory thresholds of a freshwater dolphin, *Inia Geoffrensis* Blainville. J. Acoust. Soc. Amer., 51: 530-533.

Johnson, C.S., 1967. Sound detection thresholds in marine mammals, In: "Marine Bio-Acoustics Vol. 2," W.N. Tavolga ed., Oxford: Pergammon Press.

White, M.J., Ljungblad, D., Norris, J. and Baron, K., 1977. Auditory thresholds of two beluga whales. Proceedings (abstracts) Second Conference on the Biology of Marine Mammals, San Diego, California.

Conference Proceedings

1982 IMATA Conference, Honolulu, Hawaii, USA. Many research projects require a clear way to have an animal indicate what it does or doesn't perceive. One important research training technique that can serve this function is called a "go, no-go paradigm." Here it is used in a taste experiment with dolphins. Although the explanation of training methods is not detailed, this is a good example of a go, no-go paradigm in use.

Conditioning a Pacific Bottlenose Dolphin and a California Sea Lion in a Taste Experiment

by Richard W. Hall and James L. Richards
Naval Ocean Systems Center

ABSTRACT

A dolphin and a sea lion were trained in a go-no-go response paradigm to determine their abilities to taste. The methods used in training these animals to detect substances dissolved in distilled water is examined. This methodology includes training for stationing, beaching, mouthpiece acceptance, response to acoustic tones, and the taste discrimination behavior itself. Initial taste discrimination includes training techniques of fading and trial-and-error learning while using solution flow rates as cues to standard and test solutions. Animals are trained to bite on a stimulus presentation mouthpiece while two streams of liquid are successively presented into their mouths. The first presentation is always distilled water, while the second is either distilled water or a diluted solution of distilled water plus the substance to be detected. Taste of the solution is indicated by an immediate release from the mouthpiece. Results indicate that the dolphin can detect all four primary tastes, but the sea lion can detect only the sour and salty.

A TASTE EXPERIMENT

This presentation describes the behaviors that were required in order to conduct a taste experiment at the Naval Ocean Systems Center in Kaneohe Bay, Hawaii over the past two years. When I began working with marine mammals in 1971 and, while learning about dolphins and sea lions, one fact that was generally accepted was that these animals did not possess the ability to taste or smell. That seemed rather odd to me, since both of these animals are very high on the evolutionary scale and it seemed logical that they would have some vestiges of taste. We are all aware of the tremendous amount of knowledge of marine mammals that has been accumulated over the past 15 to 20 years; however, a literature survey reveals that very little information is available on the chemoreception abilities of taste and smell. What little there is can be divided into anatomical and behavioral categories.

Anatomical evidence suggests that dolphins, at least, posses taste-bud-like structures located primarily on the back part of the tongue. These structures are located in small pits rather than being distributed on the surface of the tongue. Several researchers have located these pits and theorized that they contain taste buds.

Behavioral research is limited primarily to the findings of several Russian scientists, V.B. Kuznetsev and V.E. Sokolov. They utilized the Black Sea dolphin (*Tursiops truncatus*) and studied the four basic areas of taste: salt, sour, bitter, and sweet. In addition, they also examined many organic compounds. Their results indicate that dolphins can detect many substances.

The Russian scientists used a small database with which to draw their conclusions; their methods are difficult to duplicate and many variables were present. It was with these factors in mind that we undertook our experimental design. We also looked at the four basic areas of taste and dissolved our test substances in distilled water. Hence our test solutions were the substances to be tested in distilled water and our standard solutions were simply distilled water. Since we were working with both a Pacific bottlenose dolphin and a California sea lion, two structurally different but functionally similar delivery systems had to be designed.

The sea lion experimental equipment consisted of a bite plate mounted on a stand through which solutions could be dispensed, allowing irrigation of the mouth of the animal, especially the tongue region. A valve was installed on the back of the stand to enable the trainer to dispense either test or standard solutions. It also allowed an intertrial washing procedure to control mouthpiece contamination. A visually opaque screen was placed between the animal and the trainer to minimize inadvertent cues.

The dolphin's equipment was designed as follows. First of all, a beaching tray was used onto which the animal slid to remove him from the surrounding seawater. This was to minimize contamination of his mouth during solution testing. In addition, a mouthpiece designed to fit our dolphin was mounted on the end of the tray.

Both the sea lion and dolphin equipment were operated from an adjoining chemoreception equipment shelter that contained the necessary pumps, solution, and tubing required to conduct the experiment. An operator sat in that facility and coordinated with the trainer the sequence of events in each presentation.

The methodology used went as follows. The animal placed his mouth on the bite plate (the sea lion in response to a hand signal by the trainer and the dolphin in response to a nine-kilohertz tone), and received distilled water for a precise period of time (sea lion, five seconds; dolphin, eight seconds). At the end of this first irrigation, the animal remained holding the bite plate for several more seconds until the advent of the second irrigation. If the trial was a standard presentation, the response was to remain on the bite plate until a bridge tone was given by the trainer five seconds after the irrigation concluded. Food reinforcement followed immediately. If the trial was a test presentation, the animal received a measured amount of test solution. If he detected the presence of the substance, the correct response was to elicit a "go" and release the mouthpiece. A bridge was immediately given, and food reinforcement followed. In this manner, the animal was able to make an immediate comparison within each trial to distilled water.

With the dolphin as our example, the behaviors that were necessary to train were as follows:
1. Stationing – the animal was conditioned to remain next to a board equipped with a float during the inter-trial intervals. This controlled his behavior during this period and also, by the placement of this stationing device, aligned the animal to perform the next behavior.
2. Beaching – upon the stimulus of a nine-kilohertz tone in the water, the dolphin beached onto a fiberglass tray laying on the water's surface.
3. Mouthpiece acceptance – as he slid onto the tray he placed his mouth onto the bite plate located at the other end.
4. Standard trial performance – the animal was then conditioned to remain on the tray, mouth on the bite plate, for an entire standard presentation sequence (30 seconds). A five-kilohertz tone bridged this behavior. A baseline performance level was achieved before the next step.
5. Introduction of the test solution – a .5 molar (M) solution of citric acid was selected as our first test substance. This was a sour concentration, but diluted enough to avoid any harmful effects to the soft tissues of the tongue. The solution was introduced to the animal paired with a cue—that of a high flow volume (120 ml instead of 70 ml).

The animal responded, as hoped, by releasing the bite plate once the test solution reached his mouth. We were then able to gradually, over several sessions, reduce the flow cue to equal that of a standard trial second irrigation (70 ml). We then confirmed detection of .5M citric acid by presenting the trials in a random number series (Gellerman).

A similar procedure was used for the sea lion, who also detected citric acid in solution.

Since our goals were not only to confirm detection or non-detection of test substances, but also to locate the thresholds, we then used a bracketing procedure to approximate the threshold region. We then employed a modified method of constants and presented the animal six different molar values of the test substances which we collected over many sessions. When graphed, we had six data points representing 100 trials each (50 standard, 50 test) that illustrated our threshold curve. A 75% performance threshold line was drawn, and our threshold levels were determined. After determining the threshold for citric acid, we then studied quinine sulfate (bitter), sucrose (sweet), and finally, sodium chloride (salt).

The following comparative table outlines our result:

These results confirm other findings, both anatomical and behavioral, which indicate that dolphins have a sense of taste and establishes, for the first time, that the California sea lion can detect sour and salty substances.

Taste? Do dolphins and sea lions possess the ability to taste? Of course they do! They had the answers, we just had to figure out how to ask the questions.

Comparative Thresholds ($\underline{M}$)			
SUBSTANCE	HUMAN	DOLPHIN	SEA LION
Sodium Chloride	.01	.09	.2
Citric Acid	.0023	.017	.003
Quinine Sulfate	8.0×10^{-6}	1.36×10^{-5}	No Detection
Sucrose	.016	.07	No Detection

1990 IMATA Conference, Chicago, Illinois, USA. A common technique for gaining information from animals in a research project is to train a "matching-to-sample" task. This paper describes the methodology for training matching-to-sample. This project is all the more complex because the animal must complete the matching task through the use of echolocation rather than sight.

Echolocation for Shape, Material, and Internal Structure

by Mark J. Xitco, Jr.
The Living Seas, Epcot Center

ABSTRACT

Two adolescent male Atlantic bottlenose dolphins, *Tursiops truncatus*, were trained to perform a three alternative, echoic matching-to-sample task. A structured set of 17 three-dimensional objects were used as stimuli. These objects varied along three stimulus dimensions: shape, material composition, and internal structure. Stimuli were presented underwater behind thin sheets of black plastic. Although the sheets were visually opaque, they were virtually transparent acoustically, thus allowing echolocation. Both dolphins became highly proficient at the matching task, performing well above chance levels (probability < 0.01). An analysis of the dolphins' errors indicated that when the dolphins did make mistakes, their errors were influenced predominantly by the shape of the sample object.

INTRODUCTION

The development of echolocation has been proposed by many as a principal force behind the hypertrophy of the odontocete brain (Bullock & Gurevich, 1979; Morgane, Jacobs, & Galaburda, 1986) and the development of sophisticated cognitive capabilities in dolphins (Ayrapet'yants & Konstantinov, 1974; Herman, 1980; Jerison, 1986; Morris, 1986). The process of echolocation may be characterized as active listening. Dolphins first produce a rapid series of short, broad frequency-band "clicks", which, to the human ear, often sound like buzzing underwater. Echolocation clicks, like most dolphin vocalizations, are thought to be produced by shifting air back and forth through a system of internal air passages located within the dolphin's nasal cavity. These sounds are then directed outward in a tightly focused beam through the melon, the dolphin's bulbous, fat filled forehead. As the clicks bounce off distant targets, they produce unique, "fingerprint-like" echoes. These returning echoes reach the dolphin's inner ears by passing through fat-filled cavities located in the rear portion of the dolphin's jaw bone (Popper, 1980).

Examined primarily through the use of various discrimination studies (Popper, 1980; Ralston & Herman, 1989), the quantity and quality of sensory information provided to dolphins through echolocation is thought to at least closely approach that provided to humans through their visual system. Dolphins can ascertain, using a variety of acoustic cues, the velocity, size, form, composition and even the texture and internal structure of ensonified targets. In tests they have been able to detect the presence of a shot-put (cylindrical steel ball) more than a football field away, and have learned to discriminate between sophisticated underwater equipment. The aquarium is also home to approximately 3,000 other coral reef fish, including sharks, rays, saw fish, turtles and Orson, our 227.2 Kg (500 lb) plus grouper.

APPARATUS

The stimuli used in the present investigation were three-dimensional objects which varied along three stimulus dimensions: a) material composition, b) size and shape and c) internal structure. A structured set of 18 stimuli was fabricated for use in training the matching concept, and in generating baseline echolocation data (Table 1). The objects in this set were one of four shapes: 1) a flat, circular plate, measuring 26 cm (10.25 in) in diameter, 2) a cylinder, measuring 30.5 cm (12 in) in height and 3.8 cm (1.5 in) in diameter- 3) a grill, composed of seventeen 30.5 cm (12 in) by 6.35 mm (1/4 in) rods, with 14 vertical rods aligned across 3 horizontal rods or 4) a

Stimulus Name	Code	Supplemental Description
Aluminum Solid Plate	MSP	3.2 mm (1/8 in) thick
Aluminum Solid Cylinder	MSC	Defined in text
Aluminum Hollow Cylinder	MHC	Walls 3.2 mm (1/8 in) thick
Aluminum Solid Grill	MSG	Defined in text
Aluminum Solid Cube	MSU	Defined in text
Aluminum Hollow Cube	MHU	Walls 3.2 mm (1/8 in) thick
Clay Solid Plate	CSP	6.35 mm (1/4 in) thick, commercial glaze, 2.54 cm (1 in) depth
Clay Solid Cylinder	CSC	Walls 3.2 mm (1/8 in), filled with mortar, fiberglass resin
Clay Hollow Cylinder	CHC	Walls 3.2 mm (1/8 in) thick, fiberglass resin
Clay Solid Grill	CSG	Fiberglass resin
Clay Solid Cube	CSU	Walls 6.35 mm (1/4 in) thick, filled with mortar, commercial glaze
Clay Hollow Cube	CHU	Walls 6.35 mm (1/4 in) thick, filled with mortar, commercial glaze
Wood Solid Plate	WSP	6.35 mm (1/4 in) plywood
Wood Solid Cylinder	WSC	Hardwood
Wood Hollow Cylinder	WHC	Walls 3.2 mm (1/8 in) hardwood
Wood Solid Grill	WSG	Hardwood
Wood Solid Cube	WSU	Treated hardwood
Wood Hollow Cube	WHU	Walls 6.35 mm (1/4 in) plywood

Table 1 Description of the eighteen structured set stimuli used to train the matching concept and to generate baseline and comparison data.

cube, measuring 10. 16 cm (4 in) on each side. The objects were made of one of three materials: aluminum, wood, or low-fire clay, coated with commercial glaze or fiberglass resin. Cylinders and cubes were either solid or hollow, filled with water. The thickness of the plates and of the walls of hollow cylinders and cubes varied between objects from 3.2 mm (1/8 in) to 6.35 mm (1/4 in). The results of numerous echolocation studies (Au & Hammer, 1980; Au & Moore, 1986, 1984; and Pawloski, 1986; Au, Schusterman, & Kersting, 1980; Bagdonis, Bel'kovich, & Krushinskaya, 1970; Barta., 1969; Caine, 1976; Evans & Powell, 1967; Hammer & Au, 1980; Johnson, 1980; and Titlebaum, 1976; Murchison, 1980; Nachtigall, 1980; Nachtigall, Murchison, & Au, 1980; and Norris, 1980) suggested that the dolphins would be able to make discriminations easily within each stimulus dimension. However, no data existed to suggest how the dolphins would perform when different stimulus dimensions and combinations of stimulus values were presented on each trial.

The stimulus objects were presented to the dolphins behind thin sheets of black plastic (polyethylene, 0.004 mm (6 mil) thick), pulled taut over a frame of poly vinyl chloride (PVC) pipe. Although these plastic screens were visually opaque, their refractive and reflective properties for sound closely matched that of the surrounding water, making them acoustically transparent to the dolphins' echoic inspection of the stimuli.

PROCEDURES
Pre-training
Initially the dolphins were desensitized to a set of three stimulus objects, and trained to station on the objects when they were presented underwater one at a time. The dolphins were then required to follow this target object or sample, as it was swept through the water from side to side. In the next step, the object was first presented directly in front of the dolphin, then picked up out of the water and submerged again on either the left or the right. The dolphins were required to first station on the object in the center position, and then to station on the same object again when it was presented on either side. And lastly, as a final approximation before the full-blown matching task, the sample was presented in the center position, and then an alternative choice was gradually introduced-, by lowering a new object to one side with a duplicate sample also appearing opposite.

A large plastic screen was then introduced and the former series of approximations were presented behind the screen. The dolphins were then run on the completed matching task, using the initial training set of three objects and the single large screen. On each trial, the trainer first presented the sample object by holding it behind the center of the screen. The sample was presented until the dolphin approached the center of the screen, and made the side to side scanning head movements characteristic of echolocation. The sample was then removed, and two alternative objects were held behind the screen, one on the right and one on the left. One of the objects, the S+, was the same as the sample. The other alternative, the S-, served as a distracter. The identity and position of the S+ varied randomly from trial to trial. The dolphin's task was to station in front of the alternative which "matched" the sample. After satisfying performance criterion of 20 correct responses over 25 consecutive trials for the initial set of three stimuli, we moved on from the single screen procedure to the multiple screen configuration used throughout the remainder of the investigation.

Training the "Matching" Concept
A multiple screen procedure was used during the training of the matching concept. In this procedure, the trainer and dolphin worked from a floating platform, positioned in the middle of the main aquarium above an artificial coral mound. The trainer presented the sample stimulus approximately 15.2 -30.5 cm (6 -12 in) below the water's surface, behind a screen hanging from the platform. When the trainer withdrew the S+, the dolphin turned and dove to his alternative apparatus. Two alternative stimuli were individually housed in cube-like screens hanging approximately 3.05 m (10 ft) below the surface. The dolphins used separate sets of alternative cubes: Bob's set of cubes were positioned on one side of the coral mound, while Toby's cubes were positioned on the opposite side. The front and side faces of each cube were covered by plastic sheeting, concealing the stimuli from the trainer's and dolphin's view, while the top, bottom and back faces of the cube were open, to allow access for changing the alternatives. The dolphin's task was again to station in front of the alternative which matched the sample. The morphology of the dolphin's response was judged by a scuba diver, positioned behind the cubes, who was blind to the identity of the S+. The experimenter

Set Name	Stimuli in Set*	Dimension(s) Required	Order Presented To Bob	Toby
Training				
Initial Set	Steel Grill Chain-link HC WSC	Any two	—	—
Novel Transfers				
A	CSG CHU WSG	Material plus one	1st	5th
B	CSC WSU WHU	Solid/Hollow plus one	2nd	4th
C	MSC MSU CHC	Shape plus one	3rd	3rd
D	MSP WSP WHC	Material plus one	4th	2nd
E	MHU CSP CSU	Shape plus one	5th	1st

Table 2 Presentation of stimulus sets during matching concept training.
* See codes in Table 1.

viewed the session from the surface or from the underwater observation deck in the guest area. Based on the diver's decision, the experimenter told the trainer whether the dolphin was correct or incorrect. The trainer then reinforced the dolphin appropriately. The experimenter recorded the outcome of the trial, and then signaled the diver to change the configuration of alternatives for the next trial.

To train an abstract "matching" concept, we employed a technique originally developed by Harlow (1949) called the learning set approach for concept formation. This technique has been used successfully in many of the matching studies referenced earlier. In the learning set method, the subject is initially presented with a limited set of stimuli in the experimental paradigm. After the subject achieves some criterion level of performance with this training set, a second set of stimuli are presented. Concept formation is characterized by a decrease in the number of errors made before reaching criterion performance with these new stimuli. The subject's ability to transfer performance to novel stimuli provides evidence for the acquisition of an abstract concept (i.e., one which operates independently from any particular exemplar of a given problem).

Table 2 shows the sets of stimuli that were presented to the dolphins during the matching training. Each set contained three stimuli. Individual sets were structured so that the dolphins could not base their discriminations on any single stimulus dimension for the set. For example, in the initial training set two of the stimuli were the same shape, two were made of the same material and two of the stimuli were solid, while one was hollow. This set structure helped to ensure that the dolphins attended to each of the three stimulus dimensions at some point in their training. The same initial training set was used with both dolphins. Following the training set, the dolphins were presented with five transfer sets, presented in a counter balanced fashion to control for order effects.

To simplify the matching problem during the concept acquisition phase of the training, the dolphins were presented with only two alternative stimuli on each trial. There were therefore six possible combinations of alternatives for each set of three stimuli, and 12 possible trial types, depending on which of the two alternatives was the S+. Trials were presented to the dolphins so that a) within any string of 24 trials each of the 12 trial types was used at least once, b) no single stimulus was used as the S+ on more than three consecutive trials and c) the S+ never appeared in the same alternative position for more than three consecutive trials.

This pseudo-random presentation of trials was used to discourage the proliferation of alternative strategies, based on particular stimuli or spatial biases, which often prove successful for short strings of trials presented in truly random fashion. Dolphins often employ such strategies during initial training, and even short term success with them appears to promote their use.

The dolphins worked on each transfer set until they satisfied a performance criterion of 20 correct responses over 25 consecutive trials. They then moved on to the next set. For each set, the number of errors made before satisfying the performance criterion was recorded. A regression analysis was run to determine whether there was a significant decrease in the number of errors made by the dolphins as they reached criterion over successive transfer sets.

Baseline Echolocation Data

After the dolphins demonstrated their acquisition of a matching concept, the procedure was changed to include a third alternative stimulus. The use of three alternatives provided a more extensive corpus of data for the analysis of the dolphins' performance on complex echoic discriminations, and a greater opportunity to examine potential confusion between objects. Only 17 of the 18 objects from the matching training were used during the baseline data collection. A complete replication, presenting each of the objects as sample against all potential combinations of alternative objects would have required several thousand trials. Instead staff opted -to- run a partial replication. Each sample was paired against each of the other 16 objects four times. The combinations of distracters for each trial were selected randomly. A total of 544 trials were presented to each dolphin. Trials were presented to the dolphins so that within any string of 36 trials, each of the 17 objects served as the S+ at least once and so that the S+ never appeared in the same alternative position for more than three consecutive trials.

The dolphins' performance on the baseline procedure was tracked by recording the number of correct responses made over consecutive blocks of 25 trials. In addition, the dolphins' responses, including errors, were then examined using a log linear model. By examining the dolphins' errors in addition to their correct responses, it was hoped to more accurately determine the relative saliency that particular stimulus values or dimensions held for the dolphins.

Experimental sessions, consisting of five to 12 trials per dolphin and generally lasting about 40 minutes, were run once per day, five or six days per week. Guests at the Living Seas watched the experiment from underwater viewing windows on the Observation Deck, where staff members were on hand to answer questions and describe the events of research sessions. The experiment began on November 9, 1988. Pre-training and the single screen matching procedure were completed on December 29, 1988. Training the matching concept using the multiple screen procedure began on February 28, 1989. Toby reached criterion performance on his final novel object set on August 3, 1989, while Bob reached criterion on his final set on September 8, 1989. The dolphins began the baseline data collection phase of the study on May 1, 1990 and completed the procedure on September 27, 1990.

RESULTS AND DISCUSSION
Acquisition of the Matching Concept

The dolphins' performance on the novel transfer sets is presented in Figure 1. Errors to criterion are graphed as a function of successive stimulus sets. Toby and Bob reached criterion performance with the initial training set after 201 and 191 errors respectively. Training with these stimuli was completed over a period of approximately eight weeks. The dolphins' performance on subsequent transfer sets showed a considerable savings in learning, demonstrated by the reduction in the number of errors made before reaching criterion over successive sets. The regression analysis of the dolphins' performance indicated a significant decrease in the number of errors required by both dolphins to reach criterion performance across successive sets (for Toby, correlation coefficient $(r) = -0.78$, degrees of freedom $(df) = 5$, probability $(p) < 0.05$; for Bob, $r = -0.73$, $df = 5$, $p < 0.05$).

Baseline Echolocation Data

The dolphins' performance during the baseline procedure is presented in Figure 2. The number of correct responses per 25 trial block is graphed as a function of consecutive blocks. With the exception of the first block, the performance of both dolphins remained significantly above chance levels throughout the baseline procedure. A subsequent regression analysis indicated the performance of both dolphins was improving significantly over

Figure 1 Toby and Bob's acquisition of the matching concept.

Note: The number of errors made before reaching criterion performance is graphed as a function of stimulus set. Both dolphins were presented with the same initial training set (ITS), followed by the presentation of five novel stimulus sets (A-E). The novel sets were presented to the dolphins in a counter-balanced fashion to control for order effects. There was a significant decrease in the number of errors to criterion accross successive sets for both dolphins (for Toby: correlation coefficient (r) = -0.78, degrees of freedom (df) + 5, probability (p) < 0.05), indicating the succesful acquisition of the matching concept.

Figure 2 Toby and Bob's performance on the baseline matching procedure.

Note: The number of correct responses per block of 25 trials is graphed as a function of consecutive blocks. With the exception of the first block, the performance of both dolphins remained significantly above chance levels throughout the baseline procedure. A regression analysis indicated that performance of both dolphins was improving significantly over successive blocks (for Toby: correlation coefficient (r) = 0.86, degrees of freedom (df) = 20, probability (p) < 0.01; for Bob: r = -0.73, df = 20, p < 0.01). During the final third of the baseline procedure Toby responded correctly on 173 of 180 trials (95%, p < 0.001, summed binomial test), while Bob responded correctly on 146 of 182 trials (805, p < 0.001, summed binomial test).

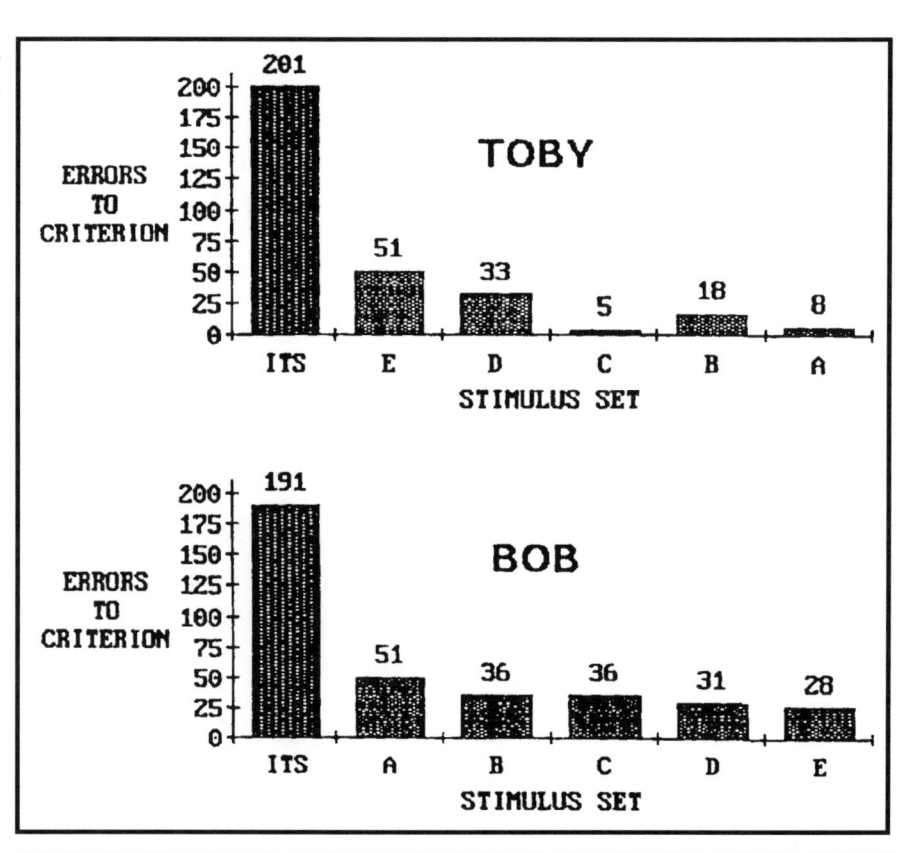

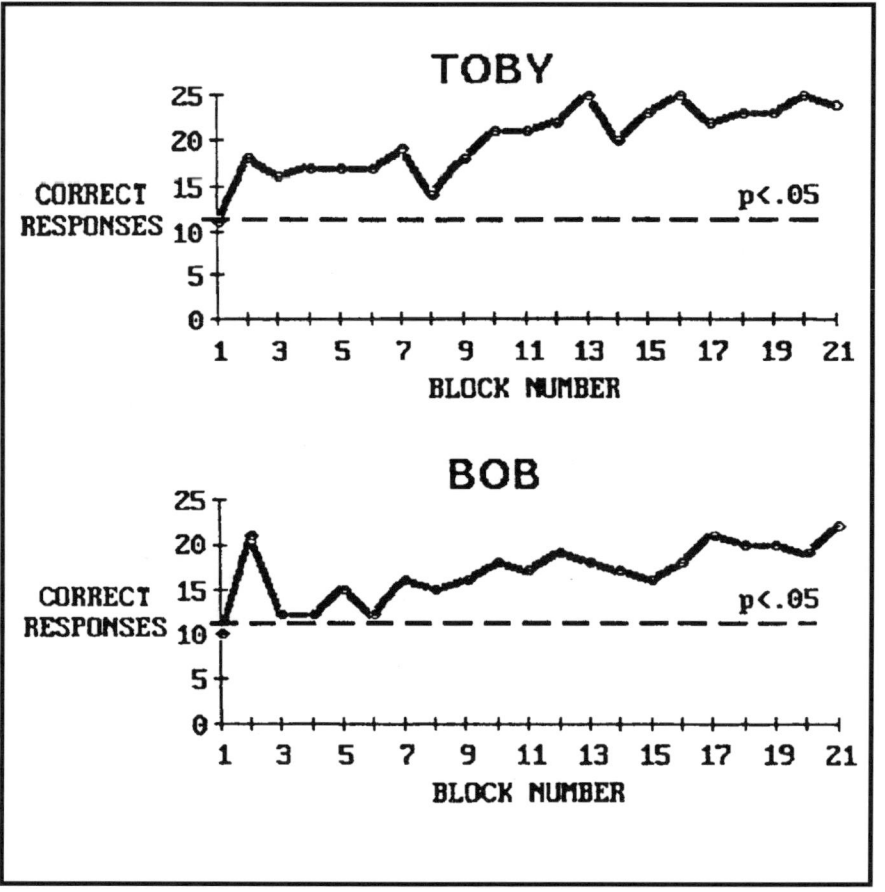

successive blocks (for Toby: r = 0.86, df = 20, p < 0.01; for Bob: r = 0.73, df = 20, p < 0.01) During the final third of the baseline procedure Toby responded correctly on 173 of 182 trials (95%, p < 0.001, summed binomial test), while Bob responded correctly on 146 of 182 trials (80%, p < 0.001, summed binomial test).

In addition, the dolphins' responses were examined, including their errors, using a log-linear model. The best fitting model showed that the dolphins' responses were based on all dimensions of the sample (i.e., shape, material, and internal structure). This simply implies that the dolphins were getting the answers right. In addition, the model indicated that Toby tended to respond to the correct shape even when he made errors. For example, when presented with a cube, Toby consistently chose a cube, although it wasn't always the correct cube. The model also showed that the dolphins were getting better on the hollow versus solid dimension over time. Perhaps this indicated that the hollow versus solid dimension was more difficult for the dolphins, and that it took them some practice to figure it out.

GENERAL DISCUSSION

The dolphins' mastery of the matching task has given our research program a flexible experimental tool for use in future studies of dolphin cognition and behavior. We have already capitalized on the dolphins' matching ability to help design and develop equipment for a communication project. Currently, we are adapting the baseline matching paradigm for use in a study which will attempt to determine whether one dolphin can listen in on another dolphin's echoic inspection of stimuli. Future studies of the dolphin's ability to integrate information across different sensory modalities will also utilize the matching task.

Participation in the research program has been the catalyst for the development of a more rigorous training program at The Living Seas. The research has taught both dolphins and trainers new skills, has provided a more variable training environment and has fostered a more sophisticated working relationship between trainers and dolphins. These developments are beneficial not only for the present research project, and others like it, but for the continuing growth of the dolphins' overall training program as well.

Our research program has become our "dolphin show." As a part of Walt Disney World and EPCOT Center, we have found ourselves to be in a unique and enviable position. We have the opportunity to present our work, and talk about dolphins, to more than six million people annually, including thousands of local Florida students who visit us on field trips. Guest reaction during our research sessions has been very positive. After only a brief explanation, the events of each trial are easily understood by our guests, who seem fascinated by the dolphins' alien capacity for echolocation. In addition, a surprising number of guests express an interest in learning more about the theory behind the study and the intricacies of the procedure. Our experience over the last two years has convinced us that the public is ready for a research-oriented presentation, and that such presentations have great potential for debunking the popular mystique surrounding these animals, while educating the public about the far more intriguing realities of dolphin behavior.

ACKNOWLEDGEMENTS

The dolphin research program at The Living Seas is funded by Wait Disney Imagineering, the research and development branch of the Wait Disney Company. I would like to thank the management of EPCOT Center and the entire staff of the Living Seas for their support and for their commitment to the development of a legitimate program of marine mammal research in the shadow of Cinderella's Castle. I would especially like to thank the members of the Marine Mammal staff for their genuine dedication to the research program, and for the openness with which they've accommodated a growing staff of visiting researchers. And lastly, I would like to thank the members of the Dive Department, and our undergraduate interns past and present, for their help in transforming the main aquarium into a working laboratory.

REFERENCES

Au, W. W. L and C. E. Hammer. 1980. *Target recognition via echolocation by the bottlenose dolphin,Tursiops truncatus.* In <u>Animal Sonar Systems</u>, ed. R. G. Busnel and J. F. Fish, 855-858. New York, NY: Plenum Press.

Au, W. W. L. and P. W. B. Moore. 1986. *The perception of complex echoes by an echolocating dolphin.* <u>The Journal of the Acoustical Society of America</u> 80 (Suppl. 1) YY8.

Au, W. W. L and P. W. B. Moore. 1984. *Receiving beam patterns and directivity indices of the Atlantic bottlenose dolphin Tursiops truncatus).* The J. of the Acous. Soc. of America 75:255-262.

Au, W. W. L., P. W. B. Moore and D. Pawloski. 1986. *Echolocation transmitting beam of the Atlantic bottlenose dolphin.* The J of the Acous. Soc. of America 80:688-691.

Au, W. W. L., R. J. Schusterman and D. A. Kersting. 1980. *Sphere-cylinder discrimination via echolocation of Tursiops truncatus.* In Animal Sonar Systems. ed. R. G. Busnel and J. F. Fish, 859-862. New York, NY: Plenum Press.

Au. W. W. L. and C. W. Turl 1983. *Target detection in reverberation by an echolocating Atlantic bottlenose dolphin Tursiops truncatus).* The Journal of the Acoustical Society of America 73:1676-1681.

Ayrapet'yants, E. S. N. and A. I. Konstantinov. 1974. *Echolocation in nature.* Nauka, Leningrad (JPRS 63328-2).

Bagdonis, A. V., M. Bel'kovich and N. L Krushinskaya. 1970. *Interaction of analyzers in dolphins during discrimination of geometrical figures.* Journal of Higher Neural Activity. 20:1070-1075. In A Collection Of Foreign Language Papers On The Subjects Of Biolog6cal Sonar System , ed. K. J. Diercks, 74-79. University of Texas, Austin: Applied Research Laboratory Tech. Rep. 1974.

Barta, R. E. 1969. *Acoustical pattern discrimination by an* Atlantic *bottlenose dolphin.* Unpublished manuscript, Naval Undersea Center, San Diego, CA.

Berryman, R., W. W., Cumming, and J. A. Nevin. 1963, *Acquisition of delayed matching in the pigeon.* Journal of the Experimental Analysis of Behavior 6:101-107.

Bullock, T. H. and V. S. Gurevich, 1979. *Soviet literature on the nervous system and psychobiology of cetacea.* International Revue of Neurobiology (21):47-127.

Caine, N. G. 1976. *Time separation pitch and the dolphin's sonar discrimination of distance.* Unpublished masters thesis, San Diego State University, San Diego, CA.

Chun, N. K. W. 1978. *Aerial visual shape discrimination and matching-to-sample problem solving ability of an Atlantic bottlenose dolphin.* Naval Oceans Systems Center, TR. 236, San Diego, CA.

D'Amato, M. R., D. P. Salmon, and M. Colombo. 1985. *Extent and limits of the matching concept in monkeys Cebus apella* Journal of Experimental Psychology, Animal Behavior Processes 11:35-51.

Evans, W. E., and B. A. Powell. 1967. *Discrimination of different metallic plates by an echolocating delphinid.* In Animal Sonar Systems, Biology and bionics ed. R. G. Busnel, (1):363-382. Jouy-en-Josas, France: Laboratorie de Physiologie Acoustique.

Fujita, K. 1983. *Formation of the sameness-difference concept by Japanese monkeys from a small number of color stimuli.* Journal of the Experimental Analysis of Behavior 40:289-300.

Hammer, C. E., and W. W. L Au. 1980. *Porpoise echo recognition., an analysis of controlling target characteristics.* Journal of The Acoustical Society of America 68:1285-1293.

Haelow, H. E. 1949. *The formation of learning sets.* Psychological Review 56:51-65.

Herman, L. M. 1980. *Cognitive characteristics of dolphins.* In Cetacean Behavior, Mechanisms and Functions, ed. L. M. Herman, 363-429. New York: Wiley-Interscience.

Herman, L. M., J. R. Hovancik, J. D. Gory and G. L. Bradshaw. 1989. *Generalization of visual matching by a bottlenose dolphin Tursiops truncatus): Evidence for invariance of cognitive performance with visual or auditory materials.* Journal of Experimental Psychology: Animal Behavior Processes 15:124-136.

Herman, L M., and R. K. R. Thompson. 1982. *Symbolic, identity and delayed matching of sounds by the bottlenose dolphin.* Animal Learning and Behavior 10:22-34.

Hunter, G. A., J. M. Osumi, J. D. Gory, H. L Roitblat, and L. M. Herman. 1987. *The bottlenose dolphin's concept of figure and ground.* Poster presented at the Seventh Biennial Conference on the Biology of Marine Mammals, Miami, Florida, December 5-9,1987.

Jerison, H. J. 1986. *The perceptual worlds of dolphins.* In Dolphin Cognition and Behavior, A Comparative Approach, ed. R. J. Schusterman, J. A. Thomas and F. G. Wood, 141-166. Hillsdale, New Jersey: Lawrence Erlbaum Associates, Inc.

Johnson, R. A. and E. L. Titlebaum. 1976. *Energy spectrum analysis., A model of echolocation processing.* Journal of the Acoustical Society of America 60:484-491.

Morgane P. J., M. S. Jacobs, and A. Galaburda. 1986. *Evolutionary morphology of the dolphin brain.* In Dolphin Cognition and Behavior, A Comparative Approach, ed. R. J. Schusterman, J. A. Thomas and F. G. Wood, 5 -30. Hillsdale, New Jersey: Lawrence Erlbaum Associates, Inc.

Morris, R. J. 1986. *The acoustic facility of dolphins.* In Research on Dolphins, ed. M. M. Bryden and R. Harrison, 369 -399. Oxford, England: Clarendon Press.

Murchison, A. E. 1980. *Detection range and range resolution of echolocating bottlenose porpoise (Tursiops truncatus).* In Animal Sonar Systems, ed. R. G. Busnel and J. F. Fish, 43-70. New York, NY: Plenum Press.

Nachtigall, P. E. 1980. *Odontocete echolocation performance on object size, shape and material.* In Animal Sonar Systems, ed. R. G. Busnel and J. F. Fish, 71-96. New York, NY, Plenum Press

Nachtigall, P. E., A. E. Murchison, and W. W. L. Au. 1980. *Cylinder and cube shape discrimination by an echolocating blindfolded bottlenose dolphin.* In Animal Sonar Systems, ed. R. G. Busnel and J. F. Fish, 945-947. New York, NY: Plenum Press.

Norris, K. S. 1980. *Peripheral sound processing in odontocetes.* In Animal Sonar Systems, ed. R. G. Busnel and J. F. Fish, 495-509. New York, NY: Plenum Press.

Premack, D. 1983. *The codes of man and beasts.* The Behavioral and Brain Sciences 6:125-167.

Premack, D. 1976. *Intelligence in ape and man.* Hillside, New Jersey: Lawrence Erlbaum Associates, Inc.

Popper, A. N. 1980. *Sound emission and detection by delphinids.* In Celacean Behavior Mechanisms and Functions, ed. L. M. Herman, *1-52.* New York: Wiley-Interscience.

Ralston, J. V. and L. M. Herman. (in press). *Dolphin auditory perception.* In The Comparative Psychology Of Complex Acoustic Perception. ed. J. R. Dooling and S. H. Hulse. Hillsdale, New Jersey: Lawrence Erlbaurn Associates, Inc.

Roitblat, H. L. 1987. *Introduction to comparative cognition.* San Francisco, CA.: Freeman.

Antiago, H. C. and A. A. Wright. 1984. *Pigeon Memory, Same/different concept learning, serial probe recognition acquisition and probe delay effects on the serial-position function.* Journal of Experimental Psychology, Animal Behavior Processes *10(4):498-512.*

Zentall. T. R., D. E. Hogan, D. E. Carter, and D. A. Eckerman. 1976. *Pigeons can learn identity difference or both.* Science *191:408-409.*

Marine Mammals: Public Display and Research

The paper presented here is interesting for several reasons. First, it describes the "two-choice paradigm" or "yes-no paradigm" that is common in many types of research. Second, the paper describes various aspects of the animals care and training beyond the actual research. Finally, it is about training manatees, which is not described in the literature very often. In fact, only a few facilities in the world house manatees, and the interest in training these animals has increased in recent years. This paper appears in Vol. 1, No. 1, 1994 of the journal *Marine Mammals: Public Display and Research.*

The Manatee Mind: Discrimination Training for Sensory Perception Testing of West Indian Manatees *(Dicheachus manatus)*

by Edmund R. Gerstein
Department of Biological Sciences . Florida Atlantic University
and
Zoological /Behavioral Consultants

ABSTRACT

In a pilot hearing study Gerstein, Patton, and Tavolga (1987) demonstrated that a captive manatee was capable of understanding discrimination tasks. Currently at the Lowry Park Zoo in Tampa and the South Florida Museum in Bradenton, several captive manatees are being trained for refined behavioral research as well as husbandry protocols.

The manatees being trained and tested show signs of complex associated learning, demonstrated through the successful conceptual transfer of generalized tasks and associated long-term memory. In a battery of two choice paradigm tests the subjects are exhibiting complex discrimination and task learning abilities on a par with dolphins and pinnipeds in similar acoustic and visual studies.

Training in a dynamic zoo setting with a community of nine manatees provides unique challenges. The animals' individual gamesmanship during training, coupled with competitive social interactions and their subtle, at times indistinguishable and deceptive behavioral indicators are discussed. Contrary to popular assumptions that manatees are impossible to motivate and train for extended behavioral studies, these manatee subjects are providing significant quantitative data on the learning and sensory abilities of this endangered species.

INTRODUCTION

The West Indian manatee is an endangered marine mammal. Though the species is of special interest and is readily observed in the wild, few behavioral studies have been undertaken. Until recently, much of the biological information available on manatees has come from morphometric and distribution surveys. Expanding radio and satellite telemetry studies are providing much needed data on manatee movements and habitat utilization (O'Shea and Kochman, 1990; Mate, Reid, and Winsor, 1987; Reid and O'Shea, 1989). With the population declining as a result of a combination of habitat degradation and direct human effects on the waterways much of the research on living animals has been focused on population biology. Little is known of how the animals perceive their environment. Questions on animal orientation, navigation, hearing, vision, taste, etc., have remained unexplored. With the exception of a few physiological evoked potential studies (Bullock, Domning, and

Best, 1980; Bullock, O'Shea, and McClune, 1982; Klishin, Diaz, Popov, and Supin, 1990) and our pilot study (Gerstein et al., 1987) no controlled quantified tests had been undertaken to measure the sensory abilities of these animals. These sensory questions are not only of academic interest but could prove vital to conservation and protection efforts.

MANATEES CAN BE TRAINED

Gerstein, Patton, and Tavolga (1987), first documented and quantified the frequency discrimination abilities of a captive manatee (Snooty). Using a simple two choice paradigm the subject was trained to discriminate between two submerged paddles: pushing one if it detected an underwater tone or the other paddle if no tone was detected. Remote event switches on paddles insured the reliable recording of test selections, while double blind and randomized on/off acoustic presentations served as precautions against experimenter bias and "Clever Hans" variants. This pilot study demonstrated the animal's discrimination abilities and indicated that manatees had greater sensitivity to lower frequencies than previous physiological evoked potential studies had measured.

The discrimination and task learning abilities demonstrated by Snooty helped to dispel commonly held professional skepticism that manatees were dull-witted and impossible to train for extended sensory or cognitive studies.

Since this pilot study, extended sensory studies on audition, memory, and pattern recognition are being conducted with Snooty at the South Florida Museum (SFM) in Bradenton, and with Stormy and Dundee at the Lowry Park Zoo (LPZ), in Tampa, Florida.

Data from more than 3000 trials and hundreds of hours of observation have been accumulated. These studies are currently in progress, and though the preliminary data is significant for the frequencies and conditions tested, results are still incomplete. Discussions of training are presented at this time.

HEARING RESEARCH RATIONALE

Defining the manatees' hearing range and overall acoustical sensitivity could prove essential to our basic understanding and protection of this endangered animal. Manatees have the physical prowess to evade boats yet many individual manatees bare the scars of repeated encounters with boats. If manatees have a sensory disadvantage in hearing or detecting the location of boats this basic research will provide valuable information which could be applied to help protect manatees in the wild. Results of this work will also provide additional insight into the effects which boat noise may have on the manatees' ability to hear intraspecies signals, localize sound sources, and navigate accordingly.

VISION AND TACTILE RATIONALE

In some of the literature, manatee vision is assumed to be poor (Wall, 1967); however, the animals' visual performance indicates otherwise. They can follow dynamic stimuli and preliminary information indicates that they can recognize shape, size, and pattern differences, as well as individual trainers. The subjects in training are accurate at detecting large visual forms and dynamic stimuli in low light conditions both above and below the water.

While some captive dolphins appear to cautiously approach new objects placed in their pool, captive manatees fearlessly approach such objects in the water. Perhaps in these situations dolphins are choosing to acoustically and or visually scan objects from a distance, while the manatees may simply need to utilize a different set of modalities to investigate objects. Once manatees swim to a new object they readily "mouth" or hold objects up to their pectoral region with their pectoral flippers. The facial vibrissae or bristles associated with the mouth are used extensively to investigate other manatees, manipulate food, and investigate their surroundings. This aggressive exploratory behavior may be the result of the animals' having, and possibly relying on, a well-developed tactile modality. The manatees' extensive musculature and specialized neurologic development associated with the mouth and facial vibrissa further denotes the animals' tactile sensory commitment.

Though physiological tests (Bullock, Domming, and Best, 1980; Bullock, O'Shea, and McClune, 1982; Klishin, Diaz, Popov, and Supin, 1990) and morphological calibrations (Cohen, Tucker, and O'Dell, 1982; Reep, Johnson, Witzer, and Welker, 1989, Johnson, Reep, Switzer, Kirsch, and Welker, 1989) have given us valuable insight into the species' potential, the sensory capabilities of the endangered West Indian manatee have yet to be determined. For a detailed bibliography on this subject see (Patton, Gerstein, Domning, Sutherland, and Perinetti, in press). Though the manatee may utilize vision, audition, tactile, and chemoreception senses, we do not know which sensory modality or weighted combination of modalities the manatee employs to navigate through the waterways. Further defining the sensory constraints of these modalities and how they integrate together to affect the manatees' perception and behavior will benefit current conservation efforts (Gerstein et al., 1987).

COGNITION RATIONALE

Though manatees appear to lack the traditional selection pressures which favor complex cognitive skills, such as threat of predation, cooperative hunting, and a recognized strong social organization, they appear to have simple to complex cognitive understanding of various discrimination tasks. The animals can execute yes and no (same-different) responses and perform matching to sample discriminations (Gerstein et al., 1987; Patton and Gerstein, 1992; D. Woodward, personal communication). The animals' ability to make cognitive choices and remember associations could prove essential to their survival in a rapidly changing environment. Manatees are long-lived and cumulative experiential learning may have always played a role in evolving higher than expected cognitive abilities. The sensory studies underway may provide further insight into the richness of this unknown mind.

Concurrent research on comparative neuroanatomy and brain morphology is finding supportive indices which compliment the acoustic discrimination and learning abilities these manatees are demonstrating (W.I. Welker, personal communication).

AGGRESSIVE BEHAVIOR

In contrast to wild populations, manatees in captivity at the LPZ appear to have strong social tendencies. I have documented organized and sustained group aggression against individuals, as well as competition, exhibited by vertical displacement, and food stealing between individuals. The social behavioral requisites for higher order cognitive abilities in manatees appear magnified in the captive community of males at the Lowry Park Zoo. The animals exhibit stable ordered relationships, male dyad and triads. They also have heightened aggressive chases with biting (mouth pinching), grasping, and tail fluke and pectoral slapping.

SUBJECTS

Stormy and Dundee, both captive-born, seven-year-old males, are housed at the LPZ. During the selection process at LPZ, I had the opportunity to work with two other manatees before choosing Stormy and Dundee--Hurricane, a nine-year-old captive born male, and Gene, a wild rehabilitated male, age unknown. Stormy was the first animal trained for these experiments and is in the testing phase of the pure tone audiogram. Dundee is the second animal currently being trained for these experiments.

Snooty, the first manatee I ever trained, is housed at the SFM, and is currently being tested for acoustic sequential matching of pure tone frequencies, visual pattern recognition, and long-term memory.

FACILITIES AND INFLUENCE ON BEHAVIOR

Two distinctly different facilities are available for these studies.

The Lowry Park Zoo (LPZ), is a new multi-pool exhibit and rehabilitation facility, which currently houses nine manatees. It consists of two large irregular-shaped exhibit pools (100,000 to 130,000 gallons). The pools have five to eight large underwater viewing panels, and irregular surface and bottom contours with rocks, ledges, logs, and other animals, such as turtles and birds The pools range from four to ten feet in depth. Long channels connect the two exhibit pools with three thirty-five foot diameter holding pools in the back area.

Separation of animals in this facility was hampered by heavy channel gates; these gates were eventually replaced with maneuverable drop gates. The size of the facility and the social mix of animals provides an enriched and dynamic environment. The complexity of this environment creates different challenges to focusing the animals' attention on the trainer and the specific learning tasks. Dominant sexual activity among males at the LPZ precipitates low levels of harassment such as undesired mounting, holding, mouthing (grubbing) or mouth pinching (biting with their bony palate), and anal penetration. However, the majority of male-to-male sexual activity is non-aggressive, and is solicited and reciprocated by all the captive males at the LPZ.

Desired intra-species social comforts are the strongest competitive distraction the trainer must contend with. Though the manatees are interested in the trainer and actually solicit underwater and surface contact, inter-species water work does not adequately satisfy the manatees need for social contact. While socialization via water work has had limited results, over correction techniques of shifting greater numbers of animals (2-3) together and providing test subjects full access to other animals when not in training or testing has reduced the strength of the manatees' social bonds. Working an animal on husbandry or control behaviors in full view of other animals also creates a competitive environment which effectively motivates the animals and has facilitated training progress.

The South Florida Museum has housed the same individual manatee, Snooty, for more than forty years. Born and orphaned in captivity, he has never been in contact with other manatees. The facility is a small 20' x 12' x 5' (6. 1 m x 3.6m x 1.5m) tile pool, and before I initiated training there were no underwater structures or physical enrichments (modular structures, rocks, scratching surfaces, or added novelties, toys, etc.). In comparison with the Lowry Park Zoo, this pool is quite spartan. The control aspects of this environment could be considered analogous to that of a simple Skinner Box. The pool is indoors with artificial lighting which can also be controlled. Training an isolated animal in such a controlled environment has enabled me to focus and motivate the animal very quickly. Criteria of 80% correct for twenty trials per session for higher order discriminations were reached in significantly shorter time by this animal than by the other manatees (Figure 1). Environment and life history are the most ominant factors influencing such dramatic differences in the learning of higher ordered discrimination tasks. Special care has been taken to train this animal to accept changes to his environment. Though his physical environment is sterile in relation to LPZ, his psychological, well-being has been attended to through a myriad of social interactions with his attentive handlers. Since the addition of behavior enrichments, training and maintaining discrimination tasks has become more challenging, as Snooty has developed new elaborate avoidance behaviors or games. Six years ago when I first trained him for a pilot study he was socially and environmentally deprived. He was extremely easy to motivate, and

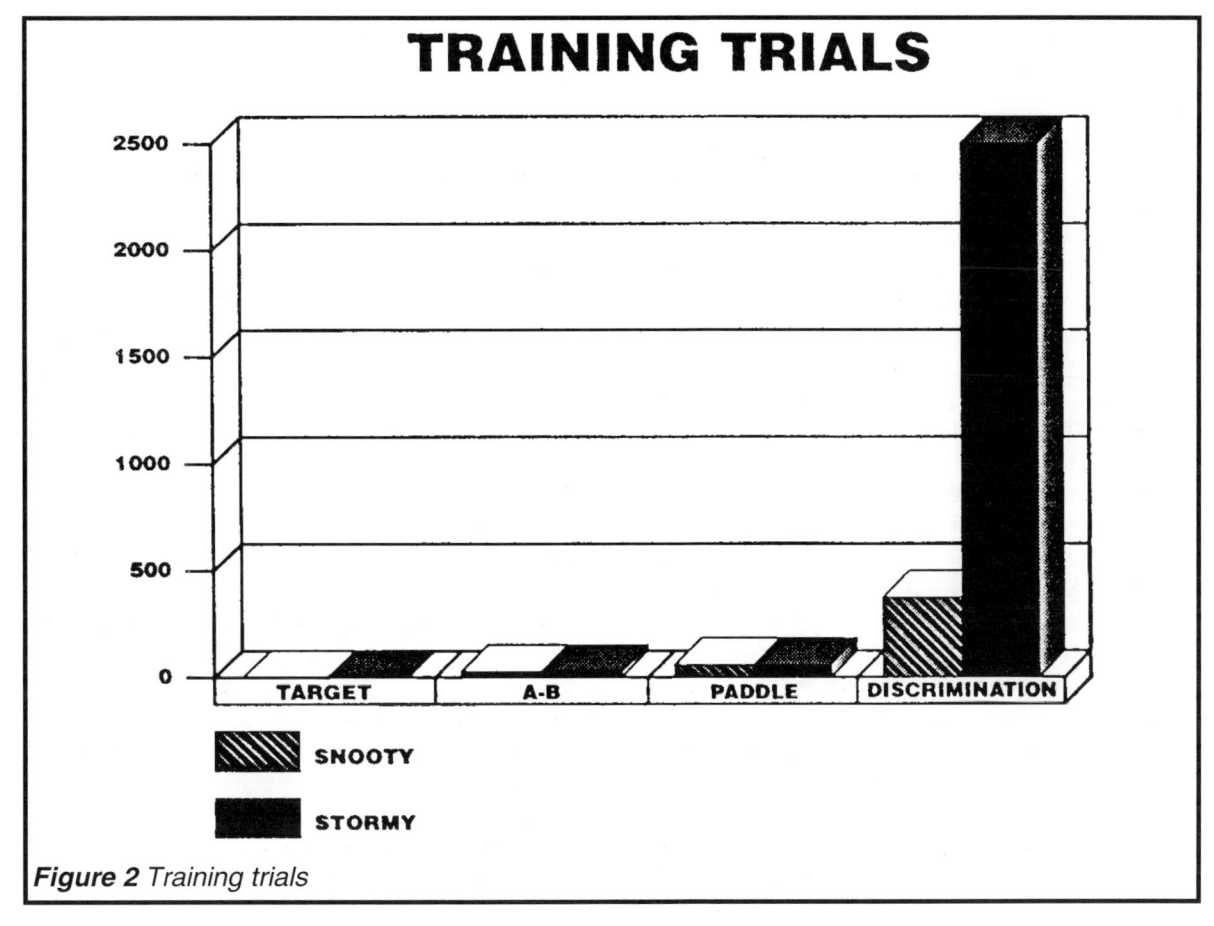

Figure 2 Training trials

learning was unencumbered by other competitive elements such as social interaction, play toys, light changes, different types of foods, and other trained behaviors. With the subsequent enrichments and attention which has followed, he has since become more independent. Though he remains a good subject, he is now more challenging to motivate.

REINFORCERS

Each subject receives up to 100 lbs. (45.5 kg) of romaine lettuce per day mixed with carrots, vitamins, and hydroponic sprouts. Preferred food items are reserved for training and testing periods; however, even lettuce can sometimes be used effectively as a reward. The manatees may have lettuce all around them, but to receive the item from the trainer is sometimes more desirable.

A variety of food rewards have been offered and tried on these animals. The most convenient and universally accepted of which is monkey chow. It should be noted that each individual animal has different preferences at varying times and it is advisable to be prepared with alternative food reinforcers in order to offer the animal a choice following bridging. I have had good success with apple and pineapple slices, bananas, water hyacinths, sprouts, hydroponic combinations, carrots, and whole fish (both smelt and capelin).

Other reinforcers include body rub downs, scratching (using the claw end of a hammer), pushing play, mouthing toys, fresh-water hose, vibrissae massage, gentle and rough caressing, slaps, water work, target touches, stationing barrel roll, body presentations, and other trained behaviors.

To avoid motivational problems due to feeding schedules, preferred food items are used exclusively during training and testing sessions. Experience has demonstrated that even with rafts of lettuce floating on the surface, manatees will still work for preferred food items.

HUSBANDRY BEHAVIORS

During the training period, control behaviors have been instituted as behavioral tools to maneuver the animals about and to keep them motivated throughout the training and testing period. Many spin-offs from the research training can be incorporated into the overall husbandry activities of the facility which house these animals. These animal are being trained for separations, fluke and flipper presentations, as well as genital presentations for future artificial insemination work.

TEST PROCEDURES

A two-paddle choice paradigm is used for testing manatee sensory abilities. My reason for a two-choice paradigm is to insure that energy requirements for the selection tasks are equal. A two-choice paradigm requires an equal demonstrative action to indicate the animal's understanding, in contrast to the go/no go paradigm. When measuring responses of marine mammals, experience has indicated that the go/no go paradigm works more effectively with more vigorously active animals such as dolphins and sea lions. Furthermore, preference for one behavior over another, such as stationing verses paddle-pushing, is avoided with the two-choice test.

The unambiguous paddle presentation facilitates a short discrimination training period (Gerstein et al., 1987). After establishing a reliable behavioral baseline for accurate paddle selections @ 80%, tests are run to quantify the hearing sensitivity, pattern recognition, memory, and sequential matching-to-sample. During the "Same-Different," experiments, a stripped paddle indicates "Different" while a white paddle indicates a "Same" discrimination.

All tests are double-blind presentations of randomized on/off, same/different trials using a modified Gellerman series. During testing, the paddles are unmanned to insure against inadvertent cueing. At the LPZ the paddles are far enough from each other that a simple touch indicates an animal's selection. The information is entered immediately on a computer. At the SFM the paddles are closer to one another so when pushed with sufficient force, electronic sensors on the paddles record the subject's choice remotely.

APPARATUS

For the acoustic tests, a stationing hoop is secured at mid-water depth, positioned two mete (6 ft.) from the transducer. A USRD H56 hydrophone (Groves, 1974) is suspended above the stationing ring to monitor the sound pressure levels and ambient noise. The stationing position insures the subject's head is the center of the projector's sound field. Two distinctly different PVC armatures are positioned on either side of the transducer. A timed strobe light releases the animal from the station after a signal or non signal has been delivered. The set-up is for the visual experiments and requires only the two paddle armature presentation and a screen presentation box at the other end of the pool.

STIMULUS

A specially configured 486 computer modified with an Aiel DSP board and Alligator Technologies multi-pass filter generates and records signals from I Hz to 50kHz. The computer is a dedicated machine designed to generate the pure tone sine waves, broad and narrow-band noise, as well as digitally store and reproduce wild noise. It will attenuate the signals and noise in prescribed Db increments, and gate rise/fall rates, monitor output signals, plot spectrums, control the release strobe and record paddle selections. The computer is the control box and signal generator in one portable unit. Having a dedicated machine makes training, testing, and real-time analysis possible. One machine alleviates the necessity of setting up a control box, independent oscillators, filters, relays, wave and noise generators, and attenuators. The signal-controlling electronics is housed in the manatee research gallery. The operator can see the animal underwater through a screen blind. Signal output is sent through a 1200 watt amplifier to one of two possible underwater transducers. For the infrasonic and lower frequencies of l0Hz to 50Hz, a modified USRD J-13 (Groves, 1974) underwater transducer is used. For the higher frequencies, a modified USRD J-9 (Groves, 1974) projects frequencies from 40Hz to 40kHz. The transducers are suspended at mid-depth, in-line with the subjects head station position at a distance of 2 meters (6 ft.).

A USRD H56 hydrophone, Rockland multi-pass filter, and dual trace oscilloscope record both ambient noise and sound pressure levels of test signals. The received signals and background noise are recorded and time stamped with a digital recorder.

At the start of each trial, the trainer/experimenter sends the manatee to station in the ring using a visual hand cue. The trainer/experimenter on the platform and researcher at the computer signal controller (keyboard) communicate with headsets. When the manatee is stationing in position, the trainer/experimenter initiates computer-controlled trials.

CURRENT PERFORMANCE

Stormy, a naive animal, learned to perform acoustic discrimination tasks with the associated stationing components in only six months of training. The two-paddle discrimination task of successfully recognizing the tone vs. no-tone paddle without the associated stationing chain of behaviors required 2500 trials to reach 80% or higher criteria for correct responses.

Training Stormy in the back pool at LPZ was initiated, knowing that the rigorous testing of his hearing would need to be conducted in the large enriched exhibit pool where the acoustic environment could be adequately controlled and monitored. His training from the onset was to prepare him for this eventual transfer. Paddles were moved about the training pool, stationing rings and spatial orientation shifts were employed throughout his training in the back pool. The transfer of the two-choice paradigm test and procedural chain of behaviors to the exhibit pool required additional equipment and a shift in spatial orientation. Upon the move to the main pool - context shift effects appeared minimal as Stormy successfully transferred the chain of behaviors and end discrimination task reaching a consistent criteria of 80% or higher for correct selections in less than ten sessions.

Snooty learned the same two-choice discrimination task, without the stationing components, six years ago in less than 400 trials over two weeks. He successfully completed a pilot study on hearing and, though his life has been enriched with increased interaction from the staff at the SFM, he was never given the opportunity to push on or see paddles since 1986. In August of 1992, Snooty successfully recognized the hand signal for paddle push during a single trial test and immediately pushed a single paddle at the opposite end of his pool. He has since been tested on the two-choice paradigm "yes-no" discrimination and has reached criteria of 80% in only forty trials done in two sessions. The original discrimination six years previously had required 400 trials. This is the first indication of long-term memory of a specific task in manatees. At this time he is learning matching-to-sample tasks for delayed short-term memory testing to follow.

The manatees' repertoire of discernable behaviors is best characterized as a gradation of intensity. Changes in intensity of swimming, head movements, grubbing, barrel rolling, scratching, breathing, squeaky vocalizations, and vibrissae extension can signal an individual's mood or motivation; however, it takes time to recognize these subtleties. Manatees offer limited facial cues and their eyes are usually cloudy and unexpressive. Their body language is rather "unibodied," although the intensity of arch, bends, and characteristic barrel rolls can telegraph an animal's intentions (slow being benign and faster being antagonistic). Despite limited overt behavioral indicators, the animals are moody and very deliberate in their behavior.

"Gamesmanship," as I define it, refers to an individual animal's strategy to achieve or maintain a desired position, be it a physical or psychological status. A game is created when the animal offers avoidance and or strings of inappropriate behaviors for known command signals (or stimuli). If the trainer continues the session the game can escalate. If the animal is skilled, or the trainer particularly unskilled, the game may go undetected. The reward is prolonged interaction with the trainer while being disobedient. The object is to maintain the interaction without fully cooperating, but to be subtle enough not to cause termination of the session (or game). Different levels of avoidance behaviors are used by animals during all forms of training. Most animals desire some control over their situation and, depending upon a trainer's criteria, certain levels or forms of control avoidance or disobedience are considered "healthy" and are tolerated. However, these occurrences may need to be checked periodically to reestablish or maintain a defined level of control or discipline to keep dominance trends from escalating. Animals can develop very subtle and cryptic behavior to try to avoid thresholds of detection which might result in a shut-down (or termination of a session) by the trainer. It is through these subtleties where the animals reveal their gamesmanship skills.

Low level avoidance behaviors associated with gamesmanship exhibited by manatees as well as other mammals can include typical head bending or turning, eye closing, and ignoring hand or tonal signals while still stationing in front of the trainer (the old "whad ya say?" "I didn't see that." tactic). It's an avoidance behavior which may work to get a repeated signal at least once in a session. A second level of avoidance is to do a different behavior slowly or the appropriate behavior lethargically, slowly drifting away from the trainer. This behavior can sometimes result in a control tap or wake-up response from the trainer and a repeated signal. A third level avoidance behavior may be to perform an incorrect response and then routinely return to the trainer. This third level is where gamesmanship becomes challenging and difficult to recognize in discrimination training. The manatees I have been training for discrimination tasks have, successfully at times, prolonged discrimination sessions by appearing not to understand discrimination tasks. Deciding if the animals were genuinely confused or just playing was at first difficult to ascertain. Their responsiveness remained constant, and no overt avoidance behaviors were displayed during sessions. Though the animals had previously reached criteria, they appeared to be genuinely confused. Eventually the animals revealed themselves by being too overt or inconsistent in their inappropriate responses. Applying a fixed schedule of timed sessions alleviated the decisions of game or no game, and sessions would be over in fifteen minutes regardless of an animas' performance. The setting of fixed training durations ended the discrimination difficulties quickly.

PERFORMANCE COMPARISONS

When comparing learning rates for discrimination tasks between individual animals it soon becomes evident that variables such as environmental setting, competitive distractions, and the life histories and training experiences of the individuals can dramatically effect the subjects' progress. All five manatees learned to target, then go, A to B, and also paddle-push with the same proficiency for these simple behaviors. However, Snooty reached 80% criteria on the higher ordered two-paddle discrimination task in only 400 trials, as compared to Stormy who required 2500 trials. No doubt environmental factors are significant.

Both manatees learned the concept of conditional right/wrong in as many or less trials than some sea lions and dolphins have in go/no-go paradigms. Though their learning elucidates aspects of higher order cognition, cross-comparisons between species are difficult to measure reliably. The variables associated with different trainers and environments are unmanageable. Success in training for refined discriminations tasks requires the trainer to force the animal to think throughout the process. Training the animals to think, might be synonymous with training the animals to attend to, as well as accept and deal with change. This can be accomplished by shifting the orientation and selection of discrimination items, and presenting objects to the anima in such a manner that the animal has to shift or modify its position to get a better vantage view o the objects. The trainer can provide challenges to the animals which they must then work through. For instance, physical obstacles can foster creative problem solving by forcing the animal to swim or climb over an object to reach a specific point in order to complete a task. These obstacles can be simple physical or positional changes in the animals' environment or more sophisticated "dynamic mazes" which require an animal to first open a gate or move a barrier to enter a pool in order to select a discrimination paddle.

UNLOCKING POTENTIAL

The cognitive potential of many animals can be unlocked through careful training and employing the animal's full range of senses to help make the discrimination process easier. With regard to the manatee, visual pattern disruption (black and white paddle vs. solid white) and acoustic and tactile information (paddles different shape and texture) are provided to help make discriminations less ambiguous.

Trainers should always remain flexible on criteria. A key to capitalizing on concept recognition events with the subjects is to be prepared to be opportunistic even if a preset criteria has not been satisfied. Criteria building is a measure of accomplished proficiency; however, the moment of recognition must be rewarded with an acceleration of choices, sometimes before standards of criteria are realized. Demonstrative scales of proficiency will come; however, it is the realization event which keeps the animal thinking--and the trainer needs to react quickly to these occurrences. Stormy successfully transferred his hearing discrimination tasks from the back pool to the exhibit pool and reached criteria of 80% correct in only ten sessions. It should be noted that I did not wait for him to reach consistent criteria in the back pool before moving him out front (he was ready). The change at the right moment set the stage for generalized transfer to the discrimination of pulsed tones in the main exhibit pool. Stormy has since run 2000 successful threshold trials, providing accurate data on manatee hearing for the frequencies tested so far.

ACKNOWLEDGEMENTS

The hearing research is funded by the U.S. Army Corps of Engineers, Waterways Experiment Station, Vicksburg, Mississippi; Florida Inland Navigational District, Jupiter Florida; the Florida Department of Natural Resources, Tallahassee, Florida; with additional technical support from the U.S. Naval Research Laboratory, Underwater Sound Reference Detachment. The hearing research on Stormy and Dundee is authorized by the U.S. Fish and Wildlife, Office of Management Authority, Washington, D. C., Endangered Species Research Permit PRT-761873.

I wish to express appreciation to the anonymous peer reviewers whose comments and suggestions help make this unorthodox communication a bit more presentable. Lex Salisbury, General Curator, and Dave Murphy, Staff Veterinarian, at the Lowry Park Zoo, Tampa, Florida for providing the unique opportunity and tremendous facility support to conduct the manatee hearing research; Jennifer Hamilton, Curator and Carol Audett, manatee keeper at the South Florida Museum, Bradenton, Florida for providing the first and continued opportunity to train and learn from Snooty; Geoffrey Patton, Anthony Finney, Susie Tapia, and Amy and Art Baum, research assistants; and to my multi-talented wife and friend, Laura Gerstein, who with her steadfast support, organizational skills, excellent animal training insights, and selfless sacrifice makes all things possible.

LITERATURE CITED

Bullock, T.H., D.P. Domning, and R.C. Best, (1980). Evoked brain potentials demonstrate hearing in a manatee *(Sirenia Trichechus inunguis)*. J. Mammalogy 61:130-133.

Bullock, T.H., T.J. O'Shea, and M.C. McClune, (1982). Auditory evoked potentials in the West Indian manatee *(Sirenia Trichechus manatus)*. J. Comp. Physiology 148:547-554.

Cohen, J.L., G.S. Tucker, and D.K. Odell, (1982). The photoreceptors of the West Indian manatee. Journal of Morphology 173:197-202.

Gerstein, E.R., G.W. Patton, and W.N. Tavolga, (1987). Preliminary underwater acoustic thresholds of a captive manatee, *Trichechus manatus*, a quantitative behavioral approach. *Proceedings of the Seventh Biennial Conference on the Biology of Marine Maninials*, Miami, Florida, December 5-9.

Groves, I.D., (1974). Twenty years of underwater electroacoustic standards. Naval Reference Lab. Rep. 7735, NRL/USRD, P.O. Box 8337, Orlando, Florida.

Johnson, J.I., R.L. Reep, R.C. Switzer 111, J.A.W. Kirsch, W.I. Welker, (1989). Well-developed auditory nuclei in manatees, *Trichechus manatus*. Society for Neuroscience Abstracts 14(l), p.491. 18th Annual Meeting, Toronto, Ontario, Canada, November 13-18.

Klishin, V.O., P. Diaz, V.V. Popov, and A.Y. Supin, (1990). Some characteristics of hearing of the Brazilian manatee, *Trichechus inunguis*. Aquatic Mammals 15.3:139-144.

Mate, B.R., J.P. Reid, and M. Winsor, (1987). Long-term tracking of manatees through the Argos satellite system. In *Proceedings of the Argos International Users Conference* (pp. 211220). Landover, Maryland: Service Argos, Inc..

O'Shea, T.J. and H.I. Kochman, (1990). Florida manatees: distribution, geographically referenced data sets, and ecological and behavioral aspects of habitat use. In J.E. Reynolds, 111, and K.D. Haddad, (Eds.), Report of the Workshop on Geographical Information Systems as an Aid to managing Habitat for West Indian manatees in Florida and Georgia (pp. 11-12). Florida Marine Research Publications 49:1-57.

Patton, GW and E.R. Gerstein, (1992). Toward understanding mammalian hearing tractability: preliminary acoustic perception thresholds in the West Indian manatee, *Trichechus manatus*. In D.B. Webster, A.N. Popper and R.R. FAy-(Eds.), *Evolutiohan, biology of hearing* (p.783). Proceedings of the First International Conference on the Evolutionary Biology of Hearing, Sararsota, Florida May 20-24, 1990. New York: Springer-Verlag.

Patton, G.W., E.R. Gerstein, D.P. Domning, M. Sutherland, and R. Perinetti, (in press). U.S. Army Corps of Engineers Technical Publication. **An Annotated Bibliography of Sirenian Hearing.***

Reep, R.J., J.I. Johnson, R.C. Witzer, and W.l. Welker, (1989). Manatee cerebral cortex: cytoarchitecture of the frontal region in *Trichechus manatus latirostris*. Brain, Behavior, and Evolution 34:365-386.

Reid, J.P. and T.J. O'Shea, (1989). Three years operational use of satellite transmitters on Florida manatees: tag improvements based on challenges from the field. In *Proceedings of the 1989 North American Argos Users Conference and Exhibit* (pp. 217-232). Landover, Maryland: Service Argos, Inc..

Walls, G.L, (1967). **The vertebrate eye.** New York: Hafner.

*This manuscript contains over 90 summarized publications referencing Sirenian auditory behavior, hearing, and related anatomy and physiology. Requests for copies should be sent to Gerstein, c/o of Florida Atlantic University or Zoological/ Behavioral Consultants.

Conference Proceedings

1991 IMATA Conference, Vallejo, California, USA. This paper describes a planned research project before training had begun. It was presented so as to get feedback from trainers at the conference. The abstract approach to this project met with quite a bit of interest and, as usual, some skepticism. However, it is creative ideas like these that continually challenge our animals and can open the door to many new concepts. Additionally, the three creative authors are at the forfront of cognitive research with marine mammals today. A domain that was once dominated primarily by the work of Lou Herman (dolphins) and Ron Schusternan (sea lions), cognitive studies with marine mammals are being conducted by many very talented scientists. At the time of the publication of this book, Mark had moved his research to the Navy's program, John was continuing at EPCOT, and Stan was working with Sea World while maintaining his affiliation with SMU.

An Introduction to the Living Sea's Dolphin Keyboard Communication System

by Mark J. Xitco Jr.[1], John D. Gory[1], and Stan A. Kuczaj II[2]
[1]The Living Seas, EPCOT Center
and
[2]Department of Psychology, Southern Methodist University

ABSTRACT

The dolphin keyboard communication system represents a new approach for interacting with dolphins. This project is modeled after a recent successful artificial language project with pygmy chimpanzees. A large, underwater keyboard serves as the communication medium between humans and dolphins. Each key contains a unique multidimensional symbol. Symbols refer to agents, objects, actions, locations, modifiers, or grammatical markers. Utterances are created by activating sequences of keys according to a specified grammar. Dolphins will learn to comprehend the symbols by observing humans modeling proper usage of the communication system within a social context. Using the keyboard, dolphins and humans can make requests or describe daily routines such as foraging for food, playing with toys, and using tools.

LIVING SEA'S DOLPHIN KEYBOARD

Today we'd like to introduce you to a project that we've been developing at The Living Seas for the past two years. We call it our Dolphin Keyboard Communication System. It is an alternative approach for interacting with dolphins, a system for research and training, for work and play. We have two related sources of motivation for this project. One is theoretical and the other practical. On a theoretical level, we have designed the system to assess our dolphins' abilities to utilize a symbol system to communicate more effectively with humans. We intend to examine their level of sophistication in using the system, looking for evidence of protolinguistic symbol usage. On a practical level, we also feel that the system holds much promise as a more sophisticated method of communicaton - between dolphins and their trainers. We ore sure that, like us, many people here have felt limited in their ability to interact and communicate with their dolphins during training sessions. The ways in which trainers and dolphins can communicate with each other arc at best crude and indirect. It is amazing how well we all do at it given the limited methods currently available to us.

All training involves communication between humans and animals. In traditional reinforcement training, humans communicate their expectations and approval by using discriminative stimuli and reinforcement contingencies. An upsweep of the trainees arm sends the dolphin off on a spectacular leap, or, perhaps, the presentation of a pair of stimuli signals the dolphin to make a similarity judgement. However, this information is generally only one-way in the form of commands from trainer to animal and concerns the performance of arbitrary responses.

In contrast, our animals often appear to attempt to communicate with us and influence our behavior. An animal vocalizes as you approach, and orients towards a toy stuck in a skimmer. You remove the toy from the skimmer and toss it to the dolphin, who plays with it. However on another occasion, in the same circumstance, the dolphin shows no interest in the toy when you throw it to him. As an even more ambiguous example, picture that in the midst of a training session a dolphin squawks and jaw claps at the trainer for no apparent reason. The information offered by the animals in these types of situations is often not very specific and is quite limited in scope. What was it that angered the dolphin in the latter case to make it squawk and jaw clap? How would we know if the dolphin in the former case wants the toy in the skimmer? Wouldn't it be desirable to have a symbol system which allows humans and dolphins to communicate more explicit information to each other about things that are important to the animals?

Previous artificial language work with dolphins at the Kewalo Basin Marine Mammal Lab (Herman, 1986, 1987; Herman, Richards, & Wolz, 1984) provides partial evidence that dolphins can learn a symbol system. The work at KBMML, which most of you are familiar with, made use of reinforcement training within a combination of symbolic matching and sequential learning paradigms to study language issues. Lou Herman and his many colleagues trained dolphins to comprehend gestural and acoustic symbols for objects, actions, and modifiers. The dolphins performance on novel and reversible symbol strings indicated an understanding of the effect of order on the interpretation of a string of symbols. Their ability to report the presence and absence of named objects provides partial evidence that the symbols may refer to objects (Herman & Forestell, 1985). In addition, the dolphin, Akeakamai, used different brain hemispheres to process symbol strings with different levels of complexity (Morrel-Samuels, Herman, Bever, & Rettig, 1989). While the degree to which this work demonstrates language-like performance will continue to be debated (Herman, 1988, 1989; Savage-Rumbaugh, in press, Schusterman, 1988, 1989), this data considered together seems to be evidence of something more than simple conditional discriminations and sequence learning, and yet less than human language.

Herman et. al.'s artificial language work used arbitrary objects and actions by design to allow objective assessment of performance, at a time when the prevailing climate surrounding animal language research was increasingly hostile amid criticisms of subjective interpretation of data by the researchers in ape language projects (for a review see Ristau & Robbins, 1982). Although this approach was fruitful, the method did not lend itself to studying some language issues because it was not conducive to communication of information pertaining to social interactions between individuals. The symbol strings functioned as commands to execute arbitrary actions with artificial objects, which outside of this context generally held little interest for the dolphins. The symbols were not used to label social interactions with trainers, which is what the dolphins seemed to be most interested in. The importance of learning to comprehend these symbol strings was probably limited to receiving a uniform reinforcement (i.e. food plus social nteraction), since comprehension had little to do with providing information useful in acquiring specific goals. The dolphins solved their symbol puzzles and discrimination games, and then got back to the real life interactions of interest, playing with humans, toys, other dolphins, and eating food. These latter interactions were governed by the same types of communication mentioned earlier and used by trainers everywhere, although Kewalo Basin trainers do make a very conscious effort to attend to and respond appropriately to the dolphins use of body movements, vocalizations, and other overt emotional signaling.

The system we've been developing is modeled after a significantly different approach. It has been most influenced by work done with chimpanzees by Sue Savage-Rumbaugh and her colleagues at the Language Research Center in Atlanta (Savage-Rumbaugh, 1988, 1991, in press; Savage-Rumbaugh, McDonald, Sevcik, Hopkins, & Rupert, 1986; Savage-Rumbaugh, Rumbaugh, & McDonald, 1985; SavageRumbaugh, Sevcik, Brakke, & Rumbaugh, 1990). Her work is designed to study symbol acquisition, referential symbol use, and symbolic communication in chimpanzees. Small, 2-dimensional lexigram symbols, arrayed on a keyboard, are used by chimps and humans to communicate about relevant interactions like finding and sharing food, playing with toys, and even doing household chores. In particular, we are modeling our approach after work done with the pygmy chimpanzee Kanzi. Kanzii learned lexigrams not through symbolic matching drills using traditional types of reinforcement, but rather, by observing humans using the symbols to communicate in a very free-form interaction about daily activities. In a typical session, Kanzi and his trainers roam through a 55 acre forest, and use symbols on a portable keyboard to discuss where they will go next, who they might visit, and where favorite food items or toys might be hidden. We have dubbed this conglomeration of activities as "a walk through the woods." Kanzi's performance far exceeds the accomplishments of animals in more traditional training paradigms. There is some evidence that Kanzi understands verbal English at the level of a young child. He produces more than a hundred lexigrams, uses them in a referential manner, and employs a simple grammar in his productions to clarify the meaning of his utterances.

Savage-Rumbaugh feels that the keys to this method's success include the use of symbols which the animals could produce, and, just as importantly, the application of symbols to label complex, non-arbitrary routines and social interactions which were self reinforcing and which the chimps desired to control. To watch Kanzi working with his trainers, Coca Cola in one hand, his other hand in a bag of Halloween candy that he had collected the night before, learning to play memory testing video games just by watching his trainers, made us very envious. It also made us ask ourselves if a similar approach could be used with dolphins. The Living Seas seemed like the perfect place to create a dolphin equivalent of the "walk through the woods." The tank is relatively large and complex because it is modeled after a Caribbean reef environment with many structures and animals of interest to the dolphins. For the past two years we've been developing a symbol system that both dolphins and humans can readily use, and we've been building a complex, self-reinforcing interaction between the dolphins and their trainers which we can describe using such symbols.

In our dolphin system the communication medium is a keyboard consisting of an irregular array of multidimensional keys. Each key is composed of a hollow plastic tube, which is open on both ends to the surrounding water to allow better echolocation of a unique 3-dimensional object mounted approximately 4 inches from the front opening of each tube. These objects function as the symbols within the communication system. The different objects are composed of a wide variety of materials, shapes and brightness. Based on visual matching to sample studies which we participated in (Herman, Hovancik, Gory, & Bradshaw, 1989), and our work at The Living Seas on echolocation with these dolphins (Xitco, 1990), we are confident that the dolphins should be able to discriminate among these symbol objects using echolocation and/or vision. We also arrayed the symbols in irregular patterns to provide spatial information to ease the discrimination of symbols. We wanted to provide as many redundant dimensions as possible in order to make the location of symbols as easy as we could for the dolphins.

The keyboard is suspended beneath a pontoon boat which houses the electronics and computer which control the keyboard and automatically record data. With the keyboard suspended beneath a boat, then it can be moved anywhere in the 200 feet diameter, 27 feet deep tank. We are currently working with the one prototype panel containing 15 keys shown in the slide. We will shortly combine that panel with three more panels on an "A" frame to give us a total of approximately 60 keys.

A symbol can be "spoken" by a dolphin or human by activating a key. An infrared sensor beam projects across the front opening of each key. The beam can easily be broken with a dolphin's rostrum or a human hand. When a sensor beam is broken, the computer turns on lights surrounding each key, thus providing immediate visual feedback as to which key was activated. As the lights turn on, the computer plays an acoustic representation of the symbol. The acoustic representations are in the form of digitized recordings of humans saying the English equivalent for the symbol,

Each time a key is activated, the identity of the symbol is recorded in a computer session file along with a time stamp giving us a complete record of everything "said" with the keyboard. An underwater observer with a SCUBA microphone makes comments about the events occur-ring during sessions with the dolphins. The observer's comments are digitized, time stamped and recorded in the data file with the key press data. The observer's comments will include the identity of the speaker activating keys each time an utterance is made by dolphin or human, as well as what events occurred before and after the key presses. This data set for each session should allow us to reconstruct the order of events and their temporal distribution. We will also be able to determine if the behavior of the dolphins bears any relation to the symbols used by either humans or dolphins. In addition, we will videotape sessions at regular sampling intervals so that we can objectively verify the reliability of our observers' comments and provide a longitudinal record for other scientists who might wish to analyze the dolphins' keyboard usage.

The set of symbols, or lexicon, is based on interactions we've established with our dolphins in our environment. The symbols will allow us to talk with the dolphins about going places in the tank, visiting others, finding food, using tools, and playing with toys. There are symbols for agents, various types of objects, locations, actions, and modifiers. The symbols are distributed randomly so that symbols in the same grammatical category are not located together in the same area on the keyboard. There are also some symbols which will function solely as grammatical markers. For example, one such key which we will add later will change the tense of the action to past tense. This would be analogous to adding the suffix "ed" to a verb. When we produce more than one symbol in an utterance, we will roughly follow syntactic conventions used by English speakers to produce sentences. However, there will also be some grammatical rules distinctly different from English. The resulting symbol strings will sound like a broken form of English. For example, imagine that I wanted to announce to our dolphin Toby my intention to go to the larger of our two underwater acrylic dive bells, which we cal igloos. In English I might say "I will go to the big igloo." In our dolphin symbol system we would say "HUMAN GO BIG IGLOO".

Our training sessions for this system will really not involve much training at all, at least not in the traditional sense of training. Humans will merely model for the dolphins how to properly use the keyboard symbols to communicate about the social activities humans and dolphins engage in together in our environment. Early on we will primarily use the symbols to announce which activities we are about to engage in. For example we might say "GO IGLOO" and then swim over to a dive bell with the keyboard following behind us. Inside the igloo there might be a diver holding a weight tool that the dolphins know how to use to open a device containing fish. We might then get the diver's attention and say "HUMAN GIVE WEIGHT" to request that the diver give the weight to us. When the diver gives it to us we might then say "USE WEIGHT" followed by "GET FOOD". We would then use the weight in-one-of the devices to obtain the fish inside. This is one of the kinds of routines that we can engage in regularly with the dolphins within this context.

During this early period when humans model proper symbol system usage, the dolphins will not be required to respond in anyway. They will simply watch humans use the system. The dolphins will voluntarily engage in the activities which follow the symbols, because the activities are themselves self reinforcing for the dolphins. They already seem to enjoy swimming about the tank with their SCUBA trainers finding food. They also seem to enjoy using their tools on their own to obtain food from various devices. Like in the pygmy chimpanzee project, we expect that overtime the dolphins will begin to learn the association between the symbols that are being used by humans and the behaviors and activities which follow. As this is happening the dolphins will also begin to experiment with the keyboard and thereby activate keys. We will not attempt to prompt the dolphins to activate keys, but rather we will wait for them to experiment on their own with the keys. At first, they will probably not understand what the symbolsrepresent on the keys they activate. Even so, the trainers will respond to this early "babbling" as if it were intentional on the dolphin's part, in a manner similar to the way human parents attribute meaning to early productions from infants. From this we expect the dolphins to learn that there are specific consequences on human behavior when specific keys are activated. The dolphins will learn that they can control and determine which activities occur by using the symbols. This is their motivation for learning the system. They can determine where we go in the tank, what we do next, which toys they can play with, when they obtain food, etc.

Early on, our utterances to the dolphins will be relatively simple containing probably only 1 to 3 symbols much like a parent might talk to a baby. As the dolphins begin to show some comprehension of our utterances and begin to produce some of their own, we will gradually increase the length and grammatical complexity of our utterances. The idea is that much of our utterances will be at a complexity which the dolphins are facile with, while some proportion will be at a slightly higher level o complexity. As the dolphins competence with increasing complexity improves we will expect them to produce or comprehend symbol strings at a their best level so far. Our utterances at the next higher level of complexity serve as models designed to pull the dolphins up to that level. At times we will act as if we do not understand exactly what the dolphin means with a symbol string in attempts to prod them into producing more complex and therefore more specific and informative utterances. For example, imagine that there ae several tools in the immediate vicinity of a dolphin and trainer. The dolphin says "GIVE" and clearly orients towards one tool, the weight. Early on in training, the trainer would likely respond by giving that tool to the dolphin. However, in a similar situation later in training after the dolphin appeared to use the single symbol, GIVE, properly, the trainer might exercise several options to prompt the dolphin into producing a more specific utterance. The trainer might give a different tool to the dolphin, or else announce his intention to give a different tool to the dolphin by producing a string like, GIVE STICK. Another option would be for the trainer to produce the string, GIVE WHAT? In each case the dolphin has the option to produce a more specific two symbol string specifying which tool it wants. For example, GIVE WEIGHT. This process of progressively increasing expectations along with maintenance of current competence levels resembles a learning process which has been described as scaffolding and used naturally by human caregivers with children acquiring language. Scaffolding may be charcterized as a sophisticated shaping process which operates during the acquisition of a symbol system, and in which the principle reinforcer is improved communication.

We intend to investigate a number of questions throughout the course of the project. In general, we want to see if the dolphins use the symbols at all. Do they use the symbols in attempts to communicate specific information to humans? Do they use them to announce their own behavior? Can they comprehend descriptions of their environment? How sophisticated can they become at comprehending and producing strings of symbols? In general, how and under what conditions do the dolphins use the system?

We are also interested to see if the dolphins learn to use the symbols in a protolinguistic manner. Will they learn to use the symbols in a referential manner? When the dolphins produce multi-symbol strings, will they use the grammatical rules which they have seen humans using? Will they invent their own rules? What kinds of errors do they make? We are sure that other questions will arise as we proceed.

We introduced the keyboard to the dolphins last week on October 31, 1991. The dolphins showed a great deal of curiosity swimming fight up to the keyboard to inspect it. They watched intently, peering over their trainer's shoulders as the humans used the keyboard for the first time to announce upcoming activities. It is much too early at this point to expect the dolphins to comprehend what the keyboard is or how the symbols function. In the weeks ahead we will be more fully integrating the keyboard into our daily expeditions into the tank. We will keep you up-dated as the project progresses.

REFERENCES

Herman, L. M. (1986). Cognition and language competencies of bottlenosed dolphins. In R. J. Schusterman, J. A. Thomas, & F. G. Wood (Eds.), *Dolphin Cognition* and behavior A comparative approach (pp. 221-252). Hillsdale, NJ: Erlbaum.

Herman, L. M. (1987). Receptive competencies of language trained animals. In J. S. Rosenblatt, C. Beer, M. C. Busnel, & P. J. B. Slater (Eds.), Advances in the study of behavior (Vol. 17, pp. 1-60). Petaluma, CA: Academic Press.

Herman, L. M. (1988). The language of animal language research: Reply to Schusterman and Gisiner. Psychological Record, 38,349-362

Herman, L. M. (1989). In which procrustean bed does the sea lion sleep tonight? Psychological Record, 39, 19-49.

Herman, L. M., & Forestell, P. H. (1985). Reporting presence or absence of named objects by a language-trained dolphin. Neuroscience and *Biobehavioral Reviews,* 9, 667-68 1.

Herman, L. M., Hovancik, J. R., Gory, J. D., & Bradshaw, G. L. (1989). Generalization of visual matching by a bottlenosed dolphin (Tursiops truncatus): Evidence for invariance of cognitive performance with visual and auditory materials. Journal of Experimental Psychology. Animal Behavioral Processes, 15, 124-136.

Herman, L. M., Richards, D. G., & Wolz J. P. (1984). Comprehension of sentences by bottlenosed dolphins. Cognition, 16, 129-219.

Morrel-Samuels, P., Herman, L. M., Bever, T. G., & Rettig, E. J. (1989). Cerebral asymmetries for gesture recognition in the dolphin. Paper presented atthe Eighth Biennial Conference on the Biology of Marine Mammals, Pacific Grove, CA.

Ristau, C. A., & Robbins, D. R. (1982). Language in the great apes: A critical review. In J. S. Rosenblatt, R. A. Hinde, C. Beer, & M. C. Busnel (Eds.), *Advances in the study of behavior (Vol* 12). New York: Academic Press.

Savage-Rumbaugh, E. S. (1988). A new look at ape language: Comprehension of vocal speech and syntax. In D. W. Leger (Ed.), Comparative perspectives *in* modem psychology. The Nebraska symposium *on* motivation, 1987, 35, 201-256.

Savage-Rumbaugh, E. S. (199 1). Language learning in the bonobo: How and why they learn. In N. Krasnegor, D. M. Rumbaugh, M. StuddertKennedy, & R. L. Schiefelbusch (Eds.), Biological and behavioral determinants of language development (pp. 209-333). Hillsdale, NJ: Erlbaum.

Savage-Rumbaugh, E. S. (in press). Language learnabilty in man, ape, and dolphin. In H. L. Roitblat (Ed.), Comparative cognition. Hillsdale, NJ: Erlbaum.

Savage-Rumbaugh, E. S., McDonald, K., Sevcik, R. A., Hopkins, W. D., & Rupert, E. (1986). Spontaneous symbol acquisition and communicative use by pygmy chimpanzees *(Pon paniscus)* Journal of Experimental Psychology: General, 115,211-235.

Savage-Rumbaugh, S., Rumbaugh, D. M., McDonald, K. (1985). Language learning in two species of apes. Neuroscience & Biobehavioral Reviews, 9, 653-665.

Savage-Rumbaugh, S., Sevcik, R. A., Brakke, K. E., Rumbaugh, D. M., & Greenfield, P. M. (1990). Symbols: Their communicative use, comprehension, and combination by bonobos (Pan paniscus). In C. Rovee-Collier & L. P. Lipsitt (Eds.), Advances in infancy research (Vol. 6, pp. 221-278). Norwood, NJ: Ablex.

Schusterman, R. J., & Gisiner, R. (1988). Artificial language comprehension in dolphins and sea lions: *The essential cognitive skills. Psychological Record.* 38, 311-348.

Schusterman, R. J., & Gisiner, R. C. (1989). Please parse the sentence: Animal cognition in the procrustean bed of linguistics. Psychological Record, 39, 3-18.

Xitco, M. J. Jr. (1990). Echolocation matching for shape, material, and internal structure. Paper presented at the Eighteenth Annual Conference of the International Marine Animal Trainers Association, Chicago.

1982 IMATA Conference, Honolulu, Hawaii, USA. Cognition training requires careful controls and various advanced techniques to be valid. Here the initial training of two sea lions for a cognition project is described.

Teaching Sea Lions that Signals Represent Objects, Object Qualities, and Behaviors

by Ronald J. Schusterman and Kathy Krieger
California State University-Hayward

ABSTRACT

Two California sea lions (a six-year-old female, Rocky, and a three-year-old male, Bucky) were trained in a symbolic matching paradigm. Gestural signs produced by movements of the trainer's arms and hands referred to types of objects, modifiers and actions. Both sea lions were eventually trained with three-sign constructions consisting of Modifier + Object + Action in that order. An example of a three-sign sequence is BLACK BALL MOUTH [glossed as "go over to the black ball (and not the gray or white balls or the black, white and gray pipes) and place your open mouth on it"]. Rocky's modifiers consisted of size and color attributes, and Bucky's modifiers consisted of different locations of the objects. After 24 months of training, Rocky had a comprehension vocabulary of 20 signs (5 modifiers, 10 objects and 5 actions), and after 20 months of training, Bucky had a comprehension vocabulary of 16 signs (2 modifiers, 8 objects and 6 actions). Semantic comprehension is considered to be demonstrated if an organism can follow directions when each sign is contrasted with every other in a series of commands. Currently, Rocky's semantic comprehension consists of 190 three-sign combinations, and Bucky's semantic comprehension consists of 64 three-sign combinations.

TEACHING SEA LIONS...

Until recently, perhaps the greatest limitation to the study of the cognitive skills of nonverbal infants, mentally handicapped individuals and animals stemmed from procedures which restricted their training to relatively simple instrumental responses to specific environmental stimulus objects (see Blough and Blough [1977], and Schusterman [1980] for critical reviews of operant methods to study the sensory and perceptual capabilities of nonverbal animals). In linguistic parlance, the nonverbal animals were trained with holophrastic commands, i.e., stimulus objects were to be acted upon in a specified way (e.g., touched or approached) when, and only when, a signal or stimulus was given (stimulus control). The command signal contained a complete phrase which included the object class, the object qualities, the location of the object and the action to be taken. There were no attempts by investigators to use stimulus control procedures in which the behavior of nonverbal animals was regulated by separate signals designating objects, object qualities, and actions. Thus the opportunity to determine whether nonverbal animals deal with instructions in which signals are recombined in different ways, i.e., whether they are capable of semantic comprehension (Premack 1976), was rarely considered. The behavior modification approach to the study of animal learning has its counterpart in the trained animal acts in zoos, circuses and oceanariums. For example, dolphins and sea lions are trained to perform a series of intricate maneuvers and subtle discriminations by Skinnerian "shaping," "changing," and "fading" techniques. However, the trainer's hand signals or rudimentary words are holophrastic commands referring to both actions, objects, and object qualities and are usually not divided into separate meanings. Thus, dolphins seem to show no understanding of retrieving the ball rather than the ring (unless the trainer points to it) or vice-versa, or leaping over the ring instead of the ball or vice-versa. Even in the training of a capuchin monkey to perform as an aide for a quadriplegic, there appears to be no use of signals to refer to various aspects of the environment. Instead, the monkey's performance seemed to depend on a series of "shaped" and "chained" behaviors primarily under the control of the trainer's verbal command "do this" or "fetch" in conjunction with a pointer (Willard et al. 1982). As Richard Soloman has recently noted, most nonverbal "animals are much smarter [and] much more capable than they appear to be, either in their natural habitat or at the hands of experimenter psychologists" (1981, p. 2), and I might add, most animal trainers.

Recently, however, these restrictive study techniques for probing an animal's cognitive capacities have been overcome. This has been particularly true in studies dealing with spatial memory (e.g., Menzel 1978), abstract reasoning, and symbolic communication (Premack 1983; Savage-Rumbaugh 1981). Gestural symbols (Gardner and Gardner 1969), plastic symbols (Premack 1983), a keyboard with symbols (Rumbaugh 1977) and computer generated acoustic symbols (Herman 1980) have been used to generate rather extensive vocabularies in chimpanzees, gorillas and bottle-nosed dolphins (*Tursiops truncatus*). In the case of an African gray parrot, the vocabulary consisted of spoken English words (Pepperberg 1981). Indeed, playback experiments in the field suggest that the "untrained" vocalizations given by vervet monkeys function in a rudimentary representational fashion, designating objects or events (Cheney and Seyfarth 1982; Seyfarth, Cheney, and Marler 1980). The present study with sea lions is most similar to Herman's studies on dolphins (Herman 1980; Herman, Richards, and Wolz, Note 1) in which the emphasis is on vocabulary comprehension rather than on a productive vocabulary. Griffin (1981) has recently reviewed this comparative psychological approach to the animal mind.

At our laboratory in Hayward and at Marine World Africa/USA, we have been training and testing two California sea lions (*Zalophus californianus*) in symbolic communication experiments in which gestural signs refer to types, attributes, and locations of objects as well as actions to betaken. The distinctive gestural signs are produced by movements of a trainer's arms and hands. The present results encompass nearly 24 months of training for Rocky and 20 months of training for Bucky. During this period, we have collected a substantial amount of data on the ability of Rocky and Bucky to comprehend signs which could be combined into a phrase made up of sequences of two or more signs or "words," with each sequence or construction conveying a unique instruction. Comprehension was measured by the accuracy and consistency of the sea lion's responses to the gestural phrases. The convention used in this paper is to identify gestures with putative meanings by capitalized words. A combination of two signs was always presented sequentially as Object + Action, e.g. FRISBEE FIIPPER-TOUCH (glossed as "go to the Frisbee and touch it with your front flipper"). Modifier signs were added before the object + Action string so that three-sign strings currently consist of Modifier + Object + Action in that order. Modifier signs that are currently comprehended by one or the other of the sea lions refer to the qualities or attributes of the objects (e.g., the shade of gray or the size of the object) and the location of the objects (located on land or i the water). An example of a three-sign sequence is BLACK BALL MOUTH [glossed as "go over to the black ball (and not the gray or white balls) and place your open mouth on it"]. Object modifiers are used when identical pairs or triads of objects are simultaneously available. In the case of color modifiers, at least six objects must be present, e.g., three balls which are colored black, white and gray, and three baseball bats which are colored black, white, and gray.

Conference Proceedings

1989 IMATA Conference, Amsterdam, Holland. It is always refreshing to see trainers presented with a challenge, then rise to meet that challenge with innovative results. This project required well planned desensitization, and an experienced and trusting animal. Although the results of the research project were inconclusive, the training was a resounding success.

Video Recording the Nasal Passage of an Echolocating Dolphin

by Debra Marrin-Cooney
Marine World Africa USA

ABSTRACT

How dolphins make their sounds has been a subject of much controversy for many years. This project's objective was to better pinpoint the origin of the echolocation clicks. In 1988, a male Atlantic bottlenose dolphin (*Tursiops truncatus*) at Marine World Africa USA was trained to accept a fiber optic scope inside his nasal passage while performing an echolocation task.

VIDEO RECORDING...

How dolphins make their sounds has been a subject of much controversy for nearly three decades. The common belief is that clicks are produced in the forehead by structures in the nasal passages. Many research projects since 1961 have supplied evidence supporting this belief. No one, however, has pinpointed the exact origin of the echolocation clicks. This presentation will deal primarily with Marine World's role in helping researchers acquire new information. First, however, I feel it is important to give you a little background information.

Ted Cranford began studying dolphin phonation in 1983. In 1985 with the use of modern x-ray technology he studied the structure of the head of a spinner dolphin (*Stenella longirostris*) by making CAT-scan images. The two dimensional images showed a lot of new detail. Through these CAT-scans Cranford discovered the dorsal bursae (rabbit ears). The rabbit ears are blobs of fat embedded in the edge of the nasal passages. Since he discovered them he thought (or hoped) that they must be important. He continued to study the rabbit ears and discovered that they were attached to the museau de singe (monkey lips) which are resilient connective tissue. In 1972 Norris and Harvey suggested that the monkey lips were the sperm whales source of sound production. This gave Cranford a more substantial reason to believe his discovery was important. Cranford did CAT-scans on ten different species of Odontocetes and in all of them he found the rabbit ears and monkey lips.

In 1986 Cranford went to Sweden and worked with Mats Amundin. They studied the structure of the head of the bottlenose dolphin (*Tursiops truncatus*) using cryomicrotomey (small frozen slices). This work made the CAT-scans easier to interpret. It showed them that the rabbit ears were on both sides of the airway and which air spaces they were near.

In 1987 Ted Cranford, Mats Amundin, and David Bain presented a paper in Miami at the Marine Mammal Society conference. They suggested that the rabbit ears and monkey lips work together to create vibrations that produce the echolocation clicks in all Odontocetes. At that time they felt they had done enough research on dead animals and that their next logical step was to find a way to see these structures in action in a live dolphin.

In 1988 Ken Norris submitted a research proposal to the Marine World Research Foundation. The proposal requested that a dolphin be trained to accept an endoscope probe into the upper nasal passages and then produce clicks. This would enable researchers to make a video and an audio recording of the clicks simultaneously. If successful this project would allow us to gain more knowledge of the origin, and hopefully see the mechanics of how the clicks are produced.

Once the proposal was approved it took several months of preparations before the research trials could start. Our first step was to go to Santa Cruz to meet with Ted Cranford, David Bain, and Ken Norris. While we were there we were shown a presentation on their previous work. After the presentation Cranford dissected the head of a common dolphin (*Delphinus delphis*) for us so we could better understand what we would be trying to record. The specimen that was dissected was different from the species we would be working with but it still gave us an idea of what we were trying to record, and how deep into the nasal passages we would have to insert the probe. The rabbit ears and monkey lips were only about one inch below the blowhole.

Later that day we went to the office of the doctor who would be lending us his equipment. Unfortunately the equipment would not be available for training sessions. We could only use it for the actual research trials. What we did was examine and measure all of the equipment. By doing this w~ learned the size of the probe, and what the animals movement limitations would be. We also found out how many people it would take to operate the equipment. This visit started us thinking about where to place all of the equipment in and around a pool that was not designed for research. By the end of the day at Santa Cruz we were ready to begin planning, and start the training for our project.

One of the most important aspects of the planning for this project was picking the right animal. The animal chosen was a male bottlenose dolphin (*Tursiops truncatus*) named Schooner. Schooner is approximately 14 years old and has been a show performer at Marine World for over 10 years. During the course of this project his routine also included performing in shows, maintenance of husbandry behaviors, and learning other new behaviors.

Schooner already knew how to wear eyecups. For over nine years the only task he did blindfolded was a ring retrieval. We had to teach him a new task that would keep him within the very limited range of the endoscope. He was trained on a tactile signal to go from the trainer to a stationing bar and hold until the bridge. Schooner had to stay within a few inches of the wall, and could only submerge a few inches below the water surface. Originally he was trained to keep his blowhole above water. Once the eyecups were added he chose to submerge his whole head. The behavior was then modified to limit his depth instead of asking him to keep his blowhole above water.

Since the endoscope probe wasn't available during training I taught Schooner to allow me to insert a 3/8" soft plastic tube in his nasal passages. This way when the trial date arrived I could slip the tube over the probe and Schooner wouldn't feel anything different during the actual trials.

After Schooner was trained to accept the tube in his nasal passages and his echolocation task was trained, the two behaviors were put together. I would put the eyecups on him, insert the tube, and give him the signal to go to the station bar.

The only things left to familiarize Schooner with at this point were the hydrophone, and the box that would house some of the equipment. These were added to the sessions and didn't seem to bother or distract him while he worked. We also had Dr. Bain doing sound checks during some sessions to make sure we could pick up the clicks on our hydrophone.

Once the training was completed and everyone involved was notified, a date was set for our first day of trials. February 27th was our first day. The park was closed so we dedicated most of our day to the research. We got a late start but still managed to do three sessions with a total of 35 trials. On March 11th we did one session. Because of equipment failure no data were recorded. The equipment was fixed over night and the next day we did three more sessions around our show schedule. A total of 19 trials were done.

We had a lot of equipment that had to be set up and in working order. Next to the pool we had a T.V. monitor, speakers, a high frequency tape recorder, and an oscilloscope. In a box just above the water on our walkway were the endoscope and video recorder. Attached to that was the fiber optic cable, the video camera, and the probe. In the water next to the equipment box was the stationing bar and the hydrophone.

When all of the equipment was set up the trials went as follows. One trainer worked with Schooner's two poolmates. Schooner stationed with myself and another trainer. The eyecups were placed on and then the probe was inserted into his nasal passages. The people watching the T.V. monitor let us know if they could see the rabbit ears. If they couldn't we would move the probe around and search for them. If the search went on too long we would release the animal and reinforce him. If we found the rabbit ears and monkey lips in view on the monitor we would give him the signal to go to the station bar. As he swam to the bar and stationed the rabbit ears and monkey lips were videoed in action as the clicks were recorded.

We discovered a couple of unforeseen problems during trials, besides equipment failure. First he was so relaxed once he reached the bar that sometimes he would sit totally blindfolded and not make a sound. On some of these trials we tried dropping objects in the water in front of him at the station bar to try to elicit more clicks enabling us to record a longer click train. Probably the biggest unforeseen problem was the slightest movement of the probe and the ears and lips were either out of view or out of focus. Lucky for us Schooner was eager to please and worked well. He performed a total of 54 trials over the two days of recording sessions. From those trials approximately seven minutes of tape provided useful information.

The video and audio recordings were taken back to Santa Cruz to be analyzed. The evaluation of the data collected has been a long process due to the difficulty of matching up the video recording to the recording of the clicks. What we have learned thus far is that the rabbit ears and monkey lips were vibrating during the production of clicks. This is consistent with the theory but not conclusive. The movement of these structures may only be incidental. It's possible that the clicks may be produced at another site.

Even though there is some disappointment in not obtaining conclusive information on the exact origin of the clicks we consider our project a successful one. Schooner allowed us to video inside his nasal passages. We learned new information pertaining to the production of clicks and the rabbit ears and monkey lips are not ruled out as a potential site for click production. More work lies ahead, with another research proposal from Ken Norris, David Bain, and Ted Cranford.

ACKNOWLEDGEMENTS

I'd like to thank the following people for their contributions. Phillip Scheinberg, M.A., Tom Boles of BLK, and Glenn Hardin of Motion Analysis for lending us equipment, and their expertise on its operation. Amy Traxler, Jim Mullen, Jon Lawrence, Paul Povey, and Terry Samansky for their advice and help during the training sessions and research trials. Sonny Allen for his help on several aspects of this project. Last but not least, Dr. David Bain for his help during all of the phases of this project.

Conference Proceedings

1988 IMATA Conference, San Antonio, Texas, USA. Teaching an animal to wear a foreign object for any length of time can be difficult. The process of designing the object and desensitizing the animal to its presence can be challenging. Whether you want a dog to wear a backpack or a dolphin an underwater camera, many of the considerations are the same.

Training an Atlantic Bottlenose Dolphin (*Tursiops truncatus*) to Wear a Harness and Remote Underwater Camera

by Gina Gouvin and Mike Wood
Theatre of the Sea

ABSTRACT

During March of this year Mike Wood and I had the pleasure of working with the British Broadcasting Corporation (BBC) on a project called "Supersense," which is a documentary of life in the animal kingdom. Theatre of the Sea was asked to train a bottlenose dolphin to wear a harness and remote control underwater camera, to obtain a dolphin's perspective of his environment. During the filming, the dolphin would be performing various tasks Including feeding on live mullet. A hydrophone was placed under water to record the dolphin's echolocation performance.

INTRODUCTION

During March of this year Mike Wood and I had the pleasure of working with the British Broadcasting Corporation (BBC) on a project called "Supersense," which is a documentary of life in the animal kingdom. It offers its viewers a visual interpretation of what the animal is experiencing through various creature's eyes and senses. Each of its six programs concentrates on one facet of an animal's awareness. For the segment "Beyond the Senses" we were asked to train a bottlenose dolphin to wear a harness and remote control underwater camera, in order to obtain a dolphin's perspective of his environment. During the filming, the dolphin would be performing various tasks including feeding on live mullet. A hydrophone was placed under water to record the dolphin's echolocation performance. These recordings were used to dub the film and are also being studied by Mr. A. D. Goodson of the Sonar and Signal Processing Group at Loughborough University in England. He is researching the correlation between the sound pulses emitted and the task being performed.

The underwater camera was attached to a harness worn by a dolphin just forward of the dorsal fin. The camera angle was such that a portion of the dolphin's head could be filmed during the echolocation tasks.

Before our training could begin we needed to choose the dolphin we felt would be best suited for wearing the harness and camera. The staff agreed that Buttons, a sixteen year old male would be the best candidate. He had always been a very tactile animal and enjoyed interacting with the trainers in the water. At approximately 2.43 m (8 ft) and 204 Kg (450 lbs.), we felt he was well suited for carrying the equipment, which weighed 5.9 Kg (13 lbs.).

Our next task was choosing a site that fit our needs for training these new behaviors. The dolphin facility at Theatre of the Sea is unique in that it is a 1.8 sq. hectometers (4.5 acre) salt water lake that was originally a quarry excavated for the construction of the Florida East Coast Railroad in the early 1900's. Salt water is pumped into the lagoon directly from the ocean at a rate of 24,605 L (6,500 gals) per minute. Various types of marine life inhabit the waters along with the dolphins.

The site we chose for our training sessions was a pen approximately 33.5 by 18.3 m (110 x 60 ft), located at the south end of the lagoon. At one side of the pen the water was 0.9-1.2 m (3-4 ft) deep which allowed the trainers to easily stand to manipulate the animal and equipment. There was also an existing dock at this location which provided us with a stationing and work area.

PHASE ONE

The station was established by having Buttons float horizontally to the dock while targeting his rostrum toward the shallow end. Once this initial behavior was consistent, a trainer would stand in the water next to the dolphin, gently turning him from side to side as well as manipulating the pectoral and dorsal fins. This helped Buttons become more comfortable with the movements necessary to take the equipment on and off. He adjusted quickly to the new stationing position and was very cooperative during the water exercises. We felt he was ready for the next phase of training.

PHASE TWO

To prepare the dolphin for wearing the harness he first had to be desensitized to wearing various straps and materials against his skin. We began by bringing a 7.6 cm (3 in) wide strap made from elastic material out during our training sessions letting Buttons touch and play with it while being reinforced. Through selective reinforcement, we gradually conditioned him to wear the strap which fastened with Velcro around his middle, forward of the dorsal fin. A second strap was then introduced in the same fashion and worn 7.6 to 10 cm (3 to 4 in) in front of the first.

Through out the next several training sessions Buttons was asked to perform specific tasks while wearing the straps. As we watched his performance it became apparent that as the material got wet it would stretch and slide down his body as he swam. In looking for a more suitable material, we found a 5 cm (2 in) wide nylon strap that fastened with a plastic snap-on buckle, perfect for our needs. Because Buttons was already familiar with the procedures necessary for putting the straps on, it only took several days for him to become comfortable wearing the new ones.

This behavior was maintained for the next four or five days as we awaited the completion of a specially designed full-length harness made from a stretchable material. It wrapped around the dolphin's body and fastened at the side with Velcro. Openings were added to accommodate the dorsal and pectoral fins. The harness fit the animal from 12.7 cm (5 in) behind the blowhole down to approximately 15 cm (6 in) behind the dorsal fin. We felt this design would provide good support to prevent the camera from slipping during filming and minimize chaffing of the animal's skin.

PROBLEMS

Through the next week of sessions as we were working with Buttons on wearing the new harness, it was becoming apparent that problems were developing. Foremost the dolphin was uncomfortable with the steps necessary to put the equipment on. For example, the time consuming task of fitting the dorsal and pectoral fins into the openings in the material. In addition, the bulkiness of the material especially when wet, was awkward to work with. After numerous, marginally successful attempts, we laid to rest the full length harness: Buttons breathed a sigh of relief.

As our filming date grew rapidly near, we turned our efforts back to the two nylon straps that the dolphin had worn so well in earlier training sessions. To attach these we designed a mounting fixture that would securely hold the camera in place. In designing the fixture several requirements were taken into consideration. First that it fit the dolphin comfortably, yet be sufficiently rigid to keep camera movements to a minimum. Secondly, the harness would also have to be adjustable to allow for proper camera angle. Last but not least, the film crew had a deadline to meet so it had to be done fast.

To construct the mounting fixture, a 43 x 35.6 cm (17 x 14 in) piece was cut from a sheet of curved plastic which would form the base. A slot was cut at one end to accommodate the dorsal fin. Two openings were added on each side for the nylon straps. Two to three layers of 7.6 cm (3 in) foam rubber were glued to any areas where the plastic might come in contact with the dolphin's skin, to maximize comfort. A foam rubber padded cylinder was secured to the plastic base. This would safely hold the camera during filming. A hinged lid on the cylinder would allow easy access to the camera for reloading.

PHASE THREE

Before introducing the dolphin to the new piece of equipment, he needed to become familiar with the sensation of carrying a weighted object on his back. To simulate the drag through the water that the camera would create, we attached a plastic jug to one of the nylon straps. Everyday we would add more water to the jug to increase the weight. After a few days of working on this we felt he was ready to be introduced to the mounting fixture. He was asked to station while a trainer held the fixture next to him as he was being reinforced. Once he was comfortable, we would gently hold the equipment on his back without fastening the straps, again with reinforcements. By the third day the fixture was in place and one strap was fastened. On day five both straps were fastened and Buttons was ready to explore his pool.

We encouraged him to swim, dive and jump to see if there were any adjustments to be made. We noted the apparatus moved considerably as he swam, creating potential problems once filming began. Because of our tight schedule any redesigning was out of the question. We found, however, that by tightening the straps, the movement was reduced to a minimum. Other adjustments included adding several more layers of foam rubber to the dorsal end of the plastic cylinder to provide the proper camera angle needed to film a portion of the dolphin's head.

PHASE FOUR

The BBC had provided us with a "mock" camera to use until the real thing arrived. It was a simple plastic cylinder of the same size and weight as the working camera. Once secured in the fixture, it would add an additional weight of 1.8 Kg (4 lbs). A day or two of carrying the mock camera and Buttons was ready for the final phase of training.

The underwater camera and housing were designed by Mr. A. D. Goodson of Loughborough University of Technology, England. The aluminum housing contained a high speed camera, battery power supply and printed circuit board. An acrylic window was attached to both ends of the housing with machine screws and sealed with standard O-rings. A 27.9 cm (11 in) ball hydrophone attached to a 45.7 cm (18 in) lead transmitted signals to the acoustic control circuit board, to control the on/off relays. In designing the control system that would operate the camera, Mr. Goodson took several factors into consideration. When using an acoustical control, there would be the possibility of the dolphin's own sonar jamming the system, which might give false commands to the circuit board. The dolphin might also deliberately mimic the control sounds, again possibly jamming the system. He considered using very high frequencies outside the dolphin's whistle spectrum, but attenuation of high frequency sounds in seawater became a factor. Mr. Goodson chose a high frequency ultrasound coded signal of 80 kHz to activate the camera.

Keeping in mind that underwater sounds won't pass through a dolphin, as air breathing mammals are acoustically opaque, Mr. Goodson designed the system to work on a multi-path reflected signal from either the bottom of the pool or from the surface of the water. An external magnet was placed over the switch on the camera when not in use to prevent accidental triggering from ambient noises. However, during a break from filming one of the crew left the camera on the edge of the dock with the ball hydrophone in the water and failed to put the magnet on the switch. When we returned the camera was running. We think Buttons got curious and buzzed the hydrophone at point blank range. This massive overload could have triggered the camera. That mistake cost the BBC a film cartridge!

PHASE FIVE

In the final stages of training, the dolphin was introduced to the actual underwater camera. We were aware that the sounds of the camera motor would be clearly audible to Buttons. To ensure that he would not be startled, we first had him station with the harness mounting fixture on while a trainer stood in the water next to him holding the camera. Beginning with very short intervals that would gradually increase, we would turn the camera on then off while reinforcing him. The first few times he seemed a little surprised but quickly became comfortable with the new sounds.

Our next training session was devoted to conditioning the animal to wear the equipment fitted with the underwater camera. Again this was done by first having him station, then securing the camera in place, again turning it on and off for short intervals. By our next training session Buttons was eager to explore his pool and perform tasks while wearing the apparatus. At this point the crew and trainers felt the time had come to load the camera for a test run.

FILMING

While the camera was filming we asked the dolphin to retrieve some weighted rings from the bottom of the pool along with other behaviors. We had considered asking him to perform some bows for the segment but after watching his somewhat clumsy attempts we decided against it, as we did not want to cause him any discomfort. For the next several days our training sessions centered around filming the dolphin feeding on live mullet. Although the lagoon at Theatre of the Sea contains live fish, there are no such delicacies as mullet. Needless to say, Buttons was more than happy to cooperate during the fish eating scenes.

CONCLUSION

By the end of the week the film crew felt they had enough footage and headed back to England. Unfortunately they are still in the process of editing the material to be used in the broadcast, so we do not yet have the finished product. Overall, we were very pleased with the project. In looking back there were several things we felt could have been improved. Foremost would be time to design a more sophisticated harness which would allow for a better camera angle. This in turn could provide a greater view of the dolphin's head during filming. From a trainer's point of view, however, we achieved our goal: successfully training a dolphin to wear a harness and an underwater camera. To work side by side with both film crews and scientists as we obtained a dolphin's perspective of his environment was an enjoyable and positive experience.

The following paper was originally presented at the 1992 IMATA conference held in the Bahamas. It was a runner up for the Outstanding Trained Behavior award. This paper is an excellent example of complex training, as it utilizes many different behaviors. One of the most challenging concepts is working with animals in the open ocean. There are several facilities around the world that work with dolphins in an open ocean setting, but the Navy program has certainly been at the forefront of this type of work. Here the animals are trained for deep dives while wearing a depth recorder and they are then required to give voluntary blood samples upon their return. This is another example of the creative ways that training can be put to good use. This paper appears in Vol. 1, No. 1, 1994 of *Marine Mammals: Public Display and Research*.

Conditioning Bottlenose Dolphins (*Tursiops truncatus gilli*) for Voluntary Diving Studies

by Steven F. Shippee, Norman K. W. Chun, Terrie M. Williams
Naval Research and Development Division of NCCOSC

ABSTRACT

The behavior and physiology of diving has been extensively studied in several species of pinnipeds and marine birds. Less is known about the diving adaptations of the most completely aquatic mammals, the cetaceans. Early investigations of the diving abilities of dolphins were conducted using forced dive conditions in the laboratory, resulting in extreme physiological responses. The investigative technique improved during the late 1960's and 70's when dolphins were trained for diving experiments in the open sea, providing initial data on the natural diving physiology of these animals. In the present study two Pacific bottlenose dolphins (*Tursiops truncatus gilli*) were trained to dive to specific depths and then return to station for fluke presentation allowing immediate post-dive blood sampling. The samples were analyzed for lactic acid content providing an indication of anaerobic effort during the graded dives. A Time-Depth Recorder worn by the animals recorded dive profiles which allowed calculation of swimming speed, bottom time, and ascent/descent rates. Additional experiments conducted in the home pen involved training the animals to allow serial blood samples to be drawn during voluntary breath holds, thus providing information on blood gas changes. Simultaneous heart rate measurements were made to verify that forced dive bradycardia did not occur. These studies demonstrate the value of conditioning voluntary responses for scientific investigation, and additional uses for "medical" behaviors.

INTRODUCTION

Over 70 species of cetaceans play an important role in marine ecosystems, having evolved a high-energy predatory life-style to survive in the challenging environment of the sea (Kanwisher and Ridgway, 1983). To thrive, these animals must be adapted to the thermal stress of the marine environment, and be able to withstand the rigors of pressure and nitrogen accumulation, which they encounter while diving to acquire food. Many cetaceans are recognized for utilizing food resources unavailable even to modern man, as is the case with sperm whales feeding on deep-sea squid (Clarke. 1980). Other cetaceans are important constituents of multi-species communities sharing common resources, for example the association between pelagic tuna and dolphins in the eastern tropical Pacific. Owing to their entirely aquatic existence and the difficulty of observing their movements while submerged, we know relatively little about the physiological ecology of free-ranging cetaceans, especially dolphins. Studies on the foraging patterns and movements of cetaceans in the pelagic environment have depended largely on radio tracking techniques and direct surface observations from shorelines and boats (Pryor and Norris, 1989; Scott, Wells, Irvine, and Mate, 1990). Yet information about the natural diving behavior of these animals remains very sketchy (Kooyman, 1989). Much of what is known about the ecology of pelagic whales and dolphins has been derived from whaling data and from specimens attained from incidental mortalities associated with human activities (Pryor, 1990). For many species, the data is entirely anecdotal.

To learn more about the diving capabilities of marine animals, laboratory studies began in earnest earlier this century (Scholander, 1940). By experimenting on a variety of different species ranging from ducks to seals, much was learned about the physiological responses to immersion and asphyxiation (Eisner, Franklin, Van Citters, and Kenny, 1966). Studies on pinnipeds using forced dive techniques led to important discoveries about these animal's diving capabilities and behaviors. However, attempts to forcibly dive a restrained porpoise (*Phocoena phocoena*) resulted in extreme cardio-

Principle Investigator(s)	Year	Species	Max. Depth Attained (m)	Type of Study
Norris, et al.	1965	*Steno bredanensis* ("Pono")	30	Diving Ability
Elsner	1966	*Tursiops t. gilli*	3	Heart Rate
Ridgway, Scronce & Kanwisher	1969	*Tursiops truncatus* ("Tuffy")	300	Diving Physiology
Hall	1970	*Lagenorhynchus obliquidens*	215	Diving Ability
Bowers & Henderson	1972	*Globicephala scammoni* *Orcinus orca*	610 265	Diving Ability
McSheehy (unpublished)	1978	*Tursiops t. gilli* ("Li'i")	535	Deep Diving Ability
Ridgway & Howard	1979	*Tursiops truncatus*	100	N_2 Uptake and Washout
Ridgway, Bowers, et al.	1984	*Delphinapterus leucas*	647	Diving Ability & Physiology

Table 1 Previous diving studies with trained delphinids.

vascular responses and then death after a fairly short duration dive (Scholander, 1940).

In the 1960's interest in the diving physiology of small odontocetes increased. With the advent of modern training techniques, it became possible to condition animals to allow handling for physiological experiments, and to induce voluntary behaviors including diving (Kooyman, 1985). This allowed measurements of telemetered heart rate from porpoises trained to wear instrumented harnesses in enclosed pools (Kanwisher, 1965; Eisner, Kenny, and Burgess, 1966; Baldwin, 1965; Ridgway, 1972). It also led to diving experiments with unrestrained animals in the open sea (Irvine, 1970; Wood, 1973). Various diving tests have been conducted with trained dolphins and whales up to the present (Table 1). Of note are the extensive physiology studies conducted by Ridgway et al. in 1969 and again in 1979. Deep dive studies conducted in 1978 demonstrated the capability of Tursiops truncarus gilli. The animal completed a trained dive in excess of 500 meters (1640 feet), a feat requiring over 6 minutes (D. McSheehy, personal communication). A significant finding was made in 1984 when a beluga whale made the deepest trained dive on record, to 647 meters (2122 feet), which took 16 minutes to complete (Ridgway et al., 1984).

Attachment of a radio tracking device in 1971 allowed measurements of dive depths to be made on a free swimming common dolphin (*Delphinus delphis*), with a maximum recorded dive of 260m (853 feet) (Evans, 1971). Other investigators have since been successful in radio tracking dolphins and whales (e.g.: harbor porpoise, spinner, dusky, white-sided, and bottlenose dolphins, pilot whales, and killer whales) (Scott et al., 1990). Nonetheless, very little actual diving data has been collected on these free ranging odontocetes.

SCOPE AND TRAINING REQUIREMENTS

Previous experiments conducted under the direction of Dr. Sam Ridgway with a trained dolphin, "Tuffy," measured O_2 and CO_2 content of expired air collected in a funnel as the animal surfaced (Ridgway and Scronce, 1969: Ridgway and Harrison, 1986). A second experiment involved training two dolphins to perform serial dives in order to test the effects of nitrogen loading in the animal's tissues, commonly known as the bends (Ridgway and Howard, 1979; Kanwisher and Ridgway, 1983). However, measurements of lactic acid buildup and blood gas values were still lacking on diving dolphins. These types of physiological values are well documented in Weddell seals and marine birds (see Kooyman, 1989 for review). In light of this, we began a further investigation of diving physiology this past year. Our study attempts to establish baseline values for unrestrained quiescent animals, and to measure lactate levels in actively diving dolphins in the open sea. The scope of our study involves two components: in pen breathhold experiments and open water diving experiments (Table 2).

ESTABLISH BASELINE VALUES
(*Home-Pen Measurements*)
• blood-gas levels of oxygen, carbon dioxide, and pH
• lactic acid buildup in blood due to breathhold
• heartrate (EKG) to validate 'voluntary' nature of dive
EXAMINE ACTIVE DIVING CONDITIONS
(*Open Ocean Measurements*)
• dive profiles using TDR
• respiration rates after dives
• blood levels of lactic acid

Table 2 Scope of study

In order to assess behavior during voluntary dives in the open sea, it was necessary to train our animals to carry instrument packages. Studies of the diving behavior of other marine animals such as seals and penguins (Kooyman, 1989; Gentry and Kooyman, 1986) have benefited from data collected on Time-Depth Recorders (TDR's). We hoped to use Table 3. Training Requirements TDR's attached to our trained dolphins to ascertain features of their diving behavior during the open water sessions.

Consequently, the training requirements included the following (Table 3): conditioning each animal to perform voluntary breathholds, which involved the use of a stationing apparatus and

Home-Pen Experiments
• trained breathhold up to 6 minutes
• station for tail presentation during breathhold
• allow attachment of heartrate electrodes
Open Ocean Experiments
• wear instrument package (TDR)
• perform voluntary dive up to 200 meters
• readily present tail flukes for immediate post-dive blood sample

Table 3 Training requirements.

depended on the animal's willingness to remain tranquil until signaled to release, to present tail flukes for blood sampling, and to accept attachment of heart rate electrodes. The animals also were required to carry instrument packages while working unrestrained in the open sea, exhibit reliable stimulus control of diving behavior, and allow a blood sample to be readily taken following a dive.

Two adult female Pacific bottlenose dolphins (*Tursiops truncatus gilli*) were chosen for the study, based on their prior open ocean conditioning, learned medical behaviors, and demonstrated diving ability. This species occurs commonly throughout the Pacific region, and is known to forage in the deep coastal waters of North and South America, Asia, and the Pacific Islands.

METHODS AND EQUIPMENT
In-pen Sampling

To provide baseline data on the breathhold limits of dolphins, it was necessary to condition the dolphins for sampling procedures conducted in the home pen. Changes in blood lactate, Ph levels, and blood O_2 and CO_2 concentrations were thus determined. To accomplish this, each animal was trained to position so that serial blood samples could be drawn during a surface breathhold. A padded biteplate mounted on a vertical board provided the animal with a means of staying motionless while in an inverted position, as well as being a focal point for attention. Its flukes were steadied by the trainer as venipuncture was accomplished on a ventral vessel using a butterfly catheter. Blood samples were drawn at timed intervals during the course of the breathhold for both lactate concentration and blood gas measurements. Blood gas samples were meticulously drawn to avoid introduction of environmental air into the heparinized syringe, requiring that the animal remain relatively still. Several repetitive sampling trails were conducted with each animal during breathholds ranging from 1 to 6 minutes. Both dolphins began to show signs of fidgeting after 3-5 minutes, but rarely released from the biteplate until signaled to do so.

To insure that the breathholds reflected voluntary dives and were not forced submersions, simultaneous heart rate measurements were taken on two occasions. This involved training both animals to accept placement of suction cup electrodes and wire leads along the sternum and side. Following a preparatory breath, the animal was inverted and positioned for tail presentation. After stationing on the biteplate, the suction cups were attached to the dolphin and adjusted for the best EKG signal. Heart rate was then monitored continuously during the breathhold. Once completed, the suction cups were removed and the animal was signaled to surface. Additional heart rate measurements were taken during normal respiration cycles with the dolphin in an upright position to give comparative values.

In addition to providing baseline diving values, this phase of our study also demonstrates an innovative application for trained medical behaviors beyond the scope of routine husbandry and health care.

Open Ocean Dives

Open water diving trials were conducted off the shores of Kaneohe Bay and the Mokapu Peninsula, on the island of Oahu, Hawaii. A variety of water depths are easily accessible within 8 km (5 miles) of the NRaD laboratory. Work stations were established for this study in depths ranging to 250 meters (820 feet). The dolphins had previously been trained to transport to the worksite in specially designed boats, thereby reducing transit times (e.g.: Shinder, 1983).

We developed two instrument packages that could be easily attached to the dolphin's pectoral fins. One housed a TDR (Wildlife Computers, Woodinville, Washington) measuring 1x4x6 cm, or roughly the size of a metal cigarette lighter. The microprocessor stored information on changes in depth, water temperature, and light level encountered during each dive. The data was later downloaded to a computer and analyzed after every session. The second package held an analog depth gauge with maximum depth of dive indicator using a bourdon pressure coil (Sierra Precision Instruments, Cucamonga, California), which provided the trainer with an immediate indication of the dolphin's dive effort. Each package was attached by a soft strap consisting of 3/4 inch nylon ribbon padded with polyvelvet cloth, a Fastex® quick-release buckle and a Velcro® adjustment tab. Fastening of the units to the animal's pectoral fins was made around the region of the axillary insertion of the fin where the circumference is the narrowest. The dolphin was trained to roll on its side and allow the watchband-like straps to be attached, adjusted, and the instruments to be inspected at any point during the work session. The compact nature of the instruments and the soft padding of the straps did not appear to cause discomfort or impede the movement of the animal during normal swimming, boat following, or diving.

In earlier dive training experiments in the 1960's and 70's, dolphins were trained to descend to a tethered pinger device which was lowered progressively deeper in the water column (Norris, 1966; Ridgway and Scronce, 1969; Ridgway and Howard, 1979; Ridgway et al., 1984; Hall, 1972). In out study, each animal was simply trained to conduct a routine dive to a buoy anchored on the bottom at a known depth and then return directly to the boat. The boat was accurately stationed above the buoy using navigational instruments. This method allowed the boat to be easily maneuvered and eliminated the time required for recovery of a pinger. Following the dive, the boat could be readily positioned to allow the animal to station for tail presentation and subsequent blood sampling.

Acoustic tones were used to signal the dolphin to dive and return to the boat. A 12 Khz pinger served as the standard recall device for instructing the animal to return to station and could be used at any point during a session. Initiation of a dive sequence needed to be controlled to prevent unwanted voluntary dives. To accomplish this, the dolphin was trained to station at the rear of the boat and await a signal from the trainer. A hand-held wand containing a hydrophone was then placed in the water, and a constant 5 Khz tone activated. The dolphin would take a final inhalation, touch the wand, and begin its descent at that location. Use of this technique allowed the trainer to control pre-dive movements, respiration, and point of dive origin. Also, the animal could anticipate the dive and make physiological and behavioral preparations beforehand.

Once the dolphin returned from a dive, an observer began to record elapsed surface time and respirations. The animal was given a one-minute recovery period, and was then asked to station for a blood sample. The trainer steadied the dolphin's tail flukes while a third member of the team drew a 10cc sample from a ventral vessel. In this position, the animal was able to float comfortably and breath normally while the blood was taken. Samples were easily obtained in this way in a variety of sea conditions.

Accurate records were made on the elapsed time of sampling and injection into the collecting tube (Vacutainer®). The tube was then placed on ice and stored for later laboratory analysis. The dolphin was always rewarded well for its efforts, yet there appeared to be little stress associated with this procedure.

To insure that previous diving exercise did not affect the sampled lactate levels, the animals were always given at least a 5 minute surface rest period prior to initiation of any sampled dives. Both dolphins were trained to make dives ranging from 60 to 200 meters (197 to 656 feet). Several training dives might be made during each session prior to and after sampling. Data was continuously collected with the TDR on these training dives, providing additional information on the normal diving behavior of our free swimming dolphins.

DISCUSSION OF PRELIMINARY FINDINGS

Our findings will be extensively summarized and published elsewhere in the near future. This discussion is included to provide a brief synopsis of the type of data collected, and how it might be applied.

By measuring heart rate and respiration rate, we can validate data taken during breathholds and trained dives as being representative of voluntary behavior. Comparisons of heart rate on the surface breathholds fit the patterns measured previously on freely swimming dolphins (Kanwisher and Sundries, 1965; Eisner, Kenney, and Burgess, 1966; Ridgway, 1972) with normal tachycardia during breathing cycles and decreased heart rate following voluntary submersion.

Our measurements of blood-gas changes during breathholds will answer questions about oxygen partitioning, CO_2 tolerance, and the metabolic processes that occur during diving in dolphins. Measurement of blood lactate levels following deep dives will give us a further indication of the diving capacity of these animals. For example, our breathhold data on blood O_2 and CO_2 levels has allowed us to calculate that the aerobic dive limit for resting dolphins is about 4.5 minutes (Williams et al., in press). By comparison, human aerobic dive limits are calculated to be around 2 minutes.

By using Time-Depth Recorders on trained dolphins, we can calculate descent/ascent rates and bottom times, and make predictions about diving efficiency, possibly answering questions about foraging strategies in diving animals (e.g.: Dolphin, 1987; Kramer, 1988; Houston and Carbone, 1992). To illustrate this, the three channels of the TDR measuring light, temperature, and depth are shown in a representative printout in Figure 1. The lower axis indicates time, with hash marks at 30-second intervals. The first dive is a search dive to the bottom in an area where there was no buoy. Prior to the second dive, the boat was repositioned above a buoy. The animal dove, first searching for, and eventually finding the buoy, which it then circled before quickly returning to the boat. Following a brief surface interval, the animal was again asked to dive to the buoy, but this time made a more direct and deliberate dive in a shorter time period. Figure 2 displays a printout of the dive profile and computer calculations for rates of descent and ascent on a trained dive to 200 meters (656 feet), with a duration of 4.3 minutes. This type of data will provide insights into the behavioral strategies employed by freely diving dolphins to balance energy expenditure against diving speed and duration (Williams et al., in press).

The combined information from these measurements may allow ecologists to interpret the observed diving behavior of wild dolphins and determine if prey aggregations at various depths are important food sources, perhaps explaining many mysteries about the niches dolphins occupy in the marine ecosystem. This knowledge will ultimately have benefits to fisheries management, and to conservation programs for marine mammals.

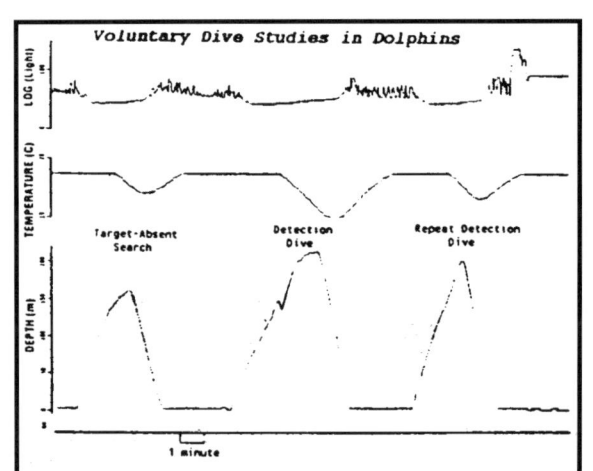

Figure 1 Representative data collected on three distinct dives using Wildlife Computer's TDR and Strip Chart Program, allowing analysis of behavioral changes for each independent dive condition.

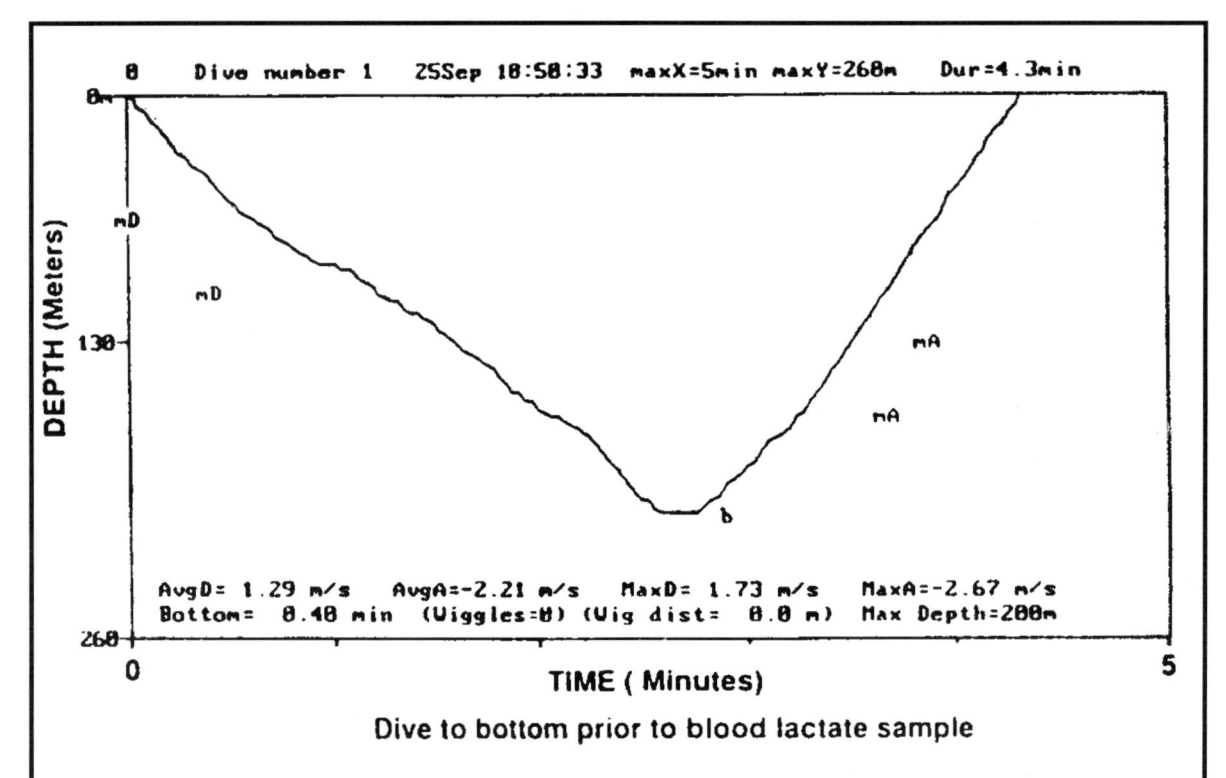

Figure 2 Swimming speed calculations and time allocation using Wildlife Computer's Dive Analysis program for data collected with the TDR on a sampled vertical dive (AvgD & AvgA - average rate of descent and ascent; MaxD & MaxA = maximum rate of descent and ascent, based on a 15% or greater portion of total dive depth; Dur = total dive duration).

CONCLUSIONS

The goal of this paper is to demonstrate the capability of behavioral conditioning for studies into the natural history of marine mammals, in this case physiological ecology. Through operant techniques, we are able to direct dolphins to voluntarily perform natural behaviors in the open sea, and to allow physiological sampling procedures to be conducted without stress. In addition to improving our understanding about the basic physiology of these animals, we are also learning about the capabilities of trained dolphins working cooperatively with man in the open ocean. We also increase man's appreciation of the natural history of marine mammals and their importance in the global ecosystem. We hope to continue with this and similar studies in the future to further investigate the adaptations of marine mammals to life in the sea.

ACKNOWLEDGEMENTS

Many individuals provided assistance with the team effort that made this study possible. Innovative training techniques, hardware designs, and logistic support were contributed by Chip Fogg, Mike Nash, Tim Sullivan, Kelly Sullivan, and Kipp Lawson. The Hawaii Lab veterinary staff, especially Dr. Pete Schroeder, Karl Keller, Eric Huber, and Eileen Rawitz, provided valuable assistance with blood collection protocols and analysis. George Lingle, and Joe Nolan assisted with visual documentation. And, of course, very special acknowledgment is made of the contribution by our two highly cooperative dolphins, Popolo and Cookie. Funding for this project has been provided through the Naval Sea Systems Command and the American Society for Engineering Education (ASEE).

LITERATURE CITED

Baldwin, H.A. (1965). Marine biotelemetry. *BioScience,* 15(2):95-97.

Bowers, C.A. and R.S. Henderson (1972). Project Deep Ops: deep object recovery with pilot and killer whales. Nav. Undersea. Cen. TP-306, San Diego CA.

Clarke, M.R. (1980). Cephalopods in the diet of sperm whales of the southern hemisphere and their bearing on sperm whale biology. *Discovery* Rep. 37:1-324.

Dolphin, W.F. (1987). Dive behavior and estimated energy expenditure of foraging humpback whales in southeast Alaska. Can. J. Zool., 65:354-362.

Elsner, R. (1969). Cardiovascular adjustments to diving. In H.T. Andersen (Ed.), **The Biology of Marine Mammals** (pp. 95-145). New York: Academic Press.

Elsner, R., D.L. Franklin, R.L. Van Citters, and D.W. Kenney (1966). Cardiovascular defense against asphyxia. *Science,* 153:941-949.

Elsner, R., D.W. Kenney, and K. Burgess (1966). Diving bradycardia in the trained dolphin. Nature (London), 212:407-408.

Evans, W.E. (1971). Orientation behavior of delphinids: radio telemetric studies. Ann. N.Y. Acad. Sci., 188:142-160.

Gentry, R.L. and G.L. Kooyman, (Eds.) (1986). **Fur Seals: Maternal strategies on land and at sea.** New Jersey: Princeton Univ. Press.

Hall, J.D. (1970). Conditioning white-striped dolphins, *Lagenorhychus obliquidens,* for open-ocean release. Nav. Undersea Cen. TP-200, San Diego CA.

Houston, A.I. and C. Carbone (1992). The optimal allocation of time during the diving cycle. Behav. Ecol., 3(3):255-265.

Irvine, B. (1970). Conditioning marine mammals to work in the sea. Mar. Tech. Soc. I., 4(3):47-52.

Kanwisher, J.W. and S.H. Ridgway (1983). The physiological ecology of whales and porpoises. Sci. Am., 248:110-120.

Kanwisher, J. and G. Sundnes (1965). Physiology of a small cetacean. Hvalradets Skr., 48:45-53.

Kooyman, G.L. (1985). Physiology without restraint in diving mammals. Marine Mammal Science, 1(2):166-178.

Kooyman, G.L. (1989). Diverse divers. Springer-Verlag, Berlin.

Kooyman, G.L. and H.T. Andersen (1969). Deep diving. In H.T. Andersen, (ed.), **The Biology of Marine Mammals** (pp. 65-94). New York: Academic Press.

Kramer, D.L. (1988). The behavioral ecology of air breathing by aquatic animals. Can. J. Zool., 66:89-94.

Norris, K.S., H.A. Baldwin, and D.J. Samson (1965). Open ocean diving test with a trained porpoise (*Steno bredanensis*). Deep-Sea Res., 12:505-509.

Pryor, K. (199 1). Mortal remains: studying dead animals. In K. Pryor and K.S. Norris (Eds.), **Dolphin Societies:** Discoveries and Puzzles (pp. 245-248). Berkeley: University of California Press.

Ridgway, S.H. (1972). Homeostasis in the aquatic environment. In S.H. Ridgway (Ed.), Mammals of the Sea: Biology and Medicine (pp. 590-747). Springfield, IL: Thomas Books.

Ridgway, S.H., C.A. Bowers, D. Miller, M.L. Schultz, C.A. Jacobs, and C.A. Dooley (1984). Diving and blood oxygen in the white whale. Can. J. Zool., 62:2349-235 1.

Ridgway, S.H. and R.J. Harrison (1986). Diving dolphins. In M.M. Bryden and R. Harrison (Eds.), Research on Dolphins (pp. 33-58). Oxford: Clarendon Press.

Ridgway, S.H. and R. Howard (1979). Dolphin lung collapse and intramuscular circulation during free diving: evidence from nitrogen washout. Science, 206:1182-1183.

Ridgway, S.H. and B.L. Scronce (1969). Respiration and deep diving in the bottlenose porpoise. Science, 166:1651-1654.

Scholander, P.F. (1940). Experimental investigations on the respiratory function in diving mammals and birds. Havlradets Skr., 22:1-131.

Scott, M.D., R.S. Wells, A.B. Irvine, and B.R. Mate (1990). Tagging and marking studies on small cetaceans. In S. Leatherwood and R. Reeves (Eds.), **The Bottlenose Dolphin** (pp. 489-514). San Diego: Academic Press.

Shinder, D. (1983). Separation and removal of marine mammals for medical examination [Abstract]. In M.T. Chunko, E. Krajniak, and J Horwich (Eds.), Proceedings of the 11th Annual IMATA Conference (p. 93). Apple Valley, MN: Minnesota Zoological Gardens.

Williams, T.M., W.A. Friedl, J.E. Haun, and NX Chun. (in press). Balancing power and speed in bottlenose dolphins (Tursiops truncatus). In I.L. Boyd (Ed.), Symposia of the Zoological Society of London, Recent Advances in Marine Mammal Science. Oxford University Press.

Wood, F.G. (1973). Marine Mammals and Man: The Navy's Porpoises and Sea Lions. New York: R.B. Luce, Inc..

DOGWORLD

AUGUST 1996 ■ VOLUME 81 ■ NO. 8 A PJS PUBLICATION

Pet owners and veterinarians are increasingly looking to animal behaviorists to help solve many pet problems. Often, it is only after a situation has become serious (like aggression) that a professional behaviorist is called in. This article looks at the growing need for certified animal behaviorists. Topics discussed include positive reinforcement, teamwork, training the family, and the dangers of anthropomorphism.

When Fido More than Misbehaves

by Fran Pennock Shaw

Aristotle, with his big doe eyes and ears that could mop the floor, hardly looked like a dangerous dog. Yet this seven-year-old cocker spaniel had bitten the two-year-old child in his family, and his owners were afraid they'd have to give up the dog they'd owned since puppyhood.

John and Teresa Monnier of Wayne. Pa., decided there was only one thing left to try. They underwent "family" counseling with specialists from the Behavior Clinic of the University of Pennsylvania Veterinary Hospital (VHUP), an option people are choosing with increasing frequency in dog loving households across the country as the science of animal behaviorism comes of age.

AN EMERGING FIELD

"Our clinic is driven by the fact that pet owners want it. Most realize they have a problem that cannot be dealt with in obedience or training classes, (and) they don't want to kill the dog," explains Karen Overall, V.M.D., director of the VHUP clinic. Meanwhile, she adds, an increasing number of neighborhood vets are being exposed to behaviorism through continuing education.

According to the American Animal Hospital Association, unwanted behavior remains the leading reason people relinquish their pets and most of those pets ultimately are euthanized. However, a 1994 survey shows the number of pets euthanized seems to be dropping, says AAHA spokesperson Amy Ashby. "Luckily, it is changing. We're getting smarter about (dealing with) animal behavior."

More and more owners seem willing to spend their time and money attempting to change a dog's behavior, even when the dog poses a real threat and even when those changes may take weeks, months or years. According to the Cornell University veterinary college's Animal Health Newsletter, one of the school's studies estimates that 60 to 85 percent of the owners who sought counseling for their aggressive dogs thought behavior modification "improved" matters.

"In the past 15 years, the focus has turned to the motivation of the animal for its behavior...as pets have become more like family members and owners have become more aware of behavior problems (and are) less likely to euthanize," agrees Wayne Hunthausen, D.V.M., Westwood Animal Hospital, Westwood, Kansas, and president of the American Veterinary Society of Animal Behavior.

The widespread interest in animal behavior is additionally fueled by an increasing number of laws-such as leash laws, noise ordinances, and breed bans-that make owners financially liable for their dogs' actions.

Animal psychology is in fact the newest specialty for veterinarians. The American College of Veterinary Behaviorists, whose board-certified members diagnose and treat problems in animal behavior, was just recognized in 1993. ACVB President Bonnie Beaver, D.V.M., Texas A&M University, says member veterinarians have backgrounds in both medicine and behavior science and complete programs most trainers do not go through.

"HE'S TOO AGGRESSIVE"

The typical problem canine usually is an aggressive dog that growls or bites whenever people ask it to sit or move, says Overall. Often this dog has completed obedience classes and performed well there; however, behavior at home is another matter.

"Gradually, over three to four weeks, you teach the dog that to get anything it wants-food, love, attention-it has to sit or lie and wait calmly a few seconds," says Overall of the general treatment process. This works well with dogs that have a need to control everything, even their master. "If you physically try to assert yourself, these dogs always get worse," she adds.

Overall says owners often misinterpret many of the signals animals use to communicate, so she teaches behavior clinic clients to read their pets' body language. Owners also can avoid many problems by recognizing situations that cause canine stress, such as moving, family arguments or a new baby.

Owners are taught reward-based obedience exercises so the dog learns to defer naturally to its owners, and at the same time, owners learn to recognize when their dog is relaxed or stressed. In Aristotle's case, for example, the family learned 15-minute behavior modification exercises to do at home each day, such as making the dog sit and wait before every walk or treat.

Hunthausen agrees the most common canine behavior problem is certainly aggression toward humans. However, he suggests people realize that "most (problem) dogs are exhibiting normal dog behaviors, like dominance, which owners simply find unacceptable." Other behaviors that most often require counseling are house soiling, anxiety and general disobedience.

CHECK FOR A MEDICAL PROBLEM

"Often these behaviors flag a medical problem," Overall says. Many times the conditions are treatable. Owners should always take their misbehaving pet for a full veterinary exam to first rule out diseases or neurological problems. But if the problem is a seriously aggressive dog, she advises immediate referral to a behaviorist rather than delaying necessary treatment.

Overall believes many dogs that end up at the VHUP clinic are not poorly behaved, but are abnormal. Dogs between the ages of 1 1/2 and 3 years old sometimes develop odd behaviors analogous to psychiatric diseases, she theorizes, such as aggressiveness, panic, phobias and self-mutilation.

Another theory is that some behavior problems are caused by a chemical or hormonal imbalance that can be controlled with medication. Obsessive-compulsive behavior, for instance, usually is treated with anti-anxiety drugs. Overall is doing research to determine if such behavior can be linked to blood metabolites.

She notes that more than half of the dogs at the VHUP clinic take tranquilizers, at least temporarily, and always in conjunction with behavior modification exercises.

In most cases of problem behavior, if a thorough medical check shows no signs of disease, a local vet simply will refer the owner to an experienced dog trainer for obedience classes or one-on-one training. Even if the owner already has tried obedience school, a vet often will recommend another trainer.

TEAMWORK IS KEY

Beaver stresses "teamwork" among the neighborhood vet, qualified trainer and certified behaviorist. "The local vet is in the best position to say that this dog needs training or needs behavior medicine," she explains. "We each have special qualifications."

Trainers work closely with Texas A&M's behavior clinic, she says. Because of the university's remote location, Beaver consults by phone with trainers across the state who are recommended by the client's local vet. Since owners typically travel to a behavior clinic only once or twice, behavior modification exercises are most often supervised by local trainers.

Pets usually come to VHUP's clinic after standard training has been tried, Overall notes. "We suggest people (first) interview two or three trainers and therapists and let them evaluate what is needed."

A behaviorist typically focuses on how each family member interacts with the aggressive dog. In addition to "leadership exercises," during which the dog is taught to defer to humans, Hunthausen says techniques often include physically controlling the dog with a muzzle or halter, recreating those situations that trigger the dog's behavior and slowly desensitizing it to those situations and reconditioning the dog to have a different reaction by rewarding desired behavior.

TRAINING THE FAMILY

Treating canine behavior problems really means training the owners. "Commonly we see people who think of their dog as a human with four legs," explains Beaver, "but dogs are not humans. They truly have different needs, and you train them differently than you do a child."

Anthropomorphizing leads owners to believe their dogs are acting out of malice when they're actually acting like dogs. "This can lead to an increasingly poor relationship, a vicious cycle," she adds.

Beaver offers two examples of this faulty reasoning: The owner who comes home from work to find the dog defecated in the house and thus rubs the dog's nose in its poop. When the dog soils again, the owner thinks the pet is being spiteful. Or an owner who shouts at the barking dog to be quiet, but it only barks louder, and the owner thinks the animal is just being stubborn.

Behavioral treatments vary with the pet and the problem. To stop the dog from barking, Beaver says, the owner could simply ignore it, use mild negative reinforcement such as spraying with the garden hose or use both commands and positive reinforcement when the pet stops barking.

By misunderstanding the way a dog thinks, people may even cause canine aggressiveness. "We commonly see dominance aggression when owners raise the dog permissively and do not take the role of leadership," she continues. "These people let the puppy sleep where it wants, do what it wants and run their life. They're surprised when as an adult dog, (it) assumes it's in control."

Not all dogs become aggressive in that situation. Beaver has studied different types of aggression and says it relates to an individual dog's disposition, genetics and breed, sex, past experiences, environment and its owner's personality. Behavior modification methods that treat one type of aggression may not be effective or may even worsen another type of aggression.

Owners can therefore aggravate matters by their actions-such as violence begetting violence. Owners also create problems by their inaction-by ignoring or being ignorant of the warning signs of behavior problems.

"We have the best chance of success when it's a misunderstanding and the owners have the right temperament and ability to reassert themselves as leaders," Beaver adds.

About 2 million people each year are bitten by dogs, according to one of Beaver's research studies reported in the Cornell University newsletter. Many of the victims are young children who simply are not taught how to interact safely with dogs. The newsletter also states that 50 to 70 percent of the canine euthanasias performed annually are due to behavior problems– chiefly aggression.

PREVENTING BEHAVIORAL PROBLEMS

- Set rules immediately for your pet and stick to them.
- Prevent opportunities for for inappropriate behavior.
- Supervise a new dog diligently, such as restricting its access to a limited area of your home or keeping it on a long leash.
- Provide attention and training.
- Encourage good behavior with praise and rewards.
- Correct bad behavior by providing alternatives.
- Never physically force compliance.
- Do not play roughly, encourage aggression, or allow play biting.
- Expose pets to different people, animals, and environments.
- See your veterinarian for existing behavior problems.

From the American Animal Hospital Association

Behavior therapy will not solve every problem, Beaver continues. "Sometimes a mismatch of personalities means (family and dog) will never get along. Other dogs are too aggressive...and euthanizing is still the only answer because of the danger."

"I don't think we cure these things," adds Overall. "We try to control it."

Although behavior modification exercises "helped a lot" in Aristotle's case, John Monnier says, the family could not tolerate the dog's continued snapping at strangers and children. "It seemed really unreasonable to have to deal with this. With our son, who was so small, we were always concerned. We couldn't imagine having to face another biting incident."

Since attempts to find other owners for Aristotle also were unsuccessful, the dog was put to sleep about one year after behavior counseling began.

"It was pretty sad...since we did get some dramatic improvement in his behavior," Monnier explains. "What (we) learned from the people at the behavior clinic (VHUP) helped us a lot. In an adult household, it probably would have been different."

The future of animal behavior medicine is

promising, but it is, admittedly, a new science. Certified behaviorists are still scarce. Less than half of the nation's 27 veterinary colleges require students to take courses in behavior science, and there are only about 10 behavior clinics in operation for the public.

The ACVB has approximately 15 members. Most of these members are teachers at veterinary colleges who are actively training new veterinary students in this field. However, Beaver says, behavior modification is the number one topic of interest among today's practicing veterinarians.

Fran Pennock Shaw is an award-winning freelancer from Lancaster, Pa., who specializes in pet and travel articles. She is currently "owned" by her "Terrapoo-Sheepcollie" mixed-breed, Tuffy.

The Professional Trainer 13

Resources and Getting a Job

Knowledge + Practice = Experience

Have I emphasized this enough? Reading this book or completing a course on training will not make you a good trainer. Reading a few books – reading 1,000 books – will not make you a good trainer. Knowledge is the start, a platform on which to build experience. Then, you have to practice what you have learned, then read some more and practice some more. It all adds up to experience – and that takes time. Technically, a trainer is a professional the moment he or she gets paid to train an animal. In the best sense of the word, however, a professional trainer is much more than that. A professional is one with knowledge and experience in applying the techniques of operant conditioning to practical situations.

Working in the Field

Every animal care facility, whether it be a zoo, an aquarium, a behavioral research laboratory, or even a circus has its own special requirements in terms of education, experience, and skill. The basics that we look for at Shedd Aquarium are outlined in an educational handout entitled *A Day in the Life of an Animal Care Specialist*, reprinted on page 527. In addition, there is a *Trainer's Forum* article (1997) that examines the subject, entitled *Getting into the Field: How to Get a Job as a Trainer*, on page 525.

Professional Zoological Organizations

Many excellent organizations can keep you current on job opportunities, trends, and developments in the animal behavior field. Many other organizations are devoted directly to the care and management of animals in a zoological setting. Because it would be impossible to list them all here, I have focused on those that I feel are most directly relevant to training and animal behavior.

IMATA

The International Marine Animal Trainers Association. Most of the articles included in this manual were reprinted from IMATA publications. This is an excellent organization that focuses specifically on training. Although the emphasis is on marine mammals, many species of animals and training in all settings are discussed. An application for membership can be found at the end of the chapter, on page 529.

    IMATA
    1200 South Lake Shore Drive
    Chicago, Illinois 60605
    http://www.imata.org

AAZK

The American Association of Zoo Keepers. This organization only recently began devoting more attention to animal training. It is an important organization for anyone working directly with animals in a zoological setting. The association's monthly publication *Animal Keeper's Forum* provides practical information for animal care professionals on a wide variety of topics.

    AAZK
    635 S.W. Gage Blvd.
    Topeka, Kansas 66606-2066

AZA

The American Zoo and Aquarium Association. This large organization represents the best zoos and aquariums in North America. AZA, too, is increasing its attention to animal behavior and enrichment.

    AZA
    8403 Colesville Road, Suite 710
    Silver Spring, Maryland 20910-3314
    http://www.aza.org

IAATE

The International Association of Avian Trainers and Educators. This is a more recent organization that, like IMATA, focuses on training. Its emphasis is on bird training in a zoo setting.

    IAATE
    c/o Minnesota Zoo
    13000 Zoo Blvd.
    Apple Valley, Minnesota 55124

EMA

The Elephant Managers Association. This international organization focuses on elephant care in a zoo setting. Although training is not the focus of the organization, it is a frequent topic in the EMA newsletter and journal.

    EMA
    1200 W. Washington St.
    Indianapolis, Indiana 46222

The Shape of Enrichment

This relatively new international organization has grown quickly by addressing the enrichment needs of animals in a zoological environment. The organization's conference and newsletter deal with enrichment strategies, devices, programs and environments. The focus is always enrichment, but the topics are as varied as the species. From the smallest tree shrew to the largest pachyderm, including the high profile aquatic-mammal to the lesser-known avian species, every animal gets equal time, and valuable, creative information is shared.

    The Shape of Enrichment
    1650 Minden Drive
    San Diego, CA 92111
    E-mail: shape@enrichment.org

The Behavior Bridge

This newsletter first appeared in 1998 and is aimed at training concerns in the zoological community. It looks at operant conditioning from the behavior analysis perspective (as a science) and applies the techniques to practical zoo applications. The newsletter, planned for a quarterly release, accepts submissions from zoos across the U.S. and plans to have a question-and-answer column in each issue as well as feature articles and at least one technical article. As a new enterprise, *The Behavior Bridge* has started small but so, too, is the subscription price ($6.00 in 1998).

    The Behavior Bridge
    2005 Sunny Lane
    Knoxville, TN 37912
    E-mail: BhvrBridge@aol.com

Other Professional Resources

A number of professional organizations focus on pet training, dog training, horse training, therapy training, companion animal training, exotic bird training . . . and the list goes on. Only a few of these organizations and resources are listed here:

Karen Pryor

Karen Pryor's *Don't Shoot the Dog* home page and her company Sunshine Books offer articles, book and video catalogs, and links to other Web sites. It should be no secret by now that I consider Karen Pryor and her publications to be a valuable resource to both the professional and amateur trainer.

Sunshine Books
49 River Street, Suite 3
Waltham, MA 02453
http://www.clickertraining.com

Gary Wilkes

If you enjoyed reading Gary's excellent articles on pet training I encourage you to order his book *A Behavior Sampler*, in which you'll find many more enjoyable and perceptive articles. You can learn about other training resources (and additional articles) from his Web site.

Click & Treat Products
2344 E. Alpine Avenue
Mesa, AZ 85204
http://www.clickandtreat.com

ABA

The Association for Behavior Analysis. This huge organization does not deal with animal training specifically, but focuses on the science and application of behavior analysis. The die-hard trainer who wants to understand the technical principles behind training may find this organization fascinating. Its annual conferences focus on behavior that ranges from mental retardation to training smokers to kick the habit. The focus is on science, and there are many disciplines involved, including a special interest group that deals with animal behavior. The special interest group is called the Animal Trainers' Forum and has a Web presence on the Cambridge Center for Behavioral Studies Web site at http://www.behavior.org.

ABA
213 West Hall
Western Michigan University
1201 Oliver Street
Kalamazoo, MI 49008-5052
http://www.wmich.edu/aba

WEB SITES

Another avenue for networking with professional and novice trainers alike is on the Internet. Many Web sites, home pages, and news groups are available and worth looking into. There are sites for almost every imaginable type of training. I recommend simply surfing the Web, you may be surprised at what you'll find. A few of my favorites:

- **Clicker List** – An Internet e-mail list that posts questions,

answers, detailed discussions, and some strong opinions about the use of operant conditioning in a wide variety of applications. It is probably wisest to subscribe in digest form:
  mailto:majordomo@listservice.net
  no subject
  message:SUB CLICK-D (no space before the SUB)

- **Clicker Journal** – The Clicker Journal is a compilation of some of the best articles from the Internet clicker list. Corally Burmaster has edited the journal and includes articles about all types of animal training. If you're computer challenged or would prefer to read a hard copy of the best from this news group, write:
  The Clicker Journal
  20146 Gleedsville Road
  Leesburg, VA 22075
- **APDT** – The Association of Pet Dog Trainers
  http://www.apdt.com
- **ARDA** – The American Rescue Dog Association
  http://www.ardainc.org/xcontent.htm
- **NASAR** – National Association for Search and Rescue
  http://www.nasar.org
- **American Dog Trainers Network** – This is a resource with links to hundreds of sites. Rescue dog associations, service dog organizations, special breed groups, etc.
  http://www.inch.com/~dogs
- **CCI** – Canine Companions for Independence
  http://www.caninecompanions.org
- **Guide Dogs for the Blind**
  http://www.guidedogs.com

I could literally list thousands of Web-sites, but the truth is once you are on the Internet, you will find favorites of your own. I have simply listed those that I have found interesting and most helpful. Most sites provide links to other sites, so if I had to give you my top-five list (addresses above), I would recommend that you start with these:
- IMATA
- AZA
- Karen Pryor
- Gary Wilkes
- American Dog Trainers Network

VOL 22, NO 2, 1997. Without a doubt this is one of the most frequently asked questions by visitors to many marine mammal facilities. Every employer has different requirements, but the two answers below may provide some useful information for those interested in pursuing a career as a trainer.

Getting into the Field: How to Get a Job as a Trainer

QUESTION: How do I get a job as a trainer, what kind of experience do I need, what do employers look for?

ANSWER 1: Undoubtedly, it seems difficult to enter the marine animal training field when you are starting out. Remembering that everyone employed as a trainer today once faced the same situation, and successfully landed a job should provide some measure of hope that you can do it too. From the onset, competition is stiff, even if simply based on the sheer number of resumes received for a single available position. That's what makes a resume such an important tool. To us, a strong candidate will list the following four qualifications on their resume:

1. A bachelor's degree in the sciences. The area of study, whether biology, zoology, conservation, marine sciences, et cetera, isn't really important. All of the areas of study can be applied to a career in marine animal training, however, your greatest amount of learning will be done on the job.
2. SCUBA certification. Because working with marine animals requires being in and around water all day long, strong swimming skills, including SCUBA certification, are highly recommended. For our facility specifically, SCUBA certification is required, as it is utilized almost daily.
3. Public speaking. Any type of exposure and/or experience with public speaking situations is desirable. Because a large part of our career is dedicated to educating the public, being comfortable presenting information to varying groups and numbers of people is very important.
4. Experience working with animals. Don't despair, this doesn't mean experience working with marine animals specifically. But experience working with any animals, including volunteering or internships, will provide the desired outcome - the realization that there is hard, sometimes dirty work and long hours involved in caring for animals. This experience on a resume lets us know that you won't be disappointed to find out there's more to the job than playing with the dolphins all day (even if that is our favorite part).

This may sound surprising, but rarely does a resume come in with all four of these qualifications. Therefore, one that does is almost guaranteed to get an interview.

Finally, there are additional areas we would advise you to pay special attention to. The first are typos! Nothing speaks worse for a candidate than a resume with misspelled words and a sloppy layout. Take the time to get it right.

The second is unrelated experience. Please do list anything that you think may have given you skills which can be applied toward your potential position. However, if you have unrelated job experiences, these may not be important. Leave these to be discussed in person when you get your interview.

Remember, we've all been there, so don't give up hope. Best of luck!
Cheryl Messinger
The Dolphin Connection

ANSWER 2: It is a common question heard again and again: "How do I get experience if no one will hire me without that experience?" It seems like a vicious Catch-22 to the eager newcomer searching for a way to get his or her foot in the door. There are many of us in the field today, so it is not an impossible situation. It does, however, require patience and persistence. In addition, it is important to remember that each facility has different requirements and expectations of applicants. Here is a summary of the advice we give interested applicants at the John G. Shedd Aquarium.

Education: Most facilities require that entry-level applicants have a minimum of a bachelor's degree in a relevant field. This may include biology, marine biology, zoology, psychology, education, as well as other disciplines. Some facilities may focus their search on applicants with a specific type of degree, but most are looking for a broad range of experiences. Often, marine mammal trainers are required to do much more than just train the animals. Backgrounds in water chemistry, nutrition, animal health, public speaking, computers, research techniques, and much more are often helpful. We recommend that students work toward a degree in an area that they enjoy, while gaining as much practical experience as possible.

Experience: Years of college and multiple degrees will not necessarily make a good trainer. Employers want to know that an applicant has the patience and full understanding of what the job entails, consequently some level of experience is usually required. Getting practical experience is not as difficult as it may seem. Too often, those interested in working with marine mammals have blinders on, and do not realize the many experiences that can prove beneficial in their quest for a job in the field. Many organizations offer internships or have volunteer programs that offer a wealth of practical experience. Almost any animal related, formal husbandry position will provide valuable experience, it does not have to be with marine mammals. Working at a veterinary office as an assistant, cleaning or groom work at a horse stable or dog kennel, as well as various jobs at animal shelters and rehabilitation centers are all excellent places to start. These animal husbandry experiences can be valuable stepping stones toward the ultimate goal of working with marine mammals. Even caring for family pets is valuable experience, but will not normally count as actual experience on a resume. An employer is usually looking for more formal experience, one where a reference can be checked; an employer never knows for sure to what extent or how well an applicant may have cared for a pet.

Special Skills: Many facilities will also look for other special skills. SCUBA diving certification, swimming skills, CPR certification, first aid training, research experience, special equipment handling skills, performing background, teaching experience, customer service background, and many other skills can be valuable. You could get hired without any of the skills just mentioned, but it never hurts to be as versatile as possible. Some facilities may specifically look for some of the skills described. It is important to include these things on a resume.

Resume: No matter how good your education is, or how experienced you may be, your resume is usually the first impression a prospective employer will get of you. If a resume is not well put together, it may also be the last impression. Often resumes are looked at by a Human Resource office before they are passed on to someone in an animal care department. Resumes should be well organized, neat, and easy to read. There is not a standard format that will guarantee that your resume stands out above the rest. Certainly there is something to be said for brevity and clarity, however, don't shortchange yourself either. The resume should represent you, and only you know your strengths and weaknesses best. Information should be easy to find, grammatically correct, and truthful. The quickest death for many a resume is false information. This is a small community, and employers will check with former employers, even when not on the reference list. It is also wise to list jobs, experiences, and hobbies that might be peripherally relevant. Waiting tables might indicate good customer service experience, an office job may include good computer skills, and many other seemingly unrelated jobs may help get you an interview.

The Interview: There are many intangibles that come into play during the interview process. It is your opportunity to sell yourself. It is impossible to know what an employer is looking for, so your best bet is to simply be yourself. Unless you are given special instructions, it is not possible to prepare for an interview other than to get plenty of rest and try to present yourself in the best light. You should think of the interview as your opportunity to ask questions also, most employers want to know what interests you. You should allow the interviewer to set the tone and guide you through the process. You should answer questions thoroughly and honestly. It is often helpful to come prepared with questions that you might want to ask if given the opportunity.

It must be obvious by now that there are no definite or sure ways to get a job as a trainer. Patience and persistence are important virtues in working toward a career with marine mammals. A solid education and as much practical animal experience as possible are extremely important qualifications. Perhaps most important, remember that experience can come in many forms. Good luck!

Ken Ramirez
John G. Shedd Aquarium

A DAY IN THE LIFE
OF AN ANIMAL CARE SPECIALIST

What is a an Animal Care Specialist?

At the John G. Shedd Aquarium the staff that works with the marine mammals and birds are called Animal Care Specialists. Each facility may have a different name or title for those who work with the animals (Trainer, Keeper, Biologist, etc.). Their job is to provide our animals with a safe, healthy, stimulating environment. Each Animal Care Specialist must understand or know:
- A. Biology, anatomy, and physiology of the animal
- B. The animals' natural history
- C. Animal nutrition and dietary needs
- D. Basic principles of veterinary care
- E. Water chemistry and filtration
- F. Animal behavior

What are the qualifications of an Animal Care Specialist?

Every facility has different qualities they look for in their animal care staff. Here are some of the most important qualifications at the John G. Shedd Aquarium:

1. B.S. or B.A. in Biology, Marine Biology, Zoology, Psychology, Education, or other related degree. Although no one single degree plan can adequately prepare an individual for a career in an animal care field, all of the mentioned backgrounds are useful.

2. Animal care experience. It is critical that anyone interested in working in a zoological environment get as much actual hands on experience as possible. This experience may come from volunteering in a zoo or aquarium, working in a veterinary clinic. at a stable, ranch, or farm. All of these experiences help an individual to find out more about the level of dedication required.

3. Team player, good communicator, dedicated and patient individual.

4. SCUBA diving certification. Not all facilities require SCUBA certification, but it is important to remember that most animal care positions are physically demanding.

5. Understand and believe in the philosophy and role of zoological institutions as education and conservation organizations.

What is a typical day like?

A typical Animal Care Specialist's day is divided as follows:

25%	Animal interaction	10%	Record keeping
20%	Cleaning	5%	Diving
20%	Food preparation	5%	Public interactions
10%	Meetings	5%	Other (Seminars, maintenance, etc.)

Sample page *This is one page of a hand-out given to those interested in finding out more about the Shedd Aquarium's Animal Care Specialist position, which is the entry level position for trainers. The next page demonstrates a few sample schedules of the type of busy days each trainer may have.*

The animal care specialist's day can be very hectic. The primary purpose behind the busy schedule is to provide the animals the very best care possible. Each day, we have at least 9 animal care specialists working. Here is half a typical day for three of them:

TIME	STAFF MEMBER #1	STAFF MEMBER #2	STAFF MEMBER #3
7:00	Arrive at work	Arrive at work	Arrive at work
7:15	Dress/look @ sched.	Dress/look @ sched.	Dress/look @ sched.
7:30	Food Preparation	Maintenance Dive	Food Preparation
7:45	↓ ↓	↓ ↓	↓ ↓
8:00	↓ ↓	↓ ↓	↓ ↓
8:15	↓ ↓	↓ ↓	Penguin Feed
8:30	New Lag Training	↓ ↓	↓ ↓
8:45	Clean & Records	↓ ↓	↓ ↓
9:00	Otter Feed	Seal Training	Pen Exhibit Clean
9:15	↓ ↓	Clean & Records	↓ ↓
9:30	Otter Window Clean	Beluga Training	↓ ↓
9:45	Otter Food Prep	↓ ↓	↓ ↓
10:00	↓ ↓	Clean & Records	Records
10:15	↓ ↓	Presentation Meet.	Presentation Meet.
10:30	↓ ↓	Lag Presentation	Lag Presentation
10:45	Records	Clean & Records	Clean & Records
11:00	Otter Training	Seal Training	Beluga Respirations
11:15	Clean & Records	Clean & Records	
11:30	New Lag Training	Freezer Duty	New Lag Training
11:45	Presentation Meet.	New Lag Play Session	Presentation Meet.
12:00	Lag Presentation	Beluga Play Session	Lag Presentation
12:15	Lunch	Lunch (On call to	Lunch
12:30	↓	Dive)	↓
12:45	↓	↓	↓
1:00	↓	↓	↓
1:15	Otter Play Session	Presentation Meet.	Beluga Training
1:30	↓ ↓	Lag Presentation	Clean & Records
1:45		Clean & Records	
2:00	Otter Area Clean	New Lag Training	Penguin Krill & Clean
2:15	↓ ↓	Snorkel Habitats	↓ ↓
2:30	↓ ↓	↓ ↓	↓ ↓
2:45	↓ ↓	Presentation Meet.	Penguin Feed

The day continues in this manner until everything is done between 6:30 and 8:30 pm each night!

JOIN IMATA

The International Marine Animal Trainers Association

Dedicated to those who serve marine mammal science through training, public display, research, husbandry, conservation, and education.

I am applying for membership in the following category (check one):

[ ] **PROFESSIONAL**- Anyone who has actively participated in the training, husbandry, and/or management of marine mammals for a total of at least three years accumulated over a period of no more than five years preceding the date of application. Requires two endorsements from Professional members in good standing, at least one of which must be from an individual whose employer is other than that of the applicant's. ANNUAL DUES $75.00 USD.

[ ] **ACTIVE**- Anyone who has actively participated in the training, husbandry and/or management of marine animals for at least one continuous year within a period of no more than three years preceding the date of application. requires two endorsements from either Professional or Active members in good standing. ANNUAL DUES $60.00 USD.

[ ] **ASSOCIATE**- Anyone who is interested in the objectives of the Association and wishes to support them. ANNUAL DUES $60.00 USD.

[ ] **STUDENT**- Anyone who is interested in the objectives of the Association, wishes to support them, and is enrolled in an accredited academic institution on a full-time basis. Proof of current status MUST be included. ANNUAL DUES $40.00 USD.

[ ] **ORGANIZATIONAL**- Any group or institution interested in supporting the obJectives of the Association. ANNUAL DUES $200.00 USD.

Name_____

Job Title_____

Organization_____

Organization Address_____

_____

Work Phone & Fax_____

Home Address_____
(Complete only if you want IMATA mail sent to home address)

List previous work experience in the marine animal field

ZOO/AQUARIUM	JOB TITLE	YEARS

Total years of experience in the marine animal field_____

List papers/posters presented, published articles, awards/honors

_____
_____
_____

How did you hear about IMATA? _Poster _Brochure _Soundings _Other

PLEASE SEE SIDE TWO

IMATA MEMBERSHIP APPLICATION
SIDE 2

I hereby make application for membership in IMATA. If accepted, I will abide by its Code of Ethics, Constitution, Bylaws, and resolutions and support its objectives. I understand that any conduct in violation of these organizational guidelines will be cause for revocation of my membership.

_____
(Applicant's signature)   (Date)

MEMBERSHIP STATUS

__Professional $75 U.S.   Please provide endorsements below or enclose appropriate letters.
__Active $60 U.S.   Please provide endorsements below or enclose appropriate letters.
__Associate $60 U.S.
__Organizational $200 U.S.
__Student $40 U.S.   Please include proof of full time status.

Payment **MUST** be sent with this application, thereafter, renewal payments will be due by 31 January of each year. Any member delinquent with dues on the 1st of February will be dropped from the IMATA membership.

Make checks payable to IMATA. Non U.S. residents, please pay by international bank draft or money order, drawn on a U.S. bank. If paying by credit card, circle one:

VISA   or   MASTERCARD

Card number:_____
                                                           EXP. DATE

Signature:_____

Print:_____

If applying for Professional or Active status, you must provide **appropriate signatures** below or enclose letters of endorsement.

I, the below signed endorser, verify that this applicant who is seeking membership into IMATA, has actively participated in the training, husbandry, and/or management of marine mammals for a total of at least 3 years accumulated over a period of no more than 5 years for Professional membership, or for at least 1 continuous year within a period of no more then 3 years for Active membership.

Endorser #1:_____   Memb status:_____

Print:_____   Date:_____

Endorser #1:_____   Memb status:_____

Print:_____   Date:_____

Mail application, dues payment, letters of endorsement, and proof of student status to:

Secretary IMATA
1200 South Lake Shore Drive
Chicago, Illinois 60605   USA

Glossary 14

Glossary

The International Marine Animal Trainers Association undertook the task of compiling a comprehensive vocabulary list of terms used in the training community. The goal was to get everybody in the training community speaking a common language. However, even respected technical references vary in their definition of certain terms. The daunting task of compiling and editing this glossary fell on the shoulders of the Animal Training and Advisory Committee. By 1997, Jennifer Hurley and Jeanine Scaramozzino had compiled multiple glossaries from different facilities and reference books, and combined them into one glossary. IMATA is trying to determine how to make the glossary most useful to its members. In the meantime, this final draft (completed in 1998) is an excellent resource. What I find most beneficial is that most terms have several definitions with a notation as to who uses that particular definition. In reading through the articles in this manual, you will find it helpful to have varied definitions as refernces. Because trainers use terms so differently, seeing various definitions in print is very helpful..

*Training and Behavioral Terms Glossary for the
International Marine Animal Trainers Association
(IMATA)*

edited by

Jenifer Anne Hurley, Ph.D. and Jeanine Marie Scaramozzino
Joseph M. Long Marine Laboratory
University of California, Santa Cruz

A

Absolute Threshold · Refers to the minimum stimulus intensity that can be perceived [27]. · Stimulus intensity to which a subject responds 50% of the time [11,16].

Abstract Control By A Stimulus · Sometimes the property of the stimulus which controls an operant performance may not be found in any single instance of the stimulus. When such is the case, the control may be through an abstract property of the stimulus, such as its shape, position or size. In each of these cases, the controlling property of the stimulus is found in a class of stimuli, and reinforcement is determined by a general rule rather than a specific form of the stimulus [9].

Abulia · Abulia is a non-technical term which describes an organism whose performances are occurring at a low frequency because the number of performances required for reinforcement is too high. It is defined as the state of an organism in which there is a loss of will power; there is an inability to act or to make decisions. The term usually refers to a performance which occurs at a low rate as a result of its schedule of reinforcement [9,25].

Accidental Reinforcement · Accidental reinforcement describes a coincidence between a performance and a reinforcer. Even though there is no intentional connection between the organism's performance and the reinforcer, there is still an increase in frequency of the performance. In accidental reinforcement, the form of the behavior that is reinforced is not fixed. With a deliberate reinforcement contingency, the organism must emit a particular performance before the reinforcer is presented. Accidental reinforcement is synonymous with spurious or superstitious conditioning and adventitious reinforcement [9].

Activation Syndrome · A large group of responses which are elicited by the environment, usually paired with emotions such as fear or anger, and characterized by flight or fight [25]. · A term to describe the effect of a large group of responses which are elicited together by certain stimuli [24].

Adaptation · The tendency of the sensory apparatus to adjust to any steady and continued level of stimulation and to stop responding [16]. · As used in connection with the senses, this refers to the fact that after continual stimulation, a sense gradually loses its ability to respond [27]. · Adjustment to new surroundings; characterized by a decrease in excitability [7].

Adjustable Stimulus · An adjustable stimulus is one which an animal may change as a result of its own behavior. A procedure where a bird may increase the length of a line by pecking at one key and decrease it by pecking at another is an example of an adjustable stimulus [9].

Adventitious Reinforcement · See Accidental Reinforcement.

Adverse · Tending to discourage, retard or make more difficult [24]. ·Moving or working in an opposite or contrary direction [21].

Affiliation · A form of integration involving the maintenance of proximity to other individuals [7]. · To connect or associate oneself with [21].

Aggression · The tendency to engage or challenge the environment; this tendency can be turned into destructive behavior by a bad environment. Normal aggressive impulse can be cultured and sent in a positive direction, or it can be frustrated and sent in a negative direction [11]. ·Behavior aimed, consciously, or unconsciously, at hurting another individual, or the impulse to do so [7]. · A type of behavior arising from hostile motives; it takes such forms as arguementiveness, scorn, sarcasm, physical and mental cruelty, and fighting [16].

Alternate Response Training · A technique used in therapy as a self-control strategy in which the individual is trained to engage in a response (e.g. relaxation) that interferes with or replaces another response to be controlled or eliminated [17].

Anti-Social Behavior · An undesirable response that is beyond the usual parameters of a specific culture [24]. · A behavior characterized by lack of conscience, sense of social responsibility, and feeling for other people; also selfishness, ruthlessness, and addiction to lying [16].

Anxiety · The emotional predisposition that is generated by a conditioned aversive stimulus. For example, a stimulus that regularly precedes pain will generate anxiety [7]. · A state of mind producing a change in behavior caused by an aversive and/or pre-aversive stimuli. The change in behavior which in the past has reduced the magnitude of the aversive stimulus may increase in frequency [9,25]. · An intrapsychic tension state with motivation characteristics: apprehensions, dread, foreboding relative to some unclear stimulus. A vague fear [27]. · The precursor to all neurotic reactions. Subject usually has a vague but intense feeling that some terrible calamity is about to occur [11].

Approach-Approach Conflict · A situation in which an organism wants something but is afraid of obtaining it; opposition between the two incompatible response tendencies of desire and fear [7]. · A conflict in which the individual has a single goal with both desirable and undesirable aspects, causing mixed feelings [16].

Approximation · One of many progressive steps from simple to more complex behavior, all leading to a finished desired behavior by gradually raising the requirement for reinforcement (successive approximation) [5]. · A single step in the refinement process of shaping. Comes from the idea that each differential or selective reinforcement selects a behavior that is a closer approximation of the endpoint behavior than the previous response [6]. · One of a series of stages measures or units calculated to achieve a desired goal [24].

Assimilation · The tendency to apply old ideas and responses to new objects or problems [2]. · The process of incorporating a new stimulus into one's existing cognitive view [16]. · A process by which new information is acquired through the application of existing rules or schemes [7].

Association · A process by which an organism connects related elements such as perceptions, memories, or ideas with each other [7,21]. · An aspect of learning in which two or more stimuli events or ideas become connected through being presented at the same time [24].

Attitude Shaping · The process of conditioning an animal's frame of mind in eliciting behavioral responses [24].

Autonomic Conditioning · An operant conditioning technique for controlling autonomic responses that are normally not under the organism's control [7].

Aversive Conditioning · A type of counterconditioning in which punishment is used in order to associate negative feelings with an undesirable response [2]. · A technique in which a painful or discomforting stimulus is paired with another stimulus in order to extinguish the undesirable response to that stimulus [7,16].

Aversive Event or Stimulus · A stimulus whose termination increases the frequency of the performance is called an aversive stimulus. Such an increase in frequency is called negative reinforcement. An aversive stimulus which increases the frequency of a performance by terminating it is called a negative reinforcer. It may decrease the frequency of the performance it follows (punishment), it may elicit reflexes (unconditioned stimulus), or it may alter the frequency of many operant performances in the ongoing repertoire (emotion or anxiety) [2,3,5,7,9]. · A stimulus that suppresses a behavior it follows, or increases a behavior that results in its termination [17].

Avoidance-Avoidance Conflict · A situation in which an organism is forced to choose one of two undesirable goals [7].

Avoidance or Avoidance Behavior · Avoidance describes a performance which increases in frequency because it postpones the appearance of an aversive stimulus. In the classical laboratory experiment, a rat postpones an electric shock for a brief interval each time it presses the lever. If the rat presses the lever frequently enough, it avoids the electric shock. Avoidance is to be contrasted with escape, when the performance actually terminates the aversive stimulus [9]. · Performance of a behavior which postpones or averts the presentation of an aversive event or stimulus [5,7,17].

Avoidance Conditioning · A response to a cue that is instrumental in avoiding a painful experience [7]

Avoidance Learning · Learning that occurs when the subject makes a particular response in order to avoid a noxious [unpleasant] stimulus [27]. · The process of learning to emit a behavior in order to prevent an aversive event, e.g., children learn to duck an oncoming ball in order to avoid being hit by it [6,7,19].

B

Baseline · The frequency that behavior is performed prior to initiating a behavior modification program. The rate of performance used to evaluate the effect of the program[17]. · In experimental work, the term is often used to refer to the control group which serves as a basis for evaluating data from the experimental group[27].

Behavior · Any observable or measurable response or act. [The terms behavior and response are used synonymously]. Behavior occasionally is broadly defined to include cognition, psychological reactions and feelings, which may not be directly observable but are defined in terms that can be measured using various assessment strategies[17]. · A specific action created by an animal. For the purposes of training, an animal action defined and named by the trainer[6]. · Any activity of animals or men which is directly observable, and where it is possible for 2 or more observers to agree upon what they saw or heard[19].

Behavioral Chain · A group of behaviors in a specific order forming a more complex behavior, and defined as a unit to the animal[6].

Behavioral Drift · A change or stray from the norm in standard of response. The result of drift over a period of time is deviation[24].

Behaviorism · The view, first expressed by John B. Watson, that psychology should focus upon the study of behavior -- overt actions capable of direct observation and measurement[2]. · A school of thought that psychologists should concentrate on the study of overt behavior rather than of "mental life" or consciousness[7,16].

Behavioral Enrichment · Stimuli and methods used as tools to increase interest in the environment and decrease the frequency of stereotypical behaviors[8]. · Stimuli presented to an animal to enrich the environment and discourage stereotypical and/or injurious behavior[18,24].

Bond · A relationship that an animal maintains with a con-specific towards which certain behavior is exclusively or preferentially directed[12,20,24,28].

Bridge · A stimulus that pinpoints in time the precise moment of a desired response and bridges the gap in time between that point and when the animal may receive further reward[15,24]. · A signal that is conditioned to be reinforcing because it is paired with other reinforces which evolves to pinpoint an instant in time for the animal in training. Intermediate Bridge signals the animal that at that instant it is on the path to success, but it has not completed the behavior yet. Terminal Bridge signals the instant at which an animal successfully completes a requested behavior[6]. · A stimulus which signals the delivery of a reinforcer. Often called a secondary or conditioned reinforcer because it acquires its effectiveness through a history of being paired with primary reinforcement, such as food to a hungry animal[7].

C

Chain or Chain Behavior · A chain consists of two or more behaviors. One behavior produces the conditions which make the next possible. The stimuli linking the behaviors together serves as both conditioned reinforces, maintaining the topography and frequency of the behaviors produced, and as stimuli setting the occasion for the following behaviors [9,25]. · A series of behaviors which are linked by stimuli that act both as conditioned reinforces and discriminative stimuli [5].

Chaining · The process of learning a sequence of behaviors that proceeds semi-automatically in a determinate order; the last previous response provides the necessary cue that determines which behavior comes next [7,24].

Classical Or Respondent Conditioning (Sometimes referred to as Pavlovian conditioning) · A form of conditioning in which stimuli associated with naturally meaningful stimuli tend to become substitutes for the stimuli themselves and to elicit similar responses. Technically, the pairing of a conditioned stimulus (CS) with a unconditioned stimulus (US) elicits a conditioned response (CR) similar to the unconditioned response (UR) originally elicited by the US [7,16]. · A basic form of learning in which stimuli initially incapable of evoking certain responses acquire the ability to do so through repeated pairing with other stimuli that are able to elicit such responses [2]. · A method originated by Pavlov in which conditioned responses are acquired. It differs from instrumental conditioning in that the behavior is clearly dependent upon particular stimulus such that it may be said to be elicited by that stimulus [27]. · Classical conditioning results in a reflex (versus a behavior) which can be elicited by a cue. A reflex is elicited by a primary stimulus - e.g., savory food elicits saliva, pain elicits rapid withdrawal, etcetera. In classical conditioning, a neutral cue is associated with an eliciting stimulus, and eventually becomes an eliciting stimulus. This type of conditioning does not involve any voluntary choices made by the animal - just a reflex response or reaction [6,17].

Communicative Delta (CD) · Communicative signal which pinpoints in time when an animal has done something incorrectly in order to provide information which will allow the animal to succeed more rapidly. Used in conjunction with a bridge stimulus has the affect of providing "hot and cold" information [15].

Conditioned Aversive Stimulus · An event which is initially neutral may acquire aversive properties by virtue of being paired with other aversive events or a signal that no reinforcement will be forth coming [17].

Conditioned Reinforcer · See Secondary Reinforcer · A reinforcer that derives its value as a result of its association with primary, innate, or unconditioned reinforcers [5,7,15]. · A stimulus which has been paired with the elements of enjoyment. A stimulus which has to be conditioned to enjoy, i.e. tactile, our dog whistles, underwater tone, playing with toys, etc. [25].

Conditioned Response (CR) · In classical conditioning, a reflex response elicited by a conditioned stimulus alone in the absence of the unconditioned stimulus after a number of pairings of the conditioned stimulus with an unconditioned stimulus. It resembles, but is not identical to, the unconditioned response [2,7,16,17,27]. · A conditioned response is the change in the organism's behavior elicited by a conditioned stimulus. In a reflex, the buzzer (conditioned stimulus), which precedes food in the dog's mouth (unconditioned stimulus), comes to elicit salivation (conditioned response) after a sufficient number of pairings [9]. · A response that is elicited by a stimulus after learning has occurred [24]

Conditioned Stimulus (CS) · A stimulus which has the property of producing a response through pairing or association [25]. · A stimulus which acquires the property of eliciting a previously unconditioned response. A buzzer (conditioned stimulus) which initially has little influence on blood pressure (unconditioned response) comes to elicit changes in blood pressure (conditioned response) when it is paired with an electric shock (unconditioned stimulus). The complete event is called a conditioned reflex [9]. · A stimulus which has a specific meaning - usually to denote the successful completion of behavioral criterion. A bridge is a conditioned stimulus. Usually denoted as S-delta [6].

Conditioning · The term conditioning is used to describe both operant and respondent behavior. It refers to a change in the frequency or form of the organism's behavior as a result of the influence of the environment. In operant conditioning the frequency of a performance changes as an organism interacts with the environment. In respondent conditioning, a neutral stimulus comes to elicit a response as a result of pairing it with an unconditioned stimulus [9]. · The operation of associating an act or object with a stimulus to modify or mold behavior [16,25]. · The process whereby an organism responds consistently to a stimulus that is presented to it periodically [19]. · The process of learning how signals, behaviors, and consequences are related [6].

Continuous Reinforcement · Continuous reinforcement is a schedule of reinforcement in which each performance is followed by the reinforcer. Continuous reinforcement is distinguished from intermittent reinforcement, which refers to schedules of reinforcement in which some performances go unreinforced [9,17]. · A schedule of reinforcement in which every selected behavior is reinforced [25]. · Conditions under which a particular form of behavior is followed by reinforcement on every occasion when it is emitted [2].

Control · The term control expresses the functional relation between a performance and the variable of which it is a function. Thus we say, "A performance is under the control of a level of deprivation," as a synonym for, "The performance is a function of the level of deprivation,"[9]. · A group in an experiment which is not exposed to the independent variable under investigation. The behavior of subjects in this condition is used as a base-line against which to evaluate the effects of experimental treatments [2,21,22].

Counter-Conditioning (Active Desensitization) · Process where normal defense reactions elicited by an aversive stimulus, such as a shock, are modified by association with a positive reinforcer[23]. · To expedite the desensitization of a novel stimulus by associating it with a reinforcer [15].

Cue · A signal which will elicit a specific behavior or reflex - as a result of a learned association [6]. · See Conditioned Stimulus.

D

Delay of Reinforcement · The interval between a behavior and the delivery of reinforcement [2,17].

Delta · See Stimulus Delta.

Deprivation · Reducing the availability of, or access to, a reinforcer [17,25].

Desensitization · Exposing an animal to a stimulus using time or experience to drive the stimulus value towards neutral [15]. · A process of changing an animal's perception of an event, negative or positive, but usually negative, to a neutral perception, as evidenced by the animals lack of response to the event when compared to a previous baseline [6]. · A process used in changing an animal's attitude against sensitivity to become more at ease in an uneasy situation [16,25]. · See Habituation and Counter-Conditioning.

Differential Reinforcement · The occurrence of reinforcement on selected occasions at or after one topography of a performance as opposed to another topography, is called differential reinforcement. For example one may differentially reinforce performances which exert a great deal of force on the lever as opposed to performances which operate it lightly [9,25]. · The reinforcement of one form magnitude of a response when other rather similar forms magnitudes are not reinforced [7]. · The process of reinforcing only those operants which are like, or increasingly like, the end-point desired behavior. Of all the operants the animal offers, approximations of the end-point desired behavior are selectively reinforced until the behavior is formed. This entire process is considered successive approximation or shaping. The trainer's strategy is selective or differential reinforcement [6]. · See Selective Reinforcement.

Differential Reinforcement of Incompatible Behavior (DRI) · Delivery of a reinforcer after a response that is incompatible or competes with a target response that is to be suppressed. The effect is to increase the frequency of the incompatible response (e.g., cooperative play) and to decrease the frequency of the undesirable target response (e.g., fighting) [17,25].

Differential Reinforcement of Other Behavior (DRO) · The DRO schedule refers to a procedure in which a reinforcer follows any performance the animal emits except a particular one. Thus, the DRO schedule specifies the performance which is to go unreinforced rather than the one which is increased in frequency. The result of such a schedule of reinforcement is a decrease in the frequency of the particular performance that is specified. This decrease in frequency usually results from an increase in frequency of an incompatible performance [9,17]. · A procedure in which any behavior is reinforced which is incompatible with a particular one. In this way, we can stop an animal from behaving in a certain way without the use of punishment [25].

Discipline · To train or develop by exercise. Functionally different from punishment [25]. · Strict control to enforce obedience as the result of such training; treatment that corrects or punishes [21].

Discrimination · Discrimination frequently refers to the control of an operant performance by a discriminative stimulus (SD). Thus, discrimination has occurred when the discriminative stimulus controls the frequency of an operant performance [9]. · Learning to react differentially to different stimuli. Such learning is brought about through reinforcement of responses to one stimulus, but not to any others [27]. · Discrimination is the ability to differentiate between stimuli attempting to have control over operant behavior, an element in both classical and operant conditioning [7,25]. · The ability to perceive differences in various aspects of the environment [5,16].

Discriminative Stimulus (SD) · A conditioned stimulus which has the property of producing a specific behavior [25]. · An antecedent event or stimulus which signals that a certain response will be reinforced. A response which is reinforced in the presence of an SD. After an event becomes an SD by being paired with reinforcement, its presence can increase the probability that the response will occur [5,17,24]. · A stimulus which has a specific meaning, in animal training, usually denoting a stimulus which elicits a specific behavior, or a cue. Usually noted as S-delta [6]. · A discriminative stimulus is the particular occasion on which a performance is reinforced, in contrast to other occasion (stimuli) on which this performance is not reinforced. The term has the connotations of the common language term to discriminate or to distinguish between stimuli. The common language term, however, refers to the state the organism who discriminates rather than to the technical properties of stimulus in the environment [9]. · See Positive Discriminative Stimulus.

Displaced Aggression(Displacement) · A mechanism in which aggression is redirected from an unassailable target to an inappropriate but assailable target [3,16]. · Aggression directed against someone or something as a substitute for the original cause of the organism's anger [7].

Distractions · Qualitative aspects of the environment - things such as bells, applause, audience, animals, the feeling of pressure, other animals, or flying objects [6].

Dominance · The social structure within a group of animals that consists of the relative status among the members of the group [3]. · The ranking of one animal over another in a fairly stable hierarchy of threats [12].

Dominant Behavior · A response that exercises controlling power, authority, or influence [21,24].

Drive · An aroused condition of an organism resulting from deprivation of the means of fulfilling a physiological need [2]. · A strong impetus to behavior or active striving [22]. · An incitement to action that has its origin in an internal bodily state (e.g. hunger), or that has been learned (e.g. the drive to obtain approval) [7].

E

Elicit · To automatically bring about a response. Respondent or reflex behaviors are elicited by unconditioned stimuli [5,9,17]. · Elicited behavior is behavior which is forcibly produced by the environment [25].

Emit · Emitted behaviors produce a change in the environment. Operant behavior is emitted. Emitted behavior is produced through willingness [25]. · We speak of operant behavior as emitted because the main variable controlling the frequency of the performance is the way in which the performance changes the environment. The emitted nature of operant behavior is to be contrasted with the elicited nature of reflex behavior. In operant behavior the main emphasis is on the stimulus which follows the performance in contrast to reflex behavior where the main emphasis is on the stimulus which precedes the response and elicits or evokes it. Because operant behavior is emitted, it has the quality of purposiveness, in contrast to the highly determined nature of the reflex [9,17]. · The act of causing an operant behavior by the presentation of a conditioned stimulus [5].

Escape or Escape Behavior · The term escape describes a relation between a performance and an aversive stimulus in which the performance terminates the aversive stimulus. Escape is to be contrasted with avoidance, where the aversive stimulus does not occur at all as long as the avoidance performance continues postpone it [9]. · The actual behavior which terminates an aversive stimulus [5,11,17,25].

Escape Learning · The process of learning to emit a behavior in order to escape an aversive event in progress, e.g., if a room is too hot, a person will leave it to escape the heat. If the person or animal can predict when the room will be too hot, they can then avoid the room when it becomes hot. Thus avoidance learning can directly follow escape learning [6]. · A conditioning technique in which the subject learns to escape or terminate an unpleasant stimulus [7].

Extinction · A procedure where the reinforcement of a previously reinforced behavior is discontinued. A behavior which has undergone extinction will decrease in frequency [25]. · Thus the effect of extinction on the organism's performance occurs as a result of each unreinforced emission of the performance. If the animal has no opportunity to engage in the behavior, then the term extinction is inappropriate. When a previously conditioned performance is extinguished (no longer reinforced), it generally occurs initially with a high frequency and then falls continuously until its rate reaches near zero. Occasionally, the rate of a performance may actually increase (although temporarily) when the performance is no longer reinforced [2,9,16,17,27].

Extinction Burst · An increase in the frequency and intensity of responding at the beginning of extinction [17,25].

F

Fading · A procedure to change one stimulus controlling a certain behavior to another stimulus [25]. · A term used to describe a procedure for gradually changing a stimulus controlling an organism's performance to another stimulus. For example, consider a pigeon which pecks at a green key and not at a red one. If a cross is superimposed on the green key and the green color is faded out, the new stimulus will control the bird's behavior without the occurrence of any unreinforced pecking. Fading, disregarding the common usage of the term, does not always refer to the disappearance of a stimulus. Sometimes in a fading procedure, a stimulus begins at a low value and is increased in magnitude. If the rate of change of the stimuli is properly paced with the organism's behavior, the control may be shifted from one stimulus to another without any instances of the bird's pecking inappropriately [9]. · The gradual removal of discriminative stimuli [SD] including prompts such as instructions or physical guidance. Yet, it is important in most situations to fade the prompt. Fading can also refer to the gradual removal of reinforcement, as in the progressive thinning of a reinforcement schedule [17].

Fine-Grain Repertoire · A fine-grain repertoire refers to an operant performance which changes under the control of small variations in the stimulus. Examples of this are drawing from copy or steering a car. The phrase, "point-to-point correspondence between changes in a stimulus and the corresponding changes in a performance," refers to a fine-grain repertoire [9].

Fixed-Interval Schedule · In a fixed-interval schedule of reinforcement, the first performance that occurs after a fixed period of time elapses is reinforced. The interval of time is measured from the preceding reinforcement. Thus, on an FI 5 schedule, reinforcement is given after the first performance which the animal emits at least five minutes after the preceding reinforcement [7,9,11,17,25]. · The application of reinforcement on a systematic time basis [27]. · A form of partial reinforcement in which a "rule" [behavior] is rewarded only after a specific period of time has elapsed since the last rewarded use, the period of time between rewards remaining constant [3].

Fixed-Ratio Schedule · A schedule of reinforcement in which the organism is reinforced after a set number of nonreinforced correct responses [2,7,27]. · In a fixed-ratio schedule of reinforcement a fixed number of performances (counted from the preceding reinforcement) are required for reinforcement. Thus on a FR 50 schedule, the fiftieth performance after the preceding reinforcement produces the next reinforcement. The term ratio refers to the ration of performances required for each reinforcement [9,25].

Frustration · Emotional behavior prompted by the thwarting or interruption of goal seeking activity [29]. · A term used in two ways. In one sense frustration refers to any interference with the satisfaction of a motive. In another sense, frustration refers to the consequences or interval state resulting from such interference with goal directed behavior [7,16,27].

G

Generalization · Before one can fade stimuli, generalization must take place. Generalization is when a stimulus acquires control of a response due to reinforcement in the presence of a similar, but different stimulus [5,25]. · The process of comparing events, consequences or objects which have some trait in common and recognizing that common trait. That trait can then be extrapolated into new situations, guiding the animal's response, without the animal being specifically taught about that new situation. For example, if a child is specifically taught not to cross a street in front of an oncoming car, bus, and/or bicycle - then the child is likely to also wait for a motorcycle to pass. Eventually, the child conceptually groups all the vehicles traveling on a road into a set - "traffic." In animal training, an animal can be taught to allow a series of specific people to touch it. Eventually, the animal will let all people pet him, even if they are strangers [6]. · The tendency to respond to a class of stimuli rather than only to the one to which the animal was originally conditioned [27].

Generalized Reinforcer · The generalized reinforcer is a type of conditioned reinforcer which has the additional property that its effectiveness does not depend upon a single kind of deprivation. It is the occasion on which many different performances may be reinforced by different kinds of reinforces. Money is a generalized reinforcer [9].

Group Contingencies ("Team behavior") · Contingencies in which the group participates. There are two major variations: 1 An individual's behavior can determine the consequences delivered to the group[2] .The behavior of a group as a whole determines the consequences that the group (each member) receives [17,25].

H

Habit · A recurrent pattern of behavior acquired through experience and made more-or-less permanent by various reinforcing events [7]. · A behavior which an animal routinely emits without a cue presented by a trainer. The behavior may have initially been taught by a trainer or the animal may have originated it. For example, a person is initially taught by his mother to brush his teeth after eating. This can become a habit which the person continues without his mother there to remind him. A person may develop certain gestures while speaking, that were not specifically taught and are not part of the actual seeking process, and continue these gesture habits indefinitely. Or a person may be conditioned to eat at a specific time. He habitually eats at that time, cued by internal body conditions [6].

Habituation (Passive Desensitization) · The lessening or disappearance of a response with repeated presentations of the stimulus [15]. · The relatively persistent waning of a response as a result of repeated stimulation which is not followed by any kind of reinforcement [14,26]. · A form of learning in that it represents a relatively permanent change in behavior that is the result of the experience of the individual and is not due to fatigue process [10]. · Instances of decrement in magnitude of unlearned response which occurs centrally in an intact organism and were due to repetitive stimulatory activation. These can be distinguished from other types of response decrement which occur as a result of receptor adaptation, loss of the effector's ability to respond, or any of the various types of inhibition [13].

High Probability Behavior · A response which is performed with a relatively high frequency when the individual is given the opportunity to select among alternate behaviors [17].

Husbandry · Long term physiological and psychological management ensuring the viability of a species [24]. · The care and raising of domesticated animals, such as cattle, horses, sheep, etc. [21]. · A branch of agriculture concerned with the breeding and feeding of domestic animals [22].

I • J • K

Immediacy of Reinforcement · A critical feature of conditioning. The act of reinforcing, exactly following the behavior which is intended to increase in frequency. If reinforcement is delayed as much as a couple of seconds, it may follow some other behavior [25].

Imprinting · The process by which a young animal forms a lasting attachment to and preference for some object, usually a parent [12]. · The very rapid development of a response or learning pattern to a stimulus at an early and usually critical period of development, particularly characteristic or some species of birds [21,22].

Incentive · Refers to goal objects employed to motivate behavior [27]. · An external inducement to act or respond in a certain way [2,7,16].

Incompatible Behavior · A behavior that is impossible to occur with another at the same time [17,25]. · A performance is incompatible with another when it is impossible for both performances to occur at the same time. Thus the behavior of clasping the hands behind the back is incompatible with reaching for an object on a table [9].

Innovative Training · Learning by which an animal is reinforced for successfully reaching appropriate approximations through a self-experimental or self-inventive process [24].

Instinct · An inborn predisposition to behave in a specific way when appropriately stimulated. Instincts are complex behaviors that are characteristic of a species [7]. · A natural and unconditioned capability shared by all members of a species [24].

Instrumental Conditioning See Operant Conditioning.

Intelligence · The ability to profit from experience, to learn new pieces of information, and to adjust to new situations [16]. · In conventional terms, the ability to adapt to new circumstances, deal with complex or abstract materials, or solve intellectual problems [2]. · Often defined as the aggregate or global ability to act purposefully, think rationally, and deal effectively with one's environment [7,27].

Inter-Stimulus Interval (ISI) · In classical conditioning, the time elapsed between the conditioned stimulus and the unconditioned stimulus [7]. · In habituation the inter-stimulus interval (ISI) is defined as the time between exposures to a stimulus [10].

Intermittent Reinforcement · A schedule of reinforcement in which a response is not reinforced every time it is performed. Only some occurrences of this response are reinforced [17,25]. · Intermittent reinforcement occurs when reinforcement is omitted following some emissions of an operant performance. The various ways in which reinforcement may be intermittent are varied in schedules of reinforcement [9]. · Any schedule of reinforcement which does not provide reinforcement following each response (partial reinforcement) [7,25].

L

Latency · The duration of time between a stimulus being presented and a response being elicited. A measure of habit strength [17,24,27]. · Refers to the interval between a stimulus and the organism's behavior which is controlled by it. In the case of a reflex, the latency may be the interval between a stimulus and the response. In the case of operant behavior, latency may refer to the interval between the appearance of discriminative stimulus and the operant performance it controls [9].

Latent Learning · Learning that takes place casually, almost as if by accident, then lies latent until reinforcement is provided [7,16,27]. · Learning that is not manifest in overt behavior at the time learning takes place, but may become evident at a later stage [24].

Law of Effect · Thorndike's conclusion that responses which produce positive consequences are strengthened, while responses which yield unpleasant consequences are weakened [2,27]. · The concept that an organism will tend to repeat and learn behavior that has a satisfying or reinforcing outcome; behaviors that cause pain or discomfort will not be repeated or learned [7].

Learned Helplessness · A condition created by exposure to inescapable aversive events. This can retard or prevent learning in subsequent situations in which escape or avoidance is possible [24,27]. · The state of considering oneself helpless because of the failure of attempts to control a situation. Some animals will eventually quit trying. This is why it is important for a trainer to set the animal up to be successful - so that it will gain confidence and believe, through generalization, that since s/he could solve any situation presented to date, s/he could solve any situation that could ever be presented. Thus s/he will work hard to meet challenges rather than give up and passively accept consequences [6].

Learning · The process in which relatively permanent changes in behavior are produced through experience [2,11,19,29]. · A significant change in behavior as a result of previous experience and reinforcement [7,24].

Learning Plateau · A period in which early progress in learning appears to have stopped and improvement is at a standstill; the plateau is followed by a new period of progress [16]. · An interval in which no improvement is observed in learning followed by further improvement as practice continues [29].

M

Matching-to-Sample · A procedure in which the choice of a stimulus that matches a sample stimulus is followed by a reinforcer. Typically, in the matching-to-sample procedure, the organism touches a key in which the sample stimulus appears. The performance on the sample stimulus is reinforced by the appearance of two stimuli on two other keys. These stimuli correspond to the sample. The final reinforcement occurs if the organism chooses the key on which the stimulus corresponding to the sample stimulus appears. A time out or the reappearance of the sample stimulus occurs if the organism chooses the key which does not correspond to the sample [9].

Method of Approximations [Incremental Learning] · A method used to shape organisms' behavior whereby successive approximations of the desired behavior are reinforced [27]. · Learning that takes place in a series of steps, in which the amount of learning increases, sometimes quickly and sometimes slowly, until the learning is complete [16].

Mimicry · The act, practice or art of copying the manner or expression of another [21,24]. · Assumption of color, form, or behavior patterns by one species of another species, for camouflage and protection [21,22].

Modeling · See Observational Learning.

Motivation · The comparatively spontaneous drive, force, or incentive, which partly determines the direction and strength of the response of a higher organism to a given situation; it arises out of the internal state of the organism [22]. · A general term referring to the forces regulating behavior that is undertaken because of drives, needs, or desires and is directed toward goals [2,16]. · The non-stimulus variables controlling behavior; the general name for the fact that an organism's acts are partly determined in direction and strength by its own nature and/or internal state [7]. · A state of mind which produces a noticeable increase in behavioral activity. The most effective way to produce this state of mind is through stimulus complexity. Through such complexity, it is difficult for the mind to maintain an unhealthy state of boredom. Deprivation may also produce motivation; however, through force, and not through willingness. Because of this, deprivation should be handled with great care [25].

Motive · Anything that initiates behavior [7]. · A desire for a goal or incentive object that has acquired value for the individual [16]. · A drive, force, or tension state within the organism that impels it to act [21,27].

Multiple Schedule · A multiple schedule is a combination of several schedules of reinforcement, each of which is accompanied by a characteristic stimulus. For example, in the presence of a red light, key pecking is reinforced on a fixed-ratio schedule and in the presence of a green light, key pecking is reinforced on a fixed-interval schedule [9].

N

Negative · To remove from the environment [6]. · Directed away from the source of a stimulus [21].

Negative Discriminative Stimulus · In operant conditioning, the stimulus to which responses are nonreinforced or negatively reinforced. Also known as a stimulus delta [7].

Negative Punishment · In operant conditioning, the removal of a positive stimulus -- something the organism seeks to encounter -- from the organism's environment following a response, thereby decreasing the frequency of that response [7].

Negative Reinforcer · The frequency of the behavior is increased by the subtraction of something the animal does not like, as an immediate result of the behavior. Not a punisher, e.g., Mother with crying baby; Mother picks up baby; It stops crying; The baby was positively reinforced for crying; The mother was negatively reinforced when the baby quit crying [2,6,19]. · Negative reinforcement refers to an operant performance whose frequency increases because it has terminated an aversive stimulus. Both negative and positive reinforcement increase the frequency of the performance. In the case of negative reinforcement, the increase comes about because of the termination of the stimulus, while in the case of positive reinforcement, the increase occurs as a result of the effect of a reinforcing stimulus [9,25]. · In operant conditioning, any stimulus that, when removed, reduced, or prevented, increases the probability of a given response over time [7].

Neutral Stimulus or Cue · Any stimulus that has no effect on behavior before conditioning [7]. · A discrete signal with no initial meaning. Its meaning is acquired through association with a primary stimulus and related reflex response [6]. · Used in the description of conditioned reflexes to indicate that the stimulus which is to be established as a conditioned stimulus did not initially evoke or elicit the unconditioned response. Such a neutral stimulus, however, may not be neutral in respect to other aspects of the organism's repertoire [9].

Novelty Affect · Innate fear provoking response associated with exposure to novel stimulus [10].

O

Observational Learning · Learning by observing another individual [a model] engaged in a behavior. To learn from a model, the observer need not perform the behavior nor receive direct consequences for his or her performance [2,17,25]. · A type of learning in which the behavior of another organism is observed and imitated [16].

Ontogenetic History · Refers to the type of behavior an organism produces, caused by its experience and interaction with the existing environment [25]. · The result of such ontogenetic experiences may produce unique behaviors in each individual because the environments generating the performances are different for each individual [9].

Operant or Operant Behavior · Emitted behavior that is controlled by its consequences [17]. · Operant behavior acts on and produces a change in the environment. It is produced through a willingness and is also emitted [25]. · Behavior that does not appear to be clearly dependent on any specific stimulus; such behavior produces some effect on the organisms environment [5,27]. · A response to the environment (a stimulus) that the animal initiates to act upon, or operate his environment. Pushing a lever is an operant, so is barking, sitting down, or biting down [6].

Operant Conditioning (Instrumental Conditioning) · The process by which, through learning, free operant behavior becomes attached to a specific stimulus [16]. · A form of conditioning in which the persistence of a response emitted by an organism depends on its effect on the environment. The conditioning procedure involves presenting an organism with a reinforcing stimulus immediately after the occurrence of a given response. The fundamental principle of operant conditioning is that behavior is determined by its consequences [7,24]. · A form of learning in which the presentation of positive or negative reinforcers alters the rate at which responses are emitted [2]. · The term "conditioning" is sometimes used synonymously with learning. May be differentiated from classical conditioning in that responses in operant conditioning appear to be emitted rather than elicited by a specific stimulus, and they produce some effect that would otherwise not occur [27]. · A type of learning in which

546 ANIMAL TRAINING

behavior are altered primarily by regulating the consequences which follow them. The frequency of operant behaviors is altered by the consequences which they produce [17].

Orienting Response · The initial phase of an organism's response to a novel stimulus, a component of the novelty affect [15]. · A response to a stimulus in which the organism, turns toward the source of the stimulus [7].

P • Q

Partial Reinforcement Maintenance · See Intermittent Reinforcement.

Perception Modification · The process of changing an animal's perception of an event or stimulus, as evidenced by his changed response to the event or stimulus when compared to a previous baseline. This is most effectively done through a conditioning process where the event/stimulus is paired with a conditioned reinforcer or punisher in order to transfer the value of the reinforcer or punisher to the event/stimulus [6].

Performance · Measures of observed behavior [7,24].

Phylogenetic History · Phylogenetic history refers to the evolutionary history of the species in which the survival of individuals with particular gene features produces a selection of genetic patterns. Thus, the inheritance of given species is determined by the evolutionary history in which other kind of animals did not survive, rather than in the ontogenetic experience of the organism [9]. · Refers to the type of behavior produced by a given species which has been determined by evolutionary history in order to survive [25].

Positive · To add to the environment [6]. · Directed toward the source of a stimulus [21].

Positive Punishment · In operant conditioning, the addition of an aversive stimulus -- something the organism seeks to avoid -- to the organism's environment following a response, thereby decreasing the frequency of that response [7,15].

Positive Reinforcement · An increase in frequency of a response which is followed by a positive reinforcer. A positive reinforcer is an event which, when presented, increases the probability of a response it follows [17,25]. · Presentation of a reinforcer following the performance of a correct response which increases the probability that a response will reoccur in the future [5,7,11]. · Any event which serves to strengthen those responses which precede the event [2]. · Frequency of the behavior increased by the addition of some thing the animal desires, immediately after the behavior [6].

Positive Transfer · The facilitation of the learning of responses in new situations as a result of past learning [7].· A process in which learning is made easier by something learned previously [16].

Pre-Aversive Stimulus · A stimulus which has been conditioned through generalization as a predecessor to an aversive stimulus [25].

Precursor Stimulus · An event that comes before another that signals its arrival [19].

Premack Principle · A principle that states that of any pair of responses or activities in which an individual freely engages, the more frequent one will reinforce the less frequent one [17,25]. · Two responses could each serve as either a reinforcer or "neutral" response with respect to the other, depending upon their independent probabilities of occurrence [11].

Primary · A quality that an animal responds to innately in a certain way, without any conditioning from a human. A primary reinforcer might be food, sex, water, or sleep. A primary punisher might be the deprivation of any of the above, fear, or pain [6]. · Any innate or unlearned perception [15].

Primary Drive · An organic drive, such as thirst; also called unlearned drive [7].

Primary Reinforcement · Reinforcement provided by a stimulus that the organism finds inherently rewarding-usually stimuli that satisfy biological drives such as hunger or thirst [5,16,24]. · A reinforcing event that does not depend on learning to achieve its reinforcing properties. Food, water and sex are primary reinforcers [17]. · Defined by some psychologists as any stimulus that reduces a need or motive [27].

Proactive Inhibition · Occurs when learning one piece of material has negative effects on future learning [27]. · Interference by something learned in the past with the ability to remember new learning [2,16]. · The process whereby the retention of new learning is interfered with by previously learned material [7].

Prompt · An antecedent event that helps initiate a response. A discriminative stimulus which occasions a response. Instructions, gestures, physical guidance, and modeling cues serve as prompts [11]. · To cause to happen [24].

Property of a Stimulus · Property of a stimulus refers to a single dimension of the stimulus which may control a performance differentially from other dimensions of the stimulus. Thus, a stimulus might be described as a large red, right triangle, and a performance may be reinforced in respect to one property of the figure, such as its size [9].

Punisher or Punishment · Anything which decreases the frequency of the behavior it immediately follows [6,7,11]. · Presentation of an aversive event or removal of a positive event contingent upon a response which decreases the probability of that response [17]. · The actual act of following an operant behavior with an aversive stimulus. Punishment can cause anxiety [9,25].

R

Recall · The process of sending or retrieving an animal from one point of station to another through the use of a conditioned sound stimulus, or to bring back to station [24].

Recognition · A retrieval process of searching memory to see if the specific situation, object, person, or event at hand has ever been experienced before [3]. · A way of measuring learning; the subject is asked to show that he recognizes what he has learned - for example, by picking out the right answer in a multiple-choice test [2,7,16]. · In ethology this term is used most frequently to describe the perception of species specific characteristics. These are recognized both between and within species [12].

Redirected Activity · A redirected activity is an activity, recognizable from its form as being usually directed toward a particular stimulus, but on this occasion directed toward another stimulus. The classic human illustration is the aggressive man slamming his fist into the table instead of into an opponent [12].

Reflex · A reflex is a relationship between an eliciting stimulus and an elicit response such as the contraction of the pupil of the eye as a result of shining light on it, the jerk of the knee as a result of tapping the patellar tendon, the excretion of sweat as a result of warm air, or the constriction of blood vessels in response to a loud noise. The reflex describes both the behavior of the organism (response) and its environment (stimulus) [9,27]. · A rapid muscular response made automatically by an organism to some appropriate stimulus; this response is controlled by the spinal cord rather than the brain [6,7,19]. · Behavior which is caused by the environment, forcing a response and producing a one-to-one relationship with its eliciting stimulus. An example being the louder the thunder, the higher you jump [25]. · An automatic and unthinking reaction to a stimulus by the organism. A reflex is inborn, not learned, and depends on inherited characteristics of the nervous system [16].

Refusal · A lack of response [24].

Regression · A retreat toward types of activity appropriate to a lower level of maturity; a result of frustration [2,16]. · Reversion to an earlier mental or behavioral level [25]. · A return to an earlier stage of learning [11,24].

Reinforcement · The event which increases the frequency of the behavior it follows [11,25]. · An increase in the frequency of a response when the response is immediately followed by a particular consequence. The consequence can be either the presentation of a positive reinforcer or the removal of a negative reinforcer [17]. · Any circumstance or event (positive or negative) that Increases the probability of a response occurring [24]. · Defined by some psychologist as any stimulus that results in the reduction of a drive; defined by other psychologists as any stimulus that brings about learning [27]. · The process of assisting learning by pairing desired behavior with something the organism finds rewarding [16].

Reinforcement Contingency · Refers to the relationship between the reinforcement and the exact properties of the performance which it follows [9].

Reinforcement Schedules · The rule denoting how many or which responses will be reinforced [25].

Reinforcer · Anything that increases the frequency of the behavior it immediately follows [6]. · The reinforcer, or the reinforcing stimulus, is the event which increases the frequency of the performance it follows. A reinforcing stimulus may also have other effects on behavior. One of these is the elicitation of an unconditioned response in a reflex [9]. · Elements of enjoyment for an organism which will increase the frequency of behavior [25].

Reintroduction · A technique used in conservation biology which uses wild-born and/or captive animals to establish or replenish wild populations in natural habitats from which the species has been extirpated by nature or man, the intent of which is to benefit populations of endangered species in the wild, not individuals of surplus or unwanted captive stocks [4,7].

Repertoire · The term repertoire is used to indicate the total number of latent performances which the organism may emit under the various conditions present in its environment and as a result of its past history [7,9,24,25]. · All the possibilities for response that an organism possesses in a given class [19].

Repression · The failure of an operant behavior caused by previous aversive consequences. A kind of forgetting; however, functionally different from either extinction or passage of time [25]. · A defense mechanism in which an individual suffering anxiety over his motives seems to banish the thoughts, pushing them into the unconscious [2,16,27].

Respondent Behavior · Behavior that is elicited or automatically controlled by antecedent stimuli. Reflexes are respondents because their performance automatically follows certain stimuli. The connection between unconditioned respondents and antecedent events which control them is unlearned. Respondents may come under the control of otherwise neutral stimuli through classical conditioning [17]. · Behavior which is produced forcibly by the environment. The environment elicits respondent behavior. Respondent behavior is not produced willingly [25]. · Behavior that appears to be clearly dependent upon a specific stimulus and elicited by that stimulus [16,19,27].

Response · An identifiable demonstration of behavior [24]. · A general term used to describe any kind of behavior produced by a stimulus [16,21].

Retroactive Inhibition · The process whereby the retention of previously learned material is interfered with by new learning [2,7,27]. · The harmful effect of new learning or other activity on the recall of what previously been learned [16,29].

Reward · A return for a correct response to a stimulus [21]. · A stimulus that when presented upon the successful performance of a task elicits within an animal the feeling of satisfaction [24]. · A satisfaction-yielding stimulus or stimulus object that is obtained upon the successful performance of a task [7].

S

Satiation · Providing an excessive amount of the reinforcer. A loss of effectiveness that occurs after a large amount of the reinforcer has been delivered [17]. · Refers to having a certain reinforcer being used excessively to the point where it no longer has reinforcing value [5,25]. · The point at which an animal no longer continues to consume an object or engage in an activity such as sex that is related to some bodily need [for food, water and so forth] [19]. · Satiation refers to the procedure of feeding an animal and is to be contrasted with deprivation, the procedure of withholding food. The effectiveness of food as a reinforcer increases with deprivation and decreases with satiation [7].

Schedule Of Reinforcement · The type, amount and frequency of the reinforcement that will be given when a task is completed. There are generally considered to be three basic schedules: continuous, fixed, variable [6]. · When the reinforcement of an operant performance occurs intermittently, the particular schedule by which reinforcement occurs is termed a schedule of reinforcement (such as fixed-ratio, fixed-interval, variable-interval, and variable-ratio schedules of reinforcement) [9]. · Refers to the various plans for applying reinforcement [27]. · Rules governing the delivery of reinforcement. When a given schedule is in effect, reinforcement can be attained only by meeting its requirements [2].

Secondary · A quality that an animal responds to because it's perception has been conditioned or learned [6].

Secondary Reinforcer · Any stimulus that acquires reinforcing properties through association with a primary reinforcement [2,11,27]. · An event which becomes reinforcing through learning. An event becomes a secondary reinforcer by being paired with other events [primary or conditioned] which are already reinforcing. Praise and attention are examples of secondary reinforcers [17]. · A stimulus which derives its reinforcing value from prior conditioning in which it has been associated with a primary reinforcer [7]. · A secondary reinforcer is something that initially had no significance to an animal and then became desired by the animal because of its association with other desired, primary reinforcers - in training this is often food. Once a secondary reinforcer is established at can be very strong - just as strong as primary reinforcers in animals that are in normal drive state (not deprived of anything) and are not driven by hormone surges at the time [6].

Selective Reinforcement · See Differential Reinforcement.

Sensitization · The enhancement of a response solicited by a stimulus with repeated presentations of that stimulus [10,15]. · The intensifying of an organism's response to stimuli that did not originally produce such strong reactions [7].

Shaping · The entire process of selectively reinforcing responses that approximate the desired response to an increasingly greater degree. A method of modifying behavior [7,11]. · Developing new behavior by reinforcing successive approximations toward the terminal response [17,25]. · The process of trying to create a behavior or put a behavior on cue by selective or differential reinforcement [6]. · A technique based on principles of operant conditioning in which an organisms' behavior is gradually molded to specific desired patterns through the careful administration of positive reinforcement [2]. · The learning of complicated tasks through operant conditioning, in which complex actions are built up from simpler ones [16].

Socialization · The process whereby an animal acquires and participates in the patterns of behavioral characteristic of its society [24]. · The teaching by whatever means, of the rules of society [conduct] to a developing child [19]. · The process of learning to behave in socially acceptable ways [27]. · The shaping of individual behavior to meet the standards of the group [29].

Spontaneous Recovery · The tendency of a conditioned response that has undergone extinction to occur again after a rest period [7,16,19,27]. · The temporary recurrence of a behavior during extinction. Even though the response has not be reinforced, it may suddenly reappear during the course of extinction. The magnitude of a response which temporarily recovers spontaneously is usually lower than its magnitude prior to extinction [17].

Station · An assigned position for an animal, designated by a trainer [24].

Stereotypic Behavior · A repetitive response that is without variation for extended periods of time. Stereotypic behavior is usually brought about through lack of stimulation [24]. · Animals (particularly active ones like monkeys and wolves) may sometimes develop stereotyped actions such as bobbing up and down or pacing out a fixed path if they are confined in small cages. It has been argued that such stereotypes can be used as an indication that the animals are suffering from their confinement [1,12].

Stimulus · Any environmental condition which impinges on the animal's sensory perception [6,11,16]. · Any physical event or condition, including the organism's own behavior. A stimulus may have many different functional relation to an organism's repertoire. It may be an eliciting stimulus for a response in a reflex. It may serve as a discriminative stimulus which precedes an operant performance. It may be a conditioned reinforcer or a primary reinforcer which follows an operant performance and increases its frequency. It may be an aversive stimulus whose termination increases the frequency of an operant performance. Finally, it may have no demonstrable effect on the organism's repertoire [9]. · An external or internal object or event which occasions an alteration in the behavior of the organism (a source of physical energy of sufficient magnitude to activate a sensory receptor) [5,7,19,25]. · A measurable event that may have an effect upon the behavior [17].

Stimulus Control · The predictability of a behavior performed in the presence of one stimulus which is not evident in the presence of another [25]. · Stimulus control refers to a differential form or frequency of a performance in the presence of one stimulus which is not evident in the presence of another [9]. · When the rate of behavioral responses changes under stimuli [5,7].

Stimulus Delta · A stimulus delta represents the particular occasion on which a performance will not be reinforced, in contrast to other occasions (discriminative stimuli) during which the performance will be reinforced [9,24]. · Signal which indicates an incorrect behavior or response and the animal should return to the trainer for further instructions [15].

Stimulus Generalization · Transfer of a trained response to situations or stimulus conditions other than those on which training has taken place. The behavior generalizes to other situations [17]. · When an organism is trained to make a response in the presence of one stimulus, there is a tendency to make the same response to other stimuli resembling the training stimulus. The amount of responding decreases as the similarity of the stimuli decreases [2,11,16].

Strain · Strain is a term used to describe the decreased frequency of a performance that occurs when the performance is reinforced on a large fixed ratio schedule. Under most conditions, strain occurs between long periods during which the performance does not occur at all and periods when there are bursts of the performance at high rates. The term abulia is also used as a synonym for strain [9]. · Synonymous with abulia. The failure of a behavior caused by a state of mind other than to physical exhaustion [25].

Successive Approximation · Successive approximation is used to condition performance which is not currently in the organism's repertoire. Some performance which is an approximation to the desired behavior and which the organism is already emitting is first reinforced. Thereafter, reinforcement occurs after those performances which are in the direction of the desire performance. Conversely, performances which are most distant from the desired behavior go unreinforced [9,25]. · The process of refining an animal's behavior, or operant, from a spontaneous initial behavior to the behavior which is planned by the trainer [2,6,7,17].

Superstitious Behavior · Behavior which results from misunderstanding. It is produced where there is no intended relation between response and reinforcement. Superstitious behavior has frequently been related to the fear of the unknown or aversive situations. However, it can also be produced through positive reinforcement [25]. · Behavior results from the chance or inadvertent reinforcement of unwanted behavior which then comes under stimulus control [5].

T

Tactile Reinforcement · Any reinforcer discernible by touch [24].

Target (Noun) · A prop which pinpoints a critical location for an animal in training. This location may be a body contact point on the stationary animal, it may be a destination point, or it may be a place where other critical information will appear. The target can be an extended finger or fist, the end of a pole, a mark on a wall or a paper, a plaque. Essentially, the trainer and the animal each extend a target contact point toward the other, meeting in the middle [6].

Target (Verb) · A "point" of behavior. The smallest unit of behavior, consists of an animal's action to touch a designated spot [6]. · The process of stimulating an animal to touch a particular object [24].

Team Bases Contingency · A group contingency in which members earn reinforcers on the basis of performance of the group. In addition, subgroups or teams are used so that there is competition to earn the reinforcers between the teams [17].

Terminal Response · The final pattern of behavior that organism's are expected to demonstrate after the completion of shaping procedures [2]. · The final goal or behavior that is achieved at the end of shaping [17].

Threshold · The threshold is the magnitude or strength of a stimulus which is just sufficient to elicit a respondent behavior or emit an operant behavior [5,9,25]. · The least amount of stimulus required to elicit a response. The point at which a stimulus becomes perceptible or is of sufficient intensity to elicit a response [16,24,27].

Time-Out · The cessation of stimulus or response from the trainer, for some interval of time. In essence, the animal receives no cues from the trainer, but also cannot influence the trainer to produce a consequence such as food or praise until the "time out" or TO has passed [6]. · Removing the situation in which an organism can get reinforcement; used to suppress incorrect responses correlated with non-reinforcement [7].

Trial and Error · An approach to problem solving that is based upon continuous attempts at a solution (trials), with each attempt pursued until it ends in failure (error) or success. This common heuristic technique is methodical rather than intuitive [2]. · A form of learning in which one response after another is tried and rejected as unsuitable, until at last a successful response is made [16]. · A type of problem-solving in which various ideas are tried until a solution is reached. It may be covert or overt [7].

U • V • W • X • Y • Z

Unconditioned Reflex · A response that is emitted on exposure to a stimulus without previous conditioning [7].

Unconditioned Reinforcer · See Primary Reinforcer.

Unconditioned Response · A response that is elicited by an unconditioned stimulus without prior training. Any display of instinct is an unconditioned response [2,7,17,19,24]. · An automatic, unlearned reaction to a stimulus [16]. · An unconditioned response (reflex behavior) is the behavior elicited by an unconditioned stimulus. Such behavior frequently influences the internal economy of the organism. The form is usually determined by the organism's phylogenetic history [9]. · In classical conditioning, this is the response that the animal manifests prior to the beginning of the conditioning procedure [27].

Unconditioned Stimulus (US) · Any stimulus possessing the capacity to elicit reactions from organisms in the absence of prior conditioning [2]. · An environmental event that automatically elicits an unconditioned response [3,19]. · A stimulus that is innately capable of causing a reflex action [16,17,27]. · In classical conditioning, a stimulus that elicits an unlearned and innate response/unconditioned response (UR) [7].

Variable Interval Schedule · A schedule of administering reinforcement. In a variable interval (VI) schedule, the first occurrence of the target response after a given time interval has elapsed is reinforced. However, the time interval changes each time, that is, it is variable. The schedule is denoted by the average time which must elapse before a response can be reinforced [17,24,25]. · A reinforcement schedule in which a reward is available after a varying amount of time has elapsed after the last reward [11]. · Involves applying reinforcement on something other than a one-to-one bases. In this case reinforcement is introduced at random time intervals regardless of what the animal does. A schedule in which the first response performed after the passage of a variable interval of time yields reinforcement. The interval which must relapse varies around some average value [2].

Variable Ratio Schedule · Variable-ratio reinforcement is a schedule of intermittent reinforcement in which reinforcement follows after a variable number of performances. The schedule is specified by the average number of performances required for reinforcement. Therefore, variable ratio 10 (VR 10) means that ten performances on the average are required for each reinforcement [2,9,11,25].
· A schedule of administering reinforcement. In all VR schedules, a number of occurrences of the target response is required for reinforcement. The number of required occurrences varies each time reinforcement is delivered [7,17,27].

Bibliography

1. Barlow, G.W. (1977) *Modal action patterns*. In **How Animals Communicate**, ed. T.A. Sebeok. Bloomington, Indiana: Indiana University Press.

2. Baron, R.A., Byrne, D. and Kantowitz, B.H. (1977) **Psychology: Understanding Behavior**. Philadelphia, Pennsylvania: W.B. Saunders Company.

3. Beach, L.R. (1973) **Psychology: Core Concepts and Special Topics**. New York, New York: Holt, Rinehart and Winston, Inc.

4. Brill, R.L. (1995) *Return to the wild...an option for managing Atlantic bottlenose dolphins*. **Soundings**. 20.3:5-6,19-20.

5. Chicago Zoological Society (1994) **Training Systems Protocol**. Chicago, Illinois: Chicago Zoological Society, Marine Mammal Programs.

6. Cover, K. (1991) **The Syn Alia Series on Animal Training, Volume I: Bridge and Target Technique Made Easy**. Sarasota, Florida: Syn Alia Animal Training Systems.

7. Dolphin Experience (1995) **Glossary**. Submitted to the International Marine Animal Trainers Association (IMATA).

8. DuBois, T. (1992) *An exhibit for drills: from drab to dazzling*. **The Shape of Enrichment**. 1.1:1-2.

9. Ferster, C.B. and Perrot, M.C. (1968) **Behavior Principles**. New York, New York: Templeton-Century-Crofts.

10. Flaherty, C. F. (1985) *Animal Learning and Cognition*. In **Habituation and Sensitization**, Chapter 2, pp. 14-29.

11. Gazzaniga, M.S. (1973) **Fundamentals of Psychology: An Introduction**. New York, New York: Academic Press.

12. Harre, R. and Lamb, R. eds. (1986) **The Dictionary of Ethology and Animal Learning**. Oxford, England: Basil Blackwell Ltd.

13. Harris, J.D. (1943) *Habituatory responses decrement in the intact organism*. **Psychological Bulletin**. 40:385-422.

14. Hinde, R. A. (1970) **Animal Behavior: A synthesis of ethology and comparative psychology**, second edition. New York, New York: McGraw-Hill.

15. Joseph M. Long Marine Laboratory (1996) **Glossary**. Submitted to the International Marine Animal Trainers Association (IMATA).

16. Kagan, J. and Havemann, E. (1976) **Psychology: An Introduction**, third edition. New York, New York: Harcourt Brace Jovanovich, Inc.

17. Kazelin, A.E. (1984) **Behavior Modification in Applied Settings**. Homewood, Illinois: The Dorsey Press.

18. Kastelein, R.A. and Wiepkema, P.R. (1989) *A digging trough as occupational therapy for Pacific walruses (Odobenus rosmarus divergens) in human care*. **Aquatic Mammals**. 15.1:9-17.

19. Lana, R. (1972) **Introduction to Contemporary Psychology**. New York, New York: Holt, Rinehart, and Winston, Inc.

20. Lorenz, K.Z. (1966) **On Aggression**. New York, New York: Harcourt, Brace and World Inc.

21. Neufeldt, V. ed. (1994) **Webster's New World Dictionary**, second college edition. New York, New York: Prentice Hall.

22. Parker, S.P., ed. (1989) **McGraw-Hill Dictionary of Scientific and Technical Terms**, fourth edition. New York, New York: McGraw-Hill Book Company.

23. Pearce, J.M. and Dickinson, A. (1977) *Pavlovian counter-conditioning: changing the suppressive properties of shock by association with food*. **Journal of Experimental Psychology: Animal Behavior Processes**. 104.2:170-177.

24. Sea World Australia (1995) **Glossary of Marine Mammal Training Terms**. Submitted to the International Marine Animal Trainers Association (IMATA).

25. Sea World of California (1994) **Animal Training Vocabulary List and Definitions**. Submitted to the International Marine Animal Trainers Association (IMATA).

26. Thorpe, W. H. (1956) **Learning and Instinct in Animals**. Methuen, London: Cambridge Press.

27. Whittaker, J.O. (1977) **Introduction to Psychology**, third edition. Philadelphia, Pennsylvania: W.B., Saunders Company.

28. Wickler, W. (1976) *The ethological analysis of attachment*. **Zeitschrift fur Tierpsychologie**. 42:12-28.

29. Williams, G.W. (1960) **Psychology: A First Course**. N.Y., N.Y.: Harcourt, Brace and Company.

Index

Index

Author – Title   559
There are over 150 authors who have written the featured articles in this manual. Their names, affiliations, and the titles of each article are included in the index beginning on the facing page. Facilities are listed as separate entries only when a facility's "training staff" is credited with authorship of an article.

Facility   568
Each facility (or affiliation) of an author is listed and each institution mentioned within an article is referenced. Page numbers indicate the starting page of an article not the actual page where the organization's name is actually located.

Subject   570
This is a standard index referencing terms or concepts when they appear in the text with some significance, or are defined, or are the main subject of an article. Words that appear in passing such as "trainer" or "S^D" are not indexed each time they appear. Page numbers indicate the starting page of an article, not the actual page where the term appears. Please note that a full glossary appears in Chapter 14 (page 531). Terms in that glossary are not indexed here.

Animal   574
This index will help the reader locate articles that focus on a particular species. Domestic animals have not been divided by breed, so that cocker spaniel or great dane would be located under *dog* in this index. Whenever an author refers to a species by a common or generic name, we have arbitrarily chosen to index them under an appropriate common name: generic references to dolphin will be indexed under *bottlenose dolphin*; seals under *harbor seal*; sea lion under *California sea lion*; porpoise under *harbor porpoise*; and whale under *cetacean*. Many species are not listed by scientific name, as the authors of many articles refer to the animal only by a common name.

Bibliography and Suggested Reading   576
Finally, there is a bibliography of references and recommended books. These books have been instrumental in my understanding of training over the years and further give background to the concepts discussed in this book.

AUTHOR – TITLE INDEX

Following the author's name is the facility each was affiliated with at the time the article was written. Because our profession often takes trainers from organization to organization, we could not update current locations for each author. Below the author's name is the title of the article(s) included in the text, followed by a series of numbers such as **1**(17). The previous notation indicates that an article is located in chapter 1, on page 17.

ABBITT, BEVERLY Theatre of the Sea
• Trainer's Forum – Interactive programs: Protocols and managing inappropriate behavior. **12**(432)

AIBEL, STEVEN M. National Aquarium in Baltimore
• Conditioning voluntary separations with beluga whales. **7**(231)

ALEXANDER, JIM St. Louis Zoo
• Trainer's Forum – Are we talking seals or sea lions? **2**(39)
• Trainer's Forum – Training phocids: A focus on husbandry behaviors. **6**(205)
• Trainer's Forum – Pinniped co-habitation: Seals, sea lions and others. **7**(253)
• Trainer's Forum – Fixing a problem behavior in the middle of a chain. **9**(352)
• Trainer's Forum – Teaching pinnipeds to work in public areas. **11**(409)
• Trainer's Forum – The case of the fish stealing sea lion. **11**(412)

ALIA–MARION, CINTHIA 1 Oregon Coast Aquarium, 2 John G. Shedd Aquarium
• 2 Using desensitization techniques to prepare animals for transport. **6**(145)
• 1 Trainer's Forum – Training phocids: A focus on husbandry behaviors. **6**(205)

ANTRIM, JENNINE San Diego Zoo
• Trainer's Forum – Polar bears and warthogs: Training in the zoo. **12**(463)
• Managing multiple elephants using protected contact at San Diego's Wild Animal Park. **12**(453)

ARTHUR, CONNIE John G Shedd Aquarium
• Using desensitization techniques to prepare animals for transport. **6**(145)

BAILEY, MARIAN BRELAND Animal Behavior Enterprises
• Every animal is the smartest: Intelligence and the ecological niche. **3**(54)

BAILEY, ROBERT Animal Behavior Enterprises
• Every animal is the smartest: Intelligence and the ecological niche. **3**(54)

BALLOU, DIERDRE San Diego Zoo
• Trainer's Forum – Fixing a problem behavior in the middle of a chain. **9**(352)

BEELER, MARK C. SAIC
• Trainer's Forum – Basic marine mammal training terminology. **4**(80)

BELLOWS, CHRISTOPHER Sea World of Texas
• Conditioning and maintaining separations with pinnipeds in a multiple animal environment. **7**(228)

BELTING, TRACI 1 Point Defiance Zoo, 2 Minnesota Zoo
• 1 Trainer's Forum – Bridging basics: How to maintain consistency. **4**(86)
• 2 Trainer's Forum – Calf mimicry, to shape or to capture? **4**(98)
• 2 Trainer's Forum - Proper use of a time out. **4**(108)
• Trainer's Forum – Teaching an old polar bear program new tricks. **7**(235)

BIEDENBACH, GREG National Aquarium in Baltimore
• Trainer's Forum – Calf mimicry, to shape or to capture? **4**(98)

BILS, JEFFREY
• Maternal feelings prevail as gorilla rescues tot at zoo. **12**(464)

BLASKO, DAN Sea World of Florida

- Trainer's Forum – Training dolphins for voluntary urine sampling. **6**(197)
- Animal separation as a trained behavior. **7**(225)

BOGDEN, ERIC Sea World of California
- Trainer's Forum - Basic marine mammal training terminology. **4**(80)

BRILL, RANDY Chicago Zoological Society, Brookfield Zoo
- The training of dolphins in a community tank. **7**(238)
- The trainer's role in the environment of the captive dolphin. **8**(262)
- R.I.R. in use at the Brookfield Zoo: Random and interrupted reinforcement redefined in perspective. **9**(320)

BROOKFIELD ZOO Seven Seas Staff
- Trainer's Forum – Bridging basics: How to maintain consistency. **4**(86)
- Trainer's Forum – How to maintain voluntary blood sampling with dolphins. **6**(169)
- Trainer's Forum – Training only one animal when others are present. **7**(241)
- Trainer's Forum – Training a behavior chain. **9**(348)
- Trainer's Forum – Training echolocation discrimination in a show. **12**(466)

BURROWS, ANNIE Pittsburgh Zoo
- Sole use of non-food reinforcers in daily training sessions with an amazon river dolphin. **9**(304)

CARTEGENA, ERIC Naval Ocean System Center
- Microcomputer-assisted training of a bottlenose dolphin. **9**(344)

CHARFAUROS, VIC San Diego Zoo
- Trainer's Forum – Training a sea lion for an ultra sound exam. **6**(201)
- Trainer's Forum – Mixing different cetacean species for the first time. **7**(248)
- Trainer's Forum – Understanding the use of recall vs. delta signals. **9**(339)
- Trainer's Forum – The case of the fish stealing sea lion. **11**(412)

CHUN, NORMAN Naval Ocean Systems Center
- Training a false killer whale for an underwater audiogram. **12**(468)

- Conditioning bottlenose dolphins for voluntary diving studies. **12**(507)

CLARKE, JAMES L. Chicago Zoological Society, Brookfield Zoo
- The training of dolphins in a community tank. **7**(238)

COVER, KAYCE
- Glossary of terms from "The Syn Alia series on animal training." **9**(307)

CURRY, CHRISTINE SAIC
- Conditioning a bottlenose dolphin for milk collection. **6**(198)

DAVEY, PETE John G Shedd Aquarium
- Trainer's Forum - Basic marine mammal training terminology. **4**(80)
- Using desensitization techniques to prepare animals for transport. **6**(145)

DE SOUSA, ROSANA Zoomarine
- Voluntary Cytoscopy – Training and mutual dedication. **6**(185)

DESMOND, TIM 1 Active Environments Inc., 2 Marineland Amusements, Inc.
- 1 Meeting behavioral objectives while maintaining healthy social behavior and dominance – a delicate balance. **7**(220)
- 1 Trainer's Forum – Mixing different cetacean species for the first time. **7**(248)
- 2 R.I.R. – A new schedule of reinforcement or a method of training trainers. **9**(335)
- 1 Protected-contact elephant training. **12**(437)
- 1 The politics of protected contact. **12**(447)

DOLPHIN CONNECTION Training Staff
- Trainer's Forum – Working tandem (or group) behaviors – when to bridge. **7**(246)
- Trainer's Forum – Handling escalating dolphin aggression: A complex problem. **10**(179)

DOLPHIN ENCOUNTERS Training Staff
- Trainer's Forum – Handling escalating dolphin aggression: A complex problem. **10**(179)

DOLPHIN EXPERIENCE Training Staff
- Trainer's Forum - Multiple bridges: Avoiding the confusion. **7**(244)

DOLPHIN QUEST BERMUDA Training Staff
• Trainer's Forum – Handling escalating dolphin aggression: A complex problem. **10**(179)

DOLPHIN QUEST HAWAII Training Staff
• Trainer's Forum – Calf mimicry – to shape or to capture? **4**(98)

DOLPHIN QUEST MOOREA Training Staff
• Trainer's Forum – Calf mimicry – to shape or to capture? **4**(98)

DOUGLAS, ALLISON Indianapolis Zoo
• Trainer's Forum – Mixing different cetacean species for the first time. **7**(248)

DUNHAM, FAITH John G Shedd Aquarium
• Using desensitization techniques to prepare animals for transport. **6**(145)

DYE, GREG 1 John G Shedd Aquarium, 2 Brookfield Zoo
• 1 Using desensitization techniques to prepare animals for transport. **6**(145)
• 2 Trainer's Forum – Training a behavior chain. **9**(348)
• 2 Passive restraint training in *Tursiops truncatus*. **6**(178)

EDMONTON DOLPHIN LAGOON
• Trainer's Forum - Multiple bridges: Avoiding the confusion. **7**(244)

ERB, LINDA Dolphin Research Center
• Trainer's Forum – Bridging basics, how to maintain consistency. **4**(86)
• Trainer's Forum – Interactive programs – protocols and managing inappropriate behavior. **12**(432)

FAD, OTTO Sea World of Florida
• Anthropomorphism: The natural enemy within? **3**(59)

FITZGERALD, NINA Sea World Australia
• Trainer's Forum - How is a recall trained and used? **9**(341)

FLYNN, TISH Marineland of the Pacific
• Trainer's Forum – Fixing a problem behavior in the middle of a chain. **9**(352)

FORCE, DAVID L. 1 Sea World of Texas, 2 Sea World of Florida
• 1 Decreasing the frequency of behavior through extinction: An application for the training of marine mammals. **4**(103)
• 1 Sea World's husbandry training program: update. **6**(160)
• 1 Conditioning and maintaining separations with pinnipeds in a multiple animal environment. **7**(228)
• 2 Trainer's Forum – Fixing a problem behavior in the middle of a chain. **9**(352)

FRANKLIN, JANE ANNE Louisville Zoo
• Trainer's Forum – Polar bears & warthogs: Training in the zoo. **12**(463)

GERSTEIN, EDMUND Florida Atlantic University
• The manatee mind: Discrimination training for sensory perception testing of West Indian manatees. **12**(484)

GIFFORD, TARA Chicago Zoological Society
• Trainer involvement in behavioral observations. **5**(125)

GILBERT, JANE San Diego Zoo
• Managing multiple elephants using protected contact at San Diego's Wild Animal Park. **12**(453)

GOFORTH, HAL Naval Ocean System Center
• Microcomputer-assisted training of a bottlenose dolphin. **9**(344)

GORY, JOHN D. The Living Seas
• An introduction to the Living Sea's dolphin keyboard communication system. **12**(493)

GOUVIN, GINA Theatre of the Sea
• Training an Atlantic bottlenose dolphin to wear a harness and remote underwater camera. **12**(504)

GULF WORLD MARINE PARK
• Trainer's Forum - Multiple bridges: avoiding the confusion. **7**(244)

HALL, RICHARD W. Naval Ocean Systems Center
• Conditioning a Pacific bottlenose dolphin and a California sea lion in a taste experiment. **12**(473)

HARE, VALERIE San Diego Zoo

• Managing multiple elephants using protected contact at San Diego's Wild Animal Park. **12**(453)

HARRIS, CHRISTIAN Dolphin Quest
• Trainer's Forum – Teaching pinnipeds to work in public areas. **11**(409)

HARSHAW, WILLIAM "CHIP" 1 John G Shedd Aquarium, 2 Virginia Marine Science Museum
• 1 Using desensitization techniques to prepare animals for transport. **6**(145)
• 2 Extended separation and targeting of north American river otters *Lontra canadensis* for sedation purposes. **6**(181)
• 2 Trainer's Forum – Training phocids, a focus on husbandry behaviors. **6**(205)

HERMANN, PAM John G Shedd Aquarium
• Using desensitization techniques to prepare animals for transport. **6**(145)

HOFFLAND, TIMOTHY Marine Animal Productions
• Trainer's Forum – Bridging basics, how to maintain consistency. **4**(86)
• Trainer's Forum - Consistency vs. predictability: Is there a difference? **8**(272)

HOLMES, NICOLE Long Marine Lab, University of California
• A review of the psychological principles and training techniques associated with desensitization. **6**(150)

HOPKINS, THOMAS The Living Seas – EPCOT
• The ethogram: present and future applications. **5**(127)

HUDSON, MEG John G Shedd Aquarium
• Using desensitization techniques to prepare animals for transport. **6**(145)
• Initiation of a sea otter training program. **6**(172)

HURLEY, JENIFER Long Marine Lab, University of California
• A review of the psychological principles and training techniques associated with desensitization. **6**(150)
• Trainer's Forum - Consistency vs. predictability: Is there a difference? **8**(272)
• Training and behavioral terms glossary for IMATA **14**(533)
• (See also Zeligs, Jennifer)

IMATA Animal Training Advisory Committee
• Trainer's Forum – Secondary reinforcers for California sea lions. **9**(300)

INDIANAPOLIS ZOO Marine Mammal Staff
• Trainer's Forum – Bridging basics, how to maintain consistency. **4**(86)
• Trainer's Forum – Pinniped co-habituation: seals, sea lions and others. **7**(253)

JACOBS, GRETCHEN S. The Living Seas - EPCOT
• The ethogram: Present and future applications. **5**(127)

JANOSEK–CHRISTAKIS, DONNAROSE John G Shedd Aquarium
• Using desensitization techniques to prepare animals for transport. **6**(145)

JOSEPH, JEAN Point Defiance Zoo
• Teaching an old polar bear program new tricks. **7**(235)

JUAREZ, DANIEL Marineland Mallorca
• Trainer's Forum - Have you lost control? **11**(418)

KAMOLNICK, TRICIA 1 SAIC, 2 SEACO, Inc.
• 1 Conditioning a bottlenose dolphin for milk collection. **6**(198)
• 2 Microcomputer-assisted training of a bottlenose dolphin. **9**(344)

KELLER, KARL V. Naval Oceans Systems Center
• Training Atlantic bottlenose dolphins for artificial insemination. **6**(203)

KIRKPATRICK-SANCHEZ, SHARON
• Positive reinforcement techniques for training controlled aggression in schutzhund and protection dogs. **10**(388)

KIRTLAND, JOHN 1 Marine Resources and Technology, 2 International Wildlife Resources
• 1 Operant definitions of reinforcement & punishment. **9**(312)
• 2 Trainer's Forum - Proper use of a time out. **4**(108)

KOMANSKI, PAUL National Aquarium in Baltimore
• Changing from a fixed ratio schedule to a variable schedule. **9**(330)

KOMAR, WENDY Brookfield Zoo
• Passive restraint training in *Tusiops truncatus*. **6**(178)

KRAMES, BUD 1 Sea World of San Diego, 2 Dolphin Quest
• 1 The conditioning of various animal husbandry behaviors with killer whales. **6**(189)
• 2 Trainer's Forum – Interactive programs – protocols and managing inappropriate behavior. **12**(432)

KRIEGER, KATHY California State University
• Trainer's Forum – Fixing a problem behavior in the middle of a chain. **9**(352)
• Teaching sea lions that signals represent objects, object qualities, and behaviors. **12**(499)

KRUEGER, JONATHAN
• Husbandry training of cats. **6**(164)

KUCZAJ, STAN 1 Sea World, 2 SMU, Center for Comparative Cognition
• 1 Training, Enrichment, and Behavior. **8**(269)
• 2 An introduction to the Living Sea's dolphin keyboard communication system. **12**(493)

LACAVE, GERALDINE Zoomarine
• Voluntary Cytoscopy – Training and mutual dedication. **6**(185)

LACINAK, CLINTON T. Sea World, Inc.
• Decreasing the frequency of behavior through extinction: an application for the training of marine mammals. **4**(103)
• Sea World's husbandry training program: update. **6**(160)
• Training, Enrichment, and Behavior. **8**(269)

LAMERE, CRAIG Gulf World
• Trainer's Forum – Understanding the use of recall vs. delta signals. **9**(339)

LATORES, SALLY Point Defiance Zoo
• 'C' is for Cindy: A case study. **12**(444)

LAULE, GAIL 1 Active Environments Inc., 2 Marineland
• 1 If my friends could see me now. **5**(119)
• 1 Meeting behavioral objectives while maintaining healthy social behavior and dominance – a delicate balance. **7**(220)
• 1 Trainer's Forum – Mixing different cetacean species for the first time. **7**(248)
• 1 What is real enrichment? **8**(267)
• 2 Trainer's Forum – Fixing a problem behavior in the middle of a chain. **9**(352)
• 1 Trainer's Forum – Dealing with aggression in a community pool. **10**(386)
• 1 Protected-contact elephant training. **12**(437)
• 1 The politics of protected contact. **12**(447)

LEHNHARDT, JOHN National Zoological Park
• Elephant handling: A problem of risk management and resource allocation. **12**(436)

LOON MOUNTAIN WILDLIFE THEATER Staff
• Proper use of a time out. **4**(108)

LOSCH, BARBARA Dolphin Research Center
• Training combination behaviors with bottlenose dolphins. **9**(354)

MARINELAND OF THE PACIFIC Staff
• Trainer's Forum – Dealing with cetacean aggression towards swimmers. **10**(378)

MARINE WORLD AFRICA USA
• Trainer's Forum – Training dolphins for voluntary urine sampling. **6**(197)
• Trainer's Forum – Dealing with aggression in a community pool. **10**(386)

MARRIN-COONEY, DEBBIE Marine World Africa
• Trainer's Forum – Calf mimicry, to shape or to capture? **4**(98)
• Trainer's Forum – How to maintain voluntary blood samples with dolphins. **6**(169)
• Video recording the nasal passage of an echolocating dolphin. **12**(501)

MCDEVITT, AUSTIN C. Minnesota Zoological Garden
• Random reinforcement of spontaneous behavior. **4**(95)

MCGEE, JENNIFER Brookfield Zoo
• Passive restraint training in *Tursiops truncatus*. **6**(178)

MCHUGH, MARK B. Sea World
• Sea World's husbandry training program: Update. **6**(160)

MESSERSMITH, MIKE Point Defiance Zoo

• Teaching an old polar bear program new tricks. **7**(235)

MESSINGER, CHERYL 1 National Aquarium in Baltimore, 2 The Dolphin Connection
• 1 Trainer's Forum – Training a blind sea lion. **11**(415)
• 2 The initiation of a dolphin interactive program. **12**(428)
• 2 Trainer's Forum – Getting into the field: how to get a training job. **13**(525)
• (See also Snyder, Cheryl)

MESSINGER, DOUG 1 Entertainment Plus, 2 The Dolphin Connection, Inc., 3 Brookfield Zoo
• 1 Trainer's Forum – Teaching pinnipeds to work in public areas. **11**(409)
• 2 The initiation of a dolphin interactive program. **12**(428)
• 3 Passive restraint training in *Tursiops truncatus*. **6**(178)

MIKA, CHERYL Brookfield Zoo
• Passive restraint training in *Tursiops truncatus*. **6**(178)

MILLER, DON
• Conditioning a bottlenose dolphin for milk collection. **6**(198)

MILLER, GARY Point Defiance Zoo
• 'C' is for Cindy: a case history. **12**(444)

MINNESOTA ZOO Training Staff
• Trainer's Forum – Enrichment devices vs. conditioned reinforcers. **9**(302)

MIRAGE DOLPHIN ENVIRONMENT Staff
• Trainer's Forum – Working tandem (or group) behaviors – when to bridge. **7**(246)

MURHPY, JEFF Sea World of Australia
• Trainers Forum – Calf mimicry, to shape or to capture? **4**(98)

MYSTIC MARINELIFE AQUARIUM Staff
• Trainer's Forum – Working tandem (or group) behaviors – when to bridge. **7**(246)
• Trainer's Forum – Pinniped co-habitation: seals, sea lions, and others. **7**(253)
• Trainer's Forum - Have you lost control? **11**(418)

NATIONAL AQUARIUM OF BALTIMORE
• Trainer's Forum – Dealing with cetacean aggression towards swimmers. **10**(378)

NATIONAL ZOO Staff
• Trainer's Forum - How is a recall trained and used? **9**(341)

NEW ENGLAND AQUARIUM Training Staff
• Trainer's Forum – How to maintain voluntary blood sampling from dolphins. **6**(169)
• Trainer's Forum - Have you lost control? **11**(418)

NEW JERSEY STATE AQUARIUM Staff
• Trainer's Forum - How is a recall trained and used? **9**(341)

NEW YORK AQUARIUM Training Staff
• Trainer's Forum - Consistency vs. predictability: Is there a difference? **8**(272)

NORDONE, LISA Point Defiance Zoo
• Teaching an old polar bear program new tricks. **7**(235)

NORTH CAROLINA ZOO Staff
• Trainer's Forum – Training phocids: A focus on husbandry behaviors. **8**(205)
• Trainer's Forum – Polar bears and warthogs: Training in the zoo. **12**(463)

OCEANS OF FUN Training Staff
• Trainer's Forum – Using an end of session signal - yes or no? **9**(358)

ONATE, MANNY John G Shedd Aquarium
• Using desensitization techniques to prepare animals for transport. **6**(145)

OSBORN, MICHAEL Sea Life Park Hawaii
• Trainer's Forum – Enrichments devices vs. conditioned reinforcers. **9**(302)
• Trainer's Forum – Training a behavior chain. **9**(348)

OTT, JACKIE St. Louis Zoo
• Trainers Forum – The case of the fish stealing sea lion. **11**(412)

PEEK, SHAWN Brookfield Zoo
• Passive restraint training in *Tursiops truncatus*. **6**(178)

PRIEST, GARY M. Zoological Society of San Diego
• Animal behavior management at the San Diego Zoo and Wild Animal Park. **11**(400)
• Managing multiple elephants using protected contact at San Diego's Wild Animal Park. **12**(453)

PRYOR, KAREN Sea Life Park
• Don't shoot the dog (*referenced throughout the manual*)
• Why porpoise trainers and not dolphin lovers. **3**(50)
• Why punishment doesn't work. **9**(315)
• The rhino likes violets. **12**(459)

PUGH, KIANA Sea Life Park
• Training a false killer whale for an underwater audiogram. **12**(468)

RAMIREZ, KEN John G Shedd Aquarium
• *Only separate articles referenced here, all chapter text and article intros authored by KR.*
• Scanning or capturing behavior: a necessary tool, an outdated technique, or a lost art? **4**(92)
• Using desensitization techniques to prepare animals for transport. **6**(145)
• Initiation of a sea otter training program. **6**(172)
• Husbandry behaviors for the care and training of a dolphin with kidney stones. **6**(192)
• Secondary reinforcers as an indispensable tool. **9**(295)
• Trainer's Forum – Understanding the use of recall vs. delta signals. **9**(339)
• Trainer's Forum – Using an end of session signal – yes or no? **9**(358)
• Trainer's Forum – Training a blind sea lion. **11**(415)
• Trainer's Forum – Getting into the field: how to get a training job. **13**(525)

RECTOR, DEIDRE The Living Seas, EPCOT
• The ethogram: present and future applications. **5**(127)

REDDY, MICHELLE SAIC
• Conditioning a bottlenose dolphin for milk collection. **6**(198)

RIDGWAY, SAM NCCOSC
• Conditioning a bottlenose dolphin for milk collection. **6**(198)

RICHARDS, JAMES L. Naval Ocean Systems Center
• Conditioning a pacific bottle-nosed dolphin and a California sea lion in a taste experiment. **12**(473)

ROBINETT, JIM John G Shedd Aquarium
• Using desensitization techniques to prepare animals for transport. **6**(145)

ROGERS, SUZANNE John G Shedd Aquarium
• Using desensitization techniques to prepare animals for transport. **6**(145)

RYAN, MARK John G Shedd Aquarium
• Using desensitization techniques to prepare animals for transport. **6**(145)

SCARAMOZZINO, JEANINE Long Marine Lab
• Training and behavioral terms glossary for IMATA. **14**(533)

SCARDINA-LUDWIG, JULIE Sea World of California
• Trainer's Forum – How to maintain voluntary blood sampling from dolphins. **6**(169)

SCARPUZZI, MICHAEL Sea World of California
• Decreasing the frequency of behavior through extinction: an application for the training of marine mammals. **4**(103)
• Sea World's husbandry training program: update. **6**(160)

SCHOFIELD, T. DAVID National Aquarium in Baltimore
• The use of operant conditioning techniques to facilitate the management of stranded marine mammals under veterinary care. **6**(207)

SCHREIB, SANDI Pittsburgh Zoo
• Sole use of non-food reinforcers in daily training sessions with an Amazon river dolphin. **9**(304)

SCHUSTERMAN, RONALD J. California State Univ.
• Teaching sea lions that signals represent objects, object qualities, and behaviors. **12**(499)

SEA LIFE PARK Training Staff
• Trainer's Forum – How to maintain voluntary blood sampling from dolphins. **6**(169)

SEA WORLD OF AUSTRALIA Staff
• Trainer's Forum – Secondary reinforcers for California sea lions. **9**(300)

SEA WORLD OF OHIO Training Staff
• Trainer's Forum – Handling escalating dolphin aggression: A complex problem. **10**(379)

SEVENICH, MARTY Brookfield Zoo
• Trainer's Forum – Training a sea lion for an ultrasound exam. **6**(201)
• Trainer's Forum – The case of the fish stealing sea lion. **11**(412)

SHAW, FRAN PENNOCK
• When Fido more than misbehaves. **12**(515)

SHEDD AQUARIUM Training Staff
• Trainer's Forum – Training a sea lion for an ultrasound exam. **6**(201)
• Trainer's Forum – Training only one animal when others are present. **7**(241)
• Trainer's Forum – Handling escalating dolphin aggression: A complex problem. **10**(379)
• Trainer's Forum – The case of the fish stealing sea lion. **11**(412)
• Trainer's Forum – Training echolocation discrimination in a show. **12**(466)

SHIPPEE, STEVEN   NCCOSC
• Conditioning bottlenose dolphins for voluntary diving studies. **12**(507)

SINGER, STACEY
• Maternal feelings prevail as gorilla rescues tot at zoo. **12**(464)

SKAAR, DEBRA SeaCo. Inc.
• Stretcher training for handling whales and dolphins. **6**(176)

SMITH, SUZANNE ZooQuarium
• Trainer's Forum - Multiple bridges: avoiding the confusion. **7**(244)
• Trainer's Forum – Pinniped co-habitation: Seals, sea lion and others. **7**(253)

SMITH, TIM Pittsburgh Zoo
• Sole use of non-food reinforcers in daily training sessions with an Amazon river dolphin. **9**(304)

SNYDER, CHERYL Entertainment Plus
• Trainer's Forum – Teaching Pinnipeds to work in public areas. **11**(409)
• (See also Messinger, Cheryl)

SOBIE, JENNIFER
• Aggression mediation in pet dogs. **10**(374)

STACEY, RITA Brookfield Zoo
• Passive restraint training in *Tursiops truncatus*. **6**(178)

STAFFORD, S. GREY Positive Innovations
• Husbandry training. **6**(159)

SULLIVAN, TIM Brookfield Zoo
• Trainer's Forum - Basic marine mammal training terminology. **4**(80)
• Passive restraint training in *Tursiops truncatus*. **6**(178)

SUSTMAN, JANET Brookfield Zoo
• Passive restraint training in *Tursiops truncatus*. **6**(178)

TAKAKI, LISA John G Shedd Aquarium
• Using desensitization techniques to prepare animals for transport. **6**(145)
• Initiation of a sea otter training program. **6**(172)
• Trainer's Forum – Enrichment devices vs. conditioned reinforcers. **9**(302)

TEUSCHER, FRAN
• Husbandry training of horses and dogs. **6**(163)

THEATER OF THE SEA Training Staff
• Trainer's Forum – Training a behavior chain. **9**(348)

THOMAS, JEANETTE Naval Ocean Systems Center
• Training a false killer whale for an underwater audiogram. **12**(468)

TOMPKINS, CHARLES D. Sea World of Florida
• Decreasing the frequency of behavior through extinction: An application for the training of marine mammals. **4**(103)
• Aggression: Exploring the causes and possible redaction techniques. **10**(366)

TRUPO, RACIE Sea World of Florida
• Animal separation as a trained behavior. **7**(225)

TURLEY, PAT (BUCKO) Marine World Africa, USA
• Trainer's Forum – Are we talking seals or sea lions? **2**(39)

TURNER, TED N. Sea World of Ohio
• Letting go of our humanism. **1**(18)
• Decreasing the frequency of behavior through extinction: An application for the training of marine mammals. **4**(103)
• Have you been too busy? **5**(122)
• Trainer's Forum – Mixing different cetacean species for the first time. **7**(248)
• Training, enrichment, and behavior. **8**(269)
• Trainer's Forum – Using an end of session signal – yes or no? **9**(358)
• Aggression: Exploring the causes and possible reduction technique. **10**(366)
• Trainer's Forum – Dealing with aggression in a community pool. **10**(386)

UPCHURCH, BRUCE Point Defiance Zoo
• 'C' is for cindy: a case history. **12**(444)

VAJDA, CRAIG Oceana
• Trainer's Forum – Using an end of session signal – yes or no? **9**(358)

VAN DER TOORN, JAAP
• Definition drift or are we monopolizing marine mammal training by changing the definitions? **9**(318)

WEINER, JACKIE Brookfield Zoo
• Passive restraint training in *Tursiops truncatus*. **6**(178)

WHITE, RANDY Sea World of Florida
• Trainer's Forum – Fixing a problem behavior in the middle of a chain. **9**(352)

WILCOX, CRAIG Point Defiance Zoo
• 'C' is for cindy: a case history. **12**(444)

WILKES, GARY
• Amazing feats of animal learning. **1**(17)

• Anthropomorphism: A case of mistaken identity. **3**(62)
• Primarily, secondary reinforcers end on a good note. **4**(84)
• Elephants go from carrot and stick to carrot and click. **4**(90)
• Training by pushing and tugging is off-target. **4**(97)
• What's in a name? **4**(100)
• Superstitious behaviors. **4**(101)
• How to get your dog into Carnegie Hall. **4**(110)
• Were you born 'good with animals' or did you learn it? **5**(118)
• Animals can make mistakes. **5**(123)
• Generalization and discrimination: fraternal twins. **6**(157)
• Monique, the one trick poodle. **9**(294)
• A look at punishment. **9**(314)
• What you teach is what you get. **11**(408)
• How the mind and body build new behaviors. **11**(411)
• Sinking your teeth into destructive chewing. **11**(414)

WILLIAMS, TERRIE NCCOSC
• Conditioning bottlenose dolphin for voluntary diving studies. **12**(507)

WINHALL, BILL Marineland
• Trainer's Forum – Fixing a behavior in the middle of a chain. **9**(352)

WOOD, MIKE Theatre of the Sea
• Training an Atlantic bottlenose dolphin to wear a harness and remote underwater camera. **12**(504)

XITCO, MARK JR. The Living Seas
• Echolocation matching for shape, material, and internal structure. **12**(475)
• An introduction to the Living Sea's dolphin keyboard communication system. **12**(493)

ZELIGS, JENNIFER
• Glossary of terms from "The Syn Alia series on animal training. **9**(307)
• (See also Hurley, Jennifer)

FACILITY - ORGANIZATION INDEX

Active Environments 119, 131, 220, 248, 267, 386, 393, 437, 444, 447
Alliance of Marine Mammal Parks and Aquariums 29
Animal Behavior Enterprises (ABE) 54
American Animal Hospital Association 515
American Association of Zoo Keepers (AAZK) 521
American College of Veterinary Behaviorists 515
American Dog Trainers Network 524
American Rescue Dog Association (ARDA) 524
American Veterinary Society of Animal Behavior 515
American Zoo and Aquarium Association (AZA) 4, 29, 436, 437, 444, 447, 521, 524
APHIS (Animal & Plant Helath Inspection Service) 29
Aquarium of Niagara Falls 330
Association for Behavior Analysis (ABA) 4, 523
Association of Pet Dog Trainers (APDT) 524
Behavior Bridge 522
Brookfield Zoo (see also Chicago Zoological Society) 80, 86, 169, 178, 201, 238, 241, 262, 348, 412, 459, 464, 466
Bronx Zoo 459
Caldwell Zoo 447
California State University 499
Cambridge University 7
Cambridge Center for Behavioral Studies 523
Chicago Tribune 464
Chicago Zoological Society 125, 246, 262, 320
Click & Treat Products 523
Columbus Zoo 220
Cornell University 515
Dog Fancy 157
Dog World 515
Dolphin Connection 246, 379, 428, 525
Dolphin Encounters 379
Dolphin Experience 244
Dolphin Quest (Bermuda, French Polynesia, Hawaii) 98, 295, 379, 409, 432
Dolphin Research Center 86, 354, 432
Edmonton Dolphin Lagoon 244
Elephant Managers Association (EMA) 521
Entertainment Plus 409
EPCOT Living Seas 127, 475, 493
Florida Atlantic University 484
Guide Dogs for the Blind 524

Gulf World 244, 339
Houston Zoological Garden 447
Indianapolis Zoo 86, 248, 253
International Association of Avian Trainers and Educators (IAATE) 521
International Marine Animal Trainers Association (IMATA) 3, 18, 39, 85, 131, 169, 197, 201, 205, 241, 244, 246, 248, 253, 272, 300, 302, 339, 341, 348, 352, 358, 378, 379, 386, 409, 412, 415, 418, 432, 463, 466, 520, 529, 533
International Wildlife Resources 108
Jersey Zoo 464
Kewalo Baisn Marine Mammal Lab 493
Language Research Center 493
Living Seas (see EPCOT)
Long Marine Lab (see University of California...)
Loon Mountain 108
Los Angeles Zoo 123, 220
Louisville Zoo 463
Lowry Park Zoo 488
Marine Animal Productions (MAP) 86, 272
Marineland Mallorca 418
Marineland of Florida 322
Marineland of the Pacific (California) 123, 189, 220, 335, 352, 378
Marine Animal Rescue Program (see also National Aquarium in Baltimore) 207
Marine Resources and Technology 312
Marine World Africa USA 39, 98, 169, 197, 386, 499, 501
Marineworld of Texas 24
Miami Seaquarium 320
Minnesota Zoological Garden 95, 98, 129, 302
Mirage Dolphin Environment 246
Mystic Marinelife Aquarium 246, 253, 418
National Aquarium in Baltimore (NAIB) 98, 207, 231, 330, 378, 415
National Association for Search and Recuse (NASAR) 524
National Marine Fisheries Service 207
National Safety Council 436
National Zoological Park 50, 341, 436, 459
Naval Ocean Systems Center (NOSC – See NRAD)
Navy (See NRAD)
NCCOSC (see NRAD)
New England Aquarium 169, 418
New Jersey State Aquarium 341

New York Academy of Science 50
New York Aquarium 272
New York Zoological Park (see Bronx Zoo)
North Carolina Zoological Park 85, 205, 463
NRAD 179, 198, 203, 344, 468, 473, 507
Oceana Cedar Point 358
Oceans of Fun 358
Oregon Coast Aquarium 205
OSHA 437
Pittsburgh Zoo 304
Point Defiance Zoo & Aquarium 86, 108, 117, 145, 235, 444
Positive Innovations 159
SAIC Maritime Division 80, 176, 198, 344
San Diego Wild Animal Park 220, 396, 400, 437, 444, 447, 453
San Diego Zoo 95, 127, 201, 248, 339, 352, 396, 400, 412, 437, 453, 463, 464
San Diego Zoological Society 400, 441, 453
San Francisco Zoo 464
Sea Life Park 169, 302, 348, 463, 468
Sea World (California, Florida, Ohio, & Texas) 18, 59, 80, 103, 122, 160, 169, 189, 197, 225, 228, 248, 269, 352, 358, 363, 366, 379, 386
Sea World of Australia 98, 300, 341
SEACO (see SAIC)
Seven Seas Panorama (see Chicago Zoological Society)
Shape of Enrichment 522

Shedd Aquarium 2, 3, 22, 30-35, 80, 92, 145, 172, 192, 201, 241, 295, 302, 339, 358, 379, 412, 415, 466, 525, 527
Southern Methodist University 493
South Florida Museum 484
St. Louis Zoo 39, 205, 253, 352, 409, 412
Sunshine Books 522
Texas A&M University 515
Theater of the Sea 348, 432, 504
University of California Santa Cruz (Long Marine Lab) 97, 145, 150, 272, 365, 533
University of Florida 131
University of Pennsylvania Veterinary Hospital (VHUP) 515
University of Texas, M.D. Anderson Cancer Center 220
US Army 54
US Bureau of Labor Statistics 436
US Customs Service 17
US Department of Agriculture (USDA) 29
US Fish and Wildlife Service 175
Virginia Marine Science Museum 181, 205
Washington Park Zoo 444
Westwood Animal Hospital 515
Woods Hole Oceanographic Institute 129
Zoological/Behavioral Consultants 484
Zoomarine 185
ZooQuarium 253

SUBJECT INDEX

aberrant behavior 394
abstract learning 73
acclimation 145
acquisition (of animals) 23
adaptive behavior 54
aerial behaviors 92, 348, 352
affection training 116, 122, 459
aggression 30, 50, 78, 90, 172, 218, 220, 238, 246, 248, 253, 304, 341, 358, 362-365, 366, 374, 378, 379, 386, 388, 394, 400, 432, 437, 444, 447, 464, 484, 515
    controlled 388
    mediation 374
    schedule induced 366
aggressive exploratory behavior 484
alternate response training (see *reinforcement: DRI & DRO*)
anesthesia 400
animal history 23
animal psychology 515
anthropomorphism 45-47, 54, 59, 62, 220, 414, 515
approximations (see *successive approximations*)
artificial insemination 203
artificial language 493
A to B 80, 136, 145, 205, 231, 379
automated feeding mechanism 400
aversive control 366, 459
aversive methods 50, 78, 447
aversive stimuli 50, 150, 164, 178, 207, 280, 281, 312, 314, 330, 339, 341, 366, 374
    conditioned 103
avoidance behavior 164, 207, 248, 307, 388, 484
avoidance learning 307

baiting 97, 164
baseline matching 475
beaching 473
behavioral control 418
behavioral drift 464
behavioral enrichment (see *enrichment*)
behavioral management program 418, 459
behavioral observations (see *ethograms*)
behavioral problems 364, 459
behavior chain (see *chains*)
behavior modification 374, 453, 499, 515
beunits 127
biopsy (voluntary) 185, 205

biting 374, 379, 388
black & white (concept of) 71, 278, 294, 428
blind animal training 415
blood taking 80, 90, 140, 160, 169, 178, 189, 192, 203, 205, 295, 400, 437, 447, 459, 507
body exams 139, 140, 143
    measurements 140
    scars & rakes 30
boredom 272, 379, 394
breath sample 189
bridge (bridging stimulus – see also *reinforcer: conditioned and secondary*) 14, 69, 76, 80, 84, 86, 92, 119, 135, 139, 160, 172, 205, 218, 235, 241, 244, 246, 280, 307, 320, 339, 341, 348, 352, 428, 453, 463, 468

cage training (see Kennel)
calf training 98, 189
call-back (see *recall*)
capturing behavior (see also *scanning*) 92, 98
cataracts 415
catheter 185
certified animal behaviorists 515
chains (behavior) 272, 290, 292, 307, 348, 352, 354, 459, 484
    common 290
    technical 290
circus 7, 97
classical conditioning 68, 150, 164, 307, 374
clever Hans 50
clicker training (see also *bridge*) 90, 163, 463
cognition training/research 43, 262, 354, 425, 484, 493, 499
co-habitation 253
combination behaviors 292, 354
communication 50
community pools (see also *group. . .*) 238
compassion 48
competition 394
conditioned "emotional" response 103
conditioned stimuli
condition(ing) 150, 185, 189, 207, 220, 228, 231, 235, 238, 241, 307, 468, 504, 507, 515
confined contact 37, 437
context shift 150, 484
continue signal 292
conservation 428
consistency 75, 86, 100, 261, 272

cooperative behavior (see also *husbandry*) 10, 215, 225, 453
cooperative feeding 220, 447
counter-conditioning 137, 150
cue (see also S^D) 15, 145, 192, 307, 437, 447, 468, 473
    tactile 140
cystoscopy 185

delta (s-delta) 103, 289-290, 330, 339, 341, 344, 352, 358
dental exam 160, 295, 459
deprivation 25, 78, 284
desensitization 119, 136, 137, 139, 140, 143, 145, 150, 159, 160, 163, 169, 172, 185, 192, 201, 225, 231, 235, 248, 257, 341, 379, 396, 400, 409, 426, 437, 447, 463, 501, 504
    active 137, 150
    passive 137, 150
diabetic 400
diet 25
discipline 400, 453
discriminate 54, 137, 157
discriminative stimulus (see S^D)
displacement behavior 248, 412
distractions 307
domestication 5, 50, 62
dominance (dominant) 50, 220, 238, 246, 248, 362, 364, 366, 394, 400, 432, 453, 515
double blind 484
DRI (see *reinforcement: differential*)
DRO (see *reinforcement: differential*)

ear exams 90, 140, 437
echolocation 425, 466, 475, 501, 504
electro-ejaculation 400
emotion 48-49, 395
end of session signal 293, 358
endoscopy 160, 501
enrichment
    behavioral 260, 267, 269, 464
    devices 261, 302
    environmental 28, 220, 267, 269, 302, 437, 447, 453
environmental conditions 26-29, 260, 393
escape-avoidance 437, 447
escape learning 307
ethograms 25, 117, 125, 127
euthanasia 515
exercise (sessions) 259
extinction 103, 110, 143, 160, 164, 189, 207, 312, 366, 374, 412

extinction burst 103, 366, 374
eye exams 140, 160, 172, 205, 437
eye contact 50, 118
eye cups 501

fading 75, 76, 178, 248, 473
fairness (being fair) 217
fecal sampling 140
fish stealing 412
fixed interval FI (see *reinforcement: schedules*)
fixed ratio FR (see *reinforcement: schedules*)
flexibility 54, 79
free contact 36, 400, 423, 437, 444, 447, 453
focal animal sampling 125
focus sessions 259
food stealing 412, 484

gamesmanship 484
gastric samples (see *endoscopy* or *stomach tube*)
gating (see also *separations*) 80, 136, 145, 172, 178, 205, 215, 225, 235, 248, 253, 428
generalization 59, 137, 157, 307
girth measurements 192
glossaries 80, 106, 307, 532
go no-go paradigm 425, 468, 473, 484
gray area 278
group behaviors 220, 225, 238, 246, 354
group training 172, 216-218, 228, 238, 241, 248, 253, 257, 341

habit 307
habitat size 26, 260
habituation 137, 150, 160, 235
hand signals 484, 499
hands-off training 37, 437
harness training 150, 504
hearing research 468, 484
heart rate monitoring 140
herpes B virus 400
holophrastic commands 499
humanism 18, 459
husbandry (behaviors, training) 90, 119, 134-144, 145, 159, 160, 163, 164, 169, 172, 176, 178, 181, 185, 189, 192, 197, 198, 201, 203, 205, 207, 220, 225, 295, 400, 415, 428, 437, 447, 459, 463, 484, 507
hydrophones 501, 504

injections 178, 181, 400
innate behavior 362
innovative sessions 92, 95, 259, 300, 320, 330
instinctive behavior 54, 101

instrumental behavior 307
instrumental conditioning (see *operant conditioning*)
interactive behavior 122
interactive programs 422, 428, 432, 459
inter-rater reliability (IRR) 127
inter-stimulus interval (ISI) 150
introduction (of new animals) 145, 218, 248, 253
intelligence 42-45, 50, 54

jackpot (see *reinforcement: magnitude*)
jaw pop study 365
job (getting a) 525

keep going signal 292
kennel training 142, 145, 160, 172
keyboard 426, 493
kidney stones 192

lay out position 140
learned helplessness 307
litter box 411
LRS (Least Reinforcing Stimulus) 77, 78, 103, 108, 244, 246, 379, 428

mammary presentation (see also *milk collection*) 189, 198
maternal care 400
matching to sample 425, 475, 484
medical behaviors (see *husbandry*)
medication administration 160, 164, 172, 178, 181, 192, 205, 207
mental welfare 6, 10
microcomputer training 344
milk collection 140, 160, 192, 198
mimicry 73, 98, 459
mixing animals 228, 248, 253
module 307
modeling 73, 97
molding (see also *modeling*) 415
motivation 25, 59, 78, 262, 285, 379, 398
mouth exams 141, 160, 172, 459
mouth piece acceptance 473
musculo-skeletal properties 39

nail clipping (trimming) 90, 159, 164, 205, 437
name recognition 145, 228, 415
natural behavior 27, 459
neurotic behavior 394
neutral cue 307
neutral response (see also *LRS*) 77, 108, 246
neutral stimulus 164

neutral zone 248
non-food reinforcer (see *reinforcers: secondary*)
"no" signal (see *punishment: conditioned*)
novel behavior 95, 150
novel stimuli 150, 169
nursing behavior 198
nutrition 25

observation (of animal, see also *ethogram*) 25, 76, 117, 125
one-stick rule 141, 192
one-on-one training 214
open ocean training 150, 426, 507
operant 307
operant conditioning 13, 50, 54, 68, 80, 103, 143, 160, 203, 207, 276, 295, 307, 312, 335, 363, 374, 378, 424, 437, 444, 453, 459, 463, 507
operant learning 164

paradigm 425, 475
parameters 307
passive restraint 178
Pavlov 68, 84
performing in shows 6
physical exercise 9
physical separation 214
play (sessions) 117, 145, 172, 259, 262, 300, 302, 378, 459
predictability 228, 231, 261, 272
pregnancy or pregnant 192, 198, 201
Premack principle 388
problem solving 279, 352, 392-399, 400, 418, 432
protected contact 37, 90, 181, 220, 235, 364, 400, 423, 436, 437, 444, 447, 453
protection dogs 365, 388
punishment 50, 78, 103, 108, 143, 280-286, 289, 307, 312, 314, 315, 366, 397, 414, 437, 447
   conditioned 290
   negative 103, 108, 282, 312, 374
   positive 103, 280, 282, 312, 374

randomized feeding mechanism 400
reactive behavior 362
reasons (to train)
   primary 9
   secondary 9, 10
recall 246, 289, 339, 341, 344, 352, 379
record keeping 29-35, 79, 364
reflex 307
regression 74, 145, 395, 475
reinforcement 134, 135, 137, 150, 159, 160, 189, 220, 225, 241, 269, 281, 282, 295, 307, 312,

reinforcement (*continued*):
   341, 453, 473, 484
  accidental 366
  conditioned (see also *reinforcement: secondary* and *bridge*) 50, 69, 80, 84, 228, 244, 262, 280, 295, 302, 320, 344, 388, 463
  continuous (see *reinforcement: schedules*)
  differential 80, 108, 248, 262, 463, 307
    DRI 108, 248, 364, 366, 378, 379, 386, 398, 428, 432
    DRO 108, 248, 364, 366, 378, 379, 386, 398, 428
  generalized 70
  intermittent (see *reinforcement: schedules*)
  magnitude 189
  natural 207
  negative 50, 78, 103, 178, 248, 280-283, 307, 312, 315, 320, 366, 397, 437, 447, 459, 515
  positive 13, 50, 69, 103, 160, 178, 220, 267, 281, 289, 307, 315, 320, 366, 388
  primary 14, 69, 78, 80, 103, 160, 163, 225, 246, 295, 307, 318, 320, 330, 341
  random 80, 95, 101, 262, 286, 320, 335, 400
  schedules of 50, 80, 103, 272, 286-289, 307, 318, 320, 330, 335
    continuous 80, 286, 307, 318, 320, 335
    fixed 80, 95, 103, 269, 318, 330
    intermittent 80, 262, 286, 318, 320
    variable 50, 80, 103, 225, 246, 269, 272, 286-289, 307, 318, 330, 335, 428
  secondary (see also *reinforcement: conditioned* and *bridge*) 14, 69, 84, 103, 163, 181, 246, 295, 300, 304, 307, 330
  selective 71, 80, 307, 453, 504
  self 412
  social 164, 453
reinforcing stimulus 207
relationship (building) 35, 38, 98, 115-117, 119, 400, 415
remote training 38, 400
respondent conditioning (see *classical*)
research 10, 127, 424, 426, 466, 468, 473, 493, 501
restraint training 178
retrievals 466
reversal level 468
rewarding 447, 453, 459, 468, 515
RIR 80, 95, 262, 286, 320, 335

scanning (see also *capturing behavior*) 14, 72, 92, 95, 205
S^D 74-75, 80, 92, 98, 100, 103, 160, 164, 231, 235, 241, 272, 307, 320, 330, 366, 388, 408

secondary stimulus 231
sedation 181
semantic comprehension 499
semen collection 140, 203, 400
semi-protected (semi-free) contact 36
sensitization 150
separation training (see also *gating*) 215-216, 225, 228, 231, 235, 248
sequential learning 493
session structure 256
session use 395
sexual activity 362, 386, 394, 432, 484
shaping 50, 71-74, 90, 92, 98, 164, 278, 320, 366, 388, 459
"shoot the animal" 315, 397
signal (see *cue* and S^D)
signature whistles 125
Skinner (see also *operant conditioning*) 8, 50, 54, 84, 101, 335, 459
slide out 143, 160, 189, 197, 473
social structure (& training) 27, 214-219, 220, 260, 267, 269, 300, 366, 386, 394, 432, 484
space (requirement, utilization) 26
spatial separation 214
spontaneous behavior 95, 150
squeeze cage (chute or crush) 143, 181, 400, 437, 447, 453
station(ing) 134, 172, 216, 235, 238, 248, 339, 341, 409, 415, 428, 468, 473, 475, 484, 501, 504, 507
"stay" behavior 228
stereotypic behavior 164, 269
stimulus (stimuli) 50, 80, 145, 150, 189, 225, 262, 267, 307, 320, 341, 352, 366, 437, 447, 463, 475, 499
stimulus control 15, 74-75, 80, 164, 178, 228, 231, 235, 269, 272, 418, 428, 499
stimulus discrimination (see S^D)
stomach tube training 192
stranded animal training 23, 207
strength conditioning 39
stressor 307
stretcher training 142, 145, 160, 176
submissiveness 394
successive approximations 15, 50, 71, 80, 90, 135, 140, 145, 159, 160, 169, 172, 176, 181, 189, 192, 207, 220, 225, 228, 231, 235, 248, 253, 307, 320
superstitious behavior 50, 76, 101, 207, 394
surgery 400
swim with dolphins (see *interactive programs*)
symbolic matching paradigm 493, 499

symbols 493, 499

tactile (taction) 136, 160, 172, 241, 295, 300, 302, 428
    bridge 86, 241
        reinforcers 134, 164, 231, 257, 295
        stimulation 145
target(ing) 15, 72, 80, 92, 97, 135-136, 140, 172, 176, 181, 189, 220, 225, 238, 241, 253, 307, 437, 444, 447, 453, 468
taste 473
teaching (training is) 8
team behavior 225, 246
technology (training is) 66, 118
terminology 66, 80, 285, 307, 312, 532
threshold training 366, 484
time out 77, 103, 108, 164, 307, 312, 320, 432, 437, 444, 447
timing 69, 86
tolerance 123
toys (see also *enrichment*) 117, 172, 231, 300, 302
training plan 32, 78, 110, 392
transport (training, preparation) 142, 145, 160, 220
trick (vs. behavior) 14
trust 13, 35, 38, 86, 92, 409, 415
two choice paradigm 425, 484

ultrasound 140, 192, 201
unison behaviors 218
up-system 262
urine collection (sample) 140, 160, 185, 189, 192, 197, 205, 400, 411

variable interval VI (see *reinforcement: schedules*)
variable ratio VR (see *reinforcement: schedules*)
variety 95, 172, 225, 256-261, 272, 289, 358
venipuncture (see also *blood taking*) 140, 203, 507
veterinary behaviors (see *husbandry*)
visual bridge 241
vitamins 26
voluntary breath holds 447, 484
vocal stimulus 228
VRRV (see also *reinforcement: schedules-variable*) 246, 287, 318

warning tone (see also *delta*) 344
water quality 27
water work 341, 378, 379
weighing (an animal) 172, 176, 459
"wrong" signal (see *punishment: conditioned*)

x-rays 160

yes-no paradigm (see also *two-choice*) 484

ANIMAL INDEX

See the introduction on page 558 for helpful notes on indexing parameters and scientific nomenclature.

Babirusa 463
Bats 54
Bears (*Ursidae*) 307
  Brown 400, 463
  Polar 50, 216, 235, 267, 269, 424, 459, 463
Bees 43, 54, 307
Birds 5, 54, 160, 459, 507, 522
  Chickens 54
  Crows 17, 43
  Hawk 123
  Ostrich 267
  Owls 59, 119
  Parrots 140, 282, 295, 499
  Penguins 24, 145, 172, 235, 269, 507
  Pigeons 17, 50, 54, 101, 320
  Puffins 235
Cats
  Cheetah 119, 400
  Cougar 119, 123
  Domestic 36, 54, 62, 97, 118, 164, 411
  Lions 59, 123, 267, 459, 463
  Tigers 97, 459
Camels 5, 422
Cetaceans 6, 140, 142, 160, 172, 176, 178, 207, 225, 248, 269, 312, 366, 378, 424, 428, 437, 444, 447, 453, 459, 466, 507

Cetaceans (*continued*):
- Amazon River dolphin (*Inia geofrensis*) 280, 304, 468
- Beluga whale (*Delphinapterus leucus*) 22, 50, 80, 95, 103, 114, 145, 172, 176, 207, 216, 231, 235, 269, 295, 320, 379, 468, 507
- Bottlenose Dolphin (*Tursiops truncatus*) 6, 17, 24, 36, 44, 50, 54, 59, 86, 95, 103, 115, 125, 134, 140, 141, 142, 143, 145, 169, 176, 178, 185, 189, 197, 198, 203, 207, 216, 220, 231, 238, 241, 248, 256, 262, 267, 269, 281, 291, 320, 330, 348, 352, 358, 365, 366, 378, 379, 386, 425, 426, 428, 432, 459, 466, 468, 473, 475, 484, 493, 499, 501, 504, 507, 525
- Common Dolphin (*Delphinus delphis*) 103, 507
- Commerson's Dolphin (*Cephalorynchus commersonii*) 103
- Dusky Dolphin (*Lagenorhynchus obscurus*) 507
- False killer whale (*Pseudorca crassidens*) 50, 103, 197, 248, 366, 425, 468
- Harbor porpoise (*Phocoena phocoena*) 459, 468, 507
- Killer whale (*Orcinus orca*) 59, 80, 103, 119, 159, 160, 189, 197, 220, 269, 320, 366, 437, 507
- Pacific white-sided dolphin (*Lagenorhynchus obliquidens*) 92, 103, 145, 172, 192, 295, 365, 507
- Pilot whale (*Globicephala sp.*) 103, 207, 335, 507
- Rough-toothed dolphin (*Steno bredanensis*) 295
- Sperm whales (*Physter macrocephalus*) 501, 507
- Spinner Dolphin (*Stenella longirostris*) 50, 501, 507
- Spotted Dolphin (*Stenella sp.*) 50, 103

Chinchilla 459
Cows 54, 59, 203
Coyote 119
Dogs 5, 17, 36, 50, 54, 62, 68, 84, 97, 100, 101, 110, 118, 157, 159, 163, 203, 282, 284, 291, 294, 312, 314, 363, 365, 374, 388, 408, 414, 418, 426, 504, 515
Dolphins (see *cetaceans*)
Elephants 50, 90, 140, 220, 400, 422, 423, 424, 436, 437, 444, 447, 453, 459, 521
Foxes 119
Giraffes 459
Goats 54
Horses 5, 50, 54, 163, 203, 282, 459, 522
Hyenas 50

Manatees 425, 428, 484
Marine Mammals 59, 119, 145, 160, 176, 192, 238, 256, 262, 363, 366, 379
Mice 54
Odontocetes (see *cetaceans*)
Opossum 119
Otters 160, 225, 358
- River 23, 143, 181, 269
- Sea 23, 142, 145, 172, 235

Oxen 5
Pandas 463
Pigs 54
Pinnipeds 22, 50, 86, 140, 142, 160, 172, 178, 181, 207, 225, 253, 358, 424, 463
- California sea lion (*Zalophus californianus*) 39, 103, 119, 150, 160, 201, 207, 220, 228, 235, 253, 280, 300, 320, 341, 358, 366, 379, 409, 412, 418, 425, 426, 428, 459, 473, 484, 493, 499
- Fur seal (*Arctocephalus sp.*) 300
- Gray seal (*Halichoerus grypus*) 207, 341
- Harbor seal (*Phoca vitulina*) 39, 145, 172, 181, 201, 205, 207, 235, 253, 341, 428, 459, 507
- Walrus (*Odobenus rosmarus*) 59, 80, 86, 103, 160, 201, 228, 235, 269

Primates (non-human) 50, 119, 447
- Baboon 220, 400, 463
- Capuchin Monkey 499
- Chimpanzee 50, 220, 267, 295, 320, 493, 499
- Gorillas 50, 220, 267, 424, 459, 464, 499
- Macaque 400
- Orangutan 50, 459
- Vervet Monkey 499

Rabbits 54, 59, 122
Raccoons 54, 119
Rats 54
Reindeer 459
Reptiles 459
Rhinoceros 424, 459
Seal (see *pinnipeds*)
Sea Lion (see *pinnipeds*)
Snail, Sea (*Aplysia californica*) 150
Squid 507
Squirrels 119
Sharks 59, 127, 314
Snakes 43, 400
Tapirs 463
Turtles 59
Warthogs 424, 463
Wolves 50, 59
Zebras 123

Bibliography and Suggested Reading

The reader may note that the bibliographic reference style is inconsistent throughout this manual. Becasue so many of the articles included in the manual are from different sources, the original bibliographic format was retained in an effort to maintain accuracy.

American Rescue Dog Association. (1991). "Search and Rescue: Training Methods." Howell Book House, New York, NY.

Bandura, Albert. (1969). "Principles of Behavior Modification." Holt, Rinehart and Winston, New York, NY.

Barlow, John A. (1968). "Stimulus and Response." Harper and Row, New York, NY.

Blackman, Derek. (1974). "Operant Conditioning: An Experimental Analysis of Behavior." Methuen and Company, Ltd., London.

Breland, Keller and Breland, Marian. (1966). "Animal Behavior." The Macmillan Company, New York, NY. 201pp.

Burmaster, Corally, ed. (1994 & 1996). "The Clicker Journal Collection, Vol 1 & 2." Sunshine Books, Inc., North Bend, WA.

Burch, Mary R. and Bailey, Jon S. (1999). "How Dogs Learn." Howell Book House, New York, NY. 188pp.

Chance, Paul. (1999). "Learning and Behavior." Fourth Edition. Brooks/Cole Publishing Company, Pacific Grove, CA.

Chance, Paul. (1997). "First Course in Applied Behavior Analysis." Brooks/Cole Publishing Company, Pacific Grove, CA.

Croke, Vicki. (1997). "The Modern Ark: The Story of Zoos, Past, Present and Future." Scribner, New York, NY. 272pp.

Curtis, Patricia. (1982). "Animal Partners: Training Animals to Help People." Lodestar Books, New York, NY. 129pp.

Daniels, Aubrey C. (1994). "Bringing Out the Best in People." McGraw Hill, Inc., New York, NY.

Davis, Kathy Diamond. (1992). "Therapy Dogs: Training Your Dog to Reach Others." Howell Book House, New York, NY. 212pp.

Doane, Bonnie Munro and Qualkinbush, Thomas. (1994). "My Parrot, My Friend." Howell Book House, New York, NY. 264pp.

Duet, Karen Freeman and Duet, George. (1995). "The Business Security K-9: Selection and Training." Howell Book House, New York.

Eames, Ed and Eames, Toni. (1997). "Partners In Independence: A Success Story of Dogs And the Disabled." Howell Book House, New York, NY. 227pp.

Ferster, Charles B. and Culbertson, Stuart A. (1982). "Behavior Principles." Prentice-Hall Inc., Englewood Cliffs, NJ.

Gardner, R. Allen, Gardner, Beatrix T. and Van Cantfort, Thomas E., eds. (1989). "Teaching Sign Language to Chimpanzees." State University of New York Press, Albany, New York.

Glen, III, Thomas B. (1997). "The Dolphin and Whale Career Guide." Omega/ Publishing Division, Chicago, IL. 360pp.

Goodenough, Judith, McGuire, Betty and Wallace, Robert. (1993). "Perspectives on Animal Behavior." John Wiley and Sons, Inc., New York, NY.

Gould, James L. and Gould, Carol Grant. (1994). "The Animal Mind." Scientific American Library, New York, NY. 236pp.

Griffin, Donald R. (1992). "Animal Minds." The University of Chicago Press, Chicago, IL. 310pp.

Griffin, Donald R. (1984). "Animal Training" Harvard University Press, Cambridge, MA. 237pp.

Hediger, H. (1968). "The Psychology and Behavior of Animals in Zoos and Circuses." Dover Publications, Inc., New York, NY. 166pp.

Hediger, H. (1964). "Wild Animals in Captivity." Dover Publications, Inc., New York. 207pp.

Herman, Louis M., ed. (1980). "Cetacean Behavior: Mechanisms and Functions." John Wiley and Sons, New York, NY.

Hoage, R.J. and Goldman, Larry, eds. (1986). "Animal Intelligence: Insights into the Animal Mind." Smithsonian Institution Press, Washington, D.C. 207pp.

Hodgson, Sarah. (1996). "The Complete Idiot's Guide to Choosing Training and Raising a Dog." Alpha Books, New York, NY. 330pp.

Holland, Vergil S. (1994). "Herding Dogs: Progressive Training." Howell Book House, New York, NY. 231pp.

Johnson, C. Scott. (1995). "How to Train Goldfish Using Dolphin Training Techniques." Vantage Press, Inc., 40pp.

Joys, Joanne Carol. (1983). "The Wild Animal Trainer in America." Pruett Publishing Company, Boulder, CO. 327pp.

Kazdin, Alan E. (1994). "Behavior Modification in Applied Settings." Fifth Edition. Brooks/Cole Publishing Co., Pacific Grove, CA.

Kleiman, Devra G., Allen, Mary E., Thompson, Katerina V. and Lumpkin, Susan, eds. (1996). "Wild Mammals in Captivity." The University of Chicago Press, Chicago, IL. 639pp.

Krames, Lester, Graham, Jeff and Alloway, Tom. (1995). "Sniffy, The Virtual Rat." Brooks/Cole Publishing Company, Pacific Grove, CA. 105pp. (Training software).

Kurland, Alexandra. (1996). "Click! Dolphin Training for Your Horse." Sunshine Books, Inc., North Bend, WA.

Kurland, Alexandra. (1998). "Clicker Training for Your Horse." Sunshine Books, Waltham, MA.

Linden, Eugene. (1974). "Apes, Men and Language." Saturday Review Press/ E.P. Dutton and Company, Inc., New York, NY. 288pp.

Logan, Jim and Logan, Amy. (1996). "Click and Reward for Llamas." Jim and Amy Logan, Chattaroy, WA. 18pp.

Macintosh, N.J. (1974). "The Psychology of Animal Learning." Academic Press, New York.

Markowitz, Hal and Stevens, Victor J., eds. (1978). "Behavior of Captive Wild Animals." Nelson Hall, Inc., Chicago, IL. 314pp.

McFarland, David. (1993). "Animal Behavior." Second Edition. Longman Scientific and Technical, Essex, England.

McFarland, David, ed. (1981). "The Oxford Companion to Animal Behavior." Oxford University Press, New York, NY. 657pp.

Michael, Jack L. (1993). "Concepts and Principles of Behavior Analysis." Western Michigan University, Kalamazoo, MI. 126pp.

Michael, Jack. (1998). "Basic Principles of Behavior." Western Michigan University, Kalamazoo, MI. 50pp.

Norris, Kenneth S. (1974). "The Porpoise Watcher." W.W. Norton and Company, Inc., New York, NY. 250pp.

Norton, Bryan G., Hutchins, Michael, Stevens, Elizabeth F. and Maple, Terry L., eds. (1995). "Ethics on the Ark." Smithsonian Institution Press, Washington D.C. 330pp.

Nye, Robert D. (1979). "What is B.F. Skinner Really Saying?" Prentice-Hall, Inc., Englewood Cliffs, NJ.

O'Connor, Karen. (1982). "Maybe You Belong in a Zoo." Dodd, Mead and Company. 141pp.

Ogden, Paul. (1992). "Chelsea, the Story of a Signal Dog." Little, Brown and Company, Boston, MA. 169pp.

Pavlov, I.P. (1941). "Lectures on Conditioned Reflexes." International Publishers, New York.

Pepper, R.L. and Defran, R.H. (1975). "Dolphin Trainer's Handbook, Part 1 Basic Training." NUC, San Diego, CA. 52pp.

Premack, David and Premack, Ann James. (1983). "The Mind of an Ape." W.W. Norton and Company, Inc., New York, NY. 165pp.

Pryor, Karen. (1975). "Lads Before the Wind." Harper and Row, New York, NY. 278pp.

Pryor, Karen. (1984). "Don't Shoot the Dog." Revised edition, 1999. Bantam Books, New York.

Pryor, Karen. (1995). "On Behavior." Sunshine Books, Inc., North Bend, WA. 385pp.

Pryor, Karen. (1996). "A Dog and a Dolphin 2.0, An Introduction to Clicker Training." Sunshine Books, Inc., North Bend, WA. 42pp.

Reed, Don C. (1981). "Notes from the Underwater Zoo." The Dial Press, New York, NY. 274pp.

Reynolds, G.S. (1975). "A Primer of Operant Conditioning." Scott, Foresman and Co., Palo Alto, CA.

Savage, Candace. (1995). "Bird Brains." Sierra Club Books, San Francisco, CA. 134pp.

Schusterman, Ronald J., Thomas, Jeanette A., Wood, Forrest G., eds. (1986). "Dolphin Cogniton and Behavior: A Comparative Approach." Lawrence Erlbaum Associates, Hillsdale, NJ. 393pp.

Scott, John Paul. (1958). "Animal Behavior." The University of Chicago Press, Chicago, IL.

Shepherdson, David J., Mellen, Jill D. and Hutchins, Michael, eds. (1998). "Second Nature: Environmental Enrichment for Captive Animals." Smithsonian Institution Press, Washington D.C. 334pp.

Sidman, Murray. (1989). "Coercion and its Fallout." Authors Cooperative, Inc., Boston, MA.

Skinner, B.F. (1974). "About Behaviorism." Vintage Books Edition, New York, NY. 291pp.

Skinner, B. F. (1938). "The Behavior of Organisms: An Experimental Analysis." The Century Psychology Series edited by Richard M. Elliott, Appleton-Century-Crofts, New York.

Spector, Morgan. (1999). "Clicker Training for Obedience." Sunshine Books, Waltham, MA. 325 pp.

Terrace, Herbert S. (1987). "Nim, A Chimpanzee Who Learned Sign Language." Columbia University Press, New York, NY. 303pp.

Thomson, Peggy. (1988). "Keepers and Creatures at the National Zoo." Thomas Y. Crowell, New York, NY. 198pp.

Tucker, Michael. (1984). "The Eyes that Lead: The Story of Guide Diogs for the Blind." Howell Book House, New York, NY. 200 pp.

Tweedie, Jan. (1998). "On the Trail: A Practical Guide to the Working Bloodhound and Other Search and Rescue Dogs." Alpine Publications, Loveland, CO. 217pp.

Twelveponies, Mary. (1982). "There are No Problem Horses, Only Problem Riders." Houghton Mifflin Company, Boston, MA. 228pp.

Wilkes, Gary. (1994). "A Behavior Sampler." Sunshine Books, Inc., North Bend, WA. 237pp.

Wilkes, Gary. (1995). "The Click and Treat Starter Kit." Sunshine Books, Inc., North Bend, WA. 36pp.

Wolman, Benjamin B. (1989). "Dictionary of Behavioral Science." Academic Press, Inc., San Diego, CA. 370pp.

Wood, Forrest G. (1973). "Marine Mammals and Man, The Navy's Porpoises and Sea Lions." Robert B. Luce, Inc., New York, NY. 264pp.